PRIVATE CAPITAL

Volume II: Investments

Eli Talmor   Florin Vasvari

www.privatecapitalbook.com

Private Capital
Volume II: Investments
Copyright © 2020 by Eli Talmor and Florin Vasvari
Edited by Kontent360
Printed in the United Kingdom

ISBN 978-1-9162110-5-6

About the Authors

Eli Talmor is professor at London Business School and founder of its Institute of Private Equity. He practices venture capital and is a serial cornerstone investor with multiple exits. He also served on the advisory board of the African Venture Capital Association. Professor Talmor is a prominent speaker to business executives worldwide. He was asked by the UK Parliament to provide a leading testimony on private equity and to advise the UK Prime Minister office. Professor Talmor was previously on the finance faculty at the University of California (UCLA and Irvine) and the Wharton School. He holds a Ph.D. from the University of North Carolina at Chapel Hill and a B.Sc. (Cum Laude) from the Technion – Israel Institute of Technology.

Florin Vasvari is professor at London Business School and head of its Accounting faculty department. He is also the Academic Director of the Private Equity Institute. His research and consulting covers private equity and debt markets, and he has published extensively in top tier academic journals. Professor Vasvari is regularly invited to present his research at major business schools in the United States and serves on the board of top academic journals. Professor Vasvari also sits on the advisory boards and investment committees of private equity firms. He holds a Ph.D. from the University of Toronto, Rotman School of Management and an M.A. from University of Toronto, Department of Economics.

To Dahlia, Yael, Lauren and my grandchildren

Eli Talmor

To Bianca, Albert and Mirela

Florin Vasvari

Contents

PREFACE TO VOLUME II

By all measures, the continuous growth and expansion of the private capital asset class has been astounding. The industry has grown over 200 times in a quarter of a century, and is estimated to triple further over the next ten years. Once regarded as a small blip at the margin of alternative investments, private equity has become an asset class of its own and moved to the centre stage of capital markets. With its long-term record of successful performance, the private equity investment model has benefited from an unprecedented increase in the capital allocation by pension, endowments and sovereign wealth funds around the world. Furthermore, the success of private equity's corporate governance model, which aligns investors with fund managers very well, has led to an expansion to other types of assets in private markets such as infrastructure, real estate and private credit, and subsequently to the rebranding of the industry as private capital. This expansion has allowed institutional investors to gain exposure to private assets on a massive scale.

From a pedagogical perspective, we continue to be amazed by the wide range of issues that are covered by the private capital asset class. Nearly all business aspects are at the heart of its matter – valuation, corporate governance, strategy, operations, financial structuring, asset allocation, risk management, entrepreneurship, reporting, tax, regulation and government policy.

The two-volume book provides a comprehensive overview of the main topics in private capital that are relevant to graduate students, investors, regulators and other professionals seeking to understand the many facets of the asset class, as well as private equity practitioners who wish to have a broader analysis of the sector. The book has grown out of our teaching the popular Private Equity and Venture Capital course and the senior executive education program at London Business School. Over the years, our focus has broadened considerably as the industry matured. Working closely with the global professional private capital community proved particularly valuable in generating up-to-date knowledge and expertise on the industry trends and best practice.

Expanding on our previous textbook *International Private Equity* published in 2011, the current book is arranged in two volumes. Volume I deals with fund level matters: fund types, structuring, due diligence, performance measurement and fund risk management. It also covers important specializations of the private capital industry such as secondaries, private debt, infrastructure, natural resources and real estate funds.

Volume II is devoted to an analysis at the investment level. It covers valuation of private equity companies, deal screening and due diligence, acquisition finance, LBO transactions and modeling, post deal execution, harvesting of private equity investments, operation in emerging markets and more.

A major part of this volume is dedicated to early-stage investing. Separate chapters deal with business angel investing, venture capital, incubators and accelerators, university technology transfers, and alternative sources of funding such as governmental support initiatives, crowdfunding, corporate venture capital and venture lending.

For each chapter we have asked a leading professional who is expert in that specific field to write a text box, commenting on practical aspects and current trends. We are thankful to all the distinguished contributors.

Our thanks go to our students, private equity partners, lawyers, scientists and other professionals who reviewed, commented and helped with research on the chapters: David Ai, Gonçalo Amorim, Tamer Bahgat,

Simone Botti, Eric Brand, Ran Dlugin, Hurley Doddy, Christopher Field, Edward Gera, Michael Glossop, Raul Gutierrez, Tim Hanford, Yoav Henis, Robyn Klinger-Vidra, Katharine Ku, Rami Lipman, Bjoern Koertner, Eric Kump, Eva Lutz, John Markland, Jon Medved, Christophe Michotte, Martin Milev, James Mitchell, Eduard Motta, Kate Mitchell, Jörg Mugrauer, Joseph Newton, Damien Olive, Justin Patrick, Dwight Poler, Carlos Ribeiro, Don Rose, Asier Rufino, Carlos Sanchez, Philipp Scheier, Alexander Schlaepfer, Yesha Sivan, Simon Sonntag, Lauren Talmor, Asher Tishler, Fernando Da Cruz Vasconcellos, Ron Yachini and Simon Webster.

The project was most effectively and professionally directed by our managing editor Michal Bohanes. Catie Phares provided exceptional editorial services. We owe them both a great deal of thanks.

Eli Talmor and Florin Vasvari, August 2020

1 Deal Screening and Due Diligence

A good beginning makes a good end ... 'Tis a great point of wisdom ... to begin at the right end.
Samuel Palmer, Moral Essays (1710)

INTRODUCTION

In March 2016, one of the world's largest generic drug makers, Teva Pharmaceutical, completed the acquisition of Rimsa, one of Mexico's largest pharmaceutical manufacturers, for $2.3 billion. Teva hailed its acquisition as a "significant platform for growth" in the second-largest market in Latin America. A few weeks later, the local transition team integrating the two companies received an anonymous email warning of alleged corruption, double paperwork, incomplete stability tests, and various irregularities in Rimsa. The plant was shut down immediately, followed by Teva filing a lawsuit against Rimsa's previous owners, the Espinosa family, stating that the company "was engaged in a years-long scheme to sell defective and unlawful products... and made up false formulations for products not yet developed or tested." In doing so, Teva claimed in its lawsuit, "Rimsa would then fraudulently launch its actual products under the guise of those made-up formulations."

For their part, the sellers argued that Teva was suffering from a classic case of "buyer's remorse" after failing to properly conduct due diligence. They argued that "Teva completely misunderstood what it was purchasing and [wanted] to undo the transaction by any desperate measure, including making false accusations of fraud. It did not understand the Rimsa Companies or the Mexican market. ... It has terminated virtually the entire management team. It unilaterally ceased manufacturing most of the Rimsa products. It has destroyed the Rimsa Companies and now wants its money back."

In August 2017, the Supreme Court of the State of New York ruled that the Espinosas did not commit fraud, but at the same time, it did not reject Teva's breach of contract claims either. The New York court ruling criticized their due diligence process. "Teva is a sophisticated entity. If it had wanted to include a carve-out that it could rely on the materials presented to it, or information included in the due diligence, or a representation that the material it viewed during due diligence was correct, it could have done so. It did not," wrote Justice Peter Sherwood in his decision. "Teva provides no reason that it could not have discovered the truth. It only states that it did not discover the truth," the judge wrote.

In this case, a leading industrial multinational had undertaken a horizontal acquisition in its own pharmaceutical sector. With a dedicated internal M&A department, Teva had proven experience, drawn from over 30 similar international acquisitions in the preceding 25 years leading. The firm had spent at least a year pursuing analysis, due diligence, legal scrutiny, and negotiations regarding the Rimsa deal, starting long before the time of the deal announcement to the NYSE in October 2015, and proceeding until completion in March 2016. Yet, the outcome had still been a disaster; was it the result of outright fraud, as the buyer claimed, or reflective of a lack of understanding about the acquired company, as the seller argued? What had gone wrong with Teva's due diligence process?

THE BIG PICTURE

Deal screening and due diligence correspond to the complex process where the GP assesses the merits of an investment before deciding whether to make a binding offer.[1] Once an investment prospect is originated, screening is a multi-stage process through which the decision to continue exploring the opportunity is revisited frequently. Only a small percentage of deals survive this process and reach the point where an investment offer is made. While strategic/business deal diligence is part of the screening process, the formal due diligence only starts after an indicative offer is accepted by the vendor, subject to a formal verification of legal, financial, technological, and other claims made regarding the status of the company. Both the economic and formal diligence processes are quite costly: they consume significant internal and external resources, as well as occupying the mind-set of both the buying and selling teams. Since most processes take place as competitive auctions, the private equity firm must constantly assess the likelihood of a successful transaction in order to reaffirm its appetite to engage further in the process.

As illustrated in Exhibit 1, deal selection in private equity is a funneling process, where the firm needs to source an ample flow of deals for the top of the funnel. Hundreds of potential targets (and sometimes even more) are sourced and then gradually narrowed down through an increasingly laborious and costly process until only a few companies get the full attention of a detailed due diligence process and, ultimately, a binding offer. Deal screening and due diligence confirm the market's and company's attractiveness, their economics, and the competitiveness of the transaction. Each assessment phase should inform the areas of value and risk to be prioritized for further investigation.

Exhibit 1: Deal screening process

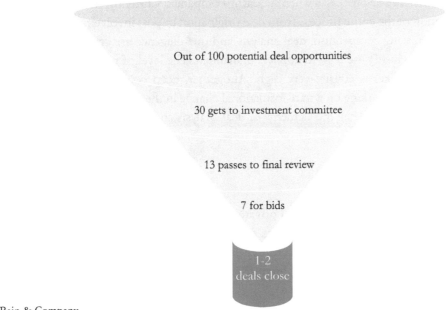

Out of 100 potential deal opportunities

30 gets to investment committee

13 passes to final review

7 for bids

1-2 deals close

Source: Bain & Company

---

[1] For expositional purposes, the expressions "deal selection," "screening," and "analysis" are used interchangeably. Similarly, "strategic/economic/business due diligence" and "commercial due diligence" have a similar meaning or are used as better fits. The latter terms are distinct, however, from a formal due diligence process, which is restricted to fact validation and verification once terms are largely agreed.

Screening investments in private equity is inherently different from the equivalent process of buying stocks of listed companies. The degree and quality of publicly available information on private companies is limited, and the seller gradually provides access to company data and communication with management as the deal progresses. The process also differs from the type of assessment conducted by a trade buyer who is interested in a strategic acquisition and thus cares foremost about complementarities and added capabilities to the existing business. Often, synergies concerning the trade buyer's sales and distribution organization and its production processes, procurement processes, or technological developments give trade buyers an ultimate advantage in evaluating investment opportunities. In private equity, the objective is not to identify synergies but to assess the potential of the private equity firm to build value in the target company on a stand-alone basis with a view to pursue an outright exit after a few years.

Even within the private equity sector, the nature of value creation has changed over the years. Until the 1990s, returns were predominantly based on the ability to spot undervalued companies and on financial leverage. The selection process was centered on paying a low entry price and then adding leverage to the structure. By the end of that decade, multiples and gearing levels started to escalate, and private equity firms had to rely increasingly on business improvements to deliver the same return to LPs, leading to more emphasis on operational aspects of the due diligence. At the same time, however, leading private equity firms became too large to make small investments where a detailed operational improvement or turnaround was the key for success. Instead, they shifted their investment thesis to identify opportunities where the driver of return was scaling the business of the target companies.

More recently, after the latest global financial crisis, the business environment took a new shape: interest rates plunged to historically low levels, creating more demand for private equity allocation, and investment multiples skyrocketed, leading to high entry bases. Simultaneously, the whole private equity industry—including not only GPs, but also intermediaries, investment banks, advisers, placement agents, leverage finance providers, and LPs—became more professionalized. As basic requirements have been outlined in many fields and standard procedures defined for many screening processes, it becomes increasingly difficult to take advantage of inefficient sale processes when acquiring companies. Currently, there is an unprecedented level of professionalization of the entire process from deal origination to post involvement. With the maturity of the sector and the increasing competition, deal analysis and due diligence are critical in order to validate the investment thesis and to justify the high multipliers demanded. The level of required resources (financial and management attention alike) is equally very high. Altogether, deep commercial and operational due diligence are required before embarking on a transformational change in the acquired company. Over the rest of this chapter, we discuss in more detail the elements of deal analysis and due diligence.

The buyer's perspective

Sourcing and screening deals is a central function of private equity GPs; it enables them to identify proprietary opportunities and apply their professional experience as well as their industry and country expertise. Due diligence on a company not only ensures that the business is financially and operationally sound, but that the buyer has assessed conceivable risks, identified potential areas for improvement (upside), and developed a robust plan to enhance value.

Before committing to an investment, the GP must answer numerous questions. Some are related to the target company and its business environment, whereas others are concerned with the transaction itself. Examples of issues to be explored in the first category include the following:

- The relevant key performance indicators and success factors of the business and how does the company compare to its competitors and peers

- The target company's opportunities and impediments to scale further

- Revenues derivers and their components. What products, regions, and customer segments drive sales growth? Are the economic environment and the market sector a safe bet?

- Barriers to entry such as intellectual property and technology issues,

- Quality and fit of existing management

- The capital expenditure (capex) requirements of the business. Are the factories safe and comparable in terms of efficiency?

- Are there hidden liabilities, such as a large amount of employee lawsuits or an unfunded pension plan?

- Are there environmental hazards or risks?

- Regulatory and tax issues.

When it comes to the transaction itself, some of the most obvious questions include the following: What is the deal competition? What share of ownership and other terms are mandatory to secure a major influence? How much leverage can the business sustain? What is the best plan to grow the business and prepare it for an exit within a few years? How can the private equity firm add value to the company?

Finding satisfactory answers to these and many other questions is the task of deal analysis and due diligence. However, note that not all of these aspects are equally important. Some are critical, and these must be flagged early in order to discuss potential solutions or mitigating measures, whereas others may only impact the way of structuring the deal or have a marginal effect on the decision of whether to invest and on the offer price. A crucial element of the screening process is to identify the few most critical aspects early on, and then to focus primarily on these matters. In this way, only limited time and resources are exerted on deals that are either not viable or not attractive enough. The process itself also has many possible forms. It can be carried out by an internal team or may involve advisers; it can range from a few weeks to many months; and it can be structured in a single phase or multiple phases. Whatever the exact pattern, the fundamental aim is the same: gaining a sufficient understanding of the risks and opportunities to get to a position where the buyer and its debt providers are prepared to make an investment.

The seller's perspective

While reasons for selling a business vary widely, there are common concerns about the process from the seller's point of view. How much information should it divulge to a prospective buyer, especially at the preliminary stages? What data controls should be placed in the due diligence process? How can the company protect trade practices and strategic and technological knowhow when competitors are among the bidders?

Sellers will wish to release as little information as possible at the start of the due diligence process (when many potential bidders may have access to this information) and only provide detailed information to a short list of bidders that have demonstrated their seriousness. In reality, sale processes very often fail to materialize, in which case, material information has been fruitlessly disseminated.

The due diligence process depends heavily on many other elements of the deal. For example, the seller will decide early on whether to conduct the transaction as an exclusive sale or an auction, which determines the number of bidders and the ones more likely to be interested in the deal. In many processes, the selling party retains advisers to collect certain data and provide an independent review of the company and its environment, referred to as a vendor due diligence (VDD) report. VDD reports are particularly generated for the financial (e.g., summarizing the historical financials and commenting on the business plan), commercial (e.g., on markets, business models, go-to-market strategies, the competitive landscape, etc.), and legal and tax aspects of the due diligence process. The benefit of a VDD report for the seller is that it may shorten the process as the data is already collected and prepared. Nevertheless, for institutional risk reasons, each private equity buyer still needs to perform its own due diligence in order to assess the risk-return profile independently.

From the first stages, the private equity firm needs to understand the motivation behind the present owners' interest in selling the company. Due diligence is essential for the buyer, while for the seller, it consists of an unwanted process that carries risks of over-disclosure and management distraction from running the business. Resolving this potential minefield often requires a careful and time-consuming process. Depending on the complexity of the deal, the seller may have to set up a physical or virtual data room to provide the buyer and its advisers with access to the company's documentation in a controlled environment for a certain period of time. There is a significant cost to prepare the documents, rent a venue (typically segregated from the company's premises for confidentiality purposes), and have advisers in place to run it during the agreed period. With document digitalization, it has become an increasingly common practice to set up a virtual data room to avoid the complexity of controlling a physical location and hard copies of documents. This alternative is more flexible and particularly preferred in cross-border deals or where there are pressures to execute the transaction efficiently.

DEAL STAGES AND THE DUE DILIGENCE PROCESS

An acquisition in the private market is highly complex by definition: years of effort and attention will be required to add value, spur the growth of the business, and improve its processes, and the asset remains illiquid for a long time. Due to such a substantial material commitment, a relatively long assessment period is required before embarking on an investment. In contrast, a purchase of traded shares by a fund manager is a binary judgment: if the asset meets certain criteria then it will be purchased, sometimes through an order executed by a robot able to apply a set of rules. Shares of listed companies can also be sold immediately if required, while the preparation and execution of a sales process takes many months, if not even a year. When acquiring a stake in an unlisted company, the process follows a funneling approach, where the option to continue the exploration and consideration can be stopped at any point before the actual investment decision is made. The choice is driven not only by the economic interest in the asset, but also by considerations such as the amount of resources available, the difficulty of conducting the analysis, the expected time required to complete the transaction, the availability of other targets, the identification of unbearable risks, any competition with other bidders, the likelihood of winning, and more.

There are three main areas of assessment covered in the screening and due diligence process, all of which are continuously re-examined as the process progresses:

- **Market and company attractiveness:** Market positioning, product mix, brand, and client portfolio are analyzed against the industry and competitive environment to determine the overall attractiveness of the target. If a company has stable revenues, for example, the market risk may be lower, but the potential upside may be moderate as well. A clear view of competitive differentials is fundamental to drive market share increase, whereas adequate capabilities need to be in place to support expansion plans. Historical performance against plans and proven management skills are parameters to assess the company's likelihood of achieving potential earnings growth. However, scaling a business necessarily requires an expansion into either new markets and/or new products, and both require adjustments to the current operation no matter how successful it has been so far.

- **Deal economics:** The fit of an investment is assessed against the fund's strategy in terms of investment expertise, size, and geography. The equity stake and power to control and influence business decisions determine the ability to add value and deliver the objectives of the investment thesis. Capital structure, capex requirements, and additional management resources to complement or replace incumbent management are considered, along with exit opportunities, to determine the required capital input and the expected return to equity holders.

- **Transaction competitiveness:** The attractiveness of the deal is determined by the level of competition, whether the process is conducted as an auction or an exclusive transaction, the seller's motivation, and the level of information transparency. When management incentives are not aligned, participation in the bid becomes unattractive. The private equity firm's competitive edge in the deal is considered and benchmarked. For example, the presence of a trade buyer who is likely to pay a significant premium for strategic synergies could render the effort in a thorough analysis unjustified. As a whole, limited human resources and partners' bandwidth prohibit pursuing as many deals as possible. Instead, targets need to be carefully selected and prioritized along a managed process so as not to overcommit resources to an opportunity that is unlikely to materialize.

Specific deal characteristics dictate the depth of the analysis at each stage. The most critical topics of analysis should be brought to the forefront in the screening process so that investment committee can identify "deal breakers" (e.g., legal constraints set by antitrust regulations, or a complex ownership structure which may trigger a large tax liability on the business) early on and avoid spending time that could be used more productively elsewhere. The more detailed and resource-intensive parts of the analysis should be left to the later stages, when there is a greater likelihood of the transaction being completed. At this stage, the bidder will have the opportunity to dig deeper into financial and operational aspects.

The analysis and due diligence process runs parallel with documentation and financing. The main stages of the due diligence process are outlined in Exhibit 2.

Deal sourcing

Deal sourcing can take multiple forms. Often, targets are identified and referred to the private equity firm through the industry network, bankers, and others. Many GPs invest heavily in creating and institutionalizing an industrial network, comprising incumbent or former corporate managers supporting the identification of targets, in order to generate proprietary deal flow—or at least have a timing and knowledge advantage in case the target is placed to be sold through an auction. Usually, these industry experts not only identify targets, but also support GPs in evaluating the companies by contributing their industrial expertise as advisers, later board members, or even buy-in managers.

Exhibit 2: Deal stages

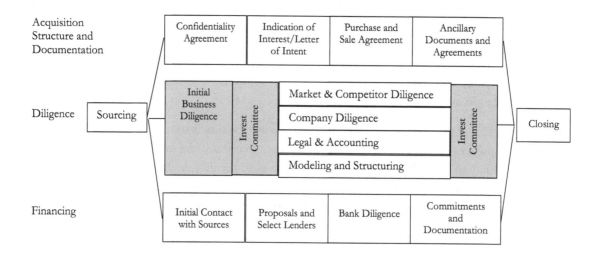

In many private equity firms, the screening process is organized vertically according to industry sectors (e.g., healthcare, services, industries, consumer goods, technology, media, etc.) in order to leverage the knowledge within a certain group of investment managers, their industry experts, and advisers. Some private equity firms cast a net of advisers who are assigned to sector-specific investment teams to focus on sourcing deal opportunities in those sectors. In other cases, the seller's shareholders decide to divest the company or a business division and approach potential buyers; in these situations, the process is originated from the sell side, through M&A advisers, with a mandate to identify potential buyers. In distress situations, banks or administrators force the sale of a company or its assets as part of a bankruptcy procedure. A common practice by leading players is to constantly track a long list of potential acquisition candidates, including, for example, aging lists of potential secondaries (portfolio companies of other private equity firms which will be sold until the end of their fund life), potential corporate carve outs, and larger family-owned businesses which may have succession issues. A top-down market screening process is used based on pre-specified criteria. While in the earlier days of the private equity industry the sourcing processes were executed "between the deal-doing," today, such processes are institutionalized, and ongoing sourcing processes lead to a short list of identified targets to track. This list is constantly revised from the larger pool based on market intelligence along certain metrics. General criteria are sector and cycle, stage, size, geography, profitability, investment theses, and ownership structure.

Depending on the origins of the process and the appetite of the parties, the initial discussions may follow different time frames, and may or may not result in a transaction. A CEO reports, "I get, on average, two approaches a week to sell this business. Even though it's a pain, I always listen politely ... after all, you never know what might be on offer."

When a deal is initiated by the company's present owners, their adviser forms a list of potential buyers who are invited to participate in an auction or to negotiate on an exclusive basis. The former option is usually preferred when multiple potential bidders exist, willingness to pay is uncertain, and there is no significant time pressure. The latter is the option of choice when there is one obvious strategic bidder, confidence about its willingness to pay is high, or when a deal needs to be executed quickly. Exclusive negotiations are always preferred by the buyers as they typically result in a lower price due to the lack of explicit competition; equally important, they enable the negotiation of special terms based on the needs of both the buyer and the seller. Such flexibility is more limited in an auction-type process, where the focus is primarily on a single measure: the price. Exclusive negotiations could also be later hailed by the private equity firm as a proprietary deal, thereby demonstrating unique origination capabilities to its investors. In reality, private equity firms participate heavily in auctions, which dominate larger-size transactions in particular. Participation also enables these firms to keep a finger on the pulse with respect to granular deal data and networks in the sector.

Teaser and information memorandum review

The seller will often commission an agent to market the deal, although larger companies may prefer to handle this task internally using their own M&A department. In structured sales processes, the first document provided by the seller's M&A adviser is a so-called "teaser," a three- to five-page summary of the business model, industrials, and key financials (e.g., only sales and EBITDA) of an asset anonymously (i.e., without disclosing the name of the asset). In case the described asset is of interest for the private equity firm, a non-disclosure agreement (NDA) is signed.

Thereafter, the first set of more detailed information is compiled and presented to one or more bidders, often in the form of an information memorandum (IM). This document specifies the assets for sale (e.g., a company or its subsidiaries) and sets out—usually in a very positive light—the company's history, prospects, target markets, competitive positioning, unique selling proposition, and basic financial situation, including a business plan. The IM provides the bidders with a sufficient amount of information to understand the business, ask follow-up questions, and form an initial opinion about their interest in moving forward to the due diligence phase. During this phase, private equity firms will reach out to their network of industry experts and advisers (so-called "experts' interviews") in order to assess the opportunity. Firms will also initiate talks with leverage finance banks and debt funds (if applicable) in order to test how much financial leverage the asset can bear according to the debt providers.

The preparation and composition of an IM may be a time-consuming process up front, and sale processes must take this into consideration. Depending on the industry knowledge of the investment bank or M&A house responsible for composing the IM, knowledge transfer between management, the seller, and the investment bank is required to draft the IM. While most larger enterprises have rolling budgets and business plans in place, many privately owned firms do not, which means they need to develop a business plan together with the investment bank and financial advisers. Depending on the complexity of the target, therefore, composing an IM may take months.

After reviewing the IM, the seller usually requires an indicative offer, comprising the identity of the potential acquirer, its rationale for the acquisition, the purchase price and its underlying assumptions, the financing of the transaction, a list of open conditions to be fulfilled in order to be able to provide a binding bid (including necessary due diligence work), and its envisaged timing.

If an initial interest is confirmed and the bidder wishes to move forward, a much greater commitment of resources will be necessary to perform a detailed analysis during the due diligence phase. At this point, the number of participants tends to be limited. A non-binding memorandum of understanding (MOU) is normally signed between the parties to formalize the interest in the deal, setting the timescale of the analysis and defining confidentiality terms. In some cases, specific exclusions or caveats are included where more information is required.

Due diligence process

Once all offers are received, the M&A adviser will compare and rank the bids with respect to purchase price, transaction certainty, time requirements, necessary due diligence steps, regulatory requirements, and other criteria. At this stage, a limited number of participants are expected, although the process may still be quite competitive. A degree of controlled access is granted to the prospective buyers through a secure data room; usually (but not always), this will be restricted to the CEO, the CFO, a few other executives, and the advisers. This stage of the process often takes between two and four weeks, although it may vary significantly depending on the size of the company, the complexity of the deal, and the number of potential acquirers. Access to the company's facilities is normally limited to those sites that are critical to understand both value and risk, and in most cases, access is only granted via structured management presentations and site visits. As institutional investors, private equity firms must document the outcome of the due diligence process for their own investment committees as well as for the credit committees of the financing bank, which will require full documentation and due diligence in order to commit irrevocably to provide debt financing. Therefore, many teams of advisers are hired simultaneously with different work streams in order to cope with the short time frame of a due diligence process. The outcome is then documented in various due diligence reports.

The due diligence process is typically segmented into several areas:

Financial

This consists of a detailed review of the target company's financial information, including historical performance, business plans, and projections. A detailed financial analysis may spot issues related to earnings quality, such as a large volume of revenue accrued up front which may not be converted into cash flow, or insufficient working capital to service short-term liabilities. Other concerns could include non-recurring revenues and earnings, impaired assets, underfunded pensions, bad debt, and capex. In a private equity investment, the current capital structure is not very important, since it will be redesigned later by the buyer. The ability to raise debt tranches at a reasonable cost depends on aspects such as collateral and creditworthiness, which are reviewed and documented during the financial due diligence.

Tax

The tax due diligence looks at the company's tax regimes, historical tax filings, intercompany relations and documentation, country-specific requirements, and the magnitude of its compliance concerning tax documentation and potential risks—particularly additional tax payments that could be claimed in the future by the tax authority after an audit concerning profits before the acquisition took place.

Commercial

This area of due diligence looks into the market in which the company participates and expands into elements of the value chain (e.g., customers, competitors, channels, and suppliers) to confirm the assumptions behind the business plan. For example, the future performance of the business may be affected by new entrants or substitute products in the near future, or a consolidation of suppliers may result in their increased bargaining power. The commercial due diligence is particularly important in a private equity investment because the ability to scale the business and deliver the expected growth within a strict window of a few years is fundamental to achieve investment returns. Any delay in reaching the expected sales or performance level will affect the IRR. Another unique private equity consideration, even before acquiring a firm, is the availability of exit routes: Are there potential trade buyers? Is there enough depth in the capital markets and IPO activity? What would be a feasible multiple to target for the exit?

Operational

The scope of the operational due diligence depends heavily on the business, and tends to be more complex in heavy industries and capital-intensive sectors. Since this area covers all operational aspects of the business, operational due diligence can quickly become unmanageable without prioritization of the areas of highest importance. Some of the elements included in the due diligence are the management team, compliance risk, IT infrastructure, human capital, supply chain, and procurement functions. It allows buyers to identify risks related to outdated production facilities, inefficient inventory management, inadequate contracts with distribution channels, or inappropriate employee incentives and reward schemes. In a private equity investment, the operational due diligence will drive decisions such as maintaining or changing the management team, reviewing assumptions on capex, scaling overseas, vertical integration strategies, bolt-on acquisitions, or asset divestitures; it also helps buyers spot opportunities to add value to the business through operational efficiencies.[2]

Legal/regulatory/insurance/environmental

These assessments aim to identify risks generated from contracts, regulation, or the ownership of certain assets and liabilities. They cover the legal structure of the company, license agreements or contracts with third parties, debt arrangements, intellectual property, real estate, labor relations, environmental risks, and pending litigation. In addition, an insurance broker will assess the incumbent insurance coverage and the corresponding premium and provide advice on improvements. As these elements influence the future ability to generate cash from assets or obligations to perform cash outflows, they have a direct impact on the prospective return on investment. All of these risks need to be accounted for in the valuation.

During the due diligence stage, teams from both sides will meet to discuss the main areas of uncertainty. Often, the scope of the diligence is limited following the preliminary analysis to those matters identified by the buyer as materially affecting value, and to key risks and potential deal breakers. Bidders will need to form their own final judgments based on the assessments received from their specific advisers in the various due diligence elements, as well as the feedback from the conversations with market participants and industry experts.

The seller will provide to the prospective buyers a draft version of the sale and purchase agreement (SPA), where price, payment method (cash, shares, or other assets), ownership transference, settlement jurisdiction, and many other details are clarified to protect the parties from unintended risks. The buyers are then asked to hand in comments or mark-ups to the SPA within the binding bid.

Further, before reaching the final bid deadline, bidders must finalize their financing. In parallel to the private equity firms, acquisition banks feed their internal credit committees with the sponsor's information (due diligence reports) and their assessment of the assets in order to get a firm approval to provide debt

---

[2] For a detailed discussion, refer to the chapter on post-deal operational improvements.

funding to the buyout. Debt financing documentation should normally be finalized before signing the transaction.

Based on the risk-return profile and the competitive situation of the auction, any risks or potential risks identified during the due diligence could be handled by (1) quantifying the risks and deducting these amounts from the purchase price, (2) trying to negotiate guarantees, warranties. or even indemnities into the SPA, (3) defining appropriate mitigating measures to cope with the risks, and, in the worst-case scenario, (4) aborting the process in the case of deal breakers. Following the analysis of the above aspects, buyers will place their confirmatory or binding bids according to the pre-specified timetable of the sellers.

The selling party will then decide with which bidder to negotiate the final SPA. Within structured auctions, sellers and their advisers sometimes negotiate SPAs in parallel to keep the competition ongoing until a definite signing of the SPA.

Deal closing

Each SPA contains closing conditions, which must be fulfilled during an agreed time period. Such closing conditions often include, for example, regulatory approvals of antitrust authorities in different countries and other governmental approvals or outstanding financing documentation (e.g., KYC documentation) in order to fund the transaction. Shortly before closing, the money from the leverage financing banks, as well as from the private equity fund's LPs, is drawn. On the closing date, the transaction will be settled, money will change hands, and the new ownership will be established. The buyer should have a post-merger/integration plan in place to be implemented immediately after the ownership transition. A good integration plan will establish the groundwork for future growth, while a poorly executed one will result in delayed benefits. The speed of execution is particularly important for private equity firms, given the pressure to realize growth and exit in a relatively short time frame.

DUE DILIGENCE BY DEAL TYPES

Each due diligence process is unique in the sense that the specific risks and opportunities of the target company and the deal itself must be identified and assessed. There is not necessarily a one-size-fits-all approach for due diligence. Therefore, different deal types lead to different focal points during the process. The unique positioning of the private equity firm and its value-added capabilities play a key role when targeting an acquisition. The injection of expensive private equity capital is only justified if the private equity firm is able to implement a well-defined strategic plan that would not be achievable by the company on its own. A very important guideline is to dig very deep into the target's business in order to identify value drivers that might be overlooked by other bidders. The question "why should I invest in this company?" must drive the analysis and due diligence at all times; if the answer is not very clear, the chance of paying too much is dangerously high. An understanding the underlying risks and a confirmation of the opportunity are only possible through diligent analysis of the deal and the business, including its operational and financial aspects.

Below are some examples of due diligence particularities driven by different deal types.

Public to private buyout in a developed market

When a private equity firm bids to gain control of a publicly quoted company, certain rules depend on the jurisdiction of the deal. Typically, the fund will need to reach a minimum stake to enable a takeover. Such a process is likely to commence with a "stalk," where the private equity firm gathers public information and develops an investment thesis and an outline valuation. One of the most critical tasks of the assessment is examining the performance and capabilities of the existing management team, which reveals whether or not a new managerial team should be appointed, and also highlights the potential sources of value creation. For deals in a developed market, finding the right skills is rarely a problem. However, managing a public company involves different demands on management than managing private equity. Managing the expectations of a large number of minority shareholders in a listed company is replaced by the need to deliver an ambitious plan as set out by the investment thesis. During this process, the private equity firm will usually perform "pre-due diligence" based on public information to spot any preliminary "red flags." Discretion is important to keep the price low: if the market becomes aware of the intention to bid then the price will almost certainly rocket, which, in this early phase, is likely to sabotage the transaction. Overall, public-to-private transactions are expensive because a sizable premium is expected to be paid over the concurrent share price—a feature that is now well recognized, and a prime reason why this type of deal is less frequent than it used to be.

Partial ownership in a family business

Such an investment is usually a growth capital investment, often for expansion internationally. A family business has particularities related to the deal process itself as well as complex management and governance matters. Often, private equity is sought by families during a generational transition phase. Succession planning must be treated carefully, as many businesses struggle when the founder steps back. Where a family company has existed for generations, it is common to find situations where family tensions divert focus from management activities; this offers the private equity firm an opportunity to win the trust of the family members so they permit to consider the deal on an exclusive basis. But even in the case of an outright exit by the current owners, their chemistry with the new investors is important, which often tilt the weight in favor of a private equity partner vis-à-vis, say, another family investing.

Decisions in family businesses are typically centralized, and there may be a high dependency on the leading individual in terms of cooperation to move the process forward during the analysis and due diligence phases. Significant effort may be required to dig into unclear areas of the business. In other situations, when multiple family members hold (or squabble over) influence in the business, it may be harder to gain a strong grip on the intended process, especially if family members are not equally committed to the deal. In addition, it may be difficult to truly know the expectations of family members regarding their continued involvement in the business, their grasp of governance, and the proactive style of a private equity partner. More than in other situations, if management stays under the control of family members, there needs to be strong confidence in it before committing capital, as well as mechanisms to enforce a change if needed, particularly if the business deteriorates over time.

When the family maintains a majority in the business or has a strong influence through its particular emerging market location, the private equity investor must create a strong governance structure that provides alignment of interests and a meaningful ability to influence decisions; this is especially true when the family maintains direct managerial involvement. Measures can include not only a strong board representation but also veto rights and detailed reporting. Another important topic is the future exit. The intentions of the family members regarding their remaining shares should be clarified and understandings about selling the business in the future may be part of the agreement. As part of the legal due diligence, the investor needs to review the existing governance rules and negotiate changes to the shareholders' agreement early on.

Finally, if the location is an emerging market, an overseas investor must consider the range of extra risks (e.g., political, regulatory, and currency risks). Ideally, a local resource team should conduct the due diligence and review internal and external aspects of the business, including exit routes.[3] The assessment will support the decision about taking the risks and the maximum price to pay.

Distressed management buy-in (MBI)

Here, the opportunity is identified when a good business in a generally healthy market is managed by a weak management team, which, for some reason, has failed to be replaced by the current owners. When a business gets close to bankruptcy, the management team may find itself "under water" and new capital will be sought. This capital could come from existing equity holders, bank loans, mezzanine providers, or new equity investors. If the buyer is a private equity firm, the management team involved in the deteriorating situation will be replaced by an external management team. The new team is assembled by the private equity investor based on its turnaround and domain expertise. Often, the new management is part of the team that carries out the due diligence, and hence commands knowledge of the situation as well as being willing to commit to deliver the turnaround strategy. This arrangement also helps speed up the transition at the helm, and retains company knowledge.

Due diligence in a distressed situation must include a focus on working capital, cash flows, and the ability to service short-term liabilities or renegotiate contracts (e.g., add new debt, review terms of existing debt, work on trade arrangements with suppliers, etc.). For a successful turnaround, decisions need to be made very quickly, as each day of delay deteriorates the business further. The deal analysis and due diligence must prioritize the prime areas of risk and be conducted promptly. The fund will require warrants in the SPA to protect itself from hidden liabilities. One of the attractions of this type of investment is the significant discount that can be negotiated and the likelihood of an exclusive negotiation, which can potentially result in high investment multiples and IRRs upon exit. However, the risk is proportionally higher as well. Negotiations are complex due to the number of parties involved (e.g., equity holders, lenders, and suppliers). Some of the parties may want to keep an equity stake and benefit from a future upside, while others just want to maximize recovery and exit. In the case of a formal liquidation procedure, the ultimate decision is made by a court, and there is a risk of not having an approval after expending great effort spent on due diligence. Even when court consent is given, sometimes debtholders have the right to appeal, which drags on the uncertainty. Therefore, only specialized distress funds engage in this type of transaction, where special skill sets and operational experience are required in order to perform turnarounds and drive returns.

Corporate carve-out management buyout (MBO)

A sponsored carve-out scenario is where a company decides to divest a division for a strategic, regulatory, or financial reason, creating the opportunity for the private equity firm to partner with the existing management team to acquire the business. In a carve-out, there is a dependency between the divested business and the

---

[3] The chapter "Private Equity in Emerging Markets" includes a detailed discussion of aspects to be considered in the deal screening and due diligence processes in these locations.

parent company, which may remain in place, requiring an in-depth operational due diligence process. The functional segregation from the parent company will likely lead to significant one-off costs, such as building stand-alone administrative and IT infrastructure. Deal modeling should also account for carve-out topics (i.e., changes in the SG&A structure where expenses that used to be shared with the wider group will be carried on a smaller scale; e.g., legal costs, human resource-related services, insurance coverage, etc.).

High confidence in the management team is necessary in this situation and incentives should be well aligned to ensure a successful transaction and high post-deal performance. The motivations for the transaction must be clearly understood. The parent's exit may be related to declining prospects of the business itself, and the commercial due diligence should assess the company's ability to grow versus the threat of increasing competition and hence, a loss of market share. Projections prepared by the management team will be carefully scrutinized to remove biases and excess optimism, and the team's historical ability to meet forecasts will also be verified. Special attention should be given to the deal structure and the stake in the upside offered to the managers for motivation and alignment of interests.

Early stage venture investment

Start-ups do not have a track record of historical performance to be validated during due diligence, so the investment analysis relies solely on the review of projections and the risk assessment. The probability of loss is high in a venture investment, given the technological and business uncertainties. Therefore, the analysis will challenge all assumptions and drill down into risks related to the market (e.g., size, timing, adoption, etc.), business model (e.g., financial structure, partnerships, operations capacity, suppliers, etc.), execution (e.g., team experience, technology availability, etc.), and legal aspects (e.g., license requirements, regulations, etc.). Management's agility in responding to changing situations and ability to steer the business as needs dictate should be assessed. In addition, the exit route may be quite distant and additional rounds of funding are likely to be required. Investors need to ensure that enough funds are in reserve to participate in future rounds as a signal to external investors, and in order to reduce their equity dilution. Terms should also be designed in a way that active founders and management will retain their economic incentives.

Secondary buyout

Direct secondary transactions, commonly referred to as "secondary buyouts" or "sponsor-to-sponsor transactions," consist of acquiring portfolio companies sold by other private equity funds. The strategic deal screening in such cases should focus on the ability to enhance value in ways that were not available to the selling GP. For that purpose, the analysis takes into consideration the underlying reasons for selling the company, such as the fund reaching the end of its life or a motivation to lock in returns. The analysis should reveal challenges in the business which may have made it difficult for the selling private equity firm to exit earlier via a trade buyer.

The process of secondary buyouts is more straightforward than other transactions. Unlike acquiring from a family or an entrepreneur, there are no emotions involved, so the negotiation centers solely on the pricing and terms of the deal. The rules of the game are understood by both parties: legal terms and the valuation metric are commonly shared and experienced by both parties, which ensures a straightforward and quick process. The mechanics of the due diligence process are also more straightforward: when buying from a reputable institutional investor, the books are in order and there are detailed business plans so that management performance can be tracked and compared to past year targets. Management has experience working with private equity, which reduces the risk of unrealistic expectations. On the other hand, if management stands to receive a significant financial reward as part of the seller's exit, its motivation to continue in full force and energy must be validated; otherwise, a managerial backup should be ready for deployment, whether from the internal management bench or external talent.

Exhibit 3 summarizes the typical characteristics of the deal types described above. While many considerations are deal specific, the table highlights the foremost characteristics for each type of transaction. The higher the overall deal attractiveness and likelihood of closing the deal, the more likely the private equity firm will commit resources to move further in the screening process.

Exhibit 3: Summary of deal attractiveness and due diligence effort by deal type

	Public to private	Family business	Distressed	Carve-out	Venture	Secondary buyout
Price attractiveness	**Lower** *Premium over the stock price. Typically auction*	**Medium** *Often exclusive negotiation*	**Higher** *Significant discount (distress)*	**Medium** *Price may reflect a shared resources*	**Higher** *Early stage discount (but venture risk)*	**Medium** *Never a bargain*
Leverage capacity	**Higher** *Depends on the sector and existing leverage*	**Higher** *Country specific and the company's balance sheet*	**Lower** *Lacking a strong balance sheet*	**Higher** *Depends on the sector Limited current debt*	**Lower** *Early stage risk No earnings*	**Medium** *Depends on the existing capital structure*
Equity stake	**Higher** *Acquisition of 100% shares*	**Unknown** *Varies deal to deal*	**Higher** *Focused and labor intensive*	**Higher** *Parent company fully separates*	**Medium** *Depends on the stage and other co-investors*	**Higher** *Typically acquisition of 100% interest together with management*
Information availability	**Higher** *Transparency standards required for listed companies*	**Lower** *Typically lower governance standards*	**Medium** *Disclosure as part of administration processes*	**Medium** *Subsidiary specific information not always available*	**Higher** *Limited historic data but typically full transparency*	**Higher** *Transparency standards dictated by the PE sponsor*
Exit route availability	**Higher** *Typically available for a formerly public company*	**Higher** *Varies with the business and the location*	**Lower** *Long holding period to complete the turnaround*	**Higher** *Typically available for a business formerly part of a conglomerate*	**Lower** *Long holding period before exit*	**Higher** *Shorter holding period before exit*

ELEMENTS OF DEAL ANALYSIS

As discussed, deal analysis commences early in the screening cycle, when the private equity firm starts to assess the potential value and risks of the targeted company based on publicly available and network information. The process should be directed throughout by an investment thesis which is, at its simplest, a summary of the reasoning behind buying the business—that is, hypotheses of how the GP can enhance the value of the enterprise. Below are descriptions of core aspects of deal analysis and strategic due diligence that form the process of private equity investments.

Investment thesis

The investment thesis is the driving force of the work undertaken during a deal, and ultimately, the investment results. Consider, for example, two private equity firms. One is looking to buy into growing IT software within the financial sector; therefore, its goal is to find growth-minded companies at an emerging stage. A second private equity house is looking to buy and build around a portfolio company that provides outsourcing services to banks. While the first firm will concentrate its analysis on market growth, management, and R&D capability, the second firm will focus on potential overlaps and synergies, emphasizing the operational aspects much more.

Building an investment thesis is a critical skill for investment professionals, and it becomes even more important as the market further matures. By constantly challenging and iteratively testing and reconfiguring the deal rationale, it guides both the market and operational company diligence. With the data available to multiple potential buyers, the investment professional that spots the right way to view the sector or the company and makes sound judgments about what can be achieved with the business has the upper hand. A good investment thesis allows a realistic estimate of the price to pay at entry as well as a clear view on what to do with the business if the purchase succeeds.

The building blocks

Deal analysis is required before formal due diligence is conducted. This analysis is the means by which investment professionals assess the potential value of a target and the purchase price they are prepared to pay. The analysis can be broken down into several elements, as follows.

Purchase and exit valuation

Determining an appropriate valuation guides the deal analysis. In essence, this process determines the price that the fund is willing to pay, which it arrives at by considering the following:

Current and projected EBITDA

One of the prime components of valuation is EBITDA, since the price is usually a multiple of that figure. Main drivers are top line growth and margin developments for both direct (COGS) and indirect costs (SG&A). Instead of the EBITDA as reported in the income statement, the analyst will prepare a normalized version, where effects of non-recurring or non-operational items are eliminated. The adjusted historical EBITDA is usually referred to as pro forma, and is often prepared for the current year and the previous two to three years in order to spot underlying trends.

Consider the example in Exhibit 4: the reported EBITDA margin is 9% in 2019 and the EBITDA compound average growth rate (CAGR) in the period is 36%. However, after stripping the effects of an acquisition in 2017 ($5 million additional revenue of a division not included in the deal) and non-recurring restructuring (other) expenses in 2016 and 2017, the EBITDA margin in 2019 is 3% and the EBITDA CAGR is -25%. The analyst will need to understand the reasons for the performance deterioration in 2019, which could be due to a churn in major customers, excessive fixed costs, or changes in the competitive landscape. These changes may be deemed temporary or permanent, and that distinction will ultimately define the attractiveness of the business. Will the private equity firm be able to implement a strategy change, or hire a more successful management team to turn around a business with negative revenue and EBITDA growth? Starting from this baseline, the most critical part of the analysis will be evaluating what the new investor can realistically achieve in terms of sales and margin growth during the ownership period.

Exhibit 4: Example of reported and normalized EBITDA (in $ millions)

Reported	2016	2017	2018	2019	Normalized	2016	2017	2018	2019
Revenue	100	105	108	112	Revenue	100	100	102	99
COGS	-60	-61	-63	-64	COGS	-60	-60	-62	-61
Gross profit		44	45	48	*Gross profit*	40	40	40	38
Admin expenses	-9	-10	-10	-11	Admin expenses	-9	-9	-9	-10
Sales expenses	-12	-13	-14	-15	Sales expenses	-12	-12	-12	-13
Other expenses	-15	-16	-12	-12	Other expenses	-12	-12	-12	-12
EBITDA	4	5	9	10	*EBITDA*	7	7	7	3
margin	4%	5%	8%	9%	*margin*	7%	7%	7%	3%
CAGR				36%	*CAGR*				-25%

Entry and exit multiple

The potential entry and exit multiples will determine the right level of consideration to be paid for the prospective company. Normally, the exit should generally follow the same multiple as the entry, unless some exceptional circumstances occur where it is possible to add value by multiple expansion. In fact, in some investments, there are multiple reductions because the growth opportunities of the company may be lower at exit.

The multiple is driven by market factors but can be heavily influenced by other factors as well, including the following:

- **The company's "story":** Creating the right positioning for a company greatly enhances the chance of a successful exit. Firms should build a strong operating platform that could be the springboard for further acquisitions. Moreover, a reduction of dependencies (e.g., broadening the customer base and hence, the addressable market, diversifying the products, or increasing the international reach) will have a positive impact on the multiple.

- **Timing:** Multiples for an industry, as a whole, rise and fall with the economy and market sentiment, particularly for companies active in highly cyclical industries. However, "catching a wave" should not be a major part of an investment thesis as predicting such waves is difficult, and will also influence the pricing decision of prospective buyers if they identify the cyclical impact on the asset.

- **Institutionalization:** Acquiring a firm coming from a family-owned business may be conceived as riskier than acquiring firms out of a secondary transaction. In most cases the long-term systems and procedures (e.g., developing ERP and reporting standards, the introduction of compliance processes, or a thoroughly developed strategy which is followed throughout the organizations) will give prospective buyers more confidence and therefore have a positive effect on the multiple.

Future cash flow

While EBITDA is considered the main source for cash flow, an investor should also account for capex, working capital needs, tax payments, and other sources and uses of cash. The cash flow profile of assets is one of the most important features analyzed. An asset-heavy business model with a lower cash conversion cycle will have different implications for the investment case than an asset-light business model with high cash conversion rates. Cash flow generation also influences the ability to use leverage (i.e., debt financing) in order to finance the funding of the transaction. In some cases, the private equity firm will prefer to return a portion of the investment through a recapitalization or by distributing profits from operations in interim periods before an outright exit, while in others, deleveraging may take priority. Clearly, the pattern of payouts directly influences the investment IRR, which is one of the main metrics of private equity performance.

Value of specific assets

Some private equity firms invest specifically in situations where particular assets—tangible or intangible—are presented as impaired or toxic but the assessment of the new investor is that their true value is higher. Finding a way to unlock this hidden value can change the valuation radically. In popular parlance, this might be referred to as "asset stripping." However, even where disposing of assets is not part of the investment thesis, a view of the underlying value of assets is critical to striking the right price. Furthermore, a disposal of non-core assets could provide funding for an early distribution or deleveraging, or be used to fund capex. If the realized selling price of such non-core assets is higher than their book value, it will result in a windfall increase in net asset value (NAV) relatively early on in the investment cycle.

Financial structure

In general, any funding structure will consist of equity, debt, and quasi-equity/debt instruments. Debt is the instrument which leverages the investment to magnify returns (positive or negative) to equity holders. The riskiness of the business and the potential risk of loss are uppermost in investors' minds and therefore play the main role in deciding on the right amount of debt. A second consideration is the cost of borrowing. Although interest is tax deductible to a certain amount (depending on the jurisdiction), net-of-tax debt service payments should be factored in the company's cash flow forecast. All of the above is iteratively considered in the analysis and the discussions with the bank.

As an example of a very simple funding structure, if a private equity firm is carrying out an all-equity deal, there is only one investment committee to be persuaded and one unique set of requirements to be satisfied during the analysis and due diligence. In contrast, if a complex and highly leveraged funding structure is created, it may require approvals of credit committees from multiple debtholders, mezzanine players, and other equity providers. In the latter case, substantial third-party consultancy support is required to generate detailed assessment and documentation, and particularly, to ensure the fund structure will provide for proper repayment to all the sources of capital under reasonable forecasting scenarios. The debt financing providers require detailed documentation of the due diligence reports produced and provided by the sponsor. Furthermore, the parties agree on an investment case with an underlying cash profile. In order to limit the risk of a payment default, debt financing providers usually require covenants. Such covenants include informative covenants (e.g., reporting), general undertakings (business behavior and restrictions), and financial covenants. The latter consists of earnings- and cash-related covenants, such as the leverage ratio, the interest coverage, the cash coverage, a capex covenant, or others. In case the actual financials deteriorate and deviate from the initial agreed investment case, a breach of covenants triggers certain actions where private equity firms together with the underlying company need to renegotiate credit agreements to the benefit of the financing providers.

The financial structure defines the sources of deal capital as a function of cost, seniority, and investment stage. Debt used to represent up to 70–80% of the investment funding, depending on the sector (e.g., cash-generating infrastructure projects tend to absorb higher project finance loan rates), although recently, it has been limited to around 50%. Equity is usually a plug figure in the structure to complete the requirements in terms of use of capital. A private equity firm may be the only equity provider, or associate with other funds or individuals (e.g., co-investment by its LPs or managers in an MBO or MBI). Equity represents the riskier and more expensive source of capital since its holders receive their claims only after all debtholders and other creditors are paid. The compensation for this risk is that equity providers get the full upside of the business.

Debt is less risky and a cheaper source as repayment is more protected, but typically with no upside. Debt is often structured in tranches of different seniority. Secured loans are cheaper but require collateral. Unsecured debt is more expensive as there are no assets in guarantee. Mezzanine is a high-yield instrument with a cash element, a paid-in-kind element, and sometimes even an equity-kicker, typically aiming to bridge cash needs for the funding. Some instruments are considered hybrid, such as preferred shares, which receive fixed dividends and have priority over ordinary shares, convertible bonds that can participate in the company's upside if exercised, and venture loans that combine debt with warrants.

Further flexibility is available for funding larger transactions. High-yield debt instruments are available where part of the interest is in payment in kind (PIK) or PIK toggle. This approach reduces the ongoing debt service burden and also diminishes the chance of default. Another instrument, "covenant-lite" debt, is widely available to finance large leveraged buyouts. Covenant-lite loans proved to be most effective in helping many firms to survive the latest global financial crisis, as harsh covenants would have triggered a default in many situations.

Building a model

Together with the valuation and the capital structure, the model will determine the basis of the transaction for all of its economic decisions (i.e., purchase price, degree of leverage, investment case, etc.). It consists of a projection of the business's future performance measured by the financial reports—income statement, balance sheet, and cash flow. By modeling these elements, the analyst will look at revenue and margin growth, working capital and capex needs, debt repayment, availability for distribution, and ratios (e.g., profitability, performance, solvency, and liquidity) over the investment period. A discounted cash flow (DCF) is typically part of the model, so that enterprise value (EV) is estimated. In a leveraged buyout, a significant amount of debt is added at the start and the model will include the schedule of partial or full repayment by the exit.

At a minimum, a model will address two scenarios—a base and a stretch case—but often, it will go further and allow for multiple possible outcomes. The stretch case also helps to determine the amount of leverage the company can bear by considering scenarios in which covenants could be broken or there could be a payment default (i.e., non-fulfilment of debt service). There are no strict rules to define the variables for the sensitivity analysis; a judgment ought to be made about what is more critical or uncertain in each deal. This judgment dictates the factors on which the due diligence should concentrate. It is only worth focusing on parameters that materially influence the soundness and potential of the transaction. With all the costs and time pressures, it is important to focus on only the most sensitive factors, even at the expense of a more superficial examination of many other parts of the business.

Ownership structure

Substantial effort will often go into designing the target company's ownership structure and modeling its changes up to the exit. The aim is to define the percentages of ownership, claims on assets, rights and obligations, and legal consequences of the structure. The ownership structure also considers tax implications for the parties, provisions for early breakup, and conditions for integration with other portfolio companies or the entry of new equity partners, to name a few examples. In terms of exit, the ownership structure impacts the stake to be sold to a strategic buyer or floated in the future. Majority ownership is typically desired to ensure control, but is not necessary. Exit-related rules (e.g., drag-along and tag-along, right of first refusals, etc.) must be aligned between the different classes of shareholders. The ability to influence the company's decisions can also be achieved through board and preferred voting rights. In some cases, another factor to consider is the dilution of shareholders in the event of exercising stock options, warrants, and convertible securities. Consequently, great importance is placed on the drawing of shareholder agreements, where the rights and obligations of all shareholders (e.g., the private equity firm, managers, board members, other shareholders, etc.) are described. At the beginning of the screening process, the main rules can be summarized in a term sheet, which is then developed over the course of the process into a fully formulated shareholder agreement before it is ultimately signed.

Integration plan

The final part of a deal analysis is the formulation of a plan to deliver the investment thesis, often as either a "100-day plan" or "full potential program." The more the deal rationale relies on operational changes, the more important is the integration plan. While an outline plan is not a formal part of due diligence, it is often prepared as an adjunct report; this is normally the case in leveraged deals where banks want to be confident that a clear plan is in place to deliver at least the base case scenario.

A typical 100-day plan would cover the actions along the first months of ownership in terms of the management team, organizational changes, and prioritized projects (e.g., cost reduction, working capital release, etc.). A full potential program focuses on the entire investment horizon (around three to five years) and sets out the priorities and requirements to achieve the investment thesis objectives from the strategic, operational, and financial perspectives. With the increasing professionalization of the private equity industry, increased documentation of a full potential program covering operational steps (e.g., how to convert a strategy into operational measures, and continued controlling of milestones and key performance indicators) has become common.

MAIN TASKS WITHIN THE DUE DILIGENCE PROCESS

As outlined above, due diligence is the assessment of all aspects of the target company, aiming to identify both opportunities and risks. Depending on the initial number of bidders, the seller will give access to a limited amount of information at a pre-due diligence stage, followed by the full due diligence, in which a shortlist of selected bidders will participate. The pre-due-diligence stage enables the private equity firm to either make a bid or decide to withdraw without bidding. During the formal due diligence process, a range of specific issues will be reviewed with full access, normally over a period of a few weeks; only in exceptional circumstances would a firm want to spend much longer than that on due diligence as it is highly distracting to both management and staff from the normal day-to-day business.

A non-exhaustive list of topics covered in a due diligence is described below.

Financial results

It is essential for the buyer to understand the target company's underlying performance in order to construct a clear picture of the company. The private equity firm may make its own determination of real results or, more often, employ external advisers to review the financial records in detail (i.e., typically full financial statements of the previous three to five years). The results are then summarized in a financial due diligence report, which is not only for the benefit of the equity sponsor but also used by external debt financing providers while preparing their credit application memoranda. The most current trading figures will be provided, along with other documentation like copies of commercial contracts. Hence, granting full open access to the books is required at some point in the due diligence process. Sources of profitability and losses, dependencies on business units, geographies, and sales channels are analyzed, which can be quite comprehensive in cases of complex international and diversified businesses.

The external adviser charged with the assessment of the performance will often demand time with the CFO and his or her team to drill down into the figures, identify unusual and one-off items, and attempt to construct a view of the true underlying results. The due diligence report will typically review each of the financial statements in detail, showing which movements are due to normal trading and which are not part of ongoing operations. The analysis will depict the trends identified, highlighting both positives and negatives.

Another aspect of the review is the assessment of the budget, forecast documents, and business plan provided by the seller. However, these materials are not always available, because while management is expected to make projections for the next few years, this may not be the case for small or family businesses. If applicable, the financial due diligence report will examine historical deviations from the financial forecasts, and the overall soundness of the figures. Generally, the private equity firm will want to check if budgets and forecasts are robustly produced and ascertain whether they are aspirational (built to create hard-to-reach objectives) or realistic (built to allow financial planning).

Commercial and operational opportunities

The investment thesis drives the due diligence process to explore opportunities along the following dimensions:

- Growth through products and services, distribution channels, geographies, or customer segments.
- Improving efficiency and growing margins through cost cutting, process improvements, and other efficiencies.
- Generating cash or releasing working capital and repaying capital sources quickly.

Growth opportunities are often investigated through the review of the markets in which the target company operates. The review aims to spot trends and the firm's relative positioning compared to its competitors. This analysis normally drills down to customer and product segment levels, enabling the projection of the top-line growth supported by concrete actions to achieve it. Therefore, such a report will review both the growth potential of the sector and the relative competitiveness of the target company.

Profit improvement opportunities are formulated through a review of the operating capabilities of the company. Conducting such a review typically involves visits at central facilities and detailed discussions on processes and organizational topics with the CEO, the COO, and other members of the management team. The review aims to identify short-, medium-, and long-term efficiency opportunities, including quick wins and required capital investments or additional human capital needed to implement the strategies. A prioritized list of such opportunities will feed into the valuation prepared by the private equity firm.

A dual strategic aspect in many sectors is exposure to the array of technological changes transforming industries in sweeping and unprecedented ways since the Industrial Revolution, particularly the digitalization of business models. Retail, automotive, banking, healthcare, entertainment, and tourism are obvious examples of industries where revolution is in full swing. Technology has to be factored into the analysis, not only in terms of product efficiency but also in order to foresee and anticipate dramatic shifts that may jeopardize the entire business or offer an opportunity.[4]

Management team

One of the most critical success factors in a private equity acquisition is the management team in charge of executing the investment plan. The due diligence will clarify whether the existing team is suitable or whether changes will be necessary. This decision will be driven by the plans for the business after acquisition. For example, a CEO who has been very successful leading the turnaround of a leading local company may not have the capabilities to expand the business internationally or to manage a conglomerate after an extensive vertical consolidation program. Similarly, in a carve-out, managers who performed very well when managing a company that was once a division of a larger enterprise may not have the right mind-set to successfully run an independent business, let alone become entrepreneurs. In many private equity firms, structural processes (e.g., assessment centers, psychological interviews, etc.) are part of an institutionalized process.

Retention of skilled talent is also a concern in a corporate restructuring. The investor should create an incentive plan to ensure that highly valuable personnel will not leave the company, or at least that this knowledge will be transferred to the new team. Typically, private equity firms will pay significant compensation packages to ensure that the right people will be in place to run the business. Incentives usually include equity and bonuses, and other provisions are likely to be added to the shareholder agreement and/or employment agreements, such as a non-compete clause for the founders or a minimum period over which key executives must remain in the company.

Risks

The risk analysis can be broken down into three broad categories:

- Market risk
- Operational risk

---

[4] Standout cases are the disappearance of the previously most prosperous Yellow Pages industry, as well as travel agencies, bookstores, toy stores, and other high street retailers.

- Environmental/legal risk

Market risks consist of systemic factors such as macro-economic cycles, political risks, and foreign exchange exposure. For example, a private equity firm may decide not to pursue a deal after concluding that the current fundamentals of an industry are fragile because of a technological transformation. Alternatively, the investors may identify promising opportunities to shift to a new growing market using the capabilities available in the current business. Whether positive or negative, a deep understanding of market risks is a fundamental part of the decision.

Assessing operational risk is often complex as it requires a detailed review of the company's capabilities, staff, and facilities. A third-party operations consultancy is often hired to conduct such a review, as a high degree of sector experience is required. The assessment will typically involve a review of the following aspects:

- **Management capability**: Are the competencies in place to deliver the business plan? Does management have credible plans and credentials to achieve short- and medium-term targets? What is management's leadership style to inspire and direct employees and delegate and complete tasks? Are the sales and marketing functions prepared to perform ambitious growth plans?

- **Facilities**: Do the factories have enough capacity for growth? Are there safety concerns? Will higher output levels trigger labor or environmental concerns? Some of these risks should be assessed through a formal review of environmental audit report as health and safety topics have become an increasingly more important compliance issue.

- **Sales and contracts**: What percentage of future revenue is already contracted? What is the actual backlog and what are the booking expectations in the sales funnel? Is the order pipeline robust? What attitude are customers likely to take upon the change of ownership? Some customer groups are loyal to the business founder, especially in the services sector. What risk is there that an important salesperson or customer will leave if new owners wish to adjust procedures or contracts? Such risks can be tested by means of customer and employee interviews.

Having full access to sites and documentation will enable the private equity firm to perform an environmental and legal risk assessment of the business and to determine the probability and impact of unfavorable events. The due diligence is the opportunity to investigate, in detail, the red flags identified during the commercial review. Permissions and regulatory compliance will be verified as part of the analysis, and areas of uncertainty may require a formal legal opinion.

It is quite common that risks identified during the due diligence can make private equity firms walk away from deals. Imagine a situation where a division of a pharmaceutical firm for sale is the subject of court actions for claimed health injuries linked to a product. If the liability is confirmed, the cost for the shareholders could be unbearable. If the current parent company was unwilling to exclude this product from the sale, would you put forward an offer, having identified this risk? Similarly, a careful risk assessment is needed in the case of a company where some of its core patents are contested or about to expire. The private equity firm wants to spot major risks like this as early as possible, before considerable resources are spent in fees and opportunity costs are sunk. Another option is to cover uncertain risks identified within the SPA under the warranties. Nowadays, so-called representations and warranties insurance (R&WI) can cover these risks, where the premium depends on the estimated likelihood of occurrence and the potential financial consequences. Such insurance is already an integral part of acquisition processes.

Strategic plan

In many cases, the target company's management will have developed a multi-year business or strategic plan. Where such a plan exists, the bidders will need to validate projections and assumptions behind the base case as well as the conservative and optimistic scenarios. A high degree of judgment and market experience is needed to challenge the views of a team that knows the business closely. The private equity firm will likely point to a different direction compared to the strategic plan because the investment thesis should differ from what the company would do itself. In other words, the GP should be able to add value through a new set of hypotheses and initiatives that the business would not consider otherwise.

PERSPECTIVES OF STAKEHOLDERS

In the discussions above, we focused on the point of view of the buyer (the private equity firm) and also touched on that of the seller. At this point, it is useful to consider other stakeholders engaged in the process in order to understand their perspectives.

Management

The interests of senior managers are rarely fully aligned with either the existing or the new owner, although they will generally have a financial interest in maximizing the sales price in case they are already existing shareholders. In fact, they have a duty to the shareholders to do so. But on the other hand, they may also expect to participate in the business going forward, which prompts a positive and congenial relationship with the bidders. In addition to playing a central role in the diligence process, senior management will consider the transaction in the broadest way. Often the consideration paid will depend largely on the company's performance (particularly revenues and the EBITDA), which creates incentives for the management to manipulate the operating figures to "look good" in the period before an acquisition.

Management usually bears the pressure to create a promising business plan and to dress up the plans in order to increase the chances of selling the company on behalf of the existing owners. On the flip side, if the potential is exaggerated, there is a risk of not meeting the target when the deal comes through, or not having space for a positive performance surprise. The bidder and its advisers will try to get to know the managers during the sales process in order to understand their level of commitment and potential biases.

Lenders

Lenders' duties in the transaction are to receive fees and interest income while carefully considering the risk exposure. Knowing that bidders will aim to present evidence that risks are low in order to borrow on the best terms, lenders will look not only at the private equity firm's reviews and due diligence reports, but also at the plans put forward by management and reports by other advisers. Independent third parties will be particularly important sources for analysis. In some processes, sellers and their advisers may make business presentations to the banks—even ahead of the sales process—in order to indicate to the prospective bidders the range of debt available for the transaction. Success in improving the initial perception of the business would lead to an increased debt capacity and hence, an improvement in the company's value.

Lenders will typically review ratios such as debt to equity and interest coverage, and demand more information as they identify business and execution risks. In the case of high perceived risk, the lenders' credit committees will decide to increase the borrowing cost or not concede credit. The more areas of concern are identified, the more lenders will want to explore the deal, leading to higher costs and time consumed during the due diligence process. As part of the borrowing negotiation, the bank will also be approached for a revolving credit facility to cover the routine business and a capex facility.

Advisers

Like other participants, advisers also have conflicts of interest to cope with. When hired by a potential buyer, the consultant's interest is to provide good advice and ample warning of key risks, but eventually, if that advice is overly cautious, a good investment opportunity may be missed. On the other hand, if a transaction takes place, there may be other services to be provided to the portfolio company as part of the restructuring process, which may lead to an adviser bias.

The consultant also bears the real and considerable risk of being sued, since any advice that it provides is usually relied upon. Providing advice on such a basis essentially means the consultant agrees to give a degree of indemnity to the recipients by ensuring it is not false or fraudulent. This degree of indemnity is a significant issue, as fees ranging around low hundreds of thousands of revenue may revert into tens or hundreds of millions of liability, which represents a disproportionate financial and reputational risk for the adviser. Therefore, advisers try to cap their liability to the sponsors. Typically, when reports are to be shared with third parties (e.g., banks) or the reliance rules are strict, the advisers' reports tend to be blander in order to minimize exposure.

In his own words: Jörg Mugrauer, Partner at Quadriga Capital, Germany

As competition increases steadily in maturing private equity markets, attractive targets are become scarce. Clearly defined and institutionalized deal sourcing, screening, and due diligence processes are a prerequisite for the success of every GP.

Over the last decade, the whole private equity universe—comprising GPs, their advisers, experts, M&A houses, financing partners, and buyout managers—has become much more professional and sophisticated, leading to higher quality standards and faster executions. "Plain vanilla" approaches, which worked well in the past, will in many cases no longer be sufficient to succeed, particularly in highly competitive auction processes.

With respect to deal sourcing, many GPs have established a broad network of senior executives and industry specialists supporting them in the identification of potential targets before they are addressed by intermediaries and investment banks. In addition to the deal flow offered through investment banks and investment boutiques, which is essential for deploying the money of LPs in a competitive environment, Quadriga Capital has a long history of generating a larger proportion of "proprietary deals" out of its network.

We exchange industrial, market, and methodological knowhow in regular institutionalized network circles. And even if the potential target is eventually sold through an auction process, the GP may have an advantage because of its proprietary knowledge and its ability to execute the transaction within a short period of time, a benefit which could be essential in getting the deal done. Many GPs in the leverage buyout asset class have organized their deal screening efforts vertically in industry sectors in order to address specific industry sectors and its needs more accurately. Some are even specializing in only one industry or a few industry niches as a differentiating factor.

While, from a private equity perspective, buy-side activities are still executed by local deal teams in most cases, on the sell side, the globalization and digitalization have led to a much broader set of potential acquirers, particularly corporates. Transnational or transcontinental deals have increased significantly in recent years.

Professionalism has also increased in due diligence processes. In conjunction with digitalization, most due diligence processes have shortened: virtual data rooms provide access to information independent from location, and decisions and assessments can be (and need to be) drawn quicker. As in the deal sourcing processes, the GPs rely on established and trusted networks of advisers. While in the past, a basic layout of a strategy and a first-100-day plan were sufficient to cover investment proposals, nowadays, the full-potential of value creation needs to be captured already during the due diligence phase; this includes, for example, long-term investment hypotheses, scenario analyses, operational improvement plans, dedicated roll-out or add-on strategies management assessment and selection, and so forth, in order to determine the best entrepreneurial decisions going forward.

During the deal screening and due diligence processes, but also during the holding period, we need to bring various nationalities, cultures, and mind-sets together. This is why we at Quadriga Capital aim to think like an industrial entrepreneur, while acting decisively and caretaking like a family business. We aim to apply systematic monitoring and structured analyses like larger corporations, while still assessing risk and return like a financial investor. Mastering these challenges with an entrepreneurial spirit is the real joy of our daily work.

2 Private Equity in Emerging Markets

The phrase "emerging markets" means different things to different people and is often reduced to the unhelpful tautology that emerging markets are "emerging" because they have not "emerged".
Anonymous

INTRODUCTION

Emerging economies represent over 80% of the world's population and landmass. While their share in the global capital market has grown quickly, this growth has been from a relatively small base. Emerging economic regions continually seek resources to fund the large demand in sectors such as infrastructure, energy, and consumer goods. Private equity plays an expanding role in these markets, alongside multinational corporations and domestic wealthy investors.

A discussion of the private equity landscape in emerging economies is inherently difficult due to the very diverse characteristics of these markets. As a result, any generalizations that we may make about the causes and consequences of the investment activity in these countries are disputable. Nevertheless, in this chapter, we attempt to provide a basic framework to describe what we think are the most important issues associated with investing in emerging markets.

Emerging markets hold several attractions for investors: growing domestic purchase power, improving macroeconomic conditions, a more developed physical and legal infrastructure, increased receptivity of governments to foreign investors, and the prospect of scalability across countries or regions. In addition, emerging markets can help institutional investors in their overall asset allocation as part of global diversification, which is why, in particular, they seek exposure to the largest and fastest-growing emerging markets (notably, China).[1]

Many investors initially dip their toe into emerging markets through public equities, which have traditionally offered exposures that were reasonably uncorrelated with developed market equities. Over time, however, returns from publicly traded emerging market securities have become more correlated with those of developed markets. Bain & Company found that cross-asset correlations between emerging market and developed market equities increased from 38% between 1990 and 1995 to 74% between 2005 and 2010. Beyond market concentration, emerging market exchanges also suffer from sector concentration. Private equity, on the other hand, offers greater diversification through access to the consumer, healthcare, industrial, energy, and IT sectors.

---

[1] The sheer growth of emerging markets is seen in the statistics of the Asian macro-economy. Within a decade, the number of "trillion-dollar" economies in Asia-Pacific grew from three to five in 2017, equalizing their number to Europe. Nearly all emerging Asian economies doubled or tripled their GDP over that decade; leading the pack was China, which grew four times, becoming the world's second-largest economy. Vietnam's economy doubled, and India's and Indonesia's economies grew by about 150% during the same 10-year period. (Source: World Bank, "World Development Indicators," September 15, 2017.)

At the same time, emerging countries are a heterogeneous group with important differences across the spectrum. The pace of political change and the size of economic gains have not been uniform. Furthermore, progress is often not inertial but rather, wildly cyclical as political instability can reverse positive trends and introduce turbulence and chaos into the economies.[2]

For these reasons, the development of market institutions and a business climate to enable effective corporate governance has been slow and difficult to achieve in many emerging economies. The lack of well-defined property rights and strong legal frameworks in some countries is an additional hurdle. However, domestic policies are becoming more market-oriented and governments are opening their countries to foreign markets and joining regional trading associations.

While offering unparalleled growth opportunities, emerging economies also present more complications in the investment decision process and the learning curve is steeper. As we discuss below, these complications should be mitigated by local knowledge, an understanding of the relevant risks, and a thorough due diligence process.

WHAT ARE EMERGING COUNTRIES?

There is no uniform and unambiguous definition of the term "emerging countries." Coined by economists at the International Finance Corporation of the World Bank (IFC) in the early 1980s, it replaced the earlier term "less developed countries," which was thought by some to be politically incorrect. Since the new label was created, it has become pervasive in the media, foreign policy debates, and capital markets, but definitions of the term vary widely. An emerging country can be defined as a country that satisfies two criteria: (1) it is in a transitional stage, typically moving from a closed to an open economy and having embarked on a reform path, and (2) it faces a rapid pace of economic development, undertaking significant efforts to improve its economic performance to catch up with the economies of more advanced nations.

The classification of "emerging countries" is most acute for multinational trade agreements, foreign aid, and capital market classifications and regulations. The main criteria used by the International Monetary Fund (IMF) to classify countries as advanced economies and developing economies were (1) per capita income level, (2) export diversification (in particular, many oil and gas exporters with a high per capita GDP would not make the advanced classification as the majority of the countries' exports are these energy resources), and (3) degree of integration into the global financial system. However, these are not the only factors in deciding the classification of countries. As stated in the WEO Statistical Appendix, "[The classification of emerging markets] is not based on strict criteria, economic or otherwise, and it has evolved over time." Reclassification only happens due to significant change, or when the case for change in terms of the three above criteria becomes overwhelming. For example, Lithuania joining the Eurozone was a significant change in circumstances that warranted a reclassification from an emerging market and developing economy to an advanced economy. Emphasizing the fluid nature of the category, political scientist Ian Bremmer defines an emerging market as "a country where politics matters at least as much as economics to the markets."

In 1988, MSCI Inc. launched the Emerging Markets Index, which originally consisted of just 10 countries representing less than 1% of world market capitalization, but has since been expanded to include 23 countries

---

[2] Notable cases where historically positive economic development trends have been recently reversed are Egypt, Ukraine, and Brazil, all on the grounds of political instability. On the other hand, Mexico, Argentina, India, and Myanmar are on a strong upswing, also purely driven by political change.

representing 10% of world market capitalization. According to MSCI, an emerging market is a country that has some characteristics of a developed market, but does not meet the standards to actually become one; this includes countries that may become developed markets in the future or were in the past. The term "frontier market" is common parlance for developing countries with economies that are too small to be considered an emerging market.

In common practice, Japan, Singapore, Taiwan, and South Korea in Asia, Canada and the United States in Northern America, Australia and New Zealand in Oceania, and Western Europe are considered "developed" regions. In international trade statistics, the Southern African Customs Union is also treated as a developed region and Israel as a developed country; countries emerging from the former Yugoslavia are treated as developing countries; and countries within Eastern Europe and the former USSR countries in Europe are not included under either developed or developing regions. The four largest emerging and developing economies by either nominal or PPP-adjusted GDP are Brazil, Russia, India, and China (the so-called "BRIC" countries). The next five largest markets are South Korea (though it is considered a developed market), Mexico, Indonesia, Turkey, and Nigeria.

GLOBAL STATISTICS

The magnitude of private equity investment in emerging markets is displayed in Exhibit 1. Total funds raised during the period from 2012 to 2015 averaged $47 billion per year. Interestingly, capital deployed during this period was lagging, with an annual average of $31 billion. Hence, there is a significant build-up of capital overhang in these markets, which is an indication of the difficulties in finding and executing suitable investments compared to fund raising. Exhibit 2 shows the total unrealized assets under management and committed but undrawn funds ("dry powder") in emerging markets; it corresponds to the previous exhibit by accumulating the funds raised over time and subtracting distributions. Exhibit 2 shows that over the last decade, the commitment by limited partners (LPs) to investment in emerging markets has grown over tenfold.

Exhibit 1: Private equity fundraising and investment in emerging markets (in US$ billions)

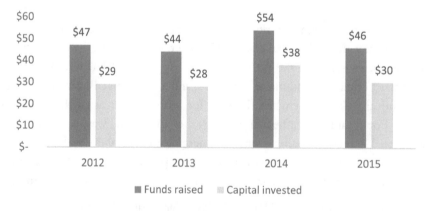

Source: EMPEA Industry Statistics Q1 2016

Exhibit 2: Emerging markets private equity assets under management, 2005–2016

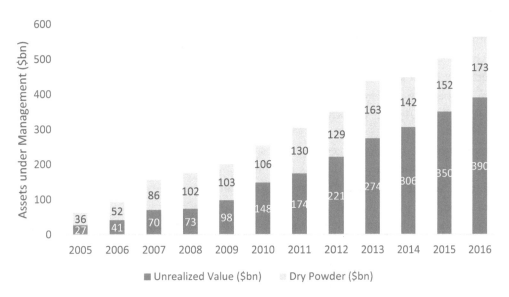

Source: Preqin Private Equity & Venture Capital Spotlight, December 2017

Exhibit 3: Number of emerging markets fund managers by region

Source: *Preqin Special Report: Private Equity in Emerging Markets*, June 2016.

As of September 2015, there have been record levels of assets under management ($208 billion) and in dry powder commitments ($89 billion). The majority of emerging markets-based private equity fund managers are located in Asia, especially Greater China, but the number of funds in other regions is also significant (see Exhibit 3). There may be an indication of some saturation in the market as the number of funds closed is declining. There has been an average of 250 emerging market-focused funds raised annually during 2008–2015, with a peak (335) in 2011 and a steady decline afterwards (only 199 funds closed during 2015).[3]

Exhibits 4 and 5 show the global geographical split of private equity fundraising and investment, respectively. Fundraising during 2011–2015 was dominated by the United States (over 50%), whereas the share of emerging markets only averaged 15%, with a significant percentage decline in recent years. Since the absolute level of emerging market fundraising has remained roughly constant, this result reflects the bullish fundraising environment in the United States and Western Europe during recent years. Within emerging markets, the vast majority of fundraising was for Asia: 80% of the funds greater than $100 billion closed in 2014–2015. The second most popular destination during the period was Latin America (9% of the total), followed by funds for Africa (5.6%), Central and Eastern Europe (4.1%), and the Middle East (the remaining 1.2%).

Not surprisingly, the average fund raised for emerging markets is smaller in size than for developed economies. For example, nearly 70% of the total funding was raised for funds below $250 million in size. The comparable figure for North American and European fund raising was 59%. As a final piece of emerging markets fundraising statistics, the allocation within private equity during the period from January 2012 through March 2016 shows that the vast majority (80%) is either replacement capital control deals or growth capital minority deals. The remaining capital went to infrastructure and real estate (11%) and private credit (9%).

Exhibit 4: Emerging markets as a percentage of global private equity fundraising (in US$ billions)

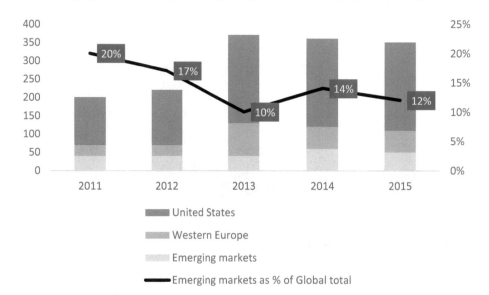

Source: EMPEA Industry Statistics Q1 2016, data as of December 31, 2015. Includes private equity, credit infrastructure, and real assets.

[3] Data in this section is drawn from *Preqin Special Report: Private Equity in Emerging Markets,* June 2016; EMPEA Industry Statistics 2015; and EMPEA Industry Statistics Q1 2016.

Exhibit 5: Emerging markets as a percentage of global private equity investment (in US$ billions)

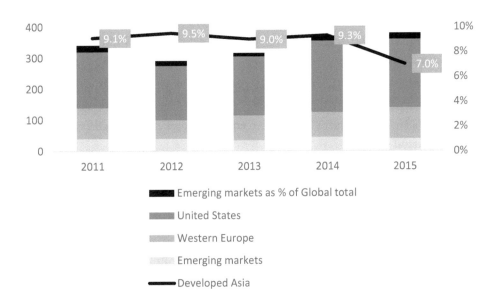

Source: EMPEA Industry Statistics Q1 2016, data as of December 31, 2015. Includes private equity, credit infrastructure, and real assets.

FUNDING SOURCES

Global pensions, endowments, and foundations are the main financial sponsors of private equity funds in emerging markets. In addition, there is a fast-growing trend of domestic pensions across Latin America, India, and Africa that invest in private equity domestically. Global governmental funding is also available for emerging markets through two important sources: sovereign wealth funds and development finance institutions.

Sovereign wealth funds

Sovereign wealth funds (SWFs) are state-owned funds which invest abroad as well as domestically and, unlike central bank reserves, are free to invest in less liquid and risker assets to seek better returns. As of March 2016, they manage $6.5 trillion of assets, over double the $3.1 trillion of assets under management in 2008.[4] Most SWFs were created through commodity exports (mainly oil) that were either taxed or owned by the government. Other SWFs were formed through transfers of assets from official foreign exchange reserves or from national budget surpluses (e.g., in China and Singapore). The largest SWFs in the world are the Government Pension Fund of Norway, Abu Dhabi Investment Authority (ADIA), China Investment Corporation (CIC), and SAMA Foreign Holdings in Saudi Arabia. Very large SWFs also exist in Singapore, South Korea, Kuwait, and Qatar.

---

[4] Preqin Private Equity Spotlight, June 2016.

Although these funds entered private equity relatively late, they have moved up quickly in their allocation to the asset class. Relative to other institutional investors, SWFs typically have a greater tolerance for illiquidity, and for the long-term horizons common in private equity. A recent survey finds that their average allocation to private equity has been 15%; however, among the more seasoned SWFs, the allocation has grown consistently to reach considerably more.[5]

Since many of the SWFs are located in Asia and the Middle East, they are more comfortable with investments in emerging markets than Western pension funds and other institutional investors. A recent survey indicates that SWFs are nearly equally attracted to emerging markets (60%) and to North America and globally in general (both stand at 65%).[6]

Development finance institutions and international financial institutions

Development finance institutions (DFIs) are specialized financial arms of developed countries to invest in developing economies. International financial institutions (IFIs) are similar to DFIs, except that they are chartered by more than one country; thus, they are subject to international law. Other multilateral institutions with a similar remit include regional development banks. The mandate of all of these institutions is to provide financing for commercial entities that promote development, and especially ones that fail to attract private investment but are important from a social or development perspective. As such, the majority of the activities of DFIs and IFIs are in developing economies.

In Europe, the advent of development banking can be traced back to the mid-19th century, when it was established to meet the demand for medium- to long-term capital by new and emerging enterprises during the Industrial Revolution. The years following the Second World War saw the establishment of DFIs in additional developed countries to provide medium- and long-term financing, which was critical in supporting the economic development agenda of these countries. There are currently 15 DFIs in Europe, which serve to implement their government's international development and cooperation policies. For example, in the United Kingdom, CDC emerged from the Colonial Development Corporation and served as a key catalyst for private equity in China, India, and other large markets long before it became a mainstream investment destiny. In 2011, there was a governmental shift in policy and the reformed mandate concentrates closely on the low- and lower middle-income countries of Sub-Saharan Africa and South Asia, where 70% of the world's poor live. Other large and very active DFIs are FMO (the Netherlands), DEG (Germany) Norfund (Norway), Proparco (France), and BIO (Belgium)—each with a somewhat different charter and criteria for qualified investments.

IFIs are also prime sponsors of private equity in emerging markets. Investments take many forms: direct, credit, as LPs, and co-investment. Prominent actors are the IFC, the European Investment Bank (EIB), the Asian Development Bank (ADB), the European Bank for Reconstruction and Development (EBRD), and the African Development Bank (AfDB).

DFIs and IFIs were crucial "first-movers" across all frontier countries; to spearhead development, they even invested in countries before the regulatory and legal frameworks were adequate for investor protection. A central objective is to make these markets more accessible to private equity investment by developing the proper infrastructure for business services, promoting domestic and pan-regional private equity associations,

---

[5] Talmor and Vasvari (2014).

[6] 2016 Preqin Sovereign Wealth Fund Review.

and educating governments on legislative barriers. Striving for sustainability takes many forms. For instance, the IFC has environmental and social (E&S) performance standards which define counterparty responsibilities for managing E&S risks; these standards have become a widespread practice.

The aim of DFIs and IFIs is not only to generate a development impact but also to deliver a financial return. They are often a cornerstone participant for both foreign and local private equity investments in frontier economies. A particular policy priority is in the SME sector, which is typically underserved, and where the potential for developmental impact is significant. In addition, DFIs set best practice standards for nascent funds, setting processes for screening and analyzing target companies as well as for structuring deals in complex regulatory, socioeconomic, and macroeconomic environments.

DFIs are generally quite flexible in terms of the vehicles for investment. Depending on the particular DFI, they may invest in companies directly, provide loans, and be LPs in funds or co-investors.

DRIVERS FOR INVESTMENTS IN EMERGING ECONOMIES

Whereas a country's attractiveness score is naturally related to the size of its population and economic growth expectations, these criteria are not sufficient to justify private equity investment. Additional favorable conditions are required to establish a vibrant private equity market, with the most obvious being the prospect of robust deal flow. Both the breadth and the quality of emerging market opportunities have improved markedly over the last decade.

Three global trends have played a fundamental role in attracting private equity investment:

- Economic liberalization policies and the movement to market-based economies since the 1990s have increased entrepreneurial and new business activity.

- The opening up of economies has increased both business opportunities to expand and competitive pressure, leading to more business owners seeking private capital.

- The close identification of family status and wealth with direct ownership of a company has reduced. This development, in turn, has lessened the reluctance to engage in third-party equity financing. The last decade has seen a gradual shift in the appetite for private equity, even by family-owned businesses.

The most important macro factors for the flow of private equity investments as follows:

Market size and growth

The size of the economy, employment levels, the diversity of the corporate sector, and the expectation of economic growth are key factors in country attractiveness. Since absolute market size is a critical determinant for most private equity investors, much attention has been focused on the BRIC countries, whose combined population constitutes more than 40% of the world's inhabitants. This huge population implies a large—and rapidly growing—consumer pool, which attracts investments to grow and scale businesses that cater to these markets. Vast and young populations are strong positive considerations for other countries, such as those in Africa and the Middle East.

Political stability

While democracy is important, political stability is even more so. China and India, for example, receive by far the largest volume of private equity investments. They are polar opposites on the political spectrum, but both have excellent track records of stable government and peaceful transitions of power. By contrast, regions that are politically unstable appear far less attractive for private equity investors.

Legal environment, investor protection, and corporate governance

Company and investment protection laws have undergone extensive revision, and codes of corporate governance practice have been introduced in many emerging markets, supported in part by assistance from multilateral development banks. Transparency and disclosure have also improved and international accounting standards (IFRS) are increasingly adopted. The legal environment and accounting and corporate governance practices have the greatest impact on the ease of conducting due diligence and enforcing governance for overseas investors. Global private equity funds are naturally drawn to environments that are better structured and supportive of foreign investors. A conducive legal framework facilitates deal screening and origination, enables shareholder protection, and permits a broader spectrum of securities. Conversely, crime, personal insecurity, corruption, black markets, or heavy bureaucracy form huge barriers to private equity. Weak property rights and investor protection are also likely to limit private equity investors' ability to steer businesses efficiently. Further, rigid labor market policies make a market less attractive. Institutional investors hesitate to invest in countries with exaggerated labor market protection and workforce immobility.

Another consideration with respect to any country's legal system is convenience. For example, funds that operate in common law countries find it easier to enforce their rights in commercial contracts.[7] Indeed, larger financings and transaction values are seen in emerging markets with a common law tradition.

Receptivity to private investments

Sometimes, certain industries are off limits to foreign investors but, on the whole, most emerging countries are receptive to private investments. As a relatively long-term asset class, private investment needs a favorable environment for new businesses to succeed; regulatory policies and entry barriers usually have a significant impact on private equity investment flows. Sectors that are high growth and less regulated (e.g., fast moving consumer goods) are naturally more attractive to private equity investment.

Depth of the capital market

Private equity activity is strongly connected to the depth of the local stock market. The ability to exit via listings on a stock exchange is a strong consideration in private equity investment. Well-developed capital markets allow for IPO exits and provide an active and liquid M&A market for deal sourcing and future divestment. Developed capital markets are also characterized by an infrastructure of key professional institutions (e.g., investment banks, accountants, law firms, M&A boutiques, consultants, etc.) required for

---

[7] Judges develop common law through the decisions of courts and similar tribunals, rather than through legislative statutes or the actions of states' executive branches (i.e., common law is based on precedent). Common law systems are usually found in emerging countries that trace their legal heritage to England as former colonies, such as Malaysia, Pakistan, India, and South Africa. Most Latin American countries, as well as Russia and China, have legal systems based on the civil code, which relies on state-initiated legislation.

successful deal transactions and execution. Lastly, the availability of debt financing, a key source of capital, is vital to the success of investments that focus on capital-intensive businesses.

Availability of skilled human capital

Countries with a relatively deep pool of skilled human capital are more attractive than those with low-wage labor alone. An emerging country with a well-regarded system of higher education (including technical disciplines) ranks highly on the list of private equity investment criteria. If university systems are deficient, this makes it difficult to recruit competent local managerial and technical personnel.

Competition for qualified talent at private equity firms is intense in most emerging markets, especially in Sub-Saharan Africa and Emerging Asia. Although the supply of qualified candidates has improved in recent years, and therefore is not as big an obstacle as it used to be, there is still fierce competition for top talent. This competition may explain why turnover of managers is higher than in developed private equity markets, leading to GP team instability except in top funds. India leads the emerging markets in terms of turnover, with more than one in five private equity employees leaving in any given year.

Operational expertise is the scarcest skill of all, and a differentiating factor across virtually all emerging markets. While there is an adequate supply of finance-related skills, it is difficult to find enough qualified managers who have operational backgrounds and private equity transaction experience, and command a strong knowledge of local markets.[8]

Which of the above factors is the most important? Although there is no clear-cut answer, some surveys rank the protection of property rights and corporate governance very highly, followed by the assessment of the capabilities of local GPs and management according to Western standards, the quality of the deal flow, and the degree of corruption. Institutional investors in private equity are not particularly swayed by government programs to stimulate local risk capital markets. They rely on the quality of the GPs they invest in, which in turn rely on the managers of the corporations they back. If investors' claims are poorly protected, or if they doubt the quality of their investees, or integrity in a host country, then they are likely to refrain from investing.

A Country Attractiveness Index for private equity investors is published annually by Groh et al. (2015), and the corresponding website provides a heat map for countries around the globe with detailed scoring of key parameters.[9]

RISKS OF INVESTING IN EMERGING ECONOMIES

Risks faced in emerging markets are significantly higher and very different from those in developed markets, particularly from the viewpoint of foreign institutional investors. These risks occur at both the country and individual company levels. At the country level, they tend to reflect political risks, economic volatility, and regulatory risks, while for individual companies, risks often relate to gaps in corporate governance, management quality, and information disclosure. We start with a discussion of the main risks at the country level (macro-level risks) and then outline the risks present at the company level (micro-level risks).

---

[8] Data is drawn from EMPEA Private Equity Talent Management in Emerging Markets Survey, September 2013.

[9] http://blog.iese.edu/vcpeindex/

Macro-level risks

While the long-term growth potential of emerging markets remains significant, the path toward this growth is often volatile. Moreover, emerging markets comprise a very heterogeneous group of countries: some will show steady long-term improvements and some will languish behind. Periods of high economic growth in emerging markets exert pressures on global commodity prices of food and mineral resources, which have at times contributed to mounting inflation in emerging markets. Conversely, plummeting energy prices hit the revenues of petroleum exporting countries such as Russia, Nigeria, and Angola. This has abated local consumption power, making the countries far less attractive to foreign investments.

Political risk

Private equity funds rarely invested in emerging markets before the 1990s due to multiple restrictions on foreign direct investment. From 1990 onwards, a series of reforms in emerging countries which resulted from major political changes have made access easier for private providers of risk capital. After years of instability, the political risks in most emerging countries are diminishing quickly. However, foreign investors are wary of political conflicts, which can generate wars, riots, or just unpredictable changes in regulations and the macroeconomic environment. Political instability can quickly erode the financial system, deepen unemployment, and harm the inflation rate and the overall growth of the economy. Since private equity involves long-term investment, a top priority before targeting a new country is a thorough analysis of the political system and its forecasted stability.

Political risks not only affect the country's macroeconomic climate, but also have direct effects on private equity. Some governments may protect local industries that create jobs and ignore international laws for political gains. What seems right for the local emergent economy may trump foreign investors' rights in court, so these investors must protect themselves at the front end by buying stakes in companies with other defenses. Lawsuits are an option, but may be expensive and ineffective, especially if the legal system is different. Therefore, private equity investors from developed countries often emphasize good relations with the local government. Backing by an influential DFI/IFI can make government commitments for regulatory and other permit approvals more reliable, and provide a competitive advantage.[10]

Currency risk

Most emerging countries' currencies fluctuate significantly, although some are tied directly to the U.S. dollar (China's yuan is a notable example). Using market forward rates and macroeconomic data, investors must form a three- to five-year view of local currency depreciation relative to the currency in which the fund has been raised. While it is difficult to make currency forecasts, they are an important input for any sensitivity tests when investing because devaluations can easily "eat'" the returns in, say, US$ or EUR at the time of exit. Forecasts can be obtained from large financial institutions or commissioned from specialist advisers.

One way to deal with this particular risk is to allocate private equity funds across different countries, in the hope that such diversification will limit the potential losses due to currency movements. An alternative is to

---

[10] Political risk is not confined to emerging markets. Turmoil in countries such as Greece and the Eurozone in general prove that risk in developed economies is the new norm. As stated in the Economist, "Britain's vote on Brexit was a reminder that impossibles may turn into improbables, and then quickly become fact" (September 17, 2016). However, the ability of a society to contain even extreme developments is clearly of a different magnitude as compared with political and economic crises in emerging economies.

hedge investments denominated in foreign currency by using derivatives that are traded in currency markets. As for debt, portfolio companies are strongly advised to borrow in the local currency (unless investing in a primarily exporting business which provides a natural hedge).

Regulatory risk

Prudent investing in emerging markets requires an understanding of cumbersome regulatory environments and licensing requirements, which can vary across national, provincial, and municipal levels. While market and industry regulations constantly change anywhere in the world, such changes are particularly troubling in developing economies where certain lines of business or activities could be drastically affected or even outlawed altogether (e.g., a sudden freeze on legal online lottery in China, which was meant to be a short-term measure but is still in force). Anticipating regulatory risks should provide guidance to avoid vulnerable sectors.

The problems of implementing legal frameworks and enforcement are accentuated in emerging markets because local business owners tend to be adept at navigating the legal changes. This adeptness puts foreign investors at a disadvantage, particularly when they need to resort to the law to resolve contractual disputes. The best way to mitigate this problem is to partner with carefully selected local agents and intermediaries as a common modus operandi at some or all stages of the deal execution.

Investors should also try to fund firms that are concentrated in one region, and seek to build relationships with local authorities in order to understand and manage the local regulatory regime that their funded firms face. Understanding and controlling the risk from regulatory institutions can become difficult and very costly if investments are geographically diverse. One proven strategy is not to expand by making many direct investments in different countries, but to scale through the portfolio companies. It is incumbent upon the management of the portfolio companies to understand in a more precise way how tariffs, customs, environmental requirements, bank facilities, and labor laws may affect cross-border commerce. Once a new country is penetrated through a portfolio company, it is far easier and safer for the private equity firm to make another investment—this time directly—in the new country.

Finally, investors often create innovative financial and legal structures that are a mix of local and Western structures. Offshore Western financial and legal structures, such as in the Cayman Islands or the British Virgin Islands, provide a legal oasis where emerging market investors can still meet the objectives of investment protection and access to liquidity while adhering to onshore local laws. The investor's limited partnership may be a permissible U.S. or U.K. entity but its portfolio companies are incorporated somewhere else. Simplistically, incorporating in efficient jurisdictions with a strong legal framework permits instruments such as preferred shares, employee stock options, and the ability to list on stock exchanges in developed markets, thus solving the lack of access to local capital markets. Singapore, Mauritius, and Dubai have also established themselves as safe harbor jurisdictions for Asia, Africa, and the Middle East.

Micro-level risks

Particularly in emerging markets where there is weak protection of investors' rights and law enforcement is often poor, investors must be alert to the quality of the management in charge of the portfolio company and to corporate governance. When the broader macroeconomic environment is stable or positive, many corporate-level risk factors may never arise. However, in more challenging environments, the quality of management and governance as well as the accuracy of the information reported by the company are likely to be key factors that differentiate successful investments.

Management risk

Managerial risk is one of the main drivers of poor investment performance. Ineffective management, lack of focus, or failure to implement strategies properly can easily transform a good deal into a loss-making investment. Other managerial issues, such as lack of integrity, may also play a role, especially in loss-making or otherwise vulnerable companies.

Emerging countries may have many talented entrepreneurs and managers, but as discussed, there is a perceived lack of professional managerial skills, particularly in sectors that require specialized knowledge. Competent and experienced managers are usually a scarce resource. Management turnover rates in some fast-growing emerging markets are high, and the pool of world-class talent can be shallow. However, there has been a "reverse brain drain" that started after the 2008 global financial crisis, spurred by the growing maturity and professional job opportunities available in emerging countries. Many educated professionals who worked abroad bring their experience back home. This phenomenon positively impacts the quality of the management teams put in place by private equity firms.

Distanced investors must always be mindful of their relationship with key managers in emerging markets. Replacing management may be more complicated in emerging markets when the loyalty of employees and possibly of customers is to key managers—not to the company as such. Non-amicable departures may trigger replacing an entire management team.

Management risk can be minimized by using a selective recruiting process with detailed reference checks. Investors also need to be aware of the changing environment, and provide competitive and timely incentives for talented managers in order to discourage them from leaving. Rapidly improving economic conditions and the limited pool of candidates combine to increase the competition for managerial talent. Aligning managerial, employee, and shareholder interests may require innovative approaches, since employee stock options—a key instrument to incentivize employees in developed markets—may simply be unavailable as a financial instrument in emerging markets.

Corporate governance risk

Introducing effective management information systems is a priority in order to minimize reliance on management intuition and retain data within the enterprise. Timely feedback on key performance indicators is a basic ingredient for informed decision making. When investing in a business run by a local entrepreneur or a family, installing and maintaining financial controls are necessary to separate the company's accounts from the entrepreneur's personal finances. Tight guidelines have to be set on the purchase of assets and unnecessary expenditures. In addition, good financial controls and receivables management can reduce the working capital requirements of the business.

While board seats are a central instrument of governance, strict shareholder agreements and articles are equally important in order to ensure the quality of information provided to the board and the investors. Information can often reach the board on a delayed basis and the influence of outside directors may be weak. An ongoing engagement with multiple managers within the enterprise ensures more granular and timely information (as opposed to depending on a board seat for such information).

Information risk

Legislation in emerging markets rarely requires the same level of public information or disclosure to the regulatory bodies as legislation in developed countries. Further, owners of private companies in these countries are used to retaining complete control of information, and are therefore more reluctant to share or disclose it. Moreover, some countries have accounting and legal rules that leave considerable room for interpretation.

When investing, valuation is more art than science in the best of circumstances, but this is particularly true in emerging markets. Forecasting future company performance is complicated by the dearth of reliable data on markets, competitors, and product pricing, and by the volatility that characterizes developing economies. It can also be hard to value a business at the time of acquisition or exit because of thin domestic equity markets, which provide minimal guidance on comparable company values. Since the ability to accurately obtain information on a firm is more constrained, due diligence in emerging markets must closely consider the entrepreneur's background and personal aspects.

Often, local managers are not educated on international business and reporting standards. A portfolio company could have one accounting book filled out according to International GAAP and one book completed according to other practices, which can make processing the information and appropriately pricing a business a daunting challenge indeed. Therefore, it is vital that private equity investors take the time to educate the owners and managers of local companies when investing. In addition, firms should be expected to produce financial reports in a form that is interpretable and easy to verify; this usually requires hiring an international accounting firm to help with the financials and audit of the firm.

Intellectual property risk

Effective management of intellectual property rights is an essential aspect of investing in emerging markets. Protecting intellectual property can involve a change in thinking for most emerging market entrepreneurs, as many think of intellectual property quite differently from their foreign counterparts. In particular, they may not consider copying a crime. Further, an entrepreneur or employee might want to split off another, independent enterprise even though it may be directly based on the knowhow of the parent company. In other cases, employees might join the organization and use the proprietary intellectual property of their former employers. To reduce these risks, investors must instill the concept of intellectual property rights in both the entrepreneur and the employees of the company. Lastly, customers (including large multinationals) sometimes reverse-engineer enterprise solutions or other software products and competitors counterfeit consumer products. While none of these matters are unique to emerging markets, the standards for data protection and intellectual property rights are far lower in these environments.

FUND OPERATION AND INVESTMENT

Fund focus

Proprietary deals are highly regarded and private equity funds in emerging markets are typically proactive in deal selection. Rather than wait for business proposals to land on their desks, or for investment bankers to make a pitch on behalf of a client, private equity funds often approach companies they find attractive; doing so also helps them avoid getting involved in a bidding auction.

Most funds still approach emerging markets with a generalist strategy, focusing on a basket of the most promising sectors, based on the size of transactions they seek. Funds with a single-sector focus are usually in infrastructure, natural resources, or agriculture.

Going local

Private equity investment into emerging markets needs to be a long-term commitment. Otherwise, competing with local private equity firms and foreign groups who have "gone local" is likely to be difficult. Given the crowded nature of private equity, investment managers must distinguish themselves. Building a local reputation for success and trust requires spending time on the ground; this enables private equity firms to cultivate strong relationships with local partners who can help navigate and source deals, and to collect local knowledge that puts them in a better position to assess the best deals.

Given that the development of local knowledge is critical, it is not enough to simply hire local partners. Private equity firms must also integrate their ongoing decision-making processes with regional or headquarter offices and build trust with these local partners. The home offices of private equity firms are challenged to bridge a wide variety of cultural and knowledge gaps in order to appreciate the logic of regional offices in certain deal aspects and ongoing work with portfolio companies.

First-time funds

First-time funds often spearhead the development of new asset classes. Historically, first-time private equity vehicles have accounted for a significant share of fundraising activity in emerging markets. Between 2008 and the first quarter of 2015, 286 first-time funds reached final closes on an aggregate $45 billion, accounting for 30% of the number of funds closed for emerging markets. New fund managers are not only inductive to a more diverse marketplace, but they also address financing gaps in many underserved markets. First-time funds play a particularly important role in frontier economies that suffer from a deficiency in investment-grade managers—for instance, in Sub-Saharan Africa, which exhibits the highest percentage of first-time funds reaching a final close, at 78% of all funds in 2014.[11]

In general, however, it is exceedingly difficult to raise a first-time fund in an emerging market. Institutional investors are reluctant to back a first-time team in a frontier economy since the risks are compounded. Even in developed markets, there are many unknowns surrounding managers of first-time funds that concern investors (e.g., Is their past experience relevant? Are the managers a good fit for the fund? How committed are they to the fund's success?). It is only natural that these concerns are amplified in emerging markets, given the increased challenges. This concern has recently given rise to a drop in the number of first-time private equity funds that reached final close in emerging markets. Instead, there has been an increase in allocations to the larger, more established private equity managers, particularly in Asia. In addition, the profile of first-time

---

[11] Data is drawn from EMPEA First time Funds in Emerging Markets Brief (August 2015).

funds has shifted, with sector-specific and venture capital vehicles each accounting for an increasing share of the number of first-time funds.

In terms of private equity performance, data from Cambridge Associates shows that within the top quartile of emerging markets funds, first-, second-, and third-time funds have outperformed later-series funds, albeit with a wider spread in performance.

In light of the difficulties highlighted above, DFIs (rather than pensions and other purely financially motivated LPs) are the largest supporters of first-time private equity funds in emerging markets.

Challenges in deal making

Typically, once a firm has passed its initial screening, investors proceed with due diligence, which includes confirmation of the nature and status of the firm's product, production capability, market demand, and status of key relationships with channels and suppliers. As discussed above, this process may be complicated in emerging markets, given the limited availability of accurate information. Local bureaucrats and business owners have significant control over information that is crucial to understanding the market, and the regulatory environment is a serious disadvantage to outside investors.

In addition, business owners in emerging markets are often reluctant to deal with foreign private equity investors. Building a certain level of comfort between local owners and fund managers so they can assess each other is a lengthy process. Learning about the founders, their colleagues, and even their families is important in the due diligence process. When working with local owners, it often becomes clear that they are more conscious of the need to factor in additional goals, such as employment, at the expense of profitability. These goals could represent positive reasons, such as relationships with relevant local governments, or negative reasons, such as nepotism. Without engagement and careful oversight, firms can end up with operational inefficiencies, such as extra employees or overproduction of goods.

Securities used in deals

On the one hand, most developed market buyouts are replacement capital control deals. On the other hand, in emerging markets, they are most often growth capital minority deals. In the not-so-distant past, minority positions were viewed as very risky but later experience shows that risk to be exaggerated. When structured properly and with the right local partners, minority positions have performed well in all forms of exit, indicating that the risks associated with them can be effectively managed.

Unlike in developed markets, where the use of convertible preferred securities is common, more than half of the transactions in emerging markets involve common stock, while a significant portion uses instruments that are essentially debt.[12] When preferred securities are not used, private equity funds are more likely to obtain a majority of the firm's equity. Another protection instrument is ratchets that increase the investor's acquired share in the business in case of underperformance.

---

[12] Some emerging countries do not allow preferred shares. Recently, there has been a revival of preferred shares in China. See Cai (2016) for a discussion of the minority common shareholders and preferred shareholders under the new regulation.

Exit strategies

When committing to invest in a business, private equity investors in emerging markets discuss the exit issue in far greater detail than those in developed economies. It is important that the local investment partner (whether a family or an entrepreneur) be entirely on board with the mindset of private equity seeking an outright exit in one form or another.

Exits through IPOs are more common in emerging markets than elsewhere, and provide a solution to the common situation where the local family or founder wishes to remain an involved shareholder. Nevertheless, there are several complications with listing companies:

- Many emerging countries still do not have proper legislation in place on securities markets, disclosure, and regulation to facilitate such IPOs.

- The selection of which firms may list on the local stock exchange might be principally a state decision (especially in China).

- Local exchanges are very small and illiquid.

Consequently, listing on a foreign exchange such as Singapore or London is a better option if it can be made viable. Looking for a strategic buyer—in particular, a multinational company—is the most readily available exit strategy. It requires selling the entire business and necessitates an upfront consent of the local partners for an outright sale.

Some private equity investors in emerging markets are willing to experiment with new, more creative approaches to exit. For example, one Latin American fund has launched a mezzanine fund that offers debt financing with many of the same characteristics as equity, but provides investors with greater assurance of a steady income stream. Another fund recapitalized some successful portfolio companies, which allows the fund to realize capital gains while waiting for an opportune time to exit.

CHINA: THE AWAKENED GIANT

Private equity in the world's second-largest economy, China, should be given specific attention, not only because of its sheer size and rate of growth but also because it is so unique, sharing very few of the principles governing domestic private equity elsewhere in the world.

Privately funded venture capital firms in China originated in 1998, when the National People's Congress allowed foreigners to invest in the country. However, there were no regulatory guidelines on the establishment of funds, so it was left to local governments and state-owned enterprises (SOEs) to develop a specific sector, typically in high technology. At that time, private equity funds were known within China as industrial investment funds. China's embryonic venture industry was not immune to global financial forces, and declined following the tech bubble collapse. To boost activity in the sector, in 2003, the government allowed foreign venture capitalists to set up investment partnerships. The legal framework was strengthened in 2006 with a much needed set of compliance rules, the Provisional Regulations for the Administration of Venture Capital Enterprises. Early stage investments were also buoyed by changes to the Company Law and the Securities Law, allowing open trading of "non-circulating" shares and facilitating an essential exit path.

Following the 2008 global financial crisis, China, as an export-oriented economy, was once again affected. Yet, the country has gradually transformed itself from a manufacturing-led economy to a mixed economy, and since 2012, the service sector has surpassed the industrial sector in terms of share of GDP.[13]

In terms of venture capital in China, a NASDAQ-style junior market, ChiNext, was launched in 2009 as part of the Shenzhen Stock Exchange, opening up a new channel for exits. This development changed the importance of the Chinese stock market for private equity firms dramatically, and became a main avenue for monetization. The private equity and venture capital sector has quickly rebounded to continue its rapid growth. China-focused funds accounted for about 8% of global funds in 2016, up from a trickle 10 years earlier. The phenomenal growth of private equity funds in China is fueled by addressing two huge voids in the Chinese financial market: a source of funds for private enterprises and an opportunity for investors. The number of funds raised flourished as a result of local and foreign opportunists. Local firms were rapidly established to capitalize on the promise of high returns, especially due to the impact of ChiNext opening up an exit channel for RMB funds. Foreign firms flocked to China en masse, eager to participate in the Chinese growth story. With China's IPO market, fund managers were confident about very attractive exit returns.

With a few ups and downs, this growth has largely continued up to the present. As of 2016, China's market for IPOs is the hottest it has ever been. The IPO process has always been strictly controlled by the China Securities Regulatory Commission (CSRC), which generally requires a minimum three-year waiting period. Hundreds of companies are still waiting for approval, and deal size and pricing are limited to avoid an oversupply of shares. This tough stance has been enforced on listings as well, both improving the standards of new offerings as well as restricting the flow of overseas-traded Chinese companies seeking backdoor listings on the mainland. As a result, there has been a spillover to listing in Hong Kong, especially for some of the larger deals.

Foreign private equity firms are now allowed to raise RMB-denominated funds, which is typically carried out by establishing a partnership with local governments or local funds. KKR, Blackstone, TPG, and Carlyle were among the funds to raise RMB funds. In addition, the domestic industry is now receiving investments from China's large social security funds and other major corporations. Generally, there is less red tape and more collaboration with the local government to raise money and identify deals. Furthermore, Beijing, Shanghai, Tianjin, Chongqing, and other local governments have issued favorable tax policies for RMB funds.

An unusual recent trend has been the acquisition of foreign companies by domestic private equity funds. The basic premise centers on the very large untapped local market of Chinese consumers. A significant number of Chinese buyout funds with billions at their disposal have been on the trail to buy technology and computer hardware companies in the United States and Europe. Unlike other private equity firms in developed and emerging markets alike, the focus is not on improving operations but rather, on leaving the companies as they are, including not moving them from their original home bases. Instead, the technology is brought inbound through joint ventures or other vehicles to build revenues and profits from the massive Chinese domestic market and to help Chinese manufacturers compete internationally. Not surprisingly, foreign regulators often find this practice difficult. Acquisitions of U.S. companies (or even foreign companies with a strong U.S. presence) require approval from the Committee on Foreign Investment in the United States (CFIUS), which blocks foreign takeovers in cases viewed as compromising U.S. national security.

As an exit strategy, investors favor an IPO in China where valuations can be the highest in the world; however, given the tedious submission process and complications discussed above, as well as the long waiting

---

[13] Source: World Bank, "World Development Indicators," September 15, 2017.

list, the more frequent form of exit is by selling to Chinese listed companies. The global private equity firms operating in China find this environment difficult. They are unwilling to pay exorbitant prices and, in many cases, lack the authority to acquire foreign companies solely for a domestic Chines operation. Instead, global private equity firms prefer to act as sellers of companies they have previously bought in the United States or Europe at frothy valuations that capture China's domestic growth potential.

CONCLUSION

Emerging markets offer growth potential and unique investment opportunities that are unparalleled in a mature economy. Despite these features, investors' enthusiasm is dampened by the fact that they also face severe challenges in these markets. First, there is a geographical bias. Geographies distant from Western Europe and North America are often viewed as risky and hazardous, thereby dictating a high risk-adjusted rate of return. Second, relative to industrial countries, emerging countries have weaker legal, institutional, and regulatory safeguards to give investors the confidence that their rights will be enforced. Third, there are extra transactional risks such as currency risk, political risk, and regulatory uncertainty that must be accounted for.

Above all, it is the weak investor protection coupled with bureaucracy and concerns with bribery and corruption that deters investments.

Most emerging markets also lack the scale to make sizable investments competitive with those in more developed markets. Consider the case of Africa. In November 2017, KKR disbanded its African private equity team, after making just a single investment in the continent.[14] As stated by the firm, "To invest our funds, we need deal flow of a certain size. It was especially the deal size that wasn't coming through. There was enough deal-flow at a smaller level." KKR never opened an office in Africa and did not raise a dedicated fund. As a result, the African deal team had to compete with European deals that were concurrently pitched to the firm's investment committee, making the bar prohibitive.

The classical Western-style model of buying out large mature companies and improving them does not work in most emerging markets where the scale and nature of the economy make such opportunities rare and the results often disappointing.[15] Indeed, the buyout market is tiny compared with the West. In 2016, there were 388 buyout deals in Sub-Saharan Africa for a combined worth of $2 billion. By contrast, there were 2,135 buyouts in North America during that year, for a combined $187 billion.[16] While there are few opportunities in emerging markets to acquire sizable mature businesses for improvement, building businesses in partnership with entrepreneurs can offer much more compelling investment opportunities.

The long-term appeal of investment in emerging markets is undisputed. There is little doubt that these economies will become increasingly integrated into the global capital markets and attract a growing share of private equity capital commitments. However, fundraising and investing in emerging markets, relative to developed markets, will remain cyclical for the foreseeable future. A gradual upward trend of private equity capital inflows will likely make these cycles less pronounced over time.

---

[14] An investment of $200 million in 2014 in Ethiopia's Afriflora, the world's largest rose farm.

[15] In 2016, Bain Capital lost control of South Africa's largest retailer, Edcon, after acquiring the business nine years earlier for $3.5 billion in the largest transaction ever in Africa. As of late 2017, shares in Nigeria's Diamond Bank have fallen almost 80% since Carlyle Group bought a $147 million stake three years earlier.

[16] Sources: Preqin and Clark and Ballard, "KKR disbands African private equity team," Financial News, November 24, 2017.

REFERENCES

Cai, W. (2016) "Use of preference shares in Chinese companies as a viable investment/financing tool, Capital Markets Law Journal, vol. 11, No. 2. pp 317-335, Oxford University Press.

Groh, A., H. Liechtenstein, K. Lieser and M. Biesinger (2015) *The venture capital and private equity country attractiveness index.*

Talmor, E. and F. Vasvari (2014) "The extent and evolution of pension funds' private equity allocations", ADVEQ Applied Research Series, Coller Institute of Private Equity London Business School.

In his own words: Hurley Doddy, Founding Partner, Emerging Capital Partners (ECP)

While the risks of investing in emerging markets are quite real and we have learned about them from hard experience, there are a number of ways to mitigate them. Moreover, there are many other risks that are less than in developed markets. Labor unions, technology obsolescence, legacy products, and cyber espionage affect more developed markets. Changes in taxation and regulation are at least as common in the developed markets, as has been particularly clear these recent quarters. Even political instability is equally potent in other geographies (Brexit, to name one case).

For the established private equity firms, teams are quite stable. At ECP, for instance, there are over 15 MDs and Directors with an average of over 10 years with the firm, and we have only lost one person at that level to a competitor in the last decade.

Investing in private equity in developed markets means generally investing in mature industries or untried business models in economies with little or no growth. In Africa, there is good underlying growth in almost every sector, and business models that have been perfected in other markets years ago can be imported. Almost all niches have a host of competitors with more popping up in developed markets, whereas in Africa, the largest restaurant chain might have 10 stores. Whole industries barely exist and competing start-ups can rarely get funding.

U.S. firms must often rely on leverage and cost cutting even though many targets have been previously owned by other private equity firms, while African firms can rely on growth. Moreover, many deals in developed markets are auctions with multiple strategic and financial bidders and limited time for differentiated due diligence. Yet in Africa, proprietary deals are still quite common.

All of these aspects make investment in emerging markets exciting, economically rewarding, and important in that the investment affects the world in a fundamental way.

3 Valuation of Private Equity Companies

Managers and investors alike must understand that accounting numbers are the beginning, not the end, of business valuation.
Warren Buffett

INTRODUCTION

Valuation involves estimating the value of a company's assets based on a series of relevant variables that are perceived to affect the future performance and success of the company. The principles of valuing private companies are similar to those of valuing public companies; however, certain estimation problems are unique to private companies. First, the valuer must deal with limited information available in terms of history and depth because private firms do not report their performance publicly, provide less granularity in their annual reports, and are not required to meet accounting and reporting standards that apply to public entities in many countries. Second, it is difficult to estimate risk parameters for discount rates that are necessary in valuation, as these estimations require equity stock prices that are not available for private firms. Third, private companies—in particular, start-ups and emerging companies—face acute uncertainties regarding their future operations, increasing the difficulty of forecasting. In fact, young private companies often have negative cash flows and earnings at the time of valuation, which makes estimating future profitability a challenging task. Finally, private companies tend to have concentrated ownership, so their reported earnings might reflect discretionary expenses (e.g., dividends in lieu of the owner-manager's salary) or be affected by tax motivations.

Managers of private equity funds assess the value of private companies at several points when they (1) invest in a financing round of the company (e.g., venture funds), (2) acquire a company (e.g., buyout funds), (3) list the company on an exchange, (4) sell the company to a third party, (5) liquidate the company, (6) report performance during ownership. Each of these points involves various valuation assumptions and approaches.

Reporting guidelines require that managers of private equity funds carry out periodic valuations of their portfolio investments as part of the reporting process to their investors. Today, private equity firms are expected to periodically mark their investments at the price at which they would be sold, regardless of whether the fund plans to hold the assets or sell them at a later date. Whereas a private equity fund manager may have a good sense of the intrinsic value of the investments in the fund's portfolio, the fair value measurement of these investments for reporting purposes relies on a series of assumptions that could lead to different outputs. Consequently, investors want greater transparency in valuations, and often expect third-party outsourced valuations that can be delivered with complete independence to avoid overstating the fund's investments. The use of an independent valuation firm signals to investors that the manager is willing to use both internal and external resources to determine the most appropriate fair value measurements. While larger fund managers have greater resources to ensure robust valuation processes, mid-size and smaller managers may find that outsourcing valuations allow for a better use of managers' scarce time and resources.

USE OF VALUATION OUTPUTS

Valuation is a combination of art and science, especially when dealing with private companies, as personal judgment always comes into play. The business plan and the extent to which the manager can achieve the milestones in light of external market forces are always sources of uncertainty. Therefore, performing the necessary due diligence on the business plan to avoid using unrealistic assumptions and unsustainable growth rates in calculations is critical. Even slight adjustments to the inputs and assumptions can cause significant differences in valuation outputs. Another highly subjective area involves the application of minority, marketability, and liquidity discounts specific to private equity transactions.

The challenge in arriving at the intrinsic value of a business to be acquired or sold is to balance the current market conditions with appropriate assumptions of transaction counterparties, given the illiquid nature and characteristics of the company being valued. A blind reliance on a particular valuation method without reconciliation to other value indicators could be a recipe for disaster.

Given these issues, one would expect valuations to be ideally provided in value ranges (with a central value) to reflect the sensitivity of the investment's value to critical assumptions. In fact, it is not really the valuation number that is relevant to the private equity fund manager but the process of reaching that number or range. The process of valuing an investment can help the private equity practitioner better understand the key factors driving the value of a company, and how sensitive the valuation is to changes in these factors. These insights can provide a key competitive advantage when negotiating deals with sellers or buyers, or when making strategic decisions for the business while it is in the portfolio.

While valuations are critical for successful private equity fund managers (who are, after all, in the business of buying and selling stakes in private companies), several caveats must be remembered:

- Valuations are quantitative but they are rarely objective or precise as they rely on a multitude of sensitive and subjective assumptions.

- Valuations age quickly and can change significantly as new information becomes available.

- Valuations can take substantial time and effort.

VALUATION APPROACHES

Guidelines

Private equity fund investments are usually reported to the investors at fair value. Fair value is relatively easy to determine when an active market exists in that asset and recent transaction prices or quotes are publicly available. However, in private equity, the majority of the investments are unquoted and no clear trading market is available. As a result, private equity funds are required to estimate what a third party might pay for the asset in their portfolio.

In order to assist private equity valuers, the International Private Equity and Venture Capital Valuation (IPEV) Board issued a set of valuation guidelines in 2009, 2012, and 2015. These guidelines are intended to promote best practice and thereby enhance investor confidence in the valuation reports. The crucially important ethos of the IPEV guidelines is that "valuation is an art, not a science." It is therefore impossible to set out prescribed rules that a valuer must follow to estimate what price a third party might consider appropriate for acquiring a particular asset. Valuers have to be allowed—and indeed, encouraged—to use their professional judgment in estimating that value.

The IPEV guidelines provide a framework within which valuers can exercise that judgment and, importantly, explain the rationale behind their valuation judgments to investors. The guidelines are based on the concept of "substance over form." It is vital that the valuation decisions are based on the expectations of the outcome and not necessarily on the strict legal form. The IPEV guidelines also focus on the estimation of the fair value, which is defined by the International Accounting Standards as "the price that would be received when an asset is sold or a liability is transferred in an orderly transaction between market participants at the measurement date." Fair value may also be defined as a value that would be determined as a fair price between a seller and a buyer acting freely in a market.

Over time, the IPEV guidelines have been updated (most recently in December 2015) to improve readability and to make certain technical clarifications. The most relevant clarifications made to the IPEV guidelines focus on valuation, highlighting the importance of calibration and backtesting of the investments. Consistency and cross-checks are also mentioned, as the revised guidelines have removed the negative bias toward the discounted cash flow (DCF) valuation methodology, affirming that it can be utilized as a cross-check.

Valuation methodologies

In private equity, the underlying portfolio investments are usually held by a relatively small number of shareholders. The value of the underlying business is commonly realized by a transaction that involves the business as a whole; it is less common for individual small stakes in a business to be realized. Accordingly, the IPEV guidelines start with the value of the firm as a whole in order to assess the value of a stake in that business.

The steps set out in the IPEV guidelines to assess the value of a stake in a business may be roughly summarized as follows:

- Determine the value of the business as a whole (i.e., enterprise value).

- Adjust for any known relevant factors such as illiquidity, control, off-balance sheet liabilities, etc.

- Deduct any amounts that rank higher (e.g., debt instruments).

- Allocate the balance among the relevant instruments and investors (e.g., allocate the amount across equity and debt instruments used by the private equity investor).

In determining the enterprise value, valuers attempt to put themselves in the position of an acquirer, considering all relevant information available. Note that due to the number of implicit or inherent judgments and potential transaction-specific dynamics (e.g., irrational escalation of commitment), proceeds on realization may differ significantly from the estimated fair value and it is unlikely that the fair value is exactly "right."

The initial step in valuing a portfolio company for reporting purposes is to select an appropriate approach and valuation methodology. The most accepted, tried-and-tested valuation approaches for valuing a portfolio company and its associated assets (i.e., both tangible and intangible assets, intellectual property, goodwill, etc.) include the following: (1) the market approach, which is based on identifying market comparators for transactions of a similar nature, where these can be found; (2) the cost approach, which is based on establishing the cost to replace the functionality of an asset, discounted for obsolescence; and (3) the future income approach, which is based on using a bespoke financial model to calculate the net present value of future cash flows or earnings attributed to a company's assets, discounted for the associated risk. Within these three approaches, there are associated valuation methodologies or techniques that may be used when valuing a portfolio company.

The methodology selected should be applied consistently over time. Six different valuation methodologies are commonly used to value holdings of private equity funds for reporting purposes:

I. Market approach

1. Price of the precedent transaction
2. Financial trading multiples
3. Industry valuation benchmarks

II. Cost approach

4. Net assets

III.   Future income approach

5. DCFs or earnings (of the underlying business)
6. DCFs (from the investment)

The valuer is required to subsequently elect an appropriate valuation methodology over the holding period of the investment. An appropriate starting basis is often to value the investment at the historical transaction price. This price might be uplifted or revised based on various milestones within the next 18 months until profits are forecasted for the next accounting period, when the valuer might shift to a trading multiple basis. Finally, an agreement will be entered to realize the sale of the asset, which may be based on a combination of industry valuation benchmarks and a DCF. This pattern of changes is expected and justifiable.

It is important that, post realization, the valuer compares the proceeds of the sale with the internal valuation model used, in order to identify and understand any differences that potentially impacted the realized sale price.

Price of the precedent transaction

On the day that a transaction takes place, the fair value of the investment is usually the price paid by the market participant. The precedent transaction methodology simply uses the evidence of the actual cost paid by the investor as the best indicator of fair value. Valuers may equally use the evidence of the subsequent price paid by another investor.

Price of the recent investment is a particularly strong evidence of fair value, since the evidence is entirely market-based, although valuers should consider whether there are any pertinent reasons why the price might not be reflective of fair value (e.g., the firm recently signed a new large contract with a customer, the firm became a defendant in a lawsuit that could trigger a large one-off payment, etc.). In the absence of such factors, the historical transaction price will most likely be an accurate reflection of the actual fair value of the asset.

The key question is, when should other valuation methodologies be used to assess the investment's fair value rather than the historical transaction price. To answer this question, valuers will need to assess whether anything has changed materially between the investment and valuation dates that could be indicative of the fair value no longer being equivalent to the cost. This type of change could occur when the investment is impacted by either internal factors (e.g., material contract renegotiations with customers or suppliers) or wider external factors (e.g., industry shocks, economic downturns, and changes in the interest rate environment).

The price of the precedent transaction is commonly used as a reference value on the day of acquisition and for early stage investments, especially prior to the generation of revenues, profits, or positive cash flows. For many venture firms or companies in development, the period between initial investment and profitable trading might be several years. During this period, the only market data available might be subsequent investments made; hence, any assessment of fair value must be at least based on the price of those investments.

The IPEV guidelines expand the concept of the price of recent investments to cover this extensive period. The guidelines encourage valuers to consider all business aspects, which is a wider category than merely financial targets and data. More specifically, key performance indicators or the achievement of certain milestones might be a useful indicator of progress, change, and potential value impact within the underlying business. However, caution is advisable as any fair value estimation based on milestones achieved post initial investment is clearly highly subjective and can work in both directions with upward and downward valuation adjustments. For example, management may advocate that achieving certain milestones in accordance with the business plan indicates that the fair value exceeds the historical cost price, even in the absence of realizing any positive financial returns.

Financial trading multiples

Arguably, the financial trading multiples approach represents the most common market-based valuation methodology. It ascertains the prices achieved for a similar asset and uses this data to support the valuer's own opinion of fair value. This methodology involves the application of a multiple of value (based on earnings or other financial measures of performance) to the company being valued. In order to perform a relative valuation, two main inputs must be determined: (1) the comparable peer universe and (2) a specific multiple. The peer group is established based on two critical matching dimensions which are growth opportunities and risk profile. In terms of multiples, several options are available:

- **Earnings multiples:** The ratio of the company's value to the company's operating income or EBITDA.

- **Revenue multiples:** The ratio of the company's value to the revenue it generates. These multiples are often used as an alternative to earnings and book value multiples (which are subject to accounting decisions). The advantage of using a sales multiple is that it facilitates the comparison between companies in different markets with different accounting rules.

- **Book value multiples:** The ratio of the company's value to the book value of assets. Book value multiples vary widely between industries, depending on the growth potential and the extent to which firms have assets recognized on their balance   sheet.[1]

Financial multiple-based methodologies could be interpreted as an abbreviation of a DCF calculation, with the key distinction being a market-based valuation (i.e., trading multiples) vis-à-vis a theoretical valuation exercise (i.e., DCF).

Industry valuation benchmarks

Some companies can be valued based on industry-specific benchmarks such as price per square foot (e.g., property), price per bed (e.g., residential care homes and hospitals), price per room (e.g., hotels), price per customer (e.g., asset management), and price per subscriber (e.g., telecommunications firms). Company valuations based on these benchmarks implicitly assume that fair value is a function of market-based factors and that overall industry profitability is not strictly relevant.

Clearly, some industry benchmarks are more valid than others but, whatever their validity, it would be unusual to use the industry valuation benchmark methodology in isolation to estimate fair value. Instead, industry valuation benchmarks are commonly used to provide a check against other methodologies in order to ensure that fair value estimations are within the range expected by the market. In addition, given the industry-specific nature of these multiples, they cannot be calculated for another sector, which may result in overvaluation or undervaluation to the rest of the market.

When using one of the three market approaches discussed above, it is crucial that the universe of comparable companies is suitable and that precedent transaction multiples relate to relevant and recent transactions.

Net assets

Many businesses trade at a value based on their reported net assets, rather than earnings or cash flow streams. This methodology is used where the inherent value of the assets may exceed the business's income-generating abilities. For example, property and resource companies are usually valued on the basis of the net asset value—the book value of the equity—of their properties and resources. This methodology may also be used as a floor when valuing a poorly performing business as tangible assets still have an inherent value, even when the company is loss-making.

Asset valuation is a bottom-up method, and the net asset value is often considered as the benchmark price for many private company deals. Negotiation of the transaction price is then mainly focused on the value of the assets and liabilities being purchased.

A variation of the net assets methodology is the adjusted book value technique, which is an attempt to reconcile the accounting values with the market values by assuming that the company will continue operating as an ongoing concern and approximating the replacement value of each asset and liability. It is common for

---

[1] For instance, in the case of technology companies, a significant proportion of the assets is intangible. Due to accounting treatments, these assets are not recognized on the balance sheet, making the book-value multiples impractical for the valuation of these companies.

valuers, in the interest of time and efficiency, to make rough estimates of the worth of each asset and liability using their best judgment.

The assets and liabilities present on a company's balance sheet can be separated into four groups:

- **Cash and cash equivalents:** Since they are normally carried on the balance sheet at market values, these items are most often left unadjusted.

- **Non-cash tangible assets:** These assets include inventories, prepaid expenses, equipment, land, buildings, notes receivables, and accounts receivables. Valuations will differ depending on the situation and whether assets are kept together or broken up.

  Book value is the starting point and the replacement cost of equivalent assets could be considered as an alternative approach. The book value of equipment, land, buildings, and other similar fixed assets is equal to the historical purchase price less the corresponding depreciation. Depreciation schedules are required by generally accepted accounting principles (GAAP) and rarely reflect the true economic life of these assets; thus, the book value does not reflect their true replacement costs. However, in some industries, the fixed assets may be the essence of the firm's competitive position and earnings potential. Therefore, in these instances, deriving the firm's value from the ownership of its fixed asset base may be very relevant. For example, the value of a strategic fixed asset with monopolistic characteristics or inherent competitive entry barriers, such as an airport, may be far greater than its historical construction cost.

  Inventories, on the other hand, are affected by the likelihood of product obsolescence and historical trends in raw material prices. Hence, their book value is typically overstated. Also, prepaid expenses should be changed to show their current value and the likelihood that the company will use them. Similarly, accounts receivable often require an adjustment for the likelihood that the company will be able to collect the amounts from their customer base. In summary, the valuer must recognize that there are no hard rules about determining the value of the tangible assets, so careful use of good judgment in each situation is recommended.

- **Intangible assets:** These items include patents, trademarks, designs, trade secrets, copyright materials, databases, proprietary knowhow, non-competition covenants, contracts, license agreements, and goodwill. In general, intangible assets should be revised periodically to reflect the value they provide during their remaining life. Goodwill is usually assumed to be of no value to the buyer, and therefore reduced to zero.

- **Liabilities:** Book values for liabilities are typically not altered, excluding distressed situations or when debt is publicly traded. However, valuers must ensure that they have a comprehensive view of the company's contracted liabilities as the company may be committed to providing a product or service in the future. The company may already have received payment from a customer, in which case the liability will be shown as deferred revenue. Commitments such as future operating lease obligations are shown in the notes to the accounts rather than represented in the balance sheet. These continuing commitments are not normally included in net asset value calculations and are regarded as ongoing rental expenses. Other liabilities, such as hedging contracts, are also shown in the notes, but the information presented in the annual accounts can be difficult to interpret, hiding the potential impact of such agreements.

Once the fair value of the company's assets and liabilities is established, the overall balance sheet structure should be considered by, for example, examining the capital employed in the business. More specifically, the valuer must address whether the company has sufficient assets to cover its requirements. When the fixed assets are not sufficient to support the ongoing business, then additional capital expenditure will be required. Alternatively, if the business is not generating sufficient cash, then additional financing will need to be found from external capital sources.

Similarly, valuers should review the working capital position by answering the following questions: (1) Is the working capital requirement and its constituents comparable relative to similar businesses? And (2) Is the working capital level representative of future needs, or can these levels be further optimized to improve free cash flow (e.g., by improving the collection of debtors, reducing inventory, or delaying payments to suppliers)?

Additionally, the valuer can make choices regarding the financing of some fixed assets. For instance, property or plants can perhaps be owned or leased. These choices do not affect the total value, but they do affect the way that value is tied up in the company (i.e., current cash requirements, future cash flows, and earnings).

Unless assets are cash or cash equivalents, there will always be a certain extent of uncertainty regarding the assets' and liabilities' value. Even when the balance sheet values are known at the date of reporting, the valuer should be aware that the balance sheet values can change as trading continues, which is why transactions are frequently subject to a review of the latest audited financials.

Discounted cash flows from the underlying business

The DCF model is a classic valuation methodology which is paradoxically extremely powerful, yet potentially very weak. In a DCF analysis, the valuer projects into the future the expected cash flows from the business and discounts those cash flows back to the present day at a certain discount rate.

The discount rate applied should reflect the cost of capital and the risks associated with the cash flows. Due to the nature of private equity and the expected risks and returns, it is common to see DCF calculations with discount rates from as low as 10% to as high as 80% for early stage investments made by venture capital funds. When applying the DCF valuation methodology, valuers must remember that the DCF calculation is quite sensitive to minor changes in the discount rate applied, so this rate must be carefully considered.

In theory, the DCF method should lead to the best estimate of the company's true value. Yet in practice, certain challenges can affect the valuer's confidence in the estimate. In a private equity context, many of the investment targets are private companies for which financial statements or forecasts may not be available (or not available in sufficient detail). This diminished availability and quality of information increases the difficulty of estimating future cash flows. Therefore, the valuer is expected to exercise good judgment, coupled with solid industry experience, when generating free cash flow estimates.

Another downside to applying a DCF valuation is the terminal value. Arguably, 70–90% of the enterprise value in a DCF valuation is derived from the terminal value. As this component is very sensitive to any change in either the discount rate or exit multiple (depending on the terminal value method), great care should be applied when estimating this metric; this holds especially true for valuing start-ups and emerging market companies.

Discounted cash flows from the investment

This methodology is similar in concept to the methodology above, but instead of considering all the cash flows from the business, it merely considers the cash flows that relate to the investment instrument itself. DCF from the investment is particularly useful when the cash flows from the investment can be predicted with a high level of certainty, such as a stand-alone mezzanine loan investment or an investment whose terms have been agreed for a future sale price (e.g., the terms of the imminent flotation of the business have been agreed).

VALUATION STEPS

In general, the valuation of a private company involves five basic steps:

Step 1: Understand the purpose of the valuation

Many private equity valuations are performed for a specific purpose. When valuing private firms, the motive for the valuation matters, as it can significantly affect the value obtained. In particular, the value of a private firm will vary dramatically depending on whether it is being valued for sale to a private trade buyer, for sale to a publicly traded firm, or for an initial public offering. If a private trade buyer is involved, then a discount might be appropriate to reflect the additional liquidity risk in holding the shares. Liquidity discounts are not necessary for publicly traded buyers or for exchange listings.

Another reason why the valuation of the company might be different is the value of control over the company. In valuations intended to value companies that are being acquired, the valuer should incorporate the effect of control. Buyers of poorly managed firms that acquire control can remove the incumbent management and change existing practices and strategies, thereby making these firms potentially more valuable. For this reason, the value per share of the same private company will be higher if a buyer acquires control. If the buyers acquire only a minority stake, then the buyers will pay less per share since they cannot influence the decision process and small stakes require a marketability discount. Buyout transactions usually reflect the value of control when valuing the targets. It is no surprise that buyout funds tend to acquire underperforming companies relative to their industry or the overall market and pay a premium for them relative to their existing market value.

Differences in tax rates across potential buyers of a private firm can also affect the valuation output. The tax rate of a buyer can vary from the corporate tax rate (if the potential buyer is a corporation) to the highest marginal tax rate for individuals (if the potential buyer is a wealthy individual). In a methodology like DCF, the tax rates affect both the cash flows (through the after-tax operating income) and the cost of capital (through the tax shields provided by leverage). Accordingly, the value of a private firm can vary across different buyers.

Step 2: Understand the industry and the company's capabilities and competitive position

Various valuation frameworks exist for companies in different industries. A deep understanding of the industry will help identify important economic drivers that affect the value of the company and highlight aspects of the business that present great challenges and opportunities and, thus, justify further scenario analysis.

Porter's (1985) five forces model is a good place to start when assessing the attractiveness of a given industry. The model posits that five forces affect the company's long-term profitability: industries with low rivalry and high barriers to entry, that create/sell products with few potential substitutes, and where both suppliers and buyers have limited power are likely to have good profitability prospects. The five forces analysis can help with a more informed estimation of the industry's growth rate, a key parameter in some valuation methodologies. Besides industry-wide prospects, the competitive position of the company within an industry, as well as its long-term strategy for overcoming any competitive pressures, will help the valuer assess whether the company's value should be higher or lower relative to its peers. The competitive position of a company can be highlighted by several measures such as market share, the company's ability to confine costs (i.e., the cost advantage relative to its peers), or its ability to produce and sell products or services with unique features or in a unique way (i.e., the differentiation advantage relative to its peers). This analysis provides an indication of the expected short-term and medium-term growth rate of the company compared to the industry average.

Important firm-specific factors affect the company's ability to meet its long-term goals and succeed in its industry segment. Valuers should take into account such factors by using as much historical information about the company or industry as possible, especially if company-level information is limited (e.g., in the case of a young firm). Time trends can reveal management's ability to run the company and adapt to different challenges, as well as the long-term potential of the industry. Information about the industry and the competitive position of the company might be difficult to find in situations when the industry is relatively young. Further, the valuation of private companies makes the information-gathering process even more challenging, given that these companies often do not have to file public reports about their financial position. Key sources include industry organizations, reports of publicly traded companies, regulatory agencies, or dedicated providers of market information.

Step 3: Select the appropriate valuation method

There are no rules as to which methodology should be used in a particular setting, but it is crucial that the methodology selected is appropriate for the private company analyzed. The selection will include a consideration of the development stage of the underlying business, the nature of the transaction (if the valuation's purpose is to help with an investment decision), the industry in which it operates, and the availability of data.

Earlier, we discussed potential methodologies that could be used. These methodologies measure value in either absolute (e.g., DCFs) or relative (e.g., price of recent investment, multiples, industry benchmarks, etc.) terms.

Step 4: Perform scenario analyses to investigate the sensitivity of the results to critical valuation assumptions.

DCF models estimate the intrinsic value of a private company but have many challenges in their application. Depending on the assumptions made, a range of values can be generated. Similarly, multiples or industry benchmark methods are characterized by a wide range of implementation choices—valuers can choose different multiples or different peer groups.

As a result, sensitivity analysis is essential. The valuer should try to value the company under different assumptions and implementations and assess how they affect the outcome. Some sensitivity analyses are common, such as different assumptions regarding growth rates and risk premiums for DCF models; others depend on the context, such as specific royalty rate benchmarks in "relief-from-royalty" techniques, and for particular assets. If the industry is competitive then the valuer should assess the sensitivity of forecasted cash flows to changes in market prices, for example, and improvements or declines in market share.

Step 5: Analyze the valuation outputs based on the purpose of the valuation.

Depending on the purpose of the valuation, the valuer can use the outputs to provide an investment recommendation or to report to private equity investors. It is important that the valuation exercise is properly described in the valuation report received by users. This report should clearly identify and provide the key assumptions and inputs used, describe relevant aspects of the macroeconomic environment and industry context, and provide some background information about the company. It should also contain a discussion about the risk factors that might negatively affect the company's value.

IMPLEMENTATION OF THE MAIN VALUATION METHODS: MULTIPLES AND DISCOUNTED CASH FLOW

The multiples (comparables) method

The multiples method is a relative valuation methodology whose objective is to value the private company based on how similar companies trade in public markets. The method relies on three basic steps.

1. First, the valuer attempts to find publicly traded firms that are similar to the private company being valued; this is difficult in many situations since no two firms are identical. Even firms in the same business and of a similar size can differ in terms of risk characteristics and growth potential.

2. Second, the valuer standardizes the market values of the similar publicly traded companies, usually by converting them into multiples of earnings, book values, or sales (revenues).

3. In the third and final step, the valuer obtains the value of the private company by multiplying its earnings, book value, or sales by the appropriate multiple computed in the second step.

The multiples method is the most common method for the valuation of a portfolio of private companies. Several factors contribute to its popularity: it requires far fewer assumptions and is quicker than the DCF methodology; it is easy to understand and present to investors; and it reflects the market's view on the value of the company.

While multiples are relatively intuitive and easy to use, the implementation of the multiples method involves several decisions.

How to pick the benchmark group of publicly traded companies or comparable transactions?

The choice of the benchmark companies or transactions (or peer group) is key to selecting an appropriate and reasonable multiple. The ideal comparable firm is one that has cash flows, growth potential, and risk characteristics similar to the firm being valued. When selecting benchmark companies, the conventional practice is to look at firms within the same industry or business area. Clearly, these should be as close as possible in nature to the entity being valued, but it is impossible to find completely identical companies. As a result, differences will always remain between the firm and its comparable firms. Once a suitable set of comparable peers is identified, these differences might impact a third party's pricing of the investment; therefore, they need to be identified and quantified. Figuring out how to adjust for such differences is a vital part of the relative valuation, and requires a significant exercise of judgment as identification and quantification of differences cannot be subject to prescribed processes and rigid formulas.

Frequently, a valuer will compare business models by considering many commercial aspects and risks, including, for example, geographical spread of the business, brand, reputation, product range, rate of growth, quality of management, currency exposures, and so on—the list is quite extensive. Comparable firms that are significantly different across dimensions deemed to be very important should be eliminated from the set of comparators.

Once a multiple is calculated for each of the remaining comparable firms, an average or median is typically computed. The idea is that remaining differences between the comparator firms and the firm valued in terms of growth, risk, or cash flows are averaged out, thus reducing the measurement error. An alternative is to modify individual peer firm multiples based on the differences observed and then use these individual ratios or an aggregate to value the company.

Valuers can also use sector multiples, which are often seen as a simple way of averaging the multiple across the entire sector. Justifying points of difference between the entity being valued and the sector as a whole are difficult tasks, though. In addition, these multiples are calculated by adding the market value of the sector and dividing it by the sum of the relevant fundamental variable (e.g., earnings, revenues) across the sector. If the sector contains a large firm with unusually good performance, the sector multiple can be mathematically calculated in excess of most of the underlying multiples, creating a large bias in the valuation.

In developed markets, it is relatively easy to find a number of suitable companies to use as comparators. However, in an emerging market, there may be no obvious local domestic comparators. In this situation, valuers need to broaden their search to other geographies. A combination of foreign company multiples and local and foreign stock exchanges over time may be a good start to points-of-difference quantification.

Which multiple to use?

A valuer could potentially measure the value of a private company based on a large set of multiples, which can be classified in two types: (1) equity price multiples (computed as ratios of equity values to some measure of fundamental value that is relevant to equity holders), and (2) enterprise value multiples (computed by dividing the total value of the company, including its debt, by measures of fundamental value of the entire company). Depending on the fundamental value used in the denominator, multiples can be classified in various categories:

Earnings multiples (price to earnings (P/E) and enterprise value to EBITDA (EV/EBITDA))

P/E multiples are regularly published for quoted companies and thus, have the advantage of being readily sourced. At the same time, they require adjustments to reflect substantially different levels of gearing commonly seen in portfolio companies acquired via buyouts. These multiples can be estimated using current earnings per share (current P/E), earnings over the last four quarters or last twelve months (LTM) earnings (trailing P/E), or expected earnings per share in the next year (forward P/E). EV/EBITDA multiples are used by many private equity practitioners, as EBITDA is seen as a proxy for cash generation within the business. EBITDA multiples usually need to be calculated from either public information or from recent acquisitions in the market. However, multiples from the latter might need to be adjusted for transaction-specific dynamics (e.g., untypical synergies or irrational escalation of commitment). These multiples are appropriate for valuing private companies with different financial leverage as EBITDA is a pre-interest earnings figure.

Revenue multiples

These multiples are computed as firm total value divided by sales. They are an extension of the earnings multiples, based on the assumption that the companies in a particular industry are all capable of generating similar margins (e.g., in highly commoditized markets). The advantage of using revenue multiples is that it becomes far easier to compare firms in different sectors with different accounting rules. Sales are less affected by distortions introduced by accounting rules than earnings or accounting book values. Revenue multiples are often used when the private company has negative or zero earnings (as is the case with many young technology companies). They are also appropriate when the private company's business is cyclical or when the company is mature. The main drawback is the inability to capture differences in cost structures and profitability.

Book value multiples (price-to-book value of equity and firm value to total assets)

The first book multiple is computed as the market price of the company's equity divided by the book value of equity (or net worth). This ratio can vary widely across industries, depending on the growth potential. When valuing a private company's entire value, the valuer should use the second ratio, which is estimated as the value of the benchmark publicly traded firm and the book value of all its assets (rather than just the equity). An alternative to the book value of all assets is to use the replacement cost of all assets (this ratio is called Tobin's Q). These multiples are appropriate for private firms that have relatively liquid assets (e.g., property, finance, and insurance), since these assets' book values are likely to be close to market values. They are also used when the private firm is not expected to be a going concern (i.e., it is expected to be liquidated in the near future).

When computing multiples, the valuer must ensure consistency between the numerator and the denominator. If the numerator is the equity value, then the denominator should be an equity measure of performance, such as net income or book value of equity. If the numerator is a firm value measure (i.e., the enterprise value, which is the sum of the values of debt and equity, net of cash), then the denominator should also reflect a firm measure (e.g., operating income, EBITDA, or book value of all assets).

Similarly, if the multiples are computed for several publicly traded firms, the valuer should make sure that the multiples are defined uniformly across different companies. Consider, for instance, the firm value to EBITDA, which is commonly used in private equity investing. The market value of equity used to compute the firm value in the numerator should be based on the stock price at the same point in time for all benchmark firms. Furthermore, not only should the market value of the debt be computed at the same point in time, but the measurement should be consistent as well (since debt is not traded or is traded infrequently, valuers typically use the book value of debt—and they need to ensure that the debt is accounted for in a similar way across all companies). Finally, EBITDA in the denominator can be from the most recent financial year (current EBITDA), from the last four quarters (trailing or last twelve month EBITDA), or expected earnings in the next financial year (forward EBITDA).

While many private equity firms use the EBITDA multiple to value companies, it is important to note that there are some limitations when using this metric. The valuer should consider at least three pitfalls of this multiple:

- It does not consider the investment needs of the business, and thus it underestimates the capital intensity and overestimates the amount of distributable cash to investors.

- It does not reflect business risks.

- It ignores taxes; this can have a significant impact if companies pay different tax rates.

As a result, when using the EBITDA multiple for valuing private companies, the valuer should consider three important factors before putting it into practice:

1) **First, understand the capital intensity of the business.** There are three main forms of investment reflected on the balance sheet:

   - **Changes in net working capital**, which do not demand a lot of investment and vary greatly between sectors.

   - **Capital expenditures (Capex) minus depreciation.** Capex represents a significant investment over time and depreciation is often used as a proxy for maintenance Capex. However, depreciation fails to consider the investment necessary to support value-creating growth. One useful measure of capital intensity is the relationship between EBIT and Depreciation, which can be defined as the EBITDA depreciation factor (EBITDA/EBIT). Companies with lower capital needs will tend to have lower EBITDA depreciation factors.

   - **Acquisitions minus Divestitures.** Acquisitions are the largest source of investment, but a common analytical mistake is that investors often extrapolate a historical EBITDA growth rate that is in part a result of acquisitions and fail to consider the necessary investments in their forecasts, thus underestimating the required capital investments to achieve that growth.

2) **Second, understand the significance of the return on incremental invested capital (ROIIC).** ROIIC compares the change in net operating profits after tax in a given year with the amount invested in the prior year. A high ROIIC means that a company can achieve its growth targets with a modest

amount of investments, and a lower amount of investments means more money to investors. Companies with low EBITDA depreciation factors tend to have higher ROIICs.

3) **Third, consider the importance of leverage.** Different capital structures reflect different tax liabilities. Capital intensive businesses tend to use more leverage to finance investment requirements because they cannot fund their growth solely with internally generated funds.

Other considerations of the EBITDA include that companies with low EBITDA depreciation factors get higher multiples (holding everything else equal) because they do not need to generate as much EBITDA to deliver the same amount of net operating profits after tax. Additionally, even though evidence shows that both P/E and EBITDA multiples are highly correlated for a large set of companies, there are some instances where the P/E multiple can vary significantly between companies with the same EV/EBITDA multiple. The core drivers of all multiples are the ROIIC and growth. Two companies with the same prospects of growth and ROIIC can have different P/E multiples because of different capital structures, tax rates, and the effects of unconsolidated businesses. In addition, various accounting adjustments further contribute to significant differences.

How to establish the benchmark multiple?

The valuer might compute several types of multiples for a group of peer firms in an effort to answer the questions of which one to select, and how to aggregate the multiples of the peer group. Each multiple computation provides some relevant information for valuing the private company; therefore, using a single valuation indicator is insufficient. In most cases, valuers compute an average multiple by type (sometimes weighted by the size of the companies). If there are outlying observations, it is more appropriate to focus on the median peer group multiple, or even to compute a harmonic mean (this mean gives more weight to low multiples and less weight to high multiples, thus mitigating the impact of large outliers and generating a more conservative valuation).

What additional adjustments are necessary?

The valuer of a private company should include a discount or premium against a comparator group to reflect any differences between the company and the comparator group. The most obvious adjustment is the discount that reflects the lower marketability and liquidity of the private company. With publicly traded firms, liquidation risks are low; the transactions costs for publicly listed stocks are usually a small percentage of the value. With equity in a private business, liquidation costs as a percentage of firm value can be substantial. Consequently, the value of equity in a private business obtained by means of a multiplier needs to be discounted for illiquidity. (We discuss the illiquidity adjustment as well as other adjustments in a later Section)

The valuer should also take into account differences between the business valued and the benchmarks used. There may be additional adjustments required for matters that fall outside the normal business model, including any matter that a prospective purchaser might consider relevant. Typically, adjustments arise from surplus assets to the business, contingencies arising from lawsuits, impending regulations which might impact the business model, and financing considerations. An adjustment may also arise from financing considerations where the valuer applies a deduction to the enterprise value to reflect the possibility that banking covenants will be breached during the next year and require renegotiation.

Valuation based on discounted cash flows

DCF valuation (also called net present value) views the intrinsic value of a private firm as the present value of its expected cash flows that will be generated in the future. The method is usually implemented by first estimating the value of the firm and then subtracting the face value of non-common stock capital (e.g., debt, stock options, preferred shares, etc.) to arrive at the value of common equity. The values of operating and non-operating assets are estimated separately, and then combined to find the firm value.

The DCF methodology can be summarized in a few steps. We discuss private equity-specific issues in the implementation in each of these steps. The first three steps compute the value of the operating assets of the company. Appendix A illustrates an implementation of the DCF valuation method.

Step 1: Calculate firm cash flows.

$$CF = EBIT * (1 - t) + DEPR - CAPEX - \Delta NWC$$

where

CF = firm cash flows (which belong to both equity and debtholders)

EBIT = earnings before interest and taxes

t = corporate tax rate

DEPR = depreciation

CAPEX = capital expenditure

ΔNWC = change in net working capital, can be negative

Capital expenditures are the current year's investments in property plant and equipment (PPE) net of depreciation of PPE. The valuer might also include in Capex acquisitions of other companies or investments in critical intangible assets via research and development expenses. Net working capital consists of the following balance sheet items: operating cash + trade receivables + other receivables + inventories + prepaid expenses - accounts payable - other current liabilities. Any change in working capital is therefore the present year's working capital minus last year's working capital.

The cash flow formula above computes cash generated by the operations of the firm, after paying taxes on operations only, and after capital expenditures and expenditures for additional working capital. These cash flows represent cash that is available for distribution to the holders of debt and equity in the firm, and/or for investment in additional excess marketable securities.

The valuer should develop forecasts for these cash flows for an initial period of 5–10 years, but also for the cash flows in perpetuity. These forecasts should be constructed based on discussions with management, bearing in mind potential managerial upward biases.

In the case of private firms, a few adjustments need to be made to the cash flow formula above:

- EBIT might be negative. In this case, the valuer needs to normalize earnings (i.e., the assumption being that negative earnings are temporary). Earnings are usually normalized based on revenue projections for which margins are estimated.

- Sustainable margins and the adjustment period may be unknown. Valuers should estimate a sustainable margin and the length of the adjustment period over which earnings turn from negative to positive.

- The salary of the owner/entrepreneur might not be reflected on the income statement of the company. Many private firms do not pay salaries to owner-managers or, if they do, the salary may not reflect the market value of the services provided to the firm; this is because in many countries the tax system does not distinguish between income earned as a salary or income from dividends for private firms, making owners indifferent between them. The valuer should treat salaries as operating expenses, or EBIT will be overstated. Appropriate salaries should be estimated based on the role the owners play in the firm and the cost of hiring replacements for them.

- Intermingling of personal and business expenses often occurs at small private businesses when there is no separation between ownership and control; for example, owners who have full control of the business may maintain offices at their homes, or make business expenses for personal activities or services they receive. The valuer should remove all of these personal expenses from EBIT to avoid creating a misleading picture of the firm's performance.

- CAPEX and ΔNWC are difficult to forecast if the private firm is in a high-growth stage. CAPEX and ΔNWC can be measured as percentages of revenues. The valuer can assume that they grow at the same rate as revenues and that their percentage of revenues will approach the industry average.

- Headline corporate tax rates may not apply. Public firms are typically valued using the marginal corporate tax rate. However, private firms may face different marginal tax rates since individual tax status and tax rates vary much more widely than corporate tax rates. Further, differences in tax rates across potential buyers of a private firm can be significant. The tax rate affects computations of both the firm's cash flows and the cost of capital.

- Other accounting adjustments may be necessary. Private firms might use inconsistent accounting rules, given that they are not expected to have high-quality audited financial statements that follow the same accounting standards as public firms. The valuer should make adjustments such that the EBIT measurement is consistent with GAAP (e.g., recognize provisions based on beliefs of future losses).

Step 2: Calculate the terminal value.

$$TVT = [CFT * (1 + g)]/(r - g)$$

where

TVT = terminal value at time T

CFT = cash flow in the terminal year (i.e., at the end of the forecasting horizon)

g = growth rate in perpetuity

r = discount rate (weighted average cost of capital) calculated as: $r = (D/V) * r_d * (1 - t) + (E/V) * r_e$; r_d is the cost of debt; r_e is the cost of equity; D is the market value of debt; E is the market value of equity; and V = D + E is the total firm value.

The terminal value captures the business value at the end of the initial forecasting period for the cash flows. It is computed based on the assumption that cash flows in the terminal year (the last year of the forecasting horizon) will continue to grow at a constant rate in perpetuity. Typically, the cash flow and discount rates are in nominal terms and are not adjusted for inflation. Estimation of both the growth and the discount rates is particularly challenging in the case of private firms, as discussed in detail below. It is important to note that the terminal value can also be computed using an EBITDA (or Sales) Multiple. Please see Appendix A for an illustration.

Growth rate: With private firms, the valuer will not have available sell-side analyst estimates of growth. Moreover, the historical growth numbers have to be used with caution, especially if the private firm is at an early stage in its life. The valuer can estimate the perpetual expected growth rate of cash flows as the product of the re-investment rate, (CAPEX + R&D - DEPR + ΔNWC)/EBIT(1 - t), and the return on capital, EBIT(1 - t)/book value of capital, at the beginning of the year. In each future year, this estimated growth rate will be a combination of inflation and real growth. In the "long run" (a factor dependent on industry maturity, firm strategy, etc.), most firms will grow at a rate between that of inflation and overall growth rate of the economy (assuming the firm operates in markets with similar economic prospects). A key point to keep in mind is that the shorter the period of forecasted cash flows (say, three years), the greater the importance of terminal value to the valuation. Valuations in which the terminal value represents a substantial majority of the value are likely to be extremely sensitive to small changes in growth rate assumptions.

Notably, with private firms, the going concern assumption must be made with extreme caution. Private firms are often younger and untested. The implication is that the terminal value of a private firm will be lower than the terminal value of a publicly traded firm. If there is a reason to believe that the private firm will cease to exist at some future point, then the valuer should use the liquidation value of the assets as the terminal value. These liquidation values are usually lower than the value of continuing operations.

Discount rate: The discount rate is the weighted average cost of capital (WACC), which is based on three important variables: the cost of equity, the cost of debt, and the debt/equity ratio. It should reflect the risk of achieving the cash flows projected given the purpose of the valuation exercise. For instance, the discount rate will be lower if the company is valued for an initial public offering versus for an acquisition or just for reporting (i.e., continuous operation as a private company). Initial public offerings are addressed to a larger group of diversified investors with lower-risk premiums. If the company remains private then its access to debt financing is more restricted than that of a similar public company; thus, its cost of debt will be higher. In general, the information disclosed about a private company is limited, introducing greater uncertainty about the quality of the cash flow projections, which in turn leads to a higher discount rate than for a public company.

- **Cost of equity:** The cost of equity for publicly traded firms is typically estimated based on the capital asset pricing model (CAPM; risk-free rate plus beta times the market risk premium) using historical stock prices. In the case of private firms, there is no historical price information and, in addition, the owners of private firms may not be diversified (diversification is a core assumption of CAPM). In a private equity setting, there are a few approaches to estimating the beta (however, all have their weaknesses due to data issues or quality of the benchmarks used): (1) accounting betas (coefficient of changes in market earnings in a regression of changes in firms earnings on market earnings); (2) fundamental betas (betas of similar publicly traded firms are related to observable variables such as earnings growth, debt ratios, and variance in earnings, and parameters of this model are then used to estimate the beta for the private firm); and (3) bottom-up betas (the beta for a private firm can be estimated by looking at the average betas for similar publicly traded companies).

- **Beta:** Whatever the method chosen to estimate the beta, valuers might need to adjust betas if the owner/potential buyer of the private company is undiversified.[2] Alternatively, valuers could consider other risk premiums specific to private firms, such as the small-stock premium, or company-specific risk premiums in addition to the market risk captured by the CAPM beta. These premiums compensate for the higher risk associated with firm size and the less diversified operations of the firm and/or its owners. The earlier the development stage of the company, the higher the company-specific risk premium.

- **Cost of debt:** For private firms, the cost of debt is measured by looking at the interest rate on the firm's debt (which is likely to be bank debt). If the private firm never used debt capital, then valuers can use the cost of debt of similar publicly traded firms and add an extra spread to reflect the incremental riskiness of the private firm relative to the public peers. If the private firm is close to an initial public offering, valuers can assume a cost of debt similar to that of publicly traded companies in the same industry without any additional adjustments.

- **Debt ratio:** When market values of equity and debt are unavailable for private firms, valuers can use the industry average or target debt ratios. If the company is valued for an acquisition, then valuers should use a ratio that reflects the likely capital structure of the target at the time of exit.

- **WACC:** While WACC is a fairly simple and straightforward evaluation of the discount rate for a firm, it relies on restrictive assumptions to get the value of the interest tax shields. With non-plain-vanilla debt securities (such as floating rate debt, high-yield debt, etc.), WACC might lead valuers to misvalue the interest tax shields.

Step 3: Calculate the value of operations.

$$EV_{operations} = [CF1/(1 + r)] + [CF2/(1 + r)^2] + [CF3/(1 + r)^3] + \cdots + [(CFT + TVT)/ (1+ r)^T]$$

All variables are defined above.

Step 4: Calculate the enterprise value.

$$EV = EV_{operations} + EV_{non-operations}$$

The value of the non-operating assets is added to the value of the operating assets computed in Step 3. Non-operating assets are defined as those assets that are not necessary for the ongoing operations of the private firm. Some examples include excess cash, marketable financial securities in which the firm invests excess cash, non-performing assets, real estate not used for operating activities, and so on.

Step 5: Adjust the enterprise value and compute the value of equity.

---

[2] Damodaran (2009) discusses the adjustment of beta for undiversified buyers/owners of private companies whereby the market beta, measured for a set of peer publicly traded firms, is divided by the correlation between the peer firm's returns and the market returns.

At this stage, valuers should adjust the total value of the enterprise for illiquidity and/or control premiums, depending on the purpose of the valuation. Finally, valuers can compute the value of the common equity by removing the value of the debt in the capital structure and that of dilutive claims. (We discuss these final adjustments separately in a subsequent section.)

The power of the DCF methodology outlined above lies in the fact that it can calculate a value for the private company in all situations. However, there are several reasons why the above DCF method might not be appropriate for private companies:

- Discount rates are difficult to estimate for many private companies given the scarcity of available publicly traded firms that are similar in terms of risk, growth, and cash flow patterns.

- The method does not deal with changing capital structures that are specific to buyout transactions. The debt ratio used to compute the discount rate is constant throughout the forecasting period.

- Forecasted cash flows might not be reliable given the high uncertainties that early stage young private companies face. In a dynamic business environment, most managers would be reasonably confident in their cash flow projections for the next 12 months, but levels of confidence fall as the period extends into the future. If a significant growth rate is projected (and particularly when it is projected from a loss-making position in the early years), most if not all of the value calculated resides in the terminal value assumptions. This result makes the outcome of the DCF valuation highly sensitive to the discount rate and growth assumptions. In addition, basing a valuation entirely on the predictability of cash flows anticipated in the period after the forecasting period lacks credibility.

- The method might not reflect actual market conditions as much as the valuer's assumptions.

We address some of the above concerns regarding the DCF method below, and present a few additional methods that are variants of the DCF methodology commonly used in private equity transactions.

The adjusted discount cash flow method

The adjusted DCF method is typically used to value buyout targets. When a firm's capital structure is changing or it has net operating losses (NOLs) that can be used to offset taxable income, an adjusted DCF method should be used. If a firm has NOLs then its effective tax rate changes over time, as NOLs are carried forward for tax purposes and netted against taxable income. The adjusted method accounts for the effect of the firm's changing tax status by valuing NOLs separately.

Under the adjusted DCF method, the valuer computes the present value of the cash flows by ignoring the capital structure. In other words, the discount rate used is the cost of equity as opposed to the weighted average cost of capital, assuming that the company is financed fully with equity (PVcash flows).

The tax benefits associated with the capital structure are then estimated separately by computing the present value of the tax savings from the tax-deductible interest payments. The interest payments will change over time as debt levels change due to repayments. By convention the discount rate for this calculation is the pre-tax cost of debt:

$$PV_{\text{interest shield}} = [I_1/(1+r_d)] + [I_2/(1+r_d)^2] + [I_3/(1+r_d)^3] + \ldots + [I_T/(1+r_d)^T]$$

where

I = Interest related tax shield in year n computed as Interest expense * tax rate (based on the debt repayment schedule)

r_d = Pre-tax cost of debt.

Finally, NOLs available to the company are quantified. They are computed as (EBIT - interest expense) * tax rate every year. Note that EBIT - interest expense must be negative in order to obtain a tax shield. The discount rate used to value NOLs is often the pre-tax rate on debt. If it is certain that NOLs will result in tax benefits, the risk-free rate can also be used as the discount rate:

$$PV_{NOL\ shield} = [NOL_1/(1+r_d)] + [NOL_2/(1+r_d)^2] + [NOL_3/(1+rd)^3] + \ldots + [NOL_T/(1+r_d)^T]$$

where

NOL$_n$ = Net operating loss related tax shield in year n computed as above

r_d = Pre-tax cost of debt.

The enterprise value is the sum of the present value of cash flows (PVcash flows), interest tax shields (PV interest shield), NOL tax shields (PV NOL shield), and non-operating assets. As with the DCF method, final adjustments of the enterprise value are necessary (illiquidity, control, etc.).

The venture capital method

The venture capital method is often applied in the private equity industry when venture capitalists provide financing to young start-up firms raising additional equity. The method starts with forecasting the earnings of the private firm in a future year when the venture capitalist expects an exit either via a public offering or a trade sale. This earnings forecast, in conjunction with an earnings multiple (estimated by looking at publicly traded firms in the same business), is used to assess the value of the firm at the time of exit. Valuers can also forecast revenues for the firm in the exit year and apply a revenue multiple to estimate the terminal exit value.

This terminal value is discounted back to the present at a target rate of return, which measures what venture capitalists believe is a justifiable return on their investment, given the risks involved:

Firm value = Exit value$_N$/(1 + Target return)^N

where

Exit value$_N$ = expected value of the firm at the time of exit

Target return = rate of return expected by the venture capital investor.

The target rate of return is usually set at a much higher level than the traditional cost of equity for the firm, and ranges from 40–75%. What can justify such a high return? Venture capitalists argue that it provides compensation for the illiquidity of their investment, the risk involved (start-up companies are at the beginning of their life and the failure rate is very high), and the valuable services they provide to the company in terms of time and advice. The target return also adjusts for the sometimes overoptimistic exit projections provided by management.

Commonly used average discount rates across different stages of company development are listed in Exhibit 1:

Exhibit 1: Average discount rates across company development stages

Stage (risk)	Description of Stage	Expected Returns
Seed	Capital to prove a concept	70–80%
Start-up	Capital to complete product development and initial marketing	50–60%
First stage	Capital to initiate full-scale manufacturing and sales	35–40%
Second stage	Working capital for the initial expansion of a company that is producing and shipping and has account receivables	25–35%
Third stage	Capital for a firm with increasing sales that is at least breaking even	25–35%
Bridge	Capital used by a company that will go public in six months to a year	20–25%

The above framework varies slightly for start-ups or early stage companies where the valuer is not seeking to undertake an outright acquisition of the firm, but instead seeking to take a minority stake in the company by injecting additional capital.

Implementing the venture capital method involves several steps, as discussed:

1. Determine the projected value of the company at a future date (usually seven to eight years ahead).

2. Discount this projected value to the present, using the investor's target internal rate of return to get what is called the post-financing valuation (V_{post}). Since this post-financing valuation includes the new capital that is being invested, valuers can calculate the implied value of the company before the financing—the pre-financing valuation (V_{pre})—by subtracting the amount of Capital (C) being invested from the post-financing valuation.

$$V_{pre} = V_{post} - C$$

3. Calculate the percentage ownership required for the investor by dividing the amount of capital being invested by the discounted terminal value.

$$\% \text{ ownership} = C/V_{post}$$

4. Adjust the percentage ownership above for the effects of adding a key employee share option pool and for potential future rounds of funding (i.e., expected dilution adjustments).

Valuation of intangible assets

Some of the most important assets of many successful companies in the present knowledge-based economy are intangible assets (IA), primarily represented by intellectual property (IP). IA are identifiable non-monetary assets that are not physical in nature (e.g., trade secrets, proprietary processes, knowhow, un-recorded inventions, market data, competitive information, etc.) which are created by businesses to perform daily activities, innovate, and create competitive advantages. For many companies, IA may account for up to 80% of their average market value. For start-ups and research-intensive companies, this figure can stretch even higher. All three elements of IA—that is, IP, intellectual assets, and intellectual capital—are vital to a sustainable business. IP refers to creations of the mind (e.g., inventions; literary and artistic works; designs; symbols, names, copyright materials (including software); databases; and images used in commerce, etc.). Intellectual capital involves, for instance, a company's positioning, branding, reputation, relationships, and contracts.

Everyone (including business owners, accountants, investors, innovators, inventors, entrepreneurs, attorneys, advisers, etc.) in an organization should understand IA and IP, because this asset fulfills its greatest potential for an organization when it is possessed by all employees collectively. For this reason, many companies spend millions of dollars to develop and/or purchase formal knowledge management systems, and to generate, organize, develop, and distribute knowledge throughout the organization.

While many managers have a good idea of how to value their tangible assets in their business, they are often less clear about when they need to assess the value of their IA. Yet, if investors, entrepreneurs, and managers can estimate the value of their IA, they can measure and manage their company's competitive position and overall IA/IP strategic roadmap much more easily and accurately, facilitating strategic decisions.

The Leveraged Buyout (LBO) valuation method

The LBO method is similar to the venture capital method, but is typically employed for firms that are relatively more mature. We cover this method very briefly here, as there is a separate LBO modeling chapter. The main steps involved in developing an LBO model are as follows (Appendix B provides also an intuitive graphical representation):

1. Build base-case projections, conduct due diligence on the industry and company, and determine model drivers and assumptions.

2. Decide on an appropriate target IRR; how much reward is needed for the risk and type of the transaction (e.g., stable buyout, growth equity, distressed/turnaround situation, management quality/need, etc.)?

3. Assume a realistic capital structure based on industry dynamics, comparable transactions, and the current state of financial markets.

4. Forecast an exit strategy and appropriate range of exit multiples.

5. Discount the exit equity valuation at the target IRRs and add the expected debt at entry based on the realistic capital structure determined at step 3 to compute the entry value of the business. Divide that value by the company's EBITDA to obtain the entry multiple that will be offered to the seller to ensure the achievement of the target IRR.

6. Stress test the model to achieve the right risk/reward profile and potentially meet the seller's price expectations. The "tension" in buyouts often centers on the feasibility of debt financing versus the adequacy of equity returns.

Thus, the method starts in an equivalent manner to a DCF analysis by projecting the company's revenues and net income over several years (usually five). Subsequently, the valuer takes some performance measure in the terminal year (e.g., year 5) and uses that to generate an exit value. The exit value may be determined using EBITDA multiples, revenue multiples, or another type of multiples. The critical element is the value that the valuer believes can be extracted at the time of exit. Selecting the right exit multiple requires considerable judgment. Current industry multiples may be helpful, but if the industry is growing very quickly at present (because it is a young industry or it is in an expansion phase), then exit multiples might be lower in the future than they are today. A recommended approach is to use the average multiple over a cycle, a substantial error may be introduced if the valuer relies on economic assumptions. Valuers may have to look at their acquisition or precedent transaction multiple as well. If valuers believe that the acquiring firm "got a good deal" because the transaction is proprietary or they purchased the firm cheaply owing to an idiosyncratic situation (e.g., short-term distress), then the exit multiple might be higher than the entry multiple. In any case, the value may be sensitized for different exit multiples.

The valuer then models an IRR based on the equity that was invested upfront today and what they believe will be received for their ownership at exit. Typically, this process requires projecting out a debt schedule, including interim debt repayments, so that the value of debt in the exit year is subtracted from the exit valuation. In essence, the private equity investor is valuing "equity in, equity out." Valuers then compare the IRR of the acquisition firm's equity investment to its "hurdle rate." Hurdle rates vary from firm to firm and also depend upon the size, stage, and industry of the investment. Most LBO hurdle rates are around 20–30%. These hurdles might be adjusted based on geography, leverage, and industry risk.

While an LBO model is similar in many respects to a DCF model, there are several important differences. First, most companies do not make extensive use of leverage and several adjustments to the basic DCF model are required to account for the substantially higher leverage that is inherent to an LBO transaction. Second, in a DCF valuation the valuer seeks to ascertain the intrinsic value of a company, which is the value of the company on an ongoing basis. By contrast, the aim of an LBO valuation is to help the valuer understand whether a target can meet its particular return requirements, which will depend largely on the purchase price. Compared to intrinsic value, a purchase price multiple reflects market value at a certain point in time.

Since an LBO model is valued from a sponsor's perspective, the cash flows used to evaluate an LBO are typically after financing cash flows, referred to as equity residual cash flows (RCFs). RCFs reflect the sponsor's perspective because, as an equity investor, a sponsor has discretion over any cash flow remaining after the commitments promised to debt holders (i.e., interest and principal payments). The conventional DCF valuation and adjusted DCF valuation are based on free cash flows (FCFs) to total capital. A comparison between the components FCFs and RCFs is detailed in Exhibit 2:

Exhibit 2: Comparison between FCFs and RCFs

Free Cash Flow to Total Capital	**Residual Cash Flow to Equity**
EBIT x $(1 - T)$, where T is the firm's marginal cash tax rate	(EBIT – Interest Expense) x $(1 - T)$ = Net income Less: Principal payments (amortization)

Items common to both:
Plus: Depreciation and amortization (D&A)
Plus: Other non-cash charges (e.g., PIK interest)
Less: Capital expenditures (CAPEX)
Less: Changes in net working capital (NWC)

The second difference between LBO valuation and the DCF method is that the DCF method assumes that the company has a fairly static capital structure. This assumption is appropriate when firms have target leverage ratios they seek to maintain. In contrast, the capital structure put in place with LBOs is designed to be transient in nature. The debt is initially high to force changes in the company, and is then paid off as operating performance improves. Thus, the firm's leverage ratio changes violate a basic assumption of the WACC method. A valuer employing the LBO valuation method avoids the issue of the discount rate and calculates an expected IRR from RCFs. The IRR is then compared against a minimum hurdle or target rate to reach a decision about the attractiveness of the deal.

Liquidation value method

In an extreme scenario where a company ceases its operations and is auctioned, a liquidation value must be computed. The following assumptions are practiced in a liquidation value scenario:

- **Cash and cash equivalent assets** are taken at nominal values.

- **Non-cash tangible assets** will be valued at below their replacement values (e.g., accounts receivable will be valued below book value because it might be difficult to collect outstanding invoices as debtors forestall their invoice payments in the hope that the business will liquidate without collecting).

- **The value of IA** (e.g., patents and licenses) is substantially reduced in a liquidation scenario.

- Since debtholders have the highest priority claims to the liquidation proceeds, **liabilities** will be valued at their normal book values.

A liquidation value method can be useful as it establishes a floor price for a business, and can be used to calculate the downside of investing in a specific company (i.e., the maximum of the downside is simply the purchase price minus the liquidation value).

Final adjustments

As discussed, once the enterprise value has been measured, regardless of the methodology, a few final adjustments are required to measure the value of the common equity in the company. These final adjustments depend on specific circumstances, such as the type of the transaction for which the company is valued, or the capital structure and other characteristics of the company.

Illiquidity discount

Given that private companies are not traded in liquid markets, private equity investors demand compensation for the risk that the acquired company may become illiquid. The magnitude of the illiquidity discount is likely to vary depending on the characteristics of the private firm; however, certain factors can guide the valuer in justifying the magnitude, such as the liquidity of the identifiable assets, the financial health of the company, the size of the firm, or the likelihood that the company may be listed on an exchange at some point in the future. Much of the practice seems to rely on rules of thumb that often set the illiquidity discount at 20–30% of estimated value. For reporting purposes, the accounting standards require that any liquidity discounts should be built into the multiple considerations or discount rates.

A number of studies have been undertaken to estimate the quantum of discount to be applied to the initial valuation of a private company to account for illiquidity risk, idiosyncratic risk, and bankruptcy risk. In essence, a typical approach to calculating the size of the discount is as follows:

1. Begin with the discount for illiquidity for a small firm with negligible revenue; empirically, this has been estimated to be approximately 30%.

2. Reduce the discount to take into account the size of the firm.

3. Increase the discount to take into account any negative earnings.

When valuing a private equity investment with the purpose of reporting to investors, an important check is comparing the size of any discount applied at the valuation date against the difference between the multiples at the date of acquisition. This will not remain constant over the holding period of the investment, but any significant movements should be explained.

Control premium

There are implications for valuation if a large portion of the private firm being valued is offered for sale. If that portion provides a controlling interest (i.e., the right to pick the firm's management), it should have a substantially higher value than if it does not provide this power. Estimation of the control premium is challenging given measurement issues, but it ranges in practice anywhere from 10%–50%. If the portion acquired provides a non-controlling small interest, then the value of the company should be smaller. For small stakes, valuers should apply marketability discounts.

Contingency-related adjustments

Contingencies represent potential future payments to the seller of a private company or the management if the company achieves a certain level of performance or certain events stipulated in the purchase agreement (e.g., if the company obtains regulatory approval for a product). The introduction of a contingent consideration introduces uncertainty when valuing the company. The valuer must estimate the probability that the events will occur, assess the magnitude of the likely future payments, and adjust downward the value of the company accordingly.

Debt-related adjustments

A typical structure for a private equity buyout transaction may result in several layers of financing, which include senior debt provided by a bank, mezzanine debt provided by another financing house, and—ranking below these—debts and/or a combination of debt and equity provided by the private equity fund. All debts that would be redeemed at the point of sale and rank higher than the private equity fund's highest-ranking interest are deducted from the enterprise value.

In a simple situation, the amount deducted would be the principal outstanding, including any accrued interest. Where redemption premiums apply, these would normally be included. The outstanding debt may be reduced by surplus cash in the investee company. Cash that is required as part of the normal working capital should not reduce the debt. Only the cash that could be used to pay down the debt without impacting the operations should reduce outstanding debt amounts.

There may be situations where the senior debt is traded and a market price, below the outstanding amount, can be observed. In theory, the private company could acquire debt in the market at the lower value and cancel it. This theory does not support the suggestion that the senior debt deduction should take place at market value, rather than the repayable amount in a liquidation scenario. Once the debt has been acquired, then the "profit" on canceling the debt might be recognized in the fair value calculation.

Dilution-related adjustments

The private equity market has developed a wide range of schemes that are intended to either incentivize the management of the investee company or favor one investor over another. Many of these schemes are as tax efficient as possible, making them enormously complicated. Typical schemes include the following:

- **Ratchets**, where the holder will receive additional equity if certain targets are achieved. "Reverse ratchets," where holders increase their percentage holding of their shares by the buyback at a fixed price of another entity's equity, are also possible.

- **Options and warrants**, which represent the rights to acquire additional equity under certain conditions.

- **Liquidation preferences**, where the holder will receive a return in preference to other investors.

- **Conversion clauses**, which stipulate the ability to switch to a different instrument.

Whatever the individual terms of these schemes, the valuer needs to determine their impact on the company valued. It would be unusual for a valuer to resort to complex derivative valuation models to separately value each derivative instrument. The valuer should assess the expected impact and consider what adjustments a prospective purchaser of the instrument might make.

Often, valuers will consider the expected outcome at the future realization date. If, for example, an option is held by the management team and the option's exercise price is below the value that would be attributed to the shares that it represents, the valuer will assume that the dilution will take place and value the remaining shares accordingly. When considering the likely outcome, it is important to recognize that the terms—particularly those affecting the management team—may need to be amended to facilitate a sale. The strict legal position may not be the expected outcome.

In the event that the private equity fund holds a significant position in derivative instruments itself, the valuer should consider using a derivative valuation model.

Transaction-related adjustments

When valuing a company for the purpose of a transaction, valuers must consider information about the potential buyer or the market conditions of the transaction.

Potential buyers can be split into two sets: strategic buyers and financial buyers. A strategic buyer is usually willing to pay a higher multiple when acquiring a company. The higher multiple reflects the lower cost of capital and the potential revenue or cost-based synergies that the strategic buyer will create after acquiring the target company. Due to their industry expertise, strategic buyers can create value internally through consolidation, innovation, and operational excellence. Therefore, the strategic buyer may use more aggressive assumptions in terms of growth that will show a higher price premium. Further, strategic buyers will determine terminal value based on a perpetual growth rate, rather than a terminal year exit multiple, as a financial buyer would. In contrast, financial buyers, such as private equity funds, have a significantly higher cost of capital and do not achieve any synergies because they are expected to run the company as a standalone entity.

Triangulating the outputs of the multiples and DCF methods

After completing the DCF and multiples valuation, the valuer has information from both the market and his/her own estimates, and can make comparisons in an effort to determine the appropriate value of the company. The most common way to triangulate the results of both valuation methodologies is by checking how values obtained from the multiples (EV/EBITDA or EV/sales) are explained by assumptions in the DCF model. In this way, valuers can determine if the assumptions implied by the DCF model make sense. In other words, valuers can see if the sales growth rates or operational margins (as well as the rest of the DCF assumptions) are too conservative or too optimistic, and make the appropriate adjustments. The advantage of plugging the valuation ranges of the multiples valuation into a DCF is that it helps valuers arrive at a more informed valuation of the company.

When this comparative analysis is careful and well reasoned, it not only serves as a useful check of the DCF assumptions, but also provides critical insights into what drives value in a given industry.

CONCLUSION

The use of multiples can make a private equity investment seem more volatile. In fact, investments are volatile and the use of multiples merely pushes the valuer toward reflecting it. That does not mean that the valuer is required to use the multiple from a comparator exactly for the valuation date. Equally, a multiple that clearly does not reflect the current market environment is unacceptable. A multiple which is reflecting the market over a short period is permissible on the basis that a third party considering acquiring an illiquid asset is unlikely to alter its pricing view of the value on the basis of daily movements in the comparators.

Valuers of private equity investments should also be aware that *cross-country differences* affect the quality of the valuation outputs. Different countries have different accounting standards; even if they use international accounting standards, the levels of implementation and enforcement are likely to vary. Thus, valuations of fund investments in different countries can be distorted and inconsistent due to variation in the recognition of revenues and expenses. Furthermore, differences in macroeconomic factors such as inflation or exchange rates can be problematic if not accounted for when reporting the net asset value of the fund to investors.

In addition, many valuation processes are affected by *accounting conservatism*, which is a fundamental accounting principle. This prudence in reporting and estimation generates undervaluation of investments in some circumstances, an effect that is exacerbated by the reaction of investors. It appears that investors would prefer to be surprised by a large uplift in the valuation, rather than the smallest loss. Accordingly, in private equity, there is no reward for overvaluing investments.

Finally, whenever assumptions and estimates are used, they should be supportable in the context of "What might a third party consider?" Such consideration might include matters that take place after the reporting date if these provide more evidence about the existing conditions as of the reporting date.

REFERENCES

Porter, M. (1985) *Competitive Advantage*, The Free Press, New York.

International Private Equity and Venture Capital Valuation Guidelines (2015).

Coller IP (2016) *IP Valuation, Realising Value from Intangible Assets*.

In his own words: Dr. Fernando Da Cruz Vasconcellos, Director, Investment Strategy & IP Valuation, Coller IP

Intangible Assets Valuation

Intangible asset (intellectual property, assets or capital) valuations can support various purposes. One of the most important aims is to support the access to investments, cash, and funding, particularly through venture capital and private equity investments, as well as via R&D tax credits, through alternative business funding schemes, or via incentives for innovation-driven companies, such as given by the U.K. Patent Box. Intangible asset valuations can also support licensing negotiations; asset refinancing, tax planning; mergers and acquisitions; insolvency, and so on.

At Coller IP, for example, our valuations of intangible assets are based on a combination of well-accepted, tried-and-tested methods using evidence-based approaches such as the market approach, cost approach, and future income approach. For the future income approach, we commonly use a DCF methodology together with a "relief from royalty" model; this is based on an estimate of the net present value of future cash flows attributable to applying a royalty rate, based on market benchmarks, to the sales of the products and services that are underpinned by the intellectual assets or property. This equation is equivalent to the royalty that the company would otherwise have to pay to a third party if it did not own the intellectual asset or property and had to pay royalty fees under a license agreement—hence the name "relief from royalty" for this modified valuation approach. This valuation technique may also provide, for instance, a direct estimate of the value of technology in a licensing model.

All three of the above approaches, properly applied, are recognized as valid and appropriate within the specialist field of intellectual asset valuation for those requiring transparency and robustness (e.g., investors, funding bodies, courts, arbitrators, regulators, and tax authorities). Intangible asset valuations are negotiation tools for strategic decisions.

So, whether you're an investor, an established business, or are just getting started, your intangible assets are key for your future success. By recognizing that these assets are part of the bigger picture of the value of your business, organization, and investment opportunities, you are sure to help increase the value of your company, and obtain more access to funding and cash, driving your business forward.

Appendix A: DCF Outputs for an Example Company

	Historical Period				Projection Period					CAGR
	2015	2016	2017	2018	2019	2020	2021	2022	2023	('18 - '23)
Revenue	1,000.0	1,100.0	1,200.0	1,400.0	1,505.0	1,595.3	1,675.1	1,742.1	1,794.3	5.1%
% growth	NA	10.0%	9.1%	16.7%	7.5%	6.0%	5.0%	4.0%	3.0%	
Cost of Goods Sold	(620.0)	(671.0)	(720.0)	(840.0)	(903.0)	(957.2)	(1,005.0)	(1,045.2)	(1,076.6)	
Gross Profit	**380.0**	**429.0**	**480.0**	**560.0**	**602.0**	**638.1**	**670.0**	**696.8**	**717.7**	5.1%
% gross margin	38.0%	39.0%	40.0%	40.0%	40.0%	40.0%	40.0%	40.0%	40.0%	
Selling, General & Administrative	(191.0)	(209.0)	(240.0)	(308.0)	(316.1)	(335.0)	(351.8)	(365.8)	(376.8)	
EBITDA	**189.0**	**220.0**	**240.0**	**252.0**	**286.0**	**303.1**	**318.3**	**331.0**	**340.9**	6.2%
% margin	18.9%	20.0%	20.0%	18.0%	19.0%	19.0%	19.0%	19.0%	19.0%	
Depreciation & Amortization	(30.0)	(33.0)	(36.0)	(42.0)	(45.2)	(47.9)	(50.3)	(52.3)	(53.8)	
EBIT	**159.0**	**187.0**	**204.0**	**210.0**	**240.8**	**255.2**	**268.0**	**278.7**	**287.1**	6.5%
% margin	15.9%	17.0%	17.0%	15.0%	16.0%	16.0%	16.0%	16.0%	16.0%	
Taxes (20%)	(31.8)	(37.4)	(40.8)	(42.0)	(48.2)	(51.0)	(53.6)	(55.7)	(57.4)	
EBIAT	**127.2**	**149.6**	**163.2**	**168.0**	**192.6**	**204.2**	**214.4**	**223.0**	**229.7**	6.5%
Plus: Depreciation & Amortization	30.0	33.0	36.0	42.0	45.2	47.9	50.3	52.3	53.8	
Less: Capital Expenditures	(44.0)	(48.4)	(52.8)	(61.6)	(67.7)	(71.8)	(75.4)	(78.4)	(80.7)	
Less: Inc./(Dec.) in Net Working Capital					(0.1)	(4.9)	(4.3)	(3.6)	(2.8)	
Unlevered Free Cash Flow					169.9	175.4	184.9	193.2	199.9	
WACC	10%									
Present Value of Free Cash Flow					162.0	152.0	145.7	138.4	130.2	
Cumulative Present Value of FCF					728.3					

Enterprise Value - Multiple Method	
Cumulative Present Value of FCF	**728.3**
Terminal Year EBITDA (2023E)	340.9
Proposed Exit Multiple	8.0x
Terminal Value	**2,727.4**
Present Value of Terminal Value	**1,693.5**
% of Enterprise Value	69.9%
Enterprise Value	**2,421.8**
Implied Perpetuity Growth Rate	**2.5%**

Enterprise Value - Perpetuity Growth Method	
Cumulative Present Value of FCF	**728.3**
Terminal Year Free Cash Flow (2023E)	199.9
WACC	10%
Perpetual Growth Rate	2%
Terminal Value	**2,549.0**
Present Value of Terminal Value	**1,582.7**
% of Enterprise Value	68.5%
Enterprise Value	**2,311.1**
Actual EBITDA (2018A)	252.0
Implied EV/EBITDA	**9.2x**

Implied Equity Value and Share Price	
Enterprise Value	**2,421.8**
Less: Total Debt	(1,000.0)
Plus: Cash and Cash Equivalents	200.0
Implied Equity Value	**1,621.8**
Fully Diluted Shares Outstanding	100.0
Implied Share Price	**16.2**

Implied Equity Value and Share Price	
Enterprise Value	**2,311.1**
Less: Total Debt	(1,000.0)
Plus: Cash and Cash Equivalents	200.0
Implied Equity Value	**1,511.1**
Fully Diluted Shares Outstanding	100.0
Implied Share Price	**15.1**

Enterprise Value | Sensitivity Analysis				
Exit Multiple				
7.0x	**7.5x**	**8.0x**	**8.5x**	**9.0x**
2,296	2,406	2,517	2,628	2,739
2,252	2,361	2,469	2,577	2,685
2,210	2,316	**2,422**	2,528	2,634
2,169	2,273	2,376	2,479	2,583
2,129	2,230	2,331	2,433	2,534

(WACC rows: 9.0%, 9.5%, 10.0%, 10.5%, 11.0%)

Enterprise Value | Sensitivity Analysis				
Perpetuity Growth Rate				
1.0%	**1.5%**	**2.0%**	**2.5%**	**3.0%**
2,296	2,408	2,537	2,686	2,859
2,203	2,303	2,417	2,546	2,695
2,121	2,211	**2,311**	2,425	2,555
2,048	2,128	2,218	2,319	2,433
1,982	2,055	2,135	2,225	2,327

(WACC rows: 9.0%, 9.5%, 10.0%, 10.5%, 11.0%)

Appendix B: Valuation Timeline for a Private Equity Transaction

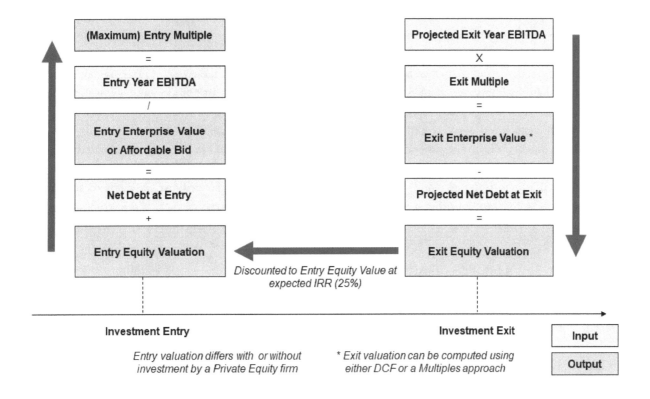

(Maximum) Entry Multiple
=
Entry Year EBITDA
/
Entry Enterprise Value or Affordable Bid
=
Net Debt at Entry
+
Entry Equity Valuation

Projected Exit Year EBITDA
X
Exit Multiple
=
Exit Enterprise Value *
-
Projected Net Debt at Exit
=
Exit Equity Valuation

Discounted to Entry Equity Value at expected IRR (25%)

Investment Entry

Investment Exit

Input

Output

Entry valuation differs with or without investment by a Private Equity firm

* Exit valuation can be computed using either DCF or a Multiples approach

4 Acquisition Finance

A banker is a fellow who lends you his umbrella when the sun is shining, but wants it back the minute it begins to rain.
Mark Twain

INTRODUCTION

Any transaction whereby borrowed funds are used to finance an acquisition involves "acquisition finance." Typically, there are several types of acquisition finance structures: those involving a financial sponsor (i.e., private equity sponsor), those that have existing management acquiring the company or business, and those involving a strategic buyer (i.e., a company in a similar line of business as the target). The targets may be private companies or public companies with securities listed on a stock exchange.

In private equity transactions, the buyer typically sets up a special purpose vehicle (SPV), which receives its funds from two main sources: equity from the buyer and debt from lenders. The equity component is primarily provided by funds managed by the private equity sponsor or other investors, and can take the form of ordinary share capital or subordinated loan notes or loan stock. The debt component is typically provided by banks, other financial institutions, institutional investors, or specialist debt funds in the form of short- and long-term debt structured as syndicated loans, second-lien loans, mezzanine loans, high-yield bonds, and other types of instruments. These instruments are often separated into senior and junior (or subordinated) debt.[1] In a private equity buyout transaction most of the overall debt package is usually used to finance the acquisition vehicle (i.e., SPV) that is "sponsored" by the private equity firm. The SPV will use its funds to acquire the shares in a target company or other assets.[2] For this reason, the debt financing part of the structure is often called "acquisition finance" and the substantial use of such debt to finance the acquisition results in "leveraged buyouts" (LBOs).

Although there is often debt financing in management buyouts and strategic acquisitions, the structures and terms of the debt financing have been developed to the largest extent in the context of private equity transactions. A portion of the debt package might, if applicable, fund the repayment of any existing debt of the target company at the time of the acquisition. The proportion of debt to the total purchase price typically varies between 40 to 75 percent depending on the profitability, sector and geography of target acquisition as well as the buyout firm. The debt is typically provided to the SPV shortly before the closing of the acquisition. Debt used in LBOs is generally rated non-investment grade debt because of the higher leverage and corresponding risk of default. The levels of debt to equity and debt multiples (i.e., debt to EBITDA ratios)

This chapter was co-authored with John Markland, Partner at Dechert LLP.

[1] Junior debt is subordinated to senior debt, and therefore provides a higher rate of return for its holders due to the increased risk profile.

[2] Most LBOs are by way of an acquisition of shares in a company, but in some cases, they represent an acquisition of other assets (e.g., in the case of the acquisition of a division of a business rather than the whole of it).

tend to peak during times when there is an oversupply of cheap credit during market booms and dip significantly during market downturns.[3]

For much of the 21st century, the private equity industry has enjoyed cheap and plentiful debt financing availability that has supported new LBOs as well as the financial engineering of existing LBOs. By borrowing at relatively low rates and then making larger returns through their investment prowess, private equity sponsors have been able to increase their equity returns substantially.

While that basic investment thesis of a leveraged private equity transaction is straightforward, its simplicity belies a complex relationship between the private equity executives, the target management, and the lenders. Whereas the classic senior debt provider abhors risk and change, private equity sponsors embrace it. Given the high risk of LBOs, driven by the amount of debt and the limited recourse in such debt financings, lenders seek to allocate every conceivable risk to the private equity sponsor. As a result, debt providers require strict repayment schedules, reporting requirements, restrictive undertakings, financial covenants, security over the assets of the target, and many other protective terms, all stipulated in comprehensive lending agreements. These requirements lead to continuous interaction with the private equity sponsors during the course of an investment. These sponsors usually need to have one or more executives that are principally focused on dealing with debt financing, and whose task it is to keep on top of developments in what is often a fast-moving market.

The key concerns for the private equity sponsor that negotiates acquisition finance with a set of lenders are that

- the cash will be there on time to complete the investment;

- lenders cannot demand repayment before it is reasonable for them to do so;

- lenders do not impose too many restrictions on how the investment is managed; and

- the private equity fund contributing equity to the investment is not liable for the borrowings, but only its investment vehicle that acquires the target (i.e., the transaction is "limited recourse").

Prior to agreeing on the terms of acquisition finance, the private equity sponsor will have drawn up a detailed business plan for the proposed acquisition, including projections for the cash flows for the life of the investment. The lenders will carry out due diligence on the target, including, of course, an analysis and validation of that business plan. Lenders will be most concerned with verifying the target company's ability to service the debt, rather than the additional upside that the private equity sponsor expects to enjoy when the portfolio company is ultimately sold. In contrast, the private equity sponsor's investment thesis will usually contemplate revenue and operational margin growth beyond the lenders' more conservative base case.

In this chapter, we consider the main documents involved in acquisition financing, their purpose and the issues concerning them that require negotiation. We discuss the various players and products involved, and the process that must be undertaken in order to conclude a deal.

---

[3] During certain times in the last 30 years (e.g., including the 2005–2007 run-up to the global financial crisis), up to 90% of the purchase price could be financed with debt, but more typically, debt levels are between 50% and 70% of the purchase price. According to Standard & Poor's Capital IQ, the leverage multiples have been hovering at around five (six) times EBITDA in Europe (the United States), up from lows of four times EBITDA in 2009 at the peak of the global financial crisis.

MARKET TRENDS

Valuations and certain funds

Today, private equity sponsors are much more focused on the acquisition financing that occurs at the formative stages of a deal than they were in the early 2000s. There are two main reasons for this increased interest. The first reason is simply that transactions are being done at significantly higher valuations now than they were 15 years ago and the component of the purchase price that is funded by third-party debt is significantly larger. These developments are partly driven by larger entry buyout valuations which penetrated the 10x EV/EBITDA mark back in 2015 (Dai, 2015). Later in this chapter, we will examine the specific risks that private equity sponsors take when funding their deals with debt, but for present purposes, suffice it to say that these risks become magnified when the debt component is larger.

The second reason for the increased interest in acquisition financing at the formative stages of a deal is that, in the modern market environment (especially in Europe), sellers of a business typically use a competitive auction mechanism that requires bidders to ensure that their bids are fully funded, with any third-party funding being committed on a certain funds basis. This so-called "certainty of funds" concept in the European documentation originated from the requirements of the City of London Code on Takeovers and Mergers (Takeover Code), which governs the takeover of any entity whose registered office is in the United Kingdom and whose securities are listed on an applicable U.K. exchange. The Takeover Code simply requires that a bidder must enter a bid for a public target company only if it is satisfied that it has sufficient available resources to satisfy any cash consideration that is being offered. Additionally (again, in U.K. public deals), a reputable financial adviser must also stand behind any bid and confirm that the relevant bidder has "certain funds," meaning funds will be available, without conditions that the bidder cannot control, upon completion of the acquisition. If the financial adviser fails to take all reasonable steps to assure itself that the cash is indeed available, it can be required to provide the missing funds itself.

In a financing transaction that is not done following the "certain funds" standard, banks might condition their commitments on the satisfaction of *conditions precedent* such as satisfactory due diligence, the absence of market conditions that make it difficult to syndicate the loans (i.e., "market out") and the absence of any material adverse change (MAC) in the target business. In a deal where the sponsor cannot persuade its lenders to eliminate conditions such as these, LBO bids would typically have a "financing condition," meaning that the bid is conditional upon being able to find lenders who would lend to fund the debt component, or upon such lenders not using their conditions to escape their commitments. Alternatively, bids that have a financing condition might be deliberately structured that way in order to allow bidders to delay doing the work required to obtain financing until after they know they have won the auction. Interestingly, in the United States, LBO bids occasionally still do have such a financing condition. In private LBO transactions and public bids in Europe, each bidder typically needs to have a full set of commitment papers signed by lenders on a "certain funds basis," thus confirming that the main due diligence and structuring conditions to closing have already been approved by the lenders (and contain no market out or business MAC conditions, as explained above).

Separately, the market in the United States developed a comparable consent to the European and U.K. "certainty of funds" concept in what has come to be known as the "SunGard approach," named after the acquisition of SunGard Data Systems (a Pennsylvania-based global software company) by a consortium of private equity sponsors in 2005. Unlike the historically more-prevalent practice in other U.S. LBOs, SunGard's merger agreement did not give the buyers a "financing out." As a result, the private equity sponsor group was incentivized to align the banks' conditions under the financing commitments with the buyer's condition under the merger agreement. The SunGard approach was subsequently followed in other LBOs in the United States (for both public and private companies), with financial sponsors closing the gap between their own limited conditionality in acquisition agreements and the somewhat broader conditionality traditionally given to banks in commitment letters. Although comparable, perhaps because of its different origin, the SunGard approach does not achieve quite the same alignment as the European certain funds approach; for example with the SunGard approach, the conditions will typically be expressed similarly in the finance documents and in the bid documents, whereas with certain funds, the conditions simply need to be removed or declared satisfied.

Developments in debt terms and documentation

Since the 2008 global financial crisis, the buyout market has seen a strong recovery, with purchase multiples (of EBITDA) rising markedly and the multiples of debt used to finance new buyouts starting to approach pre-crisis levels both in the United States and Europe.

Intense competition between banks, institutional investors, and alternative lenders, particularly over the past 10 years, has resulted in a wide array of funding products being offered to borrowers, including senior-only structures, term loan B tranches, mezzanine loans, unitranche loans, second-lien loans, high-yield instruments, and various combinations of these products (which we describe in more detail in later sections). The surge in covenant-lite loans (i.e., loans with fewer financial covenants or no financial covenants) is a direct result of the increase in financing options to borrowers at the large end of the market (where high-yield issuance is a viable alternative).[4] Covenant-lite loan transactions with lenient terms for borrowers and less protection for lenders may contribute to increased distress, perhaps in the form of lower recovery rates to lenders; this is because cash flows could potentially deteriorate to a greater degree before a default gets triggered if financial covenants are not measured periodically (in which case, payment default might be the trigger), or if such financial covenants have loose definitions or are set with a large cushion (i.e., headroom to the business case) prior to being triggered.

THE FUNDING STRUCTURE

Structuring of an LBO

Private equity deals involve a lot of careful structuring. In the context of a financing, "structuring" may involve trying to achieve various objectives, such as arranging for the financing to be achieved in jurisdictions where (1) the tax effects are less onerous, (2) there are fewer restrictions on the ability to move cash between the target company and the acquisition vehicle (e.g., in order to service the acquisition debt), or (3) the security protection that can be offered to banks is most robust.

Before discussing these objectives, one must understand the typical debt structure of an LBO deal (see Exhibit 1). The private equity sponsor (or the financial sponsor) usually establishes one or more SPVs to

---

[4] Note that high-yield bonds typically do not have financial covenants.

execute the acquisition. Typically, one entity is established as a holding company (Holdco), which receives the equity contribution from the sponsors and other investors (if any). Holdco then establishes a subsidiary (Bidco).[5] Holdco and Bidco are usually newly incorporated or "off the shelf companies": either way, they have not traded previously and are "bankruptcy remote" from the private equity fund that provides the equity in the deal.[6] To pay for the acquisition, Bidco receives equity and perhaps also shareholder debt contributions from Holdco and incurs bank or other acquisition debt. While the main equity component is commonly provided by the funds managed by the private equity sponsor sponsoring the deal, the management of the target and sometimes the vendor (the party selling the target company) may contribute to the equity as well. If there are several layers of financing instruments in the debt package, there may be additional SPVs established by the private equity sponsor in addition.

Exhibit 1: Typical Deal Structure

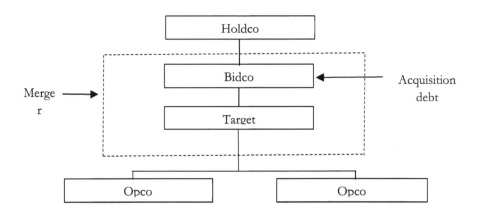

Bidco then purchases at least a majority (or controlling stake) of the outstanding shares of the Target, resulting in the Target becoming a subsidiary of Bidco. In some jurisdictions, the Target will subsequently be merged with Bidco so that the Target becomes responsible for the acquisition debt borrowed by Bidco; this might, for example, facilitate the payment of debt service (i.e., interest and amortization installments on the acquisition loans, which may be prohibited under local "financial assistance" laws as discussed below). It might also allow interest costs to be deducted from the target's profits for tax purposes, resulting in better tax efficiency.

Private equity sponsors primarily utilize debt financing to increase the expected return on equity (i.e., to create a leverage effect). To obtain debt financing for the capitalization of Bidco, the private equity sponsor often presents the potential buyout to a bank to act as lead arranger and to underwrite the debt. If the bank commits to fund Bidco with debt, it becomes the lead arranger of the financing transaction. If the transaction is unsuccessful, Bidco is unwound and the debt commitment lapses. The lead arranger typically does not provide the entire debt financing but syndicates parts of the debt to other, so-called "syndicate" or "participating" banks or institutional investors. The most common institutional investors are collateralized loan obligation (CLO) funds, pension funds, debt funds and sovereign wealth funds.

---

[5] Bidco will enter the acquisition agreement with the seller (or the shareholders) of the target company.

[6] If the transaction involves few jurisdictions, several new companies might be created to obtain the most tax-efficient treatment.

As an example, in Exhibit 2, the pay-in-kind (PIK) and high-yield debt, which is junior, is at a higher level in the corporate structure chart (Finco) than the senior or mezzanine debt (Bidco). The PIK debt is "structurally subordinated" because it is further away from the operating companies that generate the cash flows to service the debt. In other words, the direct lenders to operating subsidiaries have a stronger claim on the operating assets than lenders to holding companies and other upstream entities (which only own shares in the operating subsidiaries) because, in a bankruptcy, debt gets paid before equity. The lenders of PIK debt, or the bondholders in the case of high-yield debt, do not usually share in the security package that is given by the operating entities in the group. Instead, they are unsecured (in the case of bondholders) or only receive security over the shares in their borrower.

Exhibit 2: Deal Structure with Multiple Layers of Debt

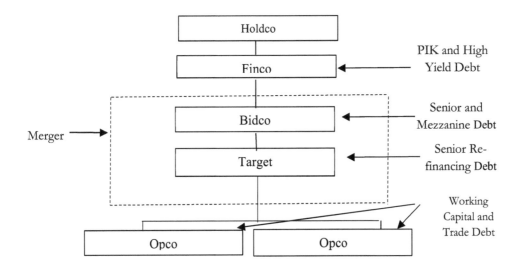

Returning to the three objectives mentioned above, the following approaches are followed by market participants:

- With regard to tax, the private equity sponsor will focus on two main issues. First, it will seek to minimize any withholding taxes on debt interest payments, or at least to ensure that if there are withholding taxes, it does not need to "gross up" the interest payments to the lenders so they are not affected;[7] the private equity sponsor can do this by various means, including, for example, by borrowing in jurisdictions where there are no (or few) withholding tax obligations. Second, the private equity sponsor will want to minimize tax on profits by deducting interest costs from the profits to the maximum extent possible, which can be achieved by, for example, borrowing or refinancing the debt at the level of the operating companies in the group or by implementing a legal merger between Bidco, the acquisition company, and the target company (this structuring technique is known as "debt pushdown"). Thus, the operating cash flow of the target company may be used for interest payments and repayments of funding received by the acquisition vehicle.
- Both the borrower side and the lender side will want to ensure that there are no impediments on the ability to "up-stream" cash from the operating companies to the companies where the debt is

---

[7] A withholding tax is a tax deducted at source, especially one levied by some countries on interest or dividends paid to an entity resident outside that country.

borrowed. If the target business is going through a significant reorganization in the first two or three years, the operating companies may have substantial costs (e.g., with redundancies) that will cause profits to be scarce, which may limit the ability of operating companies to up-stream cash by way of dividends. Lenders will want to know that even during these lean years, cash can be up-streamed one way or another to service the loans that they have made at the Bidco level. One solution is for the operating companies to provide loans to the Bidco. There are two issues with using these upstream loans to pay the debt of holding companies:

– **Corporate benefit.** Generally, directors of the operating company will be required to ensure that the transactions that they enter into are for the benefit of the company. Every jurisdiction has its own rules on this, some of which are very strict (e.g., those in France) and some which are less strict (e.g., those in the United Kingdom, which allow directors to consider their own company as benefiting from the gains that other group companies derive from the financing).

– **Financial assistance.** Many jurisdictions have laws which prohibit a company from giving "financial assistance" for the acquisition of its own shares. These laws also vary from one jurisdiction to another, but they often prevent target companies from being able to fund the debt service on the acquisition finance that was incurred by the Bidco to fund the acquisition of the target group.

• With respect to the above tax and debt service issues, there is a broad alignment of interests between the borrower and the lenders. Both sides benefit from the reduced tax burden on the borrower group, and from the greater freedom to move cash around the group. However, this freedom does not apply to the guarantee and security package that the lenders receive. The lenders, of course, want to obtain the best security package possible—after all, they typically have no recourse to the private equity fund but only to the target business (and Bidco).[8] Local rules on corporate benefit and financial assistance will also determine what security can be taken in different jurisdictions. Often, there will be a so-called "guarantor coverage test," which requires that guarantees and security are given to the lenders by group members that generate (or have) at least 80% or 90% of the group's EBITDA, revenues, and assets. The share pledge at the top of the financing group is of particular importance, because in most cases, the preferred enforcement strategy of the lenders is the sale of the whole group, "lock stock and barrel," as a going concern, rather than the sale of individual assets within the group. For this reason, it is often said that the remainder of the security package is mainly for "defensive" purposes (i.e., to prevent other parties from obtaining security rights over (or ownership of) the group's assets that will reduce the value of the group to the lenders on an enforcement).[9]

[8] Lenders typically recognize in the Senior Facilities Agreement that the security package should not impose excessively onerous restrictions on the ability of the business to operate, that they should not force security to be taken if there is a risk that the companies or their directors could face liability under corporate laws (for example laws forbidding the giving of financial assistance), and that they should only take security to the extent that it is justifiable on a cost-to-benefit basis.

[9] Contrast this with "asset-based lending" (ABL), where the lenders are lending against the value of particular assets rather than the business as a whole. In ABL, the lenders are typically much more demanding with respect to the security that they obtain over the assets they are lending against (e.g., no cost-to-benefit carve-outs).

Uses and sources of funds

The typical funding requirements as well as the sources of financing in a buyout transaction are presented in Exhibit 3.

Exhibit 3: Uses and Sources of Funds

Uses of Funds	Sources of Funds

• Purchase Price of Shares
• Debt Refinancing
• Transaction Cost
• Working Capital Needs
• CAPEX Needs
• Add-On Acquisition Costs
• Restructuring Costs
	• Acquisition Finance
	  – Senior Debt
	  – Second-Lien Debt
	  – Mezzanine Finance
	  – High-Yield Debt
	  – PIK Note Debt
	• Revolving Working Capital Debt
	• Seller/Vendor Finance
	• Sponsor's Equity
	• Co-Investor's Equity
	• Target Management's Equity

Set out below is a brief description of the main uses of funds above.

- **Purchase price of shares in the target.** This amount basically covers the purchase price that is payable to the sellers of the target company.

- **Transaction costs.** These costs include fees to lead arranging banks, consultants, accountants, and lawyers. The deal costs typically range from 2–3% for large transactions and up to 10% for smaller transactions, but ultimately depend on the negotiating position of the parties.

- **Refinancing debt on target's balance sheet.** The private equity sponsor must be ready to refinance any debt on the target's balance sheet. Usually, a change in the ownership of the target triggers an obligation to mandatory prepay the debt, thus the new owner needs to refinance it.

- **Working capital needs.** In most cases, the target business will have fluctuations in its cash income and outgoings and, to provide for the times when the outgoings exceed the income, it will have working capital needs. The size of these needs heavily depends on the type of business that is acquired.

- **CAPEX needs.** If the private equity sponsor acquires the target with the purpose of growing the company and its production capacity, then it needs to be ready to fund additional capital expenditure (CAPEX) requirements. Usually senior lenders in bank syndicates provide a separate CAPEX facility in a syndicated loan deal that covers these needs.

- **Add-on acquisitions.** Often, private equity funds will want to grow the business by making add-on acquisitions; it is common for lenders to make an acquisition facility available (or it might be combined with a CAPEX facility).

- **Restructuring costs.** If the target business is intended to be restructured (e.g., by a headcount reduction involving severance costs), the target business will need to be able to access funds associated with this (again, this is often combined with the CAPEX facility).

PROVIDERS OF ACQUISITION FINANCE

Parties involved

The sponsor

The most important player in a buyout transaction is undoubtedly the private equity sponsor that sponsors the deal. These firms invest through the private equity funds they raise and manage. The most common fund structures used by private equity sponsors are partnerships where the firm is the general partner (GP) and the investors in the fund are limited partners (LPs). If the buyout deal is very large, two or more private equity sponsors may join forces to acquire the target, or the private equity sponsor might co-invest with several of the investors (i.e., the LPs) in the private equity fund. The sponsor will invariably have legal advisers supporting the transaction, and might also receive help from a corporate finance adviser or a debt advisory firm.

The target's management team

All buyout transactions involve a management team, which may be the incumbent management of the target, a new team from an external source, or a combination of both. Often, the management team invests a reasonably large amount of its own capital in the deal, which is encouraged by all parties and ensures that its incentives are aligned with those of the sponsors. If the managers work for the target company already, prospective purchasers will be eager to get to know them, but the managers will have constraints on their ability to provide confidential information.

Senior lenders

Senior lenders typically provide the majority of the financing in buyout deals. Traditionally, the senior lenders are banks, who play a significant role in arranging and underwriting the senior loans that finance the buyout transactions as follows. Senior debt packages for mid-market and large deals are usually syndicated by lead arranging banks ("mandated lead arrangers" or MLAs).[10] Once the loans are syndicated, a lender will act as an agent for the syndicate of lenders when dealing with parties involved in the buyout. The sponsor will usually select the agent from among the mandated lead arrangers (but not necessarily—increasingly, specialist independent agencies are used). If the transaction is large, it is common to have two (or even up to four or five) MLAs that co-arrange and underwrite the debt between them before syndicating most of it to other banks, pension funds, insurance funds, hedge funds, leveraged loan (or debt) funds, or collateralized loan

---

[10] The syndication often starts soon after commitment papers are signed and the acquisition is announced.

obligations (CLOs). These alternative (i.e. non-bank) lenders are generally referred to as "institutional investors."

After the global financial crisis, when many banks were reluctant to commit large amounts of capital to private equity deals, *private debt funds* mushroomed to fill the funding gap left by the banks. Many of these debt funds are set up and operated by major private equity sponsors. Sometimes, these funds are managed by teams that spun-out of banks to exploit niches in the market such as mezzanine, unitranche, or distressed lending (see below). It is now usual for a private equity sponsors seeking acquisition finance will usually speak to both arranging banks and private debt funds and compare the options provided by each.

There are some general observations that can be made about the difference in approach between banks and the funds that provide the senior debt. First, funds tend to seek a higher return than banks do; hence, they often aim to sell the less risky part of the financing to banks or to leverage the loans that they make (i.e., by borrowing the capital they need). Second, funds are often more likely than banks to be buy-and-hold owners of the debt securities they purchase—although, of course, no two banks (or funds) are exactly alike. Certainly, funds are less likely to be in the business of arranging and then syndicating most of the debt, which is the business model for many international banks.

Some of the largest providers of senior syndicated loans are CLOs.[11] Essentially, a CLO is a fund that invests in a portfolio of different leveraged loans in order to spread the risk (across industries, borrowers, loan maturities, etc.). These investments are financed through the issuance of debt, which is "tranched" in different classes (approximately 90% of the total capital) as well as equity (about 10% of the total capital). The classes of debt are distinguished by the degree of seniority in the payment waterfall which operates if there is insufficient cash to repay everyone, with the most senior class being protected from the early losses that are borne by the investors in the junior classes. Equity investors bear the first losses and receive the residual value after all other investors in the debt tranches have been paid. During the 2008 global financial crisis, CLOs were widely accused of having simply "bought the market" without much critical review of the terms, and there was a widespread belief that this had permitted borrowers to erode important protections for the lenders as a consequence. At the height of the market prior to the global financial crisis, arranging banks did not need to worry too much about allowing borrowers more flexible terms than had been traditional (e.g., less equity cushion, less financial covenant protection, less security, larger baskets, and more generous cure rights), because they knew that CLOs would probably buy the syndicated debt regardless.

Interestingly, however, although the appetite for investing in CLOs dried up for a number of years after the 2008 financial crisis, investors in the CLO market did not suffer too badly as a result of the crisis. Moody's report 'Impairment & Loss Rates of U.S. and European CLOs: 1993-2014' notes that among all Moody's rated CLOs issued since 2009, none had become impaired to the date of the report (29 July 2015), highlighting the strong performance of CLOs. Similarly, in Moody's 'Few European CLO Tranches Likely to incur Losses' report dated 6 May 2013, Moody's state that the likelihood of senior tranches incurring principal losses is "remote" for European arbitrage cash flow CLOs. Moreover, Moody's note that this is thanks to the effectiveness of structural protections, such as over-collateralization diversion mechanisms which are inherent in CLOs (where excess spread is diverted from equity tranche investors to redeem senior notes or reinvested in new loan collateral when over-collateralization ratios are breached in order to improve such ratios to pre-default levels).

---

[11] Over the past decade, CLOs have become the dominant institutional investor in syndicated loans, reaching a 60% share in the high-yield loan market. Although new securitized loan issuance dipped during the global financial crisis, by 2013, the level of CLOs' annual investments in syndicated loans reached the pre-crisis levels (Standard and Poor's [2014]).

Second-lien lenders

These lenders are typically institutional investors such as hedge funds, leveraged loan funds, or CLOs. Often, however, second lien debt will initially be lent by the arranging banks in a deal. Second-lien loans are sometimes documented as a separate tranche in the senior facilities agreement (together with the first-lien loans) and sometimes in separate loan agreements, depending on the preference of the parties (and most importantly, depending on the arranging banks' views on the best way to market the loans at the time).

Mezzanine lenders

Mezzanine debt is usually provided by specialist mezzanine funds, hedge funds, leveraged loan funds, and other institutional investors. In fact, some banks have in-house mezzanine lending departments that can provide mezzanine facilities.

High-yield bondholders

High-yield debt securities are typically issued under a widely used exemption under the U.S. Securities Act of 1933, as amended (Securities Act), which involves a combination of Section 4(a)(2), a private placement exemption, and Rule 144A, a resale exemption, under the Securities Act. Placements under Rule144A are referred to as "Rule 144A offerings." Section 4(a)(2) provides an exemption for "transactions by an issuer not involving any public offering," and Rule 144A provides a further exemption for private resales of securities to certain types of institutional buyers (i.e., "qualified institutional buyers" (QIBs)) so long as certain conditions are met. Therefore, in a typical Rule 144A offering, the issuer will initially sell securities (the high-yield bonds) to one or more investment banks under the Section 4(a)(2) exemption. The investment bank, referred to as an "initial purchaser," will then resell those securities to QIBs under Rule 144A. QIBs are the "bondholders", which will typically be insurance funds, pension funds, mutual funds, hedge funds and other similar institutions whose portfolios meet certain size requirements and whom are permitted to invest in sub-investment grade bonds.[12] Once the securities or bonds are issued, the relationship between the bondholders and the issuer is typically managed by a "trustee" that represents the interests of the bondholders, which is documented in an indenture agreement or trust deed.

In an acquisition finance transaction in Europe, prior to issuing a high-yield bond, the private equity sponsor will usually be required by the seller to have "certain funds" (as discussed), and there is an agreed period between signing the share purchase agreement (SPA) and the acquisition or completion date. During this period, if the sponsor wishes to avoid drawing under a bridge finance facility first (and then subsequently refinancing with a bond), a high-yield bond might be issued and the proceeds held in escrow (i.e., under a special agreement between the escrow agent, which holds the funds, and the payor and ultimate recipient; within this agreement, the parties will also have agreed upon the conditions under which the funds should be released to the recipient), pending the closing of the acquisition. Should the high-yield bond fail (e.g., if market conditions are not favorable for bond issuance), then the private equity sponsor will need to draw funds from a committed bridge facility which was part of the "certain funds" package. This bridge facility is then refinanced within the next 12 months by a term loan or exchange notes (i.e., another bond issue).

---

[12] It is also common in Rule 144A offerings for a portion of the issued securities to be placed to non-U.S. persons located outside the United States by relying on a separate exemption provided by Regulation S under the Securities Act.

Vendors

The seller of a target company is sometimes another player in an acquisition financing. *Vendor financing* is primarily used when buyers and sellers have different price expectations. The economic nature of this form of financing is similar to preferred shares, but, depending on structure, the interest component might be tax-deductible for the buyout company. Vendor loans reduce the amount of acquisition finance that the private equity sponsor has to provide, and are typically used when credit markets are restrictive with LBO financing, as was the case during the 2008 global financial crisis.

Stapled finance providers

In some cases, vendors prearrange the debt package when they are planning the disposal of a company through a so-called "stapled finance" offer; this means that the vendor approaches a bank that provides acquisition finance to agree on the terms of financing for the proposed buyout. These terms are then figuratively "stapled" to the information memorandum distributed to potential buyers to enhance the prospect of the sale (i.e., to show bidders that debt is available to leverage the acquisition). Often, the financial adviser to the vendor will be best placed to provide the stapled finance offer. The staple might be a "hard" staple (substantially in agreed form) or it may be a "soft" staple (merely indicative terms).

Intercreditor agreements

A suite of finance documents with multiple tranches of creditors (whose debt claims may or may not be secured) will typically include an "intercreditor agreement." Given that in most acquisition finance transactions there are multiple layers of debt (e.g., senior debt, mezzanine debt, shareholder debt, intra-group debt, high-yield debt, etc.), an intercreditor agreement is almost invariably required. It sets out the respective rights and obligations of the lenders toward one another, including, most importantly, the ranking of the different layers of debt and the extent to which some lenders are contractually subordinated to others. Even in highly complex insolvency situations involving syndicated facilities, English courts tend to accept the validity of contractual intercreditor provisions.

A brief explanation of structural and contractual subordination is merited. Essentially, the classic method of structurally subordinating one debt to another is to lend it to a company higher in the corporate structure (i.e., to its parent company). Because, in an insolvency of the subsidiary, the liquidator will not give the parent company any return on its shares in the subsidiary until all the subsidiary company's debts are repaid (i.e., debt is paid before equity), the debt of the parent company is subordinated to the debt of the subsidiary. In Exhibit 4, the lender of Loan A is said to be "structurally subordinated" to the lender of Loan B.

Exhibit 4: Structural Subordination

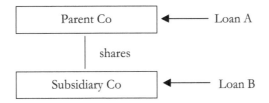

Where, as is typical, there are cross guarantees and security between the different group entities, structural subordination breaks down and the parties must resort to contractual means to create the intended subordination—this is known as "contractual subordination." (see Exhibit 5).

Exhibit 5: Contractual Subordination

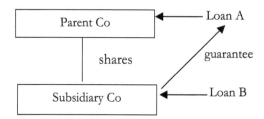

At first blush, it is not always obvious to newcomers to acquisition finance why an intercreditor is required to effect a contractual subordination; the security documents that come with acquisition finance will usually specify the first- and second-ranking nature of each debt security, respectively. This description should ensure that, for example, the senior lenders get proceeds of enforcement before the mezzanine lenders, and that the (unsecured) shareholders and intra-group lenders do not get proceeds from the enforcement of the security at all, until all secured creditors are repaid (subject to exceptions in different legal jurisdictions, of course).

However, the senior lenders do not just want to know that they get paid first; they also want to be able to control the enforcement process. Without a direct agreement between the senior lenders and the mezzanine lenders, there may be nothing to stop the mezzanine lenders from enforcing their security first. Even though the mezzanine lenders would only get paid out of the proceeds of enforcement after the senior lenders, if there were no direct agreement between them, the mezzanine lenders would, by virtue of this right to take enforcement action (i.e. to bring the stack of cards down), have an unduly strong negotiating position in the discussions that the different creditors will have to undertake to seek a consensual restructuring of the borrower's debt and equity structure. For this reason, one of the terms of the intercreditor agreement is that the mezzanine lenders agree to a "*standstill period.*" Therefore, after the mezzanine "event of default" occurs, the mezzanine lenders are forced to wait for a certain period before they are allowed to accelerate and enforce their security. In a typical agreement, this standstill period is customarily 90 days when there is a payment default, 120 days when there is a financial covenant default, and 150 days for other types of default events.

Moreover, once the senior lenders have started the enforcement, they will want to have full control over the process until they have fully recovered their loans. Only once all senior loans have been recovered will the senior lenders hand over control to the mezzanine lenders. If, for any reason, the mezzanine lenders receive any proceeds before they are permitted to, the senior lenders will want to have a direct claim against them to hand those proceeds over to the senior lender (this is called a "*turnover right*").

The intercreditor agreement will typically also contain restrictions on the different lenders' abilities to change the original terms of their respective loan agreements. Note that such restrictions are not all one-way traffic in favor of the senior lenders. It is usual for the mezzanine lenders to have a right to prevent the senior lenders from increasing the senior debt that ranks ahead of the mezzanine, beyond a certain level. This level is called the "*senior headroom*" and is usually set at about 10–15% of the amount of the original senior commitments. In this way, at least the mezzanine lenders know that they cannot be "buried" beneath an unlimited amount of higher-ranking senior debt.

The exact rights and obligations of the various creditors specified in the intercreditor agreement are especially important if the borrower ever becomes distressed and is unable to meet its obligations under the finance documents. It is at this time that the borrower and the agent will be looking to see what proportion of the lenders is required to agree to any necessary waivers and amendments to the documents so that the borrower can avoid default. In particular, if there are a number of lenders in a syndicate that provide both senior and second-lien debt, the borrower will be hoping that the adjustments to the lending agreement do not require the unanimous approval of all lenders. Typically, the so-called "money terms"—maturity date, interest rate, amounts committed, nature of security, and identity of borrower group—do, in fact, require unanimous approval. This requirement could allow small lenders (in these circumstances, often called "hold-outs") to hold up an entire restructuring in the hope of being bought out (at the face value of the debt of course, in circumstances where the debt might be trading at well below par). Distressed debt funds that are interested in trying to acquire the business at a good price (or if they see an opportunity to make a good financial return) will also be interested in studying the intercreditor rights to understand which debt securities give them the best negotiating positions.

In European deals, prior to the 2008 global financial crisis, the second-lien facility was typically structured as a "facility D" in the senior facilities agreement. As such, the second-lien creditors were entitled to vote with the other senior lenders on decisions made under the senior facilities agreement, and their specific rights were set out in that agreement. However, the second-lien lenders would rank after the other senior lenders in the payment waterfall. Since the financial crisis, second-lien facilities have more typically been documented separately, largely because the banks became less prepared to underwrite those loans. Indeed, in many deals, second lien lenders are now subordinated in a way more akin to the subordination of the mezzanine lenders.[13] Because they are subordinated, it is usual for second-lien lenders (by a vote in favor of 50% or 66 2/3% among them) to be able to trigger an acceleration of the second-lien debt and an enforcement process after a 60- or 90-day standstill period if the borrower has defaulted on payments to them. In fairness, the exact rights of the second-lien lenders vary considerably from deal to deal, partly because of the sparsity of precedents and partly because the dynamics around the establishment of the second-lien facility (including the appetite of lenders to provide it) vary so much from deal to deal.

If there is a PIK facility, it will usually be structurally subordinated (we describe these facilities later). In other words, a PIK facility will be borrowed at a higher level in the group structure, outside the senior/mezzanine group, and it does not share guarantees and security with the senior/mezzanine lenders. As such, it is not necessary for the PIK lenders to be party to an intercreditor agreement with the other senior, second-lien, and mezzanine creditors.

Deals that have a secured high-yield bond as well as bank facilities (which bank facilities may be senior or super senior, and may be by way of revolving or term debt) will have additional intercreditor issues to deal with. Apart from the priority arrangements between them in the waterfall (which will depend on whether the banks have super priority or whether they are pari passu (i.e., equal ranking)), the key issue, if at least some of the banks are to be pari passu with the bondholders, will be to decide which group makes decisions on enforcement in the case of a default. Traditionally, bank lenders take the lead, as long as their outstanding claims do not fall below a certain threshold at which they no longer have sufficient skin in the game. Below this threshold, the decision-making power switches to the trustee of the bondholders. However, this is a

---

[13] Given their status, second-lien creditors have somewhat less onerous restrictions compared to the mezzanine lenders.

critical point of negotiation and in many deals, bondholders are seen to push back on this traditional arrangement, particularly where the bonds account for a much larger portion of the capital structure than the bank debt. In the conventional U.S. LBO capital structure, however, the bonds will be unsecured; hence, no intercreditor agreement between bondholders and lenders is usually necessary.

ACQUISITION FINANCING INSTRUMENTS

As mentioned, in most modern competitive auctions for a target business there is no "financing condition" in the purchase agreement (meaning that the buyer cannot refuse to proceed with the transaction by virtue of being unable to obtain financing). For this reason, private equity sponsors often start the process of finding lenders at the early stages of the deal; this means that they commence taking soundings from potential lenders at the time of preparing initial first-round bids. Private equity sponsors often mention their potential financiers in their first-round bid letter. If they progress to the second round of bidding, then they will typically negotiate "commitment papers" with potential lenders and require the lenders to sign these just before their final bid is made, so that these papers can be included in the bid papers submitted to the vendor.

If the private equity sponsor is selected as the winning bidder in the auction, in an ideal world, private equity sponsors would delay signing the share purchase agreement until the full-form financing documents are agreed, so as to avoid the risk of an unsuccessful negotiation of the financing documents. However, such a delay is rarely possible and the sponsor will usually take the risk of proceeding on the basis of only commitment papers (but for this reason the sponsor will want to make sure that these commitment papers are as comprehensive and legally binding as is possible and that all required third party approvals are obtained).

The private equity sponsor will typically aim to generate competitive tension between prospective lenders, and make sure that the most important terms are agreed at a time when this competitive tension exists (i.e., before formally mandating the lenders). Specialist debt advisory firms are available to help with expert knowledge of the market, advising which lenders are likely to be interested in a particular deal and what terms may be achievable. In addition, specialist banking lawyers engaged by the private equity sponsor early in the process can use their deep market knowledge to maximize the advantages that can be derived from a competitive process, often (in bigger deals) holding the pen on the preparation of both commitment letters and on the full-form financing documents.

Senior financing

Types of senior facilities

Senior debt (also referred to as "senior secured debt") is an important part of the financial structure of a buyout and stands out as the largest source of acquisition finance. The senior debt package is usually syndicated by the largest and most sophisticated financial institutions operating in the main financial centers.[14] The package is typically "tranched up" into different facilities, each with a slightly different maturity and repayment terms, and hence, a slightly different pricing. These facilities are designed to appeal to different types of lenders. There are different types of loans, such as *revolving credit facilities* and *term loan facilities* (these

---

[14] This means that these banks negotiate and underwrite the senior debt package and then sell all or part of the commitments to other financial institutions in the market, a process known as "syndication." Underwriting banks receive a fee for arranging the loans.

term loans are often called "Facility A, B, C, or D"). They usually accrue interest at a floating rate above LIBOR/EURIBOR rates. The "term loan" refers to a loan which, once drawn down, is repaid in the agreed timeframe but the repaid amounts cannot be subsequently redrawn. In that way, the term loan is distinguished from a "revolving loan," which can be repaid and redrawn as and when the borrower wishes (subject to not being in default). The revolving facilities are either pari passu (equal ranking) with the term loans in the same syndicated loan deal, or can be super senior (i.e., have higher priority than the term loans).[15] Typically, commercial banks participate as revolving lenders, while term loans are traditionally provided by banks (in respect of Term Loan A (which is the amortizing tranche) and any acquisition facilities (which have a delayed-draw and then amortize after a two- to three-year availability period expires)) and by institutional investors (for the remaining facilities). The lion's share of the term facilities is used by the private equity firm to pay the acquisition price (or refinance the target debt) while the remainder can be drawn down by the target company during the holding period.[16]

Certain core facilities are present in nearly every LBO transaction. They typically comprise several term loan facilities to fund the initial acquisition, a revolving facility to fund working capital requirements on an ongoing basis, and an "acquisition or capex facility" to fund future acquisitions or capital expenditure to grow the business (if that is part of the business plan). The amount of senior loans that a given target business can carry (customarily measured as a multiple of the EBITDA of the business) depends on the appetite of lenders in the market at any particular time. Generally, senior loans are not given for more than about four or five times EBITDA. If more borrowing is needed, then the private equity sponsor must issue bonds and/or seek second-lien or mezzanine financing, which is subordinated to the senior funding. Mezzanine lenders might be prepared to lend an additional turn or 1.5 turns of EBITDA.

During the process of arranging syndicated loans, the private equity sponsor is required to provide detailed information regarding the target's business and the legal and tax structure of the proposed acquisition. This disclosure is often achieved by providing access to a data room that has been set up by the seller for the purpose of attracting bidders, and by providing due diligence reports. These reports are typically produced by independent advisers who will address their report to the sponsor and the Bidco and will, in most European deals, also be required to allow the lenders financing the acquisition to rely on the contents as if addressed to them. The exact scope of the reports varies from deal to deal, but the package usually includes the following:

- **A legal due diligence report** produced by a law firm (which explains the legal risks that the target business is exposed to).

- **A financial and tax report** produced by the accountants or tax advisers.

- **A tax structuring report** setting out the steps to be taken to effect the acquisition and any planned reorganization to be effected after completion.

- **A market report** and, sometimes, a *commercial report*, in each case produced by suitable experts. In U.S. financings, the market is less demanding of such reports; thus, lenders need to make do with having access to the data room and discussions with the sponsors' experts only. Lenders also receive an information memorandum prepared by the lead arrangers together with the private equity sponsor. In

[15] Super seniority is often designated in order to encourage clearing banks (which are most capable to provide revolving facilities) to join the syndicate of lenders.

[16] These latter facilities are the so-called "contingent facilities," such as the revolving, working capital, or CAPEX facilities.

addition, they might facilitate a credit rating to be obtained for the loans where necessary for subsequent marketing.

Private equity sponsors tend to spend a considerable amount of time and effort cultivating relationships with relevant arranging banks, so that when a deal comes along, they are able to put together the necessary underwriting quickly.

Often the underwriting is subject to a right on the part of the arrangers to increase (or "flex") the pricing, or to amend (or "tighten") some borrower-friendly terms in the finance documents if, despite their efforts, they are unable to achieve the intended syndication within the syndication period (usually 4–6 months).[17] Obviously, this flexibility that arrangers obtain is disadvantageous for the private equity sponsor, so limits on this right must be clearly specified. In addition, if the pricing is flexed, the financial covenants should be adjusted to maintain the agreed headroom over the business case. The sponsor might also ask for a "reverse flex right," which stipulates that if the arrangers find there is great demand in the market for the commitments and there is an opportunity to actually reduce pricing while still achieving a successful syndication, then the arrangers are bound to offer that to the sponsor (usually in return for an incentive fee for the arrangers, which is calculated as a portion of the first year's savings).

During the course of the borrower-lender relationship there is invariably a regular reporting regime and, in the case of loans with traditional maintenance covenants, the borrower is required to submit to the lender detailed quarterly covenant calculations. In addition, the borrower is obliged to promptly inform the lenders of material events affecting it. It is important that the private equity sponsor manages its relationships with the lenders well, because the loans usually remain in place for the duration of the investment and will almost certainly require an amendment or waiver of some terms of the documents at some point.

Below is a brief description of all loan facilities that may be present in a syndicated loan deal:

- **Facility A (the amortizing facility).** By convention, Facility A is the amortizing senior term loan facility. Amortization is the repayment of a loan in instalments. Facility A is usually all borrowed at the outset and then repaid in regular instalments every three to six months over the life of the facility, maturing between five and seven years later. It is commonly provided by commercial bank lenders, although there are some instances where non-bank institutional investors acquire Facility A loans as well.

- **Revolving credit facility (RCF).** This facility is designed to be used for working capital or other needs of the business. It can be drawn and repaid (and redrawn) during the life of the RCF. Often, it has the same maturity and pricing as facility A.

- **Facility B.** Facility B is also fully drawn down at the outset, but amortizes at a significantly lower rate than facility A (e.g., 1% per year) or is repaid in a single instalment (often referred to as a "bullet" repayment) at maturity, which typically occurs between six and eight years. Because it matures a year or so after Facility A, it carries a higher margin over LIBOR/EURIBOR rates (or other interest rate benchmarks) than facility A. The lender base for this type of facility is often a collection of non-bank institutional investors.

---

[17] During times of market stress, underwriting may not be possible (the arranging banks may not be prepared to take syndication risk). The sponsor will instead have to try to put together a number of banks who, together known as a "club," will be prepared to lend the necessary funds. These banks may subsequently syndicate their commitments when market conditions improve.

- **Facility C.** Facility C is not always included in the mix, but if it is, then it is usually on very similar terms as facility B except that it matures a year later and carries a slightly higher interest rate spread. In some cases, facilities B and C are protected by prepayment penalties and, more usually, the lenders might have rights to refuse prepayments. This feature reflects the fact that these loans are usually taken by funds or institutional lenders who prefer the loans to remain outstanding to maturity (banks, by contrast, usually regard early repayment as a good thing).

- **Acquisition/CAPEX facility.** The package may include an "acquisition facility" or "capex facility," which can be used to fund add-on acquisitions or expansionary capital expenditures to grow the business in accordance with the business plan. Such a facility is usually only available for the first two or three years of the life of the facilities, and is repaid in instalments over the remaining period to maturity. The maturity and pricing are usually the same as for RCF and facility A. The RCF and acquisition/capex facility are typically provided by banks (rather than funds or institutional lenders), which have the infrastructure and appetite to offer facilities that may be undrawn at closing and, in relation to the RCF, can be repaid and redrawn.

- **Accordion facility.** In larger deals, it may be agreed that additional financing can be added to the senior facilities (or lent on a pari passu basis in a separate agreement, sharing the same security package) after the facilities agreement is initially signed under what is known as "accordion" (or "additional" or "incremental") facilities (often up to a specified amount), so long as a pro forma leverage ratio is met. These additional debt provisions are highly negotiated, including, for example, the purpose for which this debt can be borrowed (either general purposes or for specific acquisitions and capex purposes) and the terms that can be offered to the additional debt lenders. For instance, usually, the lenders get the benefit of a "most favored nation" provision, at least for a period of time after the deal is launched, so that initial lenders are not embarrassed by the borrower raising debt with similar terms but a much higher margin shortly after the initial funds are lent.

In the U.S. asset based loan facilities (ABL) are quite common on acquisition financings, where ABL lenders typically advance against a fluctuating "borrowing base" comprised of the most liquid collateral such as receivables or stock (i.e., outstanding exposure is never permitted to exceed some agreed fraction of the borrowing base). These are much less common in Europe, where taking first priority security over a fluctuating asset pool is more complex and often burdensome in practice.

The terms for senior facilities

In Exhibit 6, we outline and explain some of the main provisions that must be negotiated and agreed in a typical acquisition financing. We then discuss some of these provisions in further detail.

Exhibit 6: The main provisions in loan contracts

Commitment	The amounts and types of credit facilities made available by the lender or syndicate of lenders.
Conditionality	The conditions that need to be met at the outset, prior to first loan drawdown, including, for example, the minimum equity contribution and all required third-party due diligence reports in a form satisfactory to the lenders.
Pricing	The margin (i.e. the interest rate payable on) of the loans, usually over LIBOR/EUROBOR rates, as well as additional loan fees, which include the upfront arranging/underwriting fee, the commitment fee (paid on the undrawn committed amount), and agency fees.
Repayment terms	Ultimately, the loans need to be fully and finally repaid on the final maturity dates for each facility. Prior to that, the amortizing loans are repaid in line with the amortization schedule, and mandatory prepayments may be required upon certain events (such as a change of control) or on the receipt of proceeds from certain disposals or claims. In addition, there is often a requirement to apply a proportion of "excess cash flow" generated by the business in mandatory prepayment of the loans—the so-called "excess cash flow sweep."
Security	Guarantees and asset security provided by the acquisition company (and its immediate parent) and the target company and its subsidiaries.
Representations and warranties	A list of statements that are warranted by the borrower to be true and accurate at the outset. Certain of these representations are typically required to be repeated at intervals throughout the life of the loans (and thus may function similarly to undertakings).
Undertakings	A list of positive and negative undertakings that the borrower agrees to maintain compliance with throughout the life of the loans, including, for example, undertakings to maintain agreed levels of security coverage and restrictions on dividends and borrowings.
Reporting	Typically, a European acquisition financing will provide for monthly management reports, quarterly financial statements, quarterly certification of compliance with financial covenants, and annual audited financial statements, plus the requirement to inform of material developments, including litigation and default. There would also normally be an annual meeting between top management and the lenders.
Financial covenants	Financial performance ratios (based on the financial accounts) that need to be complied with for the duration of the financing, tested quarterly, and confirmed annually by the auditors.
Events of default	A list of triggers, including payment default, breaches of representations, undertakings (subject to appropriate remedy periods), cross default, insolvency, and (invariably in European deals, but not in U.S. deals) material adverse change (MAC).
Transfers and assignments	The mechanics and terms dealing with the ability of lenders to transfer their loans and commitments to other financial institutions, including any restrictions on the entities permitted to be lenders and whether consent from the borrower is needed before the lender is allowed to transfer (or assign).
Waivers and amendments	The voting mechanics for decisions by the lenders, which, in most European deals, require a 66 2/3% majority to carry a decision, unless the particular matter is on the list of matters that require a unanimous vote in favor. This section may also exclude non-responding lenders from the vote (also known as the "snooze and lose" provision) and may give the borrower the right to replace (at par) non-consenting lenders with new lenders (also known as the "yank the bank" provision).

Agency and inter-lender provisions	The arrangements which regulate the positions between lenders, including, for example, their appointment of an administrative agent (often called the "facility agent") and security agent (who administers the security for the lenders) and loss-sharing provisions which require lenders who receive more than their appropriate share of repayments to redistribute appropriately.

Conditionality

The availability of the financing is subject to the prior satisfaction of so-called "conditions precedent." These (and especially the degree of "satisfaction" that the banks have already signed off on) are the subject of intense scrutiny at the point of the final bids and the closing of the acquisition—both from the seller side and from the buyer side. Everyone wants to see that the lenders' commitments are not subject to due diligence conditions, credit approvals, approval of structure, market conditions, and so on.

In many European deals, the closing conditions are required to be on a *certain funds basis*, meaning that the acquisition funding cannot be subject to lender discretions such as due diligence, market conditions, or adverse events affecting the target group (unless they are set out as conditions precedent to the acquisition itself in the acquisition agreement). Everything that remains to be satisfied needs to be under the buyers' control, as if they were using their own cash. By contrast, in the United States, tolerance remains for limited conditionality based on a material adverse change in the target and breach of specified representations, which may be referred to in the commitment papers.

In larger deals, additional comfort is often obtained at the commitment letter stage by negotiating an "*interim loan agreement*" (ILA). The ILA safeguards against execution risk, given that the commitment papers (although legally binding) are still only a summary of the terms to be included in the finance documents and are conditional upon finally negotiating the full finance agreements ("subject to contract"). Essentially, an ILA is a fully negotiated loan agreement for the full amount of acquisition funding that is needed on the closing date. However, the commitment expires shortly after funding (usually within 30–45 days) and as such, the ILA does not need to have the extensive undertakings and events of default that are in a full-term facilities agreement. Therefore, this "short form" loan agreement is relatively quick and easy to put in place. This approach is used by private equity sponsors to assure the sellers that their funding is fully committed and not still subject to contract, eliminating any disadvantage relative to trade bidders that do not need to raise debt to fund the acquisition. However, because of the short-term nature of the ILA, the parties never intend the borrower to actually borrow under it. The private equity sponsor is expected to use the time between winning the bid and closing the deal to negotiate full-form financing agreements which replace the ILA and put the financing commitments on a long-term footing.

Default and acceleration

There are two main types of loan defaults: *technical defaults* and *payment defaults*. Technical defaults occur when the issuer violates a provision of the loan agreement (other than a payment obligation). For instance, a technical default can be triggered if an issuer does not meet a financial covenant test, or fails to provide lenders with financial information. Often, there is a 15- or 20-business-day cure or grace period for the borrower group to fix the problem and get back in compliance before an "event of default" is triggered. A payment default is a more serious matter (although legally all events of default usually have the same consequence). As the name implies, this type of default occurs when a company fails to make a payment when due (most importantly either an interest payment or a principal repayment installment), and there will usually be a much shorter period of time (i.e., 3–4 days) during which an issuer can cure the payment default.

A change of control (i.e., where the borrower group ceases to be controlled by the original private equity sponsor) is rarely actually described as an event of default, but rather as a "mandatory repayment event." The reason for this distinction is to recognize that the borrower is not usually the one culpable for this happening. However, this is a nicety, because if the loans are not immediately repaid then these circumstances will quickly result in a payment default.

A breach that continues beyond any defined cure period will become an event of default. In this case, the lenders have the right to accelerate the facilities. Acceleration brings forward the maturity date and leads to the early termination of any undrawn loan commitments. The lenders will have various options at this point. They could:

- put the loans "on demand" (i.e., the loans will become repayable when, at any subsequent date at the lender's discretion, the lender asks for them to be repaid, and thus the loans are no longer "committed");

- cancel undrawn commitments;

- require the loans to be repaid immediately or at a specified date in the future;

- direct the security agent to exercise any of its rights under the security documents, including set-off rights with respect to pledged bank accounts or a full security enforcement.

Decisions by the lender-group usually require a specified majority vote of the lenders. In European deals, the majority required is customarily two-thirds (by commitments), while in the United States, it is 50.1%. Certain decisions, such as changes to the scope of the security package, require a higher majority threshold. Further, decisions that are utterly fundamental to lenders, such as changes to the pricing or repayment obligations, require unanimity from the lenders affected by the changes.

Although the lenders have the right to accelerate payments immediately upon the occurrence of an event of default, in practice, this is often just the start of a protracted negotiation between the lenders and the shareholders to see if they can reach a consensual solution. One of the most common solutions employed in restructuring loans in default involves an "*amend-to-extend*" transaction.[18] This approach allows the borrower to extend some loan maturities through an amendment, rather than a refinancing. Amend-to-extend transactions came into widespread use during the 2008 global financial crisis as borrowers preferred to push out debt maturities in the face of difficult lending conditions that made refinancing prohibitively expensive. In addition to recalibrating the capital structure, creditors' intervention after an event of default, (especially a technical default) often leads to changes in the company's financing, investing, and operating activities, particularly in the area of asset growth, capital expenditures, firm payout policy, and CEO turnover.[19]

When an event of default occurs, lenders can take control of the business by exercising rights under the security package to replace the management if it refuses to comply, or by controlling the votes in the general meeting of the borrowing group (often by using their power of attorney). However, bank lenders are typically reluctant to actually run the business, both because they usually consider it to be outside of their core competency and because they fear incurring the liabilities associated with the management of a distressed

[18] Standard and Poor's (2011).

[19] See Nini et al. (2012)

company. Instead, they usually prefer a change in management to ensure that the business is run for their benefit, pending the sale of the business as a going concern to a new owner. If the borrower has entered distress, the original lenders (particularly if they are banks) often reduce their exposure by selling their debt claims to hedge funds and distressed funds that may have more appetite to influence any turnaround or restructuring process the business is going through.

Finally, it is worth mentioning that while defaults and financial distress can be unavoidable at times, research shows that private equity-backed firms resolve their financial distress 3.5 to 4.2 months faster than non-private equity-backed firms.[20] The faster speed with which these firms complete their restructurings is consistent with private equity sponsors relying more on out-of-court restructurings and prepackaged bankruptcy filings, which typically move faster than traditional bankruptcy proceedings.[21] Additionally, even in traditional bankruptcy settings like Chapter 11 in the United States, research shows that private equity-backed firms move through such a process marginally faster than firms that are not backed by private equity.

Security

In most cases, the senior acquisition facilities are secured on the borrower group. At the target level, these assets might include fixed assets (e.g., property, plant, and equipment), but also include other assets (e.g., shares and other investments held (including in subsidiaries), inventories, raw materials, contracts, bank accounts, trade receivables, and intangible assets like copyrights, trademarks, and patents). At the level of the acquisition vehicle (which will typically be the entity that has borrowed most of the acquisition debt), the security provided will be the shares in the borrower (thus, a share pledge will be given by its parent company) and the assets of the borrower, including the shares in the target company. If lenders need to enforce their debt claim because an event of default has occurred, they will usually first aim to sell the entire business as a going concern to a third-party buyer. This sale will typically involve enforcing one of the share pledges at the top of the borrower group. An alternative to the going concern sale might be a piecemeal enforcement of the security over individual assets of the group, selling different assets in different sales; however, this option is usually more complicated (especially legally), time consuming and expensive.

Financial covenants

Financial covenants are negative undertakings in lending agreements (i.e., undertakings to not do certain things, or permit them to happen, unless lenders agree otherwise). The agreements usually specify not only the definitions of the covenants but also the remedies, in case some of the covenants are breached. Financial covenants are set and agreed with the lenders at the time of the original acquisition and are based on future forecasted financial performance. The theory is that requiring compliance with the financial covenants ensures fiscal discipline at the portfolio company level and drives operational improvements (e.g., cost-cutting measures and improved efficiencies) that are essential to meet the projected financial results.

When raising acquisition finance, private equity sponsors produce a financial model of projected earnings, taking into account the revenue enhancements and cost efficiencies that they intend to introduce to the business to increase its value over the life of the investment. Lenders receive this model as part of the business case and it is of key importance. Typically the model will be the basis for the financial covenants with which

---

[20] Hotchkiss et al. (2014).

[21] In the case of a prepackaged bankruptcy filing, a restructuring plan is submitted to the bankruptcy court at the same time when the company files its official bankruptcy petition. The court then decides whether or not to accept the proposed restructuring plan.

the borrower group will need to comply. This gives the lenders not only protection against deterioration in the business, but also early repayment if the projected improved performance is not delivered. Thus, it is important to note that having a stable, constant business model and servicing the debt is not sufficient. Performance cannot stand still when EBITDA-based covenants require improvements over time.

To monitor financial covenants, lenders require the private equity sponsor to ensure that the borrower provides annual audited financial statements and, usually, unaudited quarterly management accounts and a monthly management update as well.[22] The provision of the audited accounts must occur within a reasonable period after the end of the fiscal period (e.g., 120–180 days for annual accounts and 30–45 days for quarterly accounts). Together with the quarterly and annual accounts, the borrower needs to also deliver a *compliance certificate*, which confirms that the borrower is in compliance with the financial covenants. The financial covenants that are usually seen in senior lending agreements, and which are tested quarterly, include the following:

- **Leverage ratio.** This is the ratio of the borrower's net debt at the test date to the borrower's last 12-month cost rolling EBITDA (i.e., Total Net Debt/EBITDA). The net debt includes senior and junior commercial lender debt (indeed, it may have separate calculations for senior and total leverage) and the capital element of finance leases less cash balances (to the extent that the cash on the balance sheet is available to repay the debt). Shareholder debt is usually excluded on the basis that it will be deeply subordinated under the intercreditor agreement. EBITDA is usually defined as operating profit in the ordinary course of business before interest, tax, depreciation, and amortization. Importantly, it does not include exceptional and extraordinary items that are not recurring. The exact definition of EBITDA is often the subject of detailed negotiation. In some circumstances, EBITDA might include add-backs for impairment charges, restructuring charges, and non-cash expenses, as well as expected cost savings and synergies from the transaction. Essentially, EBITDA is supposed to represent the "pure" profit-generating capacity of the business, after stripping out one-off events, non-cash items and external factors such as the impact of the capital and ownership structure. The leverage ratio is usually tested on a rolling last 12-month (LTM) basis, and is often set to have between 20% and 30% headroom to the agreed base case in the financial model over the duration of the loan. The leverage ratio is the most commonly seen metric in acquisition finance, no doubt because it is common practice in M&A markets to also value a business as a multiple of EBITDA.

- **Interest coverage ratio.** This ratio is expressed as the borrower's EBITDA divided by the "finance charges" (interest payable with respect to acquisition finance loans and interest on capital leases) incurred during the last 12 months (i.e., EBITDA/Finance Charges). It is important to note that the finance charges are determined on an accrual basis, and are not simply the interest costs that are paid in cash. Again, this ratio is usually set at between 20% and 30% headroom to the base case, requiring that the minimum specified ratio will increase over the duration of the lending contract as debt is being repaid. This ratio is expected to provide an early warning signal about the financial situation of the borrower. When there are different layers of acquisition finance, senior interest coverage and total interest coverage ratios can be separately required.

- **Debt service coverage ratio.** This ratio is designed to check that the cash flow generated by the borrower is sufficient to cover debt payments. It is measured as a ratio of the borrower's cash flow (EBITDA adjusted for actual cash flows and working capital) to its debt service (cash interest and

---

[22] Lenders also expect disclosures about pending litigation, environmental claims, or any other information that could have a material adverse impact on the business.

scheduled principal repayments on debt outstanding and payments on finance leases (i.e., Cashflow/Debt Service). This ratio is usually set at 1:1 or 1.1:1 and is seen as a reality check to see if the business is actually producing enough real cash to fund its regular financing obligations. The debt service cover is sometimes also referred to as the "cash flow cover ratio" or the "fixed charge coverage ratio."

- **Minimum (tangible) net worth.** This balance sheet covenant is unusual in medium-sized and large acquisition financings. The covenant is most commonly calculated as the net worth of a company (total assets minus total liabilities). If a *tangible* net worth test is required, then the calculation will exclude from total assets any value derived from intangible assets (e.g., goodwill, copyrights, patents, trade names, other intellectual property, fair values of derivatives, etc.), making tangible net worth a more stringent test of corporate value than net worth. Net worth covenants are used as a backstop test against a material loss in the value of the group.

- **Capital expenditures.** Often, lenders also set limits on capital expenditures to limit overinvestments that might pose a risk to the business. Borrowers are restricted from making any capital expenditures if the aggregate cost of the fixed assets purchased exceeds a fixed amount budgeted in the original business plan during any fiscal year (plus 10–15% headroom). In deals that involve further acquisitions (i.e., "buy and build" strategies), the budget for capital expenditures might scale automatically as new acquisitions are made. Unused capital expenditures in a given year can generally be rolled over to the next year, and sometimes a portion of the following year's allowance can be brought forward to allow flexibility. This covenant is usually tested annually.

If the buyout target fails to meet any of the financial covenants when tested, the loan is in technical default. The borrower is expected to provide an immediate notice of default to the lenders. Usually, there is a 30-day grace period for breached financial covenants in senior loan agreements, giving the shareholders the ability to "equity cure." In the absence of a cure, lenders have the option to accelerate the loans (i.e., demand repayment) and enforce their claims against the borrower. However, in most cases of covenant violations, lenders do not call the loans.

If the financial sponsor has "equity cure rights" and injects more equity into the borrower group within the 30-day grace period, the financial covenants are recalculated. The impact of the new equity proceeds on the financial covenant calculations varies from deal to deal, but at a minimum, the new equity reduces debt (for the purpose of the leverage test) and finance charges (for the purpose of the interest cover test)—as if the debt had been reduced at the start of the test period. The new equity also increases the cash flow for the purpose of the debt service (cash flow) cover test. In more borrower-friendly documents the new equity is permitted to boost EBITDA, producing a much more powerful remedy. However, even the "friendliest" cure rights only fix the EBITDA for the 12-month period for which covenants are tested, and so, unless the amounts of equity required are small or the breach is seen as merely a temporary issue, the private equity sponsor will, in many cases, seek to renegotiate the debt contract in order to obtain a "covenant reset," even if this involves having to concede to additional charges in the form of amendment or waiver fees, higher interest costs and, most likely, tighter restrictions on the business.

A study that examined insolvency during the global financial crisis found that private equity-backed buyouts had a much better coverage ratio (the ability to pay interest on debt from profit and cash flow) than other companies, and were less likely to fail in the wake of the crisis. Importantly, the study found that poor management and failure to generate cash were distinguishing factors between buyouts that failed and those that survived—and not the leverage levels. One of the main factors behind this resilience is the active ownership model of the private equity funds. Due to this unique structure, buyouts that were backed by private equity funds delivered significantly higher recovery rates on debt than those that were publicly listed (62–63% compared with 26–30%, respectively).[23] Exhibit 7 presents a sample covenant test sheet that includes financial covenants in both senior and mezzanine loan agreements. As can be observed from the spreadsheet, accounting numbers are forecasted out into the future on a quarterly basis. The covenant thresholds change dynamically, becoming stricter over time as the performance of the borrower improves.

Exhibit 7: Example on the calculation of financial covenants.

COVENANT CALCULATION Transaction date: 31.12.2018	Source	FY 2019				FY 2020		
		Q2 30-Jun-19	Q3 30-Sep-19	Q2 31-Dec-19	Q1 31-Mar-20	Q2 30-Jun-20	Q3 30-Sep-20	Q2 31-Dec-20
TOTAL DEBT TO EBITDA COVENANT								
Input from Financing Case								
Total Debt	Forecast	126,788	125,771	123,800	122,776	120,758	119,686	117,461
EBITDA	Forecast	22,250	22,250	22,850	23,200	23,550	23,900	24,275
Total Debt Cover	Forecast	**5.7x**	**5.7x**	**5.4x**	**5.3x**	**5.1x**	**5.0x**	**4.8x**
Senior Debt Covenants								
Headroom (% Change in EBITDA)	Input	25%	25%	25%	25%	25%	25%	25%
Allowed EBITDA	Calc	16,688	16,688	17,138	17,400	17,663	17,925	18,206
Debt to EBITDA Covenant	Output	**7.6x**	**7.5x**	**7.2x**	**7.1x**	**6.8x**	**6.7x**	**6.5x**
Mezzanine Debt Covenants								
Headroom (% Change in EBITDA)	Input	35%	35%	35%	35%	35%	35%	35%
Allowed EBITDA	Calc	14,463	14,463	14,853	15,080	15,308	15,535	15,779
Debt to EBITDA Covenant	Output	**8.8x**	**8.7x**	**8.3x**	**8.1x**	**7.9x**	**7.7x**	**7.4x**
INTEREST COVER COVENANT								
Input from Financing Case								
EBITDA	Forecast	22,250	22,250	22,850	23,200	23,550	23,900	24,275
Finance Charges	Forecast	8,826	8,808	8,788	8,856	8,810	8,762	8,818
Interest Cover	Forecast	**2.5x**	**2.5x**	**2.6x**	**2.6x**	**2.7x**	**2.7x**	**2.8x**
Senior Debt Covenants								
Headroom (% Change in EBITDA)	Input	25%	25%	25%	25%	25%	25%	25%
Allowed EBITDA	Calc	16,688	16,688	17,138	17,400	17,663	17,925	18,206
Interest Cover Covenant	Output	**1.9x**	**1.9x**	**2.0x**	**2.0x**	**2.0x**	**2.0x**	**2.1x**
Mezzanine Debt Covenants								
Headroom (% Change in EBITDA)	Input	35%	35%	35%	35%	35%	35%	35%
Allowed EBITDA	Calc	14,463	14,463	14,853	15,080	15,308	15,535	15,779
Interest Cover Covenant	Output	**1.6x**	**1.6x**	**1.7x**	**1.7x**	**1.7x**	**1.8x**	**1.8x**

At times, when the markets are especially borrower-friendly, syndicated lenders drop some or all of the typical financial covenants from their terms in order to compete with a bond product (or with other, hungrier lenders). These covenant-lite deals are not as common in the European market as they are in the United States. Very often, European deals drop one or two covenants only (such deals are sometimes called "cov-loose"). The first covenant to be dropped is usually the cash flow coverage ratio, because it is relatively easy to manipulate (e.g., cash flow can be boosted by selling assets, which may not be in anyone's interest). The last to be dropped is usually the leverage ratio, reflecting its perceived importance as a simple measure of the value of the business relative to its debt burden.

---

[23] See Wright et al. (2014).

Second-lien facility

This facility borrows its name from a similar concept in U.S. deals. Sometimes called facility D in European deals (particularly where it is documented as an additional tranche in the senior facilities agreement), the second-lien facility ranks after the senior debt comprised by facilities A, B, and C, and the RCF and acquisition/capex facilities in the payment waterfall. It usually has a maturity of one year (or six months) after the maturity date of the senior loan facility C, and it enjoys some of the same features as a mezzanine facility (but will rank ahead of the mezzanine facility in the payments waterfall). As with a mezzanine facility, part of the second-lien facility's (higher) interest rate is typically paid on a deferred (i.e., PIK) basis, and there are usually prepayment penalties for early repayment. In the United States, the second-lien facility may be used as a substitute for high-yield bonds (e.g., in smaller transactions where a bond would not be sufficiently liquid).

Second-lien facilities are often seen as a feature of an extremely liquid market, where loans that would be lent as mezzanine facilities in more normal market conditions are squeezed into the senior facilities. Usually, second-lien facilities are relatively small, offering about half a turn of EBITDA. As their name implies, the claims on assets used as collateral, if any, of second-lien loans are junior to those of first-lien senior loans. Moreover, second-lien loans typically have a longer maturity than first-lien loans and they may, if separately documented, have less restrictive covenant packages (i.e., the financial covenant levels are set with a little more headroom relative to the first-lien senior loans). As a result, second-lien senior loans are priced at a premium to first-lien senior loans.

The largest investors in second-lien facilities are hedge funds, CDOs, CLOs, and other leveraged loan funds. Sometimes, banks that arrange for the syndication of this type of debt retain a small amount of the facility to encourage other investors to participate. Investors in second-lien loans have two main ways to document the collateral. One option is to have the second-lien loan as part of a single security agreement with first-lien loans. This agreement allocates the collateral assets, with value going first, obviously, to the first-lien claims and next to the second-lien claims. Another option is to have two entirely separate agreements. The choice between these two options is principally decided by the laws governing the relevant security agreement and the customary practices in that jurisdiction, but also partly decided by the insolvency regulations to which the borrower (Bidco or LBO target) is subject. The following is merely a hypothetical situation, to illustrate the sorts of considerations that may be in play (The exact analysis is entirely jurisdiction-dependent):

- In a single security agreement, the second-lien lenders might have a stronger argument in favor of joining the same creditor class as the first-lien lenders in the event of a bankruptcy. Thus, for adequate protection, the collateral must cover both the claims of the first and second-lien lenders. In these cases, the second-lien lenders will often have a vote as secured lenders equal to those of the first-lien lenders. One downside for second-lien lenders is that these facilities are often smaller than the first-lien loans and, therefore, when a vote comes up, first-lien lenders will usually be able to outvote second-lien lenders to promote their own interests. Contractual subordination provisions will of course be present in the intercreditor agreement.

- In the case of two separate security agreements, the first-lien and second-lien lenders are likely to be divided into two separate creditor classes. As a result, second-lien lenders may (depending on contractual, security and local law factors) not have a voice in the first-lien senior creditor committees. First-lien lenders may receive adequate protection payments if the collateral covers their claims, but does not cover the claims of the second-lien lenders.

Subordinated financing

Mezzanine financing

If there is mezzanine financing, this will typically comprise a single facility and be documented in a separate mezzanine facility agreement. The mezzanine tranches can be syndicated to institutional investors, such as banks or specialist mezzanine funds. The mezzanine (sometimes shortened to "mezz") lenders usually share the same security package as the senior lenders, with the relationship between the senior and mezzanine lenders being set out in an intercreditor agreement. The critical differentiator of the mezzanine facility is that it is subordinated to the senior facilities and ranks after them in terms of repayment. The interest margin on a mezzanine facility is commensurately higher than that on the senior facilities; to make this bearable for the borrower, the margin is often split between a cash portion, which is required to be paid on an ongoing basis, and a deferred/PIK portion, which is not paid in cash at the time that it accrues but is instead added to the loan amount (i.e., paid in kind in the form of new debt obligations). The repayment of a mezzanine facility is usually through a bullet payment at maturity, which is typically one year after senior facility C, with prepayment penalties for prepayment in the earlier years. Other than the features discussed above, the terms of the mezzanine facility agreement will normally be similar to those in the senior facilities agreement, though there may be slightly (10%) larger baskets and more headroom in the financial covenants. Importantly, however, the fact that the mezzanine is in a separate agreement means that the mezzanine lenders vote separately on any amendments and waivers requested by the borrower. The fact that they cannot be outvoted by the senior lenders can give them a powerful voice in any distressed restructuring negotiations.

Given that mezzanine financing is subordinated to senior first-lien and second-lien loans, mezzanine lenders sometimes require equity-based options such as warrants (or "equity kickers") or rights to convert/exchange to equity to enhance their returns. In some cases, mezzanine debt providers even take a minority equity position directly in the borrower. The warrants attached to mezzanine loans grant the investors the right to buy ordinary shares in the private equity investment vehicle that acquires the target company (i.e., shares in Bidco). The shares that can be purchased might be a fixed percentage of share capital or a fixed number of shares. The holders aim to exercise the warrants at a subscription share price that is as low as possible. The warrants are often transferable, allowing the investors to sell them easily in a secondary market. They are usually exercised immediately prior to the sale or listing of the portfolio company by the private equity sponsor.

Pay-in-kind financing

Sometimes a PIK facility will be put in place in addition to, or instead of, mezzanine financing. As the name implies, interest is typically not permitted to be paid in cash until the senior and mezzanine facilities are fully repaid; rather, the interest compounds and is added to the loan. This facility is usually structurally quite separate from the senior and mezzanine facilities, being lent at a parent company of the senior/mezzanine borrower and benefiting only from a parent share pledge by way of security. PIK financing is said to be "structurally subordinated" (indeed, from the senior and mezzanine lenders' perspective, it is sometimes called quasi-equity) and as such, there is usually no need for the PIK lender to be party to any intercreditor agreement (which would effect a contractual subordination). The proceeds of a PIK facility are usually used to fund a dividend to the private equity sponsor, enabling the private equity sponsor to return capital to its fund investors before a full exit takes place, thus improving the IRR of the fund. The interest rate on a PIK facility is typically high (15% is not unusual) so the private equity sponsor will usually have a plan to repay it within a short period of time (e.g., with funds received from an imminent exit).

High-yield bond financing

Most high-yield bonds have no amortization; instead, there is one bullet payment at maturity, often five to ten years after the issuance. However, interest payments are typically paid semi-annually during the entire period, and are often significantly higher than payments on bank debt (though this varies considerably with appetite for such debt in the bond markets). The interest rate in a bond is typically fixed (in contrast with syndicated loans, where it is usually (but not always) floating) and is referred to as the "coupon." The higher interest rate compensates the investors for the higher risk that follows with high-yield bonds, which are usually issued by sub-investment grade corporates. There are a few specific constraints for a high-yield bond to be issued: (a) the deal must be of a sufficiently large size (usually $150 million is seen as the minimum); (b) the issuer group must be able to show audited financial statements over the prior three years (which might not be possible if, e.g., the deal is a carve-out); (c) there must be sufficient time to complete an offering memorandum; and (d) market conditions must be favorable. Since bonds are being issued in the public markets rather than the private markets, they require extensive risk and information disclosures. The main features of high-yield bonds include the following:

- **Contractual documentation**. The legal terms of a bond are usually set out in a U.S. law "indenture" (for this reason, U.S. qualified lawyers usually lead on the transaction). English law is sometimes used but this is still relatively rare. The main document that bond investors focus on is the offering memorandum, which contains a summary of the terms of the bond (known as the description of notes, or "DoN"), a description of the business, a management discussion and analysis, risk factors relating to the business and the capital structure, as well as a full set of audited financial statements. The offering memorandum can be a very lengthy document (600 pages or more) and thus, its preparation involves considerably higher transaction costs than those incurred for bank financing agreements. In addition to the indenture and the offering memorandum, appropriate diligence must be completed by the auditors in order to provide a comfort letter confirming they have "ticked and tied" all financial numbers back to the audited financials or management financials. Lawyers need to provide appropriate legal opinions and, if the bonds are being offered to U.S. investors, *10b-5 letters* to the underwriters as part of their due diligence defense package, confirming that there are "no material misstatements or omissions that they are aware of" in the offering memorandum.

- **Restrictions**. As mentioned above, covenants are typically far less restrictive in a bond indenture than in a syndicated loan agreement. For example, whereas a syndicated loan will usually include maintenance financial covenants that are tested quarterly to confirm whether or not the business is meeting its business plan projections, bond contracts usually only have "*incurrence-based covenants*". This relative lack of restriction is one of the principal reasons why private equity sponsors on bigger deals often prefer to issue a high-yield bond rather than get syndicated debt facilities.

    A brief explanation of the difference between the incurrence based covenants that exist in high-yield bonds and the maintenance covenants that we see in traditional debt facilities:

    (i) Incurrence covenants impose limitations on certain actions that a borrower may wish to take, such as incurring additional debt, paying a dividend, disposing of an asset or making investments. They are called "incurrence covenants" even if they aren't actually concerned with "incurrence", because often in bond documents they are expressed as permitting the relevant dividend, disposal or investment if the issuer would have been permitted to incur more debt under the incurrence covenant. These may be outright prohibitions or restrictions that allow the action only if the borrower meets certain financial tests or ratios (typically a fixed charge coverage ratio for unsecured debt or some form of senior secured leverage ratio or consolidated leverage ratio). Importantly, these only trigger a default if the issuer/borrower does something to breach them (i.e. if it borrows debt that it is not permitted to incur). The issuer/borrower can avoid a default simply by not borrowing the relevant amount or doing the relevant other thing.

(ii) Maintenance covenants, on the other hand, require the borrower to meet certain financial ratio tests, such as tests pertaining to leverage, net worth, total debt, or interest coverage. These are generally tested quarterly and require the borrower to improve its financial performance over time, at least in the early years.

Some examples of incurrence-based covenants include limitations on the incurrence of additional debt, limitations on restricted payments, limitations on dividends and payments affecting subsidiaries, limitations on liens, limitations on sale and leaseback transactions, limitations on asset sales, and limitations on mergers or acquisitions. As mentioned, these actions may only be undertaken if the borrower can achieve a specific financial ratio. However, it is typical for each of the above-mentioned restrictive covenants to have exceptions (i.e., "freebie baskets" or "carve-outs") that may be used by the company, even if it is incapable of meeting the appropriate ratio threshold. In addition, the fact that such covenants are incurrence-based means that the borrower simply cannot do the relevant action if it would exceed the relevant incurrence test; therefore, failure to achieve them does not result in any breaches or defaults, unlike the maintenance financial covenants in debt facilities, which will be triggered if the required financial performance levels are not maintained.

- **Call protection.** Investors in high-yield bonds are usually institutional investors, who are more focused on yield and call protection (i.e., prohibition on early prepayment) than syndicated loan investors. A call provision on a bond sets a specific date before which the company cannot repay the bond (i.e., 2–4 years after issuance) unless it makes the bondholder "whole" (i.e., pay the interest payments that the bondholder would have been entitled to but for the early repayment), which is extremely expensive. After this date, the borrower can repay the bond at its face amount plus a premium, with such premium stepping down each year after the call period. Call protection can be extremely beneficial for bondholders when interest rates are falling, as borrowers are penalized if they want to retire the bond issue before it matures. However, note that there are often certain exemptions that permit early redemption of a portion of the bonds during the call period. For instance, early redemption can occur free from make-whole or other penalties if the company uses a portion of IPO proceeds or, in aggressive markets, if bondholders previously permitted purchasing a portion of the bonds at a discounted price.

- **Public nature.** In contrast to syndicated loans (which are "private transactions" between the borrower and the syndicate of lenders), bond issues are typically public transactions or trade in the QIB market (known as Rule 144A issues). Most issuers have only a vague idea of who their bondholders might be. For this reason, a private equity sponsor finds it much easier to negotiate with bank lenders rather than bondholders, especially if the portfolio company is facing financial difficulties and needs to amend its financing documents. Amendments or waivers to a public bond will need to be approved by the requisite percentage of bondholders as part of a public consent solicitation process. Accordingly, it is typically much more time consuming and expensive to receive appropriate waivers from bondholders than from bank lenders.

- **Flexibility and market conditions**. Public markets are more volatile than private markets and the bond market is no exception. The market can suddenly tighten and can remain effectively closed for business for extended periods. The process of book-building by the arrangers of bond financing is a laborious task (often also involving securing ratings from ratings agencies) and requires a longer lead time than a syndicated loan does. Certainty of bond funding, and the pricing and terms of this funding, is thus subject to capital market conditions. Accordingly, private equity sponsors who are planning to obtain bond financing usually run a "*dual-track process*" to line up syndicated loan commitments as one alternative and bond financing as another. Typically, in the SPA, the sponsor will ensure that a "*cooperation provision*" is negotiated that mandates the target management and vendor or seller to cooperate with the purchaser in preparing the high-yield bond, and especially that the management partakes in all required (and reasonable) diligence and book-building processes prior to the acquisition date. This clause is vital because it ensures that the offering memorandum will receive appropriate senior management time and attention prior to the bond issuance. Nonetheless, should the bond financing fail or timing be inappropriate, sponsors will then finance the original acquisition using a bridge facility provided by banks using the syndicated loan format on the usual basis (sometimes with a shorter maturity or with the margin ratcheting up materially after 12 months), and then try to refinance the bridge with a bond shortly afterwards.

- **Super senior RCF**. If the structure only has high yield bond debt, then it will also typically have a separate super senior revolving credit facility with one or more banks on more traditional bank loan terms (often with a leverage financial covenant that springs into force at a certain level of drawings).

Bank and bond debt traditionally have different covenant terms. Typically, credit agreements have both "incurrence" and "maintenance" covenants: Bonds traditionally will have only incurrence covenants, and those covenants are generally more relaxed (i.e., set at more generous levels and are more likely to be determined by reference to leverage ratio tests than fixed basket amounts) than those used in bank debt.

At this point is important to highlight important differences between acquisition loans and high-yield bonds (see Exhibit 8 for a comparative summary).

Unitranche financing

A relatively recent development is the unitranche facility, which was originally developed by leading debt fund manager, Ares Asset Management, and offered as a product in association with GE Capital.[24] As the name suggests, this instrument operates as a single facility in place of the "alphabet soup" of senior facilities, and also stretches into the space that is traditionally seen as the preserve of mezzanine lenders. Because it is a single facility (supplemented by any necessary revolving and capex/acquisition facilities), the unitranche facility presents less voluminous finance agreements to borrowers. A unitranche structure provides several key benefits, outlined below.

---

[24] Ares brought GE Capital into its offering partly because it was not set up to provide extensive undrawn facility options (revolving facilities for working capital and Capex facilities for future capital expenditure and acquisition requirements).

Exhibit 8: Comparison between a traditional European bank loan (written under English law) and a U.S.-style high-yield bond, both used in LBO structures in Europe.

Traditional European Loan (English Law)	High-Yield Bonds
Maintenance financial covenants (though move toward covenant-lite/incurrence covenants)	No maintenance financial covenants—instead there are incurrence covenants
Repayable anytime at par	Non-call periods and, thereafter, gradually decreasing prepayment premiums (2–5 years)
Documents usually based on Loan Market Association forms, though invariably customized	Documentation process is longer and more costly—requires offering memorandum, risk disclosure, and roadshow
Rating not necessarily required (though private ratings becoming more common)	Ratings required (typically two ratings from Moody's, S&P, and/or Fitch)
Amendments during the course of the investment period are relatively common and straightforward (Majority Lender consent)	Expensive to amend—requires consent solicitation and payment of consent fee, complicated by absence of a register of bondholders
Typically matures in 3–7 years	Typically matures in 5–10 years
Split between amortizing and bullet payments	Bullet payment
Includes delayed-draw facilities, such as acquisition facilities	Single issuance
Floating rate	Typically fixed rate, but can be floating rate
Private reporting (monthly and quarterly as well as annually)	Public reporting (semi-annually and annually)
Investors are banks, institutional funds	Investors are mutual funds, hedge funds, institutional funds, insurance companies, pension funds, and private wealth management accounts
Comprehensive security package over the whole borrowing group	Often just guarantees or simpler security package
Restrictions on transfer of debt without borrower consent	No restrictions on transfer

- **Reduced closing and administrative costs.** With only one credit agreement, the amount of required loan documentation is cut in half (compared to a senior and mezzanine arrangement). In addition, there is only one administrative agent and one law firm representing all of the lenders.

- **Less syndication risk.** In deals with full underwriting and no pre-closing syndication, there is no risk that the lead bank arranging the financing will be unable to syndicate the loans and, therefore, in a deal that is not fully underwritten unable to close the financing. For the same reason, unitranche deals do not usually have "flex" provisions that allow the lead bank to change pricing and other loan terms to match the demands in the market (i.e., to enable them to syndicate).

- **Often no amortization.** Many unitranche deals do not have amortization requirements, or they might only require an excess cash flow sweep repayment mechanism.

- **Easier compliance and administration.** With only one set of covenants and one reporting package to prepare, unitranche financing is easier for the borrower to administer and comply with.

In a unitranche facility, the interest rate is a "blended" rate, which is often higher than (or about the same as) the interest rate of traditional senior debt, but lower than the interest rate for traditional second-lien or subordinated debt. All lenders benefit from the same covenants and defaults and the voting provisions are similar to a non-unitranche loan agreement (that is, governed by the two-thirds vote (simple majority in the U.S.) of the lenders, with some amendments being subject to the vote of all lenders or all affected lenders). Although there remains a view that funds that specialize in lending unitranche facilities are more conservative than banks and constrained in the flexibility they can offer, they are steadily growing larger and more sophisticated over time, and increasingly they are able to match the bank market for the size of facilities and the terms that can be offered. For example, unitranche lenders have now committed to loan facilities of over €1 billion and many are now able to commit to provide delayed-draw facilities such as revolving credit facilities and capex facilities. These delayed-draw facilities will typically still be provided by a bank and will usually benefit from super-seniority in the intercreditor-arrangements (typically giving them a senior position in the payments waterfall for proceeds of enforcement, and rights to enforce after standstill periods similar to those described above for mezzanine lenders), but increasingly the unitranche lenders are prepared to front that commitment until the bank can be found (and thus this is not an impediment to the closing of the financing).

In U.S. unitranche deals, there is also no need for the borrower to see the various intercreditor relationships between the lenders of the different facilities, because these are dealt with in a separate so-called "agreement among lenders" (AAL) behind the scenes (which gives the arrangers more flexibility to "slice and dice" tranches in the facility among the lenders, but which leaves the borrower uncertain about who exactly is driving the bus). The AAL will deal with tranching, the payment waterfall, interest and fee-arrangements and voting. In European unitranche deals these AAL arrangements are rare, because of nervousness that about their enforceability in the bankruptcy courts of various jurisdictions, and instead these things are dealt with in a traditional intercreditor agreement which the borrower is a party to.

LOAN DOCUMENTATION

Commitment papers

Acquisitions that are funded through debt financings are necessarily more complex than those with consideration consisting only of the private equity fund's capital. This complexity is due to the risk that conditions precedent to the debt instruments that fund the acquisition may not be met before executing the transaction. Given this risk, it is now standard practice for an acquisition financed by debt to give the seller an opportunity to review and comment on the buyer's commitment papers. The commitment papers constitute a set of legally binding documents signed by the lenders and the buyer.

They usually consist of the following:

- **A commitment letter,** which gets signed by both the lenders and the borrower or the private equity sponsor if the borrower (Bidco) has not yet been established (with provision for transferring the commitment to the borrower in due course). The letter mandates the selected lender(s) exclusively for the deal and describes the commitment of the lender(s) to lend on the terms agreed and set out in an accompanying "term sheet" (see below). In the commitment letter, the parties agree to negotiate with each other as necessary on the basis of the basic terms set out in the term sheet, in order to develop the "full form" finance documents in the time available before the acquisition is due to be completed, which is when the cash is needed. The borrower pays the lenders' legal costs for drafting and negotiating the finance documents, as well as its own legal costs, of course.[25]

- **A term sheet**, which summarizes the main terms of the financing, including the amount and tranching of the debt into various facilities with different rankings, pricing (arrangement fees, interest margins, commitment fees, prepayment fees, etc.), and all the other important terms that are to be set out in the facilities agreements.

- **Fee letters**, which summarize the fees of the arranging banks. These fees are usually separated out into these letters (rather than being included in the term sheet or commitment letter), so that the term sheet and commitment letter can be shown by the arranging banks to potential lenders who join the lender group via the syndication process, without disclosing the fees that the arrangers will collect.

- **An interim loan agreement, ILA**, to give the seller comfort that the financing is not conditional upon the documentation being completed.

Finance documents

The main document at the heart of every financing is the credit agreement, which may go by a variety of alternative names, such as "loan agreement" (if loans are the only credit being provided) or "credit facilities agreement" (if a variety of different credit facilities are being made available). The credit agreement invariably sets out the fundamental terms presented in Exhibit 6.

If it is a syndicated loan agreement, this document will also contain detailed sections that determine the lenders' relationships with each other and with the agent, the voting arrangements for their decision making, and any approval or consultation rights that the borrower may have with respect to transfers by the lenders of the debt.

Recent developments in documentation

The syndicated loan and high-yield bond markets are continually developing. In the European syndicated loan market, the Loan Market Association (LMA) often takes the lead on developing the forms of documentation that the market uses as a basis point, and the LMA form is widely used as a starting point for negotiations. In the United States, the Loan Syndications and Trading Association (LSTA) plays a similar role, but there is a greater emphasis on the development and use of bank-specific or law firm-specific forms of credit agreements. Both the LMA and the LSTA periodically update their recommended forms of agreement and documentation. Sometimes these developments are due to changes in the law, sometimes they are due to changes in practice, and sometimes they simply needed to be improved.

One instance that revealed the need for such an improvement was the credit crunch of 2008, when the

---

[25] Note that many of the larger private equity sponsors often insist in European deals that their counsel will draft the finance documents, rather than lenders' counsel. These sponsors often also choose which law firm will represent the lenders.

syndicated loan markets suffered from the general collapse in market confidence and senior debt started being traded at below-par prices. Opportunistic sponsors deleveraged their portfolio companies by buying the debt in the market, using either new dry powder or, preferably, the portfolio companies' own cash. Surprisingly, in Europe, practitioners discovered that the LMA documentation did not deal with this issue and there was significant debate as to whether repurchasing of the loan in the secondary market was permitted or not. The LMA was initially of the view that spare cash in the business could only be used to deleverage by prepaying the loans (at par), because the documentation provided clear mechanics for that use (and did not expressly provide mechanics for buy-backs). The consequence of such buy-backs was that the sponsors were permitted all the rights of lenders in relation to the acquired debt; including for example the rights to vote in decisions of lenders, which could lead to the sponsors obtaining blocking rights. Soon, however, the LMA updated its documents to include optionality for whether or not debt buybacks were to be permitted and clear mechanics for where they are to be permitted (including, e.g., restrictions on the cash of the business that could be used, whether an auction process should be run to give all lenders a chance to participate, and the rights and obligations that lenders are governed by).

Other recent changes have included commentary and terms to address documentary implications of the U.S. Foreign Account Tax Compliance Act (FATCA), the EU Bank Recovery and Resolution Directive (acknowledging the potential of a lender "bail-in"), and Brexit in the United Kingdom.

The surging U.S. market is leading to an influx of U.S. concepts in European deals. Because liquidity is being driven by institutional lenders (a similar investor base to that which invests in high-yield bonds) rather than banks, the above-mentioned changes are facilitating a convergence between the terms of syndicated loans and high-yield bonds. As a result, there is a reduced focus on financial covenant protection, with covenant-lite deals that have no financial covenants or only a single leverage covenant becoming more common.

CONCLUSION

For borrowers, it is the rise in the number of *products* offered by alternative lenders, rather than the increase in the number of alternative lenders, that is most attractive. Borrowers have an à la carte menu of financing options available, including senior-only structures, term loan B tranches, unitranche financing, second-lien loans, mezzanine loans, high-yield securities, PIK debt, and various combinations of these products.

The reputation of a private equity sponsor plays a crucial role in the structure of acquisition financing. Reputation (which is usually reflected in persistent good performance) is an indicator of the firm's abilities to select, monitor, operate, and restructure target companies. Accordingly, borrowings by the portfolio companies owned by reputable private equity sponsors could reasonably be viewed by lenders as less risky, resulting in better lending terms. In addition, lenders might accept more favorable terms because reputable private equity sponsors conduct more and larger deals, and thus pay larger bank fees both per deal and in aggregate. Moreover, lenders price the fact that it is arguably easier to sell the loans of reputable private equity sponsors in the secondary loan markets, which improves their liquidity. These factors suggest that bankers could subsidize the loans of reputable private equity sponsors and provide other favorable non-price terms to attract future mandates from those groups. Thus, the bargaining power and prominence of reputable private equity sponsors reinforces overheating in the credit market by fostering competition among lenders and by making loans granted to reputable private equity sponsors easier to package and sell to non-bank lenders.

REFERENCES

Dai, S. (2015) "Buyout Multiples Exceed 10x, Highest Level in 20 Years," *Wall Street Journal*.

Hotchkiss, E., D. Smith and P. Strömberg (2014) "Private equity sponsors and the resolution of financial distress," Working paper.

Nini, G., D. Smith and A. Sufi (2012) "Creditor control rights, corporate governance, and firm value," *Review of Financial Studies* 25: 1713-1761.

Standard and Poor's (2011) *A guide to the loan market*.

Standard and Poor's (2014) *Leveraged Commentary & Data. A Guide To The U.S. Loan Market*.

Wright M, R. Cressy, N. Wilson, H. Farag et al. (2014), "Financial restructuring and recovery in private equity buyouts: the UK evidence," *Venture Capital* 16: 109-129.

In his own words: John Markland, Partner, Co-Head of Leveraged Finance at Dechert LLP.

Bankers and private equity executives are strange bedfellows. The former are among the most risk-averse career professionals. The latter are the modern barbarians of the buyout world. They work together to win buyouts against competition from other and similar teams, but the sharing of the risk between them is a vigorously negotiated exercise, the customs and practices of which constantly evolve with the market and which engage the minds of the smartest and most capable in the advisory world. That is the world of acquisition finance.

One of the themes in acquisition finance over the last couple of decades has been the convergence of bank lending with bond issuance. Loans and bonds are fundamentally different products, with loans being private and bonds public. Public products cost more to issue because of the regulatory requirements (i.e., the disclosure requirements for the protection of the public) but, once issued, they are much more benign in operation than bank loans. Information requirements are less onerous, restrictions on operations are more relaxed, and there are usually no financial maintenance covenants. Bonds trade freely and it can be very hard to establish who the bondholders are at any given time. Bank loans, by contrast, are a relationship product which permits only the activities that are envisaged in the business plan (with headroom), but where consents and amendments can be obtained much more readily if the parties are willing.

The United States has a deep market of institutional investors who invest in the loans and bonds market. For that reason, covenant-lite loans are relatively commonplace in there. With the contraction of the bank market following the global financial crisis of 2008–2012, Europe has seen rapid growth in its own institutional investor market, with private debt funds mushrooming and taking an ever-larger portion of the lending market, and U.S. banks able to command a bigger share of the market due to their familiarity with covenant-lite loans. As this trend continues, expect the convergence in Europe to continue likewise.

5 Deal-Specific Legal Issues

Never contract friendship with a man that is not better than thyself.
Confucius

INTRODUCTION

This chapter considers some of the main legal issues involved in the acquisition or disposal of a portfolio company by a private equity fund. It is important to note that there is no global uniformity in this regard: the structure and terms of the transaction will, to a large extent, be dictated by up to three sets of laws that apply to a particular transaction. First, the portfolio company itself is subject to the laws of each of the jurisdictions in which it conducts its business. Second, the laws of both the buyer's and seller's jurisdictions are also relevant, particularly when it comes to enforcing the terms of the transaction. Third, the transaction documentation is subject to the governing law chosen by the parties.

If the portfolio company and its operations are all located in one jurisdiction and the buyer and seller are also located in the same jurisdiction then it makes sense to have the transaction documentation governed by the laws of that jurisdiction. For example, a small German software company being sold by its German founders to a German private equity firm is likely to be sold under a sale and purchase agreement governed by German law. By contrast, if the buyer and seller are located in different jurisdictions, the parties often choose a governing law for the transaction documentation that is generally recognized to provide an established system concerning commercial transactions, even though neither party would otherwise be subject to that law. It is therefore not unusual to find a German-headquartered portfolio company with operations in few European jurisdictions, the United States and China being sold by the European office of a U.S.-headquartered private equity firm to a Chinese buyer on transaction terms governed by English law. The laws of each of those jurisdictions will, to a greater or lesser extent, have some influence on the transaction. While it is the role of the lawyers advising on the transaction to understand the legal minutiae, there are certain common themes that are likely to apply regardless of the jurisdiction, and it is those on which this chapter focuses.

We use the generic term "target" when describing the subject of the transaction; however, we make a fundamental distinction between acquiring a corporate entity on the one hand, and a collection of assets on the other hand. When acquiring a corporate entity, a buyer acquires not only all of the assets owned by that corporate entity, but all of its liabilities as well (absent a specific agreement to the contrary). By contrast, an asset acquisition allows a buyer to cherry-pick which assets are acquired and which (if any) liabilities are assumed, leaving the remainder behind for the seller.

To acquire a corporate entity, a buyer must acquire the ownership interest in that entity (e.g., shares, membership interests, units, or some other security). Accordingly, buyers should focus on ensuring the

This chapter was co-authored with Christopher Field, Partner at Dechert LLP.

acquisition of all legal rights in that ownership interest, in addition to understanding the underlying business of the corporate entity. The method of acquisition that the parties choose or the statutory procedure to effect the transaction (e.g., a merger) will depend upon a number of factors, including the time taken to complete the acquisition, the tax consequences, what approvals are required to complete the transaction, and, most importantly, the relative bargaining position of the parties.

This chapter discusses the legal processes that follow the life cycle of a portfolio company transaction from the early stages when the private equity fund identifies a target to the last stage when the fund exits it. Exhibit 1 illustrates the key documents that private equity fund managers negotiate and sign.

Exhibit 1: Key Documents

Finding the deal
- Pre-deal management arrangements
- Broker/adviser engagement letters

Executing the deal
- Confidentiality agreements
- Term sheets and letters of intent
- Sale and purchase documentation
- Funding documentation

Owning the portfolio company
- Oversight agreements
- Corporate formalities
- Management incentive contracts

Creating liquidity/exit
- Dividend recapitalization
- Trade sale/secondary sale agreements
- IPO/Dual-track processes

FINDING THE DEAL: PRE-DEAL AGREEMENTS

Once the buyer identifies and values the target, several formal and informal agreements come into play. In this section, we touch on common key documents in the early stage of an acquisition of a portfolio company. We assume that the buyer is pursuing a proprietary deal, rather than a deal in an auction process where the buyer faces competition from other bidders.

Letter of intent/memorandum of understanding

Although it is not a universal practice, a letter of intent (LOI) or memorandum of understanding (MOU) are common tools in proprietary deals to record the desires and initial expectations of both parties in writing. In so doing, the MOU acts as both an *aide-memoire* and agreement in principle on the terms of the deal. Since it is very brief, the MOU cannot cover all future issues; instead it sets formal arrangements for a partnership (albeit a somewhat adversarial one) between the private equity fund and the seller with regard to the

target. It also outlines general arrangements for the private equity fund's investment in and capitalization of the target. The MOU may consider staged funding triggered upon the base acquisition, outline anticipated key employment terms, and, if applicable, outline investment terms for the target's management.

Most parts of the MOU are non-binding and based on expectations rather than obligations. It is useful to agree on significant points and create a roadmap for the deal execution. However, a buyer may insist on several points being legally binding. One such provision is referred to as the *exclusivity* (or "no-shop") *provision*, which states that the seller and its representatives are not allowed to seek another potential buyer or negotiate with another bidder for a specific period of time.

It is also common practice for the MOU to mention costs and expenses of the transaction. Though each party bears its own costs in many MOU agreements, the buyer sometimes agrees to cover an agreed amount of fees and expenses (particularly those of management participants). Even where the entirety of the MOU is stated to be legally binding, in most jurisdictions, the courts are reluctant to enforce the MOU's terms on the basis that it does not contain the definitive terms agreed by the parties—it is merely an *agreement to agree*, providing no certainty as to what has actually been agreed, which will be contained in the definitive documentation governing the transaction.

In short, the MOU is a high-level snapshot of the deal, and in particular, of the sale and purchase agreement (which we discuss in detail in a later section).

Broker engagement letter

Where should the private equity fund source the best investment opportunities and, once they are sourced, how should they be valued? When are payments due? How are the fees split between the parties? An independent broker or investment bank is vital in addressing these questions and bringing the transaction to a successful conclusion. In an auction process, the seller of the target inevitably engages such a party to run the auction. Buyers also often use brokers to help source and execute deals. In either case, the party enters into an engagement letter with the broker that includes three key topics: (1) the scope of the broker's services, (2) the fee structure, and (3) exclusivity and preferential rights.

Scope of the services

The choice of broker is likely to have a significant impact on the overall outcome but the service of brokers may vary depending on important factors such as reputation, geographic proximity, and fees. The selection process is mainly based on a tradeoff between fees charged by the broker and its reputation.

Regardless of who is ultimately engaged, the parties need to be clear on what the broker is and is not expected to do for the fee it is being paid. One area that is often heavily negotiated is how to demarcate the scope of the transaction for which the broker is engaged. Most broker engagements contain a large success fee element, whereby the broker is only paid upon the successful completion of the *transaction* (as defined). Many brokers seek to widen that definition to cover recapitalizations, other commercial relationships, or non-acquisition-related joint ventures. For a private equity fund, the definition should exclude follow-on transactions or other portfolio company transactions. In summary, a precise definition of what constitutes the *transaction* for the purposes of the broker's engagement curtails future conflicts of interest between the private equity fund, the target, and the broker.

Fee structure

The fee structure is of particular importance. Because the broker's fee is often calculated as a percentage of the consideration achieved in the transaction, the broker is incentivized to use overbroad valuation measures. This incentive can be particularly problematic where there is a non-cash consideration that cannot be easily valued; for example, the broker may insist that an intangible benefit such as a tax asset be included when calculating its fee.

Another controversial issue in a broker engagement letter is when the broker's services may be terminated. Since the broker's fee is often dependent upon the successful completion of the transaction, the broker wants to prevent the client from avoiding payment by terminating the engagement before the transaction is completed. A broker may therefore seek to include a so-called "tail clause," under which the broker can still claim its fees if the client has terminated the engagement but the transaction thereafter completes within a specified period (usually six months or a year). To mitigate the impact of such a clause, clients try to link fee payments to progressive outcomes. For instance, in the case of a sale transaction, a minimum base fee is paid for early termination and additional fees will be a function of the broker's performance or acquisition price, giving the broker an incentive to maximize the sale price so that both parties are better off. In line with this practice, under some circumstances, both the seller of the target and the broker receive the same form of payment—if the seller is paid with a combination of shares and cash, then the same will apply to the broker.

Exclusivity

A broker often asks for an exclusive mandate. However, this can be quite costly if a seller that engaged the broker subsequently needs a second broker's services to complete the transaction. In this case, the seller has to pay another service fee. Where the broker is a full-service investment bank, it may also ask for exclusive rights on other services, such as providing the debt financing for a leveraged acquisition by its client or, at least, having a preferential right to bid for the financing. It is important to note that some jurisdictions impose limits on what the broker can demand.

Non-disclosure agreements

Non-disclosure agreements (NDAs), sometimes called confidentiality agreements, are among the first agreements to be made between the parties to a proposed transaction. On the one hand, the private equity fund and its representatives who are seeking to buy the target need access to detailed information about the target in order to properly price their bid. On the other hand, for target firms with extensive intellectual property or other intangible assets (e.g., patents, source code, and software licenses), keeping their details confidential can be particularly valuable for the business. Any leakage of sensitive material may mean a loss of competitive advantage. Confidentiality is maintained by requiring any party who is given access to the information to have first signed an NDA.

In practice, the average contractually agreed confidentiality period is about two years or less, though this is often a point of contention as the buyer wants to ensure that the NDA and the confidential information it gains access to do not hinder its ability to acquire or invest in other companies, or otherwise affect future business opportunities. Moreover, the NDA only permits the private equity fund buyer to use the confidential information for valuation purposes. An NDA may also prohibit the buyer from retaining the confidential information if it ceases to participate in the transaction process, by requiring the buyer to either destroy the confidential information or return it to the target. Occasionally, a copy of the confidential information is permitted to be retained for archival purposes only. Finally, the NDA may contain a non-solicitation provision to prevent the buyer from exploiting the access that it affords to target's employees.

EXECUTING THE DEAL: THE SALE AND PURCHASE AGREEMENT

It is an oversimplification to say that the price that buyers agree to pay for a target is dictated by what they believe they are acquiring. Buyers want certainty regarding the assets and liabilities they are acquiring and the predicted earnings of the target (absent an outside event beyond the target's control). The seller also wants certainty—certainty that the buyer will acquire the target and pay the agreed purchase price on time. However, while both parties are seeking certainty, there is an inherent tension that is driven by the different certainties they are seeking: for the seller, it is primarily deal certainty, while for the buyer, it is overcoming the lack of knowledge about the target (as compared with its owner, the seller) and obtaining certainty about exactly what it is acquiring. Thus, the parties negotiate which of them should bear the risk of not achieving the certainty each party seeks. The outcome of this negotiation (i.e., the agreed allocation of risk between the parties) is documented in the *Sale and Purchase Agreement* (SPA). Thus, the SPA lies at the heart of the transaction process because it records the terms on which the deal, as agreed between the buyer and seller, will be transacted. Its main role is to address the allocation of risk at each point in time during the transaction.

Before focusing on the SPA in more detail, it is worth exploring the concept of risk allocation between the parties further. The buyer and the seller typically use a set of (usually audited) historical accounts as a reference point by which to value the target. These accounts afford the parties greater certainty that they have correctly valued the target at that particular point in time. However, the value of the target continues to fluctuate over time. Most importantly, it continues to fluctuate between the agreed valuation date and the date on which the parties reach a legally binding agreement regarding the terms on which the target will be transferred from the seller to the buyer (i.e., the date they sign the SPA). Furthermore, while the parties may be able to complete that transfer of ownership on the same date that they sign the SPA, for reasons discussed below, it is often the case that certain conditions must be fulfilled before the completion of the transfer of ownership (also known as the *closing date*) can occur; this creates a further time gap, during which the value of the target continues to fluctuate.

Both the buyer and the seller want to ensure that the amount that is ultimately paid for the target correctly reflects any fluctuations in its value since the agreed valuation date. At the date that the SPA is signed and the parties are legally bound to undertake the transaction, either party wants the certainty that the transaction occurs on terms agreed at valuation or, if there is a sufficiently significant change, either party may want the flexibility to walk away from the transaction. Essentially, the SPA *signing* is the point in time at which the buyer is legally obliged to acquire the target, but does not yet own it, subject to fulfilment of certain requirements and actions to be undertaken by the buyer/seller/target.

The seller is generally more focused on ensuring that the sale occurs, as it owns and controls the operation of the target until the completion of the transaction, and is therefore more likely to be able to manage the attendant risks during that period. By contrast, buyers want the opportunity to walk away from, or renegotiate the terms of, the deal if those risks materialize in a way that harms them. A timeline of the transaction process is illustrated in Exhibit 2.

Exhibit 2: Transaction process timeline

It is difficult to find a modern SPA that is less than 50 pages in length, and some can exceed 300 pages (including schedules and appendices). Fortunately, there is a broad consistency across deals in the content of SPAs and, increasingly, in their layout. This consistency is due to the universal nature of the issues that SPAs address, as well as the fact that the continued march of globalization is bringing greater homogenization of deal terms. Exhibit 3 provides a typical SPA content list. We discuss in more detail each of the most important parts of the SPA in separate section below.

Exhibit 3: SPA layout

SPA contents

- The Purchase Price
  - Definitions
  - Considerations
  - Conditions
- Conditionality and Closing
  - Pre-closing covenants
  - Post-closing covenants
  - Sellers' covenants
- Representations and Warranties
- Indemnities
- Creditworthiness
- Termination
- Miscellaneous

Purchase price

The purchase price section is perhaps the most important aspect of the SPA. It answers questions such as: How much should the buyer pay the seller to acquire the target? When should the buyer pay the price? How should the buyer pay? etc.

As mentioned above, the target's historic accounts are typically used as the basis for calculating the value of the target as at the date of those accounts, which in turn allows the parties to determine the purchase price to be paid for the target.

Completion accounts (or closing balance sheet) approach

Traditionally, the parties would agree upon a price based on historic accounts and then estimate how much it should be adjusted to account for the expected change in value between the accounts date and the date on which the sale is completed. This rough-and-ready approach generally leaves more risk with buyers, as they are not in control of the operation of the target during that period. A conceptually more certain (but administratively more complex) approach is to revalue the target as at the actual sale date and, to the extent that the actual purchase price differed from the estimated purchase price, have the buyer pay the shortfall or be refunded the excess by the seller. This "true-up" methodology or completion accounts (closing balance sheet) approach is now adopted in the majority of SPAs: prior to completion of the transaction, the seller provides the buyer with an estimate of what the buyer thinks the actual purchase price will be at the completion date. Upon completion of the sale, the buyer pays that estimated amount to the seller in exchange for acquiring the target. One of the parties (usually the buyer with its auditors) then prepares updated accounts at the time of the closing showing their calculation of the actual purchase price as at the completion date. The other party has an opportunity to comment on those calculations and either agree to them or, if there is no agreement, refer the calculation to an independent expert for final determination. To the extent that the actual purchase price as so agreed differs from the estimated purchase price paid at completion, the buyer will make (or receive) the payment necessary to *true up* that difference.

In theory, it is possible to have a full net asset adjustment (i.e., every asset and liability on the balance sheet is measured and trued up). However, as there is likely to be little change in the value of non-current assets and liabilities over the measured period, the focus is on only:

- working capital (that is, current assets other than cash, less current liabilities),

- free cash not forming part of working capital, and

- long-term debt (i.e., debt that does not form part of the working capital).

These are the variables that are most likely to change between the date at which the target is priced and the date on which the sale of the target is completed.

It has therefore become conventional to refer to a target being sold on a *"cash-free, debt-free"* basis. This does not mean that the target will not have any cash or debt when it is sold, but rather, that the buyer prices the target disregarding those two variables. The purchase price is then increased on a dollar-for-dollar basis for any cash that the target actually has, and reduced on a dollar-for-dollar basis for any debt that it actually has, at the completion of the sale.

As far as working capital is concerned, the buyer needs certainty that the target has sufficient working capital at the time it is acquired to avoid having to fund the target with additional cash at acquisition. Thus, a buyer offers to acquire the target subject to it having a specified level of working capital on the date it is acquired. If there is no certainty as to the exact date on which the transaction will be completed (i.e., where the target will be in its working capital cycle on the date the buyer acquires it), the parties have to agree on a baseline normalized level of working capital for this purpose. If the actual working capital is less than that assumed level at completion of the sale, the seller is expected to *true up* the buyer (by way of a corresponding reduction in the purchase price paid by the buyer) or, if the actual working capital of the target on the date of completion of the transaction is higher than the normalized level, the buyer is expected to pay for that excess. Agreeing what this baseline normalized level of working capital should be is often a fraught and contentious negotiation, with each party carefully analyzing the working capital cycle of the target to justify its respective position. Most SPAs containing a completion accounts mechanism therefore provide for a cash, debt, and a *normalized-to-actual* working capital adjustment.

The consequence of using this purchase price true-up mechanism is that it is the seller who bears the risk of how the target trades up to the completion of the sale: if the target makes a loss during the period between when the parties originally agreed on the cash-free, debt-free price (assuming a normalized working capital level), that loss will be reflected in lower working capital, or reduced cash or increased debt, all of which will result in a lower purchase price. This risk is generally one that the seller bears, as the seller is the party who controls the target and operates its business during that interim period.

While the completion accounts approach delivers mathematical certainty as to the purchase price, there are a number of downsides:

- The adjustment takes place *after* the target has been sold. Hence, all things being equal, neither party is particularly motivated to compromise when negotiating the exact amount of the adjustment.

- Agreeing on the exact amount of the adjustment to the purchase price can be a time consuming, and thus costly, process.

If the parties cannot reach agreement, the matter needs to be referred to an independent expert for review and determination, and both parties want to ensure that the other cannot exploit that process to their advantage. This mutual desire often results in complex and lengthy drafting in the SPA to try to mitigate these risks. The seller is particularly concerned, since the buyer is in control of the target following the completion of the transaction and therefore control the trading information on which the calculation of the adjustments is based. For this reason, a completion accounts mechanism is often seen to favor the buyer.

In response to these perceived downsides, European private equity sellers have increasingly adopted a variant of the more traditional rough-and-ready approach: the so-called *"locked box"* approach.

Locked Boxes

With a locked box approach, the buyer still prices the target by reference to a historic set of accounts (which, in a locked box deal, are referred to as the "locked box" accounts). The buyer will then adjust that price for any changes in cash, debt, and working capital that are likely to occur between the date of the locked box balance sheet and the completion of the sale. Once the parties have agreed on that adjusted price, it will be recorded in the SPA and that is the price the buyer will pay on completion of the transaction. There will be no post-completion true-up regardless of how different the actual position is from that estimated by the buyer. Documenting a locked box deal in the SPA is therefore far simpler than documenting a completion accounts/closing balance sheet deal, since the SPA only records the amount of the agreed purchase price that the buyer will pay to the seller on completion of the transaction. All of the adjustments to reach that agreed purchase price will be negotiated outside of the SPA (see Exhibit 4).

Exhibit 4: Example of calculations to reach the locked box purchase price

Cash-/Debt-free price	X	Starting point for price and first-round bid
Cash-like items Debt-like items		Adjustments to bid value not shown in SPA
Permitted Leakage	(X)	
Adjusted price	X	Bid value shown in Completion Accounts SPA
Plus $ for $ Cash	X	
Less $ for $ Debt	(X)	
Net Debt adjustment	X/(X)	Adjustments to price calculated in accordance with SPA
Plus $ for Working Capital	X	
Less Normalized Working Capital	(X)	
Working Capital adjustment	X/(X)	
Purchase Price (Equity Value)	X	Price actually shown in locked box SPA
Ticking fee on Equity Value	X	Mechanism to extract cash generated between locked box date and completion
Total Consideration in Locked Box SPA	X	

We

highlight that there is not only a structural difference between a locked box approach and a completion accounts/closing balance sheet approach but also a qualitative difference in the risk allocation between parties. Since the SPA does not contain any mechanisms to adjust the purchase price for changes in cash, debt, or working capital between the locked box accounts date and the completion of transaction date, with a locked box approach the buyer (not the seller) bears the risk of how the target trades between the date of the locked box accounts and the sale's completion—even though it is the seller who is in control of the target during that period. Clearly, a buyer should only agree to such an arrangement if it has some confidence that the seller does not exploit this asymmetry in control. To help address these concerns about control, the seller will typically agree to do two things:

- To operate the target business in the ordinary course between the locked box accounts date and completion of the transaction. This should give the buyer some assurance that it is only bearing external trading risk.

- To refrain from extracting any profits or other value from the target during that period.

It is this second aspect from which the locked box approach derives its name, in that the seller agrees to "lock the box" during that period. Accordingly, if the target generates any surplus cash, it will remain trapped in the target for the benefit of the buyer, and if any is extracted or, to use the relevant jargon, any "leakage" occurs, the seller will compensate the buyer on a dollar-for-dollar basis for the amount of that leakage. The SPA therefore contains a comprehensive no-leakage undertaking by the seller, which covers not only distributions to the seller and its affiliates or other related persons, but also more subtle forms of value extraction such as transferring target assets to the seller (or one of its related persons) at prices below market value, or forcing the target to release the seller (or one of its related persons) from a liability.

Note that there are likely to be some forms of leakage that the parties anticipate and accept during the locked box period. For example, the target may be required to pay a transaction fee to the private equity seller. These known forms of leakage are documented as "permitted leakage," and the parties agree whether that permitted leakage should result in a corresponding upfront reduction to the agreed purchase price, or whether it has already been factored into the agreed purchase price (e.g., monthly salary payments to management sellers).

Even with these limited protections, why would a buyer accept a locked box structure? The short answer is competitive tension. In a hotly contested auction, a buyer may have no choice but to accept this arrangement, and may be more willing to do so where the target operates a self-contained business, such as the typical private equity portfolio company that does not have any ongoing trading relationships with other seller companies. By contrast, a locked box structure is less appropriate for a corporate carve-out where there are significant ongoing trading arrangements between the target and the remainder of the group being retained by the corporate seller; all of those trading arrangements would constitute permitted leakage creating far greater risk of value extraction by the selling group.

The advantages of a locked box approach to a seller are clear: trading risk is transferred to the buyer and there is no adjustment to the agreed purchase price (assuming the seller is confident that it has not engaged in any leakage). The absence of a post-completion purchase price adjustment is particularly attractive to a private equity seller as it allows the private equity fund to distribute the entirety of the sale proceeds to its investors on completion without any risk that they may be clawed back, thereby enhancing its IRR.

Unsurprisingly, the locked box structure continues to evolve with increased use. Sellers have focused on the fact that actual cash generation during the locked box period may exceed the amount assumed in the agreed purchase price, to the benefit of the buyer. To address this issue, sellers are increasingly asking that, in addition to the agreed purchase price, the buyer pay a *ticking fee* to compensate the seller for this additional cash generation. The ticking fee is sometimes expressed as a daily amount or as a percentage of the purchase price. Notably, the percentage is not intended to be a proxy for the seller's cost of capital but rather, for the amount of free cash that is likely to be generated over the locked box period (taking into account the working capital cycle and profit generation of the target business during that period).

Earnouts

Earnouts are another mechanism used by private equity firms to determine the purchase price of a target company. The use of earnouts has increased over time, which is unsurprising given that they provide a good compromise when the contracting parties are unable to agree on the target company's future prospects and must therefore bridge a valuation gap. Rather than paying the seller's asking price on the closing date, the buyer makes an upfront payment at closing plus an additional performance-related component, which is calculated by reference to the post-closing performance of the target business over an agreed period, and is only paid at the end of that agreed *earnout period* (typically two to four years). In essence, an earnout mechanism ensures that the seller stays active and focused on the target business after closing.

While the concept of an earnout is straightforward, it should not be seen as a panacea to bridge every valuation gap. Earnouts create a number of difficult issues that need to be carefully worked through by the parties. They can often lead to expensive and time-consuming negotiations or, if unaddressed, will almost invariably result in future disputes between the parties as to whether the earnout has been achieved. Furthermore, not every transaction lends itself to an earnout. Hence, designing an earnout structure requires diligently addressing a number of important considerations, summarized below:

- **Performance component:** The performance component of the earnout can be conditional on financial or non-financial indicators of performance. Possible *financial* metrics include EBITDA, revenue (growth), gross or net profits, and cash flows from operations, amongst others. *Non-financial* metrics can include the receipt of official approvals or licenses, the number of customers, a new product launch, achievement of manufacturing milestones, and so on. Selecting the appropriate earnout metrics will also depend, in part, on the industry and the valuation methodology used when the purchase price was determined. For example, if the target business valuation (or purchase price) was based on an EBITDA multiple and the buyer and seller disagree on the transaction multiple, then the spread can be structured as an earnout.

  The practical implementation of an earnout can be rather challenging: on the one hand, the seller wants to control the management of the target business during the earnout period to maximize the likelihood of the earnout being achieved; on the other hand, the buyer (as the new owner of the target business) does not want any restrictions on its day-to-day management of the business. Thus, the buyer prefers to leave the seller's post-closing involvement in the business open-ended, whereas the seller may even require that the target business is completely "ring-fenced" in order to ensure a clean structure for the purposes of calculating the earnout proceeds. It follows that an earnout structure is better suited to sellers who will continue to be involved in the target business after closing (e.g., a founder who continues to be employed by the target—though questions then arise as to the treatment of the earnout if the seller ceases to be employed by the target business for any reason during the earnout period). Earnouts are far more difficult to structure and measure if the buyer intends to integrate the target business into its other businesses after closing, or to add other businesses to the target business after closing (e.g., as part of a so-called "buy-and-build" strategy).

  In order to reduce the likelihood of any future disputes, earnout provisions should be detailed and specific, and address (1) the control of the post-closing entity, (2) the method of operation of the target business post closing, and (3) the method of accounting for profits, losses, and expenses.

- **Earnout measurement:** When negotiating an earnout, both parties should clearly agree on the calculation methodology, and appoint two advisors: (1) an accounting firm or other third-party expert to establish and verify the final calculations, and (2) a legal adviser to carefully draft the precise wording of the earnout clause. The parties and their advisers also need to ensure that the earnout computation methodology addresses extraordinary events (e.g., transaction expenses, sale or purchase of a division or product line, insurance proceeds or unexpected losses, etc.). As a final outcome of the earnout negotiations, a detailed earnout schedule and sample computation should be prepared by both the accountants and legal advisers to help reduce the likelihood of any future dispute regarding the actual operation of the earnout. When negotiating the earnout calculation methodology, both parties have different agendas: the seller prefers more certainty, whereas the buyer wants less specificity in order to have more wiggle room in the earnout computation. An example of intentionally including less specificity would be a simple reference to GAAP earnings as the metric for interpreting the earnout calculation, as accounting standards can be subjective and applied in different ways by different companies. The inherently dissimilar incentives of the buyer and seller can result in costly and lengthy disputes, which third party advisers should aim to prevent with well drafted earnout provisions.

- **Payment structure:** Earnout payments can be structured based on two distinct methodologies: (1) an all-or-nothing payment or (2) a graduated payment (i.e., payments based on the extent to which the earnout target is exceeded). A graduated earnout payment is the more customary practice, with buyers often negotiating an upper threshold, given that "all or nothing" payments can create a strong incentive for the buyer to miss the earnout target (to the extent the buyer is able to exert that level of control over the target business). In addition to the payment structure, a seller needs to consider the creditworthiness of the buyer and his/her ability to pay the earnout. A seller may seek a third-party guarantee or collateral to assure payment by the buyer. More specifically, the seller should also focus on the following aspects when negotiating the earnout: (1) the existence of lender or other third-party restrictions which prevent the seller from gaining control of the target company's assets for collateral purposes if the buyer defaults; (2) the existence of a parent company or third-party guarantee or funding commitment to assure the earnout payment; and (3) the availability of sufficient free cash flow at the end of the earnout period to pay the earnout.

  The earnout payment structure may also provide for an acceleration of payment under some circumstances such as when: (1) the target company is being sold, (2) the target business has been underfunded by the buyer, (3) a change in key management personnel takes place, and (4) the buyer fails to comply with its obligations to the seller, either with respect to the earnout's operation or, more generally, under the SPA. By contrast, the buyer is likely to seek the ability to offset any claim it may have against the seller under the SPA against any earnout payment that may fall due.

- **Earnout period:** The earnout period must allow for proper assessment of the target business's performance. If the earnout period is too short, the seller may be incentivized to drive revenue growth without proper consideration for metrics that impact long-term growth (e.g., lower customer creditworthiness, sub-optimal inventory levels, lower product quality, etc.). If the earnout period is too long and the earnout target(s) is set too high, then the seller might not be motivated to reach the earnout goal(s). Determining the earnout period is therefore a balancing act, given the different considerations involved (i.e., a shorter period to minimize the restrictions inherent to the earnout period, and a longer period to allow the seller more time to achieve the target(s)). Earnouts periods typically range from one to four years, depending on the business dynamics, although the majority of earnout periods end after three years. Buyers generally prefer longer earnout periods in order to feel confident about the consistency of the target company's financial situation, whereas sellers will usually prefer shorter earnout periods (as the earnout targets will likely be more conservative given the limited time period).

- **Contractual protection:** Clearly, the seller needs to ensure that it has adequate contractual protection during an earnout period as many issues can arise. Examples of potential buyer–seller conflicts include (1) the seller not receiving sufficient control to achieve the earnout target(s) due to integration efforts by the buyer, (2) the buyer investing in mainly medium to long-term growth, thereby reducing the target business's profitability during the earnout period to the detriment of the seller, and (3) the buyer reducing the seller's ability to achieve the earnout target(s) by not allocating sufficient decision-making power to the seller. These conflicts will likely arise when an earnout is poorly structured and the buyer is determined to avoid having to make additional earnout payments, potentially reducing the value of the company it has acquired. Potential conflicts in earnout agreements can be mitigated by the seller requiring protective covenants, in combination with the possible use of an escrow account and the inclusion of collateral or third-party guarantees in the earnout agreement. Protective covenants can include restrictions on disposing a division, information rights, additional protection if there is a change in key management (e.g., liquidated damages or acceleration of payments), and an express contractual requirement for good faith and fair dealing on the part of both parties.

A well structured earnout should result in an interest alignment between the buyer and seller to maximize the value of the target business. For example, if the target business achieves an increase in profitability which results in an earnout payment, then a correctly structured transaction will ensure that the buyer acquires the target company on better overall terms (i.e., a lower pro forma multiple post acquisition), while the seller achieves a higher absolute price. Therefore, the rewards for both the buyer and seller are maximized post earnout.

As an illustration of a well structured earnout, consider the example in Exhibit 5 where a purchase price of 8x EBITDA is agreed, with the target business generating an EBITDA of £1,000,000. In addition, as an earnout structuring mechanism, the following is agreed: (1) 70% of the consideration is payable on closing (i.e., the initial consideration), (2) the remaining 30% of the purchase price is payable 24 months after closing (i.e., the additional consideration, with 24 months being the earnout period), and (3) an earnout is payable as £4 for every £1 growth in profits over £1,000,000 during the earnout period (i.e., in the first 24 months).

If the EBITDA grows to £1,500,000 (i.e., a growth of £500,000) within 24 months after closing, then the earnout structure results in the following payment schedule:

Exhibit 5: Example of an earnout calculation

Payment Schedule	Initial Consideration	Additional Consideration	Earnout	Total
On Completion: £1m x 8 x 70%	£5.6m			£5.6m
After 24 Months: £1m x 8 x 30%		£2.4m		£2.4m
Earnout: £500k x 4			£2.0m	£2.0m
Total	£5.6m	£2.4m	£2.0m	£10.0m
Total Consideration Payable				**£10.0m**
EBITDA				£1.5m
Pro Forma Multiple (Post Acquisition)				**6.67x**

In the above example the EBITDA multiple (which the buyer paid for the target) was reduced from 8x to 6.7x (post acquisition), while the seller has received £2 million more for the business than the agreed purchase price. This example demonstrates that a well-structured relatively earnout can be effective in aligning the interests of all involved parties.

Conditionality and closing

The two most important issues for a seller are usually (1) obtaining the highest possible price, and (2) achieving certainty that the sale will actually happen. Until the buyer has contractually agreed to buy the target by signing the SPA, the seller has no certainty that the sale will occur. The seller may have negotiated a cost reimbursement or reverse break fee that it will receive if the deal does not proceed, but this does not fully compensate the seller for failing to sell the target. The seller's deal certainty therefore increases significantly once the SPA has been signed. In fact, absent a legal prohibition on completing the sale, the seller can be certain of the sale completing so long as any conditions to its completion contained in the SPA have been satisfied (or, if permitted, waived). Hence, the best result for a seller (or a motivated buyer) is to have no conditions on the completion of the sale in the SPA, so that the deal can complete or—to use the U.S. terminology, close—as soon as possible after signature, thereby avoiding the additional risks created by increased time between signing and closing the deal. A graphical representation of the sale process is provided in Exhibit 6.

Exhibit 6: The Sale Process

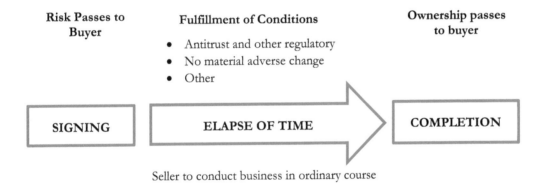

Conditions to closing

Although sellers and motivated buyers prefer it, a simultaneous signing and closing is rarely achievable with larger deals due to the regulatory requirements and filings increasingly imposed on the parties to the transaction. Some of these requirements are discussed below.

Antitrust conditions

Most jurisdictions now operate some form of merger control regime whereby parties are required to obtain clearance from the government department in charge of policing competition before transferring ownership of the target. For example, in the United States, the Hart–Scott–Rodino Antitrust Improvements Act of 1976 (commonly referred to as the HSR Act) requires business transactions of a sufficient size to be reported to the Federal Trade Commission and Department of Justice prior to completion of the transaction. The parties to the transaction must wait a specified period while these enforcement agencies review the proposed transaction to determine if it will be anticompetitive; this may mean that the buyer and seller are unable to complete the transfer of the target on the date they agreed to in the SPA.

These antitrust (or "competition") clearance conditions have become a common feature of larger deals. There are many other mandatory conditions that may also apply to a transaction, such as a certain government clearance for a change of ownership of a target operating in a heavily regulated industry. It is important that the seller understand exactly what these conditions to completion are, and how likely it is that they will be satisfied. Where the requirement to include the condition is seen to have been caused by the buyer, the seller may seek additional contractual protections to encourage the buyer to satisfy the condition; for instance, if it is the revenues of a particular buyer which have triggered an antitrust clearance in a particular jurisdiction, the seller may demand that the buyer accept a so-called "hell-or-high water" provision in the SPA, whereby the buyer agrees to take whatever steps are necessary to satisfy the competition authority—up to and including divestment of its other assets!

As noted, for most buyers, their relative lack of knowledge about the target (as compared with the seller) means that the need for deal certainty is overridden by the risk of overpaying for the target. Once the buyer has contractually agreed to acquire the target, any gap of time introduces a risk that something may occur that devalues the target. Therefore, a buyer is usually equally motivated to avoid any conditions that extend the period before which completion of the sale can occur. For example, if the target's revenues are particularly reliant on two key customers who have the right to terminate their customer contracts upon any change of control of the target, it would usually be better for the buyer to obtain confirmation that those two customers will not terminate their contracts before the SPA is signed, rather than include a condition to completion in the sale in the SPA that their consent is obtained. In the latter case, the buyer assumes the risk that, while the customers' consent is being obtained, something else happens to devalue the target; in that unfortunate situation, once the customers' consent had been obtained, the buyer would have no choice but to complete the purchase of the devalued target or breach its purchase obligation under the SPA.

It is therefore unsurprising that some of the most heavily negotiated areas of SPAs are those conditions that allow the buyer to walk away from the deal as a result of a devaluation of the target. We discuss these conditions next.

Material adverse change conditions

The most well-known type of condition that allows a buyer to not complete the acquisition if there is a devaluation in the target is the so-called *"material adverse change"* (MAC) condition (also known as the "material adverse effect" (MAE) condition).

In its simplest form, a MAC condition ensures that the buyer is not obliged to acquire the target if there is a material adverse change in the target between two specified dates (usually the date that the parties sign the SPA and the buyer accordingly becomes subject to a legal obligation to acquire the target, and the date on which completion of the acquisition occurs). Exactly what constitutes a material adverse change for these purposes is a heavily negotiated issue. Depending on the relative bargaining power of the parties, the provision may include not only material adverse changes that are unique to the target itself, but also changes in the overall economy or other events outside the scope of the target's business that result in a material adverse change in the target. The threshold for what constitutes a material adverse change may be specifically stated (e.g., an increase in liabilities, a diminution in the value of the target's assets above a specified amount, or a diminution in profitability below a specified level) or kept purposefully vague. A generic reference to MAC considerations may allow a buyer to use the threat of alleging such an event has occurred as leverage to force a price renegotiation with the seller, since the seller will not want to risk the deal being terminated in its entirety.

In addition, market practice plays a role: the vast majority of transactions undertaken on U.S. market terms contain a MAC condition; by contrast, a recent survey revealed that less than one-fifth of transactions in Europe are subject to such a condition. With the increasing internationalization of transactions, a savvy buyer or seller should take advantage of accepted market terms in the jurisdiction of the deal that work to its advantage. Accordingly, a buyer of a target located in the United States may argue that it is conventional for the seller to accept a MAC condition, particularly if the SPA is governed by U.S. law, whereas that argument would usually receive short shrift if raised in a European transaction.

Pre-closing covenants

If there is a time gap between signing and closing (i.e., "gap period"), misalignment of interests between the buyer and seller might arise as a result of seller's actions like a cash distribution or strategic decisions. To govern and manage the parties' behavior during this gap period, the SPA includes contractual provisions— sometimes referred to as covenants—that either promote an action (an affirmative covenant) or require the party to avoid or refrain from taking an action (negative covenant).

Buyers continue due diligence even after signing the SPA, and often wish to be kept updated on the seller's conduct regarding the target business. For ease of reference, we have divided covenants into (1) those concerning the due diligence process (non-operational), and (2) those concerning the conduct of the target business (operational).

Non-operational covenants

Covenants relating to due diligence during the gap period typically require the seller to provide the buyer and its representatives with full access to company filings, records, and premises if necessary. For the seller, this access may lead to concerns about the sharing of commercially sensitive information before the buyer is certain to become the owner of the target. This concern is particularly serious if the target is a competitor of the buyer (e.g., where a portfolio company of a private equity firm is trying to acquire a competitor as an add-on acquisition). It may also give rise to claims of anticompetitive "gun jumping," where competitors coordinate their conduct before the transaction has completed. The covenants usually contain provisions that enable the buyer to cross-monitor any financial statements prepared by the target during the gap period. These provisions force the seller to notify the buyer about disclosures in advance of their publication.

Restrictions on information flow from the target to outsiders are not limited to financial statements. The parties are concerned about communication and confidentiality too. Most SPAs contain bespoke agreements on these issues. Confidentiality covenants limit dissemination of proprietary information. What if the target needs to communicate with its customers and suppliers? Communication covenants kick in and require the seller and target to cooperate with the buyer in developing language for any notices about the transaction that are provided to customers, suppliers, and other third parties during the pre-closing gap period.

Operational covenants

Buyers are especially concerned with how the target business is conducted during the gap period between signing and closing, as they are legally obliged under the SPA to acquire the target. Therefore, almost all SPAs contain an affirmative covenant on the seller to run the target business in the ordinary course during the gap period. The idea is to keep the business model intact and prevent any incentives for the seller to take risks. This covenant is particularly important in a locked box deal, as the buyer acquires the trading risk during this gap period.

SPAs typically impose significant restrictive covenants on interim operations. These pre-closing covenants can be quite lengthy depending upon the business segments in which the target operates. They are usually drafted as negative covenants to avoid the risk of the buyer being found to have engaged in anticompetitive gun jumping, or being found to be a *de facto* or *shadow* director who controls the business and is therefore subject to all the duties imposed on an actual director of the target.

Operational changes to the target business do not take place overnight, and sometimes require new physical assets (e.g., new equipment or even a new plant). Restrictions on such acquisitions are common. However, firms have greater flexibility with financing decisions that can still lead to costly outcomes. Thus, buyers mostly aim to curtail such financing decisions to avoid this risk. There are three main channels through which companies can raise or redeem capital: retained earnings, external equity, and external debt. Retained earnings raise issues regarding cash and dividend policy. Most interim operational covenants prohibit (or impose significant restrictions on) the seller declaring or paying dividends and other distributions during the pre-closing gap period. For equity financing, it is very common to prohibit any issuances of target equity. Similar restrictive covenants apply to debt financing: taking or giving new loans is either not permitted or limited to certain specified levels.

Other examples of operational covenants include maintenance of the target's assets, financial accounting and tax policy, employee option plans, and compensation packages. Essentially, these covenants are meant to ensure that the target does not deviate from its ordinary course of business and its past practice.

Post-closing covenants

The buyer–seller relationship does not come to an end upon completion of the sale and purchase. Post-closing assurances are quite common in SPAs to ensure that the parties cooperate and continue to carry out the intent of the agreement. As with the pre-closing covenants, buyers are likely to restrict post-transaction activities by the sellers. Transition, non-solicitation, and non-compete covenants are some examples of such restrictions. More specifically, in transition covenants, sellers are required to refrain from any action that would discourage suppliers, customers, or other stakeholders from maintaining their same business ties with the target after the closing of the transaction. Non-solicitation and non-compete covenants prohibit the seller from soliciting suppliers, customers, or employees of the target business, or competing with the target. In this way, they help to support the purchase price paid by the buyer by preventing the seller from diminishing the goodwill in the target business.

It is vital that buyers take legal advice regarding the enforceability of these provisions (in terms of both duration and breadth), as many jurisdictions have rules against enforcing provisions that impose excessive restraint on the seller's ability to continue to trade after the transaction.

Sellers' covenants

The covenants discussed above emphasize buyer concerns; however, acquisition or disposal of a target is a bilateral transaction that carries many obligations for buyers as well. With a leveraged acquisition, the seller wants to know that the buyer's debt financing package remains available to fund the acquisition, particularly in those jurisdictions (e.g., the United States) where it is common to include a financing condition to the buyer's obligation to complete the sale and purchase of the target. Thus, the buyer's financing capacity is one of the main covenants that most sellers insert into SPAs; it requires the buyer to take reasonable best efforts (or *commercially reasonable* efforts) to arrange and obtain the required proceeds from its financing necessary to complete the transaction. This covenant ensures that the financing condition is fulfilled.

Even in those jurisdictions where it is very unusual to accept a financing condition (e.g., across Europe), the seller still wants to have visibility into the buyer's financing, given the risk posed by financing on the successful closing of the transaction.

Representations and warranties

A quick glance at a modern SPA reveals that a large portion of the document is devoted to so-called "representations and warranties" (sometimes referred to as "guarantees"). Transacting parties must understand how these terms operate under the law that governs the SPA and ask the advising legal counsel to explain them. For the purposes of this chapter which is concerned with understanding the overall risk allocation between the parties to the transaction, we assume that "representation" and "warranty" are interchangeable terms that both refer to a factual statement in the SPA regarding the condition of the target or its business.

Warranties are designed to address a fundamental point: in most jurisdictions there is no overriding law that stops the buyer agreeing to a bad bargain. The buyer acquires the target with all of its attendant defects, liabilities, and hidden problems, and must ensure that the price accurately reflects those conditions, despite the asymmetry of information about the target that typically exists between the buyer and seller. This age-old problem is best summed up by the Latin maxim *caveat emptor*—"let the buyer beware."

Buyers can mitigate these hidden risks by undertaking extensive due diligence on the target, but even this process assumes the information upon which it relies is true and accurate. Hence, buyers should ask sellers to contractually confirm that they have been given all relevant information about the target and that the information is true and accurate; it is this function that warranties fulfill.

How do warranties work in practice? For example, the seller may give a contractual statement of fact to the buyer such as: "the target is not currently engaged in any litigation." This allows the buyer to price the target on the assumption that there will be no attendant liability arising from the target being involved in litigation. If this assumption proves to be wrong, the buyer will have a claim against the seller for breach of contract, which (assuming the various legal requirements governing such a claim are satisfied) will allow the buyer to recover any loss that it suffered as a result. In this way, the breach of warranty allows the buyer to retrospectively reduce the purchase price to reflect what it would have paid had it known of the litigation liability. Therefore, representations and warranties function as a retrospective purchase price adjustment mechanism (at least in theory).

However, it is important to note that this mechanism is relatively inefficient. The buyer first needs to prove that it has a claim, and then needs to satisfy the various jurisdictional requirements for a successful claim (which may be difficult and costly). Finally, the buyer needs to recover the funds from the seller, which may also prove to be challenging. Thus, if the SPA already contains a purchase price adjustment mechanism (as discussed above), it is not unusual for the buyer to want to include as many potential liabilities within that mechanism as possible given its relative efficiency, rather than relying on warranty protection.

Continuing with the above example, what if the target is, in fact, subject to some litigation? The seller will not want to be liable to the buyer if the buyer is aware of that fact and has already priced it into the purchase price. The seller will therefore want the opportunity to tell the buyer about these exceptions to the warranty (or, to use the customary terminology, "disclose" them to the buyer), and to ensure that the buyer cannot bring a claim for any of these disclosed exceptions. For the buyer, this construct only works if the disclosure is made in sufficient time to allow it to adjust the purchase price accordingly (i.e., in advance of signing the SPA, when the buyer becomes contractually bound to pay the purchase price). The disclosure process—that is, what is treated as disclosed against a representation or warranty and when and how it may be disclosed—is heavily negotiated by the parties and depends partly upon their relative bargaining strength and partly on what is considered as acceptable risk allocation. In any event, the effect of the disclosure process is that the buyer assumes the risk for those known liabilities that have been disclosed to it and the seller retains the risk for any undisclosed and/or unknown liabilities that would breach a warranty. Since the buyer assumes the risk for the known liabilities that the seller has disclosed, it goes without saying that the private equity team involved in buying the target should be fully involved in the disclosure process to ensure that those known liabilities are taken into account when pricing the deal. In conclusion, it is often said that warranties protect a buyer against the risk of *unknown liabilities*. As will be seen below, this is not the risk allocation profile for all deals.

The discussion above highlights some of the representations and warranties that are made by sellers. However, sellers demand assurances too. For example, if the method of payment involves a stock or share issuance by the buyer, then the seller—who will become an investor in the buyer by accepting its stock or shares as payment—is likely to require investment warranties from the buyer, such as the share type, nominal values of shares, type of pre-emptive rights, options, conversion rights, capitalization of the buyer, and so on. Although sellers provide more warranties than buyers do (due to the aforementioned asymmetry of information), several components of such assurances result from common concerns. For instance, irrespective of being a buyer or a seller, both parties want assurances regarding the solvency of the other party. Other common issues that warranties address include organization and good standing of the party, and its capitalization and ability to enter into and perform the transaction.

European private equity risk allocation

There is an increasing trend in certain European jurisdictions for private equity sellers to argue that the buyer should assume the risk for unknown liabilities as well as known liabilities. In some jurisdictions, the justification behind this argument is simply that a target business under private equity ownership has good financial and governance controls in place, has identified all liabilities and other risks to the business, and (provided such information is made available to a buyer in a data room and through other due diligence materials) allows the buyer to price accurately without needing any warranty protection. The justification is typically supported through access to so-called *"vendor due diligence reports."* These reports are prepared by advisers to the seller (usually covering financial, tax, and legal aspects of the target business, but sometimes also environmental, commercial, insurance, or other aspects) and seek to identify significant issues with the target business. Vendor due diligence reports are made available for review by prospective buyers as part of their due diligence and, sometimes, afford the successful buyer limited reliance on the report—the idea being that a buyer can take comfort from the work undertaken by a third-party expert in helping to support the buyer's pricing.

In other jurisdictions, the private equity seller may argue that, as a financial owner, it has limited knowledge of the operations of the target and hence, can only provide warranties as to its ownership of the target and its ability to sell the target to the buyer. By contrast, the management of the target is better placed to identify issues with the target business, and so should provide the operational warranties regarding that business. However, since in most cases the management does not have sufficiently deep pockets to provide a meaningful recourse to the buyer if there has been a breach of warranty, the purpose of the warranties given by management should be to elicit disclosure for the buyer (i.e., to fulfill an investigative function rather than provide financial recourse). If a warranty is qualified by the warrantor's awareness (e.g., "so far as the warrantor is aware, the target is not currently engaged in any litigation"), the warranty will not be breached if the warrantor is unaware of the litigation; it will only be breached if the warrantor is aware of the litigation but fails to disclose it. In other words, the risk of unknown litigation remains with the seller. Accordingly, if all the warranties are subject to an awareness qualification, the risk of unknown liabilities passes to the buyer.

Why would the management of the target agree to a construct where it assumes the risk of giving warranties and the majority owner of the target, the private equity firm, does not? There are a number of reasons for this choice, which may include the relatively low likelihood of a breach of warranty claim where the warranties are all awareness qualified (in essence, being limited to those matters which the management forgets to disclose), and being able to achieve a lower limit on liability than would be the case if the warranties were designed to function as a purchase price adjustment mechanism.

Why would a buyer agree to such a construct? The short answer is competitive tension. In a contested auction process, a bidder may be willing to assume this risk in order to secure the target. More recently, the increased availability of representation and warranty insurance has also driven this trend.

Representation and warranty insurance

At its simplest, representation and warranty insurance (also referred to as warranty and indemnity insurance) shifts the risk of a breach of warranty from the seller to an insurer. The insurance can be purchased either by the seller, so that the seller can offset the risk of any claim by the buyer or, more commonly, by the buyer, who may make a claim on the insurer instead of the seller for any breach of warranty.

Using representation and warranty insurance offers a number of advantages for private equity sellers: it removes any credit risk that the buyer is taking on the seller vehicle; it creates a clean break for the seller upon closing of the deal, removing the risk of a subsequent warranty claim and consequent threat to the fund's IRR; and it facilitates having only the management provide the operational warranties (as discussed) with the private equity firm providing only fundamental warranties as to its ownership of the target and ability to sell it. With increased use and market confidence, representation and warranty insurance has become an integral part of the private equity deal landscape in a number of jurisdictions.

Fundamental warranties

The discussion in the sections above has focused on operational warranties regarding the target business. As discussed at the start of this chapter, most deals are structured as a sale of ownership interests in the target (shares, stock, units, etc.); this facilitates the sale of the entire target rather than just its assets. Where the target itself is sold, it is conventional for the buyer to seek *fundamental* warranties that (1) the seller has the ability (i.e., capacity and authority) to sell the target, and (2) the seller owns its ownership interests in the target. In some jurisdictions, these fundamental warranties as to capacity and title may be supplemented by additional fundamental warranties such as no transaction bonuses, commissions, or finders fees, and/or no transactions between the target and affiliates of the seller. The distinction between these fundamental warranties and the operational warranties is both quantitative (in that the cap on the seller's liability for breach of a fundamental warranty is usually set far higher and for a longer recovery period) and qualitative (in that it is very hard for any seller, even a financial owner like a private equity firm, to argue that it should not give these warranties regarding its ownership).

Post-signing risk allocation

As discussed above, a warranty is a statement of fact concerning the affairs of the target at a particular point in time. Usually, that point in time is when the SPA is signed, as that is the instant when the buyer becomes contractually obligated to acquire the target (assuming satisfaction or waiver of the conditions to completion contained in the SPA). Prior to that point, the parties are typically free to withdraw from their bargain, or to adjust the purchase price to take account of any identified issues. However, as we have seen, in many larger transactions, the buyer is not be permitted to take ownership of the target until one or more regulatory clearances have been obtained. As noted, the buyer may insist upon the ability to terminate the transaction if there is a material adverse change to the target during that period—although doing so would significantly weaken deal certainty for the seller. Alternatively (or in addition), the buyer may require the warranties to be repeated after the completion of the transaction. This requirement would mean that the seller is liable for a breach of warranty claim if an event occurs after signing the SPA and continues to subsist after the completion of the transaction. Repeating the warranties allows the buyer to retrospectively adjust the purchase price by way of a warranty claim, thereby shifting risk onto the seller.

Indemnities

We have considered how warranties generally protect a buyer against the risk of unknown liabilities; what then of known liabilities? By way of (a simplified) example, what if, in the course of its diligence on the target business, the buyer discovers that the target is the defendant in litigation proceedings that may result in the target having to pay out $500,000 damages to the claimant? The buyer could agree with the seller that the purchase price should be reduced by $500,000. That would shift the risk of the outcome of the litigation entirely onto the seller. However, unless it is certain that the target will lose the litigation and the quantum of damages awarded against it will be exactly $500,000, why should the seller bear the full $500,000 risk? What if instead the parties were to agree that, if the target were to lose the litigation, the seller would compensate the buyer for the amount of damages awarded against the target? That compensatory payment would effectively function as a post-completion purchase price adjustment and, as a contingent obligation on the seller, would allow the seller to retain the full purchase price should the liability to make the compensatory payment not arise.

An indemnity fulfills this compensatory role. Legally speaking, an indemnity is an undertaking by the party giving the indemnity, the indemnitor, to the beneficiary of the indemnity, the indemnitee, that the indemnitor will compensate the indemnitee upon the happening of an event or circumstance. An indemnity therefore functions as a mechanism by which a party can protect itself against the risk of a known contingent liability becoming an actual liability. It may be a far more attractive risk allocation between the parties than an upfront purchase price reduction, and can thus be very contentious and subject to lengthy negotiations as to the precise language used.

Creditworthiness

We have seen that the SPA creates a matrix of protections for the parties, allocating risk between them at each point in time from the date that the agreement is signed to the date that the transaction closes and the seller transfers ownership to the buyer. Parties engage in transactions because they have negotiated what they consider to be an acceptable allocation of risks between them, and they each have the certainty that those protections can be enforced against the other party. These engagements imply confidence in the legal system to which the agreement is subject, both as regards to the governing law as well as the forum where any dispute about the agreement will be adjudicated. However, even more fundamentally, the SPA assumes that the counterparty to the contract is in a position to honor any claim for which it agrees it is liable, or for which it is adjudicated to be liable. None of the carefully negotiated protections are of any use if the counterparty cannot be compelled to honor them or make a compensatory payment. Hence, it is vital to ascertain the creditworthiness of one's counterparty to the SPA.

It is worth noting in this regard that the buyer's fundamental obligation to pay the purchase price is most often completely discharged on the transfer of ownership, but the seller will continue to owe obligations to the buyer regarding the warranties and indemnities given in support of that purchase price for a period of time following the completion of the transaction. Thus, in most transactions, the question of counterparty creditworthiness is more acute for the buyer.

Ascertaining the creditworthiness of a corporate seller may be relatively straightforward, particularly where that corporate seller produces audited financial statements. If the actual selling entity is not sufficiently creditworthy, the buyer may demand that a more creditworthy affiliate (usually a parent) provide a guarantee of some or all of the selling entity's obligations. What of an individual seller, such as the founder of the business? What certainty does the buyer have that such a seller will not spend all of the sale proceeds or put them beyond the reach of the buyer? When the buyer has no such certainty, the buyer should retain a portion of the purchase price to satisfy any claims it may have against the seller or, at least, demand that those funds be escrowed to have them available to satisfy warranty claims and other claims that may arise after completing the transaction.

An escrow is a written agreement between the buyer, the seller, and an escrow agent, whereby the escrow agent establishes an account in which the buyer deposits a portion of the purchase price. The escrow agent is usually an independent entity (e.g., a bank, trust company, or another professional service provider) with specific contractually imposed duties and responsibilities, such as following the terms of the escrow agreement and ensuring that the other parties are in compliance with the terms of the escrow. In some jurisdictions, statutory duties and responsibilities are also imposed on the escrow agent.

The escrow provides certainty that the funds deposited in the escrow account are available to satisfy claims against the seller for specified breaches of the SPA—typically, the seller's representations and warranties regarding the business being sold and/or covenants regarding the company's operations between signing and closing. When the buyer successfully claims against the seller, then all or a portion of the escrow is paid to the buyer (which may include interest from the date of the claim or from the date of the loss) and any balance is repaid to the seller. When no claims are made against the escrow, then the full amount is ultimately repaid to the seller.

An escrow has many advantages (including mitigating risk for the buyer, facilitating the overall transaction execution, and removing credit risk), so the seller may receive a higher overall sale price when it is receptive to an escrow. The amount placed in escrow and the time period of the escrow depend upon the relative bargaining power of each negotiating party, the underlying obligations for which the escrow is providing credit enhancement, and the overall size of the transaction. Customary practice suggests that up to 10% of the purchase price may be subject to an escrow, and that up to 18 months is a reasonable time period for the escrow. The amount in the escrow account is often invested by the escrow agent during the time period when the funds are in the account. Both the buyer and the seller have a vested interest in the way the escrow amount is invested: the buyer likely prefers more security to ensure that the funds are available in the event of a claim while the seller may prefer more risk-taking investment behavior by the escrow agent in order to claim a possible return on the escrowed funds.

The creditworthiness issue is more complicated in private equity transactions than in the case of a corporate transaction, as the private equity fund itself is unlikely to be the selling entity. Rather, the fund will have incorporated a subsidiary or, more typically, a chain of subsidiaries at the time it acquired the target to function as special purpose acquisition vehicles. One or more of these will be the selling entity and, upon selling the target, will become a cash shell that aims to distribute the sale proceeds back to the private equity fund as quickly as possible to improve the IRR on the fund's investment. Consequently, the buyer is likely to be left with a pure shell entity as its contractual counterparty. The buyer could demand a *payment guarantee from the fund* or a *reverse equity commitment letter* under which the fund agrees to invest sufficient capital in the selling entity to allow it to satisfy a post-completion claim by the buyer. However, doing so would require the fund to maintain the selling entity in existence and bear the ongoing administrative costs of doing so. Alternatively, the buyer needs to rely on a holdback or escrow of part of the purchase price, and/or off-lay some of its risk through representation and warranty insurance.

Termination

Termination provisions give the parties the right to bring their contractual relationship under the SPA to an end in specified circumstances. Every SPA should include termination provisions when there is a time gap between the signing of the SPA and the completion of the transaction. These provisions describe the termination rights of both parties if the conditions to closing are not fulfilled by a certain deadline (often referred to colloquially as the "long-stop date"). Termination might also be exercised by mutual consent or by one of the parties if there is a specified breach of the SPA by the other party.

To avoid the risk of the SPA being terminated, both parties should carefully consider the rules of termination before entering into the contract. It is impossible to cover every potential issue that might arise and lead to termination of the contract. However, studying the termination provisions beforehand will give the parties a basic understanding of how and why the contract might come to an end.

Miscellaneous

Most SPAs have a section composed of different types of provisions that are not easily categorized but which are sometimes referred to as "boilerplate" provisions (as they contain relatively standardized language concerning the legal mechanisms for enforcing the contract in a particular jurisdiction). For example, some of these provisions address: (1) how the parties can serve notices or legal process on each other under the contract, (2) whether third parties may enforce parts of the contract, (3) the governing law of the contract, (4) the jurisdiction of enforcement and method of dispute resolution (e.g., arbitration vs. court), (5) the method of amending the contract, (6) the consequences of waiving a right under the contract, etc.

OWNING THE PORTFOLIO COMPANY

After the successful acquisition of a portfolio company, the private equity fund manager requires intensive managerial and operational planning to run the business. The discussion below highlights some key legal issues regarding board formation upon the buyout of a company.

Oversight and board seats

Having acquired the target company, the private equity fund manager will typically wish to appoint representatives to the board of directors or other governing body that is responsible for overseeing the company's management. How that body is structured and the rules under which it operates is determined primarily by the laws of the jurisdiction in which the target company is incorporated, which in turn dictate what is included in its constitutional documents. There can be wide diversity in this regard. For example, in many European civil law jurisdictions, corporate entities operate with a dual board structure, having both a *management board* whose members are tasked with managing the company and a *supervisory board* that plays an oversight role. By contrast, common law jurisdictions such as the United States and the United Kingdom operate a single unitary board structure, with management being fulfilled by officers appointed by the board (who may or may not also be members of the board). Managers are called "executive directors" (distinct from "non-executive directors," who fulfill the supervisory role) in the United Kingdom.

Given these significant structural differences between jurisdictions, it is vitally important that any individuals who are contemplating joining a board of directors or other governing body take legal advice as to their specific role(s) and the duties and liabilities that the role imposes on them. We highlight common themes so far as these duties and liabilities are concerned, but these can vary markedly depending upon the particular jurisdiction or entity:

- **Duty of loyalty**: Members of the board owe their duties to the corporate entity of which they are directors (sometimes described as a "duty to exercise [their] powers only for a proper purpose"). The corporate entity entrusts its business and assets to its directors and therefore, directors must always act for the benefit of the corporate entity and prioritize its interests ahead of their own. In practice, this means that each director is expected to act for the benefit of the current and future owners of the corporate entity. In most jurisdictions, when the entity becomes insolvent, the interests of its creditors become paramount and the directors are expected to act for the benefit of the entity's creditors rather than its owners. Exactly when and how this shift in duty occurs varies between each jurisdiction and type of corporate entity.

- **Duties of care and skill**: Members of the board must have the requisite skills to fulfill their role and suitably inform themselves prior to making any business decision. In a number of jurisdictions, these duties are assessed on a more onerous objective basis (i.e., by asking whether the individual had the care and skill that could be reasonably expected of a person in his/her position).

- **Conflicts of interest**: Because directors are required to put the interests of the corporate entity ahead of their own, they must avoid conflict between those two considerations. In the case of private equity professionals, this means balancing their duties as directors of the portfolio company with the pecuniary interests they have as equity holders and ensuring they do not misuse corporate assets, opportunities, or information. In some jurisdictions, the owners of the corporate entity are permitted to waive breaches of these duties either prospectively or retrospectively and, in some instances, merely disclosing the conflict to the board or the owners is sufficient to absolve the director from liability.

Corporate formalities

For over 125 years, it has been a basic tenet of corporate law that a corporation has a separate legal personality, and that its liabilities are separate and distinct from those of its owners. Typically, an owner's liability is limited to the amount of his/her investment. As the owner of multiple corporate entities, a private equity firm needs to understand in what circumstances a particular jurisdiction holds the firm liable for the obligations of a portfolio company. This *corporate veil* may be pierced or lifted by statute; for example, many jurisdictions have statutes that hold owners liable for environmental liabilities of their corporate entities, and owners may be held liable for fraudulent trading when the corporation is bankrupt. An owner may also contractually agree to assume the liabilities of the corporate entity (e.g., by guaranteeing the liabilities of the corporate entity).

Absent a statute or contractual agreement, most jurisdictions pierce or lift the corporate veil where it is against public policy to afford the owner the protection of limited liability; for instance, where the corporate entity is being run as a mere facade or where the owner has disregarded the separate existence of the corporation. Some of the ways to maintain a separate identity for the portfolio company are as follows:

- First, private equity funds should maintain sufficient capital in the portfolio company (note that from this perspective, leveraged buyouts can be inherently risky);

- Second, the fund should observe the requisite corporate formalities (i.e., maintain the corporate books, separate bank accounts, etc.);

- Third, holding properly constituted board meetings and maintaining written minutes helps avoid losing the benefits of limited liability;

- Fourth, the manager running the fund could elect independent directors that can make meaningful contributions to the board by allowing them to consider and approve interested party transactions; and

- Fifth, in any event, the private equity fund manager should maintain adequate liability insurance.

LIQUIDITY AND EXITING THE DEAL

Following the acquisition of a portfolio company, there are a number of strategies that the private equity fund can use to realize its investment. In this section, we focus on the key legal aspects of three such strategies: a dividend recapitalization transaction, an initial public offering (IPO), and a sale to a buyer (whether it be a trade sale to a strategic buyer or a so-called "secondary sale" to another private equity firm).

Dividend recapitalization

One of the most common strategies for private equity firms to monetize their investment in a portfolio company is a dividend recapitalization. The volume of these transactions spikes when debt markets become attractive with low interest rates. Low rates incentivize fund managers to increase the borrowings of their portfolio companies on the assumption that the portfolio company is able to service its increased debt burden due to the lower cost of borrowing. The proceeds from this debt (which are usually raised by way of a term loan or high-yield bonds if the portfolio company is relatively large) are then used to pay a special dividend to the private equity firm and other shareholders of the portfolio company. However, the increased leverage is more likely to trigger financial stress in the portfolio company and may ultimately lead to its bankruptcy. For this reason, dividend recapitalizations have attracted the ire of some politicians who—notwithstanding the fact that the steps taken by the private equity firm and its portfolio company may be perfectly legal—still regard it as one of the more egregious forms of asset stripping. In Europe, this has prompted legislative action through the introduction of the so-called "anti-asset stripping rules" contained in the Alternative Investment Fund Managers Directive (AIFMD). A dividend recapitalization therefore raises a number of legal issues:

- In European and certain other jurisdictions, most corporate entities are only permitted to pay a dividend out of *distributable profits*, effectively retained earnings; to pay a dividend out of capital is absolutely prohibited or subject to significant creditor protection requirements. These rules necessitate careful structuring by the private equity firm to effect the dividend recapitalization; this may even need to be put in place at the time of the original acquisition of the portfolio company in order to facilitate future dividend recapitalizations. For example, repayment of debt, including shareholder debt, is not subject to these restrictions or, interestingly, the anti-asset stripping rules of the AIFMD. However, in some jurisdictions, shareholder debt is treated as quasi-equity with creditor protection rules as to when it can be repaid in priority to other creditors.

- The directors of the portfolio company that pays the dividend must carefully consider their fiduciary duties and what steps they can take to protect themselves. If the portfolio company subsequently goes into bankruptcy, they may face claims for breach of fiduciary duty under a number of legal theories. One such set of claims argues that, in financing the dividend with debt, the directors and management of the portfolio company pushed the company toward insolvency and, even when it was solvent, failed to properly protect creditors' interests. Another set of claims is that the directors breached their duty of loyalty by putting their own pecuniary interests in the private equity firm ahead of those of the portfolio company. To help protect themselves, the directors often commission a solvency opinion from an independent expert to underpin their decision to pay the dividend. In the United States, such an opinion affords the directors additional protections under U.S. bankruptcy law; but even in those jurisdictions where there is no particular statutory advantage in obtaining such an opinion, it still helps the directors argue that they properly discharged their fiduciary duties.

Initial public offering

An IPO—whereby a portfolio company's shares become publicly traded—is among the most successful exit strategies. An IPO allows the private equity fund to realize at least part of its investment in the portfolio company. It also brings a number of other advantages, such as access to additional capital for the portfolio company (both at the time of the IPO and in the future), the ability to fund acquisitions using its shares rather than just cash, the perception of greater financial stability, improved management, more transparency, investor and media attention, and so on. A transition from the private to the public domain may take anywhere from a few months to over a year, and will involve investment banks, lawyers, accountants, and company representatives. A complex web of documentation will govern the process.

Registration and prospectus

Stock markets in the United States and Europe have increasingly harmonized their disclosure requirements for the IPO company and its business. To improve market efficiency and protect investors' rights, regulatory bodies such as the Securities and Exchange Commission (SEC) in the United States require an issuer to first register and publish a prospectus before its securities are admitted to trading on a stock market. Although the concept of registering securities is unique to the U.S. regulatory system, the requirement to publish a prospectus as a condition to having securities admitted to trading is almost universal. The prospectus is intended to provide prospective investors with key information about the IPO company and its business as well as the securities being offered in the IPO, so that the investors can make an informed investment decision. Where an offering is being made available to retail investors, the required level of disclosure is inevitably fulsome and lengthy, necessitating significant preparatory work on the part of the IPO company and its advisers. Given the reliance that investors will be placing on the information, substantial time will also need to be spent verifying its accuracy as well as ensuring that all required information has been included in the prospectus. For the same reason, the IPO company will be subject to significant restrictions as to the type and quality of information it can make available to the public—whether directly or through analysts—in the period leading up to its IPO. Various regulatory regimes police these matters differently.

Offering and pricing: Firm commitment versus best efforts

The IPO pricing requires diligent work because publicly available information about the portfolio company will be very limited; this not only makes the valuation process harder but also makes clearance of shares more difficult. In order to achieve greater certainty for the process, the IPO company and the private equity fund (as selling shareholder) will typically enter into an underwriting agreement with one or more underwriters. There are two main approaches in this regard:

- **Firm Commitment:** In a firm commitment agreement between the selling private equity fund and the investment bank, the underwriter purchases all shares to be offered in the IPO. The underwriter's compensation will then depend on the difference between the offer price, which is negotiated and determined by outside investors, and the purchase price. Historically, this was often done on a so-called "fixed price" basis, where the purchase price was first agreed, putting the underwriters at risk for the duration of the subsequent offering period, which could be up to three weeks. Today, the vast majority of IPOs are instead run as so-called "bookbuilt" offerings, where the underwriters first solicit interest from investors, both as to number of shares and price, and in so doing build a book of demand from which they can optimize the purchase price. This allows the underwriters to significantly reduce the period that they are at risk to less than 24 hours (i.e., the time between when they set the purchase price and the time when the investors who have expressed interest confirm their orders). Since the underwriters already know the level of demand and have priced the offering accordingly, their only real risk during that period is a sudden market downturn. For that reason, the underwriters insist on a market MAC condition in the underwriting agreement allowing them to terminate their underwriting should such a downturn occur.

- **Best Efforts:** In a best-efforts underwriting contract, the investment bank only pledges to do its best to sell the shares to cover the private equity fund's required proceeds. Under this type of contract, underwriters are relieved from responsibility for any inventory of shares they are unable to sell. They do not guarantee that they will sell the entire IPO issue thus limiting both their risk and profit potential since they only receive a flat fee for their services. Best-efforts offerings sometimes contain conditions, such as *all-or-none* and *part-or-none*. All-or-none offerings require the entire offering to sell for the deal to close. With a part-or-none offering, only a set amount of securities qualify to close the deal. Given the vastly increased risk to the private equity fund with this approach, best-efforts deals tend to be confined to smaller retail offerings.

Lock-up agreement

In order to maintain market confidence, it is common for the underwriters to insist that the private equity fund selling shares in the IPO enters into a lock-up agreement, which prohibits the fund from dumping its shares in the post-IPO period (usually 180–360 days after the IPO). Lock-ups can also contain so-called "orderly market" provisions, which limit the number of shares to be sold at any one time. Lock-up arrangements must be disclosed in the prospectus to assist the IPO marketing process.

Secondary offerings and Rule 144

An IPO is a private equity firm's first step toward exiting its investment in the portfolio company. It is unlikely that the private equity fund is allowed to sell its entire shareholding in the IPO because of a lock-up. Thereby, follow-up secondary offerings of the shares after the expiration of the lock-up periods are necessary.
Under the U.S. regulatory regime, where securities are required to be registered with the SEC, it is vital for the private equity fund to negotiate registration rights before it loses control of the portfolio company (which may occur at the time of the IPO). Alternatively, the private equity fund would need to rely on an exemption from having to register the shares for sale—such as that contained in SEC Rule 144—though this does not allow it to fully exit the portfolio company due to the limitation placed on the transaction volume.

Portfolio company sale

A sale of the portfolio company or its assets is the dominant exit strategy for private equity firms. Historically, portfolio companies were most often sold to trade buyers; however, sales to another private equity firm—referred to as secondary (or even tertiary or even quaternary) sales or, more deprecatorily, as "pass-the-parcel" deals—have become a recognized part of the deal landscape. From a regulatory and cost perspective, there are several advantages to a sale. As a privately negotiated arrangement, a sale offers the parties greater control over timing than an IPO. There are also fewer regulatory restrictions than with an IPO. Most importantly, a sale allows a complete exit by the private equity firm upon completion of the transaction.

Auction processes

To help maximize sale proceeds on a portfolio company, private equity fund managers often prefer an auction process. Though the specific approach varies across jurisdictions, most auction processes commence with the seller's corporate finance adviser or broker surveying the market for potential buyers. Once these have been identified and approached, and expressed an interest, they are invited to submit an initial bid based upon limited information. This bid is provided upon signature of the requisite NDA, and often includes access to an information memorandum prepared by the selling private equity firm and its corporate finance adviser containing key business and financial information about the portfolio company. Selected bidders are then be invited to participate in a subsequent round of the auction, at which point they are given access to more detailed information about the portfolio company, typically in the form of access to a data room (today, inevitably accessed electronically via a website). The data room provides all of the key documentation governing the operation of the portfolio company, including its financials, key contracts, employee data and so on.

The bidders may also be invited to attend a presentation by the portfolio company's management, and possibly, in the later rounds of the auction, to undertake site visits. In larger European auction processes, and increasingly in Asia, bidders may also be given access to vendor (or seller) due diligence reports. Bidders are not allowed to rely on the contents of the reports and access is provided for information purposes only; however, the successful buyer is conventionally given limited assurance by the seller's advisers, thereby supporting the accuracy and objectivity of the report. Making these reports available speeds up the auction process by allowing bidders to gain a faster understanding of a complex business and underwrite the value attributed to the portfolio company.

As part of their best and final bid, bidders are usually expected to provide a mark-up of the SPA drafted by the seller, in a form they would be prepared to sign. In a competitive auction process, the SPA will inevitably contain seller-friendly provisions (e.g., a locked box structure in European deals), with the hope that the competitive tension will force bidders to negotiate against themselves (so to speak) and minimize their changes to the draft. Following the final round of the auction, one (or more) of the preferred bidders will be selected to negotiate a legally binding transaction with the seller, ideally in the form of a contract race between the bidders. Exhibit 7 provides an example of an auction sale process with a timeline.

Dual tracks

In a so-called "dual-track" process, the private equity seller commences an IPO process for the portfolio company in parallel with a sale process, with a view to seeing which alternative will maximize its return in the later stages. Given the costs involved, a dual-track process is really only suitable for larger exits. The process places a considerable burden on the senior management of the portfolio company, making it more difficult for them to focus on actually running the business, and potentially jeopardizing the success of one or both tracks. Careful planning and coordination is therefore a prerequisite for a successful dual track. However, in the right circumstances, a successful dual track can further increase competitive tension for bidders and drive up public investor appetite for the portfolio company to come to market.

CONCLUSION

With significant values at stake, negotiating deal completion mechanisms as well as the Sale and Purchase Agreement (SPA) can be the difference between a successful and unsuccessful transaction. One of the major takeaways in today's market is that on the deal side, the current trend of limited indemnities and scaled-back representations and warranties is likely to continue. In both the European and US markets, the buyer must beware (i.e., caveat emptor). It is up to the buyer to do due diligence to assess its risk, and then price this risk into the deal to protect its investment. However competition for deals has become more intense. The usage of the locked box mechanism has increased over time and, as advisors become increasingly familiar with the mechanism, it is likely to become more popular. In addition, earnouts are now commonly used in many deals, despite taking the longest time to negotiate.

Exhibit 7: Timeline of Auction Sale Process

Step	Milestone /Workflow	Weeks
1	Seller appoints financial advisor	week -10 to 0
2	Seller commissions the vendor due diligence report	week -4 to 0
3	Seller issues round 1 process letter	week 0
4	Non-Disclosure Agreements are signed	week 1
5	Seller releases high level financial due diligence data and information memorandum	week 1
6	Bidders submit indicative offer letters	week 1 to 7
7	Seller issues round 2 process letter	week 8
8	Seller opens data room to selected bidders and shares vendor due diligence report	week 8
9	Bidders appoint advisors and commission buy side due diligence requests	week 8
10	Bidders prepare business case	week 8 to 14
11	Bidders attend one or two management meetings	weeks 10, 11
12	Bidders approach potential lenders and negotiate financing	week 8 to 14
13	Lenders sign financing commitment letters to support final bids	week 14
14	Bidders deliver final bids with marked up SPAs and signed financing papers	week 14
15	Exclusivity period or preferred bidders play-off	week 14 to 17
16	Sign SPA, disclosure letter, equity commitment letter and management term sheet	week 18
17	Competition clearances	week 18 to 22
18	Winning bidder negotiates full finance documentation	week 18 to 22
19	Closing	week 22
20	Buyer procures post-closing security over target	week 22 to 26
21	Buyer negotiates management incentives schemes	week 22 to 26

In his own words: Christopher Field, Partner at Dechert LLP

With the march of globalization, deal documentation has become more uniform in nature. As inveterate deal doers, private equity firms have been instrumental in driving this process. While the different laws in each jurisdiction will always mean that there will be differences in approach, the problems that the legal documents aim to address are universal in nature and the various methods of addressing them are being exported across the world. A lot of this thinking emanates from the United States, which is unsurprising as it is both the largest private equity market and the largest legal market in the world. However, the traffic is not all one-way. The idea of having debt financing for an acquisition provided on a "certain funds" basis originated in public company transactions in the United Kingdom, but is increasingly being seen in private equity transactions in the United States, as is the concept of selling a company on a "locked box" basis.

Increasing harmonization should lead to greater efficiencies in executing transactions, and that may well be the case for classic leveraged transactions—the existence of this text book means that everyone now has the opportunity to taste the magic private equity sauce! However, the creativity of private equity professionals and their legal advisers also means that transaction structures and deal terms will continue to evolve and almost certainly become even more complex. To succeed in that environment, you have to understand the key themes that underpin the thinking—pricing and risk allocation—and how they are translated onto the written page.

6 Leveraged Buyout Transactions

Never was anything great achieved without danger.
Niccolò Machiavelli

INTRODUCTION

A leveraged buyout (LBO) is the acquisition by a private equity (PE) buyout fund of a company, business unit, or group of assets (the target), using debt to finance the majority of the purchase price. LBO transactions take many different forms with varying levels of debt, required returns, and other dimensions. This chapter aims to describe the "typical" LBO transaction.

The amount of debt used is typically 50–70% of the target's purchase price, but has reached around 90% on some deals during the peak transaction years before the credit crisis —hence the term "leveraged buyout." The LBO buyer (also known as the "LBO sponsor") raises the debt through bonds and/or bank loans issued by the target company. The debt is either secured against the target's assets or unsecured, and the target's free cash flows are used to service and repay the debt.[1] The debt almost always includes a loan portion that is senior and secured, which is arranged by a bank or an investment bank. In the 1980s, 1990s and early 2000s, banks were the primary investors in these loans, however, over the past few years, institutional debt investors have entered the market and started to buy a large fraction of senior and secured loans.[2] The debt package used to finance LBOs often includes also a junior unsecured portion that is financed by either high-yield bonds or "mezzanine debt" (i.e., debt that is subordinated to senior debt). The equity portion of the purchase price is provided by the PE buyout fund. The new management team of the purchased company (which may or may not be identical to the pre-buyout management team) typically also contributes to the new equity, although the amount is usually a small fraction of the total equity.

The objective of the buyout fund is to hold the target for a period of about three to seven years and then sell the company with the scope of realizing a relatively high financial return on the original equity investment. The target return on equity, measured using the internal rate of return (IRR), is expected to be between 20% and 30%, depending on the perceived risk of the transaction. The buyout fund managers use a combination of three principal mechanisms to achieve this financial objective:

- Increase the target firm's value through operational improvements that boost the target's revenues and earnings.

- Pay down the debt taken to acquire the target using the target's free cash flows from operations, thereby increasing the equity portion of the capital structure of the company.

---

[1] Basically, the target company helps pay for itself (hence the term "bootstrap" acquisition).

[2] These investors include hedge fund investors and "collateralized loan obligation" managers, who combine a number of term loans into a loan portfolio.

- Sell the target company when market conditions are more favorable and therefore achieve multiple expansion.

The use of large amounts of debt to finance the acquisition of a target company has a number of risks but also some advantages. The most obvious risk is that of bringing the target company in financial distress. Many unexpected events such as changes in the regulatory environment, a worsening of the economy, more restrictive regulations or litigation can lead to a sudden decrease in the company's operational cash flows that could trigger difficulties in meeting principal and interest payments, a violation of debt covenants or outright liquidation. Further, a weak management at the target company or a misalignment of incentives between the target's management and the buyout fund professionals can exacerbate the financial distress. The main advantages to the use of leverage in acquisitions are the governance effect of debt (i.e., large interest and principal payments forces the target's management to improve performance and operating efficiency), lower tax payments and the fact that the return on the equity invested by the buyout fund is significantly higher if the deal is successful.

BACKGROUND

Historical perspective

The first LBO took place in 1901, when J.P. Morgan acquired Carnegie Steel Company for $480 million. However, using debt for acquisitions was generally considered an unusual and questionable financing technique, as most companies felt uncomfortable with high levels of debt on their balance sheets. In the years following the end of World War II, the Great Depression was still relatively fresh in the minds of America's corporate leaders, who considered it wise to keep corporate debt ratios low. As a result, very few American companies relied on debt as a significant source of funding for the first three decades following World War II.

In the early 1980s, various newly founded dedicated buyout firms emerged. These firms profited from LBOs of undervalued corporate assets and their subsequent asset stripping and financial engineering. This period saw the development of a very negative public image of PE firms that were called "corporate raiders". Books such as *Barbarians at the Gate: The Fall of RJR Nabisco* which discussed how the LBO-boutique Kohlberg, Kravis and Roberts took over and delisted RJR Nabisco in a deal valued at $31 billion, highlighted some questionable practices in the industry. Yet, a new generation of managers felt more comfortable with high levels of debt, and the buyout industry thrived. While only four deals with an aggregate value of $1.7 billion were reported in 1980, 410 buyouts with an aggregate value of $188 billion took place in 1988 (Olsen et al., 2003). The first PE boom ended in the late 1980s, after the crash of the junk bond market, which was fueled by the investment bank Drexel Burnham Lambert, and several high-profile bankruptcies of overleveraged PE-owned companies such as Federated Department Stores, the Revco drug stores, Walter Industries, FEB Trucking or Eaton Leonard .

After a short period of decline, beginning in 1992 (three years after the RJR Nabisco buyout) and continuing through the end of the 1990s the private equity buyout industry once again experienced a tremendous boom and saw the emergence of brand name firms managing multibillion-dollar sized funds. The industry began to increase in size raising approximately $20.8 billion of investor commitments in 1992 and reaching a high-water mark in 2000 of over $300 billion, outpacing the growth of almost every other asset class according to Thomson Financial's database. Although many of the acquisitions in the 1980s were unsolicited and unwelcome, buyout firms in the 1990s focused on making the transactions attractive to target companies' management and shareholders. Additionally, buyout fund managers became increasingly focused on operational activities and the long term development of the targets acquired, using less leverage in the transaction. This was partly due to the lack of lenders willing to fund these buyouts during this period. While in the 1980s leverage usually cover 85% to 95% of the purchase price of a target company, in the 1990s the average debt levels dropped below 40%.[3]

In the early 2000s, interest rates decreased, lending standards were relaxed (especially for high-yield financing), and stock markets quickly recovered from the burst of the dotcom bubble. Roxburgh et al. (2009) note that worldwide PE fundraising jumped from $71 billion in 2004 to $198 billion in 2005, $281 billion in 2006, and $301 billion in 2007. These conditions fed the second (and largest) LBO boom in history; the transactions volume jumped to $685 billion and $683 billion in 2006 and 2007, respectively. This volume was mainly driven by so-called "mega-deals" (LBOs with a transaction value in excess of $3 billion), which made up $331 billion (or 57%) of the total deal value for 2007. Some of these megadeals included the buyouts of established companies such as the Hospital Corporation of America, Alliance Boots, TXU Energy, and Chrysler.

The financial crisis in 2007-2008 and the connected collapse of the high-yield bond market ended this second LBO boom. The credit crisis dramatically reduced the availability of debt and equity. LBO fundraising fell from $266 billion in 2007 to $144 billion in 2009. Even more alarmingly, the new syndicated debt issuance to buyout funds fell to $12 billion in the fourth quarter of 2008, which represented only 4% of its peak of $283 billion in the first quarter of 2007 (Roxburgh et al., 2009). In addition, the cost of credit dramatically increased. As a consequence of these adverse factors, LBO activity dramatically decreased from close to $600 billion in 2007 to only $150 billion in 2008. Most of this decline (64%) was due to the virtual disappearance of megadeals. The global buyout transaction value dropped to about $80 billion in 2009 but, by the end of 2018, has since recovered to reach close to 600 billion.

By the end of 2018, the private equity buyout transactions reached a share of approximately 20% in the total global market for mergers and acquisitions with average EBITDA acquisition multiple reaching 11X. The purchase of expensive assets requires an increased amount of discipline for private equity fund managers, as there is little margin for error to achieve the target IRR. The recession had a lasting effect on the strategies and portfolios of PE firms. Investments made before the recession saw few exit opportunities during the down market, which forced PE firms to hold their portfolio companies beyond their entrance expectations. During this time, the average holding period for portfolio companies almost doubled—from 3.3 years in 2009 to 6.1 years in 2014—before dropping to 4.5 years by the end of 2018 (Bain & Co, 2019).

Today, with limited opportunities for multiple expansions or aggressive GDP growth in the mature American and European markets, PE firms have to invest extensively in improving their assets and focusing on long-term growth opportunities. The returns generated by buyout funds, while still good relative to the returns generated by other asset classes, have declined slowly inching toward public market averages. By the end of 2019, persistent high company valuations, volatile capital markets, US–China trade arguments, Brexit worries and the ever-present threat of a new recession have resulted in significant uncertainty for fund

---

[3] Some notable transactions in the 1990s were Thomas H. Lee Partners' acquisition of Snapple Beverages in 1992 (sold to Quaker Oats for $1.7 billion), Texas Pacific Group's acquisition of then bankrupt Continental Airlines in 1993 (generating a 1000% return), Bain Capital's acquisition of Domino's Pizza in 1998 (IPOed in 2004), etc.

managers. In addition, the increased pace of technological changes in almost every industry, started to make it difficult for managers to pick the right deals.

Outlook

Aside from the presence of a favorable regulatory treatment, the buyout industry depends predominantly on the availability of capital from LPs, affordable debt instruments as well as the continuous development of the stock market. In addition, as the overall PE industry has matured and become a lot more competitive and global, the abnormal returns that GPs could once earn on buyout transactions are more difficult to achieve. Given these developments, the PE firms are likely to follow three important trends.

Focus more on operational improvements

Due to the tightening and cyclicality of the debt markets and the commoditization of value creation by financial leverage, operational improvements are becoming increasingly important. Hence, buyout firms must increasingly attempt to differentiate themselves based on active management capabilities and industry knowledge by involving operating partners with wide industry expertise; such individuals can help transform the operational performance of the portfolio companies. Moreover, buyout firms have started to provide more advisory services to their portfolio companies. Firms, such as Vista Equity, have gone as far as to create internal consulting groups independent of the investment team to service their portfolio companies and develop robust plans to create long-term value. Some firms took this trend a step further and started to look at turnaround situations, where they acquire a company at a very low entry multiple due to, for example, potential financial distress, and then subsequently draw up a recovery plan to drastically improve the company's prospects.

Specialize on certain industries

In the early days, many PE firms were accused of achieving their returns by asset stripping and financial engineering. Because these activities are very similar across industries, the firms and their professionals were mostly generalists. However, there has been a significant shift toward achieving value creation through operational improvements that require deep industry and operational knowledge to develop a differentiating investment thesis compared to their competitors. Thus, the current trend of industry specialization of PE firms and the emergence of sector groups within large PE firms is likely to intensify in the future.[4]

Diversify their revenues away from buyouts

In the decade from 1998 to 2008, the buyout revenue share of the PE industry declined from 57% to 44%. The same period saw growth in infrastructure, real estate, private credit and other investments (such as distressed debt) as PE firms have been searching for stable yields through the various economic cycles.

---

[4] According to research from Cambridge Associates, in the period between 2001 and 2010, industry-specific funds generated an average gross IRR of 23.2%, against 17.5% from generalist funds (Cambridge Associate Private Investment Series (2014) Declaring a Major: Sector-Focused Private Investment Funds).

Types of buyout transactions

Opportunistic traditional buyouts

Opportunistic buyouts have historically comprised the majority of buyout investments made by PE funds. These are transactions where an entrepreneurial company management team is comfortable operating in a leveraged environment. Most include LBOs in situations that involve consolidation through mergers or follow-on acquisitions; carve-outs from larger organizations looking to shed non-core assets; situations requiring structured ownership to meet a seller's financial goals; or situations in which the business plan involves substantial departures from past practice to maximize the value of the company's assets.

Distressed buyouts and debt investments

These types of transactions target assets with high-quality operating businesses but low-quality balance sheets, consistent with traditional buyout strategies. The distressed securities purchased include bank debt, public high-yield debt, and privately held instruments, often with significant downside protection in the form of a senior position in the capital structure.

Corporate partner buyouts

These buyouts offer another way to capitalize on investment opportunities in environments where purchase prices for control of companies are at high multiples of earnings, making them less attractive to traditional buyout investors. Corporate partner buyouts focus on companies in need of a financial partner in order to consummate acquisitions, expand product lines, buy back stock, or pay down debt. In these investments, the PE firm does not seek control, but instead makes significant investments that typically allow it to obtain control rights similar to those that it would require in a traditional buyout (e.g., control over the direction of the business and the ultimate exit). Although corporate partner buyouts historically have not represented a large portion of overall investment activity, PE firms do engage in them selectively when circumstances make them an attractive strategy.

Other buyouts

In addition to the traditional, distressed, and corporate partner buyout activities, PE firms also maintain the flexibility to deploy capital from their funds in other types of investments, such as the creation of new companies. This approach allows them to leverage deep industry expertise and collaborate with experienced management teams to capitalize on market opportunities that have been identified, particularly in asset-intensive, distressed industries. Another alternative is to establish new entities that can acquire distressed assets at what would be attractive valuations without the burden of managing an existing portfolio of legacy assets. Like corporate partner buyout activities, these other investments (e.g., the creation of new companies) have not represented a large portion of PE companies' overall investment activities historically.

THE LBO DEAL PROCESS

The analysis of LBOs requires knowledge of many concepts, theories, and financial instruments. For example, knowledge of the various debt and equity instruments, and of ways to determine the debt capacity of a company, is needed to understand the capital structure of buyouts. Even more importantly, LBO values and financing structures are built on a huge number of assumptions and decisions that interact with each other in very complex ways. Understanding these interactions is critical to understanding and structuring an LBO.

Below, we start the discussion of the LBO deal process with a basic description of the five stages of an LBO deal transaction (see Exhibit 1).

Exhibit 1: The five stages of an LBO transaction

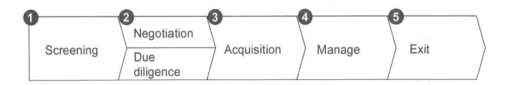

Screening

The first stage of the LBO process is to source and screen opportunities. Potential deals are sourced by the general partners in the PE firm, using personal networks that include experts, CEOs, and investment bankers. A core component of any world-class origination effort is to focus the investment generation activity through market mapping, which can be defined as identifying the key macro- and micro-economic drivers of an industry and creating a database of all the major companies in that sector. Typically, the goal of market mapping is to identify the companies and sectors that have the greatest growth potential and face limited competition. The key steps in market mapping are described in Exhibit 2 (see Teten and Farmer, 2010).

Specialization in a particular geography or industry allows for a deeper knowledge base and an enhanced network that can facilitate deal sourcing. Other ways of sourcing a deal include memberships in expert networks that can connect PE fund managers to senior industry and C-level executives to assess interest in an investment or partnerships with executives that would be willing to pursue companies jointly with the PE fund.

Once a potential deal is sourced, an initial screening is conducted to determine whether this company could be suitable for an LBO transaction. This screening is based on readily available information, which varies between public and private companies. Due to the very specific characteristics of an LBO, a potential LBO target must be able to service a high level of debt, have suitable exit opportunities within a three- to seven-year horizon, and have the potential to achieve a 20–30% IRR. Hence, choosing appropriate companies that fulfill these requirements is a central element of the work of a PE firm. A list of the main characteristics of a strong LBO candidate is presented below.

Exhibit 2: Key steps in market mapping

	Stage	Example
1	Select industry and geography	Control investing in North American telecommunication companies
2	Establish socioeconomic market thesis	Population in emerging country is very young
3	Translate into investment theme	Expected demand growth for low-risk investing products
4	Map key players in target industry/geography	Asset managers with operational expertise will likely benefit
5	Iteratively improve market map with industry experts and potential investments	Critically assess elements of market map together with experts
6	Identify priority activities along the value chain based on return potential	Invest in delivering a particular service in the value chain where there is limited market competition
7	Identify areas of future growth	Find bolt-on acquisitions while diligencing the primary target
8	Assess fit with fund's strategy	The company can benefit from synergies with other portfolio companies
9	Regularly update market map	Maintain internal database regularly with updated key market data and insights

Low current leverage

A company with low current leverage allows the PE investor to benefit from the value created by higher leverage. However, given that attracting more leverage is a commodity and every financial investor can benefit from it, the value created by financial leverage might already be reflected in the sale price; in this case, the seller (rather than the PE firm) is benefiting from it.

Predictable and strong cash flows

High leverage with acceptable interest rates and risk is only possible if the company can reliably service the interest and make principal repayments. The PE firm as well as the debt providers investigate the cash flows through due diligence. In theory, the value of the equity in the target will increase as debt is amortized. Thus, the ideal targets have strong and especially predictable free cash flows, which are usually consequences of one or more of the following characteristics:

- The firm has a long history of stable operating cash flows.

- The firm is in a mature stage where no unexpected operational expenses are required to ramp up the firm's growth trajectory.

- The firm has a leading and defensible market position, as is often the case in industries where extensive R&D, investments, technology, or patents are needed to enter the market.

- The firm owns strong brand names. Being a well known and respected brand often means a larger market share and, therefore, stronger sales figures than those of competitors.

- The firm benefits from a stable demand from customers

- The firm sells its products and services through long-term sales contracts where the revenue is guaranteed by a solid contract portfolio.

- The firm has low capital expenditure requirements to service customers.

- The firm has low customer attrition and concentration.

- The firm has stable and predictable working capital requirements.

Strong asset base

An asset base is strong if it includes a large amount of tangible and intangible assets that have a high market value and are liquid. High market values and liquidity require assets that are not too specific to the industry in which the company operates, and that have a large number of potential buyers. A strong asset base can be used as collateral when taking on bank debt, and hence, facilitates achieving high leverage at reasonable interest rates. A strong asset base also acts as a barrier to entry for competitors, thereby making cash flows more predictable and secure. However, while a strong asset base is helpful, it is not a necessary precondition for an LBO. Companies with a weak asset base might still be good LBO candidates if their cash flows are so strong and predictable that debt can be secured against these cash flows.

Operational improvement opportunities

While historically, financial leverage was the key value driver of PE funds' returns, operational improvements are becoming more important in the current market. Hence, the PE firm needs to identify opportunities for operational improvements that have not yet been exploited or that competitor buyers cannot see. Examples of operational improvements include increasing sales force effectiveness, improving IT systems, professionalizing operations, streamlining production processes, and working capital optimization.

Growth opportunities

Growth opportunities that are not entirely included in the purchase price or potentially generated by the improvements introduced by the PE firm also make a company a strong LBO candidate. Realizable growth opportunities ensure that it is possible for the company to grow during the holding period. Above-expectation growth allows early repayment of debt, generates a higher EBITDA and exit value, and might positively affect the exit multiple; it also enables the company to take on more debt and still meet debt covenants. Beyond that, high growth makes it easier for the company to benefit from economies of scale, and thus achieve better profit margins. Further, high growth increases the chances of an IPO, an often more lucrative exit option. However, this characteristic is more important for the growth capital sector of the PE industry than it is for the LBO sector. It is very common for growth equity firms to face significant difficulties in attracting acquisition financing, given that high-growth businesses have substantial operational cost requirements in order to grow the business, which subsequently results in depressed cash flows available for debt repayment.

Exit options

Because the funds raised by PE firms are usually time bound, and because their performance is largely evaluated based on the time-weighted IRRs, having a variety of potential exit options in a time horizon of two to seven years is critical. Hence, the target will be more suitable for an LBO transaction structure if (1) it is attractive to potential strategic buyers, (2) it has the potential to do an IPO (due to location, operational history, maturity of processes, etc.), or (3) it is located in an active PE market with multiple financial buyers.

Availability of a strong management team

A strong management team is critical to delivering under the high-leverage, fast-paced, and high-pressure environment of an LBO. The substantial levels of debt in the financial structure of portfolio companies after an LBO transaction places greater demands on management to operate the company more efficiently. If the existing management is disciplined enough to deliver under these conditions, the PE investor will typically keep this team and align management's incentives with large sweet equity stakes or ratchets. However, if the PE firm considers the existing management to be weak or not disciplined enough, it will bring in a new management team with experience in LBOs and the respective industry. Many PE firms prefer to continue with existing management in an LBO transaction structure, as there is always an uncertainty factor regarding how a new management team will integrate and the added pressure of a limited holding period by the PE firm.

Firm size

Strong LBO candidates exist in various sizes. The use of debt and the existence of large buyout funds enable PE firms to buy very large companies. At the same time, the maximum size of buyouts that can be financed by PE funds depends on the availability of debt and equity from LPs. In the boom buyout period between 2005 and 2007, cheap debt and abundant capital led to large LBO deals.[5] The targeted minimum and maximum size of buyouts is an element of the strategy of individual funds. The maximum size is usually limited by the size of the fund, rules that prevent managers from investing a specific percentage of the fund in one target (e.g., 10-15%), and the debt capacity of the target. The effort required to manage an LBO used to be relatively independent of the size of the buyout. Hence, PE firms—and especially the supporting investment banks that are paid based on deal value—used to prefer larger deals. However, with the emerging focus on operational improvements instead of financial leverage, the effort per deal seems to be much more size driven than before, and the preference for big deals is declining.

---

[5] For example, the buyout of TXU Energy in 2007 for $45 billion, the buyout of Equity Office Properties Trust in 2007 for $39 billion, and the buyout of the Hospital Corporation of America for $32.7 billion in 2006. In contrast, after the financial crisis in 2009, the so-called megadeals disappeared.

Ownership structure

The ownership structure of the target plays an important role in acquiring a company for a reasonable price. A suitable LBO candidate should have concentrated ownership with few major stockholders. As owners with less than 10% of the shares cannot affect the premium level of the deal, the focus of the PE firm is geared toward getting an acceptance on the bid price from the majority owners. Being able to discuss the premium with fewer shareholders increases the possibility of reaching an agreement at a lower cost.

Geography

PE firms can find strong LBO candidates in various geographies, but in practice, the United States/Canada and Europe are the regions with the most active buyout market. This state is not due to the characteristics of the targets, but to the maturity of the PE industry and the regulatory environment in these countries. For example, some emerging markets (e.g., Latin America) have only recently established a solid regulatory framework for the PE industry; therefore, LBO transactions are less prevalent in these markets.

Industry

Strong buyout candidates can, in theory, exist in nearly all industries. However, some industries show significantly higher buyout activity because they better enable the fulfillment of the first seven favorable characteristics mentioned above. For instance, consumer products/services, business products/services, telecommunications, and energy are sectors with very high LBO activity, mainly due to vast tangible assets and strong and predictable cash flows. Traditionally, high-tech companies are very rarely LBO targets due to their mainly company specific intangible assets and fast-changing business environments, which do not facilitate predictable cash flow forecasts. Growth capital firms would be more inclined to prospect high-tech companies as they look to inject equity to grow the company, but acquisition financing is often inaccessible for these types of firms. However, as tech companies continue to dominate the global markets, the PE buyout industry has invested heavily in technology. Since 2010, the technology sector has seen 120 to 170 deals annually. PE firms are also becoming increasingly specialized on one industry, or at least internally structured along industries, to assess companies based on detailed industry knowledge and to enable operational improvements after the acquisition.

Due diligence and negotiation

Due diligence is the investigation of a target's business by the potential acquirer(s). The information usually depends on the type of transaction, as shown in Exhibit 3.

Friendly deals typically involve a two-stage process consisting of an initial two-three week period to conduct due diligence and submit a non-binding offer for shortlisting, followed by a more in-depth due diligence process and, possibly, exclusivity. Hostile deals involve a shorter single-stage process without any information provided by the target. Many LBOs are hostile, in which case, the due diligence process must rely on publicly available information or expert advisers to form assumptions and forecasts for the analysis of the deal.

Due diligence is a complicated process where every aspect of the target company is evaluated to understand how the company works and what potential risks are associated with the investment. Complete due diligence is seldom done in-house. Most PE firms contract due diligence providers (e.g., McKinsey, Bain, BCG, etc.)

Exhibit 3: Due Diligence information sources by deal type

	Friendly	**Hostile**
Public	Information Management and statutory Analyst Expert	Public Annual Analyst Company
Private	Information Management Competitors Expert	Press Expert Former insider Company

to conduct commercial, financial, tax, and legal due diligence. Sometimes, PE firms have the competence to carry out certain parts of the due diligence process while others are outsourced. The process normally takes two to six months, but can be done faster (and imperfectly) if there is time pressure involved to get a deal concluded before other bidders. Because due diligence is a costly and time-consuming process, a letter of intent is written before the PE firm starts to engage in full due diligence. This letter gives the PE firm the exclusive right to buy the target during a specific time frame. The due diligence process covers four different areas (see Exhibit 4).

Exhibit 4: The four areas of due diligence

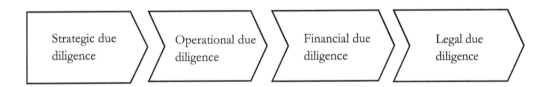

Strategic due diligence aims to understand the target's market, competitive position, and customers, with a focus on future growth, margins, and free cash flows for debt repayment. This type of due diligence could include an analysis of market size, growth rates for different products and services, the firm's life cycle (i.e., emerging, mature, or declining), and an understanding of who the firm's customers are and how they are segmented. It should analyze the competitive environment, market shares, strategy, and potential reactions to the deal as well. The PE firm will also want to understand the potential barriers to entry, such as high capital expenditure, and the potential exit opportunities or barriers to exit. Finally, there should be an analysis of regulatory and technological issues and risks. More recently, some PE firms have started taking advantage of new digital data sources and big data analytical tools. Software tools can analyze client satisfaction, geographical reach, employee compensation, organizational information, and the social media footprint of the company.

Operational due diligence (often combined with strategic due diligence under the umbrella term "commercial due diligence") aims to develop sound and defendable assumptions to support the deal structuring, and to identify potential areas for value creation through operational improvements. The latter is normally achieved using a benchmarking study of close competitors based on key ratios specific to each industry. For example, does the target have a very high cost base compared with other similar businesses? Does the high cost base present a risk which should be incorporated in the purchase price, or should this be considered as a value creation opportunity? Further, the operational due diligence process should evaluate the incumbent management team and its ability to deliver the proposed strategy for the deal, identifying any key positions that the PE firm needs to fill.

Financial and tax due diligence corroborates the target's historic financial statements and supports the development of future assumptions. The PE firm must first check the financial information the target has provided or, in the case of a hostile deal, make estimates using experts and third parties. Financial due diligence aims to verify the reasonableness of the judgments the target has made in presenting its financial statements; this is particularly important in a friendly deal where the target has prepared itself for sale. In this case, many sellers are tempted to inflate their performance by using very aggressive accounting judgments. Most PE firms look very closely at the quality of earnings and the run rate operating profit, as these will be two of the metrics on which the purchase price is determined. Taxes also constitute an important area of due diligence, as many PE firms and managers are focused on tax structuring to minimize capital gains and/or dividend taxation and avoid any potential future tax liabilities.

Legal due diligence requires great attention to detail in order to analyze the target's contractual obligations to all third parties (e.g., customers, suppliers, debtors, creditors, government, etc.) and uncover any negative aspects of the deal or potential future liabilities.

The focus of the due diligence process will vary depending on the time frame, the available information, the target's business area, and the importance of the deal to the acquirer. The combination of the different due diligence activities should be well coordinated to provide a coherent and robust analysis of the characteristics of the LBO candidate, the potential structure of the deal, and a sensitivity analysis regarding operational, entry, and exit assumptions. Most importantly, the information gleaned from the due diligence process allows the PE firm to assess the acquisition price (or the target's valuation).

In an LBO context, the acquisition price of a company is often expressed as an earnings multiple. This earnings multiple is the ratio of a company's enterprise value and an earnings or performance measure. The multiple applied to earnings measures to arrive at the valuation of the firm depends on many related factors, including:

- expectations about the growth of the economy in general, and the target's industry in particular;
- the market position, strength, and future potential of the target within its industry;
- the capital intensity of the industry;
- whether synergies or hostile takeover premiums are included in comparable transactions, and
- the current level of the risk-free rate.

Determining a target's enterprise value and its earnings multiple, with respect to a certain performance measure, is relatively easy for publicly listed companies but difficult for privately held companies. For a publicly listed company, the enterprise value is determined by the equity market value of a company plus the company's net debt. In the case of a private company, whose equity claims are not subject to a regular market valuation, the enterprise value needs to be estimated using comparable companies or transactions. Comparable companies are publicly listed companies that operate in the same, or a related, industry. Comparable transactions are recent mergers, acquisitions, or buyouts that involved companies operating in the same, or a similar, industry. From the value of those companies and transactions, earnings multiples can be derived. By applying these observed multiples to the private company's earnings measures, one can estimate the enterprise value.

However, since no two companies are directly comparable, one must carefully consider whether adjustments to the valuation multiples or the earnings measures are required. Factors to consider include (1) a control premium for a publicly traded company or an illiquidity discount for a privately held company; (2) differences in capital structure, as tax shields resulting from increased debt impact enterprise values; (3) differences in operational risk, which may result in more volatile earnings; (4) trends in the overall market since the occurrence of recent M&A or LBO transactions, etc.

Once the value of the potential target company is assessed, the PE firm must then determine the maximum purchase price it would be prepared to pay, such that the anticipated final return on investment at exit is above the firm's return expectations. The PE firm will try to bid lower than this maximum price, depending on the competitive environment it faces in the deal. This maximum purchase price is influenced by three factors:

- **Exit Valuation:** The estimated enterprise value of the target company at exit, which depends on the anticipated EBITDA growth potential and the earnings multiple at exit.

- **Debt Package:** The fraction of the purchase price that can be financed with debt, the terms and conditions of the debt, and hence, the size of the initial equity contribution.

- **The required return**: PE firms often focus on the IRR and the money multiple; an IRR of at least 25% is a common target, although it is not clear that IRRs of this magnitude may reflect the funds' cost of capital.

Acquisition

The acquisition process varies depending on the type of deal. For proprietary deals where the buyer has exclusivity, the process will involve managers of the PE fund, their buy-side advisers, and the target's management team and sell-side advisers. For competitive deals, the management team of the target company is normally less involved, but may be allied with a particular buyer.

The buyer must creatively structure financing to maximize returns and align stakeholder interests. The acquisition price will be a balance between achieving the required return of the fund and placing a competitive bid for the deal or meeting the seller's expectation. The price the buyer needs to pay is normally defined by the market conditions, the level of competition for the deal, and the relative bargaining power of the seller (e.g., a forced seller compared to a seller that is indifferent toward selling unless it receives an attractive bid). At this stage, the PE firm will create an LBO model to support the deal-structuring process and to ensure that, given the price the buyer needs to pay to close the deal, the required return on equity can be achieved (see the next chapter on LBO modeling).

To find the optimal deal structure, in-depth knowledge about common financial and legal structures and available debt instruments (sources) is required.

Financial structure

The debt structure of an LBO is determined by the nature of the target and the investor, but a typical structure is 40–70% debt and 60–30% equity, depending on market conditions. Specifically, within equity, the PE fund will own 70–90% of the common equity of the bought-out firm, with the remainder held by management, former shareholders, if any and some key executive that advise on the deal.

Another potential source of financing for LBOs is preferred equity. Preferred equity is often attractive because its dividend payments represent a minimum return on investment, while its equity ownership component allows holders to participate in any equity upside. Preferred interest is often structured as payment-in-kind (PIK) dividends, which means any interest is paid in the form of additional shares of preferred stock.[6]

Exhibit 5 illustrates a structure with 70% debt and 30% equity. The debt structure incorporates a range of instruments with varying degrees of risk and return to suit a range of different investors. In general, higher seniority and security equates to lower risk and a lower required return (interest rate) for debt investors. Investment banks typically issue bank loans that finance the LBO through a syndicate of lenders, which can include institutional investors such as hedge funds, collateralized loan obligations (i.e., vehicles that buy loans and issue bonds to finance the purchases), or pension funds.[7] Their interest rates are floating and are computed as LIBOR plus a margin that reflects a credit premium. Such spread margins are negotiated for each debt facility, and are affected by conditions in the debt market as well as the risk associated with each loan. Typically, interest rates would be around LIBOR + 3% for the revolver and senior debt, LIBOR + 6% for the subordinated debt, and higher for mezzanine debt. These levels depend on the financial health of the target company, but also on the covenants and other terms attached to each debt instrument.

The senior bank debt will contain more stringent debt covenants relative to public debt. Loan agreements require the target company to maintain a designated credit profile based on financial ratios such as the leverage ratio, interest service coverage ratio, and debt service coverage ratio. In addition, the covenants may severely restrict the operational flexibility of the company by not allowing asset divestments, additional debt, or changes in ownership. Senior debt is thus introducing less flexibility for the PE firm by requiring varying collateral and covenant packages as well as amortization schedules; it generally covers 25–50% of the total financing needed for the deal.

The issuance of corporate bonds is an additional, more expensive source of financing if senior debt facilities have reached their limit. Because of the inherently high leverage levels associated with an LBO, these bonds are usually rated non-investment grade by rating agencies. Thus, bonds issued through an LBO are often referred to as "high-yield" or, in some cases, "junk" bonds because of the relatively higher risk associated with this type of investment. The typical term of these bonds is 6–10 years, and they usually mature after the senior debt maturity ends. They have annual interest payments and principal repayment at maturity (i.e., "a bullet payments"). This form of debt is commonly structured as 20–40% of the total deal financing structure,

---

[6] Further, PE funds may opt for "participating" preferred equity, which provides additional downside coverage during a liquidation event by guaranteeing the buyers a share of any remaining liquidation proceeds in addition to their initial investment.

[7] Institutional investors have become increasingly important lenders in the past few years. Their position as buyers of leveraged PIK bonds has also been used in the financing structure. These instruments give the issuer the option of meeting interest payments either in cash or through the issuance of new bonds.

if the company can issue bonds. The main buyers of these bonds are pension funds, insurance companies, hedge funds, or other institutional and private investors.

Exhibit 5: Example of an LBO structure

Standard and Poors' computed averages for the period 1999-2008   Seniority

					High
Debt	70%	Senior	45%	Revolver facility Senior term debt Tranche A Tranche B Tranche C Tranche D	
		Junior	20%	Subordinated debt High-yield bonds	
		Mezzanine	5%	Convertible debt	
Equity	30%			Preferred stock Common stock	
					Low

Finally, the mezzanine debt is a highly negotiated instrument between PE firms and their debt providers. It is typically tailored to meet the financing needs of the specific LBO transaction, but it is also required to meet a certain return level for its investors. As such, mezzanine debt allows for great flexibility in structuring terms. It generally has embedded warrants attached to it and provides between 0% and 10% of the total funding needed. This incremental capital comes at a cost below that of equity, with the purpose of enabling PE firms to stretch the leverage level and pay a higher purchase price when alternative capital sources are inaccessible.

The equity capital in an LBO comprises 30–60% of the total capital structure. This figure varies over time and is highly dependent on the debt market conditions and preferred level of financial risk. This equity contribution provides a cushion to lenders and bondholders in the event that the financial condition of the LBO target deteriorates. A company's management often invests equity along with the PE firm. For very large LBOs, several PE firms may team up to create a consortium of buyers (i.e., a club deal), thereby reducing the percentage of each PE firm's equity contribution. Alternatively, a particular PE firm may look for co-investors to fund the total purchase price.

Exhibit 6 shows a breakdown of the debt elements of an LBO transaction into four categories: senior, revolver, subordinated, and mezzanine debt. There may also be an existing debt element, but this is usually repaid as part of the transaction due to the change of control provisions in the existing debt facilities. The exhibit shows a summary of these main debt elements with their characteristics. The financing structure is initially determined using estimates based on the breakdown presented in Exhibit 5, the determination of debt capacity rules employed by the banks, and the lenders' requirements regarding covenants and debt service ratios. The structure is then optimized using the LBO model (as described the next chapter).

Exhibit 6: Comparison of debt instruments' characteristics

	Revolver	Senior Bank Debt	Subordinated / Junior Debt	Mezzanine Debt
Description	flexible loan which can be repaid and reborrowed at any point during the facility's life	syndicated bank debt, normally has 3-4 tranches with varying risk/return profiles	high yield public debt or non-investment grade loans	hybrid instrument - between debt and equity
Source	investment and commercial banks, sometimes institutional investors	investment and commercial banks, institutional investors	investment banks, institutional investors, hedge funds	specialist mezzanine funds
Secured	yes	yes	no	no
Seniority	highest seniority	senior, after revolver	after senior debt and revolver	after any other type of debt
Financial covenants	possibly	yes, highly restrictive	no	no
Interest rate	On the drawn down portion, rates are similar to the rates on senior debt (a benchmark such as LIBOR plus a spread)	a benchmark such as LIBOR plus a spread	high coupon rates (sometimes fixed rates)	high interest rates coupled with equity warrants
Maturity and repayment schedule	ongoing facility (usually short term less than 1 year)	maturities vary from 4 to 8 years, defined repayment schedule	longer maturity than senior debt, bullet payment at maturity date	longest maturity, bullet payment at maturity, options to convert into equity
Fees	arrangement fees and commitment fees on undrawn portion	arrangement fees, agent fees	arrangement fees	arrangement fees, monitoring fees
Purpose	to fund working capital	debt repayments, M&A transactions, debt rollover	enables the issuer to increase significantly acquisition debt	quasi equity. Offers the investor the opportunity to get a share of the upside but with more protection than equityholders

Legal structure

A certain legal structure that facilitates LBO transactions has developed over time. Exhibit 7 presents this structure, where the equity contributed by the buyout fund is invested in a new "parent company." This company then purchases a 100% stake in a "sub-holding company," which, in turn, takes over the "new company." The latter company is formed for the sole purpose of acquiring the target portfolio company and is often referred to as a "special purpose vehicle" (SPV).

This legal setup facilitates the financing structure of the LBO, where different providers of debt capital in the transaction receive different levels of protection. Senior loans are granted to the new company, which makes it easier to gain quick access to the cash flows and the collateral provided by the target company. Although they are of equal rank to term loan tranches with respect to cash flow, second-lien loans entitle their holders only to subordinated claims to collateral. They are less well secured, but they are still typically granted to the new company. Subordinated and mezzanine debt instruments are the least protected, particularly since they are generally raised by the sub-holding company. Finally, if any seller loans are received, they are usually unsecured and are received by the parent company. These loans can be regarded as a deferred claim to the payment of the purchase price.

The financing structure presented in Exhibit 7 may involve the immediate merger of the Target company into the acquisition vehicle which controls it (or, if suitable, and depending on the specifics of each transaction, sometimes it is the acquisition vehicle that is merged into the Target). This operation is also referred to as a *debt push-down* structure, because the acquisition financing (obtained at the level of the new company (purchaser) and generally financed by equity and not directly by the Target) is pushed down to the merged entity level. The use of a merger with debt push-down needs to be carefully reviewed from a tax perspective to ensure it is done in a tax neutral manner (i.e., it does not raise additional tax liabilities to the PE fund investor or the company).

Management of the target

The trend toward active ownership and operational improvement has become more prevalent as a driver for LBO value creation. The ownership of the target involves several stages:[8]

Define the strategy

This first stage draws on the due diligence process to establish the full potential of the firm. It identifies strategic opportunities and strategic decisions to assess what can be achieved in the proposed holding period.

The 100-day plan

The 100-day plan is a detailed blueprint of how that potential can be achieved, from what will be done differently on Day 1 to longer-term changes in financial and operational aspects. The strength of the PE firm over many corporates is its ability to identify the "few" activities that add the most value and focus obsessively on these activities. This avoids wasting time on low-value-added activities and enables the PE firm to exit in a short time frame and maximize returns.

Operational changes

This step includes structural changes, matching talent to key initiatives, monitoring of key metrics or performance indicators (KPIs), productivity improvements, etc. PE firms should focus on just few essential metrics that measure performance and encourage value-adding activity. Many firms over-monitor too many metrics, some of which encourage management to destroy rather than add value.

---

[8] See Gadiesh and MacArthur (2008) for more details.

Exhibit 7: The legal structure of an LBO transaction

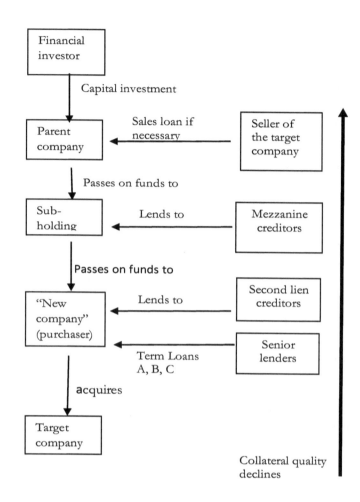

Set up incentive structures

The principal mechanism for harnessing talent is to align the investors' and managers' incentives through a rewards structure that encourages portfolio company managers to embrace the blueprint and undertake value-adding activities. This step also incentivizes management to be proactive, pre-emptive to changes in the business environment, and more agile. PE firms in LBO deals focus on earnings, margins, cash and equity returns. These performance hurdles tie to managers' compensation and are thus closely monitored and continually adjusted to provide ongoing effective incentives.

The exit

The median holding period (i.e., the time between buyout and exit) across all LBO transactions worldwide ranges from three to seven years. This holding period is relatively short because the success of a fund is measured by its IRR, which incorporates the time value of money. The decision to exit is a balance between current market conditions and additional opportunities to create future value. However, due to the time value of money and downward pressure on IRR, subsequent value creation opportunities would need to be significant to justify delaying the exit. In other words, while holding an investment longer may generate additional cash-on-cash returns, it could simultaneously reduce the IRR. A lower IRR lowers the PE firm's standing in the returns tables and could demote it from the top quartile, thus negatively affecting its ability to raise future funds.

PE firms have few key objectives to achieve before a successful exit that should fit with the initial screening and due diligence of the target:

- **increase target's EBITDA** through acquisitions, organic growth, and cost or efficiency improvements;

- **reduce target's debt** using cash flows generated during the holding period to pay down debt and increasing the equity; and

- **achieve a higher multiple valuation** through an increase in the target's size, operational improvements, improved growth opportunities and timing of the market.

We discuss exit options in more detail in a separate chapter but most LBO transactions are exited by selling the business to a strategic buyer (i.e., a *trade sale*), selling the business to another PE firm (i.e., a *secondary buyout*) or a stock listing (i.e., an *initial public offering*). In contrast to the first two options, an IPO involves only a partial monetization at the time of the transaction. An additional option is a *recapitalization*, which is not in fact an "exit" but rather, a monetization event. The company relevers and uses the debt proceeds to pay large dividends to the equity holders. This option is often utilized if the PE firm wants to partially monetize its investment and either wants to retain an upside potential in the business or cannot achieve the required value for the company due to poor market conditions.

LBO STAKEHOLDERS

Over the lifetime of an LBO, many different stakeholder groups are involved or at least are affected (Exhibit 8 shows the involvement of each stakeholder in the various phases of the typical LBO process)

Sellers/Pre-deal shareholders

The goal of pre-deal shareholders is to sell the company and potentially achieve a maximum selling price or some other objective. In the case of a private company, the ability to liquidate the otherwise illiquid shareholding in the company is the main motivation to sell. Pre-deal shareholders either actively offer their company to potential buyers, or are approached by investment banks or by PE firms. Pre-deal shareholders arrange and/or select the selling process—either a competitive auction between multiple bidders or a proprietary negotiation with only one bidder. Competitive auctions usually offer the highest potential selling price, while targeted sales usually offer a shorter and more timely process. With either process, they perform or assist with actual negotiations and bidder selection. Specialized consultancies or sell-side investment banks often support the activities of pre-deal shareholders and help put together sell-side due diligence reports for bidders.

Exhibit 8: Involvement of LBO stakeholders at different stages

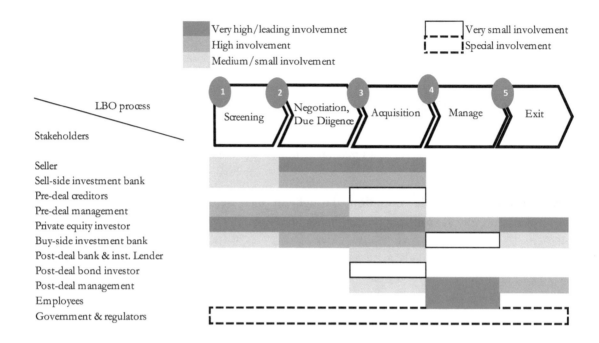

Sell-side investment banks

If the seller engages an investment bank, the bank typically markets the company to prospective buyers, sets up the selling process by conducting a (preferably) wide auction process, and acts as an adviser in the negotiations with buyers. The investment bank's goals are to make sure the deal goes through at a premium price by contacting an extensive potential buyer universe, to maximize its transaction fees, and to establish relationships with the involved parties as a potential basis for future business.

Pre-deal creditors

Pre-deal creditors do not play an active role in the LBO process, but they must ensure that existing covenants are not breached because if their covenants do not protect them, they could lose out as a result of the transaction (wealth transfer from creditors to shareholders by risk shifting); this is because pre-deal creditors receive the same return as before the LBO, but are exposed to higher credit risk due to the higher leverage.

Pre-deal management

The goals and activities of pre-deal management depend heavily on the type of deal. Depending on the involvement of the management, LBOs are classified into the following types:

- **Management buyout (MBO)**, wherein the existing management invests its own money (often a significant amount of its members' net worth) to buy the company or unit. Managers often invest alongside PE funds. They have the advantage of insider knowledge about the company. Their goal is to win the deal to be an investor in their own company and to significantly increase their net worth within a limited time frame.

- **Management buy-in (MBI)**, wherein a team of outside managers replaces the existing managers through the purchase of the company or unit. These managers invest their own money, which is, again, often a significant amount of their net worth. The goal of the existing management is typically to either stop the MBI or, if unable to do so, to negotiate a good severance package.

- **Buy-in management buyout (BIMBO)**, a combination of an MBO and MBI in which the existing management stays in place and invests its own money. However, other managers join the company and invest their own money too. If a new CEO buys in, he or she will likely take seniority over the pre-deal management team, who will now represent the second level of management.

PE firm/post-deal shareholder/financial sponsor

The PE firm is the only stakeholder that is actively involved in every phase of the LBO process. The PE firm leads the screening and due diligence, is one of the two leading stakeholders in the negotiations and deal-making process (alongside the seller), supervises and controls the management phase, and leads the efforts to find a suitable exit. The PE firm's goal is to achieve a high IRR and money multiple (while avoiding unnecessary risks), which drives the amount of carry the GPs receive on exit. Further, the PE firm's success with previous exits determines if future funds can be raised, and therefore also influences future carry options and management fees.

Buy-side investment banks

Buy-side investment banks provide a variety of services in several phases of the LBO process. Their goals are the same as those of sell-side investment banks: earn high fees and build lasting relationships to support future business. In the sourcing period, investment banks support with expertise, relationships, and resources. Afterward, they support the negotiations and might perform financial due diligence on targets. They check the target's ability to service a highly levered capital structure and validate the target's business plan using internal credit processes. Investment banks lead the construction of a financial structure tailored for the target. After the bank's internal credit team approves the financial structure, the bank can also provide a financial commitment to support the sponsor's bid and guarantee this in a sequence of documents. When using underwritten financing, investment banks guarantee to fund the debt portion of the deal. Typically, buy-side investment banks also keep in close contact with the portfolio company during the management phase and support potential refinancing rounds if necessary. Buy-side investment banks tend to support the exit at the end of the LBO process as well, where they serve as sell-side investment banks.

Post-deal banks and institutional lenders

Banks and institutional lenders act as capital providers for the debt part of the capital structure. Their goal is to invest their money with a good risk/return structure. Banks typically provide the revolver and amortizing term loans. Institutional lenders—in particular, hedge funds, collateralized loan obligations, private debt funds, pension funds, and insurance companies—typically provide longer-term loans with limited amortization. Banks and institutional lenders perform their own due diligence on the proposed transaction, and often negotiate specific covenants. So-called "bank meetings" are the platform for discussion between the portfolio company, the financial sponsor, the investment bank, and the bank or institutional lender.

Post-deal bond investors

The goal of bond investors is to achieve an attractive risk-adjusted return on their investment. Bond investors are normally high-yield mutual funds, hedge funds, pension funds, and insurance companies. They purchase high-yield bonds after attending roadshow presentations (i.e., one-on-one meetings with the company's management). Only larger LBO transactions require the issuance of bonds.

Post-deal management

In LBOs, the management of the target has high incentives, usually in the form of a large equity stake or performance-based ratchets, to align its interests with those of the PE firm. The goal of these managers is to receive high compensation and prove themselves. The management must be able to execute based on extremely ambitious plans, encourage change, and handle multiple projects at the same time. The post-deal management is highly involved in the preparation and execution of the exit phase. Additionally, certain types of managers might prefer working for a firm that has just undergone an LBO, as some managers prefer not to have the scrutiny of being in a public company or a captive division of a larger parent. Furthermore, many founders who are partly selling their company to PE funds value the ability to stay on post LBO to take advantage of a larger liquidity event without ceding operational influence or continued day-to-day involvement.

Employees

Employees do not have an active role in most phases of the LBO unless the company has unionized employees and it is based in countries where unions have a significant influence. In most cases, employees only actively take part in the management phase, when (often very ambitious) operational improvement programs are implemented. An LBO seriously affects employees if the buyer(s) plans to reduce headcount as part of its operational improvement program. However, statistical research shows that PE-owned companies do not have a higher tendency to reduce the employee headcount than non-PE owned companies (e.g., Amess and Wright, 2007).

Governments and regulators

Usually, governments and regulators are not actively involved in any of the phases of the LBO process. Yet, their laws and regulations influence each step, so their goals are very important for PE firms. The main areas of interest for governments and regulators are the effects of LBOs on employment, taxes, and strategically important industries such as defense and infrastructure. Governments around the world have varying opinions about the PE industry. Hence, PE firms must be aware of the current regulations in any country they operate in and pay close attention to the potential effect of these regulations on transactions.

VALUE CREATION IN LBOS

Measurement of LBO returns

Before discussing value creation in an LBO transaction, we present the most common measures of performance, which are the IRR and the cash-on-cash (or cash multiple) return.

Internal rate of return

The IRR measures LBO returns by factoring in the time value of money, meaning that it is important to have a relatively short holding period. However, returns are not risk adjusted, so care must be taken when comparing the performance of different LBO transactions with different levels of leverage. The IRR captures the total return during the investment period, including interim cash inflows and outflows such as dividends paid to equity holders or additional investments.

The IRR is easy to calculate using the IRR function in Excel, but users should also understand what it means. The IRR can be thought of as the discount rate that would make the net present value (NPV) zero. The equation is:

$$\sum_{n=0}^{N} \frac{CF_n}{(1+IRR)^n} = 0$$

For example, if a PE fund buys a company for $100 in Year 0 and sells it for $250 in Year 5, with no interim cash flows, the IRR return of 0.201 or 20.1% would be calculated using:

$$-100 + \frac{0}{(1+IRR)^1} + \frac{0}{(1+IRR)^2} + \frac{0}{(1+IRR)^3} + \frac{0}{(1+IRR)^4} + \frac{250}{(1+IRR)^5} = 0$$

Thus, a relatively short holding period is crucial, as a longer investment horizon puts increasing downward pressure on the IRR. In the above example, if the holding period moved to 10 years (as opposed to five), the IRR would be just 12.1% (as opposed to 20.1%).

Cash-on-cash return

The cash-on-cash (CoC) return is simply a multiple of the initial equity investment in the LBO transaction. It does not factor in the time value of money and is therefore unaffected by the investment horizon. Accordingly, CoC and IRR should be considered in combination to provide a more complete picture of the performance of a deal. In the above example where $100 was invested in Year 0 and $250 realized (after the debt repayment) in Year 5, the CoC multiple would be 2.5x.

Sources of value

Buyout funds managed by PE firms aim to achieve an IRR in excess of 20%, depending on the individual fund and its risk profile. There are three principal ways PE firms can create and capture value to achieve these return targets:

- Operational improvements
- Multiple expansion
- Financial leverage

Operational improvements

Improving the operational performance of the portfolio company is a key lever for the PE firm to create and capture value. When ignoring the effects of multiple expansion, financial leverage, and value transfers, the value created by boosting the EBITDA from $EBITDA_{before}$ (i.e., EBITDA of the company at the time of the LBO transaction or entry) to $EBITDA_{after}$ (i.e., EBITDA of the company at the time of the exit) by operational improvements can be described as

$$V_{ops} = ((EBITDA_{after} - EBITDA_{before}) * Purchase\ Multiple) / (1 + discount\ rate)^{years\ to\ exit}$$

where the purchase *multiple* is the acquisition multiple computed as the ratio of the purchase price to $EBITDA_{before}$.

As in every company, boosting the EBITDA can be achieved in three ways: (1) increasing the quantities sold, (2) increasing prices, and/or (3) cutting production and overhead costs. While all three approaches are valuable in a buyout situation, in most cases, the initial emphasis is on trimming costs and improving the efficiency of the business. The most prominent approaches to doing so include:

- cutting overhead costs;
- consolidating sourcing/suppliers;
- streamlining operations and the supply chain;
- adding new management information systems;
- controlling the working capital, especially inventory, more effectively;
- terminating low yielding investments and starting others into new markets/products;
- selling some assets;
- reducing complexity;
- investing in product development and other organic growth initiatives; and
- increasing the pace of analysis and decision making.

However, successful operational improvements are contingent on successful execution. The first step is to get the right management team—people with a track record of operational excellence—in place. In many cases, PE firms bring in project or transition teams to supplement management skill sets in key areas (i.e., those targeted for operational improvements). Often, these outside professionals are tapped to serve in interim management roles ranging from senior executives to treasury and supply chain managers. With the proper leadership structure in place, management must then focus on building support throughout the organization. Effective communication plans that allow employees to learn what the implied transaction means for them are important. The management must also determine whether the company has the right people in place that have the right capabilities and motivation to support the implementation of the strategy.

Multiple expansion

The multiple a PE firm pays when buying a company is called the "purchase or entry multiple," and the multiple the PE firm receives upon exit is called the "exit multiple." Typically, the multiples used in buyout situations are EBITDA multiples. Multiple expansion describes a situation where the exit multiple is higher than the purchase multiple. When ignoring the effects of financial leverage and operational improvements, the value captured by multiple expansion can be described as

$$V_{mult} = (EBITDA_{after} * (Exit\ multiple - Purchase\ multiple))\ /\ (1 + discount\ rate)^{years\ to\ exit}$$

Multiple expansion has two drivers with one that is highly unreliable and the other that reflects a source of value creation initiated by the managers:

- **Market timing:** The PE firm buys the company in a bearish market and sells it in a bullish market for a higher multiple. In this case, the PE firm did not create value but benefited from value arbitrage. However, consistently relying in market timing over time to generate good equity returns is not sustainable given that markets are often unpredictable.

- **Improved growth opportunities:** The multiple reflects the buyer's expectations about the future potential of a company. If the PE firm is able to improve this future potential, the multiple should increase. Multiple expansion due to improved future opportunities is much more important for PE firms that invest in fast growing companies.

As an example, Exhibit 9 illustrates a scenario in which no debt is repaid, and returns on equity are generated through an increase in enterprise value, which can be a result of operational improvements and/or multiple arbitrage.

Exhibit 9: Value creation from an increase in the multiple or EBITDA

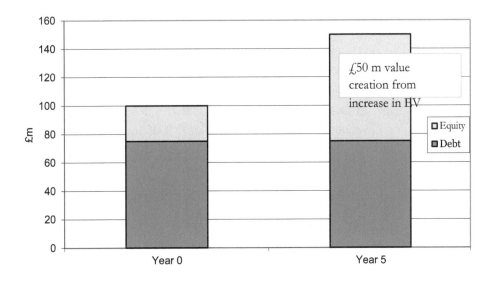

Financial leverage

Financial leverage directly affects an LBO deal's returns and risks. If the return that a company creates is higher than the cost of debt, these excess returns are captured by the PE firm and, in turn, increase its financial returns. However, it also increases the PE firm's risk. If the return of the target LBO company falls below the cost of debt, high leverage leads to lower returns for the PE firm. In terms of the effect on equity return, paying off the debt increases the firm's equity share in the target's capital structure:

$$V_{debt} = (Debt_{after} - Debt_{before}) \, / \, (1 + discount \; rate)^{years \; to \; exit}$$

The effect of debt on value creation is actually more complex. Financial leverage does affect company value by building a tax shield but also by increasing the probability of financial distress. Hence, the effect of financial leverage on the company value is positive as long as the expected tax shield exceeds the aforementioned expected cost. Exhibit 10 illustrates a scenario in which a firm is bought and sold for the same price. The firm's EBITDA is the same in Year 5, and the exit multiple is equal to the purchase multiple. The return on equity is generated through the repayment of debt from cash flows.[9]

Exhibit 10: Value creation from debt repayment (deleveraging)

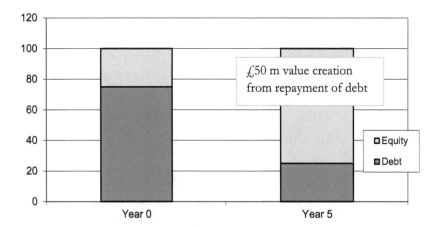

Assume that a company is bought for $100 million and sold five years later for $150 million. All free cash flows are used to service the interest on the debt, and no debt is repaid. The only difference between the two deals is the initial level of leverage. In Exhibit 11 (Scenario 1), the transaction has a low leverage of 25%, meaning an equity investment of £75 million. This deal produces an IRR of 10.8% and a return multiple of 1.7x.

In Exhibit 12 (Scenario 2), the transaction has a higher leverage of 75%, meaning an equity investment of only £25 million. The transaction is identical in all other respects. This deal produces an IRR of 24.6% and a return multiple of 3.0x.

---

[9] Note that this simplified illustration of value creation ignores the time value of money.

Exhibit 11: Leverage scenario 1 (25% debt, no debt repayment, 50% increase in firm value)

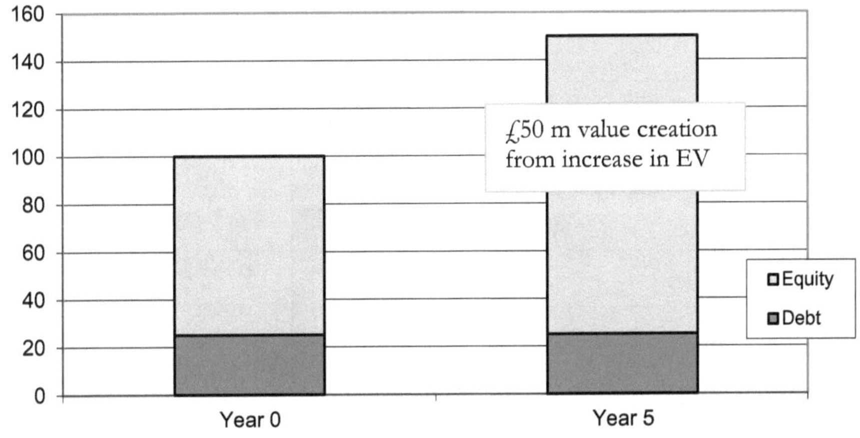

Purchase price	100
Exit Value	150
Leverage	25%
Equity Value at Entry (Year 0)	75
Equity Value at Exit (Year 5)	125
IRR	**10.80%**
COC	**1.7x**

There are two important issues to highlight when comparing these transactions. First, this comparison does not consider the potential costs of financial distress associated with higher leverage; the IRR in Scenario 2 should be adjusted for this increased risk. Second, the analysis assumes that the remaining £50 million that is not invested in Scenario 2 can be invested elsewhere for a return greater than 10.8%.

Empirical evidence

While different research undertakings attribute different proportions to the value generated by each parameter outlined above, there is a consensus that companies backed by PE firms do create value above and beyond their relevant benchmarks using all of the above parameters. According to Acharya et al. (2013) who reviewed 395 deals in Western Europe between 1991 and 2007, increased abnormal performance by PE portfolio companies is driven by stronger operating improvements in all operating measures relative to quoted peers (i.e., sales growth, EBITDA margin, and asset efficiency improvements). The evidence is consistent with the typical assertion that top, mature PE firms create economic value through operational improvements. Such improvements require skill, and the return on this skill may explain the persistent returns these funds generate for their investors.

Exhibit 12: Leverage scenario 1 (75% debt, no debt repayment, 50% increase in firm value)

Purchase price	100
Exit Value	150
Leverage	75%
Equity Value at Entry (Year 0)	25
Equity Value at Exit (Year 5)	75
IRR	**24.60%**
COC	**3.0x**

The authors also find combinations of value creation strategies and partner backgrounds that correlate with deal-level abnormal performance. Deal partners with a strong operational background (e.g., ex-consultants or ex-industry managers) generate significantly higher outperformance in "organic" deals. In other words, partners who have worked as managers in the industry or management consultants before joining a PE house appear to have accumulated skills to improve a company internally. In contrast, partners with a background in finance (e.g., ex-bankers or ex-accountants) more successfully follow an M&A-driven, "inorganic" strategy.

Consistent with the findings above, Achleitner et al (2010), who studied LBO transactions in Europe, find that two-thirds of value creation can be attributed to operational and market effects, while the remaining third is due to the leverage effect. Further, when comparing smaller to larger deals (i.e., enterprise value under and over €100 million), the leverage effect is higher for larger deals, while revenue growth plays a more important role in smaller deals. When it comes to multiple expansion, different interpretations are possible: (i) PE sponsors may simply have better market timing skills; (ii) PE sponsors may have a better sense of the improved future prospects of the company; and/or (iii) PE sellers could have better negotiation capabilities.

The differentiators of the PE approach

Unlike strategic buyers, PE firms cannot benefit from synergies unless they own similar companies in their portfolios. Moreover, the levers that PE firms use (in particular, operational improvements, high leverage, and possibly multiple expansion) are also available to the previous management. So why do top PE firms achieve relatively high returns? Do they just exploit bad management, the so-called "management arbitrage"?

While management arbitrage is indeed one reason that PE firms may achieve high returns, there are several more elements that characterize the *PE approach of managing* and underlie the success of the industry: (i) the PE governance model, (ii) PE firms' access to extraordinary talent, (iii) PE firms' knowledge and experience, and (iv) avoidance of corporate infrastructure costs.

PE governance model

The PE governance model promotes a value creation mindset, high incentives, and alignment of stakeholder interests. To achieve these aims, PE firms incentivize portfolio company managers with equity stakes and ratchets. Given that a large proportion of managers' actual or potential net worth is tied to the company's success, and the liquidity of this net worth is tied to a successful exit, managers' interests are well aligned and focused on economic value creation. PE firms often expand the system of high incentives to board members as well, thereby creating additional value (see Braun and Latham, 2007). Managers and board members are expected to also invest some of their own funds in the transaction, and their compensation is closely linked to the performance of the company. The measurement of performance is often based on cash metrics rather than on measures skewed by accounting practices or capital market trends, and is determined at the portfolio company level.

Theses focused incentives around value appreciation eliminate some non-value-adding management practices, especially in mature companies with strong disposable cash flows but without value-creating investment opportunities. Managers of these firms still tend to invest instead of paying dividends to shareholders. However, in LBO transactions, the high leverage leading to large interest and principal payments can force management to improve performance and operating efficiency instead of merely investing for the sake of investing. This "discipline of debt" can force management to focus on certain initiatives such as divesting non-core businesses, downsizing, cost cutting, or investing in technological upgrades that might otherwise be postponed or rejected outright

Beyond the above considerations, CEOs of PE firm portfolio companies are only required to report to their own board of directors. In the case of public-to-private deals, the target's management is freed from quarterly reporting duties and from the pressure of meeting analysts' short-term expectations. In the case of business unit carve-outs, the target's management is freed from the limitations imposed by headquarters, the resource drain, and the costs of reporting. Decision making is also far nimbler without convoluted bureaucratic processes to secure approval from headquarters.

There are a few basic interdependent principles known to help PE-backed firms succeed: (1) direct lines of communication between owners and top management; (2) considerable managerial autonomy under normal circumstances; and (3) willingness by the PE owners to step in and direct operations to correct unexpected problems. PE firms generally react quickly to under-performing management teams by replacing selective positions or the entire senior management team if necessary.

PE firms' access to talent

PE firms have access to highly talented employees (Gadiesh and MacArthur, 2008). Many legendary managers, such as former GE CEO Jack Welch, go on to work for PE firms. Furthermore, PE firms are among the most desirable employers for the top students from elite universities and business schools around the world due to the type of work and the compensation structures they offer. GPs in PE firms are principals, not agents, which is desirable for most high achievers, and GPs' work is diversified and interesting, covering all phases of an LBO deal and allowing them to concentrate on multiple companies at once.

Given that the bulk of PE firms' income comes from (or at least should come from) the carry (usually 20% of the appreciation of the investors' money above a specified hurdle rate), GPs are usually paid depending on the size of this carry. This structure enables GPs in PE firms to obtain very high compensation on large and successful deals.

PE firms' knowledge and experience

Over time, PE professionals become experts in change and optimization since this is their main activity once they acquire a portfolio company. By focusing the investments in a limited number of core industries, they create a platform with skills that take advantage of the benefits of portfolio relatedness. Relatedness fosters PE firms' ability to govern and support management, as well as to realize selected synergies within their investment portfolios. Leveraging the knowledge from coexisting and prior engagements gives a PE firm a stronger position in the M&A market and enables it to exercise more effective control over management decisions.

At the same time, a strong industry background can support a firm in the origination and initial negotiation of a transaction by creating trust more easily than with less informed investors, as well as by building a reputation as an investor in relevant industry networks. This important given that an increasing share of investments comes through established networks in particular industries.

Moreover, a stronghold in a selected number of industries allows a PE firm to surround itself with a group of highly skilled and experienced advisers with long-standing track records in those industries.

PE firms not only capitalize on knowledge from portfolio companies, but they have also started to exploit their scale. The proceeds of scale are captured by consolidating financial engineering, access to capital markets, and purchasing of selected core and non-core components on a level above individual portfolio companies. Some also provide an informal platform for portfolio companies to engage bilaterally and actively link senior executives of relevant firms to determine cooperation potential.

Minimization of infrastructure costs

PE firms implement their ownership models without establishing large 'corporate type' vehicles to manage their investment portfolios. The firms offer only a limited selection of services to portfolio companies, such as support in financing, strategic and operating decisions, avoiding the downside of an expensive corporate infrastructure. They also rely more on informal governance and intervention approaches, providing portfolio companies with a large degree of independence, and eliminating any opportunity for cross-subsidization of individual businesses.

VALUE DESTRUCTION IN LBOS

As a result of high leverage, poor management oversight, and changing industry conditions, defaults are possible. Nevertheless, according to Moody's, default rates are relatively similar for B-rated issuers owned by private equity firms and issuers that are not (18.8% vs. 18.7%). B rated companies comprise approximately two-thirds of all LBO issuers.

Although recovery rates were similar across LBOs and non-LBOs, a differentiating characteristic among the recovery rates resided within bank debt. Moody's research identified that bank debtholders recovered less in LBO transactions compared to non-LBO transactions, primarily due to the lower ratio of subordinated or junior debt to total debt in LBO transactions, which bears losses first. As a result of this nuance in LBOs and the sponsor's incentive to maintain favorable relationships with its banks, sponsors are likely to pursue prepackaged bankruptcies or distressed exchanges since these ultimately result in higher recovery rates for senior creditors.

In addition, the cash flow preservation to service the debt may lead to squeezed capital expenditure levels. In the long-run, postponed maintenance and investments are likely to lead to asset obsolescence, potentially yielding efficiency disadvantages and a weakened competitive position. This in turn will negatively impact firm value. The high absolute debt burden can also eventually prevent portfolio companies from investing in promising long-term projects, which the company would otherwise have undertaken (if not leveraged). Such passiveness might again result in competitive disadvantages resulting from delayed strategic repositioning, thereby also causing value destruction. This is not in the best interests of the PE fund in light of its limited investment horizon.

CONCLUSION

In the past, the media have often taken a negative view on leveraged PE transactions, perceiving them as coming at the expense of employees who suffer job cuts and salary reductions. However, nowadays, the benefits of these transactions to LBO targets are largely accepted, given the documented performance due to financial, operational and corporate governance practices implemented by PE firms. PE firms often target under-performing companies that can be transformed and where they can foster rapid corporate restructuring –enhancing productivity.

LBO transactions have moved into a mature phase. The deal multiples are bid up in the industries and companies where the activity is concentrated. The strong growth of capital available to buyout funds resulting from strong investor demand, together with readily available and cheap leverage provided by banks and other institutional investors, have increased the pressure for PE fund managers to find good new deals. As a result, the returns on LBO deals have been pushed down forcing managers need to become more creative to differentiate themselves in the marketplace.

REFERENCES

Acharya, V. V., O. F. Gottschalg, M. Hahn and C. Kehoe (2013) "Corporate governance and value creation: Evidence from private equity," *Review of Financial Studies* 26, 368–402.

Achleitner, A. K., R. Braun, N. Engel, C. Figge and F. Tappeiner (2010) "Value Creation Drivers in Private Equity Buyouts: Empirical Evidence from Europe". *Journal of Private Equity* 13, 17–27.

Amess, K. and M. Wright (2007) "The wage and employment effects of LBOs in the UK," *International Journal Economics of Business*, 14(2), 179–195.

Braun, M. R. and S. F. Latham (2007) "The governance of going private transactions: The leveraged buyout board of directors as a distinctive source of value," *Management Decision*, 45(5) 866–882.

Gadiesh, O. and H. MacArthur (2008) "Lessons from private equity any company can use," Harvard Business School Press, Boston.

Olsen, J., S. Gagliano, F. Wainwright and C. Blaydon. (2003) Note on Leveraged Buyouts, Tuck School of Business at Dartmouth Center for Private Equity and Entrepreneurship, Case d5-0004.

Roxburgh, C., S. Lund, M. Lippert, O. L. White and Y. Zhao (2009) "The New Power Brokers: How Oil, Asia, Hedge Funds, and Private Equity Are Faring the Financial Crisis", McKinsey Global Institute, San Francisco, CA.

Teten, D. and C. Farmer. 2010 "Where Are the Deals? Private Equity and Venture Capital Funds' Best Practices in Sourcing New Investments." *Journal of Private Equity* 14(1): 32–52.

In his own words: James Almond, Partner, Duke Street

Creating value beyond the returns generated through financial gearing has become increasingly important since the financial crisis of 2008. That said, the calculation and application of the right amount of debt to optimize the capital structure—as well as the debt provider's identity and its terms—are still key aspects of the LBO in current times. Each type of debt instrument tends to have different features and covenants, which need consideration when making decisions. Therefore, determining the level of debt and which sort to use is an important part of deal-making.

When considering the level of debt to apply, one must consider quantitative factors such as minimizing the cost of capital, while also bearing in mind more subjective considerations: Will there be significant operational change or restructuring in the first 18 months? Will there be another acquisition shortly after the first? Will the business plan consume cash in the early stages (e.g., capex), which may need funding through additional debt? These factors can result in a lower level of initial leverage. When making the debt decision, we perform a sensitivity analysis to see how much debt the business can service in various downside scenarios. We need to be comfortable that the business can service its debt through the economic cycle.

Increasingly, we seek to add value *pre-acquisition* by focusing on more complex deals; this might mean, for example, buying two family-owned businesses that complement each other and putting them together, buying out a business with a complex shareholding structure, or lining up target acquisitions prior to the LBO in order to complete add-ons quickly after buying the main target company. All of these activities can lead to value creation simply by being able to buy a business at a reasonable entry price.

It is also crucial to add value *during ownership* by creating an improved business. We like to create a business which is of interest to a trade buyer as trade buyers often pay the highest price, due to the potential strategic and synergistic value they can extract from acquiring an efficient and professionally run, growing business in their own sector. The operational change we apply can include improving efficiencies, implementing sales effectiveness programs, diversifying revenue streams, or acquiring smaller businesses in the same sector, typically at lower multiples of EBITDA.

During ownership, we also like to see a reduction in net debt. Depending on the debt profile and period of ownership, sometimes we can refinance the business to lever it again to make a distribution to shareholders. While the use of debt can magnify returns, a reduction in net debt tends to contribute less to the overall returns in our deals than the other factors listed above.

7 Leveraged Buyout Modeling

Analytics will never tell you everything you want to know.
Albert Einstein

INTRODUCTION

When a private equity (PE) firm structures a leveraged buyout (LBO) transaction, it must offer an equity purchase price that is acceptable to the seller and generate a minimum expected return with a manageable level of risk. In order to meet these conditions, the LBO model must take into consideration three key factors:

- **The purchase price:** This is often compared with previous recent buyout transactions based on EBITDA multiples specific to the target's industry. In public-to-private transactions, the premium over the market price is compared with premiums in prior mergers and acquisitions transactions. In the case of a competitive bid, the purchase price is benchmarked relative to other bids.

- **The IRR and money multiple:** These metrics are usually computed separately for the PE fund but also for the other investors in the deal. Some investors contribute equity while others invest through both equity and debt instruments.

- **Credit metrics:** These metrics are reflected in the financial covenants demanded by the lenders that finance the transaction and are often given by current conditions in the debt market. The typical credit metrics used by lenders are the interest coverage ratio (ICR), the debt-service coverage ratio (DSCR), the debt to EBITDA ratio, and the fixed charge coverage ratio. The PE firm needs to ensure that the covenants will be met with adequate headroom.

An LBO deal has multiple other dimensions such as the amount of leverage, the choice of debt instruments, the choice of equity instruments, or the maturity of debt instruments. These degrees of freedom influence the output measures of an LBO model in complex ways. Further, given the importance of operational improvements, it is imperative that multiple growth scenarios over the ownership period of the target are modeled and quantified. An LBO model is created by taking all of the pertinent information and dependencies into consideration via a set of inter-related Excel spreadsheets that capture a significant amount of financial information about the target (at the time of the transaction but also projected over the holding period), the financing structure of the transaction and the return expectations of the PE firm. Such a model enables the private equity professionals to test the consequences of different decisions and assumptions allowing them to make more informed bids on the target.

Without an LBO model, it would be nearly impossible to understand all of the consequences of a given set of decisions and assumptions that are necessary to make an informed bid. However, it is important to highlight that the LBO model is merely a tool that allows PE professionals to understand the sensitivity of the returns expected on a deal to different assumptions. The quality of the data imputed in the model is as important as the model itself. The due diligence process should focus on verifying the quality of the financial information used.

The LBO modeling process covers two phases (see Exhibit 1):

Exhibit 1: The big picture that characterizes an Excel based LBO model

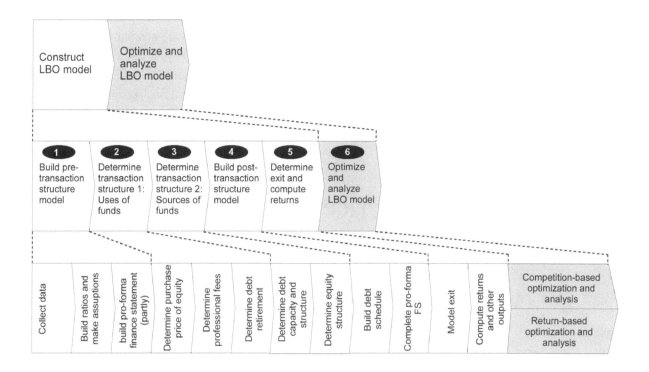

- **Construction of the LBO model:** Initially, a preliminary Excel file must be created. This phase contains multiple working steps which include: locating historic financial statements, formatting them in an appropriate way, and calculating relevant ratios based on these statements. The PE firm must make some initial assumptions to forecast the financial performance of the target (e.g., the future growth rate of a specific industry); these assumptions are reviewed and optimized in the next phase. Additional steps include assumptions about the purchasing price, the structure of the debt package and payment terms and a computation of preliminary returns given these assumptions. After this initial model construction, the PE firm has an Excel file that automatically calculates the relevant output measures based on the available information and dependencies, assumptions, and decisions.

- **Optimization and analysis of the LBO model:** The decisions are the degrees of freedom that the PE firm has to optimize the deal structure. In this phase, the PE firm analyzes output measures (e.g., expected returns, purchase price) and considers which decisions it can change to improve these measures and therefore optimize the overall deal structure and returns. As much as possible, the assumptions made must be defendable and based on facts. Assumptions are typically based on inherent industry knowledge that the PE executives might have, extensive market research, and findings from due diligence. The PE firm will also receive a set of forecasting assumptions and projections from the sell-side banks that often advise on the process; they must review these assumptions and assess whether their own assumptions are defensible. A sensitivity analysis should be done to test the effect of changes in the assumptions on returns, considering the large amount of input variables available (e.g., the purchase price or entry multiple, the debt structure, the equity structure, working capital and capex needs, sales growth rates, operational margins, etc.). The PE firm must analyze the output measures or returns of the model and evaluate whether it has to change these decisions. An efficient model will be flexible allowing the user to toggle between several deal structures and assumptions quickly.

As highlighted in Exhibit 1, the two LBO modeling phases can be broken down into six steps; these can be further broken down into thirteen steps. We describe each of the six main steps in separate sections below. Furthermore, we visualize these steps using an LBO Excel model template that we created using real-world data from Toys "R" Us, Inc. (Toys R Us). We have recreated the 2005 LBO of Toys R Us, which was bought by a consortium led by Bain Capital and KKR & Co. Inc. The consortium invested $1.3 billion of new equity to complete the $6.6 billion LBO. In our analysis, we have used historic financial data from the publicly available annual reports for 2001–2004. Toys R Us ended up filing for bankruptcy in September 2017. By the summer of 2018, the iconic American toy store closed almost all 800 of its stores. While Toys R Us was still pulling close to $800 million annually as of 2017, it could not compete with a giant like Amazon.

BUILD A PRE-TRANSACTION STRUCTURE MODEL

A pre-transaction structure model is a set of pro forma financial statements forecasting the next 7–10 years of the target.[1] These statements contain assumptions about future developments, including the expected effects of operational improvement levers that the PE firm plans to pull. However, the pre-transaction structure model does not reflect the effects of the LBO transaction —in particular, the effects of the finance structure and debt payment schedule. Hence, the pro forma financial statements that make up the pre-transaction structure model have "gaps" to will be filled later. Nevertheless, it is important to complete the structure and ensure the model balances at this point. The forecasted financial statements for Toys R Us are shown in Exhibits 2–4.

The pre-transaction structure model is built from historic financial statements and its forecasts are based on historical ratios, expert opinions, and findings from the due diligence process. It reflects the PE firm's expectations about the future operational development of the target company after the completion of the LBO transaction. Given the importance of operational improvements to generate high returns, a considerable amount of resources is devoted to the due diligence process and the pre-transaction structure model.

To create the pre-transaction structure model, the PE firms typically follow the following three sub-steps:

Step 1: Collect data

As a basis for the forecasts, information about the target's market, industry, and other macroeconomic conditions must be collected. The most important data are the historic (and audited) income statements of the company over the previous three to four years. While this data is easily accessible for public companies, it is more limited for private companies. In a friendly deal, the target company will prepare an information

---

[1] The typical time horizon of the forecast model should match the longest maturity of utilized debt instruments; usually, this is 7–10 years.

memorandum that provides historic financial statements, financial forecasts, and other information and analysis to inform potential buyers (often this is part of a sell-side due diligence report compiled by an independent third party such an accounting firm). In an auction deal process, the seller and its advisors will often provide a virtual data room that supplies historical financials, a forecast model, and other relevant key performance indicator data. Documents prepared by the seller must be treated with caution given the obvious bias towards optimistic forecasts to maximize the price; the due diligence process should verify and challenge seller's forecasts.

Step 2: Build ratios and make assumptions

Typically, PE firms calculate financial and operational ratios, and then analyze the developments of these ratios over the last three-five years. These ratios are often benchmarked to ratios of similar companies in the same industry and geography. Key ratios are calculated in the tinted boxes at the bottom of the financial statements in Exhibits 2–4. The ratios form the basis for assumptions to create the future forecasts used to build the pro forma financial statements.

These assumptions are influenced by the specific operational improvement initiatives that a PE firm plans to launch. The PE firm decides which initiatives are appropriate for the target and models the effects of these initiatives by including different operating scenarios in the forecasts. The forecasting assumption sheet for the Toys R Us model is shown in Exhibit 5. Usually, PE firms forecast several scenarios (e.g., an *expected* or *base scenario*, a *pessimistic scenario*, an *optimistic scenario*, a *management scenario*, a *sponsor scenario*). Each of these scenarios uses expected forecasts from the perspective and information set available to different players in the deal. A pessimistic scenario might be one that lenders are looking at to protect their downside risks while a management scenario might reflect the expectations of the management of the target.

Step 3: Build pro forma financial statements ready to incorporate the transaction structure

Based on forecasted financial ratios, PE firms create pro forma financial statements for the next 7–10 years (the duration should match the debt instrument with the longest maturity). In general, all three financial statements (income statement, balance sheet, and cash flow statements) are forecasted. Forecasting a full balance sheet is optional as not all balance sheet elements are required to complete an LBO model. For example, fixed asset and working capital schedules are sufficient since depreciation, capex, and working capital impact the cash flows available for debt servicing; these cash flows are the most important metric in an LBO, given the emphasis on cash flow-based returns.

At this point, the financial statements are incomplete, as the transaction structure of the deal needs to be incorporated. Hence, the pro forma financial statements in the pre-transaction structure model will have certain gaps (as shown by the white boxes in Exhibits 2–4). The gaps indicate where and at what point the inputs to these sections should be obtained.

Exhibit 2: TOYS R US pre-transaction income statement

Toys "R" Us LBO Model - Income Statement ($m)

	Hist. 2001	Hist. 2002	Hist. 2003	Hist. 2004	1 Proj. 2005	2 Proj. 2006	3 Proj. 2007	4 Proj. 2008	5 Proj. 2009	6 Proj. 2010	7 Proj. 2011	8 Proj. 2012	9 Proj. 2013	10 Proj. 2014
Sales	11,332.0	11,019.0	11,305.0	11,320.0	11,546.4	11,777.3	12,012.9	12,253.1	12,498.2	12,748.2	13,003.1	13,263.2	13,528.4	13,799.0
% growth	–	(2.8%)	2.6%	0.1%	2.0%	2.0%	2.0%	2.0%	2.0%	2.0%	2.0%	2.0%	2.0%	2.0%
Cost of Goods Sold	7,815.0	7,604.0	7,799.0	7,646.0	7,793.8	7,949.7	8,108.7	8,270.9	8,436.3	8,605.0	8,777.1	8,952.6	9,131.7	9,314.3
Gross Profit	3,517.0	3,415.0	3,506.0	3,674.0	3,752.6	3,827.6	3,904.2	3,982.3	4,061.9	4,143.2	4,226.0	4,310.5	4,396.7	4,484.7
% margin	31.0%	31.0%	31.0%	32.5%	32.5%	32.5%	32.5%	32.5%	32.5%	32.5%	32.5%	32.5%	32.5%	32.5%
Selling, General & Administrative	2,801.0	2,721.0	2,724.0	3,026.0	2,886.6	2,944.3	3,003.2	3,063.3	3,124.5	3,187.0	3,250.8	3,315.8	3,382.1	3,449.8
% sales	24.7%	24.7%	24.1%	26.7%	25.0%	25.0%	25.0%	25.0%	25.0%	25.0%	25.0%	25.0%	25.0%	25.0%
Other Expense / (Income)	–	186.0	–	63.0	115.5	117.8	120.1	122.5	125.0	127.5	130.0	132.6	135.3	138.0
EBITDA	716.0	508.0	782.0	585.0	750.5	765.5	780.8	796.5	812.4	828.6	845.2	862.1	879.3	896.9
% margin	6.3%	4.6%	6.9%	5.2%	6.5%	6.5%	6.5%	6.5%	6.5%	6.5%	6.5%	6.5%	6.5%	6.5%
Depreciation & Amortization	290.0	308.0	339.0	368.0	288.7	294.4	300.3	306.3	312.5	318.7	325.1	331.6	338.2	345.0
EBIT	426.0	200.0	443.0	217.0	461.9	471.1	480.5	490.1	499.9	509.9	520.1	530.5	541.1	552.0
% margin	3.8%	1.8%	3.9%	1.9%	4.0%	4.0%	4.0%	4.0%	4.0%	4.0%	4.0%	4.0%	4.0%	4.0%
Interest Expense														
Existing Debt														
Revolving Credit Facility														
Senior Long Term Debt														
Subordinated Debt (Mezz.)														
Commitment Fee on Unused Revolver														
Agent Fees														
Cash Interest Expense														
Amortisation of Deferred Financing Fees														
Total Interest Expense														
Interest income														
Net Interest Expense														
EBT (Earnings Before Tax)					461.9	471.1	480.5	490.1	499.9	509.9	520.1	530.5	541.1	552.0
Income Tax Expense					175.5	179.0	182.6	186.2	190.0	193.8	197.6	201.6	205.6	209.7
Net Income					286.4	292.1	297.9	303.9	310.0	316.2	322.5	328.9	335.5	342.2
% margin					2.5%	2.5%	2.5%	2.5%	2.5%	2.5%	2.5%	2.5%	2.5%	2.5%

Interest Expense section: LEAVE BLANK IN STEP 1 — TO BE COMPLETED IN STEP 4 - LINKED FROM FINANCE STRUCTURE AND DEBT SCHEDULE

Income Statement Assumptions

	Hist. 2001	Hist. 2002	Hist. 2003	Hist. 2004	2005	2006	2007	2008	2009	2010	2011	2012	2013	2014
Sales (% YoY growth)	–	(2.8%)	2.6%	0.1%	2.0%	2.0%	2.0%	2.0%	2.0%	2.0%	2.0%	2.0%	2.0%	2.0%
Cost of Goods Sold (% margin)	69.0%	69.0%	69.0%	67.5%	67.5%	67.5%	67.5%	67.5%	67.5%	67.5%	67.5%	67.5%	67.5%	67.5%
SG&A (% sales)	24.7%	24.7%	24.1%	26.7%	25.0%	25.0%	25.0%	25.0%	25.0%	25.0%	25.0%	25.0%	25.0%	25.0%
Other Expense / (Income) (% of sales)	–	1.7%	–	0.6%	1.0%	1.0%	1.0%	1.0%	1.0%	1.0%	1.0%	1.0%	1.0%	1.0%
Depreciation & Amortization (% of sales)	2.6%	2.8%	3.0%	3.3%	2.5%	2.5%	2.5%	2.5%	2.5%	2.5%	2.5%	2.5%	2.5%	2.5%
Interest Income				3.0%	4.0%	4.0%	4.0%	4.0%	4.0%	4.0%	4.0%	4.0%	4.0%	4.0%
Tax Rate					38.0%	38.0%	38.0%	38.0%	38.0%	38.0%	38.0%	38.0%	38.0%	38.0%

Exhibit 3: TOYS R US pre-transaction balance sheet

Toys "R" Us LBO Model - Balance Sheet ($m)

	Actual 2004	Incr/(Decr)	Pro Forma 2004	1 2005	2 2006	3 2007	4 2008	5 2009	6 2010	7 2011	8 2012	9 2013	10 2014
								Projection Period					
Cash and Cash Equivalents	2,003.0		2,003.0	2,326.1	2,679.4	3,039.8	3,407.4	3,782.3	4,164.7	4,554.8	4,952.7	5,358.5	5,772.5
Accounts Receivable	146.0		146.0	158.2	161.3	164.6	167.9	171.2	174.6	178.1	181.7	185.3	189.0
Inventory	2,094.0		2,094.0	2,135.3	2,178.0	2,221.6	2,266.0	2,311.3	2,357.5	2,404.7	2,452.8	2,501.8	2,551.9
Prepaid Expenses	486.0		486.0	461.9	471.1	480.5	490.1	499.9	509.9	520.1	530.5	541.1	552.0
Total Current Assets	**4,729.0**		**4,729.0**	**5,081.4**	**5,489.9**	**5,906.4**	**6,331.4**	**6,764.8**	**7,206.8**	**7,657.8**	**8,117.7**	**8,586.8**	**9,065.4**
PPE Beginning Balance	-		-	4,439.0	4,381.3	4,322.4	4,262.3	4,201.1	4,138.6	4,074.8	4,009.8	3,943.5	3,875.8
CapEx	-		-	230.9	235.5	240.3	245.1	250.0	255.0	260.1	265.3	270.6	276.0
Depreciation and Amortisation	-		-	(288.7)	(294.4)	(300.3)	(306.3)	(312.5)	(318.7)	(325.1)	(331.6)	(338.2)	(345.0)
PPE Ending Balance	4,439.0		4,439.0	4,381.3	4,322.4	4,262.3	4,201.1	4,138.6	4,074.8	4,009.8	3,943.5	3,875.8	3,806.9
Goodwill and Intangible Assets	348.0		348.0	348.0	348.0	348.0	348.0	348.0	348.0	348.0	348.0	348.0	348.0
Other Assets	749.0		749.0	749.0	749.0	749.0	749.0	749.0	749.0	749.0	749.0	749.0	749.0
Deferred Financing Fees	-		-										
Total Assets	**10,265.0**		**10,265.0**	**10,559.7**	**10,909.2**	**11,265.8**	**11,629.4**	**12,000.3**	**12,378.7**	**12,764.6**	**13,158.2**	**13,559.7**	**13,969.2**
Accounts Payable	1,022.0		1,022.0	1,024.9	1,045.4	1,066.3	1,087.7	1,109.4	1,131.6	1,154.2	1,177.3	1,200.9	1,224.9
Accrued Liabilities	866.0		866.0	923.7	942.2	961.0	980.3	999.9	1,019.9	1,040.2	1,061.1	1,082.3	1,103.9
Other Current Liabilities	976.0		976.0	923.7	942.2	961.0	980.3	999.9	1,019.9	1,040.2	1,061.1	1,082.3	1,103.9
Total Current Liabilities	**2,864.0**		**2,864.0**	**2,872.4**	**2,929.8**	**2,988.4**	**3,048.2**	**3,109.1**	**3,171.3**	**3,234.7**	**3,299.4**	**3,365.4**	**3,432.7**
Existing Debt	2,349.0		2,349.0	2,349.0	2,349.0	2,349.0	2,349.0	2,349.0	2,349.0	2,349.0	2,349.0	2,349.0	2,349.0
Revolving Credit Facility													
Senior Long Term Debt													
Subordinated Debt (Mezz)													
Other Debt													
Other LT Liabilities	1,078.0		1,078.0	1,078.0	1,078.0	1,078.0	1,078.0	1,078.0	1,078.0	1,078.0	1,078.0	1,078.0	1,078.0
Total Liabilities	**6,291.0**		**6,291.0**	**6,299.4**	**6,356.8**	**6,415.4**	**6,475.2**	**6,536.1**	**6,598.3**	**6,661.7**	**6,726.4**	**6,792.4**	**6,859.7**
Shareholders' Equity	3,974.0		3,974.0	4,260.4	4,552.4	4,850.3	5,154.2	5,464.2	5,780.3	6,102.8	6,431.7	6,767.2	7,109.5
Total Shareholders' Equity	**3,974.0**		**3,974.0**	**4,260.4**	**4,552.4**	**4,850.3**	**5,154.2**	**5,464.2**	**5,780.3**	**6,102.8**	**6,431.7**	**6,767.2**	**7,109.5**
Total Liabilities and Equity	**10,265.0**		**10,265.0**	**10,559.7**	**10,909.2**	**11,265.8**	**11,629.4**	**12,000.3**	**12,378.7**	**12,764.6**	**13,158.2**	**13,559.7**	**13,969.2**
Balance Check	0.000		0.000	0.000	0.000	0.000	0.000	0.000	0.000	0.000	0.000	0.000	0.000
Net Working Capital	(138.0)		(138.0)	(117.0)	(119.4)	(121.8)	(124.2)	(126.7)	(129.2)	(131.8)	(134.4)	(137.1)	(139.9)
(Increase)/Decrease in Net Working Capital				(21.0)	2.3	2.4	2.4	2.5	2.5	2.6	2.6	2.7	2.7
Balance Sheet Assumptions													
Current Assets													
Days Sales Outstanding (DSO)	4.7		4.7	5.0	5.0	5.0	5.0	5.0	5.0	5.0	5.0	5.0	5.0
Days Inventory Held (DIH)	100.0		100.0	100.0	100.0	100.0	100.0	100.0	100.0	100.0	100.0	100.0	100.0
Prepaid and Other Current Assets (% of sales)	4.3%		4.3%	4.0%	4.0%	4.0%	4.0%	4.0%	4.0%	4.0%	4.0%	4.0%	4.0%
Current Liabilities													
Days Payable Outstanding (DPO)	48.8		48.8	48.0	48.0	48.0	48.0	48.0	48.0	48.0	48.0	48.0	48.0
Accrued Liabilities (% of sales)	7.7%		7.7%	8.0%	8.0%	8.0%	8.0%	8.0%	8.0%	8.0%	8.0%	8.0%	8.0%
Other Current Liabilities (% of sales)	8.6%		8.6%	8.0%	8.0%	8.0%	8.0%	8.0%	8.0%	8.0%	8.0%	8.0%	8.0%

Annotations in the *Incr/(Decr)* column:
- LEAVE BLANK IN STEP 1
- TO BE COMPLETED IN STEP 3: FOLLOWING CONSTRUCTION OF SOURCES AND USES OF FUNDS
- LEAVE BLANK IN STEP 1 - TO BE COMPLETED IN STEP 4: LINKED FROM DEBT SCHEDULE

Exhibit 4: TOYS R US pre-transaction cash flow statement

Toys "R" Us LBO Model - Cash Flow Statement ($m)

	1	2	3	4	5	6	7	8	9	10
	Proj. 2005	Proj. 2006	Proj. 2007	Proj. 2008	Proj. 2009	Proj. 2010	Proj. 2011	Proj. 2012	Proj. 2013	Proj. 2014
Operating Activities										
Net Income	286.4	292.1	297.9	303.9	310.0	316.2	322.5	328.9	335.5	342.2
Depreciation & Amortization	288.7	294.4	300.3	306.3	312.5	318.7	325.1	331.6	338.2	345.0
Amortisation of Deferred Financing Fees	--	--	--	--	--	--	--	--	--	--
Sub Total	575.0	586.5	598.2	610.2	622.4	634.9	647.6	660.5	673.7	687.2
Changes in Working Capital Items										
Accounts Receivable (DSO)	(12.2)	(3.2)	(3.2)	(3.3)	(3.4)	(3.4)	(3.5)	(3.6)	(3.6)	(3.7)
Inventory (DIH)	(41.3)	(42.7)	(43.6)	(44.4)	(45.3)	(46.2)	(47.2)	(48.1)	(49.1)	(50.0)
Prepaid Expenses	24.1	(9.2)	(9.4)	(9.6)	(9.8)	(10.0)	(10.2)	(10.4)	(10.6)	(10.8)
Accounts Payable (DPO)	2.9	20.5	20.9	21.3	21.8	22.2	22.6	23.1	23.5	24.0
Accrued Liabilities	57.7	18.5	18.8	19.2	19.6	20.0	20.4	20.8	21.2	21.6
Other Current Liabilities	(52.3)	18.5	18.8	19.2	19.6	20.0	20.4	20.8	21.2	21.6
(Inc.) / Dec. in Net Working Capital	(21.0)	2.3	2.4	2.4	2.5	2.5	2.6	2.6	2.7	2.7
Cash Flow from Operating Activities	554.1	588.9	600.6	612.6	624.9	637.4	650.1	663.1	676.4	689.9
Investing Activities										
Capital Expenditures	(230.9)	(235.5)	(240.3)	(245.1)	(250.0)	(255.0)	(260.1)	(265.3)	(270.6)	(276.0)
Other Investing Activities	--	--	--	--	--	--	--	--	--	--
Cash Flow from Investing Activities	(230.9)	(235.5)	(240.3)	(245.1)	(250.0)	(255.0)	(260.1)	(265.3)	(270.6)	(276.0)
Free Cash Flows	323.1	353.3	360.4	367.6	374.9	382.4	390.1	397.9	405.8	414.0
Financing Activities										
Existing Debt					LEAVE BLANK IN STEP 1 -					
Revolving Credit Facility					TO BE COMPLETED IN STEP 4:					
Senior Long Term Debt					LINKED FROM FINANCING					
Subordinated Debt (Mezz)					STRUCTURE AND DEBT SCHEDULE					
Other Debt	--	--	--	--	--	--	--	--	--	--
Dividends	--	--	--	--	--	--	--	--	--	--
Equity Issuance / (Repurchase)	--	--	--	--	--	--	--	--	--	--
Cash Flow from Financing Activities										
Excess Cash for the Period	323.1	353.3	360.4	367.6	374.9	382.4	390.1	397.9	405.8	414.0
Beginning Cash Balance	2,003.0	2,326.1	2,679.4	3,039.8	3,407.4	3,782.3	4,164.7	4,554.8	4,952.7	5,358.5
Ending Cash Balance	2,326.1	2,679.4	3,039.8	3,407.4	3,782.3	4,164.7	4,554.8	4,952.7	5,358.5	5,772.5
Cash Flow Statement Assumptions										
Capital Expenditures (% of sales)	2.0%	2.0%	2.0%	2.0%	2.0%	2.0%	2.0%	2.0%	2.0%	2.0%

Exhibit 5: TOYS R US pre-transaction operating assumptions (income statement, balance sheet and cash flow statements)

Toys "R" Us - Forecasting Assumptions

Income Statement Assumptions

		1 Proj. 2005	2 Proj. 2006	3 Proj. 2007	4 Proj. 2008	5 Proj. 2009	6 Proj. 2010	7 Proj. 2011	8 Proj. 2012	9 Proj. 2013	10 Proj. 2014
Sales (% YoY growth)											
1	Base Case	2.0%	2.0%	2.0%	2.0%	2.0%	2.0%	2.0%	2.0%	2.0%	2.0%
2	Sponsor	3.0%	3.0%	2.0%	2.0%	2.0%	2.0%	2.0%	2.0%	2.0%	2.0%
3	Management	4.0%	4.0%	3.0%	3.0%	2.0%	2.0%	2.0%	2.0%	2.0%	2.0%
4	Optimistic	5.0%	5.0%	5.0%	4.0%	3.0%	2.0%	2.0%	2.0%	2.0%	2.0%
5	Pessimistic	1.5%	1.5%	1.5%	1.5%	1.5%	1.5%	1.5%	1.5%	1.5%	1.5%
Cost of Goods Sold (% margin)											
1	Base Case	67.5%	67.5%	67.5%	67.5%	67.5%	67.5%	67.5%	67.5%	67.5%	67.5%
2	Sponsor	67.5%	67.5%	67.5%	67.5%	67.5%	67.5%	67.5%	67.5%	67.5%	67.5%
3	Management	67.5%	67.5%	67.5%	67.5%	67.5%	67.5%	67.5%	67.5%	67.5%	67.5%
4	Optimistic	65.0%	65.0%	65.0%	65.0%	65.0%	65.0%	65.0%	65.0%	65.0%	65.0%
5	Pessimistic	68.0%	68.0%	68.0%	68.0%	68.0%	68.0%	68.0%	68.0%	68.0%	68.0%
SG&A (% sales)											
1	Base Case	25.0%	25.0%	25.0%	25.0%	25.0%	25.0%	25.0%	25.0%	25.0%	25.0%
2	Sponsor	25.0%	25.0%	25.0%	25.0%	25.0%	25.0%	25.0%	25.0%	25.0%	25.0%
3	Management	25.0%	25.0%	25.0%	25.0%	25.0%	25.0%	25.0%	25.0%	25.0%	25.0%
4	Optimistic	24.0%	24.0%	24.0%	24.0%	24.0%	24.0%	24.0%	24.0%	24.0%	24.0%
5	Pessimistic	25.5%	25.5%	25.5%	25.5%	25.5%	25.5%	25.5%	25.5%	25.5%	25.5%
Other Expense / (Income) (% of sales)											
1	Base Case	1.0%	1.0%	1.0%	1.0%	1.0%	1.0%	1.0%	1.0%	1.0%	1.0%
2	Sponsor	1.00%	1.00%	1.00%	1.00%	1.00%	1.00%	1.00%	1.00%	1.00%	1.00%
3	Management	1.00%	1.00%	1.00%	1.00%	1.00%	1.00%	1.00%	1.00%	1.00%	1.00%
4	Optimistic	0.50%	0.50%	0.50%	0.50%	0.50%	0.50%	0.50%	0.50%	0.50%	0.50%
5	Pessimistic	1.25%	1.25%	1.25%	1.25%	1.25%	1.25%	1.25%	1.25%	1.25%	1.25%
Depreciation & Amortization (% of sales)											
1	Base Case	2.5%	2.5%	2.5%	2.5%	2.5%	2.5%	2.5%	2.5%	2.5%	2.5%
2	Sponsor	2.5%	2.5%	2.5%	2.5%	2.5%	2.5%	2.5%	2.5%	2.5%	2.5%
3	Management	2.5%	2.5%	2.5%	2.5%	2.5%	2.5%	2.5%	2.5%	2.5%	2.5%
4	Optimistic	2.0%	2.0%	2.0%	2.0%	2.0%	2.0%	2.0%	2.0%	2.0%	2.0%
5	Pessimistic	3.0%	3.0%	3.0%	3.0%	3.0%	3.0%	3.0%	3.0%	3.0%	3.0%
Interest Income											
1	Base Case	4.0%	4.0%	4.0%	4.0%	4.0%	4.0%	4.0%	4.0%	4.0%	4.0%
2	Sponsor	4.0%	4.0%	4.0%	4.0%	4.0%	4.0%	4.0%	4.0%	4.0%	4.0%
3	Management	4.0%	4.0%	4.0%	4.0%	4.0%	4.0%	4.0%	4.0%	4.0%	4.0%
4	Optimistic	6.0%	6.0%	6.0%	6.0%	6.0%	6.0%	6.0%	6.0%	6.0%	6.0%
5	Pessimistic	2.0%	2.0%	2.0%	2.0%	2.0%	2.0%	2.0%	2.0%	2.0%	2.0%

Balance Sheet
Current Assets

Debtor Days - DSO (Days Sales Outstanding)

Scenario	1	2	3	4	5	6	7	8	9	10
Base Case	5.0	5.0	5.0	5.0	5.0	5.0	5.0	5.0	5.0	5.0
Sponsor	5.0	5.0	5.0	5.0	5.0	5.0	5.0	5.0	5.0	5.0
Management	5.0	5.0	5.0	5.0	5.0	5.0	5.0	5.0	5.0	5.0
Optimistic	4.0	4.0	4.0	4.0	4.0	4.0	4.0	4.0	4.0	4.0
Pessimistic	6.0	6.0	6.0	6.0	6.0	6.0	6.0	6.0	6.0	6.0

Inventory Days - DIH (Days Inventory Held)

Scenario	1	2	3	4	5	6	7	8	9	10
Base Case	100.0	100.0	100.0	100.0	100.0	100.0	100.0	100.0	100.0	100.0
Sponsor	100.0	100.0	100.0	100.0	100.0	100.0	100.0	100.0	100.0	100.0
Management	100.0	100.0	100.0	100.0	100.0	100.0	100.0	100.0	100.0	100.0
Optimistic	90.0	90.0	90.0	90.0	90.0	90.0	90.0	90.0	90.0	90.0
Pessimistic	110.0	110.0	110.0	110.0	110.0	110.0	110.0	110.0	110.0	110.0

Prepaid and other current assets (% of Sales)

Scenario	1	2	3	4	5	6	7	8	9	10
Base Case	4.0%	4.0%	4.0%	4.0%	4.0%	4.0%	4.0%	4.0%	4.0%	4.0%
Sponsor	4.0%	4.0%	4.0%	4.0%	4.0%	4.0%	4.0%	4.0%	4.0%	4.0%
Management	4.0%	4.0%	4.0%	4.0%	4.0%	4.0%	4.0%	4.0%	4.0%	4.0%
Optimistic	5.0%	5.0%	5.0%	5.0%	5.0%	5.0%	5.0%	5.0%	5.0%	5.0%
Pessimistic	3.0%	3.0%	3.0%	3.0%	3.0%	3.0%	3.0%	3.0%	3.0%	3.0%

Current Liabilities

Creditor Days - DPO (Days Payment Outstanding)

Scenario	1	2	3	4	5	6	7	8	9	10
Base Case	48.0	48.0	48.0	48.0	48.0	48.0	48.0	48.0	48.0	48.0
Sponsor	48.0	48.0	48.0	48.0	48.0	48.0	48.0	48.0	48.0	48.0
Management	48.0	48.0	48.0	48.0	48.0	48.0	48.0	48.0	48.0	48.0
Optimistic	50.0	50.0	50.0	50.0	50.0	50.0	50.0	50.0	50.0	50.0
Pessimistic	45.0	45.0	45.0	45.0	45.0	45.0	45.0	45.0	45.0	45.0

Accrued Liabilities (% of Sales)

Scenario	1	2	3	4	5	6	7	8	9	10
Base Case	8.0%	8.0%	8.0%	8.0%	8.0%	8.0%	8.0%	8.0%	8.0%	8.0%
Sponsor	8.0%	8.0%	8.0%	8.0%	8.0%	8.0%	8.0%	8.0%	8.0%	8.0%
Management	8.0%	8.0%	8.0%	8.0%	8.0%	8.0%	8.0%	8.0%	8.0%	8.0%
Optimistic	7.0%	7.0%	7.0%	7.0%	7.0%	7.0%	7.0%	7.0%	7.0%	7.0%
Pessimistic	9.0%	9.0%	9.0%	9.0%	9.0%	9.0%	9.0%	9.0%	9.0%	9.0%

Other Current Liabilities (% of Sales)

Scenario	1	2	3	4	5	6	7	8	9	10
Base Case	8.0%	8.0%	8.0%	8.0%	8.0%	8.0%	8.0%	8.0%	8.0%	8.0%
Sponsor	8.0%	8.0%	8.0%	8.0%	8.0%	8.0%	8.0%	8.0%	8.0%	8.0%
Management	8.0%	8.0%	8.0%	8.0%	8.0%	8.0%	8.0%	8.0%	8.0%	8.0%
Optimistic	7.0%	7.0%	7.0%	7.0%	7.0%	7.0%	7.0%	7.0%	7.0%	7.0%
Pessimistic	9.0%	9.0%	9.0%	9.0%	9.0%	9.0%	9.0%	9.0%	9.0%	9.0%

Cash Flow Statement

CapEx (% of Sales)

Scenario	1	2	3	4	5	6	7	8	9	10
Base Case	2.0%	2.0%	2.0%	2.0%	2.0%	2.0%	2.0%	2.0%	2.0%	2.0%
Sponsor	2.0%	2.0%	2.0%	2.0%	2.0%	2.0%	2.0%	2.0%	2.0%	2.0%
Management	2.0%	2.0%	2.0%	2.0%	2.0%	2.0%	2.0%	2.0%	2.0%	2.0%
Optimistic	1.5%	1.5%	1.5%	1.5%	1.5%	1.5%	1.5%	1.5%	1.5%	1.5%
Pessimistic	2.5%	2.5%	2.5%	2.5%	2.5%	2.5%	2.5%	2.5%	2.5%	2.5%

DETERMINE TRANSACTION STRUCTURE: USES OF FUNDS

There are three main uses of funds in an LBO deal: (i) the purchase price of equity, (ii) professional and financing fees, and (iii) retirement or refinancing of existing debt. There might some additional uses such as payments to departing executives of the target, CAPEX and working capital requirements, etc. We focus on the main uses to keep the spreadsheet more manageable.

Use 1: The purchase price of equity

Setting the purchase price of equity is a crucial decision in an LBO. The price is highly influenced by two competing objectives:

- The purchase price must be high enough to win the bid.

- The purchase price must be low enough to generate a good return for the PE fund and other investors in the LBO.

At this point in the modeling process, the purchase price decision is only an initial estimate based on EBITDA multiples or revenue multiples (if the company is running at an EBITDA loss). It could also be based on an offer price per share typical for public companies in that market. The acquisition price decision is reviewed in the optimization and analysis phase. To set the initial purchase price, firms utilize three approaches:

- **The market-based approach**, which sets the price based on previous comparable transactions, often based on EBITDA or price earnings multiples. For public companies, the purchase price can be calculated based on the share price plus a percentage premium of previous comparable transactions.

- **The expectation-based approach**, which sets the initial purchase price at the level expected by the seller. This approach requires reliable information about the seller's true expectations. The advertised price is often significantly above these expectations.

- **The value-based approach**, which sets the initial purchase price based on the intrinsic value of the company. Often, this value is approximated by using a fundamental discounted cash flow valuation methodology.

Exhibit 6 shows the calculation of the purchase price for Toys R Us using the market-based approach of both an EBITDA multiple and the share price. The model calculates the enterprise value based on a 7.5x EBITDA multiple (this multiple reflects the market conditions at the time). For the share price method, instead of adding a premium to the 2004 share price ($27), which could give an inflated valuation due to market imperfections and the share price being too high, we instead use an implied share price back-solved from the enterprise value calculated by the EBITDA multiple method. The remainder of this section assumes that the model is set up as a private transaction using the EBITDA multiple to calculate the firm's enterprise value, as we believe that this a more common methodology for calculating the target's purchase price and equity value.

Exhibit 6: Purchase Price Assumptions

Type of target (public/private)	Private
Public Entry EBITDA multiple	7.5 X
2008 EBITDA	585.0
Enterprise value	4,387.5
Less: Total debt	(2,349.0)
Less: Preferred securities	0.0
Less: Non-controlling interest	0.0
Plus: Cash and cash equivalents	2,003.0
Equity purchase price	**4,041.5**
Fully Diluted Shares Outstanding (End 2004)	214.0
Offer Price Per Share	**19.0**

Use 2: Professional and financing fees

There are three kinds of fees: investment banker and lender fees (normally calculated as a percentage of the deal value or the principal amount of each debt instrument), legal fees (based on billed hours), and consulting fees (based on billed days). While some of these fees are immediately expensed, certain categories of fees (e.g., financing fees) are accrued and amortized over the life of the deal. Depending on the desired accuracy, there are two options for modeling these fees: rules of thumb or explicit modeling:

- **Rule of thumb:** in big transactions, professional fees make up 3–6% of the uses of funds. In small deals, this figure can increase to 10%, because some work streams have the same complexity independent of the size of the deal.

- **Explicit modeling:** these are estimated by interviewing market participants and requesting quotes. It is more accurate than rules of thumb, but is also much more time consuming. Given that the differences between explicit modeling and rules of thumb are relatively small, the rule of thumb is normally sufficient (see Exhibit 7).

Use 3: Retirement or refinancing of debt

In most cases, the pre-LBO debt sitting on the target's balance sheet must be retired when the deal occurs, due to change of ownership covenants that protect existing debtholders. Therefore, the PE firm must determine not only the amount of debt that needs to be taken to acquire the equity in the target but also the early repayment of the existing debt. Usually the PE firm will ask the same lenders that finance the transaction to also provide additional debt to replace the old debt.

DETERMINING TRANSACTION STRUCTURE: SOURCES OF FUNDS

The uses of funds must be covered by the sources of funds. There are three main sources of funds: debt, new equity, and the existing cash on the balance sheet of the target. As with the uses of funds, we will not produce final numbers for the sources of funds at this stage in the modeling process. Rather, we will produce a functioning model with a reasonable starting assumption.

The three steps to determine the sources of funds are (1) determine debt capacity, (2) determine debt structure, and (3) plug in the required equity contribution.

Step 1: Determine debt capacity

The amount of debt that a company can take on is limited because the firm must be able to service the interest payments and debt repayment. In practice, debt capacity is determined by the buy-side investment bank and will be contingent on the market and regulatory conditions prevalent at that time. However, to double-check the banks' input and to better ascertain how much risk the proposal of the investment bank involves, PE firms should also use the following rules of thumb and methods:

- **Debt capacity = 5 times EBITDA multiple:** As a rule of thumb, the debt capacity of a company is approximately 5.0x its annual EBITDA. Unfortunately, this rule does not take the variability of the company's cash flows into account (the higher the variability, the lower the debt capacity) or the conditions in the debt market at the time of the transaction.

- **Debt capacity = 100% cash sweep in eight years:** Another rule of thumb states that debt capacity equals the amount of debt that the company could service and pay back in eight years, assuming a 100% cash sweep.[2] As shown in Exhibit 8, the debt structure in the Toys R Us model pays down senior debt in eight years based on 70% leverage and a 4.2x Debt/EBITDA ratio.

- **Debt capacity = ICR and DSCR:** Two other drivers of debt capacity are the interest coverage ratio (ICR) and debt-service coverage ratio (DSCR). In particular, lending institutions will require the target to remain within predefined bounds, governed by these financial ratios that are used in debt covenants. When put into relation with EBITDA or EBIT, the debt capacity can be determined by a minimum EBITDA or EBIT ICR. After determining the interest capacity by dividing EBITDA or EBIT by the minimum ICR (which is determined by the lenders or is assumed to be at industry averages), one will arrive at the maximum interest capacity. Next, dividing the maximum interest capacity by the assumed blended interest rate will provide the company's maximum debt capacity.

It should be noted that the debt capacity of two companies with equivalent annual revenue and EBITDA projections can still vary according to several factors, including their:

---

[2] A cash sweep is a debt covenant that requires the paydown of the outstanding debt with available free cash flows. A 100% cash sweep requires the use of the entire free cash flow to retire the debt with this covenant.

- **Creditworthiness:** As noted above, if the ICR is being used to determine the debt capacity, the total debt capacity is inversely related to the interest rate at which the company can borrow. Therefore, a target company with a better credit rating will generally be able to take on more debt because it will be able to borrow debt at a lower interest rate.

- **Revenue cyclicality:** When determining the amount of debt that the target company will be able to service over the course of the loan term, one must take into consideration the free cash flow generated by the company on a monthly basis during the projection period. Without significant cash reserves (as is often the case with a rapidly growing company), the company might not be able to generate the short-term cash flow to service debt during low-revenue months. Thus, when determining the debt capacity that a highly cyclical company can take on, one should be conservative when basing it on an annual EBITDA number.

- **Recurring revenue:** Recurring revenue or long-term annual customer contracts can provide visibility into the company's future revenue. The company with a larger portion of recurring revenue making up its total revenue will likely be able to take on a larger amount of debt due to its revenue being more visible and lower risk. In industries that do not have long-term customer contracts, the customer attrition rate should be analyzed. Low customer attrition rates (i.e., "customer stickiness") increase the predictability of future cash flows in a similar, but not quite identical, manner as recurring revenue.

- **Asset base:** As noted, the company with a larger asset base—especially one that is not industry specific and can be easily sold (i.e., liquid assets) —will be able to secure debt at a lower cost, and therefore might be able to take on additional debt. This factor can be considered part of the company's creditworthiness, mentioned above.

- **Industry maturity:** Long-term industry outlook and visibility are especially important to debtors, due to maturity dates often occurring seven years from the close of the transaction. Industries that are young or unstable have a higher default risk on long-term debt, and will probably have to pay a higher interest rate on the debt borrowed as a result.

Step 2: Debt structure

The PE firm must determine which debt instruments to use, as well as the amounts of these debt instruments. A typical debt structure for a large LBO contains around 30-40% bank debt, up to 10% high-yield bonds, and up to 10% mezzanine debt. An additional potential source of quasi-debt could be deferred consideration or vendor finance, which might be structured either as a lump sum payment or in tranches.

Step 3: Equity structure

Equity makes up the difference between the debt and the uses of funds; it is a plugged value in the *model*. Structuring equity involves deciding which investors to include in addition to the PE fund, how much each investor will invest, and at what valuation. Further, the exact equity instruments (e.g., common shares, preference shares, etc.) must be determined. The structuring of equity should achieve the following objectives:

- **Ensure control:** PE firms in LBOs want to control the target. However, they need to be mindful that control is influenced by both the ownership of the majority of shares and the terms and conditions of the transaction.

- **Align management incentives:** As part of the PE governance approach, management should get an equity stake that should represent a significant part of the management's net worth to align incentives. This stake can be structured as "sweet equity," where the management essentially receives a percentage of the equity for free in the form of options, performance rights, and rights to be issued further shares. Moreover, ratchets, connected to either operational performance thresholds or exit events, can be created as well.

- **Reduce risk:** Equity structuring is especially important if the buyout fails. For example, owning a significant stake of preferred shares pays off more than a significant stake of common shares (due to the position of the equity instrument in the hierarchy). Preferred shares also protect an investment in a downside exit scenario which might involve a fire sale or a liquidation.

- **Enable high returns:** Obviously, the equity structure has a direct effect on investor returns.

Exhibit 7 shows the financing structure and fees section from the Toys R Us model. This section should include the purchase price calculation, financing and other fees, and the sources and uses of funds. The sources and uses section is a summary of the cash flows required to complete the transaction. Note that there is also a functionality to include a number of alternative financing structures, which will be linked and operated by a toggle switch on the transaction summary page (see later discussion).

The final part of this stage is to link the sources and uses sections of the model to the adjustments column in the balance sheet, shown blank in Exhibit 3 (The completed adjustments section of the balance sheet is shown late in Exhibit 10). The main adjustments are as follows:

(–) Cash and cash equivalents if these have been used as part of the sources for the deal.

(+) Goodwill, which is equal to the equity purchase price minus the book value of existing shareholder equity plus any fair value adjustments.

(+) Deferred financing fees (see Exhibit 7).

(+) Cash from new debt instruments.

(–) Retirement of existing debt (if retired).

(+) Net equity contribution, which equals the equity contribution from sources of funds, less other fees and expenses.

(–) Existing shareholder equity, as the old ownership structure is no longer valid.

Exhibit 7: Financing structure and Fee Assumptions

Toys "R" Us LBO Model - Financing Structure and Fees Assumptions

Purchase Price Assumptions

Type of Target (Public/Private)	2.0	Private
Entry EBITDA Multiple		7.5x
2004 EBITDA		585.0
Enterprise Value		4,387.5
Less: Total Debt		(2,349.0)
Less: Preferred Securities		0.0
Less: Noncontrolling Interest		0.0
Plus: Cash and Cash Equivalents		2,003.0
Equity Purchase Price		4,041.5
Fully Diluted Shares Outstanding (End 2004)		214.0
Offer Price Per Share		$19.0

Financing Structure

	Structure 1	Structure 2	Structure 3	Structure 4	Structure 5	Active Case: Structure 2
Sources of Funds						
Revolving Credit Facility Available	100.0	100.0	100.0	100.0	100.0	100.0
Revolving Credit Facility Drawn Down	100.0	50.0	25.0	25.0	–	50.0
Senior Long Term Debt	1,800.0	2,000.0	2,200.0	2,400.0	1,625.0	2,000.0
Subordinated Debt (Mezz)	1,200.0	1,250.0	1,300.0	1,300.0	800.0	1,250.0
Equity Contribution	1,537.5	1,337.5	1,112.5	912.5	2,212.5	1,337.5
Cash on Hand	2,003.0	2,003.0	2,003.0	2,003.0	2,003.0	2,003.0
Total Sources	6,640.5	6,640.5	6,640.5	6,640.5	6,640.5	6,640.5
		0.70				
Uses of Funds						
Purchase Equity	4,041.5	4,041.5	4,041.5	4,041.5	4,041.5	4,041.5
Re-Pay Existing Debt	2,349.0	2,349.0	2,349.0	2,349.0	2,349.0	2,349.0
Deferred Financing Fees	100.0	100.0	100.0	100.0	100.0	100.0
Other Fees and Expenses	150.0	150.0	150.0	150.0	150.0	150.0
Total Uses	6,640.5	6,640.5	6,640.5	6,640.5	6,640.5	6,640.5
Check	0.0	0.0	0.0	0.0	0.0	0.0

Deferred Financing Fees

	Amount	Fees %	£
Revolving Credit Facility	100.0	1.75%	1.8
Senior Long Term Debt	2,000.0	1.75%	35.0
Subordinated Debt (Mezz)	1,250.0	2.25%	28.1
Other (Bridging Loan)	1,250.0	1.00%	12.5
Other Financing Fees and Expenses			22.6
Total Financing Fees			100.0

Amortisation of Deferred Financing Fees

Financing Structure 2	Year	1.0	2.0	3.0	4.0	5.0	6.0	7.0	8.0	9.0	10.0
	Term	31-Dec-05	31-Dec-06	31-Dec-07	31-Dec-08	31-Dec-09	31-Dec-10	31-Dec-11	31-Dec-12	31-Dec-13	31-Dec-14
Revolving Credit Facility	6.0	0.3	0.3	0.3	0.3	0.3	0.3	–	–	–	–
Senior Long Term Debt	7.0	0.3	0.3	0.3	0.3	0.3	0.3	0.3	–	–	–
Subordinated Debt (Mezz)	10.0	2.8	2.8	2.8	2.8	2.8	2.8	2.8	2.8	2.8	2.8
Other (Bridging Loan)	10.0	1.3	1.3	1.3	1.3	1.3	1.3	1.3	1.3	1.3	1.3
Annual Amortisation		4.4	4.4	4.4	4.4	4.4	4.4	4.4	4.1	4.1	4.1
Agent Fees (Revolver)		0.15	0.15	0.15	0.15	0.15	0.15	0.15	0.15	0.15	0.15

BUILD A POST-TRANSACTION STRUCTURE MODEL

At this stage, the effects of the financing structure must be fed back into the pre-transaction structure model to generate a post-transaction structure model. This phase does not require any assumptions or decisions. Building the post-transaction structure model involves four sub-steps:

Step 1: Build the debt schedule

The first step is to build the debt schedule, as illustrated in Exhibit 8. The debt schedule calculates the free cash flows available for mandatory and optional debt repayments. It is constructed to reflect the servicing of various debt instruments given their seniority and payment schedules. The free cash flows are computed using cash flow statement data based on the following formula:

FCF = EBIT*(1-t) + Non-Cash Expenses – Capital Expenditures +/- Working Capital

Following the mandatory debt repayments (interest and any applicable principal), the remaining funds plus cash from the balance sheet are available for optional debt repayments. A switch is added to the transaction summary options selector to enable the user to switch the cash flow sweep from the balance sheet on and off. This is a useful functionality, allowing a proportion of the excess cash to be paid out as a dividend as opposed to paying down debt, should this be allowed by the senior lenders.

The debt schedule calculates the interest and principal payments for each tranche of debt as follows:

Beginning balance (i.e., ending balance from the previous year).

(–) Mandatory repayments.

(–) Optional repayments.

(=) **Ending balance** (i.e., beginning balance for the subsequent year).

The interest rate is usually computed using either LIBOR plus a credit spread or a fixed coupon rate. The interest expense is equal to the interest rate multiplied by the average of beginning and ending debt balances.

Step 2: Complete the income statement from EBIT down to net income

Next, one must complete the cash interest expense section of the income statement from the debt schedule (see Exhibit 8) and the financing fees and assumptions sheet (see Exhibit 7). The income statement is shown in Exhibit 9.

Step 3: Complete the balance sheet

The third step involves completing the debt section of the balance sheet from the ending balances of each debt instrument on the debt schedule. Shareholders' equity is equal to the previous year's shareholders' equity plus the current year's net income from the income statement. The completed balance sheet is shown in Exhibit 10.

Step 4: Complete the cash flow statement

Finally, the financing activities section of the cash flow statement is completed by linking the optional and mandatory repayment lines for each debt instrument in the debt schedule. The completed cash flow statement is shown in Exhibit 11.

The PE firm must model the exit and calculate output measures, such as the returns for each stakeholder.

MODEL THE EXIT

To model the exit, PE firms must first decide on the most likely exit year, depending on the operational strategy to be implemented. LBOs can have a time horizon anywhere between two to seven years. Second, the PE firms must assume an expected price at exit. A typical modeling choice is to use an exit EBITDA multiple that is equal to the entry multiple. Multiple arbitrage, where a higher exit multiple is achieved at exit relative to entry, is heavily influenced by market conditions at exit therefore this assumption has been typically considered to be conservative. However, over the recent years some private equity firms started to factor in multiple regressions where the exit multiple is lower than the entry multiple. This is particularly the case if the entry multiple is higher than the historic multiple of the target's industry. It is generally not prudent to assume relatively high exit multiples to make the deal work.

To measure the performance of an equity investment in the LBO deal, three elements are included in the exit analysis:

- The valuation of the company at exit: "Implied Valuation Calculation (Exit)."

- A capitalization table: "Ownership Structure."

- The tranches of the capital structure that are measured: "Equity" and "Debt."

One could question the rationale of including "Debt" in the analysis if one is only investing in the equity. Yet, given that an LBO cannot be undertaken without having a robust and sustainable debt structure in place, it might make sense to evaluate the return that would be sufficiently attractive to the provider of this source of capital; this could also serve as a useful reference during negotiations with banks as PE firms can seek to optimize the debt structure to their requirements. Equally importantly, modeling the hypothetical returns of the management is advisable as this will again help a PE firm evaluate whether the proposed shareholding structure would be attractive to the management of the target.

As Exhibit 12 shows, the exit analysis should also account for any return that an equity investor might be able to recoup before the intended date of exit (i.e., through dividend recapitalizations or special dividends). However, one must ensure that the impact of such initiatives is modeled through the rest of the financial statements as well.

After all assumptions and decisions are included in the model, the most important output measures can finally be calculated. The return from an LBO is measured using the *IRR* and the *money multiple* or the *cash-on-cash* (CoC) return. A screenshot of how we modeled the returns for the Toys R Us deal is shown in Exhibit 12.

Assuming the base case operating scenario, 70% leverage, and entry and exit multiples of 7.5x, the Toys R Us deal would return an IRR of 24.2% and a CoC multiple of 3x, assuming an exit after five years. The first sensitivity analysis at the bottom left of Exhibit 12 shows how different entry and exit multiples affect the IRR. For example, leaving the entry multiple unchanged at 7.5x, if the exit occurs under favorable market conditions and an exit multiple of 8.5x is achieved, the IRR will increase to 28.9%. Conversely, exiting under unfavorable conditions at a multiple of 6.5x would reduce the IRR to 18.6%. The second sensitivity shows the effect of varying the exit year; this clearly shows the negative effect on IRR of a delayed exit, all other parameters remaining constant. These are the most common sensitivities for an LBO transaction, but other analyses can be added based on the PE firm's requirements.

It is worth highlighting an important warning about the use of IRR as a measure for returns: the best return is achieved in Year 1 (at 87.8%), but withdrawing at this point would only make financial sense if the amount withdrawn could be reinvested immediately at a relatively high return—higher than the five-year IRR return. In practice, putting money to work in the private equity market is not straightforward and time consuming. Investors must often commit funds for a long period of time before they are eventually drawn down to earn hopefully high returns relative to other asset classes.

Finally, a transaction summary sheet, as shown in Exhibit 13, is added to the model. This summary sheet is also known as the "*LBO model dashboard*." The transaction summary shows the most important decisions, assumptions, and output measures, and enables the user to make changes to the assumptions or scenarios and see the immediate effect on the returns and DSCR by using the toggle switches in the "options selector" box in the top right-hand corner of the sheet.

Exhibit 8: The debt schedule

Toys "R" Us LBO Model - Debt Schedule ($m)

	Pro forma 2004	1 Proj. 2005	2 Proj. 2006	3 Proj. 2007	4 Proj. 2008	5 Proj. 2009	6 Proj. 2010	7 Proj. 2011	8 Proj. 2012	9 Proj. 2013	10 Proj. 2014
LIBOR Forward Rates	3.00%	3.00%	3.15%	3.30%	3.60%	4.00%	4.35%	4.80%	4.85%	5.10%	5.25%
FCFs Available for Debt Repayment		183.6	220.1	235.2	250.2	266.4	285.1	305.7	329.5	350.0	367.0
Minimum Excess Cash on BS											
Total Mandatory Repayments		(20.0)	(20.0)	(20.0)	(20.0)	(20.0)	(20.0)	(20.0)	(20.0)	(20.0)	(20.0)
Cash from Balance Sheet		0.0	0.0	0.0	0.0	0.0	0.0	0.0	0.0	25.8	375.8
Cash Available for Optional Repayments		163.6	200.1	215.2	230.2	246.4	265.1	285.7	309.5	375.8	742.7
Revolving Credit Facility											
Amount Available (Credit Limit)	100.00										
Spread	3.25%										
Remaining Term	6 years										
Commitment Fee on Unused Portion	0.5%										
Beginning Balance		50.00	–	–	–	–	–	–	–	–	–
Drawdowns/(Repayment)		(50.00)	–	–	–	–	–	–	–	–	–
Ending Balance		–	–	–	–	–	–	–	–	–	–
Interest Rate		6.25%	6.40%	6.55%	6.85%	7.25%	7.60%	8.05%	8.10%	8.35%	8.50%
Interest Expense		1.56	–	–	–	–	–	–	–	–	–
Commitment Fee on Unused Balance on Revolver Facility		0.38	0.50	0.50	0.50	0.50	0.50	0.50	0.50	0.50	0.50
Senior Long Term Debt											
Size	2,000.00										
Spread	3.50%										
Remaining Term	8 years										
Repayment Schedule	1.0% Per Annum, Bullet at Maturity										
Beginning Balance		2,000.00	1,866.42	1,646.28	1,411.10	1,160.88	894.49	609.40	303.68	–	–
Mandatory Repayment		(20.00)	(20.00)	(20.00)	(20.00)	(20.00)	(20.00)	(20.00)	(20.00)		
Optional Repayment		(113.58)	(200.14)	(215.17)	(230.22)	(246.39)	(265.08)	(285.72)	(283.68)		
Ending Balance		1,866.42	1,646.28	1,411.10	1,160.88	894.49	609.40	303.68	–		
Interest Rate		6.50%	6.65%	6.80%	7.10%	7.50%	7.85%	8.30%	8.35%	8.60%	8.75%
Interest Expense		125.66	116.80	103.95	91.31	77.08	59.03	37.89	12.68	–	–
Existing Debt											
Spread	3.00%										
Remaining Term	0 years										
Repayment Schedule	1.0% Per Annum, Bullet at Maturity										
Beginning Balance		–	–	–	–	–	–	–	–	–	–
Mandatory Repayment		–	–	–	–	–	–	–	–	–	–
Optional Repayment		–	–	–	–	–	–	–	–	–	–
Ending Balance		–	–	–	–	–	–	–	–	–	–
Interest Rate		6.0%	6.2%	6.3%	6.6%	7.0%	7.4%	7.8%	7.9%	8.1%	8.3%
Interest Expense		–	–	–	–	–	–	–	–	–	–
Subordinated Debt (Mezz)											
Size	1,250.00										
Coupon	8.00%										
Term	10 years										
Beginning Balance		1,250.00	1,250.00	1,250.00	1,250.00	1,250.00	1,250.00	1,250.00	1,250.00	1,250.00	1,250.00
Repayment											
Ending Balance		1,250.00	1,250.00	1,250.00	1,250.00	1,250.00	1,250.00	1,250.00	1,250.00	1,250.00	1,250.00
Interest Expense		100.00	100.00	100.00	100.00	100.00	100.00	100.00	100.00	100.00	100.00

Exhibit 9: Post-transaction income statement

Toys "R" Us LBO Model - Income Statement ($m)

					1	2	3	4	5	6	7	8	9	10
	Hist. 2001	Hist. 2002	Hist. 2003	Hist. 2004	Proj. 2005	Proj. 2006	Proj. 2007	Proj. 2008	Proj. 2009	Proj. 2010	Proj. 2011	Proj. 2012	Proj. 2013	Proj. 2014
Sales	11,332.0	11,019.0	11,305.0	11,320.0	11,546.4	11,777.3	12,012.9	12,253.1	12,498.2	12,748.2	13,003.1	13,263.2	13,528.4	13,799.0
% growth	–	(2.8%)	2.6%	0.1%	2.0%	2.0%	2.0%	2.0%	2.0%	2.0%	2.0%	2.0%	2.0%	2.0%
Cost of Goods Sold	7,815.0	7,604.0	7,799.0	7,646.0	7,793.8	7,949.7	8,108.7	8,270.9	8,436.3	8,605.0	8,777.1	8,952.6	9,131.7	9,314.3
Gross Profit	3,517.0	3,415.0	3,506.0	3,674.0	3,752.6	3,827.6	3,904.2	3,982.3	4,061.9	4,143.2	4,226.0	4,310.5	4,396.7	4,484.7
% margin	31.0%	31.0%	31.0%	32.5%	32.5%	32.5%	32.5%	32.5%	32.5%	32.5%	32.5%	32.5%	32.5%	32.5%
Selling, General & Administrative	2,801.0	2,721.0	2,724.0	3,026.0	2,886.6	2,944.3	3,003.2	3,063.3	3,124.5	3,187.0	3,250.8	3,315.8	3,382.1	3,449.8
% sales	24.7%	24.7%	24.1%	26.7%	25.0%	25.0%	25.0%	25.0%	25.0%	25.0%	25.0%	25.0%	25.0%	25.0%
Other Expense / (Income)	–	186.0	–	63.0	115.5	117.8	120.1	122.5	125.0	127.5	130.0	132.6	135.3	138.0
EBITDA	716.0	508.0	782.0	585.0	750.5	765.5	780.8	796.5	812.4	828.6	845.2	862.1	879.3	896.9
% margin	6.3%	4.6%	6.9%	5.2%	6.5%	6.5%	6.5%	6.5%	6.5%	6.5%	6.5%	6.5%	6.5%	6.5%
Depreciation & Amortization	290.0	308.0	339.0	368.0	288.7	294.4	300.3	306.3	312.5	318.7	325.1	331.6	338.2	345.0
EBIT	426.0	200.0	443.0	217.0	461.9	471.1	480.5	490.1	499.9	509.9	520.1	530.5	541.1	552.0
% margin	3.8%	1.8%	3.9%	1.9%	4.0%	4.0%	4.0%	4.0%	4.0%	4.0%	4.0%	4.0%	4.0%	4.0%
Interest Expense														
Existing Debt					–	–	–	–	–	–	–	–	–	–
Revolving Credit Facility					1.6	–	–	–	–	–	–	–	–	–
Senior Long Term Debt					125.7	116.8	104.0	91.3	77.1	59.0	37.9	12.7	–	–
Subordinated Debt (Mezz)					100.0	100.0	100.0	100.0	100.0	100.0	100.0	100.0	100.0	100.0
Commitment Fee on Unused Revolver					0.4	0.5	0.5	0.5	0.5	0.5	0.5	0.5	0.5	0.5
Agent Fees					0.2	0.2	0.2	0.2	0.2	0.2	0.2	0.2	0.2	0.2
Cash Interest Expense					227.7	217.4	204.6	192.0	177.7	159.7	138.5	113.3	100.7	100.7
Amortisation of Deferred Financing Fees					4.4	4.4	4.4	4.4	4.4	4.4	4.1	4.1	4.1	4.1
Total Interest Expense					232.1	221.8	209.0	196.3	182.1	164.0	142.6	117.4	104.7	104.7
Interest income												(0.5)	(8.0)	(22.4)
Net Interest Expense					232.1	221.8	209.0	196.3	182.1	164.0	142.6	116.9	96.7	82.3
EBT (Earnings Before Tax)					229.8	249.3	271.6	293.8	317.8	345.9	377.5	413.7	444.5	469.6
Income Tax Expense					87.3	94.7	103.2	111.6	120.8	131.4	143.5	157.2	168.9	178.5
Net Income					142.4	154.6	168.4	182.2	197.1	214.5	234.1	256.5	275.6	291.2
% margin					1.2%	1.3%	1.4%	1.5%	1.6%	1.7%	1.8%	1.9%	2.0%	2.1%

Income Statement Assumptions

	Hist. 2001	Hist. 2002	Hist. 2003	Hist. 2004	Proj. 2005	Proj. 2006	Proj. 2007	Proj. 2008	Proj. 2009	Proj. 2010	Proj. 2011	Proj. 2012	Proj. 2013	Proj. 2014
Sales (% YoY growth)	–	(2.8%)	2.6%	0.1%	2.0%	2.0%	2.0%	2.0%	2.0%	2.0%	2.0%	2.0%	2.0%	2.0%
Cost of Goods Sold (% margin)	69.0%	69.0%	69.0%	67.5%	67.5%	67.5%	67.5%	67.5%	67.5%	67.5%	67.5%	67.5%	67.5%	67.5%
SG&A (% sales)	24.7%	24.7%	24.1%	25.0%	25.0%	25.0%	25.0%	25.0%	25.0%	25.0%	25.0%	25.0%	25.0%	25.0%
Other Expense / (Income) (% of sales)	–	1.7%	–	0.6%	1.0%	1.0%	1.0%	1.0%	1.0%	1.0%	1.0%	1.0%	1.0%	1.0%
Depreciation & Amortization (% of sales)	2.6%	2.8%	3.0%	3.3%	2.5%	2.5%	2.5%	2.5%	2.5%	2.5%	2.5%	2.5%	2.5%	2.5%
Interest Income				4.0%	4.0%	4.0%	4.0%	4.0%	4.0%	4.0%	4.0%	4.0%	4.0%	4.0%
Tax Rate					38.0%	38.0%	38.0%	38.0%	38.0%	38.0%	38.0%	38.0%	38.0%	38.0%

Exhibit 10: Post-transaction balance sheet

Toys "R" Us LBO Model - Balance Sheet ($m)

	Actual	Incr'l (Decr')	Pro Forma	1 Proj.	2 Proj.	3 Proj.	4 Proj.	5 Proj.	6 Proj.	7 Proj.	8 Proj.	9 Proj.	10 Proj.
	2004		2004	2005	2006	2007	2008	2009	2010	2011	2012	2013	2014
Cash and Cash Equivalents	2,003.0	(2,003.0)	--	--	--	--	--	--	--	--	25.8	375.8	742.7
Accounts Receivable	146.0		146.0	158.2	161.3	164.6	167.9	171.2	174.6	178.1	181.7	185.3	189.0
Inventory	2,094.0		2,094.0	2,135.3	2,178.0	2,221.6	2,266.0	2,311.3	2,357.5	2,404.7	2,452.8	2,501.8	2,551.9
Prepaid Expenses and Other Current Assets	486.0		486.0	461.9	471.1	480.5	490.1	499.9	509.9	520.1	530.5	541.1	552.0
Total Current Assets	**4,729.0**		**2,726.0**	**2,755.3**	**2,810.4**	**2,866.6**	**2,924.0**	**2,982.4**	**3,042.1**	**3,102.9**	**3,190.8**	**3,604.1**	**4,035.6**
PPE Beginning Balance				4,439.0	4,381.3	4,322.4	4,262.3	4,201.1	4,138.6	4,074.8	4,009.8	3,943.5	3,875.8
CapEx				230.9	235.5	240.3	245.1	250.0	255.0	260.1	265.3	270.6	276.0
Depreciation and Amortisation				(288.7)	(294.4)	(300.3)	(306.3)	(312.5)	(318.7)	(325.1)	(331.6)	(338.2)	(345.0)
PPE Ending Balance			4,439.0	4,381.3	4,322.4	4,262.3	4,201.1	4,138.6	4,074.8	4,009.8	3,943.5	3,875.8	3,806.9
Goodwill and Intangible Assets	348.0	67.5	415.5	415.5	415.5	415.5	415.5	415.5	415.5	415.5	415.5	415.5	415.5
Other Assets	749.0		749.0	749.0	749.0	749.0	749.0	749.0	749.0	749.0	749.0	749.0	749.0
Deferred Financing Fees	--	100.0	100.0	95.6	91.3	86.9	82.6	78.2	73.9	69.8	65.8	61.7	57.6
Total Assets	**10,265.0**		**8,429.5**	**8,396.7**	**8,388.6**	**8,380.4**	**8,372.1**	**8,363.7**	**8,355.3**	**8,347.1**	**8,364.5**	**8,706.1**	**9,064.6**
Accounts Payable	1,022.0		1,022.0	1,024.9	1,045.4	1,066.3	1,087.7	1,109.4	1,131.6	1,154.2	1,177.3	1,200.9	1,224.9
Accrued Liabilities	866.0		866.0	923.7	942.2	961.0	980.3	999.9	1,019.9	1,040.2	1,061.1	1,082.3	1,103.9
Other Current Liabilities	976.0		976.0	923.7	942.2	961.0	980.3	999.9	1,019.9	1,040.2	1,061.1	1,082.3	1,103.9
Total Current Liabilities	**2,864.0**		**2,864.0**	**2,872.4**	**2,929.8**	**2,988.4**	**3,048.2**	**3,109.1**	**3,171.3**	**3,234.7**	**3,299.4**	**3,365.4**	**3,432.7**
Existing Debt	2,349.0	(2,349.0)	--	--	--	--	--	--	--	--	--	--	--
Revolving Credit Facility		50.0	50.0	--	--	--	--	--	--	--	--	--	--
Senior Long Term Debt	2,000.0	2,000.0	2,000.0	1,866.4	1,646.3	1,411.1	1,160.9	894.5	609.4	303.7	--	--	--
Subordinated Debt (Mezz)	1,250.0	1,250.0	1,250.0	1,250.0	1,250.0	1,250.0	1,250.0	1,250.0	1,250.0	1,250.0	1,250.0	1,250.0	1,250.0
Other Debt													
Other LT Liabilities	1,078.0		1,078.0	1,078.0	1,078.0	1,078.0	1,078.0	1,078.0	1,078.0	1,078.0	1,078.0	1,078.0	1,078.0
Total Liabilities	**6,291.0**		**7,242.0**	**7,066.8**	**6,904.1**	**6,727.5**	**6,537.1**	**6,331.6**	**6,108.7**	**5,866.4**	**5,627.4**	**5,693.4**	**5,760.7**
Shareholders' Equity	3,974.0	(2,786.5)	1,187.5	1,329.9	1,484.5	1,652.9	1,835.0	2,032.1	2,246.6	2,480.6	2,737.1	3,012.7	3,303.8
Total Shareholders' Equity	**3,974.0**		**1,187.5**	**1,329.9**	**1,484.5**	**1,652.9**	**1,835.0**	**2,032.1**	**2,246.6**	**2,480.6**	**2,737.1**	**3,012.7**	**3,303.8**
Total Liabilities and Equity	**10,265.0**		**8,429.5**	**8,396.7**	**8,388.6**	**8,380.4**	**8,372.1**	**8,363.7**	**8,355.3**	**8,347.1**	**8,364.5**	**8,706.1**	**9,064.6**
Balance Check	0.000		0.000	0.000	0.000	0.000	0.000	0.000	0.000	0.000	0.000	0.000	0.000
Net Working Capital	(138.0)		(138.0)	(117.0)	(119.4)	(121.8)	(124.2)	(126.7)	(129.2)	(131.8)	(134.4)	(137.1)	(139.9)
(Increase) / Decrease in Net Working Capital				(21.0)	2.3	2.4	2.4	2.5	2.5	2.6	2.6	2.7	2.7
Balance Sheet Assumptions													
Current Assets													
Days Sales Outstanding (DSO)	4.7		4.7	5.0	5.0	5.0	5.0	5.0	5.0	5.0	5.0	5.0	5.0
Days Inventory Held (DIH)	100.0		100.0	100.0	100.0	100.0	100.0	100.0	100.0	100.0	100.0	100.0	100.0
Prepaid and Other Current Assets (% of sales)	4.3%		4.3%	4.0%	4.0%	4.0%	4.0%	4.0%	4.0%	4.0%	4.0%	4.0%	4.0%
Current Liabilities													
Days Payable Outstanding (DPO)	48.8		48.8	48.0	48.0	48.0	48.0	48.0	48.0	48.0	48.0	48.0	48.0
Accrued Liabilities (% of sales)	7.7%		7.7%	8.0%	8.0%	8.0%	8.0%	8.0%	8.0%	8.0%	8.0%	8.0%	8.0%
Other Current Liabilities (% of sales)	8.6%		8.6%	8.0%	8.0%	8.0%	8.0%	8.0%	8.0%	8.0%	8.0%	8.0%	8.0%

Exhibit 11: Post-transaction cash flow statement

Toys "R" Us LBO Model - Cash Flow Statement ($m)	1 Proj. 2005	2 Proj. 2006	3 Proj. 2007	4 Proj. 2008	5 Proj. 2009	6 Proj. 2010	7 Proj. 2011	8 Proj. 2012	9 Proj. 2013	10 Proj. 2014
Operating Activities										
Net Income	142.4	154.6	168.4	182.2	197.1	214.5	234.1	256.5	275.6	291.2
Depreciation & Amortization	288.7	294.4	300.3	306.3	312.5	318.7	325.1	331.6	338.2	345.0
Amortisation of Deferred Financing Fees	4.4	4.4	4.4	4.4	4.4	4.4	4.1	4.1	4.1	4.1
Sub Total	435.5	453.3	473.0	492.8	513.9	537.5	563.2	592.1	617.8	640.2
Changes in Working Capital Items										
Accounts Receivable (DSO)	(12.2)	(3.2)	(3.2)	(3.3)	(3.4)	(3.4)	(3.5)	(3.6)	(3.6)	(3.7)
Inventory (DIH)	(41.3)	(42.7)	(43.6)	(44.4)	(45.3)	(46.2)	(47.2)	(48.1)	(49.1)	(50.0)
Prepaid Expenses	24.1	(9.2)	(9.4)	(9.6)	(9.8)	(10.0)	(10.2)	(10.4)	(10.6)	(10.8)
Accounts Payable (DPO)	2.9	20.5	20.9	21.3	21.8	22.2	22.6	23.1	23.5	24.0
Accrued Liabilities	57.7	18.5	18.8	19.2	19.6	20.0	20.4	20.8	21.2	21.6
Other Current Liabilities	(52.3)	18.5	18.8	19.2	19.6	20.0	20.4	20.8	21.2	21.6
(Inc.) / Dec. in Net Working Capital	(21.0)	2.3	2.4	2.4	2.5	2.5	2.6	2.6	2.7	2.7
Cash Flow from Operating Activities	**414.5**	**455.7**	**475.4**	**495.3**	**516.4**	**540.0**	**565.8**	**594.7**	**620.5**	**642.9**
Investing Activities										
Capital Expenditures	(230.9)	(235.5)	(240.3)	(245.1)	(250.0)	(255.0)	(260.1)	(265.3)	(270.6)	(276.0)
Other Investing Activities	—	—	—	—	—	—	—	—	—	—
Cash Flow from Investing Activities	**(230.9)**	**(235.5)**	**(240.3)**	**(245.1)**	**(250.0)**	**(255.0)**	**(260.1)**	**(265.3)**	**(270.6)**	**(276.0)**
Free Cash Flows	**183.6**	**220.1**	**235.2**	**250.2**	**266.4**	**285.1**	**305.7**	**329.5**	**350.0**	**367.0**
Financing Activities										
Existing Debt	(50.0)	—	—	—	—	—	—	—	—	—
Revolving Credit Facility	(133.6)	—	—	—	—	—	—	—	—	—
Senior Long Term Debt	—	(220.1)	(235.2)	(250.2)	(266.4)	(285.1)	(305.7)	(303.7)	—	—
Subordinated Debt (Mezz)	—	—	—	—	—	—	—	—	—	—
Other Debt	—	—	—	—	—	—	—	—	—	—
Dividends	—	—	—	—	—	—	—	—	—	—
Equity Issuance / (Repurchase)	—	—	—	—	—	—	—	—	—	—
Cash Flow from Financing Activities	**(183.6)**	**(220.1)**	**(235.2)**	**(250.2)**	**(266.4)**	**(285.1)**	**(305.7)**	**(303.7)**	**—**	**—**
Excess Cash for the Period	—	—	—	—	—	—	—	25.8	350.0	367.0
Beginning Cash Balance	—	—	—	—	—	—	—	—	25.8	375.8
Ending Cash Balance	—	—	—	—	—	—	—	25.8	375.8	742.7
Cash Flow Statement Assumptions										
Capital Expenditures (% of sales)	2.0%	2.0%	2.0%	2.0%	2.0%	2.0%	2.0%	2.0%	2.0%	2.0%

Exhibit 12: Returns Analysis

Toys "R" Us LBO Model - Returns Analysis
CoC and IRR Returns

	Pro forma 2004	1 Proj. 2005	2 Proj. 2006	3 Proj. 2007	4 Proj. 2008	5 Proj. 2009	6 Proj. 2010	7 Proj. 2011	8 Proj. 2012	9 Proj. 2013	10 Proj. 2014
Entry EBITDA Multiple	7.5x										
Exit EBITDA Multiple	7.5x										
EBITDA		750.5	765.5	780.8	796.5	812.4	828.6	845.2	862.1	879.3	896.9
Enterprise Value at Exit		5,628.9	5,741.4	5,856.3	5,973.4	6,092.9	6,214.7	6,339.0	6,465.8	6,595.1	6,727.0
Total Debt		(3,116.4)	(2,896.3)	(2,661.1)	(2,410.9)	(2,144.5)	(1,859.4)	(1,553.7)	(1,250.0)	(1,250.0)	(1,250.0)
Cash and Cash Equivalents		–	–	–	–	–	–	–	25.8	375.8	742.7
Net Debt		(3,116.4)	(2,896.3)	(2,661.1)	(2,410.9)	(2,144.5)	(1,859.4)	(1,553.7)	(1,224.2)	(874.2)	(507.3)
Equity Value at Exit		2,512.5	2,845.2	3,195.2	3,562.5	3,948.4	4,355.3	4,785.3	5,241.6	5,720.9	6,219.7
Initial Equity Investment	1,337.5										
Cash on Cash (CoC) Return		1.9x	2.1x	2.4x	2.7x	3.0x	3.3x	3.6x	3.9x	4.3x	4.7x
		1 Proj. 2005	2 Proj. 2006	3 Proj. 2007	4 Proj. 2008	5 Proj. 2009	6 Proj. 2010	7 Proj. 2011	8 Proj. 2012	9 Proj. 2013	10 Proj. 2014
Initial Equity Investment		(1,337.5)	(1,337.5)	(1,337.5)	(1,337.5)	(1,337.5)	(1,337.5)	(1,337.5)	(1,337.5)	(1,337.5)	(1,337.5)
Equity Value at Exit		2,512.5	2,845.2	3,195.2	3,562.5	3,948.4	4,355.3	4,785.3	5,241.6	5,720.9	6,219.7
IRR		87.8%	45.9%	33.7%	27.8%	24.2%	21.7%	20.0%	18.6%	17.5%	16.6%

IRR Sensitivity Analysis

Assuming Exit in 2013E

0.2	Exit Multiple				
Entry Multiple	6.5	7.0	7.5	8.0	8.5
6.5	33.0%	36.3%	39.3%	42.1%	44.6%
7.0	24.6%	27.7%	30.5%	33.0%	35.4%
7.5	18.6%	21.5%	24.2%	26.6%	28.9%
8.0	14.0%	16.8%	19.4%	21.7%	23.9%
8.5	10.3%	13.0%	15.5%	17.8%	19.9%

Assuming 7.5x Exit Multiple

0.2	Exit Year				
Entry Multiple	2007	2008	2009	2010	2011
6.5	21.8%	19.9%	18.6%	17.5%	16.7%
7.0	28.0%	24.0%	21.5%	19.7%	18.4%
7.5	33.7%	27.8%	24.2%	21.7%	20.0%
8.0	38.9%	31.2%	26.6%	23.6%	21.4%
8.5	43.8%	34.4%	28.9%	25.3%	22.8%

Exhibit 13: LBO Model Dashboard

Toys "R" Us LBO Model - Transaction Summary

Financing Structure

Sources of Funds		Uses of Funds	
Revolving Credit Facility	50.0	Purchase Equity	4,041.5
Senior Long Term Debt	2,000.0	Re-Pay Existing Debt	2,349.0
Subordinated Debt (Mezz)	1,250.0	Deferred Financing Fees	100.0
Equity Contribution	1,337.5	Other Fees and Expenses	150.0
Cash on Hand	2,003.0		
Total Sources	**6,640.5**	**Total Uses**	**6,640.5**

Purchase Price

Equity Purchase Price	4,041.5
Exiting Net Debt	346.0
Enterprise Value	**4,387.5**

Returns Analysis

Exit Year	2009
Entry Multiple	7.5x
Exit Multiple	7.5x
IRR	24.2%
COC	3.0x

Options Selector

Operating Scenario	1	Base Case
Public / Private Target	2	Private
Financing Structure	2	70% Leverage
Interest Calculation	1	Average
BS Cash Flow Sweep	1	Yes

Checks

Balance Sheet	OK
Sources and Uses	OK

Summary Financial Data ($m)

	Hist. 2001	Hist. 2002	Hist. 2003	Hist. 2004	Proj. 1 2005	Proj. 2 2006	Proj. 3 2007	Proj. 4 2008	Proj. 5 2009	Proj. 6 2010	Proj. 7 2011	Proj. 8 2012	Proj. 9 2013	Proj. 10 2014
Sales	11,332.0	11,019.0	11,305.0	11,320.0	11,546.4	11,777.3	12,012.9	12,253.1	12,498.2	12,748.2	13,003.1	13,263.2	13,528.4	13,799.0
% growth	–	(2.8%)	2.6%	0.1%	2.0%	2.0%	2.0%	2.0%	2.0%	2.0%	2.0%	2.0%	2.0%	2.0%
Gross Profit	3,517.0	3,415.0	3,506.0	3,674.0	3,752.6	3,827.6	3,904.2	3,982.3	4,061.9	4,143.2	4,226.0	4,310.5	4,396.7	4,484.7
% margin	31.0%	31.0%	31.0%	32.5%	32.5%	32.5%	32.5%	32.5%	32.5%	32.5%	32.5%	32.5%	32.5%	32.5%
EBITDA	716.0	508.0	782.0	585.0	750.5	765.5	780.8	796.5	812.4	828.6	845.2	862.1	879.3	896.9
% margin	6.3%	4.6%	6.9%	5.2%	6.5%	6.5%	6.5%	6.5%	6.5%	6.5%	6.5%	6.5%	6.5%	6.5%
Capital Expenditures	402.0	705.0	395.0	262.0										
% sales	3.5%	6.4%	3.5%	2.3%										
Cash Interest Expense					227.7	217.4	204.6	192.0	177.7	159.7	138.5	113.3	100.7	100.7
Total Interest Expense					232.1	221.8	209.0	196.3	182.1	164.0	142.6	117.4	104.7	104.7

Free Cash Flow

	Proj. 1 2005	Proj. 2 2006	Proj. 3 2007	Proj. 4 2008	Proj. 5 2009	Proj. 6 2010	Proj. 7 2011	Proj. 8 2012	Proj. 9 2013	Proj. 10 2014
EBITDA	750.5	765.5	780.8	796.5	812.4	828.6	845.2	862.1	879.3	896.9
Less: Cash Interest Expense	(227.7)	(217.4)	(204.6)	(192.0)	(177.7)	(159.7)	(138.5)	(113.3)	(100.7)	(100.7)
Plus: Interest Income	0.0	0.0	0.0	0.0	0.0	0.0	0.0	(0.5)	(8.0)	(22.4)
Less: Income Taxes	(87.3)	(94.7)	(103.2)	(111.6)	(120.8)	(131.4)	(143.5)	(157.2)	(168.9)	(178.5)
Less: Capital Expenditures	(230.9)	(235.5)	(240.3)	(245.1)	(250.0)	(255.0)	(260.1)	(265.3)	(270.6)	(276.0)
Less: Increase in Net Working Capital	(21.0)	2.3	2.4	2.4	2.5	2.5	2.6	2.6	2.7	2.7
Free Cash Flow	183.6	220.1	235.2	250.2	266.4	285.1	305.7	328.4	333.9	322.2
Cumulative Free Cash Flow	183.6	403.7	638.9	889.1	1,155.5	1,440.6	1,746.3	2,074.8	2,408.7	2,730.9

Capitalisation Table

	Hist. 2004	Proj. 1 2005	Proj. 2 2006	Proj. 3 2007	Proj. 4 2008	Proj. 5 2009	Proj. 6 2010	Proj. 7 2011	Proj. 8 2012	Proj. 9 2013	Proj. 10 2014
Cash	50.00								25.80	375.76	742.72
Revolving Credit Facility	2,000.00	1,866.42	1,646.28	1,411.10	1,160.88	894.49	609.40	303.68	–	–	–
Senior Term Loans											
Existing Term Loan											
Other Debt											
Total Senior Secured Debt	2,050.00	1,866.42	1,646.28	1,411.10	1,160.88	894.49	609.40	303.68	–	–	–
Subordinated Debt	1,250.00	1,250.00	1,250.00	1,250.00	1,250.00	1,250.00	1,250.00	1,250.00	1,250.00	1,250.00	1,250.00
Total Debt	3,300.00	3,116.42	2,896.28	2,661.10	2,410.88	2,144.49	1,859.40	1,553.68	1,250.00	1,250.00	1,250.00
Shareholders' Equity	1,187.50	1,329.95	1,484.51	1,652.88	1,835.04	2,032.11	2,246.56	2,480.62	2,737.09	3,012.65	3,303.81
Total Capitalization	4,487.50	4,446.37	4,380.79	4,313.98	4,245.92	4,176.60	4,105.97	4,034.30	3,987.09	4,262.65	4,553.81

% of Bank Debt Repaid

Debt Service Coverage

	Proj. 1 2005	Proj. 2 2006	Proj. 3 2007	Proj. 4 2008	Proj. 5 2009	Proj. 6 2010	Proj. 7 2011	Proj. 8 2012	Proj. 9 2013	Proj. 10 2014
Leverage Ratio (Debt/Total Capitalisation)	70.1%	66.1%	61.7%	56.8%	51.3%	45.3%	38.5%	31.4%	29.3%	27.4%
EBIT	461.9	471.1	480.5	490.1	499.9	509.9	520.1	530.5	541.1	552.0
Interest Payments	227.2	216.8	204.0	191.3	177.1	159.0	137.9	112.7	100.0	100.0
Mandatory Principal Repayments	70.0	20.0	20.0	20.0	20.0	20.0	20.0	20.0	20.0	–
Debt Service Requirements	297.2	236.8	224.0	211.3	197.1	179.0	157.9	132.7	100.0	100.0
ISCR	2.0x	2.0x	2.4x	2.6x	2.8x	3.2x	3.8x	4.7x	5.4x	5.5x
DSCR	1.6x	2.0x	2.1x	2.3x	2.5x	2.8x	3.3x	4.0x	5.4x	5.5x
Total Debt / EBITDA	4.2x	3.8x	3.4x	3.0x	2.6x	2.2x	1.8x	1.4x	1.4x	1.4x

OPTIMIZATION AND ANALYSIS OF THE LBO MODEL

By the beginning of this phase, the LBO model should be fully functional. All relevant information is included and all decisions, assumptions, and output measures are modeled. Changes to decisions and assumptions will immediately affect the output measures. However, the modeled decisions are only preliminary so far, and have not been optimized.

This phase is about optimizing the LBO transaction structure, which is an iterative process (see Exhibit 14). In Step A, the PE firm checks the assumptions and attempts to optimize decisions regarding the purchase price, debt structure, and equity structure. In Step B, the PE firm analyzes explicit model outputs (e.g., the IRR and CoC) and risk measurements (e.g., the ICR). The PE firm will have additional considerations in mind as well, such as the probability of winning the deal and the alignment of stakeholders' incentives. Finally, if further optimizations could be achieved, the process will be repeated. If no further optimization is possible, the transaction structure is defined, and the PE firm and other stakeholders must decide whether the proposed deal is acceptable.

Exhibit 14: Optimization and analysis of the LBO model

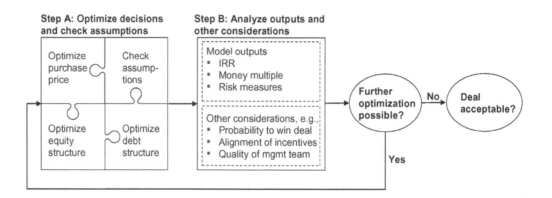

The optimization of decisions can be done following two different logics:

- **Competition-based optimization.** When following competition-based optimization, the basic question is, given the specific purchase price required to win the deal, can the PE firm make the transaction acceptable to all investors? This approach is generally used if the PE firm is aware of the approximate purchase price required to win the bid, as is often the case in public-to-private transactions or industries with many comparable PE transactions. Following this approach, the optimization of decisions in each iteration of Step A is normally done by setting the purchase price to the level that can probably win the bid, updating the debt level and debt structure and then updating the equity structure. It is very important that the initial forecasting assumptions are not optimized to "make the deal work," although this is a common bad practice in many LBO transactions. In Step B, the main focus of the PE firm is on the IRR and CoC. Typically, when deciding whether the deal is acceptable, the transaction IRR is compared with the hurdle IRR rate of the different investors in the deal.

- **Return-based optimization.** When following return-based optimization, the basic question is, given that investors want to achieve at least a specific hurdle IRR, what is the maximum price the PE firm can pay for the equity? This approach is used in the absence of any knowledge about the purchase price that is required to win the bid, which might be the case for private companies with no comparable transactions. In Step A, if the current IRR is less than the target IRR, then consider a lower purchase price, more debt, or a more investor-friendly equity structure. If the current IRR is greater than the target IRR, then consider a higher purchase price, less debt, or a less investor-friendly equity structure. In Step B: Stop if the current IRR is equal to the target IRR.

It is important to note that the main difference between PE firms and strategic buyers that target the same firms is that PE firms focus more on how the purchase price affects their returns, whereas strategics often care more about how the transaction affects their reported earnings per share.

ANALYSIS OF THE TOYS R US LBO

Was Toys R Us a good LBO candidate? Using the analytical methods outlined above, we find that, overall, Toys R Us seemed to be good target in 2005 based on the characteristics of strong LBO candidates (described in the chapter on LBO transactions); however, it did present some major risks. We discuss the characteristics of this LBO below.

Positive characteristics

- Toys R Us had strong cash flows (as shown in the historic income statement in Exhibit 2). Although growth has been stagnant, the cash flows were stable. In addition, debtor days were much lower than creditor days—4.7 versus 48.8, respectively, in 2004 (see Exhibit 3); this means Toys R Us, like most retail businesses, was cash flow positive, which is advantageous when maximizing working capital efficiency to pay down debt.

- The company had a strong asset base (as shown by the opening balance sheet in Exhibit 3). Inventory accounts receivable and Property Plant and Equipment, which are common sources of the debt security, have a book value of $6.6 billion, versus a proposed leverage of around $3 billion. This strong asset base increased the target's debt capacity.

- It is impossible to analyze the growth and operational improvement opportunities without thorough due diligence, but the company was having operational difficulties and had attempted a repositioning before the deal, which had been unsuccessful. The brand name was strong, and there was scope for a PE firm to create value using the techniques of active ownership. There may have also been a case for replacing some of the management team given the strategic problems the company has experienced just prior to the deal.

Negative characteristics

- The current leverage was very high. The company had over 2 billion of debt, which means the benefits of LBO economics may have already been included in the share price. Sensitivity analysis shows that a deal based on the 2004 closing share price of $27 would have produced a negative IRR and CoC return;

this is why our analysis is based on an EBITDA multiple, despite the fact that Toys R Us was a public company. After the transaction, Toys R Us debt jumped to $4.8 billion so the company had to make $400 million in debt payments every year— a number that was often higher than its annual profits.

- Toys R Us was not swift enough to compete with a giant like Amazon, and its brick-and-mortar stores carried huge costs as well. When the company finally decided to revamp its website in 2016, it admitted that it was 10 years behind on innovation relative to Amazon.

Operational improvements

Operational improvements could have been achieved by increasing sales (price or quantity, depending on elasticity) or reducing costs. Most PE activity is focused on cutting costs and making organizations more efficient. In the case of Toys R Us, if we assume the Cost of Goods Sold could have been reduced by 1.5% from 67.5% to 66%, the IRR would jump from 24.2% to 35.1%, and the CoC return from 3x to 4.5x. This demonstrates the powerful effect of successful operational improvement strategies. Of course, ex post, the company could not manage to cut its cost base and could not increase prices given the competition from Amazon and other online toy sellers such as eBay.

Multiple expansion

In the event that the PE firms were able to achieve multiple expansion through market timing or improved future prospects, the value creation effect could have been substantial. However, it turns out that this outcome was mostly beyond the control of the PE firm. Our base case assumed the same entry and exit multiple of 7.5x. If the exit multiple were to increase to 8.5x, the IRR would have increased from 24.2% to 28.9% and the CoC to 3.6x.

Financial leverage

The powerful effects of leverage can be illustrated by increasing it from 65% (the base case) to 80%. Making this change increases the IRR from 24.2% to 39.9%, and the CoC to 4.6x. Yet, this change does not take into account the increasing costs of financial distress, so it is only a benefit as long as the target can continue to service the debt and avoid bankruptcy. This omission is one important criticism of many LBO models; in practice, it is controlled in an LBO deal by the coverage ratios the bank sets and the debt covenants which enforce them. As discussed above, a maximum of 5x debt/EBITDA is a good guide. Leverage of 80% in this deal would lead to a debt/EBITDA ratio of 4.7x, an ICR ratio of 1.8x, and a DSCR of 1.5x, all of which were acceptable ratios in 2004 but unacceptable today.

A combination of the above value creation measures (i.e., COGS reduction, exit multiple of 8.5x, and 80% leverage), would lead to an IRR increase from 24.2% to 48%, and a CoC increase from 3x to 7.1x. This increase demonstrates the power of LBO economics and how very high relative returns can be achieved if operational improvements and fortunate market timing are included.

However, conditions can also deteriorate, as they actually did for Toys R Us following the financial crisis and the shift in consumer preferences towards online shopping. The recession had a negative effect on both the exit multiple and the sales of the company. If we assumed that the exit multiple dropped to 6x and the company's sales decreased by 3% in the two years prior to exit, the IRR would drop to 10.4% and the CoC to 1.6x—a relatively low return given the risks associated with such an investment.

CONCLUSION

The LBO modeling can be intimidating for those that are new to financial models in Excel. This is because most students of this topic or analysts are often exposed to very complex LBO models that are presented in templates that need to be populated. The purpose of this chapter is to help with the understanding of the topic and show that an LBO model is not that complicated. Basically, an LBO model is just an integrated set of financial statements adjusted to reflect a transaction (which brings source and uses of funds, balance sheet adjustments and exit analyses).

In his own words: Eric Kump, Founder, Alterra Capital Partners

The art of the Leveraged Buyout continues to evolve. At inception in the late eighties, the LBO was often characterized as financial engineering. The main source of returns was from debt pay down. LBOs at the time had a high debt funding relative to the equity contribution but not necessarily higher debt to EBITDA multiplies than today. It was the equity percentage that was lower, often as little as 10-15%. It took only a modest increase in the enterprise value (firm value) in order to get returns of 2-3x on the small portion of equity. Debt structuring was an important skill. Senior bank debt had covenants and amortization schedules and matching the cash profile of the company to these was key to prudently structuring leverage. Layering subordinated debt and even mezzanine further enhanced deal returns.

Fast forward to today. Average acquisition multiples are over 10x. Equity contributions are 40-50% in the capital structure (when equity goes above 50% it is not clear whether the transaction can still be classified as an LBO). Debt rarely has covenants or amortization schedules and many deals are done with senior-only debt structures. So how does private equity continue to generate 2x returns today on a higher proportional equity contribution? The emphasis has shifted to fundamental value creation in the form of increasing EBITDA. In the last decade, of the three basic sources of deal returns (EBITDA growth, debt pay down and multiple expansion), EBITDA growth comprised about 65% of the value creation followed by debt pay down at 20% and the multiple expansion at 15%. Therefore, the private equity industry and its practitioners have evolved into more well-rounded business improvement managers. The focus has shifted to rigorous target company senior management evaluation, recruitment and team building. This, in turn, supports detailed operating and expansion plans, both organic and acquisition led. Many private equity firms further support portfolio companies with in-house operating executives and consulting teams. Today, the art of the LBO is more about talent and operational improvement than financial engineering.

8 Post-Deal Operational Improvements

Strategy without tactics is the slowest route to victory. Tactics without strategy is the noise before defeat.
Sun Tzu

INTRODUCTION

An important change in the global private equity industry over the last few years has been the shift away from deal sourcing and financial engineering as major drivers of excess returns toward a focus on operational improvements. This paradigm shift is due to significantly increased competition in the private equity industry, which has made it vital to venture beyond leverage in order to generate abnormal returns. Currently, most private equity firms highlight their operational capabilities during fundraising as much as they highlight their track records. Many firms have built substantial dedicated in-house teams to drive operational value creation within their portfolio companies. However, despite the great importance of operational capabilities in generating returns for private equity fund investors, most firms do not provide specific details of how their operations teams add value to portfolio companies. One reason for this ambiguity is that different portfolio companies require different approaches depending on specific circumstances.

When used as a broad industry term in private equity, "operational (or operating) improvements" can be defined as non-financing-related value creation activities during the period when a private equity fund holds a company, which is typically three to five years. The term in its practical use encompasses not only value creation initiatives related to operations, but also initiatives that include adjustments to corporate governance mechanisms and a company's culture, organization, and objectives, among other areas. Operational improvements span the entire holding period, bridging the pre-acquisition due diligence phase when the investment thesis is formulated and the exit phase when additional equity value is created and realized. The execution of these improvements often starts with an intensive so-called "100-day plan" immediately post acquisition, which is followed by further initiatives that are part of a full potential plan to develop the company and increase the equity value.

The general view is that general partners (GPs) strengthen equity returns in a typical buyout deal by (1) enhancing the operational performance of the portfolio company post acquisition, (2) selling the company at a higher valuation multiple relative to the one at the time of investment, and (3) leveraging the transaction and repaying the debt before selling the portfolio company. Post-deal operational improvements are, of course, reflected in the first channel above, but they also influence the equity returns generated by the second and third channels, given that such improvements allow the firm to service its debt and increase the company's growth opportunities and margins, which, in turn, yields higher exit multiples. Over the years, GPs with funds whose performance ranks in the top quartile have consistently delivered high returns by improving their value creation activities through post-deal operational improvements. These activities are particularly important during periods with high purchasing multiples for target companies due to increased competition and excess liquidity in the mergers and acquisitions (M&A) market.

Operational improvements involve more parties than just the operational management teams of portfolio companies since an interdisciplinary approach requires complementary competencies. The larger the portfolio company, the more likely it is to need specialist advisers helping the management along the way in achieving post-deal operational improvements. These specialist advisers often include regional, functional, or industry specialists, such as the GP's investment professionals and operating partners, in-house consultants and senior advisors, the company's supervisory board as well as external consultants, industry experts, and interim managers. Since private equity investments come with active ownership, private equity professionals usually work alongside operational advisers to steer the strategic direction of the company. These professionals often form the majority in the supervisory board of the portfolio company that frequently includes external industry experts as well. The management of the portfolio company is ultimately responsible for key strategic decisions, and is the central executive entity for most operational initiatives and for day-to-day operations. The management team is both spearheaded and supported by the supervisory board, which is supposed to act as an active trusting partner.

Which operational improvements are made after a private equity deal? The answer to this question depends on the company—namely, its size, state of development, industry, geography, former ownership structure—as well as other factors, such as the investment strategy of the GP. The answer is also any and every operational improvement that facilitates the achievement of the GP's target returns assumed in the investment case that supported the deal. It is important to note that sophisticated investors in private equity funds often assess the extent to which the operational value-add activities implemented by the GP are both "effective" and "repeatable." In particular, many investors view the GP's ability to consistently implement operational plans as a sign of high future fund performance.

EVIDENCE ON PRIVATE EQUITY FIRMS' ABILITY TO IMPROVE PERFORMANCE

Several studies have documented the superior performance of private equity-owned companies in comparison to those not owned by private equity firms. Using buyout transactions in the 1980s and 1990s, Kaplan (1989), Lichtenberg, and Siegel (1990), as well as Cohn et al. (2013), provide evidence that leveraged buyouts create value by significantly improving the operating performance of acquired companies. Similarly, Davis et al. (2014) find notable increases in productivity in a large sample of U.S. buyouts that rely on leverage during the same periods. They attribute the performance to the disciplining effect of leverage used to fund the transactions, and to the better governance instituted by the GPs.

Using more recent data, Lerner et al. (2008) find significant increases in long-term innovation in a sample of 495 buyouts. Private equity-owned companies generate patents that are more frequently cited—a proxy for the novelty and the level of innovation provided by the patents. In addition, Gao et al. (2013) document that private equity-owned firms hold, on average, only about half as much cash on their balance sheets as their public counterparts, suggesting that GPs optimize the use of capital at the portfolio company level. Boucly et al. (2011) focus on a dataset of large French deals executed between 1994 and 2004 (with an average enterprise value of EUR400 million) and find that private equity targets become more profitable, grow much faster, issue additional debt, and increase capital expenditures (capex) relative to a carefully selected peer group, especially if they are credit constrained. This paper offers similar results to Acharya et al. (2013), who also analyze big deals initiated by large private equity houses. They document that the higher abnormal performance of private equity funds is due to sales and margin improvements at the portfolio company level, and that ownership by large and mature private equity houses has a positive impact on the operating performance of portfolio companies, relative to the overall performance of their sector.

Further recent evidence by Aleszczyk et al. (2016) provides new insights into how value is created at the portfolio company level, thereby offering a potential explanation for why private equity funds outperform public markets. They investigate the post-transaction performance of a large sample of European private equity deals executed between 1998 and 2014 and report that—relative to benchmark non-private equity owned firms matched by year, industry, and other characteristics—companies acquired by private equity firms increase their sales, operating profitability, and assets over the first three years of private equity ownership (see Exhibit 1). These results show that while GPs are focused on growth, they also generate other significant operational-level improvements.

Exhibit 1: Evidence on operational improvements

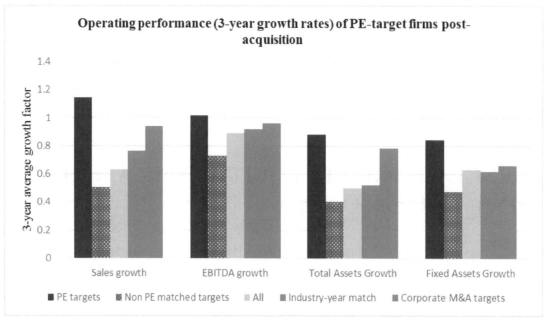

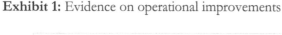

FACTORS THAT DRIVE OPERATIONAL IMPROVEMENTS

Any company encountering a change in ownership, whether public or private, will necessarily experience some form of transition. Actionable operational improvements in private equity need to take into account the constraints of the deal environment while benefiting from several enabling factors. Constraints may include a limited time frame for the holding period, implementation costs, the leveraged financing corset (if any), and the management capacity. At the other end of the spectrum, the enabling factors might consist of an active supervisory board, faster decision making, greater tolerance for risk, the three- to five-year ownership horizon (highlighting the need for rigorous implementation of value-adding initiatives), the GP's expert network, available capital, and the M&A competency of the GP (see Exhibit 2).

Exhibit 2: Actionable operational improvements

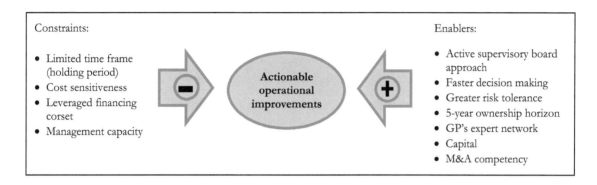

Private equity investors are medium-term temporary partners; inherent to the investment approach is the ultimate sale of the portfolio company at some point, implying a limited ownership horizon. This limited ownership time frame can be seen as a constraint on large-scale operational initiatives that may be long term in nature. Building a brand from scratch or introducing a product that requires a change in customer behavior are examples of large-scale initiatives which could potentially extend beyond the holding period of a fund. However, this time frame issue does not mean that projects with a payback period of more than five years are unattractive. Such initiatives can be used to build additional potential around the equity story at exit. At the same time, building an entire investment case on them would be challenging, as value creation initiatives are normally targeted to materialize at the time of the exit at the latest. Conversely, the three- to five-year investment horizon can also be seen as an enabler since it means that there is, in fact, a time frame, which is not available in the case of non-private equity owned companies. Relative to investors in public equity, who are more focused on quarterly results, investors in private equity funds can be more patient (yet no less demanding).

Additionally, follow-on capital is available and quick to be called if needed for projects within a portfolio company—not an infrequent occurrence for ambitious ones. Ambition also comes naturally with the high return expectations and an active supervisory board, which may contribute with relevant M&A competency and industry networks that are great enablers for growth and transformation. Such ambition can be curtailed by constraining factors such as management's limited time and capabilities for projects beyond daily operations, as well as constraints on activities that arise from the financing banks. Given that leveraged buyouts are risky, banks providing financing establish operational rules for the portfolio company in the lending agreements. For example, a bank might object to buying a complex, large but unprofitable add-on business for a portfolio company, even though it could make sense from a long-term strategic perspective. In addition, value creation projects need to reflect the cost-sensitive return-driven private equity perspective; the high cost of capital in private equity funds results in a permanent optimization of the capital invested in portfolio companies.

Post-deal operational improvements are ultimately driven by two important elements. First, the investment thesis and the business plan developed around opportunities identified at the pre-acquisition phase significantly contribute to the articulation of the post-deal operational plans.[1] Successful GPs put together a so-called "strategic roadmap" for the future of the company that identifies value creation opportunities and

---

[1] Deal screening and due diligence is covered in an earlier chapter.

how these opportunities can be exploited. Opportunities might stem from internal company-specific strategic advantages (e.g., leading market position, unique technology, geographical location, and access to knowhow) or external market factors (e.g., industry trends, macroeconomic conditions, and the legal environment) favorable to the company in the future. GPs tend to have a medium-term outlook when considering opportunities compared with publicly listed companies, which are constantly scrutinized by the capital market to deliver results on a quarterly basis. A long-term view often provides alternative unique growth options for the company, significantly enhancing the value accrued to shareholders.

The second crucial element that drives the implementation of post-deal operational improvements is the extent to which these improvements contribute to an increase in the company's value. Specifically, improvements should generate higher EBITDA growth and stimulate the expansion of valuation multiples. Every single operational activity should be measured based on its impact on the current and future EBITDA and valuation multiples. For instance, margin improvements through leaner operations or overhead cost reductions will lead to higher EBITDA growth and potentially higher valuations to the extent that these cost savings provide the firm with a long-term competitive advantage. In addition, a less obvious but no less important factor that drives increases in portfolio companies' value is the adjustment of corporate governance mechanisms and managerial incentive structures. By implementing more effective governance structures and introducing well designed incentive structures, GPs can motivate the portfolio company's management to deliver according to the investment plan. While aligning the incentives of management with those of the private equity firm or changing the firm's governance may not reflect an operational improvement activity per se, these actions are some of the most effective tools introduced by private equity firms to help achieve higher portfolio company values. Getting the management to focus, work hard, and deliver results during the holding period is a key enabler in the toolbox of operationally driven private equity firms.

We discuss operational improvement options based on these two elements. Given that most private equity firms appoint advisers and management consultants to support their post-deal operational improvement initiatives, each firm will likely have its own frameworks and methodologies to deal with the implementation of operational improvements.

THE INVESTMENT THESIS AND THE 100-DAY PLAN

High-level post-deal operational improvement plans take shape well before a purchase transaction ends. It is essential that GPs identify potential opportunities accurately by analyzing and challenging them in detail in the pre-transaction due diligence stage. As a result, the processes of deal screening, due diligence, and planning for post-deal operational improvements are closely connected.

When it comes to initiatives that specifically increase operational value, admittedly, there is no clear separation between topics. An integrated operational improvement plan must be holistic, covering various areas. At the same time, the plan should revolve around a few overarching key value drivers (e.g., internationalization, growth via acquisitions, transformation toward a system-/solution provider, digitalization, refocusing segments/products, etc.). The GPs should ask themselves the following two questions very early in the investment process: "What value can be added with our competencies?" and "What company do we want to sell at exit?" These questions support an operational improvement plan that is integrated into the broader transaction process. Exhibit 3 illustrates the overall process.

Exhibit 3: Timeline of the investment process in the context of operational improvements in private equity

Deal execution	First 100 days	Continuous value creation	Exit
• Conduct due diligence	• Conduct kick-off	• Execute strategic transformation program	• Prepare exit readiness
• Develop investment thesis	• Set up corporate governance	• Execute mid-/long-term operational initiatives	• Define buyer universe
• Identify value creation drivers and quantify impact	• Create comprehensive fact book to ensure transparency	• Track progress, reflect and adjust	• Develop equity story
• Negotiate incentives with management team and ensure alignment on strategy and value creation initiatives	• Specify strategy and value creation program		• Develop visible potentials for next owner
	• Define roadmap		
	• Install project management office		
	• Realize "quick wins," start implementing other initiatives and track progress		

The investment thesis

As shown in Exhibit 3, the first thing private equity firms should do when executing an investment in a company is formulate an *investment thesis*—a clear statement of how they will make the business more valuable within approximately three to five years. This thesis states *why* the private equity firm would want to own the company and guides every single operational action taken during the holding period. The best investment theses lay out the fundamental changes needed to transform the company in a simple and straightforward way. They provide a clear base for action that goes beyond setting financial targets, such as simply achieving increases over the previous year's profitability levels. Most top private equity professionals try to get the thesis down on paper as soon as possible, allowing them to circulate it internally and to generate reactions early and often. Effective investment theses revolve around central objectives such as

- return the company to its core business;

- replicate the business model in other geographies;

- leverage the company's core competency in other products, services, or sectors;

- roll up smaller companies to create scale;

- become the primary outlet for a particular online activity; and

- achieve operational excellence with respect to the manufacturing or provision of a product or service.

The development of an investment thesis could start by answering three basic but fundamental questions at the time of considering an investment in a potential target company:

Why this industry?

GPs must understand the long-term trends of the industry, which may be driven by demographics, environmental concerns and regulations, infrastructure constraints, input prices, or other considerations. GPs should also have a thorough understanding of the size of the market and its breakdown by geography or players, as well as the current growth drivers and dynamics.

Why this business model?

To answer this question, GPs need to first clarify the characteristics of the business model, such as its capabilities to entrench customers, be scalable, generate high growth, bring recurring revenues, be easily adopted, raise high barriers of entry for the competition, be profitable in the long term, address a key customer pain point, and so on. Second, GPs must understand the value chain to be able to identify those activities that provide more value to customers and create competitive long-term advantages for the portfolio company.

Why now?

Very often, GPs' investment strategy is driven by timing considerations. For instance, market impetus might induce a particular investment strategy during a certain period. Further, GPs should consider the deal dynamics and the situation of the selling party, as well as the time it takes to acquire the portfolio company and deliver the operational strategy, regardless of the risk profile of the portfolio company. The answer to this question also depends on the expected holding period and the anticipated point in time when the exit will occur. GP-internal considerations (e.g., regarding the risk of the current portfolio or the fundraising cycles) may also be taken into account.

An exemplary, stylized investment thesis could be as follows:

> SOFTCO is a leading security software developer that provides a proprietary solution to a blue chip customer base, operates a license business model with 75% recurring annual revenues, and has a global market share of 30% in a critical software security sub-segment which grows at 15% per annum. The investment can generate a 25% IRR and a money multiple of 3x over a period of five years if (1) the sales capacity is expanded across Europe, (2) the pricing and licensing model with existing customers is optimized, and (3) the software is deployed to enhance tangent security applications. The exit is expected to be a sale to an integrated software group as a strategic investor or via an IPO.

While GPs typically formulate the investment thesis at the time of the acquisition, they periodically evaluate the value creation potential of the portfolio company and adjust the investment thesis accordingly to adapt to potential changes in conditions.

The 100-day plan

In the due diligence phase, most target companies present a three- to five-year business plan developed by the incumbent management team. This plan often becomes the basis for calculating the company's value, formulating the investment thesis, and identifying operational synergies and growth opportunities. The typical business plan is frequently part of an extensive information memorandum that provides a detailed explanation of the corporate strategy, historical events and milestones, market and competitor overviews, and planned developments for the business over the coming years to support the projected sales growth. The incumbent management team that has created the business plan is questioned thoroughly about details in the due diligence process initiated by the private equity firm. At this stage, the GP assesses the assumptions made and the capabilities required to deliver the projected growth or strategic direction. In many cases, based on their experience and knowledge of the sector, GPs would introduce assumptions that are more conservative than those laid out in the business plan.

GPs (often with the support of their advisors) identify and formulate opportunities over and beyond those presented by the incumbent management team. A GP analysis that goes beyond the management's business plan usually leads to the articulation of the investment thesis and forms the basis of the post-deal operational strategy for the company. It is important that the investment committee of the private equity firm thoroughly scrutinize and challenge the hypotheses and assumptions behind the investment thesis. Otherwise, there is a risk of implementing an investment thesis that relies on flawed hypotheses and assumptions and misses key risk factors, potentially leading to poor performance or even value destruction.

Private equity firms often receive exclusive access to the company during the final due diligence process, allowing them to better understand the business and challenge the thinking of the company's management regarding the investment thesis and plans. The firms must ensure the feasibility of their calculated value potentials, which may or may not be shared with management at the pre-transaction stage, depending on the deal dynamics and the format of the sale process. After the identification of value potentials and their integration into the investment plan, corporate governance and management incentives are also redefined post acquisition. Most importantly, detailed planning around the execution and implementation of the strategy should start in earnest. Successful private equity firms map out the full execution strategy from deal to exit with target investment returns in mind as they complete the deal. They are usually fully ready to execute their strategy by the time the deal is complete; the "how" then becomes their main focus.

In a kick-off (or onboarding) meeting, the management team, the new supervisory board, and the private equity investment professionals establish common objectives, timelines, and responsibilities. In addition to confirming the overall value creation concept, meeting participants put into place an action plan for the first 100 days post closing (i.e., the 100-day plan mentioned above). First and foremost, this plan should aim to create full transparency. It should also specify measurable initiatives for transformation, review the organizational structure of the company, identify key hires, and set up a monitoring structure. Very often, GPs create a *project management office* (PMO) to coordinate and monitor the different operational initiatives. Below, we discuss the main areas that should be covered by the 100-day plan.

Reporting systems

A core requirement of the first 100 days of the holding period is total *transparency* regarding the current status and development of the business on an ongoing basis. Transparency is essential for an active owner (e.g., a private equity fund) as it forms the basis for any high-quality decision making and for every operational initiative. GPs expect the company to set up its reporting systems to provide monthly updates of financial and operational information and detailed quarterly reviews and forecasts. Providing *reliable data* and presenting it with a *meaningful focus* are key objectives. For instance, comparisons of actual figures with budget and prior year figures on a monthly basis allow the involved parties to obtain a clear view of the company's situation. Good reports should be analytical as well as descriptive, explaining plan deviations and recovery measures in case of a negative performance. They usually include integrated financial statements—profit and loss, balance sheet, and cash flow—with relevant performance and covenant ratios that need to be reported to lenders. Specific attention should be given to the reporting of sales, gross margin, EBITDA, operating and free cash flows, and the levels of net debt as well as their drivers.

The financial information provided should also be supplemented with reports on operating key performance indicators (KPIs), which capture the underlying performance. KPIs often provide an early warning system that flags underperformance. They are also useful in tracking the impact of operational measures and identifying areas of improvement. KPIs should be measured over time and against industry benchmarks or targets assumed in the investment thesis. It is important to note that KPIs vary significantly across business models and industries. The following list is not exhaustive, but includes some frequently used operating-level KPIs:

- For any company: Sales per employee, employee turnover rates, absenteeism rates, number of customer complaints, accident rates, and customer satisfaction.

- For manufacturing businesses: Scrap rates, overall equipment effectiveness (OEE), delivery reliability, machine uptime/downtime, manufacturing cycle time, reclamation costs, and special transport costs.

- For service providers: Customer retention, churn rates, customer acquisition cost, and agent utilization.

- For retail firms: Sales per square meter, average purchase value, average units per transaction, and conversion rate.

Regular reports are the main tool for communicating the company's performance to the private equity owner, the supervisory board, and the debt providers. The GP and the management team agree on the frequency and level of reporting detail in the 100-day plan, but, once implemented, the reporting system must prove its value by fulfilling the private equity owner's informational needs while being used in parallel by management to run the daily operations.

A vital part of any report is the executive summary, the financial and operational "cockpit." Exhibit 4 provides an example of a monthly executive summary, while acknowledging that presentation style and reporting requirements and focus can vary significantly. This summary shows the overall performance of the portfolio company and its two subsidiaries across several financial and operational dimensions.

Reporting standards differ, of course, from company to company and are often a function of many factors, such as the previous owner of the company, the industry, the size of the company, the value creation opportunities identified by the GP, and so on. For example, a mid-sized family business acquired by a private equity fund in the context of a succession solution is likely to have rather low reporting standards, while a large company being acquired in a secondary transaction will have well established, high-quality reporting systems. In the former case, a reporting system may need to be built from scratch, together with relevant controlling tools (e.g., sales, production, and capex controls) and financial forecasting and planning tools. The creation and sustainability of transparent reporting can be a major value driver in and of itself, as a transparent company is expected to attract a broader spectrum of interested parties at the time of exit.

Exhibit 4: Example of a monthly reporting summary for a portfolio company

MONTHLY SUMMARY (in €m)		Actual *Budget comparison* *Prior year comparison*	Feb 16	Cum. YTD	% Delta	FC (YTD+B)	% Delta	LTM	% Delta
Group	Sales	A / B / P	[...] %	[...] %	%	[...] %	%	[...] %	%
Subsidiary 1	Sales	A / B / P	[...] %	[...] %	%	[...] %	%	[...] %	%
Subsidiary 2	Sales	A / B / P	[...] %	[...] %	%	[...] %	%	[...] %	%
Group	EBITDA	A / B / P	[...] %	[...] %	%	[...] %	%	[...] %	%
Subs. 1	EBITDA	A / B / P	[...] %	[...] %	%	[...] %	%	[...] %	%
Subs. 2	EBITDA	A / B / P	[...] %	[...] %	%	[...] %	%	[...] %	%
Group	Capex	A / B / P	[...] %	[...] %	%	[...] %	%	[...] %	%
Group	Free Cash Flow	A / B / P	[...] %	[...] %	%	[...] %	%	[...] %	%
Group	Net financial debt	A / B / P	[...] %	N/M	N/M	N/M	N/M	N/M	%
Group	OEE	A / B / P	[...] %	[...]% %	%	[...]% %	%	[...]% %	%
Group	Scrap rate	A / B / P	[...] %	[...]% %	%	[...]% %	%	[...]% %	%
Group	Delivery reliability	A / B / P	[...] %	[...]% %	%	[...]% %	%	[...]% %	%

Monitoring measurable initiatives for transformation

Based on the investment thesis, the 100-day plan should identify the main areas of transformation, such as pricing of products and services, sales force effectiveness, corporate development strategy (e.g., "buy and build"), or internationalization of the business. Once these areas are clearly identified, feasibility is confirmed, and impacts are quantified, a detailed action plan is developed. The conceptual transformation intentions are translated into a practicable project scheme in which actions are subdivided into sequential or parallel actions. The plan includes responsibilities, timelines, budgets, milestones, and deliverables. Furthermore, the plan should put forward project KPIs that track the progress of the portfolio company's management team across each workstream in a timely, objective, and transparent manner. An effective KPI in this context is a metric that is measured at a relatively low cost in an unbiased and objective manner and is under the control of the management. Indicators with these characteristics motivate management to work hard and are perceived as fair. Examples of KPIs include targets regarding market share gains, growth, and cost reductions, or goals that are unique to a private equity transaction (e.g., EBITDA levels, return on capital, and debt paydowns).

A common—and often effective—monitoring mechanism in 100-day plans is a *balanced scorecard*. This tool defines the performance of the portfolio company and measures whether its management is achieving desired results with the respective initiatives. For each value creation project, the balanced scorecard includes a set of performance measures (or project KPIs) that can be quantified and appraised. These measures typically include categories of performance that cover (1) financial performance of the actions (e.g., incremental revenues, earnings, or cash flows, as well as return on capital invested), (2) customer value performance (e.g., market share, customer satisfaction measures, and customer loyalty), (3) internal business process performance (productivity rates, quality measures, and timelines), (4) innovation performance (percentage of revenue from new products, employee suggestions, and rate of improvement index), and (5) employee performance (morale, customer interaction, knowledge, turnover, and use of best demonstrated practices). The balanced scorecard can be supplemented with details about the project status, such as the percentage completion rate, as well as information showing whether the measure is on track in terms of its budget, timing, and targeted overall results.

Review of the organizational structure

Many private equity deals involve carve-out transactions (i.e., where the private equity fund purchases a division of a larger corporation). These divested divisions might be missing complete functions that are critical to the successful operation of the business and were handled by the seller's shared service organization structure. Therefore, the private equity firm must first identify any departments that are missing (e.g., finance and technology) and set aside the resources to build them up immediately after the transaction.

The 100-day plan should objectively identify the functions that need to be rebuilt, as well as the effort involved. GPs must base their estimates on the complexity of the business. For instance, the number of subdivisions, countries, currencies, languages, or local compliance regulations involved will play a significant role in building a new finance department. In the case of a new planning and supply chain management department, the GP should consider product configurations, production schedules, shop floor control issues, and warehouse management and distribution aspects.

Organizational structures are generally adjusted in view of the long-term development of the organization and a sale of the company at some point in the future. An effective organization in the private equity context is lean: it allows for efficient communication, gives autonomy to small units, and is flexible to learn and adapt, while also being resilient and (as much as possible) independent of any specific individual.

Identification of human resources needs

The success or failure of a portfolio company usually comes down to the people involved. The GP must ensure that the portfolio company has people with the right expertise on its board and executive management team, and on the incumbent senior management team. Moreover, an effective human resources (HR) team has to be assembled early in light of the additional management roles to be created and staffed to account for the private equity ownership situation and for the intended transformational change. For example, it is likely that a new and dedicated manager would be needed for a forceful execution of a buy-and-build acquisition strategy. In addition, a buyout brings new fields of work and aspects to be considered, especially for CFO, given the requirements from the private equity investor and financing banks. A buyout might also bring along the need for a strong controller or an interim finance manager to set up advanced reporting systems. Additional management capacities are especially necessary, for example, in succession solutions or carve-outs. In general, bringing new top managers on board can be a delicate process; thus, it is important to involve incumbent managers in the recruitment process.

Further, mid-level management must be reviewed. Often, private equity transactions lead to personnel turnover in key departmental positions that may significantly affect the success of the business. Middle management turnover in the company's HR, supply chain management, production planning, research and development (R&D), product data management, sales, or customer service functions can be very disruptive and expensive. The GP must aim to maintain continuity in these departments so that unexpected turnover does not compromise the operational plan.

Operational quick fixes

The 100-day plan also contains "quick fixes" that should be implemented immediately after closing. These normally relate to "housekeeping" issues identified in the various due diligence workstreams during the acquisition process. Working areas and tasks cover legal, tax, financing, operating, commercial, and other functions; examples include the adjustment of the insurance coverage, filling gaps in the historical legal documentation, aligning operational standards within a group, simplifying a historically grown legal group structure (e.g., liquidating "empty" legacy companies), centralizing the cash management via a cash pool, and extending the tax group according to the new group structure. Any issues of this type are mostly on a small scale. Nevertheless, they need to be fixed—especially given the aim to sell a "clean" company at the point of exit.

OPERATIONAL ACTIVITIES THAT IMPROVE PORTFOLIO COMPANY VALUE

Private equity firms with the ability to improve the performance of portfolio companies on a consistent basis typically establish an in-house group of *operational (or operating) partners*. These are individuals with extensive experience (e.g., former senior executives in the corporate or consulting world, or from other private equity firms). They act as portfolio company board members or consultants, and adopt a hands-on role in the strategic planning and supervision of the company by applying their industry knowledge and analytic skills to any issues facing the company.[2] Operating partners accumulate experience working with multiple portfolio companies in different industries, and can therefore offer a broader perspective than that of a portfolio company CEO.

Operating partners are expected to collaborate closely with the portfolio company's management team in order to show their trust in management and gain greater support for operational improvement initiatives from the company's employees. In an ideal situation, rather than replacing the management team or imposing external decisions upon the company, operating partners should engage with the management team to take ownership of operational initiatives. However, sometimes, the operating partners might reach the conclusion that the current senior management team (or an individual member of the team) is in fact, part of the company's problems. In these instances, the operational partners are expected to hire new managers with the help of external recruitment agencies.

The operational partners and the management team should share a primary focus: *improving the valuation* of the acquired company. Compared to the typical corporate situation, private equity ownership places a stronger emphasis on cash flow generation, while the time frame for tackling important issues is greatly compressed. Thus, all operational initiatives pursued are continuously evaluated based on how they contribute to growing the company's EBITDA and valuation multiples. These evaluations dictate the selection and priority of implementation given the limited time frame.[3] Identifying the priorities ensures a successful strategy, as the operational partners often face an overwhelming number of potential improvement opportunities that can be acted upon.

As noted, there is no single formula for creating an operational advantage in private equity. Competing private equity firms target deals of all sizes, in a variety of industries, using many different investment strategies. As such, the most effective methods for implementing operational changes to increase the value of portfolio companies vary according to the strategies set out in the investment thesis. Exhibit 5 presents some of the areas for strategic and operational value creation initiatives that are covered by private equity firms. Some of these topics overlap as they are interrelated. Given the large number of issues that could be covered, we discuss only the most pertinent ones here.

Sales growth

Organic sales growth

An acquired business that has shown solid organic growth over recent years and projects similarly strong growth in the future could be an attractive investment for a private equity fund.[4] If the sales growth story is accepted during the due diligence process, the operational partners' immediate concern will be to ensure the long-term sustainability of the organic sales growth; this could be achieved through several approaches:

---

[2] Private equity firms have adopted different operational models that vary with the operational partners' level of involvement. Some firms (e.g., Clayton, Dubilier & Rice) use a fully integrated operating partner model, where the operational partner spends significant time with the portfolio company as an active chairman dealing with the company's investment opportunities and day-to-day operations. The in-house consultant model, where a group of internal consultants rotate across portfolio companies to work on specific projects, is another alternative (e.g., Cerberus). The third model is the adviser model, where an internal or an external professional provides operational and strategic advice to the company as a board member or as a consultant hired on a project basis.

[3] Banks that provide financing for the deal also monitor the impact of operational improvements on the EBITDA and free cash flows as the financial performance of the company needs to meet financial covenants stipulated in the lending agreements.

[4] To some extent, high growth expectations would normally be reflected in the acquisition price/multiple.

Exhibit 5: Overview of areas for strategic and operational value creation initiatives

Sales: • Sales force effectiveness • Sales channels • Pricing review • Customer retention • Marketing strategy • Key account management • Ancillary offerings	**Profitability:** • Supply chain management • Procurement /gross margin improvement • SG&A cost reduction	**Capital management:** • Factoring/receivable management • Inventory management • Payables management • Asset sales/sale and leaseback
Strategy/transformation: • Competitive benchmarking • Strategy review and adjustment • Key strategic value drivers/ transformation path	**Product/technology:** • Product differentiation • Customer needs • Technology development	**Environmental and social issues:** • Normative systems • Health and safety • Contingency plan • Corporate social responsibility
Financing: • Hedging • Refinancing	**Culture:** • Results-driven culture • Sense of urgency • Common value ground	**Organizational efficiency:** • Simplification of legal structure • Internal communication • Knowledge management
Operational processes: • Operational structure • Lean management • Project management • Quality management • Certifications • Documentation • Standardization • Make or buy/outsourcing	**Information technology:** • ERP • CRM software • Electronic data interchange • System-integration • IT security	**HR:** • Individual objectives and incentives • Schedule of responsibilities • Recruiting key people • Talent management • Successions • Coaching, retention
Transparency: • Regular reporting • KPIs • Budgeting/forecasting • Controlling best-practice (sales, capex, production, etc.)	**Corporate development:** • Bolt-on acquisitions • Complementary add-on acquisitions • Buy and build • Joint ventures/partnerships • Non-core disposals	**Internationalization:** • Operations footprint optimization (LCC production, proximity to customers, etc.) • Sales offices • Relocation/ optimization of resources
Corporate governance: • Management incentives • Supervisory board • Two-person integrity • Checks and balances • Rules of procedure	**Innovation:** • Digitalization • Automation • Disruptive technologies • Innovation and IP management	**Exit readiness:** • Equity story development • Buyer universe • Pre-exit discussions with strategic buyers

- **Business expansion.** Business expansion is the most common approach to organic sales growth. While the underlying business may remain the same, gross margins and profitability could be improved by scaling up the business. The expansion must be carefully planned and managed in light of the investment requirements (e.g., land, building, factories, or machinery), market demand, risks, and HR needs in the context of the returns to investment that can be achieved. The expansion of the business can be refined through a customer segmentation analysis that can identify unmet customer demand. Detecting separate segments can lead to investments of resources that are tailored to match the needs of each segment. Business expansion can also be achieved by innovating in new products and services, as well as internationalization.

- **Sales force effectiveness.** A subtler approach to increasing sales without the requirement of major upfront investment is by increasing sales force effectiveness. The performance of the sales team can have an immediate and direct impact on the top line. Is the number of sales people sufficient? Do they have the right tools and information to sell and are they in the right locations? Do they have the right marketing support? How are they managed? Are they incentivized to be successful? Can they sell more? Are they selling the right products or services? Can they cross-sell a mix of other products and services? There are plenty of questions that need to be answered to ensure that a business has an effective sales force. Market research and analysis are required to form the best approach to improving sales effectiveness.

    Adequate KPIs need to be in place to measure sales force efficiency, while benchmarking with the sales force of best-in-class competitors could provide relevant information on the effectiveness of the sales force. The objective of benchmarking to competitors is to find examples of superior sales performance and understand the sales practices driving that performance.

- **Pricing.** Revenue can also be increased by optimizing the pricing models. Every company has a logical pricing matrix used to sell its products and services, but there could be a more advantageous pricing model to directly boost revenues. For instance, using mathematical modeling, management can calculate how demand varies at different price levels. Combining that data with information on costs and inventory levels allows companies to identify optimal prices that improve sales and profitability. Understanding how customers respond to price changes enables management to tailor the pricing of products and services for different customer segments. Since pricing is a data-driven approach, access to detailed historical data is essential.

- **Addressing customer churn rates.** In a business with recurring sales, growing the top line only works if current customers return to buy further products and services. If there is a high customer churn rate, management should identify its root causes to stop customer defections and revenue loss; this often involves designing loyalty schemes that grow revenues and profits by improving retention among customers, boosting their allegiance and ultimately turning them into advocates for the company's products and services. Management should regularly assess customer loyalty levels and design ways to distinguish between mere customer satisfaction and true loyalty. Loyalty levels should be benchmarked against those of competitors to identify opportunities for improvement.

Acquisition-based sales growth

Sales growth in portfolio companies can also be achieved through a strategy of acquisitions by the portfolio company.[5] This so-called "roll-up" or "buy-and-build" strategy is a common practice to grow a portfolio company much faster than via a purely organic route. Additionally, this approach is a natural fit since all private equity funds inherently have a strong in-house M&A skillset. Given these skills, many private equity firms apply a proactive and systematic corporate development approach; this starts with a comprehensive search field analysis to identify potential target companies. Often, a long-list is already being created during the due diligence phase. This list is then narrowed down to a focused short list with several high-priority targets. In this context, the portfolio company acts like a strategic investor that can offer synergistic benefits to a target company, while from the ownership structure, the portfolio company benefits from the potential for co-investment opportunities that are offered to key senior people.

For such add-on acquisitions to existing portfolio companies, private equity funds are normally less restricted in their investment criteria. While they have a clearly defined investment focus when it comes to investment style, industries, or geographies, funds often have substantial flexibility regarding add-on investing in terms of a target's geography, profitability, or size. Thus, relatively small or large investments that would not be possible on a stand-alone basis can be made to strengthen existing portfolio companies. To be able to bring the portfolio company into a position to lift large acquisitions, private equity funds can make follow-on equity investments. At the same time, private equity professionals can draw down opportunistically on leveraged finance loan contracts with predefined acquisition lines that were signed at the time of the acquisition of the portfolio company.

A portfolio company can add similar operations to its business (i.e., *horizontal bolt-ons*) or expand to additional stages within the value chain (*vertical* or *complementary add-ons*). Strategic rationales behind an add-on acquisition include an increased market share, diversification, cost benefits, access to new products or geographical markets, access to new customers or valuable assets (e.g., specific technologies), and even acquiring a new management team. From a fund perspective, another rationale could be to add to a platform in a fragmented industry of small competitors that can normally be acquired at lower acquisition multiples. Acquiring multiple small corporations at low valuations typically brings down the average acquisition multiple of the total investment, and can thus increase the multiple expansion potential. Relatedly, larger companies trade at statistically higher valuation multiples, which even creates room for a multiple expansion at exit.

Active corporate development initiatives normally start early in the holding period of a portfolio company. One reason for this timing is that execution (e.g., target identification, approach, due diligence, acquisition, and integration) absorbs substantial amounts of time. Accordingly, corporate development initiatives are usually mid to long-term in nature. Moreover, given a typical holding horizon of three to five years, cumulative benefits from acquisitions are higher when they are closed earlier. Furthermore, if an add-on has been part of the portfolio company for a while, and has been integrated successfully and consolidated group financial figures are available, the portfolio company has a more credible equity story at the time of the exit.

After an add-on acquisition has been closed, it is usually followed by a thorough post-merger integration project.[6] Such an integration project has multiple workstreams, including the streamlining of systems and processes, the establishment of group-wide standards, and the extraction of synergy potentials. It often

---

[5] In addition to acquisitions, a proactive corporate development strategy can also include joint ventures, strategic alliances, and disposals of non-core or underperforming entities.

[6] IT harmonization often requires significant investments of time and money.

includes external consultants, but full oversight and responsibility lies with top management. In practice, a comprehensive post-merger integration roadmap can be very detailed, including project costs, quantified benefits of synergies, and specific timelines for each workstream. Exhibit 6 shows a sample high-level overview with select key topics.

If the acquisition involves employees, employment laws in the applicable jurisdictions need to be considered while pursuing the most optimal solution with the highest return on investment. This solution could involve site closures and integration or migration of multiple sites. Alternatively, management may conclude that keeping the businesses separate and undertaking very little integration work is the best option for the combined entity. The latter conclusion is fairly common (potentially because of cost savings), but it can lead to potential criticism later about not acting sooner to avoid higher costs and duplication of processes. Cultural issues could also arise if two businesses are not integrated well. Therefore, management should address operational integration issues immediately, rather than taking too long and allowing these issues to fester.

Exhibit 6: Post-merger integration topics

Issues/ drivers	Status	Priority	Aim	Impact (est. € million gain p.a.)	Next steps	Project end
Transaction communication	Done	A	Internal communication (employees)	Mitigate uncertainty	Meeting with labor unions and employees	T
	Done	A	External communication (customers, suppliers, and other stakeholders)	Sustain and foster relationships	Public statement followed by customer meetings	T
Procurement	On track	A	Joint, centralized procurement	Reduce purchasing costs (100)	Cost analysis	T + 3 months
Financial management	On track	A	Integration of financial function, combine reporting and forecasts and review business plans	Combine financial management and reporting	Working session between CFOs	T + 3 months
Marketing	Delay	A	Review and integrate marketing strategies (combined brands, pricing review, and promotion materials)	Optimize marketing strategy (10)	Define joint objectives	T + 3 months
Distribution/ sales	Delay	A	Define sales reps' responsibilities and eliminate overlaps; extract and share best practices	Increase sales efficiency (200)	Specify plan with external consultant	T + 6 months
Other	Delay	B	Implement tax group structure, synchronize insurance contracts	Cost reduction (10)	Approach external consultant	T + 6 months
Logistics	To start	B	Harmonizing inventories and logistics, consolidate locations	Optimize logistics (30)	Initial meeting logistics managers	T + 9 months
Org. integration	On track	B	Synchronizing business processes (operations, admin, HR, finance department, etc.)	Increase organizational efficiency (100)	Define processes/ responsibilities	T + 4 months
	On track	B	Migration and integration of IT systems	Integrate IT (10)	Feasibility study	T + 1 year

	On track	A	Review organizational chart and definition of responsibilities and tasks	Optimal use of internal competencies	Definition of common aims and values	T + 1 month

Margin (or profitability) improvements

Private equity firms regularly identify opportunities to immediately improve margins by having leaner and better managed operations. Again, such opportunities are identified at the pre-acquisition stage by benchmarking gross margins and overhead costs against those of close competitors, or identifying cost-cutting opportunities by changing existing operating models and processes. If some cost-reduction opportunities are evident at the outset, these will be the first to be implemented post transaction, in parallel with top-priority sales growth efforts.

Profitability improvements involve many different types of opportunities, such as identifying overhead cost savings or improvements in the supply chain, manufacturing, procurement, or internal operational processes. Some of these opportunities are discussed in greater detail below.

Overhead cost reductions

Usually, there is no single cost-cutting idea that would radically change the cost structure of the portfolio company, thereby solving all of its cost problems at once. Instead, operational partners, together with the portfolio company management team, should plan to reach their cost targets with a combination of actions. An important question that always hangs over every cost-cutting effort is, "Are we cutting enough or too much?" In other words, "What is the right level of overhead?" Reducing overhead costs is probably the most common form of post-acquisition "quick win" in larger companies. The actions taken could be as minimal as implementing a hiring freeze and waiting for natural attrition in headcount, or as drastic as introducing shared services where internal consolidation of back offices would contribute to headcount reductions and cost savings. Moreover, reorganizations of back-office functions (e.g., basic payroll, financial controlling, or information technology (IT) functions) can decrease the need for management layers, accelerate information flows, and eliminate errors caused by multiple handoffs, further reducing overheads. For example, IT overhead can be reduced by consolidating data centers, eliminating redundant networks, and standardizing software applications. Back-office functions could even be outsourced if doing so reduces overall costs.

All back-office functions usually have unresolved personnel issues—even those that have been through previous rounds of cost optimization. Thus, under-utilized functions should be reassessed, while underperformers should be challenged. When looking at the possibility of a reduction in headcount, local employment laws must be considered to understand what can and cannot be done. The cost of involuntary redundancy also needs to be incorporated into the economics of such decisions. However, even above economic considerations, management must consider the overall impact of draconian cost cutting on an organization and its employees. People are the most important productive asset of a business. Therefore, when considering changes (however small those changes may be), management has to assess the impact of those changes on people's morale and commitment to the business.[7]

---

[7] Proper communication is crucial and headcount cuts are ideally done as "one-time" events, as soon as possible (within 15 to 30 days) after the transaction closing. Taking longer than 30 days, or doing more than one cut, increases uncertainty and morale "recovery time."

Reducing marketing is another option if these costs are proving to be too high for the company or divergence losses are too significant. Better usage of marketing expenditures could be explored by measuring the effectiveness and contribution of marketing initiatives to sales. For example, accurately measuring the return on individual promotional programs and the effects of integrated marketing activities can provide insights that could lead to lower marketing expenditures or a redirection of the spending to alternative programs.

Another significant cost for many companies is R&D. Analyzing the investment returns of R&D expenditures can result in a better understanding of their importance. It may be that the existing R&D capabilities are so weak and ineffective that, in the long run, it would be more economical to buy externally or acquire relevant licenses. Operational partners can mitigate R&D costs by supporting cross-functional team collaborations. The portfolio company could engage sourcing, sales, marketing, and even finance departments early in the product development process to ensure better alignment of incentives, leverage analytical capabilities, consider supply sources, and simply execute more effectively. Early cross-functional engagement is an important criterion that enhances the likelihood that new ideas developed by the R&D department will make their way to implementation. Removing top layers of management and having a direct report between mid-layer management and the CEO (or COO) can further increase agility and R&D efficiency.

Supply chain management and procurement

Optimizing the supply chain could lead to substantial savings for a portfolio company; doing so involves the synchronization of suppliers, manufacturers, distributors, retailers, customers, and so on. This synchronization is usually achieved by relying on technologies that enable seamless exchanges of information, goods, and services across the company's organizational boundaries.[8] As a result, the company should be able to deliver the right products and services to the right locations on time and at a low cost. For instance, the management team could optimize the geographical distance between the company's facilities and its suppliers or markets, leading to lower transportation costs and time from end to end. Management could also limit the number of parties involved in the supply chain—the fewer parties involved, the higher the efficiency gains are likely to be. Lastly, the operational partners and the management team might jointly conclude that some processes should be brought in-house to save costs and improve efficiency, while others should be outsourced to more cost-effective third parties.

The procurement department is crucial to a portfolio company given that in today's environment, volatile commodity prices and fluctuating supply and demand affect both the price and availability of critical components and materials that the company might need. Procurement should be centralized and fully integrated (i.e., disparate procurement systems should be combined). It should operate across corporate functions and deal with the full range of products and services provided, with a wide vision over the entire supply chain. This approach enables operational partners and the management team to drive the agenda for managing strategic suppliers and working with other parts of the business. Procurement managers are expected to negotiate the best prices possible when purchasing from suppliers. The timing, quantity of purchases, and currency exchange rates all affect a company's ability to secure the best prices and procurement costs. Immediately after a portfolio company is acquired, GPs should ask several basic questions: Is the procurement function efficient? Are the materials bought at the best prices possible? Is the business

---

[8] Relevant information that is exchanged may involve more accurate and up-to-date demand forecasts, inventory levels, capacity utilization, production schedules, delivery dates, and other data.

susceptible to fluctuations in commodity prices or is it hedged to protect itself? Should it implement long-term contracts at fixed prices?

Operational partners should consider setting up procurement dashboards that ensure a link between the objectives set in the investment thesis and category-specific savings opportunities. These dashboards allow greater visibility of key costs, quality, and service performance in real time and at different levels in the portfolio company. Such insights facilitate continuous improvements of processes. For example, a procurement dashboard model could collect information on (1) cost metrics (e.g., cost per unit, transportation costs, supply chain costs, and procurement cost per amount invested), (2) quality metrics (e.g., percentage of orders completed, returns, or defects; number of complaints; etc.), (3) service metrics (e.g., percentage of on-time deliveries/jobs, response times, procurement cycle time, etc.), and (4) operational metrics (e.g., personnel assignments, personnel status, and open sourcing projects).

Both supply chain and procurement functions need to have in-depth capabilities to make the most of technological advancements. Investments in systems that automate sourcing, purchases, invoicing, or supplier collaborations often provide significant efficiency improvements and cost savings.

Operational structure and processes

From an early point, operational partners should try to gain a thorough understanding of the organization's structure. This structure provides a blueprint of the overall value chain and the way work gets done in the organization. It is broadly about grouping individuals into various departments/functions and organizing these according to an appropriate hierarchy and spans of control, as well as ensuring optimal communication, coordination, and integration across departments/functions.

Portfolio companies with multiple divisions may have a separate set of support functions for each division. The operational partners should ensure that the support functions service the specific and differentiated requirements of the respective division.

If the requirements are not greatly differentiated, however, having a separate set of support functions is probably unnecessarily expensive because of role duplication across divisions. In these situations, operational partners, together with the management team, should aim to create a centralized pool of such support functions, and to lend their services as and when required to eliminate unnecessary role duplication.

Toward the complex end of operational structure optimization, operational partners might need to implement major transformational projects for the portfolio company, such as site closures, site integrations, or site migrations to other locations. To avoid disappointment after the work is completed, these projects should involve complex program management and careful financial planning to ensure that synergies and savings are not overestimated. Clearly, transformational changes are not unique to private equity-backed companies. For instance, the portfolio company may operate out of multiple small sites, and synergies could be identified by consolidating these into one big facility.

As businesses grow, they tend to shift from a dispersed localized model to a centralized model or a hub-and-spoke model. Yet, operational partners need to understand why the company has been operating in such a fragmented manner to begin with; was this due to past acquisitions and post-merger integration being left unaddressed, or was it a strategic decision to be close to a fragmented market? If the latter is true, does the business need to remain operating as it is, or are there elements that could be consolidated while leaving crucial elements near the fragmented markets? Could the company outsource elements of the process for greater efficiency? Could it reduce headcount? There are many questions to ask and decisions to be made prior to execution. Alternatively, there might not be a need to change the status quo if the additional return resulting from the change is minimal. Ultimately, the following key question has to be answered: Is the existing business model and infrastructure the optimal solution now and for the long term?

In recent years, site migrations or outsourcing to low-cost countries have become more common. Outsourcing in particular is meant to enable companies to focus their efforts on their core competencies. Often, very high savings are initially estimated based on low labor costs but, with more case examples and lessons learned, it has become clear that cost savings from outsourcing to low-cost countries must be properly analyzed to arrive at a more realistic estimate of savings. Import and export tariffs, transportation costs, cross-border treaties, and trade agreements should all be taken into account before actual migration takes place. Operational partners often engage with external advisers to support the decision-making and implementation processes involved in site migration.

It is important to note that changes to the business operation model are likely to cause significant disruption to the day-to-day business, and therefore need to be analyzed, planned, and implemented very carefully in order to reap the benefits of a major transition.

Digitalization and information technology (IT) systems

IT systems and the data they generate have become an integral part of running most businesses. Assessing whether the portfolio company has adequate IT systems in place is a must, as adopting the right systems can yield significant cost savings. The journey to big data and the industrial internet of things (IIoT) started in manufacturing and service industries few decades ago. The era of digitalization began when the companies upgraded from analog and paper-based systems to digital instrumentation and distributed control systems, triggering the generation of vast amounts of data that supported the first wave of digital applications, such as just in time manufacturing and advanced process control.

Today, best practice private equity firms pursue the next big digital transformation by making use of new technologies such as high-performance computing, artificial intelligence, machine learning, cloud solutions, internet connectivity, mobility, robust cybersecurity, etc. These technologies have come together to generate deeper insights from analyzing the data generated by portfolio companies. Thus digital transformations are making it possible to derive insights not afforded before, to capture even greater value through improvements in operations and reliability, and ultimately to maximize margins through operational excellence programs. The ability to leverage the massive collection of data to extend the life of productive assets and maximize the return on capital employed represents one of the greatest sources of additional profit still available in the marketplace.

As a result, top private equity firms pursue digital transformations by integrating digital technologies from the very beginning of the ownership period into the strategy and operations of the portfolio company. These transformations involve setting up systems that merge the best of the digital and physical worlds and provide notable cost savings by optimizing workflows. For example, a system might be created to track each step in the customer experience chain to personalize marketing campaigns, provide better product customization, or help customers discover and purchase new products. In a manufacturing or logistics business, one can install sensors in various assets and link them to the enterprise or cloud-based systems to better understand their use and efficiency and generate predictive analytics.

Investments in IT systems must facilitate big data analytics, which involves the rapid extraction, transformation, search, analysis, and sharing of massive datasets. Such systems must have new capabilities in the speed and power of computers. Only these capabilities can allow the processing of millions of data points on an almost real-time basis. While in the past such a system was prohibitive, now, with the cloud and high-performance computing, managers can readily access the server capacity to perform the necessary analysis and allow the portfolio company's management to identify previously unseen correlations and patterns that improve decision making.

To successfully implement a value creation strategy that involves digitalization, private equity firms should aim to:

- hire operational partners with technology backgrounds from successful technology firms. Such partners should be able to advise the management of portfolio companies on the purchase or internal development of new hardware and software and on the hiring of data scientists with the necessary skills.

- verify data integrity. Even though the portfolio company might have been collecting data for many years, when the digitalization project begins, operational partners may find that the data quality is not what they expected. Thus an initial effort, must focus on determining the scope of data and examining its quality. Data integrity is the foundation of a successful digital transformation process.

- build data management capabilities. The process of collecting, aggregating, structuring, conditioning, safeguarding and then using massive amounts of data is complex. Portfolio companies need to be advised to acquire data management skills or access them through third party technology providers.

- be pragmatic. Operational partners should start small and avoid solving everything at once. Trying to implement too many technological changes too soon in a portfolio company can end up in failure with a significant loss of capital. Being pragmatic does not mean going after small profit opportunities but after a significant technology shortcoming that could represent a major source of value creation.

- use digital technologies to drive sustainability and high environmental standards. Sustainability and environmental responsibilities have become a top priority for many investors in private equity funds.

Capital management

Another key area of potential value lies in the active management of the portfolio company's capital. Capital management improvements start with an assessment of the company's net working capital and tangible assets.

Many companies give insufficient attention to managing their working capital processes because they are too focused on the top-line growth. They chase revenues and, in the process, they loosen credit and return policies, build up inventories, and allow the quality of their receivables to deteriorate. Poor net working capital management might also be due to a weak reporting system, a failure to track and resolve disputes with customers, or administrative errors. The management team can strengthen the working capital platform by looking at inventory, receivables, and payables in terms of absolute levels and relative to sales. Computing metrics such as days-inventory-outstanding, days-sales-outstanding, inventory-days, and net-working-capital-days help in understanding how much cash is tied up in working capital—cash that could potentially be used more effectively in other areas of the business. In this context, benchmarking the above metrics against historical performance and industry peers can provide an indication on the financial upside potential of various improvements:

- Optimized receivables management could encompass the implementation of more strict payment terms, incentives to customers for early payments, systematic collection of late payments, or even the sale of receivables at a discount to third parties through factoring transactions.

- Inventory-level optimization should be targeted to be at the highest delivery reliability with a minimum capital lockup; it starts with physical stock-taking to create transparency and continues with reviewing warehouse locations and the logistics setup. Depending on the situation, customers should be challenged as to what degree consignment stock volumes should be sold, as customers sometimes use such instruments to keep a safety stock at the expense of the portfolio company. Overall, inventory initiatives can range from selective reductions to substantial improvements as part of a transformation to a just-in-time model.

- Account payables management includes the renegotiation of payment terms with suppliers (e.g., early payment and volume discounts as well as due dates for payments). In the daily payables management, the optimization issue is given by the trade-off of having cash (late payments) versus receiving discounts (early payments). The latter aspect should not be underestimated as early payment discounts (e.g., 3–4%) directly add to the EBITDA of the company. When considering the exit EBITDA multiple on the absolute value of such discounts, this can have a substantial effect on the company's value.

Efficient capital management should also consider asset optimization in terms of tangible fixed assets. Optimization can free up significant cash flows by divesting unnecessary and redundant assets, especially in the case of companies that rely on capital-intensive business models (e.g., manufacturing or utilities). To achieve greater fixed asset productivity, the analysis should begin by identifying the company's *core assets*—the assets that give the company its competitive advantage. Core assets are assets (1) whose operation relies on proprietary processes or technologies, (2) that are in close proximity to customers, and (3) that are flexible and/or have significant cost advantages. At the same time, these assets should sustain growth, be profitable, and have further potential for efficiency improvements. These assets should be kept on the portfolio company's balance sheet and be further developed, while non-core assets—as well as assets that are obsolete or underutilized—should be divested. If some non-core assets are still needed, the company could sell them and then lease them back. Such a practice needs to be discussed and approved by the lending banks in a leverage finance context. Sometimes, moving to an *asset-light business model* through partnerships, contract manufacturing, or outsourcing is the best way forward for companies whose core capabilities lie in product development, design, marketing, or sales (Apple and Nike are prime examples of such companies).

The final step in the analysis of fixed assets is to forecast capex based on (1) the cash generated by each asset that contributes to the production of each good and service, location, or value-added step, (2) the economic cycle, (3) the competitive industry environment, and (4) expected technological advances. Data on cash contributions of each asset should be compared with industry standards or close competitors in the industry to obtain a better view of the overall productivity of the assets and their potential for improvement. Capital spending should be prioritized to the top investment areas in the company's core businesses where it will have the largest impact. Two factors should be carefully considered when setting out capex plans:

- Spending on new assets or on maintaining old assets can be limited if the portfolio of products and customers is streamlined. For instance, complex product portfolios result in frequent changes, ramp-ups, and ramp-downs that can lead to a larger set of assets dedicated to specific products. Most importantly, by reducing complexity in the manufacturing process, companies can respond more quickly to sudden shocks in the demand for products and services or in the supply of raw materials.

- Spending can be more effective if asset characteristics are matched carefully with the needs of specific customers or products. Plants might be designed to produce a small number of products in large volumes, or to be very flexible to suit the production of goods with unpredictable demand. Matching is also achieved by consolidating products with similar features that require similar production processes into the same production facility.

Operational partners are expected to develop a long-term fixed asset strategy given that the full benefits of fixed asset productivity are usually realized over time. Notably, this long-term strategy should involve commitments only to assets that support the core business of the portfolio company. Ultimately, the key to riding a downturn or winning in an upturn (both of which often occur before an exit) is having a critical base of core assets that enhance the portfolio company's competitiveness and profitability.

Adjustments to corporate governance and incentive structures

Corporate governance

Private equity investment professionals who usually take up supervisory board positions in portfolio companies are likely to have been involved in the transaction execution, with a clear understanding of the historical performance, future plans, and vision of the company. They are responsible for monitoring the newly acquired business, bringing professional rigor and experience, and, with the help of the company's management team, steering the strategic direction of the company. As a result, they are expected to take an active approach at the board level, especially given that there is no intermediate level between the management and the owner. Such an active and professional ownership approach immediately strengthens the corporate governance processes and decision quality.

Board memberships allow private equity firms to quickly identify and act on early warning signs when problems occur. Private equity firms also identify and introduce key leaders from the industry in which the portfolio company operates to join them on the board. Such industry and/or subject matter expert board members are often involved in leading or monitoring specific value creation initiatives, bringing in their own expertise and network of contacts. Thus, in the case of private equity ownership, the supervisory board functions not only as a monitor but also as an active equal partner in the portfolio company's management.

The supervisory board of the portfolio company usually approves major strategic topics, critical investment decisions, annual accounts, and budgets, as well as changes in key personnel. Besides monthly reports, calls, and informal discussions, typically four to six formal supervisory board meetings are held annually. Productive cooperation in this context is a socially complex topic, as it brings together different mindsets and roles. Therefore, supervisory board members need to be agile and take on varying roles according to the specific situation, from partnering with to intervening against (or with) the management, or from taking charge to stepping back. In this way, disciplined, professional, and decisive boards are a key element of value creation in private equity. Academic evidence that focuses on public-to-private transactions by private equity funds suggests that the boards of private equity companies experience significant changes under their new private equity owners that potentially make them more efficient.[9]

The active involvement of all parties—including the management team, the supervisory board, and the private equity investor—is necessary as operational improvement initiatives encompass multiple disciplines. At the same time, alignment of interests is strengthened by the equity participation of the portfolio company's managers, which makes them co-owners of the company. A frictionless corporate governance structure and a strong alignment of interests are major enablers of value creation for private equity investors.

Incentive structures

Unraveling how private equity firms (particularly the large and mature ones) make handsome returns and grow has become a focus of academic debate. Acharya et al. (2013) quantify value creation at the enterprise level and attribute it to financial engineering, systematic risk, and operational engineering. Their research finds "abnormal performance"—compared with quoted peers, in particular—in "organic" deals that focus exclusively on internal value creation programs and margin improvements. However, "inorganic" deals with an M&A focus also grow portfolio company values substantially. They conclude that abnormal performance is partly due to differences in human capital factors. GPs with an operational background (ex-consultants or ex-industry managers) generate significantly higher outperformance in organic deals. In contrast, GPs with a background in finance (ex-bankers or ex-accountants) generate higher outperformance in deals with M&A events, suggesting that GP background is correlated with deal performance.

If post-deal outperformance is indeed correlated with GP background, the success should be attributable to the investment thesis that the GPs developed for the target portfolio company. Further, in the current environment of increased competition, GPs are even more likely to apply an industry-rooted, strategic investment approach, working with management and industry experts while setting clear value creation priorities. While any other company has access to the same value creation tools, private equity firms can exploit the value of control and alignment of interest in this context, meaning that operational initiatives can be approved quickly and effectively. Specifically, private equity firms place a strong emphasis on selecting the right portfolio company management team, and align these managers to their benefit beyond other ownership models.

Relationship with the management team

Assessing the incumbent management team is an important aspect of any acquisition. Many GPs choose not to proceed with a transaction if they find the incumbent management team has a weak performance track record or seems incapable of steering the future of the company based on the proposed strategy. Alternatively, prior to acquisition, GPs may identify a new management leadership team to take over. Many transactions are a mix of a management buyout with the incumbent management as co-investors and a management buy-in, which requires bringing in new managers. Both terms imply the financial participation of the management team in the form of an *equity co-investment* in the transaction; this is seen as a sign of managers' confidence in the business and their own managerial capabilities, and highlights managers' entrepreneurial spirit.

---

[9] Cornelli and Karakas (2008) find that (1) board size and the presence of outside directors are drastically reduced; (2) in leveraged buyouts, outside directors are replaced by private equity professionals, whereas in management buyouts, outside directors disappear and only management is left; (3) private equity board members are most active in complex and challenging transactions; and (4) companies with more need for supervision or advice have more private equity professionals in the board.

The GP's relationship with the portfolio company's management is a fundamental factor in successful ownership. If the incumbent management team has a strong performance track record, brings along managerial talent, is transparent, and is capable of implementing operational value creation initiatives, there may be a case for the private equity firm to remain "hands-off" and allow the incumbent management to progress with the changes. At the same time, every specific development stage of a company brings its own challenges. Thus, different management types are often needed over time as a company evolves. In this sense, during the holding period, it can be appropriate for new managers to come on board with complementary skills, or even to replace existing managers. In some cases, the GP's board membership could be the only involvement it has if it decides not to become actively involved with the company's operations, as long as the company is meeting the agreed financial targets. In contrast to publicly held companies, ownership is concentrated in private equity, while there is constant interaction between the private equity owner and the management without any intermediate layer between them. In such a governance model, a trust-based relationship between the parties involved is crucial. Mutual respect, transparency, fairness, and responsiveness are just a few of the parameters that define an effective partnership approach in this regard. To emphasize this trusting relationship, many GPs define the common value ground between the business leaders and themselves in a charter at the beginning of the holding period.

The operating partner from a private equity firm is not expected to dedicate most of his/her time to one portfolio company and take on an executive function there as this can be quite disruptive to the management team. Invading the portfolio company management's sphere of responsibility could be interpreted as a sign of mistrust. A good operating partner should act as a sounding board and a coach to the CEO of the portfolio company. The private equity firm should either have confidence that the company's management team is up to the task, or it should replace that team. The latter course of action often occurs when the new private equity owner of the business is looking to change the strategy, and thus, the interests of the owner and the management team cannot be aligned.

The actual operational improvements made within portfolio companies may not be unique to private equity-owned businesses, and could be applied to businesses with other ownership models. The focus on an exit plan from day one, however, gives companies under private equity ownership a unique sense of urgency and a strict culture of delivery, where failure is clearly unacceptable. If the portfolio company has a high level of debt with covenants and repayment schedules, management will be working hard to deliver agreed results according to projections.

GPs may suggest the appointment of consulting and advisory firms to support management in implementing the full potential plans set out for the company, whether they focus on cost reduction, procurement and supply chain improvements, and/or a multitude of other EBITDA improvement efforts. These appointments would allow management to continue with their current responsibilities of running the business while operational improvements are being made with minimal disruption and time involvement. Many private equity firms have created internal operational teams that operate among the portfolio companies. Although operational management of companies is not the core function of a private equity firm, its importance has increased as private equity expands in more challenging deals.

Incentivizing management

Incentive schemes are introduced as effective tools to ensure that management is driven to succeed and is only rewarded when agreed targets are met. They draw out managers' entrepreneurial behavior by clarifying their responsibility and accountability. Incentive tools do not stop at the management of the portfolio company but apply to the private equity firms as well. It may be naive to stereotype private equity investment professionals but, in general, they are well educated, competitive, and demanding individuals. They are unlikely to accept mediocrity and are unforgiving of failure. They too are heavily incentivized to bring success to their private equity funds, and this would require the portfolio companies under their responsibility to perform and generate returns for their shareholders. The portfolio company managers will constantly remain under the scrutiny of the GP, and are likely to receive regular calls and requests for financial performance information, keeping them "on their toes."

Management incentive structures are normally focused on equity value increases, the major interest of the private equity fund, during the three to five years of the holding period. The focus is on a frictionless alignment of interests between the private equity owner and the managers, and often involves several instruments:

- First, in many cases, the *fixed base salary* of managers is increased post acquisition. It is common for managers of private equity-owned companies to receive more than the respective peer market remuneration; this shows the new owner's confidence in the managers, and also motivates them from the start while compensating for a potentially increased workload in the new setup: as managers of a management buyout, they will have to run the daily business while managing several operational improvement initiatives in parallel. An additional argument for an increased fixed salary for managers is the fact that before closing, during the transaction execution, they are a key success factor and have to be convinced by the potential new owner to come on board.

- Second, *bonus schemes* are realigned. These can vary in their form and relative amount to the fixed salary from one private equity owner to another. Usually, they focus on the company's equity value enhancement—that is, the amount of the bonus depends on the actual increase of the equity value that year. The equity value calculation is predefined in the bonus agreement. For example, the fixed purchase multiple is applied to the actual EBITDA (before bonus payments) achieved in the respective year in order to calculate the enterprise value. From the enterprise value, net financial debt, including shareholder loans (to neutralize refinancing effects), is deducted in order to quantify the equity value. On the absolute amount of the equity value increase from the last year (to the bonus year), a predefined percentage ratio is applied that determines the actual bonus, which is normally capped at a specific maximum amount. The input variables of the calculation usually stem from the business plan of the company; the percentage ratio applied to the amount of the equity value increase is chosen in a way that the maximum bonus is paid when the plan is achieved. If the calculated bonus exceeds the maximum amount or the equity value development is negative, the exceeding bonus amount or negative bonus will be carried forward to the next year. Regularly, individual performance is compensated by a further bonus element, which can be 50% of the total bonus. This amount can be discretionary, depending fully on the decision of the supervisory board, or it can be clearly defined and quantified in an agreement.

- A third and even more powerful incentive instrument is the *equity participation* of the managers. Through their co-investment in the equity of the company, they become co-owner-managers and entrepreneurs themselves. The equity participation of managers is a prerequisite for most GPs as it aligns interests between the management and the new private equity owner. Additionally, it is a strong sign of confidence of the managers in their own skills and the success of the company. Equity participations are structured differently. Some funds give low-interest credit to the managers, while others only want them to invest their own capital as credit-financed participations could put substantial pressure on managers during times of underperformance, distorting the positive incentive. A rule of thumb is that around one annual gross salary is expected as a co-investment – however, amounts vary and differ substantially, depending on the situation. For instance, in a secondary buyout, co-investment amounts are expected to be much higher as managers already cashed-in significantly in the first transaction.

Managers normally also receive so-called "sweet equity" (sometimes also called "sweat equity"). That is, management participates in the equity value increase over-proportionately, relative to the private equity fund. This can be achieved in a structure where the management invests only in pure nominal equity, while the private equity fund often invests in equity, capital reserves and shareholder loans. The so-called "envy ratio" normally shows how much more, on a relative basis, the management earns at exit compared to the private equity fund. While the fund may generate two to three times its invested capital at exit, it is not unusual that managers earn an investment multiple of this. Such management participation is in some cases even further "sweetened" via an IRR participation. That is, if the fund generates for example a minimum 25% IRR with a money multiple of for example minimum 1.8 times, managers receive an additional pre-defined stake in the absolute return amount beyond the 25% IRR. Such additional IRR participation gives the managers further incentives to fully support an exit process. As they are in the spotlight during the sale of the company and thus have substantial influence on the exit performance, it is important that interests are fully aligned.

Depending on the situation, the equity participation is also being extended to mid-level managers and key people via employee stock option plans, or the issuance of virtual shares or simple equity.

Prioritization of execution

Post-deal operational plans are unlikely to involve a single change but rather, a list of initiatives that should be undertaken to access the full potential of the portfolio company. These typically range from quick wins that can be implemented in the short to medium term to more complex, long-term transitions. Carrying out a full plan is by no means an easy transition and requires both financial and operational knowhow. Management should decide if it will first tackle low-risk and easy-to-implement initiatives or high-risk and difficult projects; alternatively, both types of initiatives could be tackled simultaneously. These decisions need careful consideration in the implementation of operational improvements. Timely and swift execution is critical for the new ownership to signal necessary change across the organization, and to lay out expectations for the future. While several initiatives can usually run simultaneously, their objectives must be ambitious but realistic to avoid demotivating managers. Clear milestones and transparent status update reports need to be defined as part of an overall project management strategy.

Private equity is capital with a long-term vision that brings along a short-term sense of urgency as the "IRR clock" is ticking for the capital invested. Involving short- and long-term initiatives, value creation plans are front-loaded by nature when it comes to implementation. From a private equity perspective, it is preferable to have extraordinary project costs at the beginning of the holding period, as these costs are under less scrutiny by a potential buyer at the time of an exit, while the value impact can be reaped over a longer period until the exit. At the same time, large, complex initiatives need time and room for adjustments in between. The following schematic overview (see Exhibit 7) can help to prioritize value creation initiatives, given their equity value impact and implementation time needs.

MEASUREMENT OF OPERATIONAL IMPROVEMENTS

The returns generated by private equity funds at the portfolio company level are driven by multiple factors, such as operational improvements implemented, timing of the investments, or simply favorable industry and overall market trends. An appropriate measurement system should be able to isolate all these factors to help the investors identify performance patterns across the full set of portfolio companies of a GP's funds and assess the extent to which the GP has operational skills that are unique in the marketplace. Private equity professionals often refer to this analysis as the "value attribution analysis" (VAA).

Exhibit 7: Value impact versus implementation time

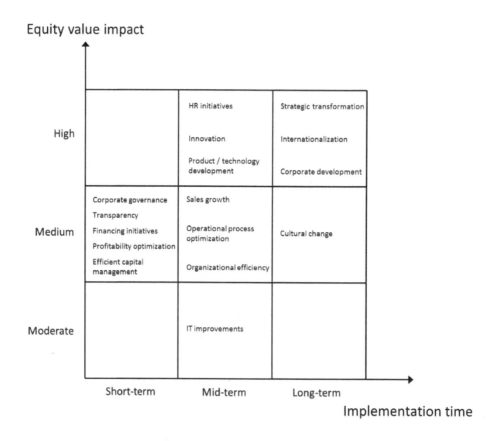

The typical VAA framework used to measure the drivers of value creation in portfolio companies identifies (1) the change in a company's enterprise value and (2) the net cash flow generated for shareholders during the holding period. The value of a portfolio company might change because of deviations in the reported EBITDA and the EBITDA valuation multiple. The net cash flow generated by shareholders is typically captured by the change in the company's net debt during the holding period under the assumption that cash flows generated by the company during the holding period can be either accumulated on the balance sheet or used to pay back the lenders.[10] Therefore, the value created on a private equity investment can be measured quantitatively using the following formula:

$$
\textbf{Value Created} \; \vdots \; \Delta \text{ Company Value} + \Delta \text{ Net Cash Flows}
$$

$$
\vdots \; \Delta \text{ EBITDA} * \text{Multiple}_{\text{Entry}} + \Delta \text{ Multiple} * \text{EBITDA}_{\text{Exit}} + \Delta \text{ NetDebt}
$$

$$
\vdots \; \text{EBITDA Effect} + \text{Multiple Effect} + \text{Leverage Effect}
$$

EBITDA Effect

The EBITDA effect quantifies the portion of value creation attributable to changes in operating performance that affect the company's reported EBITDA during the ownership period, holding the EBITDA valuation multiple constant (i.e., under the assumption that the exit valuation multiple is the same as the entry valuation multiple). EBITDA is conventionally used as a proxy for the company's operating cash flows, potentially providing a measure of company performance unaffected by accounting reporting standards or the company's capital structure. Increases in EBITDA are viewed positively to the extent that they reflect an improvement in the operations of the portfolio company. However, the focus on EBITDA changes carries some significant downsides:

- EBITDA does not capture a company's performance in the context of its industry peers. Thus, it is unclear whether the performance is driven by company-specific operational improvements or by industry (or macroeconomic) trends.

- EBITDA is an aggregated accounting number that does not provide any insight into the sources of changing operating performance. Therefore, it is impossible to know whether the performance improvements were achieved through changes in revenues or in cost structure.

- EBITDA changes distort the operational performance if the portfolio company engages in acquisitions and disposals. EBITDA growth usually leads to an overstatement of the magnitude of operating improvements in the context of acquisitions and to an understatement of the performance if the portfolio company divests some of its subsidiaries.

Multiple effect

The multiple effect measures the change in the price paid by the market per unit of EBITDA at exit, between the time of investing in the portfolio company and the time of selling it. The private equity industry typically uses EBITDA multiples to value companies, although, in the context of early stage companies or companies with negative profitability, sales multiples or non-financial based multiples are also used. The change in the EBITDA valuation multiples is commonly viewed as value creation driven by market, industry, or macroeconomic factors that are beyond control of the GP once the company is acquired. However, this simplistic view is certainly wrong, given that valuation multiples also capture growth opportunities specific to

---

[10] Typically, lenders do not allow payments of dividends to shareholders before their claims are paid off to mitigate wealth expropriation. Lending agreements include covenants that restrict distributions to shareholders.

the company that are the result of operational improvements pursued by the GP. As a result, the change in the valuation multiple presents certain problems:

- It does not differentiate between changes in valuation attributable to market cycles, industry performance, or company-specific changes that lead to higher growth opportunities relative to peers. Market and industry factors that affect valuation multiples are beyond the control of the GP and the management of the portfolio company.

- Change in the valuation multiple fails to capture the evolution of the company's multiple in the context of acquisitions, or the value captured in the context of a roll-up strategy, which involves the M&A of small companies in the same market to reduce costs through economies of scale.

- It does not distinguish between changes in the expectations about the company's future prospects and changes in the recent performance of the company. For example, a low valuation multiple might not be bad news if it is due to an increase in the recent performance of the company.

Leverage effect

The change in a company's net debt position is measured in dollar/euro terms and represents the free cash flow generated for shareholders during the holding period. This cash can be used to pay down debt or pay dividends to shareholders if permitted, or it can be retained on the balance sheet. It is important to note that all dividends paid to shareholders *before* the exit contribute to the leverage effect (i.e., they should be added to the final exit value of the firm and subtracted from the net debt). Thus, net debt might decrease because the company generates more operational cash flows that are kept on the balance sheet or are paid out in dividends, and not necessarily because the company actually pays down the debt. Measuring changes in net debt is particularly relevant for a leveraged private equity transaction, with the cash flow generated by the portfolio company expected to service the acquisition debt. The measurement of equity value creation generated by a decrease in the net debt reported by the company also has inherent drawbacks:

- It does not quantify the direct impact of financial leverage on the investment returns because it captures only debt repayments. As a result, a highly leveraged transaction where very little debt is paid back by the time of the exit will show a small leverage contribution to value creation. Nevertheless, it is clear that the high level of leverage magnifies the equity returns if the firm value increases.

- It does not provide any insight into the underlying sources and uses of operational cash flows during the holding period. Historical cash flows can be obscured by financial engineering, or by how the portfolio company's acquisitions are financed.

It is essential to understand how the measurement of value creation is achieved for a basic transaction. For example, assume that a private equity firm buys 100% of the shares of OILSERVICECO, a company that provides services to the oil industry, for which it pays US$1 billion (assume also that the company does not have any cash on its balance sheet). The transaction is financed with $500 million in equity and the remaining $500 million is borrowed from a bank syndicate (i.e., the net debt at the time of acquisition is $500 million). At the time of the acquisition, OILSERVICECO's EBITDA was $100 million, so the private equity firm paid a multiple of 10 times EBITDA for the company. Then after five years, OILSERVICECO is sold to a trade buyer that values the company at $1.8 billion. Over the five years, the EBITDA of

OILSERVICECO has increased by 40% to $140 million, and the net debt has dropped to $200 million. On this basis, the exit multiple was 12.85 times the EBITDA and the value of the private equity firm's investment in OILSERVICECO was $1.6 billion. This valuation generates an absolute return of $1.1 billion on the initial investment of $500 million. Thus, the multiple on the investment is 2.2 times the invested amount. Exhibit 8 provides the value attribution analysis for this transaction.

As can be seen, value captured by the EBITDA growth reflects a significant portion of the equity value created by the transaction. However, it is unclear whether the EBITDA growth reflects operational improvements implemented by the private equity firm or increases in the overall industry performance. This measure overestimates the impact of the private equity fund managers if the industry performance improves over the same period. Similarly, the multiple effect generates significant value, but the improvement in the valuation multiple might not be due to the repositioning of the company by its new owner to exploit additional growth opportunities, but rather, to a more optimistic sentiment in the M&A market at the time of exit. In addition, it is unclear what impact OILSERVICECO's potential acquisitions/divestitures during the holding period have on the value drivers.

Exhibit 8: Value attribution analysis calculations (basic framework)

(in US$ millions)	At Acquisition	At Exit	Changes
EBITDA	100	140	40
Net Debt	500	200	(300)
Equity	500	1,600	1,100
Enterprise Value	1,000	1,800	800
Valuation Multiple	10x	12.85x	2.85x
		Percent in Total	Multiple Contribution
EBITDA Effect	40 * 10 = 400	36.36%	0.8x
Multiple Effect	2.85 * 140= 400	36.36%	0.8x
Leverage Effect	500 – 200 = 300	27.27%	0.6x
Total Equity Change	**1,100**	**100%**	**2.2x**

A very basic solution to these drawbacks is to disaggregate the EBITDA and multiple effects to capture the impact of M&A activities as well as the industry trends. One could split the EBITDA growth into three components: (1) EBITDA growth due to industry performance (i.e., apply the industry growth rate to EBITDA at entry); (2) EBITDA growth from acquisitions/divestitures during the holding period; and (3) residual EBITDA growth, which is likely driven by operational enhancements executed by the private equity firm. If more detail is needed about the components of EBITDA, the three numbers above could be further split based on revenues and costs. A similar adjustment could be made to the multiple effect by deducting the change in transaction multiples for a group of comparable companies in the same industry and geography.

Thus, the multiple growth can be decomposed into (1) industry multiple growth over the same period and (2) residual multiple growth, which potentially reflects the extent to which the portfolio company's growth opportunities have improved over and above industry trends. This second component reflects the operational activities initiated by the private equity firm over the ownership period.

Finally, the leverage effect can be further split by measuring the components of growth in net cash flows as (1) changes in cash generated over the holding period, (2) changes in net debt due to acquisitions/divestitures, (3) changes in working capital debt taken by the company during the holding period, and (4) residual debt change, which likely captures the repayment of the debt used to acquire the portfolio company.

We extend the OILSERVICECO example to illustrate the importance of the issues highlighted above by making the following assumptions for the five-year ownership period:

- The industry average EBITDA growth rate was 25%.

- The average valuation multiple of the industry increased from 9 to 10 times the EBITDA (i.e., the industry valuation multiples increased by 11%).

- The company had $30 million in cash on the balance sheet at the time of sale.

- OILSERVICECO acquired another smaller company whose EBITDA was $5 million. It paid $20 million for the company and financed the transaction fully with a term loan. At the time of the sale, none of the principal of this debt was paid.

- OILSERVICECO took an additional $10 million working capital revolving facility from its bank to finance its operations. At the time of the sale, $5 million of this debt had been repaid.

This is modelled in Exhibit 9 and as can be seen there, the operational improvements implemented by the private equity firm have added $345 million in equity returns for investors in the private equity fund (i.e., $100 million from the EBITDA effect and $245 million from the multiple effect), or 31.36% of the overall increase in the equity investment, which was $1.1 billion.

Exhibit 9: Value attribution analysis calculations (extended framework)

(in US$ millions)		Percent in Total	Multiple Contribution
EBITDA Effect	40 * 10 = 400	36.36%	0.8x
Industry EBITDA Effect	25 * 10 = 250	22.72%	0.5x
Acquisition EBITDA Effect	5 * 10 = 50	4.55%	0.1x
Operational EBITDA Effect	10 * 10 = 100	9.09%	0.2x
Multiple Effect	2.85 * 140= 400	36.36%	0.8x
Industry Multiple Effect	1.1 * 140= 155	14.09%	0.3x
Operational Multiple Effect	1.75 * 140= 245	22.27%	0.5x
Leverage Effect	500 – 200 = 300	27.27%	0.6x
Increase in Cash on Balance Sheet	30	2.72%	0.06x

Increase in Debt for Acq./Divest	-20	-1.81%	-0.04x
Increase in Operational Debt	-5	-0.45%	-0.01x
Decrease in Acquisition Debt[11]	295	26.81%	0.59x
Total Equity Change	**1,100**	**100%**	**2.2x**

Several adjustments to the above analysis are worth mentioning, depending on the situation:

- If the private equity firm had provided equity to the portfolio company's management, the absolute return to the fund's investors would have been lower. If, say, management received 10% of the equity (which is reasonable, given industry practices), then the overall equity return to the investors would have been only $940 million. Accordingly, all dollar numbers in the exhibit above should also be adjusted downward by 10%.

- If the company distributed some dividends to the shareholders over the holding period, a new line item with a positive amount should be disclosed in the leverage effect section to illustrate the payment of these dividends. Simultaneously, the decrease in the acquisition debt should be lower by the amount of dividends paid (the assumption is that the cash used to pay dividends could have been used to retire the debt).

Very often, investors prefer to see a graphical representation of these numbers; this allows investors to benchmark the performance of various private equity managers when allocating their capital to private equity. In the case of our example, the components of the multiple achieved (i.e., 2.2x the initial investment) could be shown as follows (see Exhibit 10).

Exhibit 10: Graphical representation of the value attribution analysis

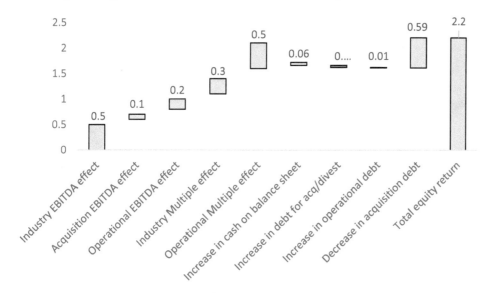

---

[11] Given the numbers provided above, if the company has a net debt of $200 million at exit and a cash balance of $30 million, then the outstanding debt is $230 million. This debt includes the working capital facility still outstanding ($5 million) and the term loan used to acquire the subsidiary ($20 million). Therefore, the remaining balance of $205 million is the outstanding amount for the debt used to acquire the company by the private equity firm. In other words, the acquisition debt has dropped by $295 million (from $500 million to $205 million).

WHEN OPERATIONAL IMPROVEMENTS FAIL

Even if they have created and implemented an excellent operational improvement plan, some portfolio companies still fail. The most likely cause of this failure is mismanagement, although some failures are due to influences beyond management's control, and to sheer bad luck. Mismanagement is most often caused by managerial overextension, ineffective communication, high turnover and neglect of HR, inadequate analysis of markets and strategies, misunderstood company goals, and many other factors. When a portfolio company fails, the GP is typically faced with a binary choice: walk away from the company or try to engineer a successful turnaround.

Implementing a turnaround requires a unique set of skills. If these are not available in-house, the GP needs to find turnaround professionals that can determine what is wrong with the company, develop strategies that no one has tried before, and implement plans to restructure the company quickly. Because the current managers of the portfolio company have allowed problems to emerge and bring the company to its depressed state, they are usually not equipped to be part of the turnaround process. Therefore, the first stage in the turnaround is often to fire the management and hire a new CEO who can successfully lead the turnaround; this is usually an individual from outside the portfolio company with a proven track record and the ability to assemble a new management team that can implement the strategies to turn the company around. The new CEO's job is to stabilize the situation, implement effective plans to transform the company, and then hire a replacement before the GP needs to exit the investment.

One of the CEO's first objectives should be to gain control of the cash situation of the company and establish breakeven. Stopping the cash bleed is as important as raising cash immediately—whether from a third-party equity investor, from the same private equity fund (if possible), or by securing asset-backed loans from lenders. The second objective should be to restructure the debt on the company's balance sheet to lower the interest payments to a level the company can afford. At the next stage, the company will likely need to be resized by selling off assets and laying off employees, if necessary. The remaining operations must be made profitable.

Overall, the process of turning around a troubled portfolio company is quite complex. Further, this process is made more difficult by the multiple constituencies involved, all of whom have different agendas. Board members will want to avoid risk and litigation, employees will demand job guarantees and benefits, lenders will request a return of invested capital (preferably with interest), suppliers will want their money in exchange for goods and services they provided, and the private equity firm will want to recover the capital invested. All of these desires can conflict and hamper the turnaround effort. Therefore, in most situations, the GP is likely to decide that other investors with specialized turnaround skills will be more successful, and walk away from the deal.

CONCLUSION

Successful private equity firms diligently identify attractive opportunities and invest in companies by means of a strategic plan and roadmap for their exit. Their investment thesis develops into a detailed execution of operational improvements or organizational changes, which lie at the core of value creation in private equity.

The operational improvement plans may not be too different from those that could be implemented for any publicly owned peer company, but they can be executed without distraction from constant market speculation impacting share prices. Successful private equity firms have repeatedly demonstrated the importance of the following to extract value for the company and its shareholders: (1) maintaining a pure focus and drive to create a lean and efficient mode of business; (2) not wasting time in setting up a target model; and (3) avoiding bureaucratic systems or internal politics that slow down the decision-making process.

Clear articulation of the investment strategy, careful and detailed operational planning, and a results-driven culture with incentive schemes aligning the interests of the private equity firm with those of company management are all essential components of the formula for private equity success.

REFERENCES

Acharya, V. V., O. F. Gottschalg, M. Hahn and C. Kehoe (2013) "Corporate governance and value creation: Evidence from private equity," *Review of Financial Studies* 26: 368–402.

Aleszczyk, A., E. T. De George, A. Ertan and F. Vasvari (2016) "Value Creation in Buyout Deals: European Evidence," *Adveq Research Series on Private Equity*, London Business School.

Boucly, Q., D. Sraer and D. Thesmar (2011) "Growth LBOs," *Journal of Financial Economics* 102.2: 432-453.

Cohn, J. B., L. F. Mills and E. M. Towery (2014) "The evolution of capital structure and operating performance after leveraged buyouts: Evidence from US corporate tax returns," *Journal of Financial Economics* 111(2): 469-494.

Davis, S. J., J. Haltiwanger, K. H., R. Jarmin, J. Lerner and J. Miranda (2014) "Private equity, jobs, and productivity," *American Economic Review* 104(12): 3956-3990.

Gao, H., J. Harford and K. Li (2013) "Determinants of corporate cash policy: Insights from private firms," *Journal of Financial Economics* 109(3): 623-639.

Kaplan, S. (1989) "The effects of management buyouts on operating performance and value," *Journal of Financial Economics* 24(2): 217-254.

Lerner, J, M. Sorensen and P. Strömberg (2011) "Private equity and long-run investment: The case of innovation," *Journal of Finance* 66(2): 445-477.

Lichtenberg, F. R. and D. Siegel (1990) "The effects of leveraged buyouts on productivity and related aspects of firm behavior," *Journal of Financial Economics* 27(1): 165-194.

In his own words: Philipp Scheier, Partner, Halder

Operational value creation in family-owned businesses

Family-owned businesses can be attractive targets for financial investors. However, they have frequently developed over a long history into complex organizations that are difficult to manage. For the new private equity owner, implementing organizational, HR, and corporate governance changes is necessary to have a basis for any further operational value creation—a foundation to be laid prudently to last sustainably.

Even during the due diligence process, underdeveloped management functions and HR gaps need to be identified. They are filled post closing, with internal promotions or external hires. For instance, family-owned firms often lack a solid internal finance function. Given the leveraged buyout-induced complexity, bringing in a CFO can be a top priority. Furthermore, if the owner-manager is departing as part of a succession solution, a critical vacuum must be filled. To ensure continuity and a controlled handover of knowhow as well as stakeholder contacts, the former owner-manager should be retained for a well defined transitional period. Otherwise, it can become difficult to dismount obsolete working patterns and implement change. Top-level leadership transformation often requires a high-caliber external director to come in via a holistic, investor-led recruitment process that needs to involve incumbent management as well. Although time is of the essence, hiring decisions should not be rushed. If the wrong manager is hired, a new recruitment process will have to be started, which means losing more time while the IRR clock is ticking. An active chairman of the supervisory board, who acts as a coach and sparring partner to managers, can foster stability.

In primary deal situations, new corporate governance requirements from private equity, including supervisory board meetings, might lead to resistance from managers. To mitigate concerns, management should be able to appoint a supervisory board member. This role could also be occupied by a former owner-manager or an industry expert. A strong management team will appreciate expert inputs and might be motivated by high-quality board discussions.

Working with former family-owned businesses often means that private equity professionals need to be more "hands on." However, they also need to remember their role as owners, not managers. They need to be prudent and empathic as well; a trust-based, transparent approach wins! Private equity—particularly in previously family-owned companies—has the best chance of success in the form of partnership capital.

9 Harvesting Private Equity Investments

Profits are an opinion, cash is a fact.
Alfred Rappaport

INTRODUCTION

The ethos underlying private equity, as a transitional form of capital, is to invest in assets for a limited number of years before seeking monetization through an exit. Investments in portfolio companies are made by looking for ways to unlock value—whether by growing the business or through operational improvement. Irrespective of the degree of success, it is never the intention of the fund managers to hold the assets for the very long term. Instead, the GP seeks to harvest the investment through an outright sale of the portfolio companies. Within a standard 10-year fund structure, the search for an exit starts much earlier. Considering that acquisitions are made approximately evenly during the first five years of the fund (the so-called "investment phase"), a time frame from investment to exit could be as short as one or two years or as long as 10+ years, with an average holding period of five years.

Once the investments are harvested by selling the portfolio companies, proceeds are then distributed back to the investors in the fund, the LPs. Distributions are made progressively, as portfolio companies are sold one by one, until the fund is ultimately extinguished. As serial sellers of businesses, private equity firms have well developed sales skills and are able to draw upon a variety of exit routes to maximize cash returns to investors. Given the requirement to sell every investment within a finite horizon, the exit is a key part of any investment case.

Exiting the investments not only enables a financial return to private equity investors, but also allows the portfolio companies to consider a different strategic direction from their new investors.[1] In most cases, the entire equity stake is sold at once; however, partial exits are also observed, mainly when the private equity fund lists the company on the stock market. If, by the time defined in the limited partnership agreement, a portfolio company has not yet been sold, the fund life can be extended for a few further years.[2] Alternatively, in some cases, the remainder of a fund is sold in the secondary market in order to close the fund, in what is called a tail-end transaction.[3]

Until the exit, the value created is estimated through the periodic "mark to market," an estimate of net asset value. This estimation enables the LP to record a value on the balance sheet, though an actual return is crystallized only after a liquidity event and cash distribution. The mandatory need to exit shapes every aspect

---

[1] The portfolio company's articles specify drag-along rights, which indicate that when the private equity fund sells its shareholding, management and other investors in the company need to sell their holdings at the same time and on similar terms.

[2] Rather than forcing the sale of all portfolio companies to take place within the limited life of the fund even if this is undesirable for some, the GP can seek approval from the LPs to add a year (and later, even a second year) to the life of the fund in order to keep one or two remaining companies for a longer period; this is approved on a case by case basis and no management fees are charged in such instances.

[3] The other possibility of repayment to the LPs is with illiquid shares of the portfolio companies; however, this is highly undesirable and is not used as liquidity and control would be limited.

of the private equity investment, from capital raised to deal screening and execution. A successful track record of exits has direct influence on the GP's ability to raise follow-on funds, which is of major importance for the firm. Therefore, potential exit opportunities are identified early in the deal analysis and reviewed regularly throughout the value-adding phase. For the same reason, during the harvesting period itself, the GP will build an exit plan to maximize the value generated on the investment, balancing both the multiple of money invested and IRR.

Harvesting an investment under favorable terms depends firstly on the company's own parameters, such as its core competencies, financial performance, size, and growth potential. However, a successful exit is also strongly influenced by external forces: the business cycle, sector prospects, and capital markets sentiment. Looking at the private equity industry, it is possible to identify two different exit trends over the last decade. Between 2007 and 2010, the proportion of capital calls was higher than distributions, as private equity firms intensified their capital deployment to benefit from depressed valuation levels following the global financial crisis, and due to the dearth of public or private exit opportunities. This situation led to average negative net capital flows of $80 billion per year. The funds that had invested at high valuations before the 2008 global financial crisis were forced to delay their exits, further contributing to distributions lagging behind capital calls. From 2011 onward, sale markets much improved and distributions became stronger. A dramatic indicator of the performance of the asset class is that the ratio of distributions to contributions exceeded 2:1 in each of the years from 2013 to 2017, where net capital flows reached a peak of $217 billion in 2015.[4] The intense harvesting period was fueled by exits from the attractive investments after the global financial crisis, strong operational improvements, and a favorable buying appetite in the financial markets, all resulting in strong distribution flows. Over the next few years, the volume of distributions is likely to stay at high levels as long as capital markets remain highly liquid, and exit opportunities could fetch near historically high multiples.

There are material differences between venture capital and buyout funds in terms of exit strategy and monetization. Although both types of investment are generally made via a limited partnership structure, venture capital investment is often injected in stages, in response to capital needs and the progression of the venture business. On the exit side, early stage investors may sometimes wish to realize their investment at an interim point by selling to a secondary buyer. However, this approach usually applies to founders and business angels, and not to venture capital (VC) funds. It is most unusual for an involved VC fund to sell its position before reaching an exit for the entire company, other than in a public offering. As the start-up enterprise gains maturity, the VC firm leads the process of cultivating an outright liquidity event through either a sale to a strategic buyer or by listing the company on a stock exchange.

In contrast to venture capital, buyouts often involve control interests in mature businesses, where the initial acquisition is funded by a structure of debt and equity. Because the business is more stable and better understood, there is more flexibility in terms of monetization, which may include a recapitalization or a secondary transaction. Further, given the value of control, the whole stake is typically sold to maximize value of the control premium, except in an initial public offering (IPO). Detailed descriptions of the possible exit routes are provided below.

---

[4] Bain & Co. Global Private Equity Report 2018 and Cambridge Associates.

STEPS TO EXITING A PRIVATE EQUITY INVESTMENT

Planning how to exit an investment is only one part of the original investment thesis, and initially most of the focus is on the business fundamentals, the GP's ability and plan to add value, and the financial structure. However, exit becomes a growing consideration during the transformation of the business as it gains maturity and prominence. Exit planning should start early, with considerable thought being given to structuring and positioning the business to make it attractive to likely buyers. Private equity firms consider timing in the context of the market, in order to exit when conditions are viewed as favorable. Once these firms have decided to sell, they consider all possible exit route options and proactively conduct pre-sale due diligence to expedite the transaction, create credibility, and enhance the attainable value. Efforts should be made to "warm up" the market by making potential buyers aware of the upcoming sale months before the formal process actually starts. Significant preparation takes place behind the scenes by which the GP reviews management plans, re-examine the financial structure, and conduct a pre-due diligence.

Strategic considerations

Studying the divestment potential of a business early on not only allows the GP to model potential financial returns, but also to understand elements of the investment strategy that may actually detract from value creation. When deciding whether to exit or keep the company in the portfolio for a longer period, a GP should consider several strategic factors:

- **What are the financial motives behind the pursuit of an exit strategy?** A successful exit strategy balances the company's need for additional growth capital with the need to provide returns on capital to the fund's LPs. The private equity fund should evaluate the timing of the exit and assess whether it would be more beneficial to keep strengthening the company and fetch a higher valuation at a later time, or exit right away for optimal time to exit.

- **Does the GP see the company approaching the potential exit from a position of strength or weakness?** A company is in a position of strength if its track record shows that it consistently meets or beats its goals and performance targets, and if the market environment reflects strong buyer presence and appetite.

- **Is the company prepared to execute the exit strategy?** Managing the sales process involves substantial time and adviser fees, especially during an IPO. Is the company ready for the intense disruption of management and operations that accompanies the exit process? Before conducting a sale strategy, a company will be subjected to a stringent due diligence exercise to ensure that all of the proper systems and controls are in place. Surprises can diminish buyer confidence and impact value.

- **What is the state of the market?** How accessible is the market, given the current conditions and market sentiment? For instance, public markets can be volatile, and a successful exit strategy depends largely on market timing. Many IPOs have been pulled at the last minute at a high cost because of unfavorable market conditions. Similarly, if a sale is pitched to specific buyers (e.g., Chinese corporations) it is important to know about any constraints that would affect potential transactions and outbound acquisitions (e.g., Chinese limitations on foreign currency transactions, such as those that were in place at the end of 2016).

- **How will the exit affect the company?** Even sellers need to assess how the exit may enhance the company's core competencies. Can the new owners provide the company with new opportunities to expand and gain additional market share? How will the company's management and employees be affected? Retention of key management and personnel can be critical to the buyer. Furthermore, employees often become nervous upon hearing rumors of a sale, which is often associated with downsizing and layoffs.

Sell-side due diligence

Preparing for the exit improves the achievable transaction value and reduces its completion uncertainty. Before divesting, the private equity firm typically performs a thorough sell-side or vendor due diligence process to anticipate any risks and issues that might disrupt the deal or lower its value. Taking an in-depth look at the company in advance helps prevent unwanted surprises and allows the GP to proactively address transaction risks; it may even expedite the transaction, as there will be a lower probability of unexpected issues requiring resolution between the parties.

Sell-side due diligence facilitates the buy-side due diligence of a broad buyer group by limiting the time demands on management during the sale process, and avoiding surprises. Sometimes, companies that are put up for sale are unprepared or lack the resources to address the critical pressures that accompany the transaction process. For instance, a small company might lack the financial and accounting infrastructure to respond to the buyers' informational needs. These and other issues can be identified during sell-side due diligence, giving the seller the opportunity to proactively fix or improve them before the buyer's assessment. Some aspects usually covered in sell-side due diligence include the following:

- Profitability of the company, including quality of earnings, impact of non-recurring items, and sustainability of projections. Revenues and EBITDA trends, as well as capital expenditure and working capital requirements, determine the future performance of the business.

- Validation of the management plan by a third party (albeit one that is hired by the sell-side team), typically comprising accountants and/or consultants who note any areas of higher or lower confidence in the projections.

- Management and operational weaknesses and any potential transition issues.

- Income tax risk exposure, value-added tax (VAT) or sales tax obligation, as well as the optimal tax structure and its impact on potential buyers.

- Impact of regulations on the company by the time of exit. For instance, an IPO in the United States requires compliance with the Sarbanes–Oxley Act, which can require significant effort and preparation in advance. Similarly, exposure to environmental hazards must also be investigated.

Accounting estimates—such as bad debt reserves, inventory reserves, unfunded pension accruals, and other contingencies—should be carefully reviewed. GPs should be aware that buyers may have differing views of what constitutes an appropriate estimate for these reserves and accruals, which may lead to a post-closing purchase price adjustment dispute.

The effect of taxes

Whether the exit is through an IPO, recapitalization, or a strategic/financial acquisition, tax matters have a significant impact on valuation, particularly when valuable tax assets such as net operating losses and tax credits exist. Two primary areas require attention: the proposed deal structure and optimization of the underlying tax assets residing within the acquired entity.

It is essential that the selling party considers income tax effects when structuring an exit. For instance, a sale can often be structured as either an asset or a stock sale. If it is structured as an asset sale, the buyer will frequently take a higher, fair market value basis in each asset (known as a "stepped-up basis"), which can dramatically lower the buyer's taxes in the future. This situation often results in a stepped-up basis premium being included in the purchase price. However, if the target company is a corporation, an asset sale will usually result in double taxation of gains, first at the company level and again at the owner level, which makes asset sales unattractive relative to stock sales, notwithstanding this premium. In a stock sale, there is only one level of tax (at the owner level), and the company's asset bases remain the same.

It is equally important that GPs consider tax assets, such as net operating loss carryforward, and tax liabilities prior to the sale. The seller and the buyer have to agree to terms for each party to be responsible for all unfiled tax returns. The analysis might result in a requirement for an escrow account for potential taxes.

An agreement should be drafted between the parties to address tax attributes on a post-transaction basis. Tax issues related to the tax basis of assets, net operating losses, and credits may come up several years after transactions are completed, so identifying the responsibilities of both the seller and the buyer is vital.

The buyer should also consider any plans to break up the asset into divisional or subsidiary sales in the future, as proper structuring at the time of entry may mitigate tax consequences later upon partial sale. It is critical for the buyer to obtain advice specific to the jurisdiction in advance.

EXIT STRATEGIES

There are multiple routes available to a private equity fund to monetize all or a portion of its investment in a portfolio company; the main ones are outlined below.

- **Trade sale:** The portfolio company is acquired by another company, either public or private.

- **IPO:** The portfolio company's shares are offered to the general public on a public stock exchange. Proceeds that stay in the company for debt reduction or growth capital are called primary proceeds; Proceeds that provide cash to the sellers for their shares are called secondary proceeds.

- **Secondary buyout:** The portfolio company is sold to another private equity fund or an institutional investor in a *sponsor-to-sponsor* transaction.

- **Recapitalization:** The portfolio company assumes an additional debt, and possibly raises additional outside investors' equity capital in order to pay a dividend to the existing equity holders of the portfolio company and re-leverage the entity going forward.

- **Share repurchase:** The shares of the private equity fund in the company are bought back either by the company itself and/or its management and other investors.

- **Breakup and liquidation:** The portfolio company is liquidated and sold piecemeal; this is usually the case when the company fails and becomes a drain on the private equity fund's resources.

The choice of the desirable harvesting method depends on a variety of factors, the prevalence of which changes over time. Statistics for 2017–2018 show that trade sales accounted for 44% of all global buyout exits, while secondary buyout transactions accounted for 42% of the cases and IPOs for 14%.[5] These figures are remarkably similar for both the United States and Europe but they fluctuate over time especially with respect to public listings.

The seller must weigh several considerations when choosing the optimal exit route, including valuation, the ability to divest entirely, the likelihood of completing the transaction, deal complexity and timeliness, and management's personal objectives. The buyer's objectives should also be considered as part of the assessment of alternatives, as they provide insight about which parts of the business are likely to be perceived as more attractive.

With respect to venture investments, trade sales constitute the overwhelming majority of the successful exit means, whereby nearly 75% of exits take place through a sale to a strategic buyer. By their very nature, few start-ups reach sufficient scale to be viable candidates for an IPO. However, when a VC-backed business does go through an IPO process, it often attracts high valuations, particularly in a "hot" IPO market. The method for exit depends heavily on the nature of the business. Technology companies with a strong intellectual property and knowhow but without recurring large revenues would find it difficult to attract the public, and are therefore most likely to exit through a sale to a strategic buyer. A transatlantic comparison shows an interesting difference: trade sales are essentially the only viable exit route possible for European venture companies, whereas in the United States, a larger proportion of ventures also exit through IPOs.

Each type of exit has different implications for the LPs, the GP, and the company's management. As mentioned, an IPO may result in the highest valuation of a company, but the private equity firm is unlikely to be able to liquidate its entire position at the time of the primary listing. A trade sale can be a very attractive harvesting method for the private equity fund, as it provides payment in cash or marketable securities and a full divestiture. Managers may sway either way in terms of their preferences. They may be reluctant to become a public company because of the complexity and burden of reporting and the need to constantly focus on analyst expectations, which often forces myopia and hampers long-term business performance. On the other hand, management may favor being listed over a trade sale in order to preserve the firm's independence and avoid becoming a mere division of a larger enterprise. If possible, the management team may prefer selling the company to another financial sponsor (i.e., a secondary buyout) in order to maintain independence, avoid listing, and retain the ability to boost the next phase of the company's development. Open discussion with managers about their personal objectives is critical to avoid conflicts of strategy in an exit.

When the economy is vulnerable and the primary listing market exhibits low activity, or when many willing buyers exist, sellers frequently seek to explore multiple exit options simultaneously. They elect to employ a so-called *dual-track* strategy, whereby one team looks for potential acquirers while the other team prepares for a public listing. Under this strategy, the company tries to better position itself to take advantage of the most attractive opportunity available.

There are certain scenarios when the M&A market becomes buoyed, such as when a sector or product reaches sufficient maturity to seek consolidation, when cash-rich trade buyers look for valuable assets to

---

[5] Preqin 2019 Global PEVC

support their expansion, or when new technologies enable operating improvement breakthroughs. Similarly, the IPO market improves with an increase in investor confidence and appetite for private companies that have reached sizable growth and revenues.

As noted, the divestment phase is crucial for the overall performance of a private equity investment—and fund. Recognizing the difficulty of ensuring a successful and timely exit, private equity funds sometimes build arrangements into the financing structure of the unsold company to allow a payout even in the absence of an outright exit. One approach is to secure a subordinated debt tranche with an interest and repayment schedule that at least provides for a minimally acceptable return. The debt is coupled with warrants, which allow the investors to realize an equity-like return if the investment is successful.

Another approach for investors purchasing a minority interest in a business is to demand an equity put or a "drag" right from the majority holder under certain stated conditions. For example, such a right to put the shares, or force the sale or listing of the company, might be exercisable if the majority holder refuses to accept a bona fide offer from a prospective buyer to acquire the company. These devices, which are common in developed markets, may not be available or enforceable under the laws of some emerging countries. Put rights are typically matched with a call right to the majority holder; together, these may be attractive to the majority owner who wants to retain control of the enterprise in any event.

In the following subsections, we review the main harvesting mechanisms and their various and their associated benefits and risks.

TRADE SALE

Trade sales consist of selling the entire share capital or the assets of a portfolio company to another firm that is often in the same industry—a strategic investor. A trade sale can be structured as a share sale, where common stock is traded, or an asset sale, where assets and liabilities are purchased. Whereas a share sale comes with all assets and liabilities on the balance sheet of the holding entity, an asset deal can specify which assets and liabilities are assumed. Each has different tax consequences to the seller and a different risk profile to the buyer.

As outlined above, a trade sale is the most common exit route for both buyout and venture deals. Private equity firms may prefer a trade sale over other methods, as it provides more control over the process and often extracts the highest sale price from a buyer inclined to obtain operational synergies.

When pursuing a trade sale, the private equity firm should seek to understand the needs that motivate the buyer to make the acquisition. Common motives can be strategic (e.g., access to a technology, patent, product, or talent), defensive (e.g., to reduce competition), or growth related (e.g., access new locations, increase market share in existing markets, or incorporating capabilities to expand). A strategic buyer seeks to achieve synergies and will therefore assess whether the target is a good fit with its existing business. The target will normally enhance the existing business of the buyer in a way that is cheaper and faster than if it was to be developed organically. In some cases, the acquisition will consist of a vertical or horizontal integration, leading to different types of synergies (e.g., control over strategic supplies or economies of scale). When the companies operate in different sectors and the buyer aims to build a diversified operation, cost synergies tend to be limited to administrative functions, and possibly customer synergies, but provide entry into new markets. Either way, the seller should identify the value of synergies to the buyer in order to gauge its leverage in the deal negotiation and its potential to share in that value creation at sale, as well as to assess the likelihood of the transaction's completion.

The acquirer's deal motivation also has an impact on the business strategy in the period leading up to the transaction itself. A trade buyer integrates the acquired company into its own organization and places value on particular key strengths, whether these are technological capabilities, geographical presence, or other complementarities. Once a particular strategic buyer is identified and enters into serious negotiations, it calls to consider a reduced resource allocation to areas that would likely be discontinued after the operational consolidation. For example, if a U.S. corporation is about to acquire a European one in order to gain rapid traction there, it would make little sense for the target to deploy resources to establish a presence in the American market where the likely buyer is already well positioned.

Preparing for a sale

Preparation for an outright sale involves appointing external experts, carrying out pre-due diligence, and preparing the transaction documentation. Bankers and advisers are retained to provide services including valuation, buyer finding, and an auction sale. A law firm will prepare the data room (i.e., to provide access to the documents that the purchaser might use to analyze the business being sold) and draft the sale and purchase agreement. This document includes information such as consideration, representations and warranties, indemnities, conditions precedent, restrictive covenants, completion arrangements, transfer of pension rights, and other matters.

The private equity firm should decide whether or not it will pursue an *auction sale*. In an auction sale, the seller seeks competing bids for the company before entering into exclusive discussions with the most attractive and qualified buyer. Upon receipt of a signed confidentiality agreement from interested parties, the company will circulate an information memorandum summarizing investment considerations, financial information, sales analyses, and other key information about the company. Recipients of the memorandum may then submit indicative bids. A shortlist of bidders is given access to the electronic data room to complete their due diligence, and offers are submitted with a marked-up version of the seller's proposed share purchase agreement. Auction sales can be attractive to private equity funds, as competition reduces the buyers' bargaining position and a higher valuation of the company can be achieved. However, auctions are best suited to the sale of more attractive and "easier to understand" businesses; the more complicated the asset, the narrower the typical buyer list and process.

Warranties and indemnities

The seller usually produces a disclosure letter to the buyer late in the process, the contents of which qualify the warranties, if any are provided. Private equity firms often try to resist giving broad warranties on a sale (other than as a title to the shares, and capacity and authority to enter into the sale agreement), primarily because it prevents distribution of the full amount to the LPs in the fund. In other words, the sale proceeds cannot be distributed, due to fear of any clawbacks. Corporate sellers that will remain in existence post asset sale are often more willing to provide warranty cover and thus avoid pricing discounts. Practices vary greatly across countries.[6] Since some purchasers are unwilling to proceed without warranties, the management team normally provides warranties regarding having made full disclosure of all material information and reasonable care in preparing the business plan.

Indemnities are a common mechanism in the transaction to deal with price adjustments. The acquired company is valued by reference to a balance sheet at a date prior to closing (usually an audited balance sheet from the last year-end, or a specific one drawn up for the deal). The mechanism is based on the idea that the economic interest in the business effectively transfers at that date, after which the buyer assumes the risk. The private equity seller is expected to provide a contractual indemnity that no cash or other benefits have been taken out of the business since that balance sheet.

Alternatives to management warranties can include (1) escrow arrangements, where all existing shareholders participate in funding any claim pro rata, subject to the limit of the escrow; (2) the purchase of warranty and indemnity insurance by the selling shareholders on behalf of the purchaser; and (3) the provision of further financial incentives to management to take greater contingent risk on the warranties. Insurance removes uncertainty from the transaction, covers pre-specified costs, and provides settlement protection at a fixed price.

Advantages and disadvantages of a trade sale

The general advantages of trade sales include the following:

- **The possibility of a fast exit:** Negotiations with one strategic buyer can progress rapidly, especially in an exclusive deal, where there is only one buyer to negotiate with. Moreover, because a strategic buyer is knowledgeable about the business, the due diligence process may be smoother.

- **Attractive valuation:** A trade buyer may be willing to pay a premium to have access to synergies, increased market share, or new markets.

- **Improvement of the business:** Operating synergies with the buying company can lead to significant business improvement. Further, strategic acquisition usually gives the target company access to resources that it did not have as a standalone entity, resulting in more opportunity for growth.

- **Fewer restrictions compared with IPOs:** Trade sales do not involve the extensive regulatory requirements and disclosures necessary to go public at a stock exchange, and thus save additional cost and effort.

However, a trade sale may also be less attractive for several reasons:

- **Disclosure of strategic information:** At times, potential buyers are competitors who will gain access to confidential information during the due diligence. Regardless of a confidentiality agreement being in place, this represents a competitive disadvantage if the deal falls through, or if "runner up" bidders still gain proprietary knowledge.

---

[6] In the United Kingdom, established private equity houses do not provide contractual comfort to purchasers, other than the minimal warranties stated above. On the other hand, in the United States, private equity sellers may often need to concede a reasonably full warranty package. Elsewhere in the world, the picture is mixed depending on the relative bargaining strength of the parties.

- **Management personal concerns:** Some managers are likely to lose their position post acquisition, and for others, the level of responsibility will be diminished if the two management teams are consolidated after the acquisition.

- **Job loss across the company:** After a merger or acquisition, the entity may attempt to achieve synergies resulting from the combination by downsizing in areas, leading to facility closures and job losses; this is likely to have a negative effect on company culture and morale.

- **Culture shock:** In some situations, the involved corporate cultures are so different that a combination may raise issues or even damage customer loyalty. Because the company becomes part of a larger group, additional bureaucracy may reduce the competitiveness of the business.

- **Approval process:** This process may be slower, and potentially less certain, for a corporate acquirer that is not as experienced in M&A as a sponsor.

INITIAL PUBLIC OFFERING

Companies intending to list on an exchange must file a detailed registration statement with the local securities regulatory body, which usually includes in-depth financial, management, and operational information about the company. Because of the extent of the requirements and validation, an initial public offering is a costly and time-consuming process. Being publicly listed also brings significant exposure to the company, which will likely attract research coverage and monitoring of quarterly results.

Preparation for an IPO

There are several requirements that a portfolio company must fulfil, and several steps that it can take to better position itself for a potential IPO. Depending on the exchange, the company will have to meet a minimum market valuation. The ability to raise a sufficient amount of capital in its offering and a growth track record are also essential for a successful listing. If a portfolio company is planning to conduct an IPO, it needs to begin operating like a public company well in advance. Some GPs note that it should be fully functional as a public company at least two quarters before the IPO, as surprises to public investors can be costly indeed via stock price reactions. The company must have tight accounting, financial, and legal internal controls in place as well. Some actions the private equity fund can take prior to conducting the IPO process include the following:

- Rearranging the company's capital structure by replacing the preferred shares and shareholders' loans with a single class of common equity.

- Cleaning up the company's financial records by ensuring they are free of material misstatements, and comparable on a year-to-year basis.

- Creating an investor relations unit to deal with investors and analysts.

- Establishing controls to ensure a timely and accurate preparation of the upcoming disclosures required of a public company.

- Restructuring the board of directors. Depending on the exchange, a public company must adhere to different corporate governance requisites.[7] Mandatory rules might specify the number of directors that must be independent. GPs who serve on boards of portfolio companies may need to resign as they do not meet independence standards.

- Strengthening the company's management team. Different skill sets and teams may be required to manage a public company. It is important to anticipate these managerial needs, rather than waiting until it is too late.

In addition to preparing the company, the private equity fund's managers should give consideration to the optimal structure of the public offering at the outset of the discussions, identifying how soon the capital is required, and the best time of year for strong demand in the IPO market. Factors to consider when deciding the terms of the offering and the stock exchange on which to commence trading include the size and growth rate of the company and its sector, the breadth of the shareholder base being sought, and the likely level of demand for the company's shares. Another factor is the amount of money that will go out to selling shareholders, vis-à-vis capital injected into the company. There is an interesting duality in the act of listing—even a kind of "double-talk": whereas existing shareholders view it as an exit, an IPO is just a first step to liquidity as the company is staged to the investment community for the purpose of raising money to advance its growth.

An IPO could be structured as (1) an institutional offering where shares are placed privately to a selected base of qualifying institutional investors, after which trade resumes; or (2) a retail offering where the shares are offered to members of the public who are resident in selected jurisdictions and satisfy certain criteria. Retail offerings entail significantly higher transactional costs, as a result of the increased complexity of the compliance requirements. Thus, they are undertaken only for larger transactions, particularly where the company already has a high public profile. Both institutional and retail offerings are usually coupled with an employee offering that rewards and incentivizes key personnel in the company.

The IPO process

One of the first steps before conducting a public listing is to select an underwriting firm or independent adviser to assist throughout the whole endeavor, from preparing the registration statement to setting a price for the company's shares. With its access to capital markets, the underwriting firm can help with distributing the company's shares to institutional and retail clients. GPs usually select the underwriter to lead the process, given their expertise and past experience, as well as their desire to reduce the time demands on the company's management team. Nevertheless, both the IPO and M&A processes are very distracting to management, taking much of their time away from the more routine tasks.

When evaluating an underwriting firm, GPs must consider the size and types of IPOs the firm has handled in the past, as well as its client base. The underwriter needs to have experience in the relevant industry sector and access to a wide client base in order to achieve the desired distribution of shares to a range of institutional

---

[7] In the United States, the Sarbanes–Oxley Act has created stricter rules for listed companies; for instance, five of a company's directors must be financially literate and at least two must have had a CPA license at one point.

and individual investors. Other important factors include the pricing of the company, the sell-side coverage offered by the underwriter, and the proposed strategy of how to position the company.

Depending on the size of the portfolio company, the GP might hire more than one underwriter in order to gain access to a larger pool of investors. The group of underwriters working on a deal is called a syndicate. One firm is usually designated as the "lead left" underwriter (i.e., the true leader is listed on the far-left side of the prospectus), with heightened responsibilities, including setting the final price before the IPO, entering into the underwriting agreement, and controlling advertising.

Once the underwriter or underwriting syndicate has been selected, a non-binding letter of intent is drafted. This includes a description of the security, the tentative number of shares to be issued, a tentative price range, underwriters' compensation, the type of underwriting (firm commitment or best efforts), and which expenses the company will be responsible for if the offering does not succeed.

The portfolio company also develops a share prospectus, which is essentially a document to present itself to investors. It should provide a full representation of the company, including its vision, products, and competitors. The prospectus also contains historical financial information (typically for five years) that will assist investors and others in learning more about the company's profitability, financial position, and future potential. This very detailed document is highly scrutinized by regulators to protect public investors.

Pros and cons of IPOs

The general advantages of an IPO include the following:

- **It can provide an exceptional return:** If an IPO is very successful, the private equity firm may generate greater returns than in a trade sale, as well as the opportunity for the sponsor to continue to "ride the upside" going forward.

- **Future financial flexibility:** An IPO creates public awareness about the company, giving it access to a larger pool of capital to use. For instance, the company will be able to issue more shares to be used as consideration for making future acquisitions.

- **Share compensation:** Floating makes employee stock options liquid, thereby improving their value significantly.

- **Greater visibility:** By generating media and analyst coverage of public companies, an IPO results in increased visibility for both the company itself and the private equity firm that has listed it.

At the same time, IPOs can present several disadvantages:

- **Uncertain offering price:** The valuation is not set until the very end of the process, and can change dramatically from original expectations.

- **Lock-up agreements:** Typically, the private equity firm will be required by the underwriting firm to maintain a substantial part of its holdings for a certain period (the so-called lockup period); this postpones the time until the investment in the portfolio company is fully realized through *follow-on sales*, exposing the private equity fund to the risk of a drop in the share price, including by uncontrolled factors such as general market conditions. The fluctuation in the residual value of the holdings is quite significant. From 2011 to 2017, follow-on sales amounted to double to triple the annual IPO value for buyout-backed companies.[8]

- **Significant initial and ongoing costs:** Preparation of documents and the pre-IPO road show is a long, arduous task that takes up a great deal of management's time. Further, advisers such as lawyers, accountants, underwriters, and other counsel charge fees to assist with the process. The company also needs to meet costly regulatory requirements like the Sarbanes–Oxley Act, and these regulations are becoming more stringent in the wake of the latest global financial crisis.

- **Increased scrutiny:** Public companies are required to disclose more about their operations through press releases, filings with regulators, and annual reports, which reduces strategic and operational confidentiality. With this increased visibility comes intense scrutiny of financial information and management behavior, including pressure for short-term performance and earnings management at the expense of the long-term wellbeing of the company.

Dual-track process

A dual-track process is an exit strategy that combines an IPO process with a track toward finding an outright buyer, typically a strategic investor or financial sponsor. This route creates a competitive tension between stock market investors and outright buyers, which can improve the price and sale terms. The seller engages in this dual-track strategy until it becomes clear which exit route will achieve better terms and is more certain to be completed. Although this strategy is potentially very attractive, it may take longer to achieve results; hence, it is only suitable in a limited number of cases where the company has strong fundamentals (e.g., brand, financials, and growth). Moreover, it must be noted that either side could lose momentum out of fear of competing with the other.

SECONDARY BUYOUTS

Secondary buyouts refer to the sale of portfolio companies by one financial private equity investor to another. Also known as *sponsor-to-sponsor deals*, secondary buyouts are seen as a less preferable option for private equity funds, and are associated with periods during which other exit mechanisms are less accessible. When secondary buyouts were introduced, there was originally a stigma of failure associated with not being able to take a company public or sell it to a strategic partner. However, investors have since accepted that a secondary buyout may be appropriate for both the acquiring and selling funds in certain situations, such as an expansion phase of a portfolio company, and returns to LPs have proven attractive. The selling fund may not have additional capital to commit or the geographical reach to further expand the business. As a result, the acquiring fund may be better off using its expertise and dry powder to grow the business and create value.

The exit timing is also influenced by the need to pay out LPs when a fund is close to the end of its life, which presents an opportunity for a secondary buyout private equity acquirer. In a growing market and low-cost-of-debt environment, secondary investors can buy a target in a sought-after industry with a proven management team, even at high multiples, and finance the deal on convenient terms. With an industry-driven

---

[8] Source Dealogic and Bain & Co. Global Private Equity Report 2018.

multiple expansion, the target may later be sold at the same (or a higher) multiple, after having paid down part of the debt. The attractiveness of this strategy is enhanced by a positive operational record of the target company, which has already proven to be able to cope with stringent financing. Additionally, the management has already gained expertise in dealing with private-equity-style governance where tight monitoring systems are already in place. If equipped with a differential operational expertise or exposure to new geographical markets, secondary buyouts can provide follow-up private equity buyers with a less risky, quicker, and potentially lucrative deal.

Another reason for selling in the secondary market is to shorten the investment lifetime by exiting relatively early. For the original private equity firm, it may be an opportunity to lock in returns or enhance the IRR by reducing the holding period. In some situations, a secondary buyout represents an opportunity to recapitalize the business to attend to the liquidity needs of LPs or to incentivize the management team to deliver the next stage of growth. A secondary transaction may also be an opportunity to sell the remainder of a fund (tail-end) before its closure.

From the LPs' perspective, a secondary exit may be considered suboptimal if it has commitments on both sides of the transaction—that is, interests in the exiting and the acquiring funds. Given that they are already invested in the company, these investors will bear transaction costs to sell and re-buy the same business, while maintaining with about the same long-term exposure.[9]

A secondary buyout highlights an inherent conflict faced by the company's management team in relation to a new acquirer. The management team must handle the relationship with both the selling and the acquiring private equity funds, which adds complexity. Management has to present attractive business prospects and representations, dressing up the target company in order to achieve optimal terms for the seller. Yet, it exacerbates the pressure to deliver future growth and sets high expectations for post-acquisition budgets. Alignment with the seller is enhanced through management monetization as part of the exit distribution. One way to achieve alignment with the buying party is to defer part of this consideration or to provide future performance-based remuneration.

Secondary buyouts are the same as trade sales with respect to the buyer's demand for protection against unknown liabilities that could diminish the value of the target after acquisition. As discussed, the selling private equity fund will likely be reluctant to provide full warranty and indemnity insurance. The target's management will normally agree to provide it, except in cases where managers will not participate in the business going forward. In this case, the seller may agree to put a proportion of the proceeds into an escrow account for an agreed period of time, although an escrow is rare in secondary transactions.

RECAPITALIZATION

A private company recapitalization, in its simplest form, involves the company borrowing money and using the proceeds to purchase some of the outstanding equity or pay a special dividend. A leveraged recapitalization involves re-levering the company based on, for example, the company's earnings or a more attractive financial markets sentiment. In such transactions, the private equity fund that owns the company pulls out some or all of its original investment without selling the business. Since special dividends generate tax consequences,

---

[9] For example, the pension funds of New York State, San Francisco Employees, Los Angeles Employees, and Illinois Teachers were all LPs in both the selling and buying funds in the 2016 sale of the software company Vertafone by TPG to Bain Capital and Vista Equity Partners for $1.4 billion.

private equity investors may prefer share repurchases; however, some companies use a combination of the two, repurchasing some shares and distributing the remainder of the recap as a special dividend.

Leveraged recapitalizations are highly controversial in some countries. For example, some labor unions are concerned that payment of special dividends, especially from the companies' cash reserves or financed by borrowings, might make their employment positions more vulnerable or impair pension value. In some countries, there is a minimum capital regime in place to protect against insolvency that may make recapitalizations difficult to implement. One way around limitations on distributions is by making a large part of the original private equity investment in the form of shareholders loan notes. Doing so adds significant flexibility since loan redemption is more straightforward, and is particularly attractive to materialize investments in countries with limitations on equity repatriation.

Leveraged recapitalizations are financed based on the future potential of a company, and are especially suitable for companies that generate high free cash flows. However, not every business is a viable candidate for leveraged recapitalization. The primary requirement is the ability to utilize debt, including asset-based and cash-flow-based (mezzanine) financing, to fund the transaction. Companies that already have a highly leveraged capital structure or operate in an industry where debt is difficult to obtain will not be able to pursue a recapitalization transaction.

Debt used for recapitalizations

Re-leveraging a portfolio company can also be executed via securitizations, high-yield debt offerings, or sales and leasebacks. Thus, a recapitalization can be seen as a way of recycling capital, since no new "real" value is added by the transaction.

Most recaps rely on bonds, but some private equity funds turn to bank debt or mezzanine debt as an alternative (or in addition) to bonds. When used for a recap, bonds often include buyer protections absent in most bond issuances. In certain circumstances, immediate redemption can be triggered at slightly above face value. The bond's interest rate can be tied to credit ratings or to changes in control. Although the company faces downside risk if conditions worsen, these investor protections make financing cheaper and are attractive for solidly profitable companies. Convertibles may also be used to reduce costs, although they pose the additional risk that investors will exercise their right to acquire stock. Bank debt is used less often than bonds but it can be pre-paid, which offers flexibility when the GP does not wish the company to be tied up for a fixed term.

Pros and cons of recapitalizations

Recapitalizations offer certain advantages:

- **Earlier returns and liquidity:** The proceeds of a recapitalization are distributed through share repurchase plans, shareholders loan redemption, and special dividends before the company is sold. In this way, recapitalizations enable private equity owners to achieve partial liquidity without having to sell their ownership.

- **Tax-related benefits:** All things being equal, debt beats other sources of financing, because its interest is tax deductible, though this is being revisited in some jurisdictions.

- **Disciplining management:** With additional debt, management tends to act in a more focused and disciplined manner than if it had excess cash or a pure equity capital structure.

However, recapitalizations also have some disadvantages:

- **Higher financial risk:** After a recapitalization, the company is left with more leverage, which increases financial risk. Highly leveraged companies could struggle if economic conditions unexpectedly worsen, which could trigger insolvency.

- **Loss of flexibility:** The leverage associated with recapitalization decreases the flexibility of the company because of restrictive covenants attached to the debt instruments. For instance, the company may not be allowed to sell assets, or a change in the company's ownership might trigger forced repayment of the debt.

REPURCHASES

A repurchase is a special form of recapitalization in which no new debt is being raised. In a repurchase, the company buys back the private equity shares and/or its other shareholders, such as an original family owner who is still in management and in control of the majority of the shares. The repurchase may also be a mandatory redemption in the case of preferred shares, where private equity investors have demanded exit options to the company owners at the time of the initial investment. Buyback rights cause the company to buy back the private equity investors' shares, whereas put option rights cause the co-owner of the company to purchase the private equity investors' stake at an agreed return. For many investments, however, share buybacks are considered a backup exit route and are used primarily when the investment has been unsuccessful.

Usually the firm's co-owners and management specify a price at which they will buy back shares, the number of shares they intend to repurchase, and the period of time for which they will keep the offer open. Equity repurchases may offer tax advantages to the private equity fund, since dividends are usually taxed at higher rates.

EXITING DEFAULTING INVESTMENTS: LIQUIDATIONS AND REAKUPS

Despite all good intentions and efforts, underperforming investments do occur from time to time and, sooner or later, must be written down or written off. Hence, this exit category has to be regarded as a necessary evil rather than a choice. The approach to liquidations can vary widely by jurisdiction as each country has very different schemes in place to address failing companies.

Liquidations are sales in circumstances where the lenders have taken control because the company has been unable to service the debt. These tend to be relatively rare, because insolvency usually results in a *workout* or restructuring, whereby the capital structure is renegotiated to make debt serviceable. The *breakup* exit strategy involves reorganizing the company and separating it into independent businesses, which are then sold by distinct trade sales. This divestment strategy can be a lengthier process, but sometimes the total disposal proceeds can still end up producing a positive return to the private equity fund, especially if there were prior recapitalizations.

Certain factors are taken into consideration when determining whether the company is suitable for breakup. Subsidiaries that operate as separate legal entities, or are individually financed and self-contained, are easier to sell. Alternatively, a reorganization of the company can be undertaken to divide a group into separate disposable companies. Running simultaneous sell-offs may improve efficiency and a standardized approach for all of the disposals should further reduce fees, expenses and the time taken on the entire sell-off. The legal position of owners and directors must be addressed, as this can be a major issue.

CONCLUSION

Harvesting culminates in and provides the finishing accolade to the long-term process of investing and value creation. All private equity funds should conduct an exit review as early as possible—even at the time of considering making an investment. This review provides a view of who the likely buyers will be and how best to steer and build the company in that general direction. The value created by the private equity fund is reflected in the sale price of the portfolio company. IPOs are infrequent but can result in eye-popping valuations. While secondary buyouts have become a frequent means of exit, trade sales remain the natural route for most private equity investors.

In his own words: Dwight Poler, Managing Partner and Head of Bain Capital Europe.

A Bain Capital Perspective

The exit decision is increasingly a fundamental component of the ingoing investment thesis. At time of purchase, because the market has become more competitive, the optionality and risks of potential exit outcomes must to be priced to some degree into the original purchase price. Since the exit horizon is typically well into the future and is thus uncertain, a range of scenarios should be considered—trade sale, IPO, secondary sale, dividend recap, or restructuring—and the associated return and probability of each then discounted back into the purchase value. Given the often high cost of the control premium paid by PE funds to gain an asset, the ability to determine, and time, the best exit needs to be seen as a fundamental source of value that comes with control of the company. Further, any due diligence work that can refine the buyers' understanding of those potential exit outcomes, before signing the purchase, will enhance the ability to price the asset in the same way (or potentially with more impact) as the diligence work that goes into business plan validation.

As we consider strategies to enhance exit value during the ownership period, our experience is that the key drivers of an exit multiple are forward growth at exit, predictability of future cash flows, strength of competitive positioning, and scale, in addition to the critical state of the markets at the time of the actual exit. While the latter cannot be predicted until the point of sale, each of the former factors can be influenced by the owner during the hold period and must be optimized if maximum sale proceeds are to be realized. Additionally, building understanding and demand for the asset among potential buyers well in advance of any sale process is fundamental to a strong exit outcome.

At the time of the actual exit decision, valuation can and should be treated with the same rigor as the original investment decision; the sale is, in effect, just a decision to buy cash at that moment using the currency of the asset currently owned. Our approach is to convene an exit committee which will consider the rate of return of an investment based on: (a) our internal view of the forward business plan; (b) assumed to be "purchased" at the price we feel can be achieved in a current sale; (c) with the capital structure then available in the market; and (d) as an exit multiple five years hence that reflects the then forward growth opportunities. If the resultant return would be at or above our fund hurdle rate for a new investment, or even within a few hundred basis points given the lower risk of a "known asset" versus a new buy, we will hold the asset as it will offer us a better risk-adjusted return than finding a new company with the sale proceeds. If the return to us would be well below our investment hurdle (i.e., the buyer has placed a lower discount rate on the forward cash flows than we have) we will sell the asset. In between those two bands, we will further debate whether to sell or hold, or potentially structure an ongoing participation.

The last key factor which must be taken into account is the resulting impact on overall portfolio construction either way, considering concentrations and correlations of risks in the portfolio (e.g., exposure to foreign exchange, country, or sector risk; dependence on capital markets to realize liquidity, or other fundamental risks that have emerged and may diminish fund level returns).

In sum, the harvest decision is a more important, and less considered, risk factor (positive or negative) than many investors realize. The value of understanding and quantifying that risk at the entry cannot be overstated.

10 Search Fund Investing

He who would search for pearls must dive below.
John Dryden

INTRODUCTION

A search fund is an investment vehicle in which a small group of investors provide financial support to an entrepreneur, while the entrepreneur seeks to identify, acquire, and manage a privately-held company.[1] Each fund is a unique vehicle formed with the purpose of acquiring a single company, with a typical price of between $5 million and $30 million. Investors are able to invest pro-rata in the target company acquired by the fund, depending on their individual preferences. Once the company is acquired, the entrepreneur who is running the fund takes an operating role in the acquired company, usually as a CEO. Initially popular only among recent business school graduates, the search fund model has expanded to include mid-level managers looking to pursue an entrepreneurial career.

Numerous funds were started in the United States in the 1990s and the investment model continued to become more prevalent throughout the 2000s, spreading into various geographies. The expansion of these types of investment vehicles was mainly due to their overall performance over time. According to the latest investigation on performance, search funds achieved pre-tax internal rates of return of 37% and money multiples of 8.4x through year-end 2015, although about 27% close without making an investment.[2]

Search funds are typically started by young and motivated entrepreneurs (or "searchers") with limited direct experience in the target industry, and sometimes little or no operational experience. Most, if not all, searchers are unable to secure backing from a traditional private equity management buy-in. They are also likely to have just finished an MBA, meaning they are often unable to put down any significant amount of capital to demonstrate that they have "skin in the game." In these situations, the search fund model is appealing because it provides an effective and quick route for these young individuals from a variety of backgrounds, but without financial resources, to run and build an equity stake in a company. While the individuals' lack of experience is a risk and may be a contributing factor to failure, the significant successes achieved through well-managed investment processes keep investors interested in the model. The "lack of experience" risk is partially mitigated by the fact that investors in the search fund prefer stable and profitable companies and are willing to share their own expertise to support the entrepreneur.

The main goal of the investor group is to back promising, motivated entrepreneurs in an environment with a high probability for success while monitoring and mentoring them. Investors rarely have a preference for entrepreneurs with a particular professional background, but rather aim to back those with the requisite skill set to source investment opportunities with high potential to create value. All investors in a search fund are equal in terms of their return economics. Investors who prefer to be close to the entrepreneur by serving on the board of the acquired company and providing mentoring do not receive any additional returns. Some

---

[1] This is a relatively new private equity sub-asset class, which traces its origins back to H. Irving Grousbeck, a professor at the Stanford Graduate School of Business, who originated the concept in 1984.

[2] See Pohlmeyer and Rosenthal (2016).

prolific search fund investors have day jobs at private equity firms although they invest their own personal capital. Like venture capitalists, angel investors, and growth equity investors, search fund investors enjoy the opportunity to work with young entrepreneurs and focus on building companies from a foundation of existing products, services, or customers.

The life cycle of a search fund tends to go through four important phases: (1) *fundraising* (2–6 months), (2) *search and acquisition* (2–30 months), (3) *operation* (4–7+ years), and (4) *exit* (6 months). The time period for each of these phases varies depending on the fund, characteristics of the target, investors, and economic conditions, with the most significant variation taking place in the operation phase. Some noteworthy successes have had long holding periods of over 10 years. Often, investors are happy to stay in a good deal far longer than a private equity fund because money returned early to them incurs taxes and requires redeployment to new opportunities, which are not easy to find. The exit is usually led by the entrepreneur rather than the investors. In the event that no suitable targets are found and the search fund runs out of money, the fund is closed and investors will write off their capital.

In the private capital universe, search funds occupy a unique space somewhere between venture capital (VC) investing and private equity investing. While VC funds often end up with many loss-making investments but a handful of spectacular successes, and private equity funds realize few failures but also achieve fewer "home runs," search funds balance these two profiles by achieving relatively few failures with a broad distribution of profitable returns. One explanation for this low rate of failure is that entrepreneurs target profitable businesses with recurring revenue and benefit from mentoring from seasoned investors.

WHY START A SEARCH FUND?

Most entrepreneurs consider starting a search fund because they aspire to run an established business, work for themselves, and benefit from equity ownership. They want to be a CEO and a key player in both day-to-day operations and the strategic development of the company. Such individuals do not want to start a new company as start-ups require innovative ideas or products that are not proven in the market and have a high risk of failure. Instead, they prefer to improve and grow a business that is undermanaged and thus offers opportunities for additional value creation. The typical target of a search fund is a cash-generative, stable, and high-margin business that often has an older founder looking to retire, a middle-aged founder looking to hand over the reins, or a warring pair of co-founders that elects to bring in new management.

Another motivational factor for entrepreneurs is the possibility of achieving higher financial payoffs relative to the payoff that could be obtained as an employee of a company. While, over the duration of the process, the searcher usually lives on a relatively lower income than the income from a well-paying job at a large company, there is potential for a major payoff when the target company is eventually exited. Unlike the manager of a private equity fund, whose compensation is affected by a more diversified portfolio of companies, the searcher relies only on one business (sometimes for a decade or longer) to generate a healthy payout.

Searchers must be able to handle the pressure of raising money. The proposition is quite challenging as many investors are reluctant to invest money in a young professional who has not run a company before and may have no experience in the target industry. Essentially, investors are taking an option on an individual who they think will be able to succeed. Despite their relative inexperience, the entrepreneurs need to be resilient to the many adverse factors encountered while running the search fund. The ability to successfully navigate an environment with high levels of uncertainty and new challenges is critical. Searching for, acquiring, and operating a small or middle-market firm requires a significant amount of physical, intellectual, and emotional energy. Further, given that the search and acquisition period may be a very slow process, the searchers must be prepared to be patient and determined as they progress through the different stages. For the average searcher, this move is a career decision rather than a job. Investors, too, must be patient and supportive as there is no liquidity during the duration of the fund.

ECONOMICS AND STRUCTURING

The structure of a search fund directly impacts the split of benefits between the searcher (via his/her share ownership in the company) and the investor group. Most search funds are structured to provide the investors with a liquidity preference over the searcher, who typically does not have cash to invest. This arrangement allows investors some downside protection while maintaining their potential for uncapped gains. If the entrepreneur puts cash in the deal then it is likely to rank side by side (i.e., pari passu) with the investors' cash. The searcher is rewarded by investors with common equity in the acquired business. This compensation structure ensures that incentives are aligned for the duration of the deal. Therefore, as with any management buy-in executed by private equity funds, the manager (in this case, the searcher) does not realize a return until the investors realize their return. The equity return usually occurs when the business is sold.

Investors choose search funds for several reasons. First, they have the ability to invest limited amounts of money and stage their investments over time. Investors can pool their capital with others that have varying levels of experience.[3] Moreover, as we discuss below, investors initially provide a relatively small amount of capital to fund the search for targets before providing a more significant amount of capital for the targets' acquisition; doing so allows them to limit the risk of a capital loss by learning more about the entrepreneur and the business to be acquired. Second, investors are often eager to pursue personal interests via search fund investments. They may prefer to invest in particular sectors, or simply find it appealing to support and mentor a young team.

Usually, entrepreneurs running a search fund attempt to assemble a mixed group of investors with complementary skills in terms of search fund investment, operational, and industry expertise. Ideally, some of these investors should also have deal execution experience to support the searcher in the negotiation and terms of the purchase. Entrepreneurs often build personal relationships with some investors that prove very valuable during difficult times. Such investors become mentors and advisors and understand when things do not go according to the original plan. This personal connection between the entrepreneur and the investors is one of the main differences between classic private equity funds and a search fund.

Capital structure

The capital structure of the search fund encompasses two key inputs: investors' capital and searcher's compensation.

---

[3] Depending on the size of the target company, a search fund might have anywhere from 5 to 20 investors.

Investors' capital

Investors' capital is provided in two different stages: the search stage and the acquisition stage. *Search capital* is most often raised in a form of units, typically priced at $30,000 to $40,000 per unit in a U.S.-based fund, although some (usually influential or very useful) investors have been able to purchase half units, increasing the average number of investors per fund.[4] With this initial investment, investors receive the right (not the obligation) to participate with additional capital to fund the acquisition of the target company. The amount of search capital needed is usually the searcher's salary over the target search period plus other expenses such as legal fees to set up the fund, travel costs, logistics costs (office, phone, etc.), some due diligence fees, and contingency costs. According to a survey by Kolarova et al. (2016), the median search capital raised by international search funds is $391,195. Further, the median number of investors per fund is about 15, while raising the search fund takes between four and five months, on average. Search capital is supposed to fund the search of the target company for a determined period—typically 24 to 30 months.

Upon completion of an acquisition, search capital traditionally converts into the same securities as the securities issued for taking over the target company with the acquisition capital. However, the conversion (or rollover) is always at a stepped-up rate of 1.5x to account for the fact that the search period is the riskiest period of the fund. For example, if an investor is investing $200,000 in the acquisition and this is split 50% into preferred shares at a 5% coupon and 50% into ordinary shares, then the rollover of the investor's search capital will be inflated by 1.5x and roll into the same instruments in the same proportion.

Acquisition capital is the funding required to acquire the target company. Kolarova et al. (2016) find that target companies have an EBITDA of $1.5 million and a purchase price/EBITDA multiple of 5.2X. While investors' capital can come in many forms, investors usually structure the acquisition capital to gain preference over the searcher's share ownership; this is achieved through capital structure seniority and a preferred rate of return in the form of subordinated debt or preferred equity (see Exhibit 1 below for a discussion of the pros and cons of each):

- **Subordinated debt:** In some rare circumstances, the deal involves a layer of high-coupon subordinated debt provided by investors, which is usually short term on the basis that the entrepreneur has committed to replace it with bank debt. The high-coupon aspect encourages this debt refinancing.

- **Preferred equity:** Preferred equity is junior to all debt, but senior to common equity. It can be structured as *participating* preferred stock to offer investors the right to the initial value plus accumulated and unpaid preferred dividends plus 100% of the common equity less the searcher's vested equity upon sale or liquidation. Preferred equity can either be issued as redeemable (i.e., investors can redeem prior to a sale, recapitalization, or liquidation) or non-redeemable. It can also be structured as *convertible* preferred stock to offer investors the right to either (1) the initial value plus accumulated and unpaid preferred dividends, or (2) a predetermined number of common equity shares. The latter approach allows for a natural hedge. If the underlying common equity value of convertible preferred stock is less than the accreted face value, the investors keep the preferred stock and are paid out before the common equity has any value. The investors' return is capped at the dividend rate of the convertible preferred stock, granting a return similar to subordinated debt. Conversely, if the underlying common equity value is greater than the accreted value, the investors convert into common equity and have the ability to receive uncapped capital gains.

---

[4] Some searchers also invest their own money to buy a unit (or more) as a way of showing a commitment to the company by becoming a co-investor.

Exhibit 1: Pros and cons of subordinated debt and preferred equity

	Subordinated Debt	Preferred Equity
Investor	Pros • Mitigates downside risk through early return of capital • Provides an opportunity to reinvest redeemed capital elsewhere • Early capital redemptions can boost the internal rate of return on the investment Cons • Caps investment upside to coupon rate • Repayment of the subordinated debt may allow searchers to vest common equity earlier	Pros • Maintains prospect of uncapped returns • Investment is senior to searchers' equity and provides downside protection Cons • May lead to misalignment of interests between investors and searchers. If the company is not doing well, searchers (who own common equity) might take excessive risks to increase the chance that they get a return.
Searcher	Pros • Allows the repayment of the expensive capital component • Creates value for common equity • Early return of capital can boost internal rate of return so the searcher vests into common equity Cons • Better suited for companies with strong free-cash-flow-generative abilities	Pros • Cheaper capital over a longer investment horizon if the company does not generate free cash flows in the early years of the investment Cons • No ability to pay down the expensive components of the capital structure • In mid-growth scenarios, accretion of preferred equity prevents growth to common equity

It is worth noting that search funds structured with 100% preferred equity can result in demotivation for searchers who are unable to deliver on projections, because the value of their common equity is reduced by the compounding of investors' dividends on their preferred equity, which is senior to the searchers' common equity.

Searchers' compensation

Searchers are not permitted to draw a salary from the search fund until the full amount of targeted search capital is raised. As a result, searchers must live on their own savings during the fundraising period, which can last up to one year. Yet, the fact that the entrepreneur does not receive a salary during the fundraising period proves the individual's commitment to the fund and ensures that the money raised is spent on searching for a company rather than searching for investors.

In addition to a salary, searchers typically earn 25–30% of the common equity in the target company. However, the equity entitlement for the searcher is awarded based on a vesting schedule. Vesting usually occurs in three equal tranches:

- **Tranche 1:** Vested upon the acquisition of the company;

- **Tranche 2:** Vested over time (4–5 years) with acceleration upon a liquidity event (e.g., sale of the company sooner than expected); and

- **Tranche 3:** Vested when performance hurdles are achieved (e.g., internal rate of return hurdles, return on invested capital targets, etc.). When based on the internal rate of return (IRR), the vesting schedule uses a sliding scale with increments based on minimum IRR thresholds that typically start at 15–20% IRR to investors. The maximum thresholds reach 30–40% IRR.

Many search fund contracts include a clause stating that from years one to five the fund will target an IRR of between 20% and 35%. After year five, the hurdle rate becomes the return on investment (ROI), usually between 4x and 6x. This rate is amended in the contract with the sole purpose of incentivizing ownership of the company for a longer period of time if future growth prospects remain strong. Even though a 30% IRR could be harder to sustain over longer periods, a combination of both IRR and ROI can support the decision to extend the holding period beyond five years.

Performance

Traditionally, search funds' performance has been measured from the perspective of the investors that provided the initial search capital using two measures, IRR and ROI. IRR represents the annual compounded rate of return achieved by the investors on their search and acquisition capital invested; this is only relevant for investments that return a positive return above the initial investment. An ROI represents a multiple of the investment that is returned to investors; for instance, if they invested $50,000 and received $100,000 in return, they would attain an ROI multiple of 2.0x. Kolarova et al. (2016) note that the average international search fund in their relatively limited sample achieved an IRR of 33.4% and an ROI of 2.8x.

In addition, using a sample of 258 *first-time* search funds, Pohlmeyer and Rosenthal (2016) show that the funds achieved an IRR of 37% and a money multiple of 8.4x for the investors that provided the initial search capital. The calculation includes funds that quit the search, sold the company, or still operate the company. If the company is not sold yet, its valuation for the purpose of computing performance is based on the searcher's estimates of market value. Exhibit 2 illustrates the distribution of the funds in this sample and their performance over their life cycle.

The study finds that a large percentage of the search fund entrepreneurs had recently graduated from an MBA program and that, in terms of their background, the largest cohort (29%) had a background in private equity. The median amount of initial search capital raised was approximately $420,000, and about 27% of all search funds closed down without completing an acquisition.

Exhibit 2: Search funds in each phase of the life cycle

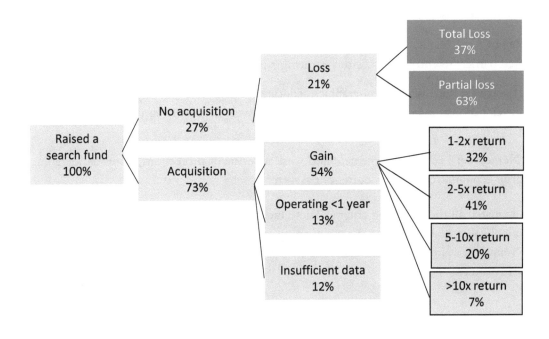

Source: Pohlmeyer and Rosenthal (2016)

THE INVESTMENT PHASE

Establishing investment criteria

Search fund principals start by first allocating considerable time to set the appropriate investment criteria for the new search fund. This set of criteria drives the framework for the search process and for evaluating acquisition opportunities. The criteria should serve to maximize the chance that, within a reasonable amount of time, the searcher will find a solid business that can be financed and acquired but also protects investors from weak investment proposals. Common search fund investment criteria include the following measures:[5]

- **Company Positives:** Recurring revenues and sustainable profit margins (>15% EBIT margins), low CAPEX and working capital requirements, competitive advantage, high barriers of entry, motivated seller for non-business reasons, multiple avenues for growth, solid middle management, available financing, reasonable valuation (appropriate size and EBITDA), realistic liquidity options in three to six years, etc.

- **Company Negatives:** Turnaround situation, high customer concentration/churn rate, limited or no management bench strength, competitive auction, public-to-private transaction, etc.

---

[5] See Rozenrot (2005).

- **Industry Positives:** Fragmented and industry, sizable industry (both in terms of revenues and number of companies), relatively early in industry life cycle, high number of companies in target size range, straightforward industry operations, etc.

- **Industry Negatives:** Highly consolidated industry, declining industry, high competitive intensity/limited barriers to entry, high customer pricing power, unpredictable exogenous factors, etc.

- **Geography Positives:** Favorable demographics, educated workforce, developed entrepreneurial culture, well developed institutions and legal systems, strong levels of growth, sizable number of small businesses, etc.

- **Geography Negatives:** Lack of enforcement and weak investment protections, poor demographic dynamic, difficult economic conditions, currency risks, etc.

Targets very rarely match all the screening criteria. These measures are viewed as a framework of ideal circumstances and not absolute restrictions on the target company. However, establishing these acquisition criteria before establishing the search fund helps align the entrepreneurs' and investors' expectations for the general nature of the investment.

Fundraising for the search

Before raising the fund, the entrepreneur must be able to articulate a compelling investment proposition. In particular, the entrepreneur needs to identify the focus of the fund and how the target company's characteristics align with his/her experience and expertise. In order to begin the journey towards acquiring a target, entrepreneurs must raise capital to fund expenses associated with the search (i.e., the search capital). Search capital is usually raised from people who have already invested in other search funds and have more confidence in the search fund model. Attracting capital from investors who are not familiar with the model can be difficult, but as the search fund community has grown, interest from these investors has grown as well. Typically, two or three investors who commit money for search capital will become advisors during the search process and later join the board of the acquired company, so it is vital that entrepreneurs try to engage with experienced investors.

One of the first steps that searchers take before contacting investors is to create a private placement memorandum (PPM), which highlights, among other things (1) the searcher's background, (2) the search strategy, including specific search criteria, (3) industries of interest, (4) a detailed timeline with expected completion dates, (5) the structure of the search fund, including types of financing required, (6) a detailed breakdown of the use of investors' capital, and (7) the expected terms of a deal. Once a potential investor has reviewed the PPM and is interested, a meeting is scheduled with the searcher to discuss further details.

In most search funds, investors purchase *units of initial search capital.* When the searcher has gathered all the units from all investors to cover the necessary search capital, a contract is signed and the money is deposited in the search fund's bank account. It is important to note here that the searcher must fund the period of search capital raising. Investors' capital cannot be spent to raise money from other investors or to provide for some backlog of "salary."

Search capital usually lasts for a period of two years. It is used to pay the searcher a salary and to cover administrative expenses such as office space and travel costs, as well as due diligence costs.

Searching for a target

For entrepreneurs, the search process is typically the most stressful stage in the life cycle of the search fund, as the success of the entire fund hinges on the quality of the final target company selected. Ultimately, entrepreneurs want to run a company, not search for a company to buy, so this might be a new area outside their career focus. Moreover, if the two-year search period expires without an acquisition, it is highly unlikely that the investors will put up any additional capital to extend the search period. In most cases, when the search fails, the entrepreneur spends the search capital received in full. The potential to fail influences the early decision-making process of the entrepreneur, adding further stress and pressure.

Searchers either take an industry approach (i.e., target specific industries) or an opportunistic approach (i.e., source deals from intermediaries in an industry-agnostic or opportunistic fashion) when looking for investments. Most searchers follow a mixture of both approaches, dedicating the majority of their time to screening companies in select target industries, but remaining open to considering companies from other industries. This methodology is discussed with investors during the initial screening criteria conversation. Due to the significant time constraint associated with the search fund model, adopting a succinct and efficient search strategy is important to ensure that the entrepreneur prioritizes targets with meaningful potential.

Searchers choose different search methodologies depending on whether an industry-focused approach or an opportunistic approach are used. Deciding between these two approaches depends primarily on the entrepreneur's background and skill set, as well as the search fund investors.

- **Industry approach:** In an industry-focused search, the searcher uses a number of techniques, including accessing the relevant trade organization, attending industry trade shows, utilizing search databases, and outsourcing services. Search databases are used to screen for appropriate targets that generally fall within the predetermined investment criteria.[6] Usually, the industry approach involves searches in more than one industry (e.g., three or four industries or sectors at the same time). Once the search fund has built a sufficient list of potential targets, there are various ways to contact the business owners.

- **Opportunistic approach:** Opportunistic searches target companies that are actively looking to engage in a sale process. This method helps limit the number of companies contacted whose owners are ultimately unwilling to sell. It relies heavily on third parties such as business brokers, investment banks, accounting firms, and law firms that refer companies available for sale. These parties potentially provide a constant stream of relevant targets to the search fund. Given the reliance on information provided by third parties, these investment opportunities tend to be more competitive (and therefore expensive) as more potential buyers are likely to see them; this explains why most searchers tend to source potential acquisitions on their own, looking for companies that are not marketed.

A critical step in the deal sourcing process is finding "qualifying sellers"—that is, determining if the company is truly an attractive target and the seller is willing to sell in the near future. While searchers may build an extensive list of potential targets and contact as many as possible, they must also be very stringent in allocating their time to any potential targets. Given their limited resources, searchers cannot afford to spend time, money, and energy getting to know a company, only to find out that the owner is not truly committed

---

[6] Searchers in Europe have a huge advantage over those in the United States because private and small European companies are required by law to submit their annual financial data to governments (in the United Kingdom, it must be submitted to Companies House). This data can then be accessed by searchers at a low cost.

to a sale, but is rather looking for a free valuation service. Approaching companies that are not for sale forces searchers to devote more time and effort to the process, as getting the attention of the owners/management and gaining access to financial information can be a very complex process. It is thus vital that searchers establish key criteria for walking away from unfavorable potential targets in order to prioritize worthy opportunities. To increase the chances of success it is advisable that searchers:

- focus on one or two industries at any given time,

- know those industries well to gain credibility with the seller (talking to anyone in the industry would help),

- develop a close relationship with the seller, and

- focus on proprietary deals.

Targeted letters, cold calling, emailing, warm references from industry insiders or other personal and professional contacts, and meeting at industry conferences and tradeshows are all common techniques used by managers to make initial contact. As a first contact, the most common approach to a potential seller is through email. A relatively successful approach is to start with a personalized e-mail and follow up with a phone call less than a week later. Regardless of the reach-out method utilized, a searcher should aim to meet with the owner in person as soon as possible. Once the first contact is established and the potential seller is interested to meet, then the clock starts ticking: any time spent on a potential deal means less time available to continue the search somewhere else and thus missed opportunities. As the searchers have limited resources, they need to assess quickly the potential seller and decide if it is worth moving on as soon as possible.

The searcher should have contact with both investors and advisors throughout this process to keep the relevant parties up to date on significant developments. Once a target company has been identified, the searcher will send a proposed *deal summary* to the investors. This summary serves as the basis for a discussion among the searcher and investors to determine if the proposed acquisition matches the original target criteria and warrants further diligence. It also allows investors to develop a holistic understanding of the business. Some of the elements in the deal summary include:

- an overview of the business and the market (e.g., products and services provided, management, key assets, customer base and concentration, key suppliers, geographic presence, market size and trends, market segments, etc.);

- the value proposition (e.g., benefits to customers, competitive advantages, etc.);

- a financial summary (e.g., revenues, profits, financial ratios, capital structure, etc.);

- main deal points (e.g., investment highlights, value of the deal, sources and uses of funds, seller motivation, expected returns, equity participations, transaction timeline, etc.);

- a financing plan (e.g., amount of financing and repayment schedules, the types of financing instruments used, cost of financing by instrument, seniority of each instrument, etc.);

- key risks and mitigating factors (e.g., potential liabilities, adverse industry and macroeconomic trends, regulation and compliance, competition, loss of key people, etc.); and

- any other important issues related to the acquisition (e.g., technology, tax implications, governance issues, involvement of incumbent management, etc.).

The foremost ingredients in a successful search process include an entrepreneur with relentless drive and discipline, creativity in finding sellers, sourcing deals, and negotiating deal terms. In addition, the searcher should show diligent tracking and planning of all activities throughout the search process. However, ultimately, searching for a target is a demanding numbers game: the more time and effort searchers put in the greater the chance of success.

What happens if the search turns out to be unsuccessful? Statistics indicate that as much as a quarter of the searchers fail to find a target. One option is to ask investors for an extension. An extension could be granted if the investors feel that the searcher is close to acquiring a target; this would justify the extra time and money invested. The other option is to move on. Although the search fund may have failed, searchers gain valuable skills and the knowledge to acquire and grow a successful business and a better understanding of the industries covered. Such knowledge can allow them to carry on in a new career (or to just go back to their previous employment) with more maturity and experience.

Executing the acquisition of the target

As the search process provides potential target companies, the searcher usually sends regular information updates to the fund's investors to inform them about the interest in those companies. Since most search fund entrepreneurs have never purchased a company before, it is important that they discuss the potential targets with the fund's investors (especially those who have expertise in the industry) to avoid buying a bad business. Subsequently, searchers submit letters of intent (LOIs) to the target companies to formalize their interest in them. After an LOI is signed by both parties, searchers can initiate the due diligence process.

Entrepreneurs are expected to conduct due diligence on few acquisition opportunities during the search process. Typically, they make a quick evaluation of both the company and the industry, looking for potential "deal killers" while assessing how closely the opportunities align with the investment criteria agreed upon with the investors. In the second stage of evaluation, the entrepreneurs perform additional analyses on the industry and company to more accurately value the business, set out the major terms of the acquisition, and identify issues that require further investigation.

At this point, a comprehensive due diligence process begins. Upon completion of the due diligence and negotiations, the entrepreneur will submit a formal *investment memorandum* for the target company to the fund's investors for their final review and decision. This document will be much more comprehensive than the initial proposed deal summary. It should include additional information from the due diligence process, such as: (1) the rationale for the sale, (2) key industry trends, (3) customer information, (4) supplier information, (5) an overview of staff and management, (6) a competitive positioning analysis, (7) a transaction summary, (8) sources and uses of capital, (9) an investor return profile, (10) a detailed post-acquisition plan, (11) an exit strategy, and so on. The fund investors are then given the right of first refusal to participate in the deal and become the new owners of the company alongside the search fund entrepreneur. If all goes to plan, the search fund acquires the target company through various financing methods and enters the operational phase of its life cycle.

As soon as a target is identified, the searcher enters into *simultaneous negotiations* with the seller of the company, as well as the providers of capital, to acquire the business. Acquisition financing for the target company typically includes a combination of new investor capital, bank debt, and seller financing.

- **Investor capital:** A transaction is usually structured with offerings of preferred and common equity to investors. In rare instances, subordinated debt could also be offered, although this type of debt is used temporarily until it is replaced with bank debt. Preferred equity allows investors to participate in the upside from the eventual growth and sale of the company while providing priority over common equity.

- **Bank debt:** Senior bank debt, including term loans and revolving facilities, comprises a significant portion of the acquisition financing. The actual percentage varies with the asset intensity or the cash flow of the company, interest coverage ratios, and general banking climate at the time of transaction. The bank that has historically provided loans and other services to the target company can sometimes become the lead lender for the transition to new ownership.

- **Seller financing:** Sellers often stay involved after the deal via seller loans or earnouts, either of which can provide substantial funding that is considered relatively "friendly" financing. Thus, such funding may be relatively cheaper, and would also help align the seller's incentives with that of the investors. In particular, seller loans are common. These instruments are subordinated to senior loans and are frequently used as warranties for indemnity claims (i.e., the loan is used to cover unexpected warranty claims that occur after the acquisition). They could also bear interest that can be paid annually or at more frequent intervals. Notably, the availability and extent of seller financing is influenced by the seller's needs for liquidity, tax liabilities, and interest in staying engaged with the business.

Often, the structure and terms of a transaction and other non-financial concerns are as important to the seller as the price paid. Hence, by listening closely to the seller, the searcher may be able to offer more flexibility than a private equity or strategic buyer and win the bid despite paying a lower price.

Note that investors in a search fund have no obligation to provide capital for any potential acquisition after the search, as they have the right of first refusal. If any investor decides not to participate in the acquisition, the searcher will usually ask existing investors to provide additional capital, or obtain it from a new source. In addition, when an investor walks away from the acquisition, he/she will receive the initial search capital provided plus the 1.5x step-up, either in cash or as equity in the acquired company. The entrepreneur can mitigate the risk of individual investors walking away from a deal by maintaining regular communications with them.

When the acquisition is completed, the structure of the search fund adjusts to reflect the transformation of the venture. Typically, the search fund ceases to exist, with the remaining search capital being converted into securities issued for taking over the target company with acquisition capital. This conversion (or rollover) is always at a stepped-up rate of 1.5x to compensate the initial investors for participating in the riskiest part of the process. The target company will then be owned and operated as a stand-alone entity with the new investors as owners alongside the searcher. In some circumstances, depending on tax needs, the fund may continue to exist as a holding entity for the acquired company.

THE OPERATIONAL PHASE

Search funds follow an investment strategy that provides a direct pathway to manage a growing company without having to develop an idea or company from scratch. In this section, we focus on management of the acquisition from post transaction until the exit. This period can be split into two sub-periods: (1) the transition and (2) the operation of the business. Successfully managing the business in both of these periods will improve the business's growth trajectory and (hopefully) achieve a sufficient exit return multiple for both investors and searcher.

The Transition

Once the search fund has acquired the target, the new manager and investors must tackle the questions of whether the seller should stay involved, the form of that involvement, and for how long; these can be contentious issues among searchers and investors. In some cases, the seller will exit the business on the day of acquisition and the searcher will assume his or her new duties as CEO. In other cases, the searcher may arrange for the seller to be retained in an active management position for a period of transition, depending on the seller's existing customer relationships, any continuing economic stake the seller retains in the business (e.g., seller debt, earnout, etc.), and the searcher's relationship with the seller. However, the search fund principal should ensure the relationship is structured so that he/she retains full control over the company.

In light of searchers' general lack of management experience, it can be extremely beneficial to retain the seller in a management role. This strategy can also provide some confidence to the business's current employees, customers, suppliers, and other stakeholders. At the same time, it can be destructive to retain the seller; doing so may impede the transition of the business and prevent a change in strategy or culture of the firm by fostering confusion around decision-making authority. Moreover, the seller might not be motivated or willing to turn over authority to the searcher. A common tool to guard against these situations and define a clear transition between the seller and the entrepreneur is a *transition services agreement*, which explicitly details the roles, responsibilities, time commitments, and compensation agreements between the seller and the searcher.

As part of the due diligence process, the searcher may have identified issues that require mitigation plans and opportunities for operational improvement in the target company. The entrepreneur can utilize these issues to create a 100-day road map, focusing on developing a deeper understanding of the issues rather than attempting to create organizational change immediately. During the first 100 days, the entrepreneur should aim to learn the ropes, not change anything unless absolutely necessary. Since the due diligence process is often more constrained for search funds than traditional private equity funds due to scarce financial resources and smaller teams, the 100-day plan should seek to uncover further issues and manage the transition by focusing on the following factors:

- **Communication:** The entrepreneur must communicate effectively with all involved stakeholders throughout the transition. A consistent and clear message backed by a transparent timeline will keep stakeholders aware of the transition and prepare them for the proposed changes.

- **Education:** The entrepreneur should concentrate on learning the ins and outs of the business (e.g., by meeting with customers, employees, suppliers, the community, and industry groups).

- **Evaluation:** The entrepreneur must continually evaluate each part of the business to provide a more in-depth roadmap for necessary operational improvements in the future.

- **Governance:** The entrepreneur should set out an enhanced governance plan for the company, identifying and selecting the board, ensuring key controls are in place, and evaluating the current governance structures in place.

Operating the business

Once the transition is complete, the entrepreneur should focus on creating value in the operation. There are three key drivers that a searcher can use to create equity value in the acquired company:

- **Operations:** Grow revenue through sales, marketing, strategic initiatives, new business developments (e.g., new products, geographic expansion, pricing and promotions, tangential market entry, etc.), inorganic activities, improvements of products or services. Operations can also involve margin expansions through cost minimizations or operating leverage.

- **Financing:** Reduce the capital intensity, minimize the cost of capital, and optimize the capital structure

- **Multiple expansion:** Pursue the adage of buy low, sell high and facilitate growth opportunities beyond those open to other firms in the same industry.

Given that search funds usually pursue moderately profitable, smaller businesses, entrepreneurs traditionally focus on improving the growth trajectory through both organic and inorganic activities to drive value creation in the investment. However, growth is not the only avenue to value creation, and entrepreneurs must be able to match their personal risk aversion and their capabilities to drive equity value in their investment using one (and hopefully more) of the three drivers above.

THE EXIT PHASE

While the initial phases (i.e., investment and operations) create and grow the value of the acquired company, the exit phase finally allows searchers and investors to harvest the majority of their financial returns. Due to the lengthy period from initial fundraising to liquidity (usually 5–8 years), the exit phase commands a high level of importance. Typical exit methods are similar to those of regular private equity funds, and include

- sale of the company to a strategic or financial buyer;

- stock purchased by new or current shareholders (including management);

- recapitalization of debt structure and dividend payout;

- initial public offering; and

- stock repurchased by the company.[7]

---

[7] This is usually not a realistic alternative as the price will not be good for the investors. A low price can also affect the searcher's performance-based equity allocation.

Although search funds are established with a long-term outlook (five-year asset holding period), entrepreneurs should constantly re-evaluate their exit strategy throughout the operations phase in order to satisfy expected returns. The single asset nature of the model and the timeline requirements leave search fund returns heavily reliant on industry conditions and exit opportunities. Only after seller and bank debt is paid down and the company is on a good trajectory can exit opportunities be explored. By this stage, the entrepreneurs have created significant value for themselves.

The final exit event represents the end payout. As such, this process necessitates considerable effort and focus from the searcher to ensure that the search fund has been a financially rewarding endeavor. The equity earned by the searchers throughout the search fund's life cycle makes up the majority of the remuneration received, and serves to keep them aligned with their investors. Searchers or principals can earn a sizable share of the total equity in several ways:[8]

- **Equity grant upon acquisition:** Upon successful closure of acquisition, the principals receive an initial equity stake.

- **Time vesting:** The principals can receive a portion of prescribed equity monthly or quarterly, with accelerated vesting in the case of an early exit.

- **Performance based:** If the company achieves certain goals, the principals receive an additional equity stake.

Often, these options are combined in order to create a structure that best aligns the respective incentives of entrepreneurs and investors. The cash distribution or "waterfall" is done strictly following the pecking order: any outstanding debt must be paid first; after paying down debt comes the preferred equity and its coupon (preferred equity holders are the investors); finally, the common equity is left to pay both investors and the entrepreneur. The common equity is usually split between investors and the entrepreneurs at a ratio of 75/25 in the case of a single searcher, or 70/30 in the case of dual searchers. The exact outcome will vary depending on the achievement of the performance hurdle rates.

The search fund model is attractive to investors because of the alignment of interests between the searcher and investors, as the investors receive a return of their cash invested *before* the searcher receives a return. As a result, searchers will always try to maximize returns without taking unnecessary risks, as they rely on a good exit to profit.

CONCLUSION

Search funds target companies that are not attractive to private equity funds. Once a searcher acquires a company, he/she will aim to create value through operational enhancements and capital structure optimization which might not have been possible under the original management.

The world of entrepreneurship has continued to attract individuals who are motivated by the desire to build and manage their own business. Yet the search fund model has allowed access to this arena for many

---

[8] See Rozenrot (2005).

who may lack their own business idea or the desire to start a company from scratch, offering instead the chance to acquire a small business with the help of experienced investors. It is an undeniable fact that some people are better at starting a business and others are better at managing and growing a business. Thus, many young professionals continue to gravitate towards the search fund model as an effective avenue to managing a company in which they have a meaningful ownership position. As the search fund model has grown in popularity since the 1980s, it has been deployed in various industries and geographies. While it has become more common in the United States, the concept is still very nascent in most of Europe. However, as search funds continue to report strong returns relative to other private capital investment vehicles, the model will undoubtedly gain more traction.

REFERENCES

Kolarova, L., P. Kelly, A. Davila and R. Johnson (2016) *International Search Funds - 2016 Selected Observations*, Working paper, *IESE*

Rozenrot, E. (2005) Note on Search Funds, Tuck School of Business, Center for Private Equity and Entrepreneurship.

Pohlmeyer, S. and S. Rosenthal (2016) "Search fund study: Selected observations," Case: E605, Center for Entrepreneurial Studies, Stanford University.

In his own words: Simon Webster, Founder of Ivy Partners, Entrepreneur, and Serial Investor in Search Funds

I first heard about search funds in 1991. At the time, only a few people had raised search funds and they had all been in the United States. Would it work in the United Kingdom where culturally we were more conservative and less entrepreneurial? It took me six months to raise the initial search fund money and over three years to acquire the first company, which I ran as a CEO. Raising the initial search fund is the hardest fundraising most search funders will ever do. Investors are asked to back an idea from an unproven, but enthusiastic, individual. As a result, they ask penetrating questions, forcing the searcher to ask questions of themselves, their ambitions, and their motivation. This first stage tests the sales skills of the searcher, which are essential for a budding CEO.

Finding a good quality business at an attractive price and negotiating a good financial structure is the next big challenge. Most searchers see themselves as CEOs, not deal sourcers and negotiators. Good deals are hard to find and this is reflected in the numbers, as 20% fail to find a deal. The search requires dogged determination, relationship building, negotiation, analysis, fundraising, investigation, etc. The way the searcher conducts the search process and briefs investors builds experience for the searcher while providing direct feedback to investors, who need to decide whether to back the acquisition.

The greatest value is normally created by growing the business. This task is never easy but it is made easier by sticking to the criteria for selecting a business highlighted in this chapter (a profitable business, in a growing sector, with a high level of recurring revenue) so both the searcher and investors can maximize the prospects for success. Things rarely go completely to plan. Timescales are often longer than expected and surprises come in many forms. There will be people, finance, customer, technical, and a host of other issues to address. The strength of a good board, drawn from the investor group, and a knowledgeable group of supportive investors can prove key to the searcher and to the success of the business.

Successful search funders will often go on to mentor and invest in younger searchers. They have practical experience and knowledge to draw from. Helping young people is satisfying in itself but investing in search funds can also be financially rewarding.

A final thought: Raising a search fund is a fantastic career choice for the right person. However, it will not suit the majority of MBA graduates. Only the individual can determine if it is right for him or her but selecting the wrong career choice, whatever it is, can be a very uncomfortable experience.

11 Venture Investing – An Overview

Imagination is the beginning of creation. You imagine what you desire, you will what you imagine, and at last you create what you will.
George Bernard Shaw

INTRODUCTION

Start-ups, early stage companies, and new ventures are synonymous terms in reference to new and innovative high-growth companies. Almost exclusively, these firms are also technological companies or have a very strong technological component, such as e-commerce platforms. Perhaps more than any other asset class in the 21st century, this sector has been subject to unparalleled fluctuations in response to global macro events. The burst of the dotcom bubble shortly after 2000 and the 2008 global financial crisis both resulted in a free fall in terms of funding start-up activities, only to be followed by a steady recovery and the rise of new venture companies to global leadership: Facebook, Alibaba, Airbnb, and Tesla, to name a few. In addition, there have been landmark developments in the types of vehicles that fund entrepreneurs.

Investing in an innovative high-growth start-up is both a risky and long-term undertaking, sometimes taking up to 10 years to go from concept inception to product development, growing revenues, and ultimately, becoming a sustainable enterprise. It is often unclear how much funding a company will require and when. In order to reduce the risk, investments are made in stages. At each stage, only a limited amount of funding is provided until the next milestone is achieved at a desired/higher valuation. Needless to say, each phase carries its own technological, operational, and market uncertainties and challenges. Hence, neither the amount of funding required for going forward nor the company valuation can be predicted. To address these matters, funding is done on an incremental basis, using what a set-up known as "investment rounds."

Entrepreneurs typically self-fund the initial development, be it technology or any other new product concept. To attract additional investment, an entrepreneur will usually seek seed capital, whether by partnering with a business angel investor or by engaging in an incubator or accelerator. Chapter 12 details the process and nature of angel investing, including types, best practice, legal documentation, angel networks, and market trends.

Once a start-up grows and progresses, it requires more capital to facilitate research and development (R&D), hire a management team with a versatile skill set, and expand its operations and marketing. Exhibit 1 outlines the main sources of funding based on the stage of the company. As shown, venture capital (VC), as the first institutional funding of start-ups, is filling the funding void between seed-level finance and the capital markets. Chapter 13 delves into the nature and process of VC funding: deal screening, stages of funding, involvement and governance, type of securities, terms and preferences, and some technical computations.

Exhibit 1: Sources for funding a start-up

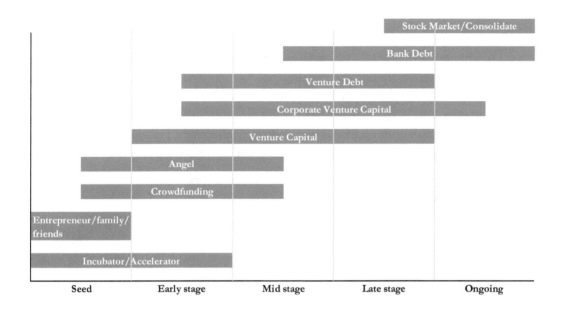

Building a successful enterprise requires multiple rounds of funding until revenues can support self-sustainability, or there is an exit event through an initial public offering (IPO) or a strategic acquisition. Investment rounds can be classified into pre-revenue (i.e., seed and early stages) and post-revenue (i.e., mid and late stages). These stages roughly correspond to investment series; preferred Series A for an early stage round, Series B for a mid-stage round, and so on. Each series is structured and negotiated with new or existing investors on an arms-length basis. Series may differ from one another in terms of size, type of securities, company valuation, and certain rights and terms (e.g., voting and cash flow preferences).

A common feature of start-ups is that funding goes into the company, and not toward buying shares of the founder or other existing shareholders; this differs from private equity buyouts of mature or distressed companies where existing owners are paid directly in return for selling their shares. In start-ups, the cash is required for the business and there is no intention to provide the entrepreneur with an early monetization. On the contrary, entrepreneurs are expected to remain committed to the business, and should only be rewarded at a later stage if plans are materialized and the business succeeds. From a technical point of view, the company needs to issue new shares to follow-on investors; whereas secondary transactions in start-up shares are rare.

Chapter 14 reviews corporate venture capital (CVC), a distinct form of venture investment which has become a dominant player in the venture capital arena. Notably, about 50% of the amount invested in late-stage deals is by non-traditional venture capitalists, of which corporate venture capital constituted a major part.[1] Essentially, CVC is when a large corporation decides to broaden itself by being exposed to the entrepreneurial, start-up ecosystem through minority equity investments. The key distinction between CVC and traditional VC is that the considerations for investing are not only financial but also strategic. It is the blend of these two separate objectives that gives rise to the numerous permutations by which CVC may be structured. The chapter also outlines the prerequisites and challenges involved in the correct implementation of CVC, and the wide spectrum of possible outcomes. Not surprisingly, the mortality rate of these programs

---

[1] Late stage is considered as VC-backed $20 million+ rounds.

(including remaining dormant) is staggering, and the sector as a whole is characterized by swings and cycles. Having said that, there are impressive success stories in CVC—for instance, Intel Capital Corp and GV (formerly Google Ventures).

Chapter 14 also presents the strategic objectives for setting up a corporate venture program side by side with more traditional corporate venturing activities such as internal R&D and acquisitions. It then contrasts the main forms of vehicles: direct investment, an internal GP model, and an external LP model. Implementation and reasons for failure are covered in some detail, followed by the unequivocal academic evidence on the positive effect of CVC on growth and governance. It is also an effective instrument for multinational corporations to execute impact investing and corporate social responsibility missions, and indeed, many make strong use of it. Notable cases of CVC programs complete the chapter.

The scarcity of exit possibilities on top of an already high degree of technological and business risk, makes investment in start-ups unattractive to many institutional investors particularly after the 2000 crash of the dot com bubble and until about 2013. This long dry spell of funding was termed the "equity gap," reaching such an alarming magnitude that it prompted academic scholars and industry thought leaders to question the overall business sense and legitimacy of early stage investments.[2] Several sources of financing have emerged to augment the funding of high-growth start-ups in their most embryonic stage.

Chapter 15 presents crowdfunding, an innovative and pronounced source of early stage funding that originated from the transformative informational reach offered by the digital force. Crowdfunding allows entrepreneurs to appeal to a broad audience through online platforms and social networks in order to get their innovative ideas off the ground. Both reward-based and equity crowdfunding are discussed.

Chapter 16 reviews seed incubators and accelerators, which are founded and backed by a wide range of hosts: corporations (e.g., Microsoft), individuals (e.g., Y Combinator), government agencies, universities, and cities in support of the venture ecosystem. This form of support includes a strong element of training and mentorship and there are many hybrids and variations, which depend on the goals set and the core competency of the sponsoring organization.

Policymakers recognize venture enterprises as a prime engine of economic growth through innovation, employment, and export. As such, governments around the globe increasingly design and implement methods to support an entrepreneurial ecosystem. In Chapter 17 we review direct and indirect funding programs, tax subsidies to investors, and funneling resources to create an accommodating environment by funding education and building clusters of innovation, financial and technological infrastructure, and more. However, public sector support of venture investment has not been without criticisms, including on the allocation of risk and economic return between the public and private sectors. This controversy and the track record of government intervention is also discussed in the chapter.

Chapter 18 is dedicated to university-led venturing. There is a general consensus on the centrality of universities to disruptive technology, innovation, and venture activity. Recognizing these unique capabilities, private sector companies are attracted to form strategic alliances with technological and science-based research institutes. Universities, in turn, also seek to engage proactively in the commercialization of new discoveries

---

[2] Two highly influential references on the severity of the equity gap are a book by J. Lerner (2012) entitled *"Boulevard of Broken Dreams"* and a Kauffman Foundation research report (2012) "We have met the enemy … and he is us." An equity gap still exists today in drug discovery and other basic research areas of deep innovation (see www.collerinstituteofventure.org/ research-strands/deep-innovation). In these fields, the required degree of investments is so large that only a small percentage of promising projects are funded. Unfortunately, the fields that are most impaired by the equity gap, such as medicine and cleantech, are the ones with the most potential to positively impact humankind.

and increasingly enable decentralized faculty and student-led initiatives. The process of commercializing scientific discoveries is known as technology transfer, whereby university-born intellectual property is either licensed to established commercial companies or is spun off by creating a start-up. Other forms of commercialization include a collaboration with external VC funds and raising a dedicated fund for investment in its technology transfer opportunities. The chapter reviews a variety of university initiatives around the globe starting with ARCH Venture Partners, which was monumental in changing the mind-set of universities toward commercializing their intellectual property. The chapter also examines university science parks at Stanford and Korea, university-based accelerators, and other current initiatives in the United States, Europe, India, Kenya, and Japan.

Venture lending (also referred to as "venture debt" or "venture loans") is the last topic in the segment on venture investing. The use of venture lending for funding technology start-ups is far from obvious and even paradoxical. It would seem that for anyone who wishes to be exposed to start-ups, doing it through an equity investment better matches the high-risk/high-reward venture profile. Chapter 19 compares venture loans to traditional forms of debt and goes through the components of return, including warrants, fees, and prepayments. Detailed attention is given to the right way to structure the loan in order to mitigate as much risk as possible. The roles of IP and of the equity investors are particularly important as loans are not returned from internal cash flows but from subsequent fund raising. The main motivation of the borrower is to "buy" time in order to build more value in the business prior to the next round of equity funding, and thus minimize dilution. For the loan provider, the focus is on the diligence of both the company and its investors. As a whole, the business model of venture lending places a great deal of importance on the venture capital firms (choosing strong VC firms minimizes the chance of default) as well as on due diligence materials and overseeing the business on an ongoing basis. With venture capitalists, the relationships with of the debt providers are long-term; hence, reputation and credibility of all parties increase the value of venture loans, and renegotiations, if needed, are more amicable.

DATA AND TRENDS

Exhibit 2 provides 2019 statistics for the different investment series: average (median) round size and company (pre-money) value at each stage. These figures are considerably larger than the equivalent ones in previous years, due to the incredible business success of an increasing number of technology companies. With respect to frequency of transactions, seed and early stage transactions are by far the most frequent. Presumably, later companies are either shut down or sold at increasing frequencies.

The growth of the global venture capital fund industry as an asset class is portrayed in Exhibit 3. Both fundraising (denoted by contributions) and cash distributions from exits are on the rise. Of particular interest is that distributions outpaced capital calls for the last 7 consecutive years thereby generating a positive net cash flow for the LPs.

Exhibit 2: Median round sizes and pre-money valuation by stage in 2019 (in US$ millions)

	Concept	Product	Customers	Expansion	
	Seed	Early stage /Series A	Mid stage /Series B	Late stages	
				Series C	Series D+
Round size	2.0	8	19	30	55
Pre-money valuation	7.5	22	73	107	250+

Sources: PitchBook Private Market PlayBook Q2 2020, PwC / CB Insights MoneyTree Report 2019 and KPMG Enterprise Venture Pulse 2019.

Exhibit 3: Global annual VC fund cash flows, 2000-2018

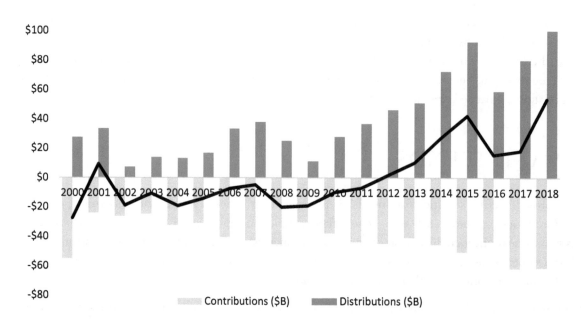

Source: PitchBook Global PE & VC Fund Performance Report Q3 2018

Exhibit 4 summarizes the level of venture capital activity around the globe. There has been a massive expansion in Asia over the last 20 years as well as elsewhere in the world, however the United States maintains an undisputed leading position. Another trend is the so-called mega deals, i.e., deal rounds of $100 million or more. There was a record 184 mega rounds in 2018, by US VC-backed companies, a dramatic increase from previous years.[3] For one institutional investor, Softbank, $100 million+ mega rounds became almost routine.

Exhibit 4: Major venture deal activity in 2018 by location

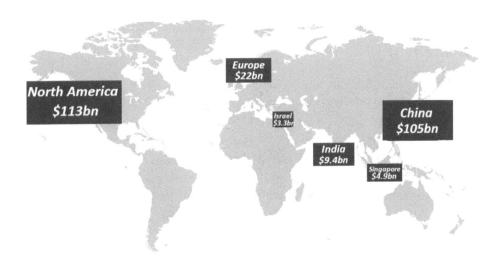

Source: 2019 Preqin Global Private Equity and Venture Capital Report.

We conclude with data on exits. For successful start-ups, the vast majority (70%) of exits are in the form of an outright sale to a strategic (trade) buyer. The rest is equally divided between an acquisition by a financial investor and a public listing. In 2018, global venture-backed exit activity reached an unparalleled record of over $350 billion equity value, in great part through initial public listings of unicorns (i.e., companies with a valuation above $1 billion dollar). This trend was not limited to the U.S. but also prevailed in Asia and Europe.[4]

More global statistics are presented in Chapter 13 on venture capital.

---

[3] Source: CB Insights 2019.

[4] Sources: KPMG Enterprise Venture Pulse Q1 2019, Pitchbook-NVCA Venture Monitor 2Q 2019 and Pitchbook 2018 Annual European Venture Report.

12 Angel Investing

I can accept failure. Everyone fails at something. But I cannot accept not trying.
Michael Jordan

INTRODUCTION

Business angels play a key role in venture finance as they represent one of the oldest and largest sources of seed equity capital. The growing number of start-ups and the venture capital (VC) preference for larger deals have widened the so-called "equity gap" in early stage investment. With entrepreneurial access to other funds being limited, angel investing has gained greater prominence than ever. Although it is difficult to estimate the total size of the angel investing market, owing to its informality, most studies estimate that angels invest at least as much as the entire venture capital market does every year. Moreover, since individual angel investments back earlier stage companies, there is about a 10:1 ratio between the number of companies that receive angel-backing for every one company that receives venture capital financing.[1]

The size of the business angel market in the United States has significantly increased in recent years to approximately $24 billion of annual investments, poured into 70,000 companies by 300,000 individuals. Similarly, the capital deployed by angel groups has doubled (or more) over the recent decade in Europe. In 2017, there were €7.3 billion of angel investments in Europe, and the community grew to 337,500 investors which closed 40,000 deals during that year. Adding other early stage investors, like venture capital and equity crowdfunding, brings the European volume of early stage investment to €11.4 billion in 2017; further adding capital raised through initial coin offerings (ICOs) brings the overall European early stage investments to €13.2 billion.[2]

For most VC funds, making seed investments in early stage companies does not fit their mindset, nor is it economic. First, given that venture capitalists are engaged institutional investors, the magnitude of capital deployed by these investors has to be meaningful. An investment size below a couple million dollars is rarely worth putting it to work; as even a small fund size of $100 million would result in an unmanageable number of portfolio companies. Further, the cost of due diligence would represent a significant proportion of the investment made. Second, an embryonic business rarely enables investors to perform a material due diligence analysis. Instead, venture capitalists prefer to let individuals make seed investments in order to flush out the early risks from opportunities. Whereas the so-called "friends and family" remain the first circle of attainable capital for companies in their initial pre-seed stages, investments by angel investors represent the most common second circle of financing for such companies. In this way, angels fill a critical equity gap until companies reach the minimal scale and feasibility to warrant venture capital consideration.

The fast decline in the cost of starting a digital technology company has facilitated a less formal investment process, in particular for business angels backing companies in early stages. Data by CB Insights (2015) shows

---

[1] May and Liu (2016); http://www.forbes.com/sites/tanyaprive/2013/03/12/angels-investors-how-the-rich-invest/2/#7ce c635e6831

[2] Sources: The Angel Capital Association website for the United States https://www.angelcapitalassociation.org/, EBAN Activity Report 2018 for Europe (http://www.eban.org/wp-content/uploads/2018/11/EBAN-Activity-Report-June-2017-June-2018.pdf), both retrieved July 31, 2019.

that the average cost of starting a software company was $5 million in 2000. With the development of open source and horizontal scaling, this was reduced to $500,000 by 2005. Cloud computing drove the essential cost of launching many start-ups to $50,000 in 2010 and to a bare-bones cost of $5,000 in 2015. The cost of hardware components has dropped in a similar manner.[3] As a result, founders' own resources (known as "bootstrapping")—along with those of family, friends, and angel investors—are increasingly expected to fund the seed stage until a proof of concept and a clear indication of sizable traction are achieved. Funding by angels has become even more critical in recent years, as U.S. and U.K. venture capitalists have been shifting their investment focus away from start-ups and early stage firms in favor of more developed growth stage ventures.[4]

Supporting small firms and ventures is equally important in both developed and emerging markets. National job creation and economic prosperity continue to become less dependent upon large firms as the small-firm sector provides the main vehicle for recovery from recessions. Thus, the economic importance of small firms is receiving increased consideration. Special attention is given to the procurement of capital, which plays a key role in the transformational process of entrepreneurial ideas into revenue-generating companies. As detailed below, academic evidence on global angel investments has invariably documented the positive impact on the growth, performance, and survival of the firms that these angels fund.

WHAT IS ANGEL INVESTING?

An angel investor is typically a high-net-worth individual (HNWI) who provides capital in the form of debt or equity from his or her own funds to a small private business, owned and operated by someone who is not an immediate family member. The term "angel investor" originates from the financiers of Broadway shows in the early 1900s. These were wealthy individuals who provided capital to help launch new theatrical productions. As patrons of the arts, these investors were considered "angels" among theater professionals. While angels are informal investors, not every informal investor constitutes an "angel." Informal investors are made up of two different groups: angels, and a group colloquially known as "friends and family."[5]

Entrepreneurs identify business angels first through their personal networks that include relatives, friends, colleagues, and university alumni networks. A later form of angel money is raised through "angel networks," where one person brings along others to co-invest. Increasingly, formal angel networks are being supported by government and regional funds that co-invest side by side with pre-approved angel network groups, usually on similar terms.

---

[3] Average cost of Wi-Fi, Bluetooth, and GPS components decreased by 50% in the period from 2010 to 2015. For the same five-year period, the average cost of accelerometer components decreased by 30%, thermometers by 25%, and processor components by 15% (Source: CB Insights 2015).

[4] Migrating the focus of venture capital towards growth stage and away from the seed stage could be noted for example in the case of Accel, a traditionally leading early stage investor which raised $2 billion in 2016, of which only one-quarter was allocated to early stage growth investments whereas the rest was for late stage growth investments. In addition, Accel co-manages a technology-focused $1.3 billion buyout fund (Accel-KKR Capital Partners V) raised in 2015, and a $685 million minority equity fund (Accel-KKR Growth Capital Partners III) raised in 2018. Altogether, only one in seven dollars invested in the Unites States is allocated to early stage growth. Interestingly, the case is different in Accel's other geographies where 70% of the latest Accel India fund raised in 2016 is invested at $2 million or less. (https://tech.economictimes. indiatimes.com/news/startups/accel-promotes-three-execs-to-bulk-up-partnership-in-india/68191037).

[5] Recently, another group of informal investors have emerged, known as "crowd investors." This form of investment will be reviewed in a later chapter.

Angel investors are a heterogeneous group and come from diverse backgrounds: some are technologically savvy, whereas others have strong legal or general business acumen. Informality is common in angel investment. Typically, angels do not incur the same ongoing overhead costs as VC firms do, potentially because they do not have anyone to report to but to themselves. Angels are able to make smaller seed and start-up stage investments, well below the minimum deal size considered by VC fund managers, and execute the investments faster and without excessive formalities. In this way, angels provide an important bridge between investments made by friends and family and those made by VC firms. Friends, family, and the entrepreneur's own saving may provide some funding (up to $200,000 or so). Despite the aforementioned decline in starting costs, this is hardly enough to sustain a rapidly growing start-up enterprise for very long, especially when there is a need to recruit additional employees to grow the business. As long as the start-up costs are below about $10 million, angels provide the most viable source of capital. Recent data covering the U.S. market indicates that the median round size when only angels invest stands at $270,000.[6] This level of funding is below the radar of most VC funds since they aim at institutional investors who seek to make meaningful capital commitments. To deploy their funds efficiently, these fund managers are induced to seek larger investments than may be appropriate for nascent companies.[7]

In addition to size and stage, there are other differences between venture capital and angel investing. The former type of investors tend to focus on high-tech and medical industries, while angels are active across a wide spectrum of sectors, including traditional low-tech industries.[8] Several low-tech start-up companies have generated extremely high financial returns on angel investments (e.g., Starbucks). Business angels are also characterized by being more geographically dispersed than VC funds. The majority of venture funds are located in leading financial or technological hubs. By contrast, angels are spread geographically, and make most of their investments within their domestic region. Moreover, business angels differ by their impetus for investment, the structural vehicle that is used, their selection criteria, and a host of other considerations. We discuss some of the main classifications in greater detail below.

Active versus passive angels

An active angel is often a cashed-out entrepreneur or venture capitalist who continues to seek out the next high-growth venture. The angel could also be a retired executive from a large company who remains active in the domain of his or her previous sector. Active angels perform their own due diligence, typically invest in start-ups in industries they are familiar with, and get actively involved with the companies that they finance. This type of investor has relevant industry expertise, a strong network of contacts, or another form of experience that adds value to the company. In addition to making a financial investment, active angels usually offer assistance in the development of the companies they back: informal advice and counseling on commercial matters and, in particular, referral to further funding sources. This assistance can occur either by devoting time informally or by participating in the corporate governance through a board seat. Sometimes, these angels may also enter into a formal employment or consulting relationship with the venture, which can bring value, but also governance issues.

---

[6] Source: Halo Annual Report 2017. Note though that the median investment size of all seed rounds (i.e., including when a venture capitalist participates) is $1 million and the pre-money valuation in 2017 was $3.5 million.

[7] An exception is the wave of micro venture capital funds with capital below $50 million, primarily in Silicon Valley which also aim at early stage investing (these are discussed in the venture capital chapter).

[8] For the 2012–2017 period, 30% of angel investments were outside the technology and biotech sectors (Halo Annual report 2017).

Active angels are similar to venture capitalists in providing value-added services to the companies in which they invest. Because they are often either ex-entrepreneurs themselves or serial investors, they can offer seasoned advice and empathize with the significant hurdles that entrepreneurs face in building an early stage venture. Many entrepreneurs believe that an active angel's advice and industry connections are just as important as his or her financial capital.

In contrast, passive angels limit their involvement with their financial investment, and may avoid participating in follow-on founding rounds. A passive angel is often a wealthy professional (e.g., a physician, attorney, etc.) who chooses to remain focused on his or her day-to-day career or hobbies. While willing to invest, these investors usually do not have the interest or specific expertise to get involved in the start-up. Before making their investment, they rarely examine the business plan in detail or perform thorough due diligence. Instead, they tend to follow others who act as lead investors and are personally known and trusted by them. Because they are less involved, the investment propensity of passive angels is low. They often treat their investment as buying a "lottery ticket," and do not tend to invest in subsequent rounds. In some cases, they are also not allowed to participate through limitation of the pre-emptive rights, which are set to require a certain threshold percentage of holding.

The rise of the super angels

The term "super angel" is relatively new, and refers to investors who are prolific in their early stage investment activities. These serial investors are particularly sophisticated and well connected in the start-up business community. They are HNWIs who typically made their wealth from prior exits either as investors, or as founders of other companies. Another category of super angels is that of wealthy families or individuals of an unrelated background who opt to become serial investors and devote considerable time to backing young companies.

Unlike ordinary angels, whose investment activity is a small part of their daily work, super angels dedicate the majority of their time to managing their venture investments. Many invest in a large number of companies in order to reduce the risk of the asset class, and often create a professionally managed office to oversee their investment portfolio. Whether they participate in the form of a corporation or create a fund jointly with other investors, super angels are able to instill rigor into the practice and procedures while maintaining a rapid and informal decision-making process.[9] Super angels' funding rounds tend to be larger than those made by other angels, although they are smaller than rounds involving venture capitalists.

Well known Silicon Valley super angels include Reid Hoffman, the founder of LinkedIn (until he joined the VC firm Greylock Partners), Marc Andreessen, the founder of Netscape and LoudCloud (until he formed Andreessen Horowitz), and Peter Thiel, the co-founder of PayPal and an early backer of Facebook. However, every few years, a new breed of highly sophisticated and well connected angel investors emerges in Silicon Valley. What differentiates these investors from other super angels is their unique access to a superior deal flow. Many of them are viewed in their communities as a having a "Midas touch," and hence, investors are eager to co-invest with them. By pooling capital from friends and business associates, these investors control a sizable amount of commitments from which they make their investments.

---

[9] May and Liu (2016).

Lastly, a hybrid between a super angel and an early stage venture fund is Innovation Endeavors. Although formally called an "early stage venture fund," it is solely backed by Eric Schmidt, the executive chairman and past CEO of Google (now Alphabet). Through Innovation Endeavors, Schmidt has made dozens of early stage investments in cutting-edge companies, such as Uber. Of course, super angels are not limited to California but can be found around the globe, where they gain recognition as popular speakers.[10]

BUSINESS ANGEL ACCREDITATION

There are regulations and restrictions on offerings of securities in private companies. In particular, in most countries, there are requirements to make private offerings only to accredited/qualified investors. The purpose of this status designation is to protect potentially unsophisticated investors from assuming unintended risks. The assumption underlying accreditation is that individuals or organizations who qualify will have sufficient financial knowledge to understand and take on the risks associated with private investment offerings. The qualifications to become an accredited or qualified investor vary across jurisdictions, and there are differences as to what type of fundraising process can be allowed from either accredited or non-accredited investors. These regulations have great importance to the size of the business angel community.

Accredited angel investors in the United States should meet the Securities and Exchange Commission (SEC) accreditation requirements. According to **SEC Rule 501 of Regulation D**, an accredited investor must have a net worth of more than $1 million or an expected individual annual income of more than $200,000 (or $300,000 per household). Whereas entrepreneurs can approach accredited investors more or less freely, Regulation D stipulates that only a maximum of 35 non-accredited investors are allowed to be solicited into a private offering.

In the United Kingdom, the Financial Conduct Authority (FCA) rules released in March 2015 allow individuals meeting the income (£100,000) and net worth (£250,000, excluding their primary residence) thresholds to invest. However, unlike the SEC, the FCA also allows "sophisticated" individuals, regardless of income or net worth, to invest. To qualify, an individual must pass a questionnaire to demonstrate sufficient knowledge of the risks associated with an investment solicitation.

The definition of accredited investors has to strike a fine balance between encouraging early stage investing and protecting the general public from taking uncalculated risks. The Dodd-Frank Act requires the SEC to re-examine the definition of an accredited investor every four years to determine whether it should be modified. Proposals under current discussion suggest increasing the net worth and income benchmarks to account for past inflation. If adopted, these proposals could more than double the current financial benchmarks, which would seriously reduce the pool of accredited investors.[11] A proposal with a potential opposite effect is to follow the U.K. example by considering and allowing professional accreditations (e.g., certified public accountants, chartered financial analysts, brokers, traders, and legal counselors) regardless of whether an individual satisfies the income or net worth tests.[12]

---

[10] Some super angels have even reached a celebrity status beyond the investment community, appearing on reality television shows such as Money Tigers (Japan), Shark Tank (United States), and Dragons' Den (international).

[11] The U.S. Government Accountability Office (GAO) July 2013 report identifies that increasing the net worth and income benchmarks along the proposed lines would potentially exclude 60% of currently accredited investors.

[12] http://www.crowdfundinsider.com/2014/06/42279-changes-accredited-investor-definition-clip-wings-angel -investors.

WHAT MOTIVATES BUSINESS ANGELS?

Angel investing fosters the growth of early stage companies and helps them reach the milestones necessary for attracting further capital infusion, primarily venture capital. These milestones include proof of concept through product development, marketing objectives, securing customers, and obtaining patent protection.

Business angels are motivated to invest by a multitude of factors. Understandably, they are attracted by the prospect of high financial returns, fueled by media stories about successful individuals who invested early in mega start-up successes.[13] Some angels are looking to be engaged on an ongoing basis in their investments. Often, they allocate considerable time to helping entrepreneurs through challenging issues, making angel investment more personal to both parties. Many angels also enjoy transferring their knowhow by helping young entrepreneurs build their business. For angels who were entrepreneurs themselves, they may express the desire to "give back" to the entrepreneurial community that made them wealthy while doing what they love(d). This involvement can take the form of assisting emerging entrepreneurs and helping them become successful, investing in start-ups seeking to commercialize socially beneficial technologies (e.g., green/clean technologies), or aiding start-ups that create jobs in the local community.

Last but not least, tax incentives make for an additional motivation for business angels. Many governments and other public entities have implemented various policy initiatives to improve access to informal equity financing for high-risk small and new technology businesses. The most common policy—and one that has an immediate effect on the annual income tax of the angel investor—is to offer tax relief on the amount invested in early stage ventures. A large number of countries are also abolishing capital gains tax for this type of investment.[14] In a recent U.K. study, nearly 90% of angels surveyed had made use of either the Enterprise Investment Scheme (EIS) or the Seed Enterprise Investment Scheme (SEIS) at least once. Nearly 80% of the total angel investments were made under one of these schemes, with over half (55%) investing in EIS and a quarter investing in SEIS (see Wright et al. 2015).

THE ANGEL INVESTING PROCESS

Given that business angels invest in smaller amounts and at earlier stages of a company's development, they undertake particularly high risks, including the following:

- A high degree of uncertainty exists as to how the company will develop over time.

- The quality and motivation of the entrepreneur cannot be accurately assessed.

- Time and financial resource constraints inhibit the ability to undertake extensive due diligence.

---

[13] A famous angel investment was the $100,000 check that Sun Microsystems co-founder Andy Bechtolsheim made out to Google after watching Larry Page and Sergey Brin demonstrate their search engine software. The check was uncashable at first (as Google did not yet exist as a legal entity), but ultimately made hundreds of millions of dollars for its investor.

[14] The tax incentive program in France to facilitate investment by individuals in small and young companies is SUIR (Société Unipersonnelle d'Investissements à Risque) (translated as "Individual Company for Risk Capital Investments"). In the Netherlands, the Tante Agaath ("Aunt Agatha") scheme, set up in 1996, also proved popular with business angel investors.

- Other sources of financing are largely absent.

Yet business angels have less costly structures, even if they operate in syndicates, and hence, face low transaction costs. Since they do not invest others' capital, the decision-making process is straightforward, requiring no stringent involvement committees or administrative compliance. These factors result in a much shorter and less formal decision cycle.

Investment process

Raising capital for a start-up company is an arduous process. Interactions with external investors, both in the initial round and in the subsequent rounds of funding, take significant time and often incur complications along the way. The process can easily stall due to any number of factors. For example, raising the full amount of capital needed to get the business to a healthy start may require funding from several angels, of which some may be more reluctant or uncomfortable with the terms than others. An investor may also delay the process in order to carry out more screening or for personal unrelated reasons. Finally, an angel can easily withdraw from the process by terminating discussions with the entrepreneur at any time prior to making an investment. We discuss the stages of the process below, while highlighting the importance of an angel's personal investment objectives.

Screening stage

This stage of the process involves learning about the opportunity and meeting the entrepreneur. The origination of investment opportunities may come through various sources, such as friends, colleagues, business associates, accountants, lawyers, or organized angel networks. At this early stage in the process, potential investors usually receive a summary business plan. A formal non-disclosure agreement (NDA) is rarely required, although information is expected to remain confidential. The opportunity is analyzed, based on preference for industry sector and other considerations. Although globalization and data accessibility have broadened the spectrum of potential investors, angels still prefer to invest close to home and in familiar industries. However, they are also open to considering proposals outside of their core interest if a trusted and informed person is co-investing.

In the early stages of a start-up company, assets and knowhow are typically intangible. Moreover, there is no trading track record to examine whether the company is at a pre-revenue stage. Thus, business angels often work with no historical performance data, and must their judgments solely on indirect general market information. Against such a backdrop, they have little option but to place relatively greater weight on the personal attributes of the founders of the new business. While more information should be gathered about the business opportunity, assessment at this stage focuses heavily on the entrepreneur or team behind the business. Entrepreneurs need to be able to present not only their ideas but also themselves effectively. Even if the business idea is exciting, the person and team who run the business are the key to success. Angels use their own business networks to check the background of the entrepreneur.

In addition to technological capabilities applicable to the relevant business domain, investors look for entrepreneurs who show passion. Entrepreneurs who demonstrate this quality often receive more interest than those who may have a better business model or product, but lack enthusiasm. Entrepreneurs without great commitment and endurance are less likely to succeed. Angels also appreciate when entrepreneurs are willing to put up a significant amount of their own money or other type of strong commitment to get the company going. At the other extreme, it does not look promising for an entrepreneur to maintain partial employment elsewhere, which demonstrates an unwillingness to commit to the new endeavor. Besides signals, interactions between entrepreneurs and investors, like most human interactions, are based on trust. Accountability and transparency go a long way to creating this trust. In contrast, entrepreneurs who appear to provide contradictory answers lose credibility and trust.

One personal quality that it is difficult to track down in early stage businesses is the ability to be flexible and prepared to change business strategies as competition intensifies or circumstances change. It is not realistic or even advisable to buy into an investment solely on the basis of a superb entrepreneur without considering the original business concept. Yet, the reality is that even for successful business outcomes, it is typically not the original idea that proves right, but the so-called second or even third "bounce of the ball" that lead to a company's success. Often, the adaptations to the business model and strategic maneuvering over time lead the final business concept quite far from the original idea. The entrepreneur's prior leadership track record (whether in commercial arenas or others, such as military service) may provide strong clues as to a future ability to improvise and reinvigorate a business, as well as endure under difficult business and funding conditions.

At the screening stage, angels should also try to look down the road and understand who may be the potential acquirers one day. A start-up might demonstrate profitability, have a solid business plan, and be led by an entrepreneur with a proven managerial track record, but it still may not be a good investment opportunity if there is no clear exit path. The focus should be on who might want to purchase the start-up and why. One crucial consideration is scalability. Companies that provide a solution that only addresses a niche market are not able to attract external funding. Further, start-ups where the time required for technological and product development is very long (e.g., more than five years) before any interim indications of success are quite unattractive and unlikely to receive funding from angels.

Overall, the angel investing screening process is far less rigorous than the one employed by VC firms. Nevertheless, angel investors query the plan, and different business and financial aspects emerge during the process of investigation. Strategic and operational considerations that angels might assess include barriers to entry from competitors, intellectual property (IP) quality and protection, the size of the market, profit margins, entrepreneurs' knowledge, solidity of the management team, and more.

Negotiation stage

While studying the business plan, angels are also likely to be assessing how they can contribute to the enterprise beyond the scope of their financial investment. Foreseeing a satisfactory post-investment role can be a key factor in ensuring that the investment process unfolds smoothly, as consideration of this issue makes it more likely that angels will achieve a good "match" with appropriate entrepreneurs.

At this stage, some form of due diligence also occurs. Frequently, this process is conducted by the angels themselves, and is not formalized. The actual level of due diligence varies, depending upon factors such as the size of the investment, the nature of the business, the prior trading history of the company, and the angel's level of familiarity with such deals. A basic due diligence process commonly covers legal, financial, and commercial aspects:

- **Legal due diligence** examines whether the company has been properly incorporated and whether it runs in compliance with the legal requirements of such a business.

- **Financial due diligence** is conducted in order to ensure that there are no errors or missing numbers in the accounts or the company's future projections and forecasts.

- **Commercial due diligence** entails reviewing any major commercial contracts that are in place, checking whether employees are working under appropriate employment contracts, and ascertaining ownership of IP (this is particularly important for companies operating in the technology sector).

Negotiations are highly centered on valuation and terms. A key issue is how much (and what type of) equity angel investors should receive for their capital commitment. Valuation at this stage is particularly challenging as there is little to value at the infant stage of a firm's development. Factors that have a positive impact on the initial value are the amount of investment already made by entrepreneurs using their own personal finances or family money, existing IP and special knowledge, initial signs of market tractions, and the intensity of the perceived competition.

The initial valuation has a significant impact on the investment's return, because committing capital at an early stage implies that the venture, if successful, will attract follow-on rounds of equity financing from the venture capital industry or from other investors. Each of the subsequent rounds requires a process of negotiation of terms and valuation, which typically involves new investors. If the valuation at the seed or start-up stage is set too high, then subsequent rounds are more likely to be done at a lower valuation; this could excessively dilute the early stage investor, leading to bitterness and negative knock-on effects down the road. On the other hand, an initial valuation that is set too low overly dilutes the founders. To the extent that the company depends on them, this factor would have to be reconsidered in future rounds to ensure that the founders' motivation remains high and their incentives continue to be strongly aligned with the investors' interests.

In addition to the pre-money investment valuation, there are three more factors that directly influence the value of the shares purchased by the business angel. First, the size of the round matters, because as more funding is raised, the percentage of equity in the business is reduced. Second, the value of the shares is lower if the investment is made in the form of common equity, thereby on pari passu terms with the entrepreneur. The value of the shares is higher if the investor receives preferred shares, thereby getting priority and an extra return when selling or liquidating the investment. Third, investors receive a higher value per share if they agree on a valuation that takes into account the allocation of the option pool for the company's current and future employees. If an option pool is not agreed on at the time of the investment, then future option pool allocations will dilute investors' ownership; this is particularly relevant and justified when the management rank is not completed.

Subsequent rounds of capital, whether they are injected by angels or venture capitalists, are somewhat easier to value, given that the company is more mature and there are more tangible indicators to review and assess. Further, company valuations in previous rounds can be used as benchmarks. Any step up in the valuation relative to a previous round will mainly consider the incremental technological and commercial progress since that round.

Value creation stage

Angel investors are usually experienced in business and new enterprises, and many are fairly active with their investments. Given that most of their investments are made locally, angels are able to make a contribution to the growth of the business either through a formal active post-investment role in it, or through informal counsel and network benefits.

The role of the angels in guiding the start-up company is most important at the early stage before institutional investments from VC funds or corporates. During this stage, angels typically expect to take a role that enables them to contribute strategically through a board position and to interact with the entrepreneur on an ongoing basis, participating in decision making and observing venture performance in real time.

Angels should always try to understand whether the entrepreneur or the managing team is adequate for the particular stage of the business. Angels are usually less concerned about the entrepreneur when it comes to start-ups that are not very far along. However, as the company grows, the entrepreneur is not expected to be able to do everything. As a team is built up, the entrepreneur should be aware of the shortcomings of the current employees—in particular, members of the management team—and understand which roles may need to be added. An important aspect that should be discussed is the team's commitment to the company's long-term success. Angel investors like teams that show perseverance by struggling through hard times.

English being the international language of business implies that a flawless command of the language is essential in terms of oral and presentation skills. However, since many businesses are global, some e-commerce, social media, and entertainment platforms may require the ability to interact with retail customers and channels in other languages. Therefore, a team's cultural and national diversity can be a plus—and is even essential sometimes.

Horizon and exit considerations

Business angels invest at a presumably low valuation, but it is coupled with some high costs. First, they are exposed to the early stage risk—where proof of concept, technological, and market risks are at their zenith. Second, they are also at risk of significant dilution and losses if subsequent investments take place on harsh terms. Third, business angels are subject to the longest holding period until the investment is harvested.

Interestingly, the investment horizon is not an objective matter. It is guided by psychology rather than economics. Moreover, it is not a function of the length of the period since inception or even the stage of the business's maturity. Rather, every investor counts the time since his or her moment of investing. Being the earliest and longest investors may generate a conflict of interest with later ones, in particular with venture capital investors. The latter are willing to endure a longer time till exit, not only because they invest later but also because they are mentally prepared to aim for "homerun exits." Targeting homeruns nurtures a tolerance for a longer investment horizon and avoidance of selling beforehand at a lower value; this often clashes with the disposition of business angels who are content to sell earlier at a lower exit price to avoid further ups and downs, the dilution of their equity share at subsequent equity rounds, and the uncertainly at the time of harvesting. At this stage, angels rarely have a say in the governance of the business and must therefore go along with the decisions of the VC investors and management. A partial remedy to this inherent misalignment of interests is to allow early investors to sell through a secondary transaction. When such a transaction takes place, it is done as part of a late stage round where, in addition to injecting capital into the company, new investors offer to buy shares from existing shareholders.[15]

The misaligned horizon and exit expectations of venture capitalists and angels are responsible for the increasing number of start-ups backed by super angels and other private money aiming to get to get through exit without seeking venture capital funding.

ANGEL INVESTMENT CONTRACTS

Business angels rarely obtain a majority ownership of their portfolio companies. Most studies show that participants in the initial financing round of a start-up collectively acquire 20–35% of the company in which they are investing. An angel investment usually results in the following documents:

- **Investment and shareholders' agreement:** This document sets out the terms of the investment and regulates the relationships between the shareholders once the investment has been completed. It addresses the specific rights of the angel investor(s), such as rights to appoint directors, to receive information on the business, and to veto certain actions of the company.

- **Articles of association:** The document sets out its internal regulations for a company's operations and defines the company's purpose. It defines the process of appointing directors, and the means by which the shareholders exert control.

As a whole, the documentation is quite simple at this early stage in the life of the company, and a single lawyer is usually used to represent all parties to the transaction. Even if preferred (and not common) shares are used, waterfalls and capitalization tables are still very simple at this stage of the life of the company. It is not the investors' intention to introduce layers of legal ink and documentation. One exception is investment rounds which involve business angel networks (BANs) or government support co-investment funds. In this case, more legal scrutiny and documentation are required, adding requirements of periodic reporting, veto rights to investors' directors on the board, and other internal practices to ensure transparency and an orderly code of conduct.

Stock received

Angels may receive common rather than preferred stock in exchange for their investment. Common equity claims do not provide any protection in the event of bankruptcy or liquidation. Traditionally, common shares were typically issued to put the business angels on the same footing as the founders (in terms of liquidating distributions). Over the years, the terms have changed as angels from organized syndicates have pushed harder for preferred shares.

---

[15] Buying shares of existing investors as part of a new round is relatively rare due to their lower preference in the capital structure waterfall. A new innovative tool to address the excessive dilution of early stage investors is transferring the preemption rights to a third party. A notable example is Alpha Venture Partners, which co-invests alongside top-tier VC firms in late stage companies through the acquisition of preemption rights from existing investors, offering them, in return, a split of the upside at the time of a successful exit.

Board seats

It is now commonplace for the principal angels ("anchor" angels) to demand board seats, and upon subsequent rounds, for all investors to make up the majority of the board. For certain decisions, anchor angels may require a board majority voting where founders and other non-investor board members are excluded from voting.

Pre-emption and anti-dilution clauses

Pre-emption and anti-dilution protection are provisions, usually included in the articles of association, which protect an investor from future dilutions of his or her shareholding. Dilutions occur when additional shares in the company are issued after the date of the investor's contribution. With pre-emptive rights, no new shares can be issued until they have first been offered to the existing shareholders on a pro rata basis. This enables earlier investors to maintain their share ownership by participating in the new round, at least up to their current ownership percentage.

Dilution is of a particular concern if the new round of funding is at a lower price per share than the previous one (known as a "down round"). In such a case, there is a further protection through a specific anti-dilution provision. In practice, the usage of anti-dilution clauses is more common in venture capital contracts than in angel investments. However, sophisticated angels use anti-dilution protection in the form of a ratchet mechanism that retroactively reprices the investor's stake if further shares are issued by the company at a lower price.[16]

Liquidation preference

Liquidation preference provisions are designed to protect angel investors' capital committed, and to align interests. These provisions establish that angel investors get paid ahead of the entrepreneur and earlier investors, as well as how much they get paid if an exit event occurs (e.g., the sale or liquidation of the company). Liquidation preferences mitigate the downside by making sure they get their initial investments back before other parties. If the company is sold at a profit, liquidation preference can also help investors boost their share in the proceeds. Traditionally, angel investment agreements were much less likely to include a liquidation provision than VC investment contracts. While this is still the case, today it is more common for investment agreements to stipulate a liquidation preference of around 1x (i.e., one times their original investment), and occasionally more.

Angels' mindset in designing investment terms

Why do angels demand fewer rights than venture capitalists, despite investing at a more embryonic, risky stage? A first possible explanation is that angels are unsophisticated investors, who are willing to settle for few

---

[16] The precise format of the ratchet mechanism as well as the liquidation preferences below are described in more detail in the venture capital chapter. The chapter also covers bridge financing through a convertible loan agreement (CLA) and the mechanics of round capitalization.

protections because they do not know any better. However, although complacence or a lack of sophistication may partially explain the angel contract design, it is unlikely to be the primary explanation for two reasons: first, many angels are HNWIs or "accredited" investors who are not the sort of capital providers that are generally considered unsophisticated; second, they are often ex-entrepreneurs or serial investors, which suggests that they are not only knowledgeable about investments in general, but also have a good understanding of start-up investments in particular.

A more plausible explanation as to why angels demand fewer rights than venture capitalists has to do with the timing of their investment in relation to the development of the start-up. Angels usually provide the first, but not the last, source of outside funding for start-ups. Their capital builds the financial bridge from the funds received from friends and family to venture capital. Angels must entice venture capitalists to follow their investments in order to have any hope of profit. This need for venture capital sets de facto limits on the terms of the angel investment contract. Established VC firms are flooded with funding proposals and accept only a tiny percentage of them. Funding proposals might be rejected in the presence of aggressive or overreaching early investors. Angels must keep the terms of their equity simple, because nothing prevents follow-on funding more than an overly complicated angel investment contract that venture capitalists have to untangle.

A third explanation as to why angel investors demand fewer rights is a simple cost-benefit consideration. Angels might rationally choose to forgo preference-laden contracts because the costs entailed would be disproportionately high relative to the amount of investment, and because they do not have the same need for some provisions (e.g., regarding an exit, they do not face the same downstream pressures as venture capitalists). Not only is there a cost of negotiating with the entrepreneur, but it is also quite costly to prepare a contract that is verifiable by a third party, such as a judge, if it is violated or in dispute. In addition, the potential ex-post legal costs related to having the contract verified and enforced by a third party might be prohibitive in the case of a start-up.

In contrast, because venture capitalists have a fiduciary duty to their limited partners, they need to have formal procedures that are implemented when making investments (e.g., formal due diligence reports, legally sound shareholder agreements, reporting requirements, etc.). Therefore, venture capitalists spend more on contracting costs and screening before making investments.

ANGEL INVESTMENT PERFORMANCE

By using their own wealth, angels directly expose themselves to both the risk and the reward of their investments. Indirectly, they may also commit capital that belongs to their trust or on behalf of others. Beholden mainly to themselves, they usually do not have fixed targets in terms of return and timescales. Consequently, business angels are willing to invest in infant and unproved concepts. One reason for these preferences is that, as discussed above, angels have the flexibility to invest for non-financial as well as financial reasons if they so choose.

Only a minor portion of angel investments have a positive exit. Their financial payoff comes from a small number of start-ups that go on to attract venture capital and then exit through a sale to a strategic buyer, and rarely from listing through an initial public offering (IPO). Although the best financial returns for investors in start-ups tend to come from companies that go public, only a small proportion of angel-backed companies achieve this. To make matters worse, success is severely biased in favor of the few elites who have their pick of the best technological start-ups in Silicon Valley or other major tech/fintech/cyber clusters.[17]

There are only a few systematic studies on angel investment performance. Wiltbank and Brooks (2016) examine the investment returns of angel investors in the United States, where the overwhelming majority of the data is for 2010–2016. They find that the overall investment return is very positive: a cash multiple of 2.5x capital and an IRR of 22%. However, as may be expected, the outcomes are highly skewed, whereby 10% of all exits generated 85% of all cash. The median angel investment is a loss and the failure rate is 70%.

Kerr et al. (2014) study two prominent U.S. angel groups and their effects on the start-ups in which they invest. Their findings suggest that angel investments enhance the outcomes and performance of the firms that are funded. Angels improve (1) the likelihood of survival of the firm by four or more years, (2) key operational factors such as the level of employment, patenting, and web traffic, and (3) the likelihood of achieving successful exits. Lerner et al. (2016) extend the testing by looking at business angels globally. Their study of 1,680 companies across 21 countries provides evidence that angels have a positive impact on the growth (e.g., more employment, larger management teams, etc.) and survival of the companies they fund.[18]

ANGEL BEST PRACTICE

Given the constantly changing environment in which firms receiving angel investments operate, and the high overall risk of early stage companies, it is difficult to draw definitive conclusions about the ability to succeed when making angel investments. There are, however, some factors that correlate with better outcomes and that improve the odds, including the following:

A strong network to source good deals

One way to capture this advantage is to become a member of an angel network (see below) or an informal network. These networks facilitate contact and the exchange of best practices and experience between angels, venture capitalists, and other sources of early stage funding through networking events, regular communication, and government support schemes.

Domain expertise

Angel investors who are familiar with an industry are more likely to realize when major trends are shifting, and to foresee possible risks. They are also better able to add value along the way.

---

[17] For instance, the so-called "PayPal Mafia," a group of former PayPal employees and founders who have since founded and developed very successful technology companies like Tesla Motors, LinkedIn, Matterport, Palantir Technologies, SpaceX, YouTube, Yelp, and Yammer. The former PayPal CEO, Peter Thiel, estimates the PayPal Mafia to comprise around 220 people.

[18] Lerner et al. (2016) also report that an early stage company that is located in a relatively entrepreneur-friendly nation is more likely to survive, to patent more innovations, and to raise additional funding.

Due diligence

Expertise is relevant only when it is used to evaluate the details and potential of alternative opportunities before choosing the most attractive ones. Indeed, Kerr et al. (2014) document that the engagement levels of angels at the stages of the initial presentation and due diligence are predictive of investment success.

Involvement

Projections, teams, and competitors change the most successful companies and make radical adjustments to their initial business plans, as entrepreneurs discover the reality of the situation compared with their original expectations. Angel investors are expected to play a role in helping management teams to make these adjustments and prepare for venture funding. Involvement is attained through coaching, board membership, making introductions, advice on operational matters, and so on.

Judging the people

In the early stages of a venture, assets are intangible and knowledge based. Since the products and ideas are untested in the market, angels must place a significant weight on the attributes of the founders of the business and the team running it. They are ultimately investing in people.

Risk diversification

Angels should limit their exposure to each early stage company to only a very small fraction of their net wealth, and put a cap on their overall allocation to their portfolio of early stage investments. To mitigate dilution, they should also factor in resources for possible follow-on participation in future funding rounds if the company becomes successful. Another way to diversify risks is to invest as part of an angel syndicate.

BUSINESS ANGEL NETWORKS

Along with the proliferation of business angel activities, individuals in strong entrepreneurial hubs have also started to organize themselves into informal groups, typically made up of 10 to 150 accredited investors interested in early stage investing. Angel groups are formed with the goal of sharing deal flow and due diligence work, and pooling individual funds in order to make larger investments. These groups vary in the degree of their formality. They could be informal personal networks to which an angel may turn for advice. At the other side of the spectrum, there are formal BANs and syndicates that are more tightly managed and supported by government or regional development agencies.

In choosing to invest through a group, individuals abandon informal origination and screening in favor of a more professional process, by pooling their investments through regional angel groups. These BANs combine the seed investment activities of multiple accredited investors. There are various advantages of working in groups, including networking, easier access to pre-qualified deal flow, leveraging the intellectual capital and expertise of individual members, a more rigorous diligence process, and more formal reporting requirements.

BANs provide a channel of communication between investors and entrepreneurs that minimizes the cost of the entrepreneurs' search for capital. They also enable investors to examine a larger number of investment opportunities, thereby facilitating their access to proposals that meet their investment criteria. Further, BANs are important instruments for raising awareness about the market, both for entrepreneurs seeking external capital and for potential investors.

Major angel groups

As of August 2015, there were 470 angel networks in the United States alone.[19] The oldest organized angel group, the Band of Angels, started in 1994 in Silicon Valley. With more than 150 current members and a focus on North California, the network examines more than 1,000 plans a year, out of which approximately 5% are selected to be presented before the group as a whole. So far, the group has invested $231 million in over 277 companies. Of these, 61 firms have been acquired for a gain and 11 have gone public, generating an impressive return since inception.[20]

Originating from the activities of the Kauffman Foundation, angel groups banded together to form an Angel Capital Association (ACA). This association acts as the official industry alliance of over 100 of the largest angel investor groups in the United States. Since its founding in 2004, ACA has played a significant role in facilitating information exchange among angel groups, networking, and the development of best practice guidance and practices as related to early stage investing.

The idea of formally organizing regional angels has caught on throughout the world. When EBAN was created as the European Business Angel Network in 1999, only 50 angel networks were operating in Europe, half of which were located in the United Kingdom. Today, there is a clear interest from business angels to look at collaboration (including joint investment) in different countries throughout Europe and beyond. As of 2017, the number of known networks and groups in Europe was 475.[21]

Unlike individual angels, BANs are not difficult to find. Most have websites that provide information about the organization for potential members and entrepreneurs. However, members' identities are more carefully guarded. In terms of membership, some BANs require members to be accredited investors. Others, including the Band of Angels, require technical knowledge and expertise, and therefore exclude the likes of lawyers and accountants. Industry-specific BANs, unsurprisingly, require substantial knowledge of the industry.

How BANs function

BANs introduce a more "arm's length" relationship with entrepreneurs; due to their prescreening, fewer entrepreneurs and business plans will be known by the angel beforehand. Thus, BANs potentially sacrifice some of the familiarity and intimacy that such pre-existing knowledge brings. Moreover, most BAN-affiliated angels are less active participants in venture development post investment than traditional angels may be.

Many of the BANs run on a non-regulated basis whereby a gatekeeper acts as a facilitator between the entrepreneurs and angels. The gatekeeper reads the business plans and meets the entrepreneurs, and

---

[19] May and Liu (2016).
[20] Band of Angels website as of August 2018.
[21] http://www.eban.org/wp-content/uploads/2018/07/EBAN-Statistics-Compendium-2017.pdf

subsequently decides which proposals should be presented to the investors, but does not get engaged in the deal process or give investment advice.

Some groups require that a member meet with the entrepreneur and determine whether the plan is viable before allowing the entrepreneur to present it to the group. Other groups allow the administrative staff and managing director to review the plan and invite the entrepreneur to present without a "champion." Once the presentation has been made (usually in 10–45 minutes, including a question and answer period), the entrepreneur is asked to leave the room. The angels discuss the opportunity and, if one or more angels are interested, then, depending on the group, either the entrepreneur is invited back at a later date for a more thorough review of the plan or an initial term sheet is developed within a week and presented to the entrepreneur. The investors can then make their own individual decisions, or in other cases, act as a syndicate.

What BANs provide to business angels

Although most of their members remain passive following the investment, the BANs themselves have elements that resemble venture capital funds, especially in the process leading to the investment itself. They act more professionally than standard angels and allow for higher capital commitments and later stage investments. They provide several benefits to angel investors, including

- a steady stream of deal flow to angel members;

- interactions between angels, venture capitalists, and service providers like lawyers and consultants;

- funding for larger deals through the pooling of member angels' resources;

- harmonization of the due diligence process;

- consulting services to start-up companies in order to make them "investment ready";

- promotions of angels as a key source of capital for new and high-growth firms;

- a regular dialogue with government agencies, to help shape policies for the benefit of the industry; and

- development of codes of conduct for angels to promote best practice.

Government support

Policymakers recognize the equity gap in early stage financing as an acute problem, and view BANs as an important vehicle to improve the flow of funding from the private sector. The European Commission runs a significant effort to foster the creation of angel networks. Indeed, angel groups have been growing consistently in terms of the number of new members and investments all across Europe.

The newest way of intervention to support the business angel market comes in the form of *co-investment schemes*. These are primarily regional programs which complement the scarce financing available from active angels by matching government funds. It is neither manageable nor wise to use taxpayer funding to co-invest alongside individuals. Hence, the best practice is to co-invest through committed pools along prescreened and approved angel networks.[22]

---

[22] See for example the London Co-investment Fund: www.lep.london/funding-and-support/funding

CONCLUSION

The market for angel investing emerged to bridge the gap between the capital provided by the entrepreneur or his friends and family and the capital provided by venture capital funds. Angels are typically HNWIs who invest their personal funds in early stage companies. In addition to providing capital, these investors also tend to contribute business and industry expertise to start-up firms.

Angels are a diverse group and they vary in their investment motivation, degree of engagement, depth of due diligence, and accreditation. In recent years, super angels and angel networks have played increasingly important roles, providing maturity and structure in an otherwise vastly opaque investment landscape. Recognizing the key role of technology, innovation, and start-up companies to economic growth, policymakers around the globe provide incentives to stimulate angels to invest by improving the appeal of early stage deals; this has become an acute priority, given the recent widening of the equity gap as venture capital funds' preferences have drifted toward larger deals. Incentives to angels include personal tax concessions as well support to the ecosystem of angel groups.

Considering the dependency of start-up firms on angel financing, understanding their mindset and modus operandi has crucial implications for the efficient allocation of private capital and the success of new small businesses.

REFERENCES

Kerr, W.R., J. Lerner and A. Schoar (2014) "The Consequences of entrepreneurial finance: Evidence from angel financings," *Review of Financial Studies* 27 (1): 20-55.

Lerner, J., A. Schoar, S. Sokolinski and K. Wilson (2016) "The Globalization of angel investments: Evidence across countries," working paper, Harvard Business School, February.

May, J. and M. M. Liu (2016) "Angels without borders: Trends and policies shaping angel investment worldwide", World Scientific.

Klingler-Vidra, R. (2014) "All politics is local: Sources of variance in the diffusion of venture capital policies." PhD thesis, London School of Economics. A synopsis appears in *Venture Findings* 1: 37-42.

Wiltbank, R. E. and Brook, W. T. (2016) "Tracking angel returns," Ewing Marion Kauffman Foundation manuscript.

Wright, M., M. Hart and K. Fu (2015) "A Nation of angels: Assessing the impact of angel investing across the UK," U.K. Business Angels Association, Enterprise Research Centre, January.

In her own words: Kate Mitchell, Co-founder & Partner, Scale Venture Partners; Former Chairperson, National Venture Capital Association; Board Member, Silicon Valley Bank

Lessons learned from Silicon Valley about angel investing

Angel investing is a less frequently examined but increasingly important investment sector. It has become large enough to be identified as a distinct asset class. The first lesson to learn about angel investing is that success does not come easily. In fact, this earliest stage carries the highest risk within the continuum of start-up investing. Savvy entrants into angel investing become highly educated before writing the first check. They are prepared to be patient as the road to success is a long one.

The first step before building an angel portfolio is to set clear investment objectives.

- Are you investing for gain? Most angel investments fail; therefore, your return expectations should be modest. Only invest capital you can afford to lose and diversify your portfolio.

- Are you investing for a purpose? Your motivation may be to support the next generation of leaders, a cause, or your community. Build your portfolio around these goals.

Most angels invest for a combination of profit and purpose. Experienced angel investors value the opportunity to coach entrepreneurs as well as to continue their own education about emerging trends. Financial success is only expected as an upside benefit.

The best investments are usually not those seen by a wide group of investors. Good ideas are hard to find and will get picked up quickly by experienced angels. Source your deal flow by leveraging your professional network. An investment within your area of expertise means you will better underwrite and guide a company, given it is a business you understand.

Pattern recognition is a phrase often used in venture capital. We invest in a sector with inherent uncertainty and where success is based on constant change; and yet, truisms emerge. First, the founder is the most important determinant of success. At this stage, that is what you are investing in. Does he or she have the vision, relevant expertise, and grit that it takes to succeed? Second, does this person have the temperament to be a successful leader? Our most successful CEOs are passionate about their ideas but also objective about soliciting feedback. They can confidently convince teammates and customers to sign on to their vision, but are humble enough to listen to constructive criticism and market feedback.

Founders often start companies early in their careers. Consider being an informal or formal advisor to your start-ups. You may be surprised how valuable your general business experience can be. If a specific expertise led you to this investment, sharing advice and contacts with founders increases their chance of success.

At Scale Venture Partners, we invest after the angel round and co-invest with angels of all kinds. While well-known angels in Silicon Valley rival venture firms in resources and expertise, many angels have limited experience with venture-backed companies. There are important considerations about your role and financial position once venture investors join in.

The biggest concern an angel has is the alignment with the later investors, particularly when it comes to subsequent financing rounds and an eventual exit. You are now investing alongside professional investors. VC funds manage capital on behalf of pension funds, endowments, and foundations which have expectations about the timing and return on a portfolio of investments. As a result, venture decision making may be different than yours.

Venture investors are expected to recognize losses early and focus resources on the winners in their portfolios. Typically, only a minority of investments grow into successful investments. That means we will sell or close a company at a loss if it is not meeting expectations. That can be difficult for an angel who is less accustomed to taking these early losses. At this stage, expect to become increasingly objective about the performance of your portfolio.

If successful, start-ups require multiple rounds of capital to grow. In each round, at least a portion is designated to be filled by existing investors on a pro rata basis. It is critical that angels reserve a significant amount of additional capital to support future funding requirements. The penalty for not funding your pro rata share may vary, but it will certainly include dilution of your ownership. A rule of thumb used by many angels is to reserve 50–100% of an initial investment for follow-on rounds. The right level of reserves will be a function of the stage of the company and the capital required to get to cash flow break-even.

An angel and a VC may also have very different investment horizons. While we may decide to exit sooner than you might like, we may also determine that the optimal path is to stay private longer to give the company more time to grow. Angels may have already tied up their capital for the good part of a decade, and may prefer to take their winnings sooner. One of the recent changes to the private capital market has been the increase in liquidity alternatives for private shares. It is increasingly common for internal or external investors who want to own more of the start-up to offer to purchase your shares. The price is agreed upon privately and is, therefore, easiest to execute when there is a new round being priced by another investment professional.

Finally, be patient. Failures in your portfolio become evident before successes. One of the tenets for entrepreneurs taught by Eric Ries, author of *The Lean Startup,* is to "fail fast and fail cheap." The same advice applies to investing. If something isn't working, the best investors cut their losses, preserving resources for another promising innovation. A successful IPO or M&A exit takes a decade or more to be realized.

Angel investing can be rewarding from the start. There is nothing as thrilling as watching a team and an idea come to fruition. In the process, you can learn as much as you teach, and help sow the seeds of the next successful start-up.

13 Venture Capital

"Someone, somewhere, is making a product that will make your product obsolete."
Georges F. Doriot, America's first institutional venture capitalist

INTRODUCTION

Venture capital (VC) is the first form of institutional capital that is invested in high-growth private companies. Similar to other private equity funds, it is a vehicle that pools together capital from financial sponsors (limited partners (LPs)) and deploys it in ventures that are too risky to be financed by more traditional forms of equity capital or by banks. Venture capital funds are managed by venture capital firms, whose *general partners* (GPs) work closely with the management of the start-ups by injecting both funding and experience into these new businesses. It is the purpose of venture capital to invest only in innovative growth companies that show a strong and viable commercial potential. These companies are usually technology based, whether pre revenue or post revenue. VC firms intend to remain invested for a certain number of years, with a typical horizon expectation of 5–10 years, until a rewarding exit is attainable. As with other private equity funds, the investment is solely for the purpose of a financial gain, and there are no deliberate strategic considerations as a motivation.[1]

In consideration for funding, a venture capital firm receives a portion of a company's equity along with certain preferred terms over prior investors. Venture capitalists, especially early stage ones, tend to nurture their investments by being heavily involved in their portfolio companies, guiding the management with their experience and network and setting the strategic direction. It is the VC commitment to an active governance and involvement that differentiates these investors from other types of early stage equity investors, who are usually more passive.

The role of venture capital in the economy cannot be overstated. Venture capital investments have been credited with creating more employment, driving more innovation, generating more revenues, and contributing more to economic growth than their counterparts, even after their VC investors exit.[2] Over the past 50 years, VC-backed innovations have created new industries in fields ranging from biotechnology and medical devices to big data, financial technology (fintech), social media, and cybersecurity. These newly-developing fields have transformed other sectors as well, generating quality jobs in the process. For example, numerous graphic designers, copywriters, and artists are now employed by web design and other Internet and software companies. With their focus on high growth and innovation, venture-backed companies often follow a distinct development path that prevails long after the venture capitalist exits an investment.

---

[1] An exception is corporate venture capital (CVC), where corporations have a strategic motivation for investing on top of the financial interest; CVC is discussed in the following chapter.

[2] Gornall and Strebulaev (2015) and Popov and Roosenboom (2009) document the long-term impact of venture capital on R&D in the United States and Europe, respectively. Paglia and Harjoto (2014) provide evidence on the growth of sales and employment in small and mid-size companies backed by venture capital. For the role of venture capital in the diffusion of innovation, see Gonzalez-Uribe (2014).

Notably, venture-backed companies have grown into some of the largest companies in the world. Five of the six largest U.S. companies by market capitalization were backed by venture capital: Apple, Google, Microsoft, Amazon, and Facebook—all formed after 1975.[3] According to the National Venture Capital Association, in 2015, companies which were initially VC backed accounted for 11% of private sector jobs in the United States and 21% of the country's $18 trillion GDP.

Major institutional investors—especially pension funds, endowments, and foundations—have long been backers of venture capital as LPs. This involvement has been motivated by several considerations: financial returns, a low correlation with other investments, and the desire to support macro objectives of innovation and economic development. Exhibit 1 displays the performance of U.S. venture capital as compared to other asset classes, and shows its long-term outperformance over the public stock market.

Exhibit 1: U.S. Venture Capital performance against benchmarks for periods ending September 30 , 2017

	5 years	10 years	20 years	25 years
Cambridge Associates U.S. Venture Capital Index	14.8%	9.1%	22.3%	28.2%
Russell 2000	13.8%	7.8%	7.5%	10.0%
S&P 500	14.2%	7.4%	7.0%	9.6%

Source: Cambridge Associates Q3 2017 data.

However, because of its cyclicality, the venture capital asset class has seen significant swings in investor sentiment and overall activity.[4] It suffered a slowdown following the burst of the dotcom bubble in 2000, but since then, there venture capital activity, especially in recent years has broken every record. Whereas in 2009, $27 billion of capital was directed to venture capital investment in the United States, the average investment in 2018–2019 quintupled to $140 billion per annum owing to a steep increase in the number of mega deals (defined as funding rounds above $100 million). The sharp growth of the last several years is even more pronounced when considered on a worldwide basis. Global venture capital deals in 2009 totaled $37 billion, which surged to an average of $233 billion in 2017–2018. As for GP fundraising, the growth trend continues with a high of $88 billion raised in 2018 by a total of 450 VC funds.[5]

---

[3] The remaining company in the top six is Berkshire Hathaway, ranked fourth. Data excludes financial and oil and gas companies and is based on values as of January 2016.

[4] At the extreme side of the spectrum, Yale University's most successful endowment had a 14% allocation to venture capital in 2016, compared with just 4% to publicly-listed domestic equity.

[5] U.S. data is taken from from Pitchbook Private Market PlayBook Q2 2020; global data is taken from Preqin Global PEVC 2019 and KPMG Enterprise Venture Pulse Q1 2019. Of interest to note that the top 5 VCs have raised over $55 billion during 2015-2019, led by Sequoia Capital ($17.5 billion) and Insight Partners ($12.5 billion). Andreessen Horowitz, Summit Partners and NEA complete the top 5.

HISTORICAL OVERVIEW

At its genesis, venture capital served a rather informal function and was dominated by angel-style investments from wealthy families until it grew into its modern organizational form immediately after the Second World War. The first institutional venture capital firm, American Research and Development Corporation (ARD), was founded in Boston in 1946 by General Georges Doriot, Director of the U.S. Army's Military Planning Division. It was created to encourage private sector investments in small firms in order to facilitate the development of technology and aid the economic revival of New England in the wake of the Great Depression. ARD was the first public VC firm that did not depend on wealthy individuals for capital. It is credited with making Boston a leading venture hub, and for spurring many others to create VC firms. Importantly, ARD formalized the model of due diligence and post-investment monitoring.[6]

A second industry trailblazer and a contender to the title of first venture capital firm is J.H. Whitney & Co., also formed in 1946 by John Hay Whitney and Benno Schmidt. Whitney and Schmidt's goal was to finance entrepreneurs that could not get banks to finance their plans, claiming that "our business is the adventure."[7]

On the opposite coast of the United States, Silicon Valley in the southern portion of the San Francisco Bay Area is the undisputed global hotbed for innovation and technology. Home to the world's largest technology corporations as well as thousands of high-tech start-up companies, the area has become synonymous with venture capital. The title *Father of Silicon Valley* belongs to Fred Terman, Dean of Stanford's School of Engineering who spearheaded the creation of Stanford Industrial Park in 1951 by leasing land to attract large technological companies such as General Electric, Hewlett-Packard, and Lockheed. Subsequently, in order to make the area a viable cluster, Terman had the further vision to propel the development of residential neighborhoods, shopping malls, and services to bolster the area to become a desirable and vibrant social community.

A milestone in the history of Silicon Valley was the foundation of Fairchild Semiconductors in 1957 by the "traitorous eight" leading engineers of Shockley Semiconductor Laboratory, who resigned together.[8] Founded with $1.5 million capital from Arthur Rock, an early and successful VC investor, Fairchild invented the first commercially practical integrated circuit and was subsequently responsible for much of the progress of the industry in the following decade. Its eight founders became figureheads in the history of semiconductors and venture, including Gordon Moore (author of Moore's law) and Robert Noyce, co-founders of Intel, Eugene Kleiner, who co-founded the renowned VC firm Kleiner Perkins Caufield & Byers, and others.

Nonetheless, even 10 years after its establishment, the venture capital landscape remained desolate. The U.S. government eventually stepped in and enacted the Small Business Act of 1958, which allowed the licensing of private *small business investment companies* (SBICs) to support the development of small-growth businesses in the United States. Draper, Gaither & Anderson was formed in 1959 as the first venture capital limited partnership, which essentially remained the standard format of the industry to date. During the 1960s

---

[6] By historical measures, venture capital is still in its infancy, at the third generation of its birth in the United States and younger everywhere else. To illustrate, Reid Hoffman, founder of LinkedIn and a first-round investor in Facebook, is currently a partner at Greylock, which was founded by Bill Elfers and Charlie Waite in 1965, who worked for General Doriot at ARD.

[7] Benno Schmidt is credited with coining the phrase "venture capital," an abbreviation of "private adventure capital." He instructed his firm to describe it that way, opposing the *New York Times* referral to J.H. Whitney & Co. as an investment banking firm.

[8] William Shockley was a co-inventor of the transistor and 1956 Nobel laureate with a unique ability to spot top talent, but a catastrophic manager.

and 1970s, VC firms focused their investment activity primarily in the electronic, medical, and data-processing industries; this led to venture capital becoming almost synonymous with technology financing.

Up until the 1970s, investments were primarily provided by wealthy individuals and banks. As such, the industry developed slowly until 1978, when the Employee Retirement Income Security Act (ERISA) was amended by the U.S. Department of Labor, allowing the venture capital industry to take off. By applying a "prudent person" standard on the diversification of investments, the revision enabled pension funds to make high-risk investments in private companies as long as the investment portfolio was diversified. This boosted the funds' participation level, making them the predominant suppliers of financing to venture capitalists. To this day, pension funds are by far the largest provider of capital to the venture industry, supplying nearly half of all the money for U.S. VC funds. Moreover, since pension funds are considered prudent institutional investors, their commitment has paved the way for, and hastened the participation of, other financial sponsors as well.

During the late 1970s, several headline success stories attracted a flow of entrants to the industry—both new VC firms and a greater asset allocation by the financial sponsors. Particularly in the United States, returns skyrocketed during the 1995–2000 dotcom boom, when valuations peaked in line with public markets due to investor focus on the Internet and other technological innovations (as depicted in Exhibit 2). In the post dotcom crash years, once the dry powder of commitments dwindled, the venture capital industry reached a standstill. Many portfolio companies founded in the boom era were unable to receive more funding and exits were few and far between. It caused many to wonder about the long-term viability of early stage investing. There has been significant academic public policy debate and concern summarized by a reference to an "equity gap," as well and the recurring question: Is the VC model broken?[9]

However, the last several years have seen a resurgence of VC activity to unprecedented level surpassing all historical records. This is largely attributable to technology breakthroughs in fields such as nanomaterials, cloud computing, cybersecurity, communication, bid data, artificial intelligence and computer vision. In parallel, there has been a surge of interest in business models such as software as a service (SaaS), personalized medicine and fintech. While venture capital has always been impacted by the inherent cyclicality of exit markets and LPs' appetite to make commitments, it has continued to attract investors and is well developed, particularly in North America.

Elsewhere in the world, venture capital is much younger—certainly within the context of the technology sector. While the term "venture capital" has been used for quite some time, it did not mean technology venturing as in the United States; instead it referred to investments in brownfield and traditional non-disruptive sectors, and as such, has been synonymous with private equity to date.[10]

The first VC fund in Britain was the Industrial and Commercial Financial Corporation (later rebranded as 3i). It was established in 1945 to fund small and medium-sized businesses. Funding was exclusively provided by large banks to rebuild the British industry following the Second World War. While the fund did have LPs, it lacked today's key finite fund structure element and was not aimed at new companies.

---

[9] Another expression along the same line was the "boulevard of broken dreams," followed by the public policy book by J. Lerner with the same title. A much publicized case of this industry soul-searching is the Kauffman Foundation report by Mulcahy et al. (2012). From its title, the study leaves no ambiguity that much of the responsibility for the equity gap is on the industry itself.

[10] For historical and pragmatic reasons, the private equity associations around the globe still follow the acronym of venture capital: AVCA, AVCAL, BVCA, IVCA, LAVCA for the African, Australian, British, Indian, and Latin American associations, respectively.

Exhibit 2: U.S. Venture capital investments, 1995–2018 (in US$ billions)

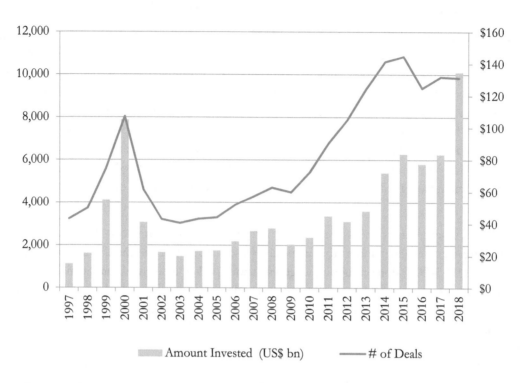

Source: PitchBook 2019.

Apax Partners, one of Europe's leading private equity firms, has its origins in venture capital on both sides of the Atlantic. It pioneered the American VC style across Europe, raising its first European fund in 1981 before moving exclusively upstream to leverage buyouts. Quester Venture Partners, founded in 1984, was another lead source of finance for young and growing technology companies in the United Kingdom. However, the vast majority of U.K. technology start-ups were not led by venture capital. Rather, they emerged from Cambridge and other universities and were financed by corporations and individuals.

Continental Europe was often criticized for lacking an entrepreneurial spirit needed for start-ups, thereby inhibiting the economic growth in most European economies. Although the popular view is that this feature is a cultural matter (i.e., a cultural aversion to risk and disdain of the capitalistic drive it represents), there are actually more practical causes, primarily related to the evolution of the financial systems. The first "American-style" VC firm established in France and probably in the entire continent was Sofinnova Ventures. Founded in 1972 with the backing of several French financial institutions (most notably, Crédit National), it specialized in early stage biotechnology companies. Two years later, the firm became the first European venture company to enter the U.S. market. In the Netherlands, Atlas Venture was founded in 1980 as a subsidiary of NMB Bank, and since then, has also focused exclusively on early stage life sciences and technology companies. Sofinnova and Atlas Venture typify a common theme among many VC firms in the early years in Europe in that they were originated by banks, then expanded to form an American subsidiary, and were finally carved out from the banks by either remaining private or going public.

Germany's first venture capital attempt was the foundation of WFG in 1975 by a large consortium of German financial institutions; however, the group failed before it funded its first investment. Other VC firms were founded (primarily by banks) across West Germany in the early 1980s, but struggled to produce acceptable returns. In most cases, the structure ensured that the government, rather than the investors, bore most of the losses. Yet in Berlin, the Innovationsfonds des Landes Berlin, founded in 1982, actually succeeded rather well. Altogether, the government and the regional savings and loans banks were the primary drivers for the promotion of innovation in small and medium-sized businesses by creating VC vehicles and assisting companies directly.[11]

Asian venture capital was pioneered in Japan, first by using public funds in 1963 to create firms like the U.S. SBICs.[12] In 1972, Nippon Enterprise Development was formed by a group of 39 firms, and a year later, Nomura Holding established JAFCO. In the early 1980s, other Japanese banks followed by forming venture capital subsidiaries, but their purpose was to use the investment to build relationships with small and medium-sized firms in order to sell them other services. In 1982, JAFCO introduced the first Asian limited partnership format and an American subsidiary was formed in 1984 in San Francisco. In Korea, the first government-led VC firm, KTAC was established in 1974; however it was more of a technology transfer organization. Korea Technology Development Corporation (KTDC), founded in 1981, was yet another technology commercialization intermediary. In Taiwan, venture capital started in 1984 by an Acer subsidiary, Multiventure Investment Inc., which made its first investment in a Silicon Valley start-up that year. Not much later, the Silicon Valley investment bank of Hambrecht & Quist launched its fund with investors from prominent industrial groups in Taiwan and the government-controlled banks and agencies. In India, the venture capital industry officially began in 1988, with the World Bank helping to set up four state-owned funds with an initial capital of $45 million. Notably, however, these funds provided passive investment and were not focused on the technology sector.

In mainland China, it was only in the late 1980s that the Chinese government allowed the formation of the first VC firm, which was a government-foreign joint venture. It was followed in the 1990s by a proliferation of venture capital operations backed by state and local governments. To decentralize the decision making, three major centers of Chinese venture capital were formed in Beijing, Shanghai and Shenzhen. Four distinct types of venture capital firms operated: local government firms, corporation subsidiaries, university-affiliated firms, and foreign firms. Fast forwarding, the success of ventures in Southeast Asia culminated in the 2014 NYSE listing of Alibaba Group. Founded by Jack Ma in 1999, the initial public offering (IPO) of the gigantic Chinese ecommerce company ranks as the largest ever at $25 billion, for a total market value at issuance of $231 billion. The growth of Asian venture capital has continued in 2015-2019 with a volume of deals as much as 4 times that of Europe, and with Chinese deals being the main drivers of activity.[13] As an interesting reference to the sheer magnitude of China's venture capital, the three largest global exits during 2018 were all China-based ecommerce and electronic companies (Meituan Dianping, Xiaomi, and Pinduoduo).

There is no country that depends on innovation and entrepreneurship as much as Israel, earning it the nickname "the start-up nation."[14] The first Israeli VC fund, Athena Venture Partners, was formed in 1985. But the true catalyst for the growth of the industry was Yozma, a disruptive 1993 government initiative, which provided risk-reduction incentives to private sector and foreign funds for setting up venture capital vehicles

---

[11] For the history of venture capital in Germany, see Fohlin (2006).

[12] An important source on the history of venture capital in Asia is Kenney et al. (2007).

[13] Source: PwC / CB Insights MoneyTree Report Q2 2019.

[14] The expression comes from the bestseller 2009 book *Start-Up Nation: The Story of Israel's Economic Miracle* by Dan Senor and Saul Singer.

to invest in Israeli start-ups. Within just a few years, this resulted in an unprecedented share of growth that is attributable to high-tech ventures.[15]

MARKET STRUCTURE

Similar to other private equity vehicles, VC funds are typically structured as partnerships, with the GPs serving as managers and investment advisers to the VC funds. The funding is provided by the LPs, who themselves play a passive role in the investments, which are managed in their entirety by the GPs. LPs are comprised of high-net-worth individuals and institutions with large amounts of available capital: pension funds, insurance companies, endowments, foundations, and sovereign wealth funds. Each VC fund builds a strategic focus to differentiate itself from other funds in the competitive process of raising capital from institutional investors. The differentiating factors could be the industry or sector of the targeted companies, investment size, development stage of the target, and geographical location.

As in other segments of private equity, most VC funds are structured using a fixed 10-year lifetime, with potential extensions to liquidate unrealized investments. Once a fund is formed, investor commitments are called in as suitable investments are identified, and to cover the G&A expenses through the management fee. There is the usual period of five years to source and complete investments. Throughout the fund life, the VC firm is committed to building value in its portfolio companies with the main goal of preparing them for an exit via selling to a strategic buyer or an IPO.

While there are significant similarities between VC funds and buyout funds, there are also some noticeable differences. First, there is a difference in the amount of funds being managed: a VC fund rarely exceeds $500 million due to the smaller deal size (yet equally extensive post-investment involvement) of the portfolio companies. Second, given the riskiness of venture deals, leveraging is not a common way of financing these deals. Even in cases where a venture loan is taken by a company, it is limited to a small fraction of its overall financing. Third, lacking a positive operational cash flow, exits in venture deals are outright. In contrast, it is common to have recapitalization as a form of monetization in buyout transactions.

Market trends and the impact of the COVID-19 pandemic

The trends across global VC deal activity are portrayed in Exhibit 3. According to Preqin, there were nearly 15,000 VC deals globally in 2018, for a total investment of $274 billion. The years 2015-2018 saw the highest number of portfolio companies receiving large rounds of financing at high valuations. An unprecedented rise in the valuation of later stage companies led to a steep increase in the size of the investment rounds. There were 187 mega rounds—each above $100 million—totaled up to $55 billion in funding. Hence, the pattern in the venture data is very skewed, with 1.2% of the 2018 deals accounting for nearly 50% of the investment capital. Another important trend is the somewhat decreasing share of North America, which stabilizes around 60% of the global deals.[16]

---

[15] http://city-journal.org/html/silicon-israel-13208.html.

[16] Sources: PwC / CB Insights MoneyTree Report Q2 2019 and KPMG Enterprise Venture Pulse Q1 2019.

Exhibit 3: Global venture capital deals, 2007–2018

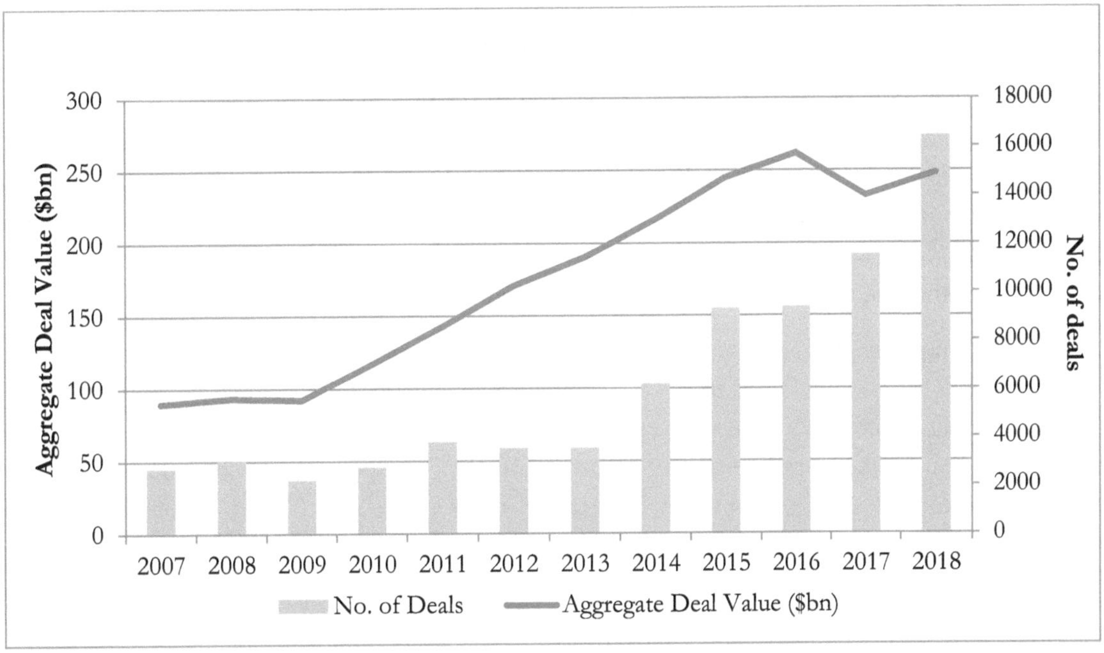

Source: Preqin Global PEVC 2019

During the 2010-2019 decade, venture capital enjoyed an unparalleled period of growth, expansion and maturity. Then, the COVID-19 pandemic struck, and global chaos to human life did not spare the venture economy. Generally, during market downturns, investors tend to be cautious about making new investments and focus instead on protecting their existing portfolio. Indeed, venture capitalists are more conservative in committing to new endeavours during times of an economic contraction. They scrutinize deals more closely and focus on the vulnerability of the start-up company within the new global disruption. The nature of the current crisis—a pandemic that has decimated entire industries for an indeterminate period—adds incalculable complexity.

Early stage companies are especially vulnerable when the economy weakens. They face far greater challenges to ramp up production and sales when demand is weak and customers are scarce. Business plans must be redrawn, revenue forecasts extended with time to reach profitability far longer than was envisioned.

Late-stage start-ups with significant revenues are generally more resilient to an economic downturn. They may actually benefit by using the crisis to trim salaries and headcount as well as to renegotiate terms with vendors who have relaxed payment terms in the current crisis and occasionally provided free services. Organizational flexibility and agility have become the name of the game for survival. Having completed several rounds of investments, late stage companies also enjoy a more robust investor base which is less likely to stop backing them. However, they may see significant valuation reductions when reaching out to new investors. In such cases, these firms will have to contend with complicated down-round pressures and conflicts among existing investors due to liquidation preferences, thereby making larger deals harder to close.

During COVID-19, countries offer government grants or stimulus-related debt instruments to assist their high-tech industries. These stimulus efforts are very valuable lifelines for late-stage companies as they are more likely to qualify for government aid schemes. On the other hand, early stage start-ups are rarely able to demonstrate a proven market traction and therefore lack access to these facilities.

Despite the market-wide uncertainty, there are several mitigating factors worth noting. Relative to previous downturns, the current venture capital industry is larger, better understood and more liquid. It includes a significant number of non-traditional investors who invest directly in venture-backed companies, especially in late stage rounds, such as pension funds, equity hedge funds and corporate venture capital (CVC). Second, the digital revolution over the past decade makes it easier for start-ups to continue operations remotely, as well as to introduce new products via digital channels.

On the deal making front, indeed late stage investments have outpaced early-stage rounds since the beginning of the crisis. Mega-rounds and mega-funds have seen an increase in popularity, with VCs and LPs pumping an increasing percentage of their cash into established names. At the same time, first-time funding is tracking their lowest annual total in 10 years. Together, these trends illustrate how investors are willing to back more established portfolio companies while being reluctant to make new, riskier investments, particularly when in-person meetings with new founders are more difficult than ever.

At the fund level, firms have closed 24 different mega venture funds of $500 million or more during the first six months of 2020, nearly equaling the previous year's total. The result has been a surprising fundraising boom amid an otherwise turbulent market. Firms closed $42.7 billion worth of venture vehicles in the first half of 2020, by itself a higher sum than all but three of the past 15 full years.[17]

Exits are generally more distanced and less attractive. Expected valuations of future IPOs is reduced from the previous heights. As far as M&A transactions are concerned, there are less strategic buyers since multinational companies must concentrate on their core businesses and find it difficult to justify great sums on acquisitions while having internal labor layoffs. It is also politically impossible to defend an acquisition of a company overseas at time of dependency on government aid to industries most severely affected by the crisis such as retail, hospitality and automotive. Additionally, restrictions on international travel abruptly inhibits the ability of potential buyers to conduct an on-site due diligence, leading to dropping the process altogether.

At the sector level, retail transactional businesses have a harder time finding investors given the massive pullback in consumer activity and the nature of the pandemic in keeping people at home. On the positive side those that gain from the crisis include:

- Enterprise start-ups that offer longer-term SaaS contracts and easy remote onboarding.
- COVID-19 accelerated the digital transformation in numerous industries, notably distanced learning.
- Digital medicine and healthcare services more broadly.
- Cyber security to defend enterprises in the new working from home environment.

Lastly, we should point out the growing trend of countries to be less cosmopolitan, thereby creating more dependency on local supply chains, customer base and strategic partnerships. Becoming localized

---

[17] See K. Dowd, PitchBook News & Analysis, July 19, 2020.

was a concept that was unimaginable until recently.

Venture ecosystem

Venture capital is the key medium for institutional funding of start-up companies. Therefore, governments find it crucial to maintain an ecosystem that nurtures the development and growth of venture investments. A vital factor in creating a supportive ecosystem is the structuring of appropriate tax rates for capital gains and carried interest to fund managers. A stable and investment-friendly regulatory framework can also encourage venture capital activity through programs to fund research and development. Given the relatively early stage and long-term horizon, venture capital is disproportionally exposed to higher risk than other types of investment. Further, pension funds are the largest LPs that sponsor venture capital thus, their regulation is imperative for the industry. As mentioned above, the revision of ERISA to apply a prudent person standard that encourages diversification into alternative investments had a transformative effect on the allocation to private equity in general, and to venture capital more specifically. Another factor which has a large bearing on the level of venture capital activity is the existence of a healthy exit market. Since private equity is transitional capital, investors must ensure from the outset the existence of as many exit outlets as possible: a functioning and liquid stock market, an active M&A market for larger companies to acquire smaller ones, and an efficient fundraising environment. Geographies where government policies are more conducive to venture capital have been able to raise more capital and invest in more new ventures. As such, the U.S. VC industry has been able to attract by far the largest share of institutional funding. In fact, according to the MoneyTree Report, nearly all of the most active technology-oriented VC funds worldwide are based in the United States.

High-tech clusters

Legendary Silicon Valley investor John Doerr said that in venture capital one has to be able to bike to the deal. Years later, this statement still captures much of the essence of venture capital secret sauce. The industry commonly operates in geographical areas known as "business clusters." Broadly defined, a cluster is a local concentration of related companies that both cooperate and compete. Most clusters are situated in geographical areas characterized by high levels of education, research, and entrepreneurship.

A geographical proximity to the companies enables the venture capitalists to be close to management, and to actively watch the ongoing operation. Being in a technological hub also provides access to an ample source of new start-up opportunities. The *spillover effect* (or *ripple effect*) supports not only the VC industry but the entire entrepreneurial community by generating jobs, venture opportunities, and other positive economic ramifications. The concentration of talent in an area attracts others to follow, resulting in a high availability of qualified people to staff managerial and engineering roles in the companies. The value of networking is also much stronger in a tight geographical region. The VC industry benefits from sharing unique service provider resources such as intellectual property attorneys, specialized labs for biotech research, boutique technology investment bankers, specialized media experts, and so on.

Further synergisms develop as a cluster matures. Retired venture capitalists—as well as entrepreneurs and executives who experienced a successful exit—often become angel investors, thereby further growing and supporting the local investment community. Last but not least, there is already a mature ecosystem of companies who grew over time to become leading technological corporations. These enterprises are as important (if not more so) than the factor which originated the cluster in their particular location.

Unsurprisingly, the most well-known venture clusters exist in the United States. Some of the largest and most famous hubs are Silicon Valley, Route 128 near Boston, and New York City. Indeed, nearly half of all U.S. VC-backed companies are located in these three areas.[18] Other clusters have also blossomed in areas such as Austin, Seattle, and the Research Triangle in North Carolina. Outside the major U.S. clusters, hubs can be found in London, Stockholm, Tel Aviv, and Bangalore. In more recent years, there has been rapid expansion of clusters in an increasing number of other cities across the world: Berlin, Dublin, Zurich, Toronto, Hong Kong, Singapore, and many more.[19]

VENTURE CAPITAL INVESTMENT FORMS AND STAGES

Venture capital expertise

In contrast to banks and other mainstream capital providers that do not get involved with companies beyond providing them with funding, venture capitalists are expected to nurture the companies in which they invest. They engage with their portfolio companies and groom them to achieve and scale revenues, aiming to "bend the growth curve," thereby increasing the likelihood of reaching a profitable exit. In order to achieve their primary objective of monetizing their investment for a higher value, venture capitalists utilize their expertise in all stages of the investment—allowing them not only to assess the merit of an opportunity relatively quickly, but also to provide help to the founder after the investment has taken place.[20]

Venture capitalists steer the direction of the business and influence management both formally and informally. Formally, steering is done through board seats and preferred voting rights. Less formal but equally critical engagement involves things like making introductions to strategic partners and investors, networking, recruiting staff to key managerial positions, and providing strategic and commercial input to the business. VC firms often second key personnel for a limited time to help the business in a specific role, and in some cases, remove individuals from executive positions (including, at times, the founder). This hands-on approach and continued monitoring, together with the venture capitalists' experience in professionalizing a business, are crucial elements in the value creation process. These types of mentoring roles are important in any business, but particularly so in disruptive high-growth businesses, where management is typically young and inexperienced.

VC firms whose reputation precedes them have historically been able to produce more successful exits, strengthening the argument that professional venture capitalism is not just about providing capital to early stage companies but also about adding value—something that is especially expected from investors who lead the investment round. Therefore, an investment offer from a more successful VC firm is far more likely to be accepted by an entrepreneur than an offer from a less reputable investor. Being affiliated with a successful VC firm carries tangible benefits in terms of credibility, networking opportunities, an ability to secure further

---

[18] Chen et al. (2010).

[19] For instance, in Europe, cities such as Berlin, Zurich, and Paris are noted for start-ups in artificial intelligence, big data, and virtual reality; and London and Dublin are noted for fintech.

[20] For academic evidence on the channels through which venture capital drives operational efficiency in portfolio companies, see Chemmanur et al. (2011). Tian and Wang (2014) find evidence that venture capital motivates corporate innovation through a higher failure tolerance.

funding, and an ultimate exit. These considerations ought to weigh heavily alongside those of deal terms and company valuation.

Investment forms

From the concept inception to product development, to growing revenues and ultimately becoming a sustainable enterprise, investment in an innovative high-growth start-up is a long-term and risky undertaking. It is often unclear how much funding a company will require and when. In order to reduce the risk, investments are made on an incremental basis using what are known as "investment rounds." At each round or stage, only a limited amount of funding is provided until the next milestone is achieved, and with it a higher company valuation. Needless to say, each phase carries its own technological, operational, and market uncertainties and challenges.

As matters progress, the process of building value will require multiple rounds until revenues can support self-sustainability. Within the investment process, the multiple rounds of funding can be broadly split into pre-revenue and post-revenue stages; or be classified more specifically as seed, early stage, expansion, and late stage financing. Typically, the seed and early stages are pre revenue, while the expansion and late stages are post revenue (see Exhibit 4).[21]

Exhibit 4: Series of investment rounds

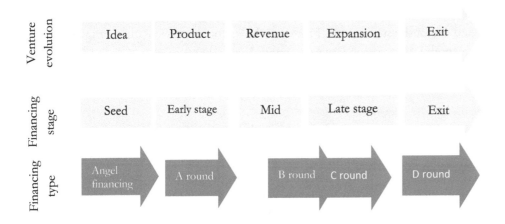

Each round of funding is structured and negotiated with new or existing investors on an arm's length basis. Terms are naturally influenced (and often even dictated) by the terms of the previous rounds. Negotiation centers on valuation, round size, type of securities, and their terms. Within a round, an investment can occur in multiple forms. First, it is possible to commit funding based on milestones, in which case, the investor contractually commits to provide additional future funding contingent upon the company meeting specific financial or non-financial hurdles (e.g., revenue hurdles, clinical test FDA approvals, licensing agreements, etc.). This arrangement can be beneficial to the company since it alleviates some of the onus to

---

[21] An even earlier stage for a start-up is pre-seed, where the financing is by the founder and the immediate family or friends.

raise subsequent funding once the capital from the current round is exhausted; it also benefits the new investors since it reduces the risk by tranching the capital committed and making some of it contingent on achieving a certain milestone. In the case of milestones, pricing is agreed in advance for the future tranches. Should the company fail to meet the agreed milestone, the investor is relieved from its obligation to provide the subsequent tranche of capital.

A second feature of a round is its extension terms. Often, the investors agree to an extended period during which further capital could be raised (usually under the same terms), in addition to the capital already raised in the round.

Third, instead of a round, it is possible to secure funding through a bridge investment. The bridge takes the form of a convertible loan agreement (CLA), whereby the bridge funds automatically convert into equity once a round is closed. This mechanism is particularly suitable for existing investors or others who are not willing to set the price and terms for the upcoming round, and would instead prefer to wait for a lead investor (typically a venture capital investor) to set arm's length terms. In designing a bridge, the main terms are (1) its size, (2) defining what makes a round trigger a mandatory conversion (minimum round size and for how long the company is allowed to raise it), (3) terms to induce investment in the CLA, which is more risky than the round itself (thus, sweeteners typically include a discount to the round price and (more rarely) warrants), and (4) terms should a qualifying round fail to happen.

One common feature of investment in early stage companies is that the investment is always into the company, and not in buying shares from the founder. This detail differs from the case of mature or distressed companies where current owners are often paid cash for their shares. In start-ups, the cash is required by the business and there is no intention to provide the entrepreneur with an early monetization route. On the contrary, entrepreneurs should remain committed to the business and only be rewarded at a much later stage if plans are materialized and the business succeeds. From a technical point of view, the company needs to issue new shares to subsequent investors; secondary transactions in the shares of a start-up are rare.

Investment stages

Pre-seed and seed

The pre-seed and seed stages are aimed at funding the initial concept developed by the entrepreneur. These are the earliest rounds of financing needed to prove an invention or an idea, and are typically provided through bootstrapping by the founder, funding from friends and family, business angels, or other seed investors. As of 2019, the global median size of a seed round was $2.2 million, with an average valuation before the new investment (known as "pre-money") of $7.5 million.[22] However, the average size of seed rounds only by angels without a venture capitalist participation is considerably small, will below $1 million. Historically, VC firms did not invest in such earlier stages since the amounts of capital required were not significant and the risk extremely high. They considered the stage of development altogether too early to warrant their attention and involvement. However, recent years have seen a new form of financing in the United States, known as "micro venture capital," which focuses on seed investing.

---

[22] Sources: PwC / CB Insights MoneyTree Report Q2 2019 for round sizes and KPMG Enterprise Venture Pulse Q1 2019 for pre-money valuations. Same sources are also used for the round size and valuation data of the other investment stages.

Micro venture capital funds with committed capital below $50 million are concentrated in Silicon Valley and make investments in seed rounds.[23] Over 200 new first-time micro-venture capital funds were raised during the 2012-2015 period for a total of $2.5 billion.[24] These funds were driven by the growing number of start-ups with founders and management who have a proven track record in advancing technology companies. Notably, the initial costs of starting a software or ecommerce business have been significantly reduced, lowering the financial risk of seed-level start-ups. This new environment attracted a wave of fledgling funds backed by family offices and high-net-worth veterans of the high-tech industry. Micro venture capital funds are capable of not only making the initial investment, but also investing in follow-on rounds.

Early stage

The early stage round (labeled the "Series A" round) is often the first round in which institutional investors such as venture capital funds invest. This initial stage of financing incurs a very high level of risk. Even with positive indications from the seed stage, visibility into the company's future prospects is still very low, making it difficult to evaluate its potential for success. Moreover, the amount of capital provided in the early stage tends to be relatively small (in comparison to later rounds) as the business is still unproven, so capital is supplied more cautiously. The investment at this stage is pre-revenue; typically, no sales or other sources of revenue have materialized. It is no wonder that this period between a start-up's initial funding and when it starts generating revenue has been called the "valley of death"—where additional financing is usually scarce, leaving the firm vulnerable to a short cash runway.

The amount of capital to be committed by a VC firm at the early stage is reflective of the size of the fund itself and the number of portfolio companies it intends to have. This number rarely exceeds 20 portfolio companies per fund, and is usually much less. The global median round size Series A in 2019 was $8 million, which is double the round size 5 years earlier. Pre-money valuation that has risen over the same period from $10.5 million to $22 million. The capital provided in the A round is expected to finance the company for a period of 12–18 months. The proceeds are intended to be used for hiring additional professionals, building a distribution network to execute the sales plan, and marketing the product or services. At this stage, a company's management team will already be in place and a preliminary product will be ready or nearly ready for distribution. The goal of the funding is therefore to enable the build-up of a revenue-generating enterprise.

Expansion stage

The purpose of investment at this stage (known as the "B round"), is to extend the cash runway of the business by providing follow-on capital to previous rounds. The key objective of the B round of financing is further development, as well as product sales. Existing or new investors are approached to provide capital directed at either the same applications as invested into in the A round, or the creation of new revenue streams and making the enterprise more sustainable. B round pre-money valuation has surged too in recent years, from a global median of $31 million in 2014 to $73 million in 2019. Equally, the size of the B round deal has gone up during that time from $6.3 million to $18 million.

---

[23] Extremely successful seed investments by micro VC funds include SV Angel's investment in Dropbox and Lowercase Capital's investment in Uber.

[24] The total amount of funding raised by micro venture capital during the four-year period was $5.9 billion across 478 existing and new funds. Data: PitchBook 2015 Annual PE & VC Fundraising & Capital Overhang Report. According to Preqin 2016 reports, funds below $50 million are 22% of the total number of funds raised in the market, with the majority of them in North America (58%), followed by Asia (19%).

Late stage

A later stage financing is commonly classified as "Series C" or higher, and is often the last round before monetizing the investment. By that time, the company has generated consistent sales, shows strong signs of revenue (and possibly profit growth), and hence, is being groomed for a potential exit. Existing investors may already have clear visibility to the targeted type of exit: in particular, whether to list the company or sell it to a strategic buyer. The decision of how to use the proceeds raised from the late stage funding will be affected by whether the intention is to keep the business independent or not.

Global median pre-money valuation at the C round has gone from $57 million in 2014 to $107 million in 2019, and the deal size of the round from $9 million to $26 million over the same years. For companies for which there is a D round or higher, valuations have kept increasing over time, averaging pre-money valuation of $250 million during 2014-2019. The amount of capital injected in a D round increased over the same period from $12 million to $45 million.

The United States dominates the venture space, not only in terms of the size of the U.S venture capital funds or the number of start-ups acquired by American companies, but also in overseas investments. For instance, a significant amount of the capital invested in European start-ups comes from U.S. VC firms; unsurprisingly, this figure increases as the company matures and the size of the round grows, accounting for 5% of the seed stage, 11% of Series A investment, 25% of Series B, 42% of the growth stage, and a staggering 81% of the mega European rounds (above $100 million).[25]

Syndication

Each round of financing typically involves between one and three VC firms, with one operating as lead investor and the others as co-investors. Multiple VC firms offer more perspectives and increased industry contacts. Clubbing together also provides more capital and facilitates independent verification and valuation processes.

Syndication alleviates the funding constraints of investors, and is particularly relevant to VC firms. Upon investing in a new company, VC firms also factor in resources for potential follow-on participation in subsequent rounds in order to mitigate future dilution. Hence, any undertaking of a new portfolio company must balance the allocation between the initial investment and reserve funds for the incremental financial needs of the company. In this way, the need for follow-on investments restrains the resources available to invest in a given round and caps the number of portfolio companies within a fund.

The participation of existing venture capital investors in future rounds is almost a prerequisite to attract new funding. Otherwise, in the new round, investors become suspicious about the company's prospects, resulting in either no financing or a less attractive valuation if they do invest. Syndicating increases the likelihood of at least some existing VC supporters to follow on in subsequent rounds.

Naturally, there is a trade-off in involving more than one VC firm. Negotiation and transaction terms can become increasingly protracted and complex when involving multiple institutional parties. This complexity becomes more pronounced in a challenging exit environment, which results in more financing rounds and further complexities of terms with multiple parties.

---

[25] CB Insights (2015).

There is one more factor that makes the number of involved venture funds larger than perhaps ideal. Most VC firms not only have a limit on the amount they can invest in each portfolio company per fund, but also will not use a subsequent fund for follow-on investments—the primary reason being the obvious conflict of interest centering on valuation between related parties. There would be a mandatory requirement to justify to the LPs in the younger/new entering fund that the valuation is not too high and that they are not being asked to rescue a portfolio company of a preceding fund. In the few cases where a cross-fund investment occurs, the GP is expected to engage a third-party valuation to substantiate the proposed investment.

SCREENING AND SELECTION PROCESS

Venture investments are risky and illiquid in nature, and require an extended time frame to harvest. Recognizing that a majority of early stage disruptive companies will fail and investments will be written off, venture capitalists are expected to carry out in-depth due diligence prior to committing funding and effort.

The high failure rate of innovative venture companies highlights the importance of the portfolio approach in venture capital—that is, a reliance on a small number of very successful companies to return several times the original investment in order to make up for those that fail or do not meet the required return metrics. While business angels may be content even with a more modest payoff, VC firms are only willing to commit if they confirm a groundbreaking potential and a chance for a very high payoff. The screening and due diligence processes must be thorough and exhaustive in order to select companies that meet such a high standard. The decision of which companies to invest in for the long haul is the most pivotal one, and is made based on the attributes and management of the target company. Considerations such as valuation and related terms cannot sway the principal investment decision—they only come afterwards.

For an investment to take place, both parties need to agree on several issues. First, it is important to set the company's valuation on the eve of the investment (the firm's *pre-money* or *pre-investment* valuation); the uncertainty of future cash flow projections makes this a difficult exercise. Second, both parties must decide on the amount and terms of the equity investment. Third, both parties need to agree on the future commercial strategy of the company. Fourth, both parties must agree on the extent to which the investor will be involved in the governance of the company. These negotiations can be protracted and difficult, as entrepreneurs often have preconceptions that are very different from the far harsher venture capital terms. In practice, broad term negotiation often takes place in parallel to the screening and diligence part so to build a mutual trust and ensure that both the entrepreneur and existing capital providers have appropriate expectations. This negotiation may also involve early conversations about rejigging the board, and other terms that early investors would need to accept for the deal to be consummated.

During the due diligence process, venture capitalists often look for prospects of innovation, a competent management team, and a well-defined business strategy that controls for operational and execution risk. The company must offer an innovative product with the potential for a significant market size, protected by barriers to entry such as proprietary technology, a first-mover advantage, or another unique selling proposition. A company may be taking advantage of a dislocation in a market that has customers demanding the new service or product. Investors look for indications of a likely demand and to understand the cost and revenue drivers of how a certain product can satisfy that void in the market. There is a need to identify to what degree the product is differentiated from other solutions in the marketplace, and to what degree it addresses customers' pain (e.g., does it enable material cost cutting, genuinely simplify or improve processes and bottlenecks, etc.?).

Additionally, product- or service-specific factors should be examined, such as the length of the sales cycle, transactional costs for customers switching to the venture's products, repeat sales record, and client attrition. These and other factors must be weighed during the overall analysis. A comprehensive due diligence process will allow the VC firm to examine the company's business strategy and quantify the potential for growth and scalability.

The VC firm must have full confidence in the competence of the management team, which should be comprised of individuals with solid subject matter expertise. VC firms also seek signs of managerial and leadership capability beyond pure engineering or scientific innovation. Naturally, expectations vary with the stage of the business, as the profile of founders in early stage companies may well be more technical and less managerial. In later stage companies, there are strong expectations for a professional team to be in place. The management team must be committed and dedicated to the venture in order to ensure continuity through the ups and down of any high-tech business. For this reason, seasoned management teams with a proven entrepreneurial track record are more trusted by venture capitalists to be successful than first-time entrepreneurs. On the other hand, management teams should also be driven and willing to make personal sacrifices in terms of lifestyle.

Another important element in the analysis is the rate at which a start-up company is consuming cash, known as its "burn rate." Burn rate describes the current rate of operational cash flow spending and is indicative of the length of time the company is able to continue without further capital injection. Investors are discouraged by companies who burn sizable amounts of monthly cash, whether through large payroll, overhead, or (especially) marketing costs. A high burn rate prompts the company to continuously require additional sources of funding, which may not be sustainable. Furthermore, since the due diligence process and investment negotiation may take time, start-up companies often find themselves running out of cash while still in a stage of investment negotiation. Not only is this situation unhealthy for the business, but it also makes negotiations with new investors unpredictable and difficult. Once a term sheet from a VC firm has been received and signed, the company enters a *no-shop* period, which covers the entire period of due diligence and reaching a definitive agreement. The no-shop period leaves no other way for new funding to come in except from current investors who might be unable, uncoordinated, or slow in response. Therefore, wherever possible, a company should seek venture capital or other investment funding when the cash situation is relatively healthy. The cliché "raise money when you can, not when you need to" applies.

TYPES OF SECURITIES AND KEY INVESTMENT TERMS

Investing in early stage companies requires balancing economic rights to cash flow distributions with risks and rewards that are properly and carefully set through structural payoffs. Accordingly, venture capitalists structure their investment contract so it specifies cash flow rights (how residual cash flows will be split), liquidation (priority of payment upon an exit), and control rights (voting rights and board rights) of the founder, previous investors, and themselves. Information rights, and frequency and type of reporting are also set.

When investing in a new company, the VC firm submits an initial term sheet, which indicates a willingness to invest. Prior to and after the submission of a term sheet, there are discussions and negotiations of the investment terms with the leading parties that have been involved up to that stage—VC firms who invested in prior rounds, business angels, founders, and the CEO (if this is someone other than a founder). These negotiations are centered on the valuation and preference terms.

Ordinary shares (common stock)

Common stock is the basic equity interest in a company and the type of stock held by the founders. Employee stock option plans (ESOPs) also convert into ordinary shares. Typically, there is only one class of common stock; however, there could be situations where certain types of ordinary shareholders are not entitled to vote. For example, it is not desirable that ex-employees who own common shares from exercising their vested employee stock options have information or voting rights.

Preferred shares

Preferred stock has many advantageous terms over common stock. Venture capitalists nearly always insist on receiving preferred stock for their investment. Preferences vary across the different investment rounds, and therefore, preferred shares are bundled in groups and referred to as Series A, Series B, and so forth. Preferences can be with respect to liquidation priority, dividends, redemption, share conversion, voting, and other special rights.

Liquidation preference

The key difference across the various series of preferred shares is in the seniority to cash flows in the event of sale or liquidation of the business. Terms are set such that the latest investment series have a priority to pre-defined cash flows that "go ahead" in the event of liquidation. Liquidation preference defines the amount that a holder of a preferred stock receives, and the pecking order in relation to other preferred and common shareholders. The liquidation preference amount can be paid in cash or in the stock of an acquirer.

The most common liquidation preference is to receive back one time the original amount invested, but new round investors may require a stronger liquidation preference, known as a "multiple preference"—that is, a multiple of the amount invested (1.5x, 2x, etc.). Whether one time or more, the multiple preference is almost always set as a senior liquidation preference before the more junior preferred series and common stockholders receive any distribution. In rare cases, the seniority of multiple liquidation preference only applies to one time the original investment, relegating the additional liquidation preference down the distribution waterfall; for example, after all preferred shareholders have received one time their investment, but before a distribution to common stock.

The liquidation preference should be structured with extreme caution and forward thinking. It can be tempting to demand a multiple preference when investing in a new round of preferred shares. However, the flip side is that "terms stick," and any such preference would be matched or exceeded in each future round; this would quickly clog the capital structure (i.e., seriously dilute the economic interest of the past investors and founders). While management interests could be rectified, there is a zero-sum game with past investors, whether business angels, prior VC firms, or others. Facing such a severe impairment of their economic interest may cause these investors to object to the proposed new financing round, favoring other means instead (e.g., reducing spending or even a fire sale of the business).

It should be noted that although the word "liquidation" carries a negative connotation, in this case, it does not necessarily mean a bad outcome. Liquidation preferences apply both to a disposition of the company's assets upon dissolution or bankruptcy, and to a sale of the company (whether via stock, assets or merger) to a third party or a change of control. Most venture capital exits take place through an outright trade sale to a strategic buyer, which qualifies as a liquidation event, but this could be an extremely profitable event.

Convertible preferred shares

Preferred shares rank higher in the capital structure than ordinary shares, and thus offer a downside risk mitigation. Yet, they also allow the holder to participate in the upside by converting the shares into ordinary shares upon exit. In the event of an IPO, these shares must automatically convert into ordinary shares. A convertible preferred share is the most common structure for venture capital investment in companies.

Participation

In addition to the liquidation preference, participating preferred stock also entitles the holders to share pro rata with the common stock in the remaining amount available for distribution. In other words, when a company is acquired, the proceeds available for distribution to shareholders pay the liquidation preferences first, and then are shared by both preferred and common shareholders alike.

Participation rights are usually capped so that they limit the upside to the preferred stock by stopping the participation in the proceeds of a sale (or other distribution) after receiving back a predetermined amount. Caps are set to a level of several times the original amount invested, usually three to five times. The purpose of a cap is to rearrange the cash flow distribution in the event of a very successful exit. In such a case, participating convertible preferred stockholders are better off giving up the liquidation preferences and converting to common stock in order to eliminate their return cap. Although they give up the liquidation preference, receiving a pro rata share on a fully converted basis would result in a higher payoff than a preferred return subject to a capped participation. The economic rationale for having a cap on participation is to incentivize entrepreneurs by boosting their economic share in the case of a highly successful outcome through the removal of the investors' preferred liquidation preference.

Cumulative dividends

Holders of preferred stock have an entitlement to dividends. Dividends are not paid in cash annually, but accrue until the time of exit. The typical dividend right is 4–8% per annum, which is accumulated to be paid at the time the company is sold. The reason it is accrued rather than paid annually is simply because young high-growth companies lack profits and are lean on cash.

Warrants

A warrant is an option to purchase a certain number of ordinary shares at a predetermined price. Warrants could accompany preferred stock to increase their upside return participation. In other situations, warrants are given to bridge investors to compensate for the additional risk they bear. Warrant coverage is also an important consideration in the fee terms of venture lenders. Lastly, warrants are a common currency to provide equity participation to either ad hoc parties (e.g., equity introducers) or ongoing service providers (e.g., law firms).

Bridge financing

In venture capital investment, a bridge loan is used to inject short-term financing into a company, thereby allowing an extension of its cash runway and continuation of business activities until a finance round is secured. An advantage of bridge financing is that it bears no price per share, which circumvents the need to set a valuation for the company, and hence enables prior investors to provide urgent funding before an external financing round is secured and in the absence of an arm's length valuation.

Once a so-called "qualified round" is raised, the bridge is automatically converted into that round on fundamentally the same terms. However, a bridge is inherently more risky than the round that follows since there is no guarantee that such a round will occur. To compensate for this risk, additional economic incentives are offered to the bridge investors. The main one is a discount to the round share price; sometimes warrants are also offered. The terms that define a qualified round are set in advance: a minimal size to be raised and a maximum time for it to happen. Otherwise, debt-type terms apply to the bridge financing, the conversion is not mandatory, and there are multiple liquidation preferences (typically twice the principal bridge loan amount plus interest). From a legal perspective, the bridge financing takes the form of a CLA.

Pay to play

As a last resort, when no external financing is available, existing shareholders may attempt to save the company by injecting cash on ultra-favorable terms denoted as "pay to play." Pay-to-play provisions impose penalties on previous investors who select not to participate with their pro rata share in the round. Penalties take place through extraordinarily generous liquidation preferences to the participating shareholders (e.g., four times the cash amount of the new round) as well as a very low round price. In extreme cases, penalties to shareholders who do not participate also revoke their existing preference by converting their preferred stock into common stock.

A pay-to-play round results in a drastic dilution of the economic rights of non-participating shareholders. Such a situation is also known as a "cram down round." Because of the traumatic impact on the ownership structure of the company, the pay-to-play process can take place through a sequence of offers until a right pricing can be found. However, it has to take place swiftly within the minimal time required for the pre-emptive rights as set in the shareholders agreement; otherwise, the company is likely to run out of cash.

Vesting rights

For an early stage company where the founding team's motivation or other credentials are unproven, it is possible to have a vesting schedule for the founders' shares in the company (i.e., shares are only awarded in tranches, where each tranche becomes vested after a pre-agreed time period). If an entrepreneur were to leave the company, the unvested shares would be transferred to the investors.

Drag-along and tag-along rights

Drag-along rights (also known as "bring-along rights") are the rights to force all other shareholders to agree to an outright sale of the company by dragging their shares along. All the liquidation and participation preferences discussed above remain intact whether the decision to sell the entire company is made through a drag-along process or unanimously desired.

The flip side term is "tag-along rights," meaning the rights of the minority shareholders to sell their shares together with the larger investors (also known as a "co-sale").

It is important to be alert to the danger of a manipulated and deeply structured term sheet. As most colorfully expressed by Benchmark's Bill Gurley, sophisticated investors are better and quicker to understand the massive consequences of liquidation and participation preferences, and the biases they introduce to an otherwise fully converted shareholding ownership basis. A series of terms that are hidden deeper in the document can easily capture the majority of the economic gains independent of the headline valuation. Acting in such an opportunistic and short-sighted way at the expense of naïve or desperate entrepreneurs can backfire badly in the future—not only in terms of a collegial partnership between the investors and the entrepreneur, but also by making future financing impossible without a precarious restructuring.[26]

MECHANICS OF ROUND CAPITALIZATION

Pre- and post-money valuation

Once the company valuation is negotiated and agreed between the existing and new shareholders, it is typically stated in pre-money terms (i.e., before the capital of the new investment round is accounted for). Post-money valuation reflects the value of the company after the financing has been provided and is the sum of the pre-money round valuation plus the investment amount of the current round. The ownership stake of the new investors is calculated by taking the new amount of funding and dividing it by the post-money valuation.

Often, valuation is determined in a reverse-order process when new investors demand a certain equity share for a set amount of investment. For example, a VC firm may state its terms as a $5 million investment for 25% of the business. This figure corresponds to a post-money valuation of $20 million; therefore, the VC firm values the company at $15 million pre-money.

A previous chapter has discussed the so-called "VC Method" to evaluate companies. In essence, this approach makes assumptions concerning the exit value, the amount of further funding required until exit, the required discount rate, and the time expected to elapse until reaching an exit. Running such scenarios forms a basis to decide the ownership percentage required for a given investment ticket size. While the technique may well be applicable to a late stage investment, this is rarely doable for an early stage start-up. Valuing an early stage company is more of an art than an exact science. In practice, such a valuation reverts to the usual economic forces of supply and demand. On the demand side, the valuation depends on how the company compares to alternative investment opportunities, as well as the prevailing market sentiment at that time; on the supply side, it depends on the available cash runway of the company and the willingness of existing investors to provide further funding. Both the VC firm that invests and the previous shareholders who are concerned about their equity dilution are more comfortable using market benchmarks from similar companies in the sector. Much attention is also given to the post-money valuation of the company at the last investment round, and its progress since then.

Finally, when negotiating round terms and valuation, VC firms require the targeted company to have a sizable ESOP reserve for management ahead of their investment. An ESOP pool allocation is a natural

---

[26] "The Sharks Arrive with Dirty Term Sheets" in the *Above the Crowd* blog by Bill Gurley, April 21, 2016.

mechanism for rewarding current management and employees, including a reserve for future ones. However, venture capitalists wish to ensure that the ESOP's dilutive effect on ownership does not come at their expense. Once the allocation is computed on a pre-round basis, then for any agreed company valuation, the price per share paid by the new investors drops, and so their equity percentage share in the company is larger. For example, setting a 10% ESOP in advance of computing the new round would prevent a similar dilution compared to a case where the ESOP pool is set after the new shares are allocated.

Capitalization table

The capitalization table (or "cap table") summarizes key information about the ownership structure of a VC-backed company, including the following:

- Shares of founders and other common holders such as those awarded to early stage advisers or board members.

- For each investment series,

  - names of participants in the round and number of shares that each owns.

  - types of security (common, preferred, etc.).

  - price per share.

  - percentage of ownership on a fully diluted basis.

- Shares reserved for the ESOP (allocated and unallocated).

- Number of warrants to which certain investors, intermediaries, or bankers are entitled.

- Approved allocation to future investors (e.g., if there is an open round or an approved extension to the last round).

The cap table is a visualization of the evolution of the company's financing and current ownership under two polar scenarios: as it stands and on a fully diluted basis (i.e., if all warrants are exercised and preferred shares converted to common).[27] To illustrate the computation, consider a simplified case of two investment rounds, first by angel investors in common shares and then a round by venture capital in convertible preferred shares. When founding the company, all common shares are held by the founder. Subsequently, business angels pour in $1.2 million in the same type of common shares as the founder at a pre-money valuation of $4 million. They are therefore entitled to 23.1% of the company, diluting the founder to 76.9% of the shares. Assuming an arbitrary number of 5,000,000 initial shares, then 1,500,000 new common shares ought to be issued to the round investors at a price per share of $0.80. After adding the amount of round capital provided to the negotiated pre-money value, the company post-money value is $5.2 million.

A year later, a Series A preferred round is negotiated with a VC firm at a pre-money value of $7 million. The investment size is $3 million in return for convertible preferred shares accumulating interest, liquidation protection, and other rights. In addition, the VC firm requires the company to set a 12% ESOP prior to the current new equity allocation. The latter requires an issuance of 886,364 new shares, which reduces the

---

[27] A practical Excel worksheet cap table template is downloadable from the S3 Ventures website: http://www.s3vc.com/resources/s3-venture-cap-table-template/.

ownership percentages of the founder and angel investors to 67.7% and 20.3%, respectively. Since there are already 7,386,364 shares outstanding, then 3,165,584 Series A shares are to be issued for 30% of the company on a converted basis, post-money value of $10 million and at a $0.95 price per share. Ownership on a fully converted basis is distributed 47.4% to the founder, 14.2% to angel investors, 8.4% ESOP, and 30% Series A preferred.

A key principle that the cap table does *not* account for is the impact of the preferences of each class of securities. In particular, it does not reflect the liquidation preferences, since it only displays the two extreme cases of either no preferences or a fully diluted basis, and both cases ignore this important consideration, effectively assuming that preferred shareholders have given up their preference by opting to convert to common stock. The effect of liquidation preferences can be gauged by calculating the so-called "cash waterfall" under alternative exit values. The waterfall shows the priority and magnitude of cash entitlement of each of the preferred classes (both liquidation preferences and accumulated interest), and the residual amount for distribution among common and preferred shareholders. The waterfall calculation only applies to the cash to which shareholders are entitled. Hence, when considering the payoff return under various exit scenarios, one should also consider any outstanding loans to banks and other non-converted claims. Once all liquidation preferences, accumulated interest, and loans are accounted for, it is striking to see how high the value of an exit should be before founders and early investors can be meaningfully rewarded.

ANTI-DILUTION PROTECTION

Once a new investment round takes place, existing shareholders are generally able to maintain their percentage ownership through pre-emptive rights which enable them to participate in a new round by investing up to their current pro rata share. Of particular concern is whether the new round of funding is at a lower price per share, known as a "down round." This situation is viewed as an "unfair" one, in which existing shareholders assume more risk in investing earlier and end up paying a higher price than later-round investors. To protect against such a situation, the investment agreement includes a specific anti-dilution clause, which provides not only pre-emption rights but also an adjustment to the price per share that the investors originally paid. The difference between the original price per share and the down round price per share is applied later according to a conversion formula, and results in allocating additional shares to the protected investors. These shares come at the expense of common shareholders, including the founders, as well as unprotected preferred investors.

There are two main types of anti-dilution protection: a full ratchet and a weighted average ratchet. A full ratchet is a more onerous form of anti-dilution protection. Although it is extremely rare today, it is helpful to review it first. In essence, a full ratchet states that regardless of how few or how many new shares are issued at the lower price, the conversion price of the protected preferred shareholders drops fully to the new price. For example, assume that the founder and early investors own 3,000,000 shares of common stock at $1.00 per share and that they then negotiated with new investors an A round of $1.2 million at a post-money valuation of $5 million (i.e., for 24% of the company). Series A is in the form of 947,368 convertible preferred stock at a price of $1.27 per share. Then, in a time of a crisis, the company raises an interim $200,000 at $3 million pre-money valuation. This interim down round (denoted for simplicity as Series B), for which its investors receive 6.25% of the equity of the company.

Under a full anti-dilution ratchet, the Series B price per share also becomes the conversion price for the protected Series A. Having originally invested $1.2 million, Series A investors are entitled to six times the share of Series B (i.e., 37.5%). With Series A investors increasing their holdings from 24% to 37.5%, common shareholders are commensurable diluted from 76% to 56.25% ownership.[28] Without any anti-dilution mechanism, common shareholders would have been entitled to 71.25% of the shares and Series A investors to 22.5%. The impact of a full ratchet is a transfer of 15% of the equity from common to Series A. Altogether, common shareholders were diluted by a whopping 19.75% of the company for $200,000, not only because of the low round B valuation but primarily because of the harsh ratchet.

Weighted average anti-dilution provisions are a milder form of protection, and they are the pervasive mechanism today. Under these provisions, the conversion rate of the preferred stock is increased based on a formula that takes into account the overall economic effect of the sale of new stock by the company. Although the formulae used can differ in some ways, the basic approach is to adjust the conversion price to the average price received by the company for stock issuances, taking into consideration the relative size of the down round as well. A typical formula is as follows:

$$NCP = \frac{(OB * OCP) + New\$}{OA}$$

where:

NCP	=	New conversion price
OB	=	All outstanding shares before offering
OCP	=	Old conversion price
New$	=	Amount raised in offering
OA	=	All outstanding shares after new offering, before ratchet

Continuing the same numerical example, first consider the allocation without the extra shares issued to Series A under the anti-dilution protection. In such a case, there are 3,947,368 shares before the new round, and 263,158 Series B shares are issued for 6.25% of the company. Under the weighted average formula, the numerator is computed by summing the 947,368 Series A shares plus the 3,000,000 common shares, and then multiplying by $1.27. Adding the $200,000 paid in Series B gives a sum of $5,213,157. This amount is divided by the total number of shares outstanding after the B round but before ratchet—4,210,526—to yield $1.24, which becomes the new average price for Series A. Investors in Series A are thus entitled to a total of 969,207 shares, which requires issuing 21,839 new shares under the weighted average ratchet. With a total of 3,969,207 shares to common and Series A shareholders post the anti-dilution protection, Series B investors need to receive 264,620 shares in order to have 6.25% of the company. The total number of shares by all classes is 4,233,821. Series A now owns 22.89% of the shares, common shareholders 70.86%, and Series B 6.25%. In this case of a more flexible anti-dilution mechanism, common shareholders are only diluted by 0.4% of

---

[28] The number of shares in the B round is computed on the basis that 3,000,000 common shares comprise 56.25%, implying 2,000,000 Series A shares (of which 1,052,632 are newly issued) and 333,333 shares issued to Series B. The corresponding price per share of the round is therefore $0.60.

compensation to price-protected Series A investors, as compared to a transfer of 15% of the company in the case of a full ratchet.

Beyond the mechanics of the anti-dilution protection, it is important to emphasize two economic principles which are often overlooked. First, as stated earlier, terms stick. Preferred terms and protections that are negotiated by earlier investors are then also expected by subsequent investors (or even harsher ones). Onerous anti-dilution ratchet terms made earlier in the life of the company make it more risky to agree on future terms, negatively affecting the ability to raise new capital without entering into a dangerous pay-to-play spiral. Second, new investors are not quite indifferent to the degree of dilution of existing shareholders in case of a down round. They may worry about legal issues if certain shareholders are wiped out, and in particular, they are concerned that founders (to the degree that they are still relevant to the business) may lose their economic interest, causing in turn a founder dilution to early investors.

EXIT

Upon considering the methods by which VC firms can harvest their investments, it soon becomes evident that start-up companies are rarely able to reach profitability within a pragmatic investment horizon, and even if it happens, the funds from operation are required to keep growing the business. Unlike in traditional sectors, therefore, dividend payout is not a viable means of monetization. Refinancing through debt is also not a realistic option in the absence of positive cash flow from operation. Moreover, as the lead financiers, VC firms cannot liquidate their position through a secondary sale of shares to other investors. Hence, the menu of successful exit strategies is limited to either an outright sale of the company to a strategic or financial buyer or listing it for public trading on a stock exchange.

The number of venture exits globally for the seven years ending in 2018 has averaged 1,500 annually, of which 60% were in the United States, followed by Europe, China, India, and Israel.[29] Classifying exits by sectors, the four major ones are Internet, software and gaming, healthcare, and telecom, in that order, and they add up to 75% of the total exits.

The majority of exits take place through an acquisition by a strategic corporate buyer, which account to about 70% of the cases globally.[30] The remaining is split evenly between buyout sales to financial investors and IPOs. Although less frequent, IPOs are the most rewarding type of exit. In 2019, the median pre-money valuation of U.S. Venture-Backed IPOs was $367 million compared to a median valuation of $105 million for an exit through a sale to a trade buyer compared.[31] Of the 15 largest VC-backed technology exits between 2011 and 2015, only two were through an acquisition (WhatsApp and Skype). The remaining 13 were via listing on a stock exchange, led by Facebook. Interestingly, it was more balanced in the healthcare sector: of the top VC-backed healthcare exits during the same period, eight were by an acquisition and seven through an IPO. This remained the case in subsequent years. There were 26 companies globally that exited in 2018 at above $1 billion equity valuations (commonly termed as Unicorns); of which 20 companies went public. Only

---

[29] Sources: KPMG Enterprise Venture Pulse Q1 2019 and Pitchbook-NVCA Venture Monitor 2Q 2019.

[30] Source: KPMG Enterprise Venture Pulse Q1 2019.

[31] Source: PitchBook – NVCA Venture Monitor Q1 2020.

6 companies were sold to a corporate buyer (AT&T, Walmart, Cisco, PayPal, Microsoft and Flutter Entertainment).[32]

The method for exit depends very much on the nature of the business, the appetite of the buyers, and the macro-economic environment at the time prior to exit. Technology companies capable of developing strong IP and knowhow but without recurring large revenues would find it difficult to attract the public and hence, are most likely to exit through a sale to a strategic buyer. Timing also plays a key role. It is exceedingly difficult to go public at a desirable valuation in times of a flat market sentiment.[33] It is also very difficult to exit through an IPO in geographies that have less established markets and smaller cap companies. However, exits through an IPO have become more difficult even in the United States. Regulatory changes in the stock market have further reduced the share of listing companies and the Sarbanes–Oxley Act of 2002 has made going public less appealing.

Regarding the identity of the acquirers, U.S. technology companies clearly dominate strategic acquisitions across the globe. For example, 40% of successful start-ups in the European Union get acquired by U.S. companies.[34]

A Silicon Valley survey reports some further illuminating statistics on exits through an IPO for 2014–2015, including

- a median price per share increase of 36% from the last financing round;

- 20% of the IPOs triggered ratchet-type protections that resulted in the companies' late stage investors receiving additional equity (however, the additional equity only averaged to 3% of the company's pre-IPO value); and

- about 20% of the IPOs had major pre-IPO institutional investors purchasing shares in the IPO (primarily mutual and hedge funds that invest in both private and public companies).

In 2018, global venture-backed exit activity reached an unparalleled record of over $350 billion equity value, in large part through initial public listings of Unicorns. Important, this trend was not limited to the U.S. but also prevailed in Asia and Europe.[35]

Rate of return to investors is not only determined by the exit value but also by investment time. It is insightful to consider time to liquidation for both acquisitions and IPO exits. U.S. data for Q1 2018 to Q2 2020 shows that the median number of years to liquidate from first funding was 6.7 years when exit took place through an acquisition. The median time to exit via listing on a stock exchange was about the same, however it was more varied according to the waves of IPO flurry and often longer time to exit.[36] This indicates a pattern of waiting for strong IPO market sentiment particularly by more mature companies, either because they are more difficult to list otherwise, or lack willing to compromise on a fully desired valuation.

---

[32] https://www.cbinsights.com/research/unicorns-exits-2018/

[33] The cyclicality of IPOs is very dramatic. During the 2006–2015 decade, the numbers of IPOs ranged over twelvefold from a low of nine cases in 2009 to a peak of 121 occurrences in 2014. In contrast, the range of exits via an acquisition only varied twofold between the lowest and the highest years of occurrence (434 in 2006 and 865 in 2014).

[34] Source: CB Insights 2015.

[35] Sources: KPMG Enterprise Venture Pulse Q1 2019, Pitchbook-NVCA Venture Monitor 2Q 2019 and Pitchbook 2018 Annual European Venture Report.

[36] Source: PwC / CB Insights MoneyTree Report Q2 2020.

The role of VC firms is pivotal to achieve a successful exit. They bring a wealth of experience into the sale process and are typically more networked with the banking community than management and early stage investors. Venture capitalists can weigh the pros and cons regarding the timing and desired method for exit and plot accordingly. They are also the main party that negotiates the exit terms and facilitates the process.

CONCLUSION

Since its creation, the venture capital industry has been instrumental in driving innovation and economic growth and creating high-skilled jobs. VC-backed companies have developed many products that have become household names and are now considered essential to daily life. What is particularly remarkable is the pace at which these companies have evolved from early stage businesses to large organizations, and at which the new products and services have been accepted and incorporated into the mainstay of society. VC-backed firms in areas such as biotech and enterprise software have equally found their way into services and products that are embedded in organizations, manufacturing facilities, and healthcare, to name a few applications.

The ability of the industry to add value to early stage companies can be demonstrated in a number of ways. First, it has funded and guided most of the major and successful technology companies in existence today; this has been carried out through the professional, operational, and financial expertise that venture capitalists offer—expertise that is built on seeing so many companies transitioning through similar challenges. VC firms are willing to take far greater risks than other funding sources, and to support their position for a relatively long period in order to achieve a sizable return. Third, being an institutional investor, VC imposes a strict corporate governance structure compared with other capital providers. Fourth, empirical evidence shows that companies funded by venture capital grow more rapidly and generally bring products to market faster than similar companies funded through other means.[37]

In recognizing the abovementioned points, governments across the globe view the venture capital industry as a driver of innovation, a powerful economic engine, and an essential asset class for institutional investors.

REFERENCES

Chemmanur, T.J., K. Krishnan and D.K. Nandy (2011) "How does venture capital financing improve efficiency in private firms? A look beneath the surface," *Review of Financial Studies* 24: 4037-4090.

Chen, H., P. Gompers, A. Kovner and J. Lerner (2010) "Buy local? The geography of successful and unsuccessful venture capital expansion," *Journal of Urban Economics* 67: 90-102.

Fohlin, C. (2006) "Venture capital revolutions: Germany and the United States in the post-war era," working paper, John Hopkins University, October.

Gonzalez-Uribe, J. (2014) "Venture capital and the diffusion of knowledge," working paper, London School of Economics, February.

---

[37] See Puri and Zarutskie (2012) for evidence that VC-backed companies grow quicker and have a lower failure rate than matched non-VC-financed companies.

Gornall, W. and I. A. Strebulaev (2015) "The economic impact of venture capital: Evidence from public companies," working paper, Stanford University, November.

Lerner, J. (2012) *Boulevard of Broken Dreams: Why Public Efforts to Boost Entrepreneurship and Venture Capital Have Failed--and What to Do About It*, Princeton University Press.

Mulcahy, D., B. Weeks and H.S. Bradley (2012) "We have met the enemy … and he is us," Ewing Marion Kauffman Foundation, May.

Paglia, J. and M. A. Harjoto (2014) "The effects of private equity and venture capital on sales and employment growth in small and medium sized businesses," *Journal of Banking and Finance* 47: 177-197.

Popov, A. and P. Roosenboom (2009) "Does private equity investment spur innovation? Evidence from Europe," working paper No. 1063, European Central Bank, June.

Puri, M. and R. Zarutskie (2012) "On the life cycle dynamics of venture-capital- and non-venture-capital-financed firms," *Journal of Finance* 67: 2247–2293.

Kenny, M., K. Han and S. Tanaka (2007) "Venture Capital in Asia," in *Making IT: The rise of Asia in high tech*, Rowen et al, Editors, Stanford University Press.

Tian, X. and T.Y. Wang (2014) "Tolerance for failure and corporate innovation," *Review of Financial Studies* 27: 211-255.

In his own words: Tim Hanford, Managing Director and Head for Europe, J.C. Flowers & Co.

Lessons learned on venture investments and financial services start-ups (fintech)

Venture capital investing is rightly regarded as a specialist investment strategy. The investor capabilities that go into making successful early stage investments are not unique, but the emphasis on specific capabilities is distinct. Most private investing strategies are a team game, combining the efforts of managers with those of the investors. Disciplines like venture investing are closer to an extreme sport, associated with higher risk and higher reward, and requiring specialist reflexes.

With venture capital the emotional connections between the (founder) entrepreneurs, the investors, and the employees are intense, while at the same time, the governance is often not straightforward. When this complex set of relationships is well managed in combination with the right people with an understanding of each other's perspective then the results can be very powerful—otherwise the situation can become messy to the point of being self-destructive. Team risks of one form or another are the key element to ensure consistent execution, and this requires constant investor vigilance.

The investment process starts with defining the diligence and valuation work that will support the hypothesis and the underwriting of a deliverable business plan that balances execution risks and time frame against the value of the addressable opportunity. This diligence work has a different emphasis compared to the diligence of an established company where there are generally many more facts to verify and data to work on. Valuation inputs such as projected margin progression or unit economics will necessarily need to draw on analogues and experience to compensate for lack of company information.

Venture diligence focuses on operational plans, specific value creation (or "intellectual property," broadly defined), and management assessment and selection. Short and long-term operational plans should be created with detailed planning for the immediate horizon and scenario analysis to test different outcomes. Through intense discussion of these plans, the management and investors develop a common understanding, create trust and appreciation of each other's working style and expectations, and establish a communication framework for the entrepreneurial decisions to come.

As venture markets have become more competitive, and the volumes of capital available at an early stage to support growth ambitions have increased, it has become more important to work closely with the management team to identify sources of differentiated value creation. The investor will need to look at valuation through a number of different lenses in order to develop an opinion on the value of a company that may be some distance from the creation of positive operating cash flow. In an activity where some degree of failure is inevitable, and where failure frequently means total loss of investment capital, it is also necessary to understand how the new venture fits into the overall portfolio and to carefully construct a portfolio which avoids correlation between points of weakness in individual business models.

At this early stage of plan diligence and validation, it is important to understand the alignments between team capabilities, target customer segments and the product or service proposition, and the expected exit strategy. Everyone should understand up front the exit objectives and time frames in the context of likely future capital needs. These objectives will inform subsequent execution decisions as the business is built for a specific type of strategic acquirer or for longer-term independence in private or public ownership, and will be part of a lens through which to view the sometimes conflicting directions desired by the shareholders and the expectations of the entrepreneurs whose passion and commitment has built the company.

Having concentrated knowledge of a sector with associated global and local networks—in other words, investing in areas you understand—is clearly important to all investment activities and particularly so with early stage and venture investing, where you are making hard-to-test assessments of execution pace and market adoption. Combined with the detailed domain knowledge of the founding team, these sector networks enable an understanding of the competitive landscape in which the team is going to build value. Through this understanding of the proposition, environment, sales cycle, technology, and regulation, the investor is able to assist in the execution challenge.

In our sector of financial services, technology has been integral to a competitive service offering for decades, but recently, there has been a proliferation of technology-enabled start-ups, or fintech companies, that are building upon a robust global technology architecture and changes in consumer behavior to offer alternatives. These challengers are encouraged by a political and regulatory agenda that promotes competition and innovation; hence, they are able to penetrate the most regulated and capital-intensive sectors of financial services. These sectors were previously left largely to the incumbents due to the advantages of scale, the barriers of regulation, and the capital requirements necessary to compete. The scale of the opportunity is huge for those ventures that can harness technological innovation with compliant and cost-effective customer acquisition.

During the ownership period, different investors adopt different approaches to involvement. At J.C. Flowers, our approach is to be heavily involved within a structured governance framework, something which prepares for the "early maturity" often required within a regulated sector. Good governance and strong boards enable disciplined decisions to be made with pace, but a balance is required to ensure that planning and decision support becomes a valued contribution and is not burdensome. Other venture firms allow looser governance with more entrepreneur-led decisions about direction. Whatever the approach, most investors seek to support the management team in a number of key ways, including the following examples:

- **Finding and attracting talent:** A challenge for all companies (and one that can be particularly acute for young companies, particularly in certain cultures and sectors. The network and presence of recognized investors with substantial capital resources), finding the right talent can greatly assist with profile, prestige, and recruitment. The hiring and firing decisions associated with different functional disciplines at different growth points are critical, and can have significant cultural impact. For example, the style and experience required of a sales leader at one point in time may be very different from that required a relatively short period later.

- **Building through a sustained growth phase:** This is often the key challenge for early stage companies, and one where there is no substitute for experience and having the right people around the table focused on planning, anticipating the issues, and solving the problems associated with scaling an organization and its processes. Shortcuts, trade-offs, and prioritization decisions are facts of life and important judgments with consequences and payback at a later stage ("technical debt," as Ben Horowitz likes to call it). Not achieving growth can be equally challenging of course, introducing a need to clinically assess the underlying reasons during a stressful period when cash may continue to be consumed at a significant rate. When and how to pivot the model, when to persevere, and when to walk away are vexing questions that are also an integral part of venture investing.

- **Access to capital:** This is the lifeblood of ventures during their cash consumptive phase. Few companies are funded up front for their entire plan, and so most will need to go through successive funding rounds. Different investors approach this in different ways, but we typically like to lead the rounds and to have a clear understanding of the necessary signs of value increase required to support further capital contributions. Experience is essential to structure these funding rounds, set valuations, balance shareholder rights, and establish appropriate terms and governance. Similarly, an investor's corporate finance expertise and broad networks will aid the negotiation of partnerships that accelerate delivery, support international expansion, and assist with M&A or any positioning required on the path to exit.

Overcoming the challenges of establishing a new venture—especially as part of a motivated team whose ambitions and entrepreneurial spirit have the potential to create value from a life dream—is the real pleasure of this investment strategy. The journey can be long but the rewards come in many forms and can be significant.

14 Corporate Venture Capital

Global trends are having a "Pac Man effect" on business models, and those who are not paying attention are being up-ended.
Deborah Hopkins, Citi Ventures

INTRODUCTION

Simply put, corporate venture capital (CVC) is when a corporation becomes an investor in start-ups while keeping them outside the corporation's walls. Corporations achieve this degree of separation by not being the sole investor—and typically, not even being a leading one—in the start-up firms. Unlike venture capital (VC) firms, which act as general partners that manage the capital of others, corporate venture capital usually deploy internal funding resources. In addition, whereas the motivation of venture capital is purely financial, in the case of corporate venture capital the considerations are both financial and strategic.

Corporate venture investing has evolved into a crucial tool for gaining access to future innovations and new markets. It can be viewed as one approach to corporate development (alongside internal R&D, strategic acquisitions, joint ventures and other alliances) rather than as a stand-alone activity. Within CVC, there are three main forms: direct investment, internal general partner (GP) investment, and external limited partner (LP) investment, where direct investment sometimes complements an internal or external VC program. For an internal GP structure, the objective is to enable the CVC unit to have relative autonomy, to build venture capital capabilities inside the organization, and to more directly balance the financial and strategic considerations in the selection of investment targets and during the path of growing the activities of the venture arm.[1]

Although Corporate venture capital has undergone dramatic swings in terms of its overall cycle of activity, the trend is clearly growing and a significant number of the top programs are in their second decade of investing. Globally, the number of active CVC programs has surged in the last decade to about 800 in 2018. The number of global deals reached a record high of 2,740 in 2018, with the total amount invested increasing from $10 billion in 2013 to $53 billion in 2017.[2]

CVC deals are a growing source of competition to traditional VC firms and participates in over 20% of all VC deals. In the United States, there were over 1,800 CVC investments in 2019. They invested across all investment stages, and their funding participation increased from $5.5 million in 2013 to $26 billion in 2019. The rate of growth in Europe was equally pronounced: from $1.1 billion in 2013 to $5.5 billion in 2018, with the UK, Germany and France take the lion share of the European activity. In Asia the participation was even larger—nearly one in every three deals involved CVC. In fact, by 2018, Asia made up 38% of the global CVC share, whereas North America's share decreased from 64% dominance in 2013 to 41% in 2018; Europe accounts for nearly all of the remaining global activity (17% in 2018).

---

[1] For comprehensive and insightful reports on corporate venture capital, see the Volans Report (2014) and the BVCA Guide to Corporate Venture Capital (2014).

[2] Source for the data in this section: CB Insights – 2018 Global CVC Report and PitchBook-NVCA Venture Monitor Q1 2020.

In terms of investment size, CVC funds generally write larger participation checks, averaging $26 million per deal versus an average of $21 million for a VC fund. The larger average deal size holds true for both early stage and late stage rounds. In particular, 20% of CVC deals by count are invested in rounds sized $50 million or more, and about 50% of new technological companies above $1 billion (known as "unicorns") are backed by them. At the other side of the spectrum, there is also more willingness to invest at the seed stage. In 2018 332 unique CVC groups participated in at least one seed financing round, which amounts to a three-fold increase over a period of five years. With respect to investment style, CVC funds rarely lead a round, but have been increasingly willing to engage with start-ups directly, whether through their contacts or in a strategic partnership.

Leading the pack in recent years were, GV (formerly Google Ventures), Salesforce Ventures, Intel Capital, Qualcomm Ventures, GE Ventures, and China-based Baidu Ventures and Legend Capital. The pace of technological advancement has pushed corporations to find new paths for innovation, which resulted in new entrants into the field such as Unilever, Kellogg, Campbell Soup, the Israeli secret services Mossad, low-cost airline JetBlue and children's programming company Sesame Street.

Despite the positive momentum, there are certain non-trivial challenges that compromise the trend of CVC growth and account for its historical volatility.

OBJECTIVES, PREREQUISITES, AND TRACK RECORD

Multinational corporations and start-ups have much to learn from each other. Corporations can open doors for start-ups, offer a breadth of industry experience, and provide valuable infrastructure such as access to distribution channels. In the other direction, investing in start-ups provides corporations with access to innovation that occurs at the peripheries of their core business. This investment can be used as an "agent of change," identifying cutting-edge technologies for protecting the future competitive position of the core business units and acting as a catalyst for further growth.

CVC is an integral part of a broader effort to develop the strategic capabilities of the sponsoring corporation; yet, at the same time, it is an investment for a direct financial return. It is a hybrid between the VC model and pure corporate development, and should be tied to the corporation's overall future goals and offerings. While strategic consideration should be heavily weighted, financial returns are also a prerequisite for any potential investment in a start-up.

Specific strategic objectives vary across the sponsoring corporations and can shift over time. Operational and budgetary constraints may also get tighter, which explains the radical fluctuations in organizations' commitment to CVC. Wide variations in implementation forms are common as well, as some corporations deploy a more ambitious plan of multiple CVC units aimed to achieve a large number of objectives over a shorter time period.

For these reasons, CVC only fits a specific set of companies: typically, multinational corporations with substantial financial resources, an open managerial attitude, and internal process capabilities. As a non-core activity, CVC requires significant untied cash at hand. Increasingly, over the last decade, corporations (especially large U.S. technology giants) with exceptionally high cash balances have emerged. Indeed, these companies are heavily committed to CVC (e.g., Google, Microsoft, Intel).[3] Capital availability also depends on the company being in a state known as "peacetime." A company in peacetime is stable and secure, so it can look to improve its internal structure, expand its R&D capabilities, and create new products (e.g., Google, which has long enjoyed market leadership). On the other hand, a company in "wartime" must funnel its entire cash flow into ensuring its survival and pursuing a competitive edge.[4]

Another requirement for CVC is that the corporation should already have a strong R&D department; this ensures good knowledge transfer and integration between the start-up companies and the corporation. Ideally, over time, the internal R&D department will be able to support the venture company through resources and expertise, thereby shortening time to market and reducing risk while the start-up company maintains an independent and undisrupted build-up.

A checkered track record

Strategic logic and good intentions notwithstanding, the track record of CVC is seriously problematic. The sector has experienced extreme fluctuations—waves of rapid growth during economic upswings and massive shutdowns when performance fails to materialize. These fluctuations have led to a proliferation of so-called "zombies". Park and Vermeulen (2015) find that nearly half of the 419 venture units initiated over the four years from mid-2010 to mid-2014 were inactive and had not made a single deal by the end of 2014.[5] The evidence of Lerner (2013) is also quite startling: for decades, many corporations either saw their venture initiatives failing outright or gave up on them rather quickly. The median life span of CVC programs has traditionally hovered around one year, inducing the historical swings in corporate venture activity. However, that said, there are notable exceptions of corporations that have perfected CVC, such as Intel and Google.

STRATEGIC CONSIDERATIONS AND VEHICLES OF INVESTING

The strategic goals for employing CVC vary widely. CVC keeps corporations in touch with emerging technologies, and can bridge a gap between internal R&D activities and full acquisition of start-up technology companies. In this way, CVC offers a more capital-efficient way to identify disruptive technologies without making a full commitment. While CVC tends to focus mainly on new technologies, it can also be used on the distribution side; for example, investing in a foreign selling channel in order to "test the waters" in new markets. Moreover, it can be used to encourage a culture of innovation within the parent organization. Corporate employees who work closely with, or are seconded to, a start-up portfolio company are directly exposed to an entrepreneurially minded work environment, where timeliness and an enthusiastic spirit play key roles.

Chesbrough (2002) discusses four distinct investment strategies that can be accomplished via the hybrid CVC structure of strategic and financial objectives:

---

[3] Extreme examples are Google and Microsoft, both with cash reserves roughly equal to their annual revenues during 2013–2018.

[4] See Ben Horowitz (2014) on the notion of peacetime versus wartime management and operation in organization.

[5] Data was collected from the Global Corporate Venturing Magazine.

- **Driving investments:** These investments are made for strategic alignment. The CVC fund identifies start-up companies that are closely linked (technologically or otherwise) to the core corporate business for a potential later integration into the parent company. This approach is not useful if the company is looking to "transcend current strategies and processes." A recent extension of this strategic objective is to invest in start-ups that fundamentally utilize the technological solutions of the parent company; for example, Microsoft invests in companies that commit to its technology as their core.

- **Enabling investments:** Here the purpose is also strategic, but there is no close link between the operations of the start-up and the parent company. Rather, the intention is to exploit complementary products or capabilities in order to enhance the strategy of the current business.

- **Emergent investments:** While they do not promote current strategies, these investments do link with the company's operations. If the business environment changes, the start-up in which the investment is made could become very valuable strategically. This design helps create an option strategy that is independent of financial returns, and allows the company to explore new untapped markets outside the core markets that it already serves. If the intelligence gathered during the investment period and overall experience is promising, the parent corporation could look to expand in that new direction. In summary, emergent investments are initially made for financial gains, but can ultimately result in strategic gains as well.

- **Passive investments:** Passive investments are not connected to the investing company's strategy nor its operations. Thus, these investments do not help the investing company to actively advance its own business and can only provide financial returns. Essentially, passive investments are no different than any other class of financial assets. Lacking any strategic advantages, passive investments are not practical or valuable.

As noted, there are three forms by which CVC may be structured:

- **Direct**, aimed at getting business and tech experience in emerging areas. Mostly strategic, this structure often carries a precondition to have a business unit as an internal champion. This structure fits the driving and emergent investment cases outlined above.

- **Internal GP**, in which the fund has more autonomy for step-out options for start-ups. Its goals are mostly financial, with a strategic element as well. This structure fits the enabling and emergent investment cases above.

- **External LP**, which is aimed at gaining a wider exposure to markets and understanding of venture capital best practice processes. Its goals are ROI/financial, and it may fit the emergent and passive investment cases mentioned above.

Exhibit 1 outlines and contrasts the key structure and performance criteria for each of the forms.

Corporations will invest in VC-backed firms directly from their balance sheet in two scenarios: (1) when the corporation does not have a CVC program, or (2) outside it if involves development cooperation such a non-recurring revenues (NRE) program or a joint venture (JV). The motivation in these cases is to advance a joint product or technological solution that crosses over between the start-up's new capability and the existing technologies of the corporation. There has been a steep surge in the global number of deals where corporations deployed funding directly into VC-backed start-ups (a four times growth between 2013 and 2018). Furthermore, corporate direct investment into ventures surpassed the number of CVC deals in every year since 2015: 4,383 corporate direct deals during 2018 compared to 2,740 CVC investments.[6]. However, in terms of deployed capital, the figures are comparable, which indicate that corporate direct investment is, on average, smaller and in earlier stage companies where joint development programs are easier to negotiate.

Exhibit 1: Types of CVC vehicles

	Corporate/Direct Investment (Balance Sheet)	Internal Dedicated Fund (GP Model)	External Fund (LP Model)
Purpose	Gain direct business and technology experience in emerging areas	Emerging business and technology with more autonomy for step-out options	Develop internal VC capabilities while gaining market awareness and understanding
Structure	Direct investment, funding each deal, closely related to business divisions and future business opportunities	Corporate acts as LP in a 100% captive fund. Greater fund autonomy	External GP firm Corporate functions as LP Decision on investment GP in fund parameters
Talent	Internal corporate talent	Mixture of external VC hired and internal corporate talent	Experienced VCs and potential secondees from corporate
Success Measures	Measurement of direct strategic inputs	Primarily financial with a level of strategic exposure	Predominantly ROI
Examples	BP, Bosch, Panasonic	Bloomberg Beta, Unilever Ventures, Reed Elsevier Ventures	Siemens Venture Capital (SVC), Physic (Unilever)

Source: BVCA Guide to Corporate Venture Capital, 2014.

WHY DOES CVC FAIL?

As stated, nearly half of all CVC units set up in recent years are idle, and as a whole, the financial performance of the sector has been lukewarm if not poor. Reasons for this lack of success are plentiful, ranging from an absence of internal knowhow to minimal interest in actually engaging with start-ups as a legitimate partner (Lerner, 2012). In addition, there is a failure to match between corporations and start-ups in terms of how they operate and what they expect from the partnership.

The reality is that mature companies and start-ups are inherently different creatures. As Park and Vermeulen (2014) discuss, too many corporations unreasonably expect that the rules of the game for a 50-year-old company should also apply to a recently formed enterprise. The diligent and comprehensive way that large companies operate can be crippling for a new venture. Whereas Fortune 500 companies operate in

---

[6] Source: CB Insights – 2018 Global CVC Report.

relatively stable markets that are somewhat predictable, start-ups usually operate in environments that are far less defined and highly uncertain. The "deep dive" strategic research that global multinationals conduct is largely useless in the context of the start-up world, and is even counterproductive if speed (a critical component to start-up viability) is compromised.

Along the same line of reasoning, mature companies measure progress and success according to very different metrics than those used by start-ups. It is the job of a good corporate venture capitalist to ensure that expectations are recalibrated between the two different corporate cultures.

A misalignment in goals is another thorny aspect: when both sides have their own business interests beyond a purely financial goal, conflicts can arise, and they typically do. A common case of misalignment is if part of the investment is in the form an NRE program or JV, as mentioned above. Friction may also result if the corporation demands a first right of refusal upon a trade exit of the start-up. Furthermore, the corporation often enters a clause that forbids the start-up from dealing commercially with its competitors. Similarly, as part of the investment, the corporation could either require product exclusivity on the use of the technology (e.g., mobile phones) and/or a territorial exclusivity (e.g., China).

IMPLEMENTING AN INTERNALLY DEDICATED FUND STRUCTURE

Once a business case is made for an internal CVC fund with clear goals, there is a need to develop a structure to deliver on these targets. First, a strong buy-in from top management is required, or else the program will not take off. An annual investment budget has to be set out and the internal boundaries should be defined. The latter refers to the formal hierarchy and relationships between the business units (particularly the R&D and business development departments). Further, the degree of autonomy granted to the CVC unit must be decided; this degree may be different for each organization and is often very difficult to get right (e.g., should the CVC operation be separate from, or very close to, the parent company?).

Past experience shows that CVC funds benefit from a large degree of autonomy at the beginning, which allows rapid and independent decisions to be made. An autonomous environment is also powerful for recruiting external VC talent. Once the CVC program is established and functioning independently, closer ties should be formed with the divisions of the parent company to maximize potential synergies with the start-ups in order to facilitate organizational learning, access to IP, and insight into broader market developments.

For the autonomy to succeed, the CVC management needs to truly understand the products and long-term strategy of the parent corporation to ensure that the correct investment decisions are made. Once closer ties are forged, the CVC unit still needs a high degree of autonomy. Therefore, a single investment committee composed of top management from the parent organization along with partners from the venture arm is ideal. This structure streamlines approval and avoids duplication of effort from internal R&D. Needless to say, even if the venture unit is highly autonomous, it should still have regular communication with the parent R&D department, acting as a scouter for new technology and product developments. As a matter of pragmatism, several iterations may be needed to achieve the correct composition for each organization.

Forming the GP team requires balancing a mixed set of capabilities and ensuring that the culture is not dominated by a single company. Talent should be recruited from outside as well as within the company based on domain expertise and complementary skills. The team needs to have technological and business acumen in order to be able to analyze investments, perform due diligence, and form sound judgments. Having persons with prior venture capital experience is also hugely important. In addition to bringing relevant practices from the VC industry, these individuals have different (and most likely larger) networks to benefit the fund and the portfolio companies alike. Those individuals who transfer from within the organization must have a strong rapport with, and be highly respected by, their corporate peers. In combination, meeting these objectives will nurture a supporting relational context with three levels of executives: parent firm executives, business unit managers, and members of the venture capital community.[7]

There is a strong rationale for growing in stages, starting by making small minority investments. This approach builds team harmony and diverse knowledge. In particular, it is helpful to invest as part of a syndicate or when there are already venture capitalists on the board of the start-up, which enables direct engagement with these individuals to share knowledge about operational requirements, processes, and extending the network for deal origination. When investing side by side with others, the CVC funds rarely take an active role in the governance, and usually have observer seats on the board instead. This arrangement is not necessarily problematic, but it does limit the CVC partners' active engagement. On the other hand, it is much more efficient and allows for scaling up by undertaking more investments with the same set of professionals.

While setting targets and tracking the financial performance of the fund is reasonably straightforward, measuring the strategic element is much more complex. Accordingly, it is crucial that the financial metrics be set using both quantitative measures and strategic synergies in qualitative measures. The use of financial metrics is essential for taking a disciplined approach to valuing potential new ventures and the performance of current ventures. Another disciplinary feature is a fixed fund duration, which forms a goal and a mindset of seeking monetization. Although corporate venture capital rarely has such a mandatory time horizon, independent VC funds have a limited fund life (typically 10 years) and hence, a time pressure to exit. While different horizons among investors may generate misalignment of interest regarding the optimal time to exit, in practice, it benefits the CVC to have an investor who is structurally disciplined to build value in the start-up in a timely fashion.

As for the remuneration of the venture partners, in order to attract and retain top talent, CVC units need to offer similar incentives as traditional venture capitalists—in particular, a sizable carry. This incentive is very challenging to achieve, since the venture arm often works closely with staff members in the parent corporation who have no such financial incentives. Many past breakdowns of CVC programs are attributed to the mismatch of remuneration structures between sets of teams in the same organization. Therefore, a trade-off is required to fit the culture of each corporation. For instance, whereas BP Ventures does not offer such financial rewards, most others CVC funds do.[8]

THE IMPACT OF CVC: THE ACADEMIC EVIDENCE

Despite its inherent limitations, corporate venture capital has several strong advantages over the classic, stand-alone venture capital model. Being backed by a reputable multinational is a strong certification, and allows the start-up to ride on the parent brand when dealing with other parties in its business environment (e.g., commercial banks, suppliers, etc.). Sometimes, the parent offers its corporate procurement to the start-up (e.g., negotiated wholesale pricing, suppliers with proven quality control, priority for timely scarce resources

---

[7] Hill and Birkinshaw (2014).

[8] For reference see the BVCA Guide to Corporate Venture Capital (2014), p. 9.

such as laboratories, etc.). Corporate venture capital programs can provide a significant balance sheet and the ability to serve as a patient investor. As a result, they invest larger sums at higher valuations, and are more tolerant of failure. The academic literature provides unequivocal support for these observations. Chemmanur et al. (2014) find that CVC-backed firms are more innovative, as measured by patenting output, although they are younger, riskier, and less profitable than VC-backed firms. The impact continues at a remarkable rate post IPO. Specifically, CVC-backed firms produce 27% more patents in the three years before IPO than other VC-backed firms do, and these patents receive 17.6% more citations; and in the first four years following the IPO, CVC-backed firms produce 44.9% more patents that receive 13.2% more citations.

In terms of going public, companies backed by CVC attract higher-quality underwriters and analysts and larger holdings from institutional investors. Moreover, CVC-backed firms obtain higher valuations at the IPO as well as higher acquisitions premiums, but only if there is technological complementarity with the CVC parent (Ivanov and Xie 2010).

Corporate venture capital can play an important role in those sectors where the parent corporation offers unique benefits. Often, these parents can provide technological and engineering input and advice that is instrumental to smaller start-ups. Yet, the nature of such contributions is not limited to technical support. In the biotechnology sector, for example, pharmaceutical firms can extend their expertise in navigating FDA regulations and processes. Indeed, Alvarez and Dushnitsky (2016) find that corporate-backed biotech start-ups are more productive whenever the parent firm possesses relevant regulatory experience.[9] The contribution of such non-technical—yet critical—experience extends well beyond the life sciences sector. For instance, consider the recent hurdles faced by Uber and Airbnb. While both companies have solved complex technological challenges and pioneered new business models, they continue to experience threats to their growth due to regulatory pressures; Uber's relationship with its drivers is contested in multiple jurisdictions, and Airbnb is forced to curate its participant pool so as to adhere to hospitality and tax laws. It follows that regulation-intense sectors (e.g., life sciences, aerospace, finance, and insurance) may be particularly fertile ground for CVC funds and the companies they back.

SOCIAL RESPONSIBILITY AND ACCELERATORS

Multinational corporate executives are becoming increasingly conscious of the need to implement impact investing policies to drive change within their organizations. Blending corporate venturing with sustainability agendas is a powerful tool for translating this need into action, producing far greater benefits than those produced by corporate social responsibility (CSR) policies in isolation. This trend has led to an array of dedicated CVC investments in environmental initiatives, healthcare, and impact/social venturing.

Cleantech and healthcare have grown to become part of the general venture capital arena. However, CVC funds are a more natural approach to impact investing compared to independent venture firms. Once a corporation adopts a social and environmental agenda as part of its strategic goals, the translation into the non-financial criteria of the CVC unit is relatively straightforward.

A notable case is GE Ventures, one of the most active corporate venture capital firms worldwide. "Ecomagination" is GE Ventures' growth funding strategy to reduce its global environmental footprint (due

---

[9] Using a wide array of innovation factors (e.g., FDA approvals, patents, publications, and technological experience), Alvarez and Dushnitsky (2016) find CVC backing is associated with more than double the innovative output of ventures compared to sole VC backing.

to both customers' choices and the company's own operations) by devoting funding to cleaner technology, reducing water consumption, and more. This initiative was closely followed by "Healthymagination," an initiative to improve the quality and affordability of healthcare globally. In 2013, GE Ventures brought these funds under one umbrella to leverage insights and connections.

Identifying and nurturing promising start-ups is a top priority among corporate and independent venture capitalists alike. Incubators and accelerators, such as Y Combinator, provide early stage investment and mentorship to participating entrepreneurs. CVC funds are very active in developing a healthy ecosystem for their investment programs. For example, IBM Ventures combines innovation centers with a global entrepreneurship program. Google runs a very comprehensive operation in this space through Google Ventures (GV), Google Capital, and Google for Startups Campus. The latter operates facilities in six locations: London, Tel Aviv, Seoul, Madrid, Warsaw, and São Paulo. These are community hubs where entrepreneurs can learn, share ideas, and launch their start-ups. Fostering entrepreneurial innovation has both a social impact and allows to identify potential new ventures to pass on to Google Ventures.

The corporate incubator model is especially effective in the life sciences. Biopharma in particular is very different from sectors where revenue comes long before the full maturity of a company, even in regulated markets (e.g., the automotive industry). Nearly all early stage biopharma start-ups depend on partnerships with large pharmaceutical companies for their continued sustainability, and having a CVC fund as their shareholder significantly increases the likelihood of a successful partnership.[10]

GlaxoSmithKline (GSK) illustrates another model by which corporate venturing plays a role in innovation and incubation—one that involves the government and a major endowment. A joint partnership created between GSK; the U.K. Department for Business, Innovation and Skills; the Wellcome Trust; and Innovate UK provides both incubator and accelerator space at the Stevenage Bioscience Catalyst. At GSK's Stevenage site, start-ups have access to lab space and offices, and can draw upon world-leading expertise, networks, and scientific facilities.[11] In addition to participating in this close collaboration, SR One (GSK's venture arm) invests in start-ups housed in that incubator space. Overall, knowledge sharing is made to work both ways – from the corporate to the start-ups and vice versa.

NOTABLE CASES

Below are five leading cases that illustrate the various possible structures of corporate venture capital. Each serves as a kind of role model in its own unique way: GV in the scale and leadership of its activity; 3M New Ventures, which showcases more than any other company the potential of venturing empowered from inside the organization and the structural form to fit it; Cisco Investments' specific acquisition strategy and the fit of its venture to originate potential targets using both an internal GP and external GPs; Tencent Investment's massive scale of activity in China and elsewhere; and the financial services sector on venture activity around fintech, big data, and cybersecurity.

GV (Google Ventures)

---

[10] For a further discussion of incubators in biopharma, see Dr. Simone Botti's comments in an expert text box below.

[11] As a further support, GE also provides a lab on the same site with dedicated staff and advanced equipment that can be used by start-ups for running costly biotech R&D.

Launched with a single $15 million investment in 2009, GV has since completed more than 500 investments in over 300 companies and swelled its portfolio to $1.5 billion assets under management. The fund has a particular interest in big data applications, digital health, and cybersecurity, but has also invested in a coffee roasting company. Recently, GV has been the most active CVC fund in the world, investing in over 70 unique companies in 2017. GV often syndicates with lead VC firms such as Kleiner Perkins, SV Angel, and Andreessen Horowitz. Y Combinator also feeds many deals to GV. Until 2015, nearly half of its investments were seed and Series A, 25% Series B, and the rest in later rounds; however, as of 2016, GV has been less active as a seed investor, shifting its attention to more mature companies instead. Notable investments include Uber, Nest, and Jet to name a few. CapitalG (formerly Google Capital), a cousin of GV, was launched in 2013, and focuses on investing in late stage growth companies. Its investments include Survey Monkey, Lending Club, Airbnb, Lyft, and Snap.

3M New Ventures

Originally a mining company, 3M has been dramatically transformed by growth due to its culture of encouraging employees to suggest new products, ultimately becoming a $30 billion business that sells over 50,000 products. 3M New Ventures is the firm's corporate venturing arm. It uses a unique CVC model of internally funded investment opportunities that do not fall into a particular operational area. 3M's success demonstrates how workers on the ground often have excellent ideas but need a platform to nurture them with an opportunity to spin out.

Cisco Investments

The CVC arm of Cisco Systems, Cisco Investments, started investing in 1993, and uses both the internal GP and external LP investment models. The underlying premise has been that when Cisco could not develop a product internally, it looked for smaller external companies that were easier to integrate into the corporation. This so-called "spin-in" strategy favors minority investments that give the company insight into new technologies without too much risk. These form a base to target acquisitions later. Since inception, Cisco Investments has taken positions in hundreds of companies. As of 2018, the fund invests $200 to $300 million annually, from series A to late stage growth investments, and has an active portfolio with over 120 portfolio companies as well as LP positions in over 35 funds globally. Main directions include big data and analytics, the Internet of Things, enterprise networking, security, connected mobility, and storage. Cisco Investments is managed by over 45 investment professionals located across the globe; four geographies—North America, China, Israel, and India—are formally emphasized.

Tencent Investment

Headquartered in Shenzhen, Tencent Holdings Limited is one of the largest Internet companies in the world and has the same market value as Alibaba. It offers web portals, mobile applications, telecommunications, ecommerce, social network applications, and much more.[12] Tencent Investment, the CVC arm of Tencent Holdings, acts as an internal GP and is among the most active funds globally. It invested in 163 companies during 2018, ranging from several $2 million seed investments to as much as $4 billion for 13% of Meituan-Dianping.

---

[12] As of July 2019, both Tencent's market cap and that of Alibaba were each about $450 billion.

Financial institutions

Historically, banks invested in VC before floating through an IPO. This approach has largely disappeared since the dotcom crash, aided by the poor financial returns from investing in VC over the subsequent decade, as well as the increased regulatory restrictions and bank capital adequacy requirements. Attention has shifted to fintech as an attempt to combat the trend of disintermediation—where financial services such as foreign exchange transactions are bypassed—and the overall surge in Internet banking. In addition, algorithmic trading, big data, and cybersecurity have become hot-button issues. Corporate venturing activity in fintech is now globally widespread across numerous financial institutions, including hedge funds, insurance companies, and data service providers. Citigroup has emerged as a leader in corporate venturing through Citi Ventures, which most frequently invests in late stage rounds with a strong emphasis on fintech and technological solutions.

REFERENCES

Alvarez, G. E. and G. Dushnitsky (2016) "Are Entrepreneurial venture's innovation rates sensitive to investor complementary assets? Comparing biotech ventures backed by corporate and independent VCs", *Strategic Management Journal* 37: 819–834, May.

Chemmanur, T.J., E. Loutskina and X. Tian (2014) "Corporate venture capital, value creation, and innovation", *Review of Financial Studies* 27: 2434-2473, August.

Chesbrough, H. (2002) "Making Sense of Corporate Venture Capital", *Harvard Business Review* 80(3), March.

Hill, S.A. and J. Birkinshaw (2014) "Ambidexterity and survival in Corporate Venture Units", *Journal of Management* 40(7), 1899-1931.

Horowitz, B. (2014) *The Hard Thing about Hard Things*, HarperCollins Publishers, New York.

Ivanov, V.I. and F. Xie (2010) "Do corporate venture capitalists add value to start-up firms? Evidence from IPOs and acquisitions of VC-backed companies financial", *Financial Management* 39: 129–152, Spring.

Lerner, J. (2012) *The architecture of innovation: The economics of creative organizations*, Harvard Business Review Press.

Lerner, J. (2013) "Corporate venturing", *Harvard Business Review*: 86-94, October.

Park, B. and E.P.M. Vermeulen (2015) "Debunking myths in corporate venture capital: What works, what does not, and how to make it happen", *Journal of US-China Public Administration* 12(10): 764-776, October.

Volans Ventures Ltd. (2014) *Investing in breakthrough corporate venture capital*, Research Report: http://archive.volans.com/wp-content/uploads/2014/05/BreakthroughCVC.pdf

In his own words: Alexander Schlaepfer, Partner at Swisscom Ventures

New structures to avoid CVC failure

CVC failure is not only a matter of difficulty on the level of collaboration between start-ups and large corporates (and therefore poor "innovation" results for the corporate) but also an issue in financial performance that often leads to shutting-down. Many CVC arms do not have clear financial objectives and are – in the best case – expected "not to lose the money" as they are driven primarily as another R&D effort. Obviously, such CVC units are cut down quickly when the mother-company moves into cost-cutting mode during an economic slow-down as they are unable to demonstrate a positive financial contribution. At the same time, demonstrating "innovation benefits" is very difficult. Many such open-innovation use-cases that are good for PR but provide little to the bottom-line.

There is an increasing realization in the CVC industry that you must be able to demonstrate financial returns at the level of the company's weighted average cost of capital to be sustainable over a longer period of time. This is, among other, the reason why more mature CVC's have taken the GP or the LP-model as this makes financial performance more transparent and allows CVC teams to be compensated performance-based in line with VC industry standards.

Is there a new model of CVC emerging? A handful of CVC units have demonstrated sustained financial returns over the last decade and have built a track record that matches the one of top decile Silicon Valley funds. Intel Capital is such an example, Softbank (a Japanese Telco at its origin) is another and, we like to believe, ourselves – Swisscom Ventures – as well.

These CVC units have shifted from being a mere "innovation enabler" to what can be described as a corporate venture investment centre of competence with a clear focus on producing financial returns to the mother-company – Softbank with their Vision Fund is taking that to the extreme in the sense that Softbank is now perceived an investment fund manager rather than a Telco - at least internationally. South Africa's Naspers – who hold a 31% stake in Tencent for an original investment of $32 million in 2001 is a similar case.

In the new CVC model, corporate management has realized, that the collective competencies and resources of the mother-company can be leveraged to a) make better investment decisions and b) accelerate the growth of the portfolio companies post-investment (with channel partnerships, sourcing agreements and just hands-on support like introducing other corporates to the start-up). Hence, corporate resources create value in the portfolio which – hopefully – results in better investment outcomes.

Interestingly, several CVC in the Telecom space have embraced this model. Besides Softbank mentioned above, Deutsche Telekom Capital Partners, Telstra and ourselves, Swisscom clearly pursue this strategy of being a "value adding" investor and we have structured ourselves accordingly (with independent funds).

At Swisscom Ventures, we have closed in 2018 a CHF 200 million co-investment fund with 14 Swiss institutional investors (pensions funds, family offices) that now invests systematically along Swisscom Ventures in every new investment we are making (2018-2027). Swisscom set up the GP and is receiving fees and carried interest from this fund. Testra and DTCP are in the process of setting up similar structures.

In his own words: Dr. Simone Botti, Co-Founder and former Head of the Israel Bioincubator Fund—Merck Ventures

On the powerful role of corporate incubators in life sciences

Merck Ventures is the strategic, CVC arm of the biopharmaceutical division of Merck KGaA, Darmstadt, Germany.

A corporate incubator fund fills a real gap in life sciences. It is not necessarily the best solution, for example, for mobile applications or for the Internet economy. In those cases, an incubator or an accelerator is mainly a place to generate ideas and to go around and meet people that may have interesting outlooks, but ultimately, the time to market is so quick that an incubator fund is probably not necessary. However, in the life sciences industry, there is an undeniable and very large gap to fill between the first instance of a particular technology and the final product. The classic example is moving from a potentially interesting biological insight developed in an academic lab to an approved drug. In such cases (and in other similar cases), there is a need for a very hands-on approach to validate and develop the technology, and an incubator fund might be what is missing to bring academic discoveries to a stage where a biotech company can be further funded.

Ours is a VC incubator, similar to the ones of Pfizer, Johnson & Johnson, and other biotech companies. We all invest in an incubator because we believe that there is a definite gap, where attention to detail and a hands-on approach might make the difference to bring a technology from the level of academic science to clinical trials and further.

However, our incubator model only fits regions with a very high density of technological innovation. It works well in places where you have strong tech clusters, a venture infrastructure, and enough modules of the ecosystem that can also take part in the relay race, picking up what has been produced in the incubator and moving it forward—like passing the baton on to the next person.

15 Crowdfunding

The crowd is not led by the head but by the heart
Hungarian Proverb

INTRODUCTION

Crowdfunding is the practice of raising small amounts of capital from a large number of individuals to finance a project or business venture. Due to the increasing difficulty of attracting conventional sources of early stage capital, crowdfunding has emerged as an alternative source of financing. Using an online platform and spreading through social networks, it enables the entrepreneur to expand the pool of potential investors from whom funds can be raised beyond the traditional circle of relatives, business angels, and venture capital. Over the last few years, crowdfunding has gone from marginal to mainstream, complementing the funding and aiding to bridge the equity gap in early stage ventures.

While our main focus in this chapter is on equity, crowdfunding campaigns actually have a broader set of purposes. Most of the statistics refer to four crowdfunding models: donations, rewards, lending, and equity. However, in the last couple years, a fifth category has emerged: real estate crowdfunding.

Averaging over 500 new project launches a day, many of these ventures are technologically oriented, but an overwhelming number of projects come from the music and film industries. In fact, one of the pioneers of online crowdfunding is Electric Eel Shock, a Japanese rock band, which raised £10,000 in 2004 in order to fund the making of a music record. In return, they offered their backers a lifetime membership on the band's guest list. The record for the highest reported crowdfunded project to date belongs to Star Citizen, an online space flight simulation game which reportedly raised over $139 million from 1.7 million individual backers between 2012 and 2016.[1] In November 2015, Glowforge's "3D laser printer" attracted $27.9 million in pre-order sales, breaking the record for the most crowdfunded sales in 30 days.[2]

According to the Massolution Crowdfunding 2015 Report, the global crowdfunding industry has grown immensely in recent years, especially after the financial crisis of 2008.[3] It more than doubled annually between 2012 and 2015, raising $2.7 billion of investments worldwide in 2012 versus $34.4 billion in 2015. However, as stated by the crowdfunding industry itself, there is a tendency to parade exaggerated statistics by including peer-to-peer (P2P) marketplace lending as a form of crowdfunding, as it makes up 70% of the total crowdfunded amount. Most companies in the P2P lending space do not view themselves as crowdfunding vehicles. Yet, even without P2P, $10 billion is an impressive figure. The breakdown for the 2015 data is $25.1 billion of lending, followed by $2.85 billion in donations, $2.68 billion for rewards, $2.56 billion of equity

---

[1] https://robertsspaceindustries.com/funding-goals. In return, backers receive virtual rewards in the form of tiered pledge packages, which include a spaceship and credits to buy additional equipment and to cover initial costs in the virtual economy, like fuel and rental fees.

[2] Another record of a sort belongs to Zack Brown, whose initial campaign goal was only $10 but the campaign raised around $55,000 in 2014 for making a bowl of potato salad. After the campaign went viral, Brown ended up making a 3,000-pound potato salad.

[3] 2015CF Crowdfunding Industry Report, Massolution, 2016.

(start-ups and real estate), and the rest are hybrids. North America is estimated to comprise 50% of global crowdfunding activity, followed by Asia (30%), and Europe (20%). More granular data is tracked for the United States, where equity offerings for start-ups raised $1.2 billion in 2015 and real estate offerings were $900 million.[4]

HOW IT WORKS

While the term crowdfunding has only been in use for the last decade or so, the practice dates back centuries.[5] Crowdfunding in its various forms began as early as the 1700s when authors and publishers would advertise literary projects for the public to subscribe to. A book would then be written and published only if enough subscribers indicated their readiness to purchase it. Although the actual flow of cash would not begin until the publication was released, the list of subscribers created the necessary confidence among writers and publishers to undertake the venture's risk.

A boost to new-era crowdfunding came in the form of the Jumpstart Our Business Startups (JOBS) Act in the United States, which lifted the ban on "general solicitation" and advertising in private placements of securities. Designed to encourage funding of small businesses by easing various securities regulations, it was passed and signed in 2012, and the final rules and forms went into effect in May 2016. The JOBS Act substantially changed a number of laws and regulations, thereby making it easier for companies to raise capital privately. Small offerings through crowdfunding were exempted from the requirement to register public offerings with the SEC, with the condition that any Internet funding platform be certified by the government. Importantly, participation is not restricted to accredited investors, although they do need to meet certain criteria.[6]

Over time, crowdfunding has continued to evolve into different forms. In recent years, investors are most often attracted via Internet-mediated platforms and social networks, thereby creating a three-person dialogue between (1) project initiators who propose the venture to be funded, (2) individuals who support the idea, and (3) a moderating organization (the "platform") that brings the parties together to launch the project. Individuals (the "crowd") indicate a willingness to back projects they believe in, triggering the herding process. Project initiators benefit as they obtain low-cost capital, exposure, and feedback on their venture projects. Many start-ups will crowdfund a small amount of capital purely for the exposure it brings. For instance, numerous crowdfunding videos have gone viral on social media, and these can provide a vast amount of low-cost publicity for start-ups.

It is estimated that up to 85% of the individuals who back projects are not serial investors, but backers who invested in only one campaign.[7] Indeed, successful campaigns are typically those that created a critical mass of funding by first mobilizing the entrepreneurs' own close social circles—friends, family and their immediate networks. Once certain traction has been attained, then the intermediary harnesses its platform to

---

[4] Real estate crowdfunding in Asia only started in 2016.

[5] The earliest recorded use of the word was in 2006 by Michael Sullivan in fundavlog (http://wordspy.com/index.php?word=crowdfunding).

[6] One of the conditions of this exemption in the United States is an annual aggregate limit on the amount each person invests in offerings of this type, tiered by the person's net worth or annual income. The limits are $2,000 or 5% (whichever is greater) for people earning up to $100,000, and $10,000 or 10% (whichever is less) for people earning above $100,000.

[7] Dushnitsky and Marom (2013).

leverage the initial interest further by approaching the general crowd of potential backers. Hence, this model is built on driving all effort and social networks to a single specific campaign launched on a single platform.

TYPES OF CROWDFUNDING

Donations

Donation-based crowdfunding is essentially the collective effort of individuals to raise money for a charitable cause. An array of platforms has emerged in order to facilitate philanthropic contributions without the need to commit each backer to a large donation.

Rewards

In reward-based crowdfunding, entrepreneurs offer to pre-sell a product or service to individuals in exchange for funding. This source of funding is particularly helpful, for example, when a community wishes to support a local store in exchange for discounts or users want to prepay for the development of a product. It is a non-dilutive source of capital, whereby persons with creative ideas do not have to incur debt or sell equity in order to launch the venture. In fact, on many occasions, project initiators do not have to follow through with their initiatives at all if the goal is not met.[8]

Lending

Other forms of crowdfunding take on a somewhat different arrangement. P2P lending creates a platform for individuals to apply for loans and for investors to buy securities in funds that provide these micro loans. In recent years, the industry has grown substantially, attracting institutional investors. For instance, in 2013, Google invested $125 million in Lending Club, a platform for P2P lending, which went public in December 2014, raising almost $900 million in what was the largest U.S. technology IPO of 2014.[9]

Equity

In equity crowdfunding, individuals receive equity in exchange for their support of a venture. Here the entrepreneur is not only expected to make the product or service for which the capital is raised, but is also expected to establish the company through which equity will be distributed to investors. This approach has been called "crowdfund investing," "hyperfunding," and "crowd investing," among other terms, but the term "equity crowdfunding" has become standard.

Equity crowdfunding fills in the gap in the nascent phases of setting up a business, often at the idea or prototype stage. Unlike the traditional model of business angels, it uses social networking for intermediated capital. This type of crowdfunding is strongly linked to the stage prior to business angels where funding is obtained from friends and family. Given its position as a shareholding type investment, equity crowdfunding is dealt at length below.

---

[8] Reward-based crowdfunding may take the form of a "Keep-It-All" or "All-or-Nothing" campaign. In the former model, a project initiator sets a fundraising goal and keeps the entire amount raised regardless of whether or not the goal is met; in the latter, the amount raised is kept only if the campaign goal is met.

[9] http://www.forbes.com/sites/navathwal/2014/12/18/lendingclub-ondeck-ipos-billion-dollar-valuations-are-just-the-beginning-for-the-online-lending-market/#17401364240e

Real estate

Another application of crowdfunding is in the real estate market. Real estate crowdfunding helps to fund mortgages, home buyer down payments, and financing of commercial projects. It also bundles investors to create equity real estate purchases. Real estate is one of the fastest growing segments of the crowdfunding phenomenon, with more than 150 platforms launched worldwide over the past couple years.

EQUITY CROWDFUNDING

As noted, the key differentiator in equity-based crowdfunding is that members of the crowd become actual investors, acquiring equity stakes in private companies. Examples of equity crowdfunding platforms are Crowdcube in the United Kingdom, AngelList in the United States, and OurCrowd, based in Israel. As of 2017, 25 funding portals have registered with the SEC and FINRA to operate in the United States.[10] In the United Kingdom, the equity crowdfunding leader territory in Europe, this investment form represented 15% of all seed and venture funding in 2016.[11] Looking forward, Crowdfund Research reported projections that equity crowdfunding might exceed standard venture capital models in volume by 2020.[12]

Vulkan et al. (2016) performed an in-depth study of equity crowdfunding by examining over 600 U.K. equity campaigns, encompassing over 1,700 investors and 65,000 investments. They found that equity crowdfunding differs from the typical reward-based crowdfunding in a number of important ways, including much higher campaign goals and much higher amounts pledged. The average campaign goal was £138,000 with a wide heterogeneity in the amount asked by individual projects—from £2,500 to more than £1 million. The level of desired investment has climbed substantially over the past several years, reaching an average of over £200,000 in 2015 and an average pre-money valuation of about £1.6 million; this is in sharp contrast to reward-based campaigns, which had an average goal of less than $10,000.[13] Transaction fees in equity crowdfunding reported by Vulkan et al. (2016) were a one-off fee of up to 7.5% from successfully funded businesses, and an additional success fee from investors equal to 7.5% of the profits made as a result of their investment.

In terms of the number of backers per equity crowdfunding campaign, successful campaigns had an average of 158 backers, more than five times the average number of investors in failed campaigns. In each calendar month, about 8.5% of the running campaigns reach their target. This success rate has consistently improved over time, doubling from 5% in 2012 to more than 11% in 2015.

An important effect of such platforms is the opportunity they represent both for investors and for entrepreneurial companies. These platforms are disrupting how start-up companies are funded, "democratizing" both sides of the marketplace. By opening up opportunities to investors from around the world, the phenomenon is breaking down the geographic barriers that plague many entrepreneurial

---

[10] https://www.finra.org/about/funding-portals-we-regulate.

[11] https://www.crowdfundinsider.com/2016/10/91794-rise-equity-crowdfunding-report-crowdfundinghub

[12] https://medium.com/crowdfund-research/top-trends-in-equity-crowdfunding-7db76efd7cae.

[13] Mollick (2014).

companies, particularly those in areas where venture capital funding is scarce. Investors across the globe can now access an asset class previously only available to large institutional investors and experienced angels.[14]

As venture capital and private equity have effectively captured large portions of the overall value creation in the economy, individual investors have increasingly sought exposure to these asset classes. Equity crowdfunding allows the individual investor to tap into investment opportunities once reserved only for larger players like venture capital firms. Investing in private companies allows investors to diversify their investment portfolios with potential ROI unavailable from other asset classes, while supporting innovative technologies that are shaping the future.

FORMS OF EQUITY CROWDFUNDING

Equity crowdfunding platforms can be broadly categorized into two groups: those open to all investors, and those open only to accredited investors. Further, most platforms provide access to investments but do not perform the same level of due diligence that a venture capital firm does, nor do they invest alongside the investor.

Crowdcube, founded in 2011 to advance British start-ups, raised over £200 million from more than 330,000 unaccredited investors by the end of 2016; two of its start-ups have had exits. San Francisco-based CircleUp, also founded in 2011, brought $285 million in capital from accredited investors to emerging consumer products brands and had 66 portfolio companies during that period. In the United States as a whole, during the period from May 2016 to October 2017, 61,000 investors funded $52 million in 168 successful Regulation CF offerings that reached their minimum funding target.[15] OurCrowd, founded in 2013, raised and invested $440 million in 120 companies from within a community of 20,000 accredited investors from 112 countries by the end of 2016.[16]

In addition, platforms may vary in terms of portfolio company sector and stage. AngelList, for instance, tends to focus more on hardware and software high-tech solutions. Others, such as OurCrowd, are sector and stage agnostic.

While providing potential benefits to the average sophisticated investor, the choice of platform can significantly affect the investment outcome. An equity crowdfunding platform that is basically an online brokerage may not perform more than perfunctory due diligence on an investment opportunity, nor provide much help post investment. Investors must take steps to understand the risks and potential of their investment. Likewise, the companies on the receiving end of investments from such platforms do not receive marketing and other business support. Those platforms that provide professional-level involvement can reduce risk for a private investor's portfolio, providing an extra layer of due diligence before investment, and valuable support after.

A new direction in equity crowdfunding is the development of products that aggregate investments into funds. These hold the promise of reducing risk through diversification and traditional portfolio management. But here too, the true efficacy and popularity of such vehicles will only become known over time.

---

[14] OurCrowd, for instance, has received deal flow from 46 different countries and made investments in six of them, funded by active investors in 37 different countries.

[15] https://wefinder.com/stat accessed on November 8, 2017.

[16] https://www.israel21c.org/ourcrowd-marks-4-years-320m-raised-100-startups-9-exits/

INITIAL COIN OFFERINGS

Initial Coin Offerings (ICOs) are fundraising campaigns using cryptocurrencies as a mechanism to pre-sell a company or service. The ICO approach has recently become a massive new source of funding for start-ups in the cryptocurrency ecosystem, enabling them to potentially raise hundreds of millions of dollars, often on the basis of nothing but white papers. Between 2014 and May 2018, over 650 entities originating from more than 50 countries issued tokens and raised approximately $13 billion from investors by selling their own virtual currencies to investors.[17] During these years, ICOs dwarfed other forms of crowdfunding campaigns by a great measure.

Coins can be classified into three types.[18] The first type of coins is "cryptocurrencies," which are broadly inspired by Bitcoin. Through technical innovation, cryptocurrencies attempt to function either more easily, more securely, or more rapidly (e.g., by reducing transaction verification times) than fiat currencies and other competing cryptocurrencies. Other examples besides Bitcoin are Litecoin, Bitcoin Cash, Monero, and Bytecoin. The second type of coins is "infrastructure coins," which aim to offer a platform for developing smart contracts (i.e., hosting the development and launching of new cryptocurrencies and tokens based on blockchain technology); examples include Ethereum, NEO, and NXT. The third and final type of coins is "utility coins," more generally referred to as "tokens." These tokens entitle their holders to receive specific products or services from a wide range of the same, including real estate, insurance, cloud storage, and media and entertainment, among others. Tokens represent a large and growing portion of the trading volume in the cryptocurrency market.

During the ICO process, companies exchange tokens against fiat currencies (e.g., USD) or cryptocurrencies (e.g., Bitcoin) in order to fund the development of their products or services. ICOs have the form of reward-based crowdfunding campaigns since they are generally designed so that investors do not get an ownership stake in the cryptocurrency-based start-ups. These companies create and sell their own virtual currency, generally under rules similar to those used for well-known virtual currencies like Bitcoin and Ether (the virtual currency inside the Ethereum network). The new tokens are usually designed so that they can only be used on a computing service that the company is building.

After the ICO is completed, all subsequent exchanges of coins or tokens are transacted with their own free-floating value on the cryptocurrency market, which operates on the blockchain to enable verification, security, and data integrity. The main public cryptocurrency exchanges on which tokens are listed include Binance, Bitfinex, and Kraken.

ICOs share characteristics with both crowdfunding and virtual currencies: they are generally pre-revenue; retail investors buy substantial fractions of these offerings; and the volatility of the offerings is extreme. Investors seem to be highly motivated by speculation in the value of the cryptocurrency or token rather than investing in the underlying company growth, leading regulators across the globe to watch this matter with some concern. China first issued a blanket ban on all domestic ICO platforms in late 2017, closing down all platforms and cryptocurrency exchanges in the country. Similarly, Korea placed a ban on domestic ICOs. In the United States, grave concerns were expressed by both regulators and lawmakers, leading the SEC to

---

[17] Source: www.coinschedule.com.
[18] Based on Bourveau et al. (2018), who also provide a thorough review of blockchain, cryptocurrencies, and Initial Coin Offerings.

declare in 2018 that the ICO ecosystem is what "the wider securities marketplace would look like without regulation," thereby hinting the direction regulators lean to take.[19]

While the underlying blockchain technology itself is a system of record that has much promise, ICOs are very speculative and have strongly utilized the hype around cryptocurrencies.

CONCLUSION

Crowdfunding is a form of financing that is part of a larger trend on alternative sources of capital that will likely continue to grow and evolve over the next few years. It allows entrepreneurs to appeal to a broad audience through an online platform in order to get their innovative ideas off the ground. Although the goal is to reach out to the general public, for a campaign to be successful, the initial traction has to come from the direct social network of the entrepreneur. Crowdfunding has now gained general acceptance and appears to not be controversial. P2P lending and real estate crowdfunding keep expanding. Crowdfunding, being centered on social networking, is also a very natural platform for donations and rewards-based campaigns.

However, the verdict is still out with respect to our prime focus, which is equity campaigns. As yet, there are no definitive statistics on their success in comparison to other forms of early stage financing such as angel investing. The approach is novel by allowing retail investors access to early stage companies side by side with high-net-worth investors and professional venture capitalists. But this novel approach is accompanied by substantial risks as well, both for specific investors and for entrepreneurs. First, the dynamics of campaigns are often centered on trust and a herding behavior of the crowd. Second, due diligence may be absent given the very early stage of the business and the modest investment size of each campaign. Third, in cases where the investor base is small and diverse, governance is rarely considered and negotiated. Fourth, early crowd backers are unlikely to keep investing in future rounds and hence, may be washed away and lose their economics as liquidation preferences are dictated by future investors and, in the event of a future down round. A fifth type of risk is the health of the platform itself. As the industry matures, the risk of failure seems to be decreasing. In 2016, only one crowdfunding platform went out of business when it did not meet the mandatory statutory requirements of U.S. regulators.[20]

Although there are no definitive statistics yet on exits, in light of the overall grim odds with respect to early stage investments and the additional considerations above, the financial performance of investors in equity crowdfunding may prove disheartening. What can improve the odds is a choice of platform that can perform material due diligence on the individual investment. A proper diversification can also significantly reduce the risk of loss. As noted, it is only over time that the efficacy and reliability of this investing approach will become apparent.

---

[19] Speaking to CNBC, SEC Commissioner Robert Jackson made the comparison when talking about the agency's role in regulating cryptocurrencies and ICO-derived tokens, and the prospect of tighter controls in the market: "If you want to know what our markets would look like with no securities regulation, what it would look like if the SEC didn't do its job? The answer is the ICO market. Investors are having a hard time telling the difference between investments and fraud." (April 30, 2018)

[20] https://medium.com/crowdfund-research/top-trends-in-equity-crowdfunding-7db76efd7cae.

REFERENCES

Bourveau, T., E. T. De George, A. Ellahie and D. Macciocchi (2018) "Initial Coin Offerings: Early Evidence on the Role of Disclosure in the Unregulated Crypto Market," Working Paper, June 2018 (https://papers.ssrn.com/sol3/papers.cfm?abstract_id=3193392).

Dushnitsky, G. and D. Marom (2013) "Crowd monogamy," *Business Strategy Review* 24: 24-26.

Mollick, E. (2014) The dynamics of crowdfunding: An exploratory study. *Journal of Business Venturing* 29(1): 1-16.

Vulkan, N., T. Astebro and M. F. Sierra (2016) "Equity crowdfunding: A new phenomena," *Journal of Business Venturing* 5: 37-49.

In his own words: Jon Medved, Founder and CEO of OurCrowd

We're at a special time in history. One industry after another is being disrupted by online technologies—and the stakes are huge. People are concerned about losing their jobs or their businesses, while at the same time they're afraid of missing out on potentially incredible opportunities. Equity crowdfunding itself is a disruptive force, yet if done right, it has the potential for democratizing venture capital and fostering innovation in a way that is unprecedented.

What do I mean by "done right"? Although I think it is a good thing that there are multiple models for equity crowdfunding, and I have great respect for the pioneers in this field—particularly those in the United Kingdom—many platforms do not perform appropriate due diligence on investments, and investors are buying common shares with no board representation and no post-investment management.

OurCrowd sources and vets prospective deals from around the world, investing in two or three out of over 150 prospects each month. We commit our own capital into every deal, alongside leading institutional and venture investors, and it is then offered to the 20,000 accredited investors on our platform. They may invest either in individual companies, or through a pre-funded account allowing default allocation, or through index and sector funds. This diversifies our portfolio and offers investors a variety of options to facilitate diversification.

We like to take a healthy minority stake between 10% and 25% and be part of a syndicate. We aggregate our investors into a limited partnership special purpose vehicle (SPV). The SPV then buys preferred stock in the company with the same rights and benefits as the large investors, such as anti-dilution rights, pre-emptive rights, information rights, and board seats. The SPV also prevents the capitalization table of the company from being overloaded with numerous uninvolved investors; this makes other venture capital or corporate investors more comfortable. OurCrowd's economics are based on charging its platform investors a post-investment management fee and a success fee at exit. By not charging a placement fee from the investee companies, we align ourselves solely with our investors.

Our model of crowdfunding attempts to extend beyond funding by working closely with the companies post investment on matters from marketing strategy to recruitment to connecting with potential partners or acquisition targets. We mobilize the crowd not just to raise money, but to act as a force multiplier, drawing on the network for ideas and connections. Likewise, the crowd acts as a second level of assessment in our due diligence process. We might decide to put $2 million into a company, with 5% of OurCrowd's own capital at the same terms as our investors, then offer it on our platform. Sometimes, the crowd says, "No, thank you"!

Our investor base covers well over 100 countries, and while the majority of our portfolio companies are Israeli, a large and growing minority are based around the world. We work with global partners for both sourcing and distribution, such as an accelerator with Reliance Industries in India and Motorola in the United States, and offerings on the platforms of UOB in Singapore and NAB in Australia. This range greatly extends the number of small investors who have the chance to capture potential opportunities unavailable from other asset classes, while also supporting innovative technologies that are shaping the future.

Finally, for early stage investors planning their capital allocation, it is crucial to manage expectations as it is the norm for growing businesses to take more time and money than originally planned for. Avoiding dilution requires investing multiples of capital in subsequent funding rounds compared to the initial early stage investment. While the anticipation is for future investors to pay higher share prices, the notional dilution is actually a good thing. As the cake becomes bigger, it is difficult—and perhaps unwise—to maintain the same percentage slice. The focus should be on total return and the stake in terms of value rather than on the percentages.

16 Incubators and Accelerators

Not houses finely roofed, nor the stones of walls well built, nor canals, nor dockyards make the city, but men able to use their opportunity.
Alcaeus (600 BCE)

INTRODUCTION

Pre-seed and seed companies require far more than just an innovative idea and funding to get off the ground. Over the years, the venture toolkit has expanded to include accelerators, incubators, and hybrids of all sorts in order to fill in this gap. The terms "incubators" and "accelerators" are often used interchangeably; however, they are very different models.[1] In this chapter, we elaborate on these two venture support tools, explaining their modus operandi, histories of development, and differences.

Essentially, accelerators support early stage companies through mentorship and exposure to the wider entrepreneurial ecosystem. Programs are typically a few months long and highly competitive, and they accept participants on a cohort-basis. Incubators support early to late stage companies by providing services such as office space, administrative services, and business advice. Entry is generally less competitive and participants are accepted one at a time, so that development benchmarks and "graduation" requirements are tailored on an individual basis, and not as part of a cohort.

INCUBATORS

In 1956, the largest industrial company in Batavia, New York closed down, leaving a 20-acre multi-storey building complex vacant. The Mancuso family then purchased the complex and, after having trouble finding a single company willing to rent, decided to pursue a different model. The family divided and rented the space to separate businesses, offering shared office services, business mentoring, and assistance with raising capital. Known as Batavia Industrial Center, this complex soon became the world's first, and longest-running, incubator. Since then, the concept of incubation gradually expanded to the rest of the United States in the 1980s, and later to Europe and the rest of the world. Estimates for the total number of incubators globally vary but are in the thousands.[2] By comparison, in 1980, there were only 12 incubators in North America.

Business incubators generally take the form of publicly or privately funded programs that support early to late stage ventures by providing office space and shared administrative services. Incubators typically do not take the same "hands-on" approach that characterizes accelerators, nor do they offer the proliferation of opportunities in a high-paced entrepreneurial environment. As noted, participants are accepted one at a time

---

This chapter was written by Lauren Talmor, Duke University School of Law.

[1] The term accelerator is more commonly used today as incubator sounds to many outdated and "sleepy."

[2] The National Business Incubation Association (NBIA) has more than 1,400 members in the United States and a total 1,900 members in 60 nations (source: https://www.entrepreneur.com/article/52802, retrieved July 29, 2019).

and usually remain in the program for one to five years. The duration of residency is tailored to fit individual development benchmarks and "graduation" requirements are linked to revenue goals or staffing levels rather than time, offering longer stays for ventures with lengthier R&D cycles, such as those in life sciences. Entry is less competitive than in accelerators, and participants are sometimes asked to pay a small monthly fee.

Many for-profit incubators were launched in the late 1990s seeking to "hatch" businesses quickly and bring profits. Over time, however, and especially in the aftermath of the dotcom burst, the majority of these programs closed, and financial sponsors turned to creating accelerators instead. As such, incubators today often take the form of either government or university incubation programs. The majority of the programs are sponsored by government entities and economic development organizations, such as the World Bank programs. Incubator programs typically concentrate on socioeconomic policy needs, including fostering a community's entrepreneurial climate, building local industry clusters, and encouraging ventures founded by women and minority individuals. University incubators differ in that they have developed out of an increasing effort to generate financial return on scientific output, and are aimed at helping technology start-ups. Since researchers are not entrepreneurs by nature, this model has allowed universities to link academics, alumni, and students to resources in order to facilitate the commercialization of technological innovations. Joining forces with entrepreneurs has enabled scientists and other academics to essentially take ideas from the lab to the shelf, transferring knowledge and expertise to the economy at large.

ACCELERATORS

As the name suggests, accelerator programs are designed to accelerate the entrepreneur's learning process by compressing years of experience into a three- to six-month period in a high-paced and venture-vibrant environment. These programs support early stage companies through training, mentorship, and financing within a fixed-term, cohort-based setting. Entry to the programs is very competitive, with application acceptance rates of around 1–3% for some of the top accelerators. Although there is no magic number, 20 to 25 teams (80 to 100 individuals) per batch form a critical mass, allowing for sector diversity and for a number of exceptional teams to lead the group discussions and interaction, thereby generating a positive effect on the rest of the cohort.[3] Programs typically culminate in a public pitch event and a "demo day," where the start-ups present their ideas to a large audience of qualified investors.

Broadly speaking, accelerators help early stage companies define and build their initial products, identify promising customer segments, and secure capital and human resources. In addition, many accelerator programs make a small seed investment ($22,000 on average, but this could range up to $150,000) in their start-ups at the beginning of the program and receive 5–7% of the company's equity in return.[4] Equally important, accelerators offer intensive mentoring and a profusion of networking opportunities with both peer start-ups and successful entrepreneurs, program graduates, venture capitalists, and angel investors. Participating start-ups are also linked early on with corporations that could help with technology development, distribution channels, or funding; this may be achieved through speakers and discussions on corporate-specific innovation needs.

[3] Public Policy Forum on Venture Capital and Innovation, Quebec City, 2012. Main Conclusions, p. 17.
[4] Fehder and Hochberg (2014).

Unlike incubators, accelerators are a relatively new phenomenon. The first seed accelerator program was launched in Boston, Massachusetts in 2005 by Y Combinator. Since it launched, the program has funded over 2,000 start-ups with a combined valuation of over $100 billion.[5] Y Combinator has maintained its prominence in the field, and is responsible for the rise of unicorns such as Airbnb, Stripe and Dropbox. In 2006, another worldwide network, TechStars, was launched in Boulder, Colorado. Since its inception, TechStars has funded nearly 1,600 start-ups, with staggering success rates (87% of them are still active).[6]

The two programs have evolved differently over the years, with Y Combinator consolidating its activities to a single Silicon Valley location in 2009, while TechStars has spread globally with thousands of events and over 10,000 mentors worldwide. To date, the two remain some of the most prestigious accelerator programs, along with names such as 500 Startups, MassChallenge, SOSV and Start-Up Chile. Unsurprisingly, many accelerator programs are concentrated in start-up hubs—Silicon Valley, London, Boston, New York, Berlin, and Tel Aviv, to name a few. In North America, there were 178 accelerator programs by the end of 2016.[7] Many of these were concentrated in Silicon Valley, Boston, New York, and Vancouver, accounting for almost half of all accelerators in the United States and nearly two-thirds of accelerator investments in the last decade.[8]

The rapid growth of the market since Y Combinator's early days has led to an influx of investments, with 3,000 U.S.-based start-ups having received investments with a median investment of $100,000. Overall, these companies raised a total of $107 billion in funding, most of which came from additional venture capital and other financial sources. Further attesting to the success of the accelerator model is the fact that the median and average valuation of these companies upon graduation from the program reached $5.5 million and $7.1 million, respectively. For the 10 years of data till 2015, ventures that went on to raise additional capital had a median valuation of $15.6 million and an average valuation of $90 million. In 2015, these figures reached $30 million and $196 million, respectively.[9]

With the growing popularity of accelerator programs in the United States, it did not take long until the idea crossed the pond and gathered support in Europe's growing start-up ecosystem. In 2007, Seedcamp was founded as a pan-European accelerator program by a group of veteran European entrepreneurs and venture capital firms. Startupbootcamp followed in 2010, and today hosts a network of programs across Europe, the Middle East, and Asia. In total, there were 193 main accelerator programs in Europe in 2016, led by the United Kingdom (44), Spain (26), and France (23). Combined, they raised €47 billion in funding, which was invested in 3,700 start-ups.[10] While the number of accelerators and participating start-ups is comparable in Europe and North America, programs in Europe seem to receive, on average, half the funds invested in their North American counterparts.

Nearly two-thirds of the accelerators in North America are for-profit, whereas the remaining third are not-for-profit. Of all these programs, 56% are funded only with private capital while the remainder are funded in full or in part by public funding. Private capital is provided by high-net-worth individuals, angel groups, venture capital funds, and corporations, all of which are rewarded for their investments through equity in the start-ups. Public funding typically comes in the form of government grants.

---

[5] Y Combinator. Retrieved July 25, 2019, from https://www.ycombinator.com/

[6] TechStars. Retrieved July 25, 2019, from http://www.techstars.com/

[7] http://gust.com/accelerator_reports/2016/us_and_canada/

[8] Hathaway (2016).

[9] http://gust.com/usa-canada-accelerator-report-2015/

[10] http://gust.com/accelerator_reports/2016/europe/

Recent years have witnessed accelerator programs opening around the world, with giants like Google launching accelerator programs in Indonesia, Brazil, and India, and Microsoft starting programs in India, China, and Brazil. Exhibit 1 portrays the geographical spread of accelerator activity in 2015/6 in terms of number of accelerators, number of participating start-ups, and total invested capital.

Exhibit 1: Global overview: Number of accelerator programs and participating start-ups in 2015/6*

	Accelerators	Participating Start-Ups	Total Investment (in US$ millions)
North America	111	3,269	$107
Europe	113	3,701	$50
Latin America	62	1,795	$24
Middle East	47	1,172	$8
Asia Pacific	54	1,368	$18

* Number of accelerators is taken from the Gust 2015 report whereas the rest of the table has been updated in the Gust 2016 report (both referenced above).

It is important to emphasize that not all accelerators are created equal, and quality matters and varies greatly between programs. While the top programs seem to accelerate start-up development, most programs do not seem to live up to their intended purpose. The academic evidence suggests that the impact of many programs on participating ventures is ambiguous at best, and sometimes even harmful.[11] This diversity results in fierce competition among entrepreneurs for admission to strong accelerator programs. Nonetheless, in comparison to start-ups funded by top angel investment groups, accelerator graduates are more likely to receive their next round of funding significantly sooner.[12] Moreover, accelerators appear to have a positive impact on their broader ecosystems, attracting seed and early stage financing activity which spills over to non-accelerated companies as well.[13] By stimulating entrepreneurial growth in the wider regional economy, accelerators have attracted the attention of policymakers at all levels, from central government to municipalities.

DISCERNING BETWEEN ACCELERATORS, INCUBATORS, AND HYBRIDS

Incubator and accelerator programs engage differently with the ventures they host. Incubators support and collaborate with a small number of start-ups for as long as five years. Accelerator programs aim at rapidly screening a large number of start-ups focused in a particular region or technology for a fixed term (usually three months). Four distinct factors make accelerators unique: they are fixed term, cohort based, and mentorship driven, and typically culminate in a graduation or demo day. None of the other early stage

[11] Hallen et al. (2014).

[12] Winston-Smith and Hannigan (2015).

[13] Fehder and Hochberg (2014).

sponsors (i.e., incubators, angel investors, or seed stage venture capitalists) have these collective elements. While all may share the goal of cultivating early stage start-ups, each has its own distinct business model and incentive structure. Some of the supporting features that characterize accelerators are also common to incubators, which often results in a mistaken undifferentiated meaning. To compound this confusion, most organizations today are considered "hybrids" of accelerators and incubators, though they usually refer to themselves as accelerators. These businesses more resemble what might be called "angel investors plus" (i.e., angel investor services plus an additional element such as on-site office space and support services), rather than true accelerators. Exhibit 2 summarizes the key differences between incubators, angel investors, accelerators, and hybrid set-ups.

Accelerators have been dubbed the "gold standard" for mentoring and accrediting toward potential future funding. Their overall acceptance rates are low, their networks can help entrepreneurs reach innovation "superstars," and their equity share provides a greater alignment of interests with start-ups. Nevertheless, both incubators and accelerators rarely invest alone. Instead, they form partnerships with corporations or team up with other organizations in order to gain access to a greater number of high-quality start-ups.

Exhibit 2: A comparison of incubators, accelerators, and hybrids

	Incubators	**Angel Investors**	**Accelerators**	**Hybrid**
Duration	1–5 years	Ongoing	3–6 months	3 months to 2 years
Cohorts	No	No	Yes	No
Business Model	Rent; non-profit	Investment	Investment; can also be non-profit	Investment; can also be non-profit
Selection	Non-competitive	Competitive, ongoing	Competitive, cyclical	Competitive, ongoing
Venture Stage	Early or late	Early	Early	Early
Education	Ad hoc, human resources, legal	None	Seminars	Various incubator and accelerator practices
Mentorship	Minimal, tactical	As needed, by investor	Intense, by self and others	Staff expert support, some mentoring
Venture Location	On-site	Off-site	On-site	On-site

Source: Hathaway (2016)

THE CORPORATE INNOVATION TOOLKIT

We turn next to review the corporate angle in promoting incubators and accelerators. Corporations perceive growth through innovation as the surest, straightest route to maintain leadership. In search of new game-changing ideas and disruptive technologies, modern-day corporate venturing goes beyond traditional R&D efforts and M&A activities. As the search for innovation intensifies, companies are seeking new approaches to facilitate their growth. Expanding the venture toolkit has allowed for strategic and financial benefits as corporations are exposed to a wider range of new ideas than they could generate internally. Exhibit 3 summarizes the key distinctions between the different venture tools that facilitate growth from the corporate perspective.

Exhibit 3: Venture toolkit from the corporate perspective

	Business Incubation			
	Corporate Incubator	**Corporate Accelerator**	**Corporate Venture Capital**	**Corporate Strategic Partnerships**
Objective	Support start-ups with an array of business support resources and services, orchestrated by incubator	Support start-ups with a structured program along fixed curricula	Support existing companies with capital in exchange for equity shares	Partner with existing companies to drive joint value creation
Benefits to start-up partner	• Office space, hardware • Business skills training • Professional networks • Management support • Potential funding support	• Office space, hardware • Skilled mentorship and coaching • Start-up network • Technical support • Potential funding support	• Financial support • In many cases, close cooperation with corporate unit as equal partner • Mentorship (in some cases)	• Extend market potential • Close missing IP gap • Limit investments in noncore corporate capabilities • Create competitive advantage
Benefits to company	• Outsourced R&D function • Wider corporate growth options and investment opportunities • Enhanced employee recruitment and retention	• Wider search field for corporate development and growth options • "First pick" potential in case of promising start-up business	• Equity share in company with strong growth and profit potential • Portfolio extension, especially in advanced technologies and products	• Extend market potential • Close missing IP gap • Save investments in noncore corporate capabilities • Create competitive advantage
Investment	Up to 25 percent of equity	Partly without equity; in some cases up to 5 percent	20 percent or less	Possible equity exchange, depending on partnership format
Start-up stage	Early-stage, without existing business	Start-ups technically ready to "spread wings"	Small existing companies with high growth potential	Innovative companies but not necessarily new players
Time frame	12–36 months	Typically 3 months	5–7 years	Depends on product cycle

Source: BCG analysis.

Source: Brigl et al. (2014)

Accelerators and incubators have reached a very high level of popularity and acceptance, and they are now in use in over 40% of the top firms examined across seven innovation-intensive industries (up from a mere 2% in 2010).[14] In particular, financial services, consumer goods, and telecommunications companies rely on accelerators and incubators to search for innovations in adjacent industries. Working essentially as in-house start-ups, they complement conventional R&D by interacting with the outside entrepreneurial world.

The choice between the use of incubators and accelerators to complement traditional R&D efforts varies between industries and their business development schemes. Two models best explain best the corporate dilemma in the pursuit of growth through innovation: the tight-focus model and the wide-angle model.

The tight-focus model is designed to strengthen the core business by targeting innovations in adjacent fields as well as in the core itself. Most companies that follow this model opt for incubators rather than accelerators due to the relatively large equity investments involved in incubation, which promote close cooperation between the corporation and the participating start-ups. To facilitate the cooperation, incubators

---

[14] Brigl et al. (2014).

are typically located in close proximity to the corporate R&D facilities. The tight-focus model is employed by automotive, chemical, and some consumer goods companies as innovation of their core products is key.

Alternatively, companies that wish to tap into innovation across a broad spread of domains often follow the wide-angle model. This approach seeks to promote business development by emphasizing the transfer of expertise and practices, rather than cash, which is usually achieved through the use of accelerators. This model is particularly relevant to technology, media, telecommunications, and other fast-changing industries that continuously seek access to disruptive technologies. To cast their net as wide as possible, companies often locate their accelerator programs in a major science park or technological cluster.

However, there are many possible permutations, joint ventures, and innovative structures. For example, consider Paris-based MD Start, which was created in 2010 as the first collaboration between venture capital institutional investors and industry to accelerate the development of innovative medical technology ideas in Europe. Medtronic and LiveNova, both world leaders in medical device technology, alongside Sofinnova Partners, a leading life sciences venture capital firm, and Bpifrance, a French governmental development bank, joined forces to create an independent entity in order to provide financial and strategic resources to accelerate innovative medical technologies. Altogether, accelerators and innovators have been identified by large corporations as an essential vehicle to stay abreast on disruptive technological innovation, business development and for identifying potential acquisitions and joint ventures, however the particular approach is custom tailored based on the internal set up and the external environment.

REFERENCES

Brigl, M., A. Roos, F. Schmieg and D. Watten (2014) "Incubators, accelerators, venturing, and more: How leading companies search for their next big thing," Winning with Growth series, The Boston Consulting Group, June.

Fehder, D.C. and Y. Hochberg (2014) "Accelerators and the regional supply of venture capital investment," MIT working paper, September.

Hallen, B. L., C. B. Bingham and S. L. Cohen (2014) "Do accelerators accelerate? A study of venture accelerators as a path to success," Academy of Management Annual Meeting Proceedings, January.

Hathaway, I. (2016) "Accelerating growth: Startup accelerator programs in the United States," Brookings Institution: Advanced Industries Series 81, February.

Winston-Smith, S. and T. J. Hannigan (2015) "Swinging for the fences: How do top accelerators impact the trajectories of new ventures?" Temple University working paper, June.

In his own words: Gonçalo Amorim, Executive Director, Building Global Innovators

Building Global Innovators—IUL MIT Portugal Accelerator

Building Global Innovators (BGI) is a transnational, deep tech accelerator, based jointly in Lisbon, Portugal, and in Cambridge, Massachusetts. The initiative was originally part of the broader MIT Portugal program that was launched by the government in 2006 to advance Science and IP commercialization in the country's leading engineering and science universities, targeting key areas for economic development such as bioengineering, Engineering, Design and Advanced and Smart cities. This MIT Portugal Innovation & Entrepreneurship Initiative (MPP-IEI) was itself officially launched in 2010, with an aim to aspire technology entrepreneurs. It selects a cohort of start-ups in each so-called "edition" of the program, helping them scale up their ventures and preparing them for a global market launch. BGI is a spinoff of the MPP-IEI, incorporated in 2013 as a For Profit entity, providing support to its participating deep tech start-ups, relying on a core full-time team with a diverse set of relevant skills as well as a large network of global, highly vetted experts, both from Portugal and abroad. Originally founded by a Top rank #66 FT Business School (IBS - ISCTE Business School) and a leading VC Fund in Portugal (Caixa Capital), in 2018, BGI did an MBO and is today owned by 18 shareholders including international investors. Since its inception, BGI has followed an equity-based model in the ventures that it supports. In the period of 2013-2016 in the form of straight equity or convertible notes and since then in the form of SAFEs.

Ventures that are selected and invited to join the BGI accelerator have access to significant resources embedded in BGI and the opportunities including venture financing. It also provides structured mentoring programs by sector experts, training, and entrepreneurial development. Structured over 9 months, on average, the teams make four trips to Lisbon, each for several intense days. The program involves a rigorous process of workshops, structured feedback from coaches, and semi-structured cohort group practices before participants present to potential investors—an approach that avoids a premature scaling of ventures without thoughtful validation of their technology, business concepts and market opportunities. In addition, they spend 1 to 2 weeks in the Boston/MIT ecosystem with a particular focus on global market penetration, i.e. access to market and access to funding (scale-ups).

A core of over 200 experts is available to be intensively involved in the process of idea clarification and validation. Altogether, each venture invited to join BGI is exposed to over 1,000 hours of expert mentoring aimed at fine-tuning their value proposition.

Seed funding is also part of the accelerator offering, originally with up to €1 million allocated among the top 4 ventures per cohort of each edition. BGI has an overall acceptance rate of 12% across four core verticals.

Once ventures graduate from the acceleration program - similarly to a VC fund, BGI provides support to its alumni until they exit or fail. Since 2010, BGI has accelerated nearly 200 start-ups from all over the globe, with over €206 million raised. Featuring a start-up survival rate of 63% and

17 Government Venture Financing

Civilization advances by extending the number of important operations which we can perform without thinking of them.
Alfred North Whitehead

INTRODUCTION

In 1994, when Internet search tools were rudimentary catalogues based on keywords, the National Science Foundation (a U.S. federal agency established to promote science) funded an innovative project carried out by Stanford student Larry Page. Its aim was to build a web search structure as a collection of links between pages, which would fix gaps in page rankings. Page's project was joined by Sergey Brin to jointly develop the PageRank method. By 1998, both had obtained the funding to incorporate their company, Google, in a garage in California, using PageRank as one of its main search engine components. In this way, the government provided early stage funding to build the technology behind of one of the largest technology companies in the world.

Innovate UK is a British agency established in 2004 with the goal of accelerating sustainable economic growth by investing in scientific and technological innovation. It provides an array of programs to assist with funding, knowhow, and networking to venture businesses. One of the agency's investments was an Internet of Things business called AlertMe, founded in 2006 as a platform to connect multiple devices, allowing corporate partners to offer remote monitoring and control to its customers. The company was bought by British Gas for $65 million in 2015, and promises to expand its smart home services to millions of households in the United Kingdom and worldwide. Innovate UK's support was crucial to AlertMe when the company developed its initial projects of fully integrated home services.

BACKGROUND

Venture enterprises are a prime engine of economic growth via innovation, employment, and export. Yet, inevitably, start-ups' foremost concern is funding. Accordingly, governments around the globe increasingly design and implement schemes to create and support an entrepreneurial ecosystem through methods that include financial aid, tax subsidies, regulatory breaks, logistic support, and a generally accommodating environment. These efforts may be advanced at a national government level, regional agencies, and municipalities. Private sector financing is often very hard to raise for seed and early stage companies given their high failure rate, leading to what has been known as the *equity gap*. The main objective of public sector venture funding and other forms of incentives is to help bridge the equity gap for these early stage firms.

The origin of government venture support goes back to the 1930s, when the U.S. government initiated new ways to fund small businesses and support economic recovery after the Great Depression and again more forcefully after World War II. American Research and Development Corporation was then created as the first known venture capital (VC) firm. Another important milestone came with the Small Business Investment Company (SBIC) program, enacted in 1958 to support and fund small enterprises. Despite serious flaws in its design which led to abuse and corruption,[1] the program stimulated small businesses and had a major role in the proliferation of venture companies in the newly emerged technology centers of Silicon Valley and Massachusetts Route 128. Combining funding with specialized legal and accounting services acted as a catalyst for the expansion of the venture industry. Companies like Apple and Intel received support from SBIC in their early stages, and the program later became a model for similar initiatives in other parts of the world, such as China and Singapore.

Other milestones included changes to the capital gains tax rate in the 1970s, and when the U.S. Department of Labor (DoL) provided a clarification of the Employee Retirement Income Security Act (ERISA). Known as the *Prudent Man Rule*, this allowed pension funds to allocate capital to venture investments, opening an important channel to a large pool of institutional investors.

In the United Kingdom, the Industrial and Commercial Finance Corporation (ICFC) was founded in 1945 to provide long-term capital to small and medium-sized firms, with the aim of helping domestic industry recover from World War II. The Bank of England and the five major clearing banks at the time funded the effort with £10 million in equity ownership. Following a merger, ICFC was rebranded in the 1980s as Investors In Industry, which was shortened at the time of its London Stock Exchange flotation to 3i (as it is known today). For many years, the firm dominated the British venture capital and private equity arena. Over the years, other funds emerged to lead British and European activities in this space, benefitting nonetheless from the pioneering role of ICFC.

POLICY CONSIDERATIONS

It is commonly recognized that sole government financing generally fails to reach its goals due to a lack of knowhow and providing the wrong incentives. Instead, investments are either made through grants and loans or, when in the form of equity, side by side with private sector investors. In the latter case of equity co-investment, there are incentives and subsidies that reduce the cost of capital through mechanisms such as a cap on government return or tax incentives to investors. Notwithstanding a few exceptions, the object of venture funding is not equity return to the government in and of itself, but facilitating a vibrant venture environment. On top of high risk exposure to embryonic technologies and businesses, government funding may be subject to further risk when aims to achieve other social goals (e.g., prioritizing remote or deprived regions) are included.

While the empirical evidence on the impact of government venture financing is mixed, the majority of academic studies demonstrate that in markets where both government and private sponsors are present, more venture enterprises receive funding and the average funding per enterprise is higher. There is also a positive correlation between the ability to reach a successful exit and access to a mix of government and private venture funding, attributable largely to the additional investment.[2]

---

[1] See Bean (2001) for evidence on "sweetheart" financing of real estate development and corrupt funds to businesses run by friends, relatives, and even organized crime syndicates. Nine out of ten SBICs violated federal regulations in some way. For further criticism of the SBIC program, see Eyal-Cohen (2011–12).

[2] See Brander et al. (2015) study based on a dataset of ca 20,000 early stage enterprises in 56 countries. For additional evidence see Alperovych et al. (2016).

Public sector sponsorship of ventures is a widespread global phenomenon. It is estimated that over one-quarter of VC-backed companies have some type of government support.[3] Efforts have been spreading globally since the initial programs in the United States, with countries launching their own venture funds, creating science or industrial parks, and providing subsidies.[4] Their objectives varied from supporting specific industries of strategic interest to the development of local Silicon Valley-like innovation centers. An OECD (2013) survey revealed that out of 32 respondent member states, nearly all have grant, loan, or guarantee schemes, of which the majority have fund of funds or co-investment schemes. Front-end or back-end tax incentives are also quite common. Apart from VC funding, governments often provide funding and incentives for research and development (R&D), which may impact entrepreneurial projects but are not limited to venture firms.

At the same time, public sector intervention in venture investment has been subject to several criticisms, mostly based on concerns about an eventual crowding out effect. According to this argument, government venture sponsoring could result in the displacement of private venture capitalists, especially if capital is provided at a lower cost. However, the comprehensive study by Brander et al. (2015) found that markets where government venture financing exists show higher private venture funding per enterprise, which indicates a complementary effect.[5] Complementarity may be attributed to a stricter investment screening process carried out at two levels in cases of dual funding, or enhanced business support when both public and private institutions are involved.

Another argument advanced against government intervention suggests that policymakers' key motivation is a social return on investment (e.g., economic growth, job creation, and boosting deprived regions). Such a goal is not aligned with a pure financial return, which focuses on picking the most suitable and promising start-ups, irrespective of social goals. If anything, objectives actually clash since the likelihood of a start-up succeeding in an environment that is remote or socially weak is rather low. Finally, government priorities are often viewed as distorted, being subjected to political pressures and partisan interests.

Although it lies slightly outside the scope of this work, it would be a gross oversight not to mention the foremost contribution of the public sector to venture activities: basic research. After all, nearly all major technological and medical achievements emerge from the sciences:

- Led by the ingenuity of Alan Turing, Bletchley Park was the birthplace of the first computer in 1943 and where cryptology was developed (the Enigma machine).

- Numerous commercial applications emerged from NASA and most likely also from its Soviet counterpart.

- It is estimated that the U.S. government, via the National Institutes of Health (NIH) is funding 75% of all revolutionary new drugs.

- The Human Genome Project was a $3 billion U.S. government initiative in 1990.

---

[3] Ibid. In Europe, the European Investment Fund (EIF) was single-handedly responsible for funding 26% of the total capital raised in 2016 (source: https://blog.dealroom.co/wp-content/uploads/2017/09/European FundsFINAL.pdf). Country-specific public sector programs such as KfW (Germany), BPI (France), and ECF (UK) add significantly to that figure.

[4] Outside of the United States, an early government initiative was Taiwan's creation of the Hsinchu Science Park in 1980.

[5] Afonso and St. Aubyn (2015) report more mixed results in their study of 17 OECD economies. Using over 50 years of data, they find that public investment led to the crowding out of private investment in six countries, and a positive crowding in effect in the other 11 countries.

- The Internet and the microprocessor were invented by DARPA.

- Cellular technology and GPS by the U.S. military.

- The technology that formed the basis for Apple's iPod, iPhone, iPad, and touch-screen was developed by government-backed scientists and engineers.

- All cyber and big data companies in Israel are led by engineers who gained knowledge and experience while serving with military intelligence.

The list could go on and on.[6]

The monumental contribution of governments to technological break-through discoveries brings up an interesting issue, first raised by Block (2008). It is widely agreed that the role of government is to provide infrastructure to the private sector and to regulate markets. However, in the examples above, the public sector also invested in areas of high risk and uncertainty, leading to some of the most disruptive technologies. In contrast, the private sector reaps all the economic profit by creating new products that are based on an incremental contribution. As Mazzucato (2013) asserts, when the state drives innovation, the allocation of risk and reward between the public and private sectors is grossly distorted, with the private sector cherry-picking the most lucrative opportunities.[7]

FORMS OF PUBLIC SECTOR FUNDING

Government financial support of innovation and start-ups may take multiple forms. These are presented below: first the forms of direct funding, then indirect funding, and finally, supporting tax schemes to investors.[8]

Direct funding

In general, governments refrain from making direct equity investments in start-up companies, and instead prefer the use of grants or loans. Grants are awarded through competitive bidding, or are decided on a project-level basis without taking any equity stake. For example, the U.S. Small Business Innovation Research (SBIR) program was established in 1982 to stimulate technological innovation by supporting R&D with a budget of over $2 billion annually. Since then, through contracts and grants, SBIR programs have awarded over $40 billion to research-intensive American small businesses. A sister program, Small Technology Transfer Research (STTR), uses a similar approach to expand public/private sector partnerships by facilitating cooperative R&D between small businesses and U.S. research institutions.[9]

Israel also has several long-running and successful schemes of direct financial assistance. Its Office of the Chief Scientist offers loans to develop innovative technologies to projects that pass a rigorous technological

---

[6] The NIH statistics and the information on the Apple products are based on Mazzucato (2013).

[7] For a further, more detailed analysis, see Weiss (2014).

[8] For a taxonomy and discussion of government policies to assist venture firms, see Klinger-Vidra (2014).

[9] Direct investment is often targeted to specific areas of importance or core competency. For example, Tekes, the Finnish funding agency for innovation, targets R&D in areas such as arctic seas, customer experience, industrial Internet, smart cities, and more.

review.[10] Moreover, the country has signed several bilateral investment fund agreements to support innovative projects through international collaboration. Applications for loans are jointly submitted by a pair of companies, one from each country.[11] The original and longest-running bilateral program has been BIRD with the United States. Established in 1977, this program has since backed nearly 1,000 projects by providing half of the funding on an approved project basis. Similar bi-national programs were later launched with Canada, Korea, and Singapore.

On the debt side, governments sometimes offer collateral or guarantees for entrepreneurs to obtain bank loans or trade finance that would otherwise not be approved by banks (or would be excessively expensive).

Another form of direct financial support is through sponsoring outreach activities, such as funding travel to trade shows and exhibitions overseas. While these sponsorships are often modest sums, the activities they fund are nevertheless significant in providing global exposure to companies at a nascent stage.

Indirect funding

Equity funding by governments is not done directly but as co-investors in collaboration with private sector investors. Lacking expertise to screen and select quality early stage companies, governments offer funding through a variety of co-investment schemes alongside pre-approved investors. Qualified private parties can take the form of a VC fund, with many examples across the globe. Most notably, in 1992, the Israeli government set up Yozma Venture Capital, a $100 million fund. At the time, there was virtually no VC activity in the country and the goal was to attract foreign venture capitalists to establish funds there so that the local start-ups would benefit from the knowhow and networking of the foreign VCs. To entice the foreign funds to establish an Israeli fund, Yozma committed to invest and take a minority equity position in each of them. The incentive for the investors came in the form of a significantly enhanced return structure since Yozma granted each partner a five-year option to buy back its share at the original cost plus interest. The program has since exceeded all expectations and attracted 10 groups to set up venture funds, of which eight have exercised their option to purchase the Yozma shares. A decade after the program's inception, these groups were managing a combined venture portfolio of $2.9 billion, bringing the Israeli technological entrepreneurial surge to global prominence and earning the country the nickname "the start-up nation."[12]

The Yozma model highlighted two important concepts: co-investment led by the private sector, and an asymmetric structure that improves the risk/return profile to private investors. A core principle of the model was that the government was a passive investor, and did not interfere on the professional side (e.g., on investment strategy, a veto at the investment committee, or in overseeing the portfolio companies). The model was later replicated around the world with various types of return enhancement structures such as differential cash flow timing, capped return for public sector investment, and private equity seniority; examples include the UK Enterprise Capital Funds, Singapore's Technopreneurship Investment Fund and Early-Stage Venturing Fund, the $ 1 billion Russian Venture Corporation, and the Brazilian Development Bank, which has deployed capital to boost the entrepreneurship market in Brazil.

---

[10] An interesting matter is the restriction on moving the developed IP outside the country and if so at what cost to the company.

[11] To qualify, the two companies must demonstrate a combined capability to develop, manufacture, sell, and support an innovative product or service. The business relationship has to involve sharing both the product development and the commercialization (i.e., it cannot be that one company develops and one commercializes the product).

[12] "Start-up Nation: The Story of Israel's Economic Miracle" by Dan Senor and Saul Singer, 2011.

By aiming at the seed and early stages of companies—that is, where the scarcity of equity is most significant—governments or regional development agencies also co-invest side by side with pre-approved business angel network groups and syndicates, typically on the same terms. They also commit funding to VC funds that aim to bridge the early stage gap. For example, in 2016, Germany and France announced their plan to create a joint €1 billion fund to help their start-ups grow beyond the seed stage. A year earlier, the two governments committed €75 million to the French VC fund Partech Growth through the public investment bank Bpifrance, the European Investment Fund (EIF), and the German public bank KfW.[13]

Tax relief

Tax incentives can be offered to the start-up firm, its investors (VC funds, individual investors, etc.), or both. For the start-up firm, the incentive may take the form of a lower corporate tax rate applicable to small companies; for individuals, it can allow a tax deduction on investment capital, or reduced capital gains tax upon exit. Similarly, for venture funds, the applicable tax rate could be smaller. For example, in the United Kingdom a Venture Capital Trust (VCT) is a tax-efficient type of listed company that invests in small private companies, while the Enterprise Investment Scheme (EIS) and the Seed Enterprise Investment Scheme (SEIS) have proven most popular as they provide income and capital gains tax relief to investors in qualifying companies. Singapore has ruled tax exemption for qualifying VC funds. In France, SUIR (translated as "Individual Company for Risk Capital Investments") is a tax incentive program to facilitate investment by individuals in small and young companies. Australia introduced a package of 24 measures to facilitate innovation across the economy in 2016.[14] Apart from differentiated tax rates, incentives may also come in the form of tax credits or tax deferral such as corporate incentives for investment in R&D.

BUILDING AN ECOSYSTEM

Exhibit 1 presents the components of a well-functioning innovation system as presented by the World Economic Forum. In addition to financial incentives, governments must foster a supportive environment for fledgling businesses. Below, we discuss some of the most critical policy aspects: regulation, science parks and clusters of innovation, talent and investment attraction, initial public offering (IPO) access, technology infrastructure, and education.

---

[13] Source: *Forbes*, December 19, 2016.

[14] The U.K. SEIS and EIS programs allow 50% and 30% personal tax offsets, respectively, on investment in qualified start-ups subject to certain limitations. The measures by the Australian government include a 20% tax offset on the amount of the investment, capped at $200,000 per investor per year. In both schemes there is a tax exemption on capital gains for investments held over three years.

Exhibit 1: World Economic Forum components of entrepreneurial ecosystem pillars

Accessible Markets	Human Capital/Workforce
• Domestic market – large companies as customers • Domestic market – small/medium companies as customers • Domestic market – governments as customers • Foreign market – large companies as customers • Foreign market – small/medium companies as customers • Foreign market – governments as customers	• Management talent • Technical talent • Entrepreneurial company experience • Outsourcing availability • Access to immigrant workforce

Funding and Finance	Support System
• Friends and family • Angel investors • Private equity • Venture capital • Access to debt	• Mentors/advisors • Professional services • Incubators/accelerators • Network of entrepreneurial peers

Regulatory Framework and Infrastructure	Education and Training
• Ease of starting a business • Tax Incentives • Business-friendly legislation/policies • Access to basic infrastructure (e.g., water, electricity) • Access to telecommunications/broadband • Access to transport	• Available workforce with pre-university education • Available workforce with university education • Entrepreneur-specific training

Major Universities as Catalysts	Cultural Support
• Major universities promoting a culture of respect for entrepreneurship • Major universities playing a key role in idea-formation for new companies • Major universities playing a key role in providing graduates for new companies	• Tolerance of risk and failure • Preference for self-employment • Success stories/role models • Research culture • Positive image of entrepreneurship • Celebration of innovation

Source: World Economic Forum, "Entrepreneurial Ecosystems around the Globe and Company Growth Dynamics," downloaded June 2017.

Regulation

Governments can assist in entrepreneurial activities by lifting some of the regulatory requirements and by making fundraising hurdles less onerous. Legal structures such as limited partnerships and regulation on disseminating fundraising materials enable a more efficient fundraising process without the more stringent requirement in the mature parts of the capital markets. Funding restrictions could be simplified by eliminating limitations on international investment, ownership, and especially during exit time (e.g., enabling repatriation of the principal and allowing the transfer of intellectual property overseas).

Bankruptcy law provides personal protection in case of business distress. Japan and Singapore have changed their bankruptcy laws to make it easier for companies and investors to exit bankruptcy situations, thus reducing the occurrence of so-called "zombie companies," in which entrepreneurs cannot efficiently wind down failing enterprises. Law enforcement and the existence of intellectual property rights reduce the risk of intangible assets, whether innovations, technologies, or commercial knowhow are infringed. The cost of business can be reduced by implementing flexible labor rules, such as those that make it easier to hire new employees or make employees redundant if the economic situation worsens.

Science parks and clusters of innovation

Governments can promote entrepreneurship by creating social environments institutions focused on innovation, such as science parks and research institutes dedicated to developing new technologies. The Hsinchu Science Park, established in 1980 by the Taiwanese government to boost innovation, has become one of the most important centers for developing semiconductor, computer, and industrial technologies. Entrepreneurs at seed and early stages also need programs like business training, incubators, accelerators, and co-working spaces that provide the basic infrastructure and information to establish their start-ups. Regional agencies can play a key role in closing the early stage financing gap by facilitating the creation of angel networks. When there is already a product in the market, governments can use their procurement power and buy from smaller firms, providing them scale for growth from early stages. Finally, establishing manufacturing and export zones can ensure competitiveness for venture firms and support their ability to scale. For example, Vietnam started creating manufacturing zones in the 1990s, including hi-tech, industrial, economic, and export processing zones.

Talent and investment attraction

Government immigration and work permit policies have a direct impact on the development of local ventures and the country's attractiveness to new businesses. Incentivizing the immigration of talented professionals and/or qualified workers can benefit a country's entrepreneurial environment; for instance, the U.K. Entrepreneur visa, La French Tech in France, LaunchPad Denmark, the Global Investor Program in Singapore, and Start-Up Chile are all designed to attract early stage, high-potential entrepreneurs to bootstrap their start-ups in the respective country as a platform to go global. The schemes provide grants, accelerator programs, and in some cases a permanent residence for international investors to create their start-ups in the country. Indeed, even in Silicon Valley and other industrial parks in the United States, the prevailing entrepreneurial ethos centers on stories of immigrants who achieve the American dream through ingenuity and hard work.

Trade and capital liberalization policies can also serve as tools to enable cross-border investment, export of domestically manufactured goods, and import of key production inputs (e.g., European Union, NAFTA, MERCOSUR). The constitution of investment agencies plays an important role in promoting the country internationally and attracting foreign direct investment (FDI), while the multilateral investment funds mentioned above can support the cross-border deployment of capital to start-ups and assist in their international outreach.

Accessing the stock market

Young firms find it more difficult to comply with the requirements set by the stock markets for listing and ongoing trade. For example, listed companies face stiff and expensive reporting requirements that young companies find too onerous for their size. While recognizing the importance of protecting public interests, regulators and stock exchanges around the world are often sympathetic to this cause, and understand the need to find the right balance. As the first electronic stock market, the NASDAQ attracted new growth companies such as Microsoft, Apple, Cisco, Oracle, and Dell, and helped modernize the IPO. More recently, the U.S. Jumpstart Our Business Startups Act (JOBS Act) was signed into law by President Obama in 2012, and final rules went into effect in May 2016. The legislation simplifies the path to IPO registration for emerging growth companies by relieving regulatory and disclosure requirements in the registration statement that is filed when going public, and most significantly, certain regulations that originated with the Sarbanes–Oxley Act and related rules.

The Brazilian Exchange allows for different listing segments according to the company's profile. Similarly, the Singapore Exchange offers the Catalist listing board for fast-growing enterprises seeking a primary listing, and the Korea Exchange launched the KOSDAQ for listing small and medium companies. By allowing a second-tier listing scheme, policymakers grant earlier access to a large pool of investors while promoting a healthy balance of governance and accessibility. Softening conditions for listing on a second-tier exchange include waiving the requirement to show a certain number of consecutive years of profitability before listing, as is the case in Taiwan. In other countries, by allowing dual listing on local and foreign stock exchanges, regulators have promoted access to international liquidity and visibility.

Access to the stock market has an additional virtue. In many cases, after a company proves to be worthy of going public, or even after filing for the IPO, it is acquired by a larger company for strategic reasons. The availability of an alternative to the merger and acquisition process improves exit valuations and thus enhances the return to investors.

Technology infrastructure

Another method for governments to support start-ups is by making technological infrastructure available, including high-speed Internet or specific hardware (e.g., 3D printers). The Korean ETRI offers a comprehensive range of smartphones for entrepreneurs to test their apps, on top of other services for start-ups. Most recently, Korea has also been investing in establishing a 5G network, which will be five times faster than 4G. Offering public access to relevant data sets, especially online, can be invaluable as well.

Entrepreneurs can use this data to conduct market and technological research in building new businesses. The U.K. Open Data Institute aims to provide support for entrepreneurs to innovate with data. At times, the public sector partners with the private sector to create research and innovation ecosystems like living labs—typically through universities and research institutes—in order to develop and test new ideas.

Education

Governments can encourage entrepreneurial activity by introducing technology education from an early age in the primary school curriculum, or by offering specific readiness programs to prepare entrepreneurs for investor pitching. The U.K., Vietnamese, and Estonian governments are examples of those that have introduced programming classes into the school curriculum, even for very young children. Entrepreneurship education is provided by Australia and France through their respective Commercialisation and Investissement programs. At public and private universities, opening technology centers and facilitating grants are tools to encourage innovation and support faculty, postdoctoral researchers and students to develop and commercialize their innovations. Some of these institutions also offer internship programs at start-ups, allowing students to experience a venture environment, and companies to inexpensively access qualified talent and a platform to recruit.

In practice, combining a number of these initiatives tends to produce the best results and reach a broader range of entrepreneurial needs. Measures with cash impact, such as taxation, funding, and stock market access, tend to have a shorter-term impact—from one to five years. In contrast, initiatives aimed at creating an entrepreneurial-friendly environment, such as regulatory flexibility, innovation institutions, talent-attracting schemes, and infrastructure, are expected to bring results in three to seven years. Education also tends to bring longer-term benefits (i.e., a five- to ten-year horizon). Most importantly, the policy mix should not inhibit the private sector with excess intervention. A wide variety of factors affect policy decisions, including sector-specific strategic relevance, budget, technical capabilities, the country's development level, and specific risks or obstacles.

LOCAL INITIATIVES: THE CASE OF CHICAGO

A prime example of how to build a unified entrepreneurial ecosystem is the city of Chicago, Illinois.[15] In 2003, the Chicagoland Entrepreneurial Center (CEC) was formed by notable business leaders with backing from the city government. In 2012, it launched an innovation incubator with financial backing from the State of Illinois and a highly visible exposure by the state governor. The incubator was named "1871" after the Great Chicago Fire of that year, which had been followed by the city's "Great Rebuilding." The CEC allocated a large, centrally located space as a hub for entrepreneurial activities serving Chicago's start-up community. It partnered with large corporations and service firms, the financial community, non-profit organizations, and academic institutions—many of which also had their own incubators and accelerators.

This concerted effort to build the Chicago venture ecosystem aimed to leverage the strong industrial base and mix of services in the city. The initiative was further enhanced by forming ChicagoNEXT, a council of technology leaders to work with city government officers and other parties. ChicagoNEXT formed World

---

[15] For a thorough review of the design and implementation of Chicago's entrepreneurial ecosystem, see Applegate et al. (2017).

Business Chicago as a public-private partnership chaired by Chicago's mayor, whereas ChicagoNext was chaired by J.B. Pritzker, a prominent Chicago businessman and philanthropist. Adding to that, the University of Illinois established UI Labs with a focus on collaborative experience in digital manufacturing and urban innovation. Ultimately, Chicago achieved a unique public-private sector collaboration and an entrepreneurial hotbed tailor-made to the local conditions.

FAILURE OF GOVERNMENT INITIATIVES

Too often, government programs to promote innovation and nascent enterprises are unsuccessful. In her comprehensive study of government venture programs worldwide, Karsai (2015) points out that direct participation could result in distorting market processes. Lerner (2009) distinguishes between two main causes of government program failure: flaws in their design and flaws in the implementation. The former includes a lack of continuous commitment over a sufficiently long period, inadequate size of the funds provided (either too small to make an impact or too large, resulting in crowding out private funding), or the absence of expertise or flexibility to embrace business shifts that are natural for innovative start-ups. For investment in industrial parks to be beyond buildings, it is essential to develop and link together people, science, culture and ambiance for such a place to flourish and become a community. In the 2000s, the Malaysian government invested in a large biotechnology complex called BioValley (inspired by Singapore's Biopolis) without thoroughly researching the attractiveness of the region for companies. Eventually, the initiative failed to create an innovation ecosystem, leading to the project's new nickname, "the Valley of Bio-Ghosts." Similarly, the European Seed Capital Fund Scheme is another example of an undercapitalized program that was not able to build successful enterprises.

The second cause for failure of government venture support programs stems from implementation flaws. At times, insufficient attention is given to incentives; for example, when the financing scheme permits early cash-out to the entrepreneur, or if private investors are ensured an unconditional return. Lerner (2009) refers to the Heartland Seed Capital Fund from Iowa to illustrate this issue. To start, the fund applied a traditional procurement process to select its fund manager, a venture firm with little local knowledge. The fund was set with a generous management fee of 3%, which resulted in a dispute when after three years, the fund managers had collected $1.4 million in fees after making one single investment of $1 million. In other instances, government programs fail to be timely and attuned to changes in investors' sentiments. For instance, the U.S. Advanced Technology Program decided to focus on Internet and genome projects in the late 1990s, although these sectors were already overfunded by the private sector.

CONCLUSION

Innovative early stage enterprises have been identified by governments across the world as prime drivers for economic growth. Yet, the risk/return trade-off is not sufficiently attractive for private sector investors, leading to the so-called equity gap in early stage enterprises. Supporting technology start-ups has therefore become an acute priority for policymakers in order to propel innovation and foster economic growth. Over the years, numerous government programs have been launched, varying in their design and implementation.

However, most have yielded poor results and failed to reach their objective of building an entrepreneurial environment.

To succeed where these programs have failed, governments and regional agencies must build a supportive ecosystem that reduces the complexity of running a fledgling business; doing so requires a less bureaucratic legal and regulatory system and a well-developed technological infrastructure. Other helpful factors include a cluster of similar companies to attract investors, technological expertise (e.g., intellectual property), corporate sponsors, and special facilities (e.g., testing laboratories). Clusters should offer attractive living conditions and aim to become communities that bolster an entrepreneurial spirit. Government support is critical at the nascent stages of market development, as well as during times of market downturn, such as the dot-com crash.

In terms of creating financial incentives with government funding, it is crucial that any public sector funding of new business ventures is only invested alongside private sector investors who has their own skin in the game. The inclusion of the private sector is important primarily because of their expertise in identifying qualified investments, and the capabilities they offer via mentoring and stewardship along the way. The form of government support could be through a tax relief or through return enhancements such as a capped return for the public sector investment.

Finally, for a country to be successful in fostering early stage entrepreneurship, it must build a critical mass of success stories, to create a society of serial entrepreneurs who have broad expertise and feed into the culture of risk taking. In addition to building a thriving venture ecosystem, such serial entrepreneurs could also help dealing with crisis times during market downturn such as the dot com crash.

REFERENCES

Afonso. A. and M. St. Aubyn (2015) "Economic growth and public and private investment returns", working paper, University of Lisbon, November.

Alperovych, Y., A. P. Groh and A. Quas (2016) "When can government venture capital funds bridge the equity gap?" working paper, EMLYON Business School, January.

Applegate, L. M., A. Meyer and T. Varley (2017) "Rising from the ashes: The emergence of Chicago's entrepreneurial ecosystem," Harvard Business School Case Study 9-817-061.

Bean, J. J (2001) *Big government and affirmative action: The scandalous history of the Small Business Administration,* University of Kentucky Press.

Block, F. (2008) "Swimming against the current: The rise of a hidden developmental state in the United States," *Politics and Society* 36(2): 169-206.

Brander, J. A., Q. Du and T. F. Hellmann (2015) "The effects of government sponsored venture capital: International evidence," *Review of Finance* 19: 571-618.

Eyal-Cohen, M. (2011/12) "Why is small business the chief business of Congress?" *Rutgers Law Journal* 43(1): 1-57.

Karsai, J. (2015) "Squaring the circle? Government as venture capital investor," *Studies in International Economics* 1(1): 62–93.

Klingler-Vidra, R. (2014) "The public venture policy menu," *Coller Venture Review* 1: 36-43.

Lerner, J. (2009) *Boulevard of broken dreams: Why public efforts to boost entrepreneurship and venture capital have failed--and what to do about it*, Princeton University Press.

Mazzucato, M. (2013) "*The entrepreneurial state: Debunking public vs. private sector myths*, Anthem Press.

OECD (2013) *Policies for seed and early stage finance: Findings from the 2012 OECD financing questionnaire.*

Weiss, L. (2014) *America Inc.? Innovation and enterprise in the national security state*, Cornell University Press.

18 University Venturing

The machine does not isolate man from the great problems of nature but plunges him more deeply into them.
Antoine de Saint-Exupéry in Wind, Sand and Stars (1939)

INTRODUCTION

While universities were originally formed as a bastion for the preservation of the past, the modern university has emerged with the introduction of forward-looking scientific research and the dissemination of knowledge. University research is geared more toward these altruistic aims rather than commercial goals; however, it is a fact that commercial technology and innovation are born as an outgrowth from science. Although the path to commercial developments is usually incremental and non-linear, economists agree that universities and government-sponsored research labs are central to innovation and venture activity.

This theme was well summarized in a keynote address by philanthropist Gerald Chan:

> For the everyday man, science is esoteric and can be baffling. Technological innovation became the means whereby the everyday man gets to enjoy the new discoveries of science. He need not understand Bernoulli's principle and the Navier-Stokes equations in fluid mechanics in order to enjoy air travel in a plane. … It is by technology that science becomes palpable to the everyday man, and thus, progress becomes experiential to him. … Being in the biotechnology business, I can assure you that without university research the pipeline for new medicines would dry up. The same can be said of many other industries, from transportation to communication, from manufacturing to robotics, from energy to new materials. There is no doubt that university research is now the most powerful impulse for human progress.[1]

The list of disruptive innovations and technologies developed at universities is endless, and they stem not only from the most prominent research institutions, such as the Massachusetts Institute of Technology (MIT), Stanford University, and the University of Cambridge, but from all across the scientific world. Scattered examples include the discovery of penicillin (Imperial College London), Vitamins A and B and the enrichment of Vitamin D content (University of Wisconsin-Madison), MRI scanners (SUNY Downstate and University of Nottingham), the artificial heart (Wayne State University) and the first fully functioning digital computer, ENIAC (University of Pennsylvania), to name a few.[2]

University-led innovation relies on three core, interconnected aspects to further research activity and knowledge transfer across medicine, engineering, and the sciences: infrastructure, faculty, and students. As will be discussed below, some of the most successful universities have developed their entrepreneurial

---

[1] Keynote address at University College London, 14 July 2016 (www.geraldchan.net/2016/07/14/university-college-london-july-14-2016/).

[2] Prominent national laboratories in the United States include the Fermi National Accelerator, Lawrence Livermore, Los Alamos, and Sandia. Of note in Europe is CERN; although its main function is to provide the particle accelerators and other infrastructure needed for high-energy physics research, it is also the birthplace of the World Wide Web. For additional major discoveries see Appendix.

capabilities by building bridges with industry, being proactive in the commercialization of new discoveries, and enabling decentralized faculty- and student-led initiatives. The fluid nature of ventures requires universities to adopt an evolving approach to deal with potential issues such as intellectual property (IP) and faculty time commitment, among others. In some cases, the research centers and technology business units within a university partner together to anticipate the challenges inherent in converting technological innovation into a successful business. In other situations, the dedicated technology transfer units take a leading role. University accelerators also play an increasing role in technology transfer.

The unique capabilities of universities attract private companies interested in strategic alliances; because equipment and budgets to conduct cutting-edge experiments are limited, this type of alliance can be a win-win collaboration if designed and carried out properly. For university projects, such partnerships are undoubtedly beneficial, as the industry brings a practical perspective of how to translate new technologies into marketable products. Other benefits from university-industry partnerships include access to corporate funding, usage of private sector R&D facilities, market knowledge databases, and an avenue for commercialization.

The transformation of universities from "ivory towers" to a market-oriented innovation settings is no trivial matter. It is a transformation that does not fit with all research disciplines, and even in fields such as engineering and computer science, not all faculty wish to (or can or should) devote time away from pure research. Matters of equality and balance have to be carefully addressed. In addition, there is the inevitable threat of top researchers migrating away from university engagement, either in favor of lucrative full-time positions in major corporations, or in order to participate further in a project/start-up activity if it gains sufficient momentum.

TECHNOLOGY TRANSFER

The process by universities and other public research institutes (e.g., national laboratories and public hospitals) to commercialize their scientific discoveries is known as "technology transfer" or "technology translation." Bringing university-born IP to the marketplace is accomplished in several ways but mainly through licensing to companies that have the strategic fit and resources to incorporate the IP in their own technological developments. In return, universities receive payments in the form of cash payments from licensing fees, royalties on earned revenues, or equity in a newly formed company.[3] Universities then allocate a share of the proceeds according to their own policies to the scientists who are responsible for the discovery while feeding back the remaining proceeds to the university research budget.

Most universities have a technology transfer office (TTO) that is responsible for protecting and commercializing the IP developed. The remit of the TTO is to identify within the research departments the discoveries with the most direct commercial applications, to protect them legally, and to engage in the commercial transactions. It provides a central resource of trained and experienced professionals to carry out the registration of IP, check freedom to operate, negotiate license agreements, oversee spin-off formation and investments, collect income, and distribute it to the beneficiaries.

---

[3] Licensing fees could be structured purely up front or by instalments based on reaching milestones (either technological (e.g., reaching a certain technology readiness level, obtaining a certification, etc.) or commercial (e.g., reaching a certain level of sales)).

The TTO also works closely with the university research office (or a similar title). In some universities, the research office establishes ownership of university IP which is then passed on to the TTO for commercialization. Each university develops its own organizational structure for managing research grant applications, equipment services, and technology transfer. TTOs are either part of the university administration, a wholly owned subsidiary company, or, more rarely, an outsourced service.

Establishing the source, ownership, and consent of IP can be complicated since the initial research usually involves governmental or other public funding. Scientific work often involves multiple researchers and funding bodies, sometime stretching back over many years. It may also involve a collaboration of several universities, which results in a need to obtain the right permissions and establish economic rights.

While a licensing agreement in return for royalties is the most common way to commercialize, there is also the possibility of setting up a spin-off company around the IP (along with the academic founders as partners) before investors are involved. Setting an appropriate equity split between the founders and the institution is a matter of internal policy. Some universities choose to have fixed pre-set terms in order to minimize the level of internal negotiation, while others opt for flexibility to account for differing circumstances.

Since scientific research often involves public funding, technology transfer may be subject to further stipulations and procedures. In the United States, a 1980 amendment to the Patent and Trademark Law Amendments Act, frequently referred to as the Bayh–Dole Act, was described twenty years later by the *Economist* as "possibly the most inspired piece of legislation to be enacted in America over the past half century."[4] It mandates universities to have certain responsibilities such as reporting inventions to the funding authority in a timely manner and sharing income from those inventions with the responsible scientists. The government also retains certain rights, including a non-exclusive license to use the IP or to license it to third parties under exceptional circumstances, such as critical unmet public health needs.

Governments directly support the commercialization of university IP as well. The European Union's Horizon 2020 program provides grants for university research subject to an obligatory participation of a commercial company or VC fund. Israel's government programs Nofar and Magneton are similar, and Kamin grants funding for university research that is close to, but not yet ripe for, commercialization.

COLLABORATION WITH EXTERNAL VENTURE CAPITAL FIRMS

Over the years, universities have experimented with various models of collaboration with external venture capital funds. VC firms are the most natural party to objectively identify innovative products that are ripe for commercialization, with added capabilities and proven experience in overseeing and steering technological start-ups. Committing their own funds to university-born start-ups incentivizes VC firms to maximize the potential from the innovations they select to back. Yet, many of the original collaborations did not work well. Often, the collaboration was with a single venture capitalist after a selection process. Whether because there were not many qualified projects, or because of reasons specific to the venture capitalists (e.g., they found better or easier deals elsewhere, a change of taste, etc.), very few investments were actually made, leading to a great difficulty in raising money from alternative sources as well. With a first right to invest, a collaboration

---

[4] https://www.economist.com/technology-quarterly/2002/12/12/innovations-golden-goose

with a selected VC firm caused a delay to the inventors and the university when looking for alternative funding. Moreover, it also signaled to the market that the innovation had passed by the key partnering VC working with the university. Until the early 1990s, terms were largely skewed in favor of the venture capital firm, until universities gained the relevant experience and formed TTOs. Since then, collaborations and cooperation have taken varying forms, often with syndicates or multinational corporations.

ARCH Venture Partners, spun off the University of Chicago, represented a turning point in university venture initiatives. In 1986, ARCH Development Corporation was formed as a not-for-profit affiliate corporation dedicated to commercializing technology developed at the University of Chicago and the Argonne National Laboratory, with a broad mandate to license innovation and promote the formation of spin-off companies. An area of legal concern was the nature of the relationships with the researchers. Although they were allowed by the university and the national lab to serve as directors and consultants to spin-off companies, they were not allowed to hold equity in these entities. ARCH Development Corporation was monumental in changing this mindset by strongly advocating for the researchers to own 25% of the spin-off businesses and a large share of royalties from other commercialized activities.

Within a few years, a need was recognized to separate the technology transfer function from the investment part. ARCH Development Corporation remained within the university as its technology transfer arm, while a VC fund was created to support the formation of spin-off companies, as the region did not have a strong early stage VC community at the time. ARCH Venture Partners was formed and raised its first $9 million fund, and in 1992 it spun off while the University of Chicago became a cornerstone investor. Over the subsequent years, ARCH Venture Partners signed agreements with numerous other universities to become their strategic partner for investing in their technological innovations. Expansion took place both in terms of managed capital and in the organization's geographical reach to universities and national labs such as the University of Washington, Sandia, Los Alamos, Columbia University, and Boston University. To date, ARCH Venture Partners has made early stage investments in more than 200 companies through nine funds including in Ireland, Iceland and China.

Interestingly, ARCH Venture Partners' first success did not come from life sciences or engineering but from the Department of Education of the University of Chicago. Originally staffed with a few students and operating out of the basement of the department, the Everyday Learning project aimed at reforming the mathematics curriculum in the United States for kindergarten through to the sixth grade. Material was made available through what was called summer boot camps to mathematics coordinators across the country. With a total investment of $1.5 million by ARCH Venture Partners and others, Everyday Learning was structured as a company in 1989 and an external CEO was recruited. The business broke even early in its second year of operation, although additional capital was raised later for the development of new product lines. ARCH Venture Partners exited the investment in 1995 when Everyday Learning was sold to the Chicago Tribune for $26 million. The university, which had substantial ownership for having licensed that product to the company, received a return in excess of $10 million, an enormous success at the time. Subsequently, in 2000, Everyday Learning was sold to McGraw-Hill while remaining the top-selling elementary mathematics curriculum.[5]

In a slightly different model, IP2IPO Group plc was formed in the United Kingdom in the early 2000s, pioneering long-term partnerships with several universities and university departments and securing first

---

[5] Information on ARCH Venture Partners and Everyday Learning is drawn from Lerner (2000) and the websites of ARCH Venture Partner, Crunchbase (https://news.crunchbase.com/news/chicago-based-arch-venture partners-targets-600m-for-tenth-deep-tech-fund/) and the Illinois Venture Capital Association (IVCA) all retrieved on 25 February 2019.

rights on investment opportunities in spin-off companies.[6] Within a few years, six IP2IPO companies were listed on AIM, the London Stock Exchange's market for smaller growing companies, of which three were in the biotech sector. Later rebranded as IP Group, its investments to date comprise around 80 portfolio companies, of which 17 are listed.

UNIVERSITY-RAISED FUNDS

A recent growing trend at universities is raising a fund dedicated to investment in its technology transfer opportunities. Often there is an anchor investor in the form of a multinational corporation which is capable of helping with outreach and market knowledge. In December 2016, Temasek, the giant Singapore state investment company, announced an investment in the University of Oxford's science and technology fund, Oxford Sciences Innovation (OSI). OSI develops and commercializes disruptive IP of university researchers. This investment is part of a new £230 million funding round (mainly backed by Asian investors) that comes on top of a similarly sized 2015 round to fund spin-off companies from the university's mathematical, physical, life sciences, and medical sciences divisions. Investors included asset management firms, endowments, and wealthy entrepreneurs such as artificial intelligence pioneer Demis Hassabis of Google's DeepMind.

Two recent funds raised by University College London (UCL) show diversity in structure and collaborating partnerships. The £50 million UCL Technology Fund was launched in 2016 to commercialize scientific research with funding provided equally by the listed company Imperial Innovations Group plc and by the European Investment Fund (EIF), and externally managed by the VC firm, Albion Ventures, which also contributed to the fund.[7] A second 2016 fund, Apollo Therapeutics, puts together a consortium of three "Golden Triangle" universities—the University of Cambridge, Imperial College London, and UCL—with three leading pharmaceutical companies—GlaxoSmithKline, AstraZeneca, and Johnson & Johnson Innovation. Apollo Therapeutics's mandate is to work with the TTOs of the universities to commercialize novel medicines. This is a unique multi-partisan cooperation between academia and "Big Pharma." The pharma companies are slotted to contribute £10 million each over six years, and the universities to contribute £3.3 million each. The rules agreed by the partners are also innovative: "The aim of Apollo is to advance academic pre-clinical research from these universities to a stage at which it can either be taken forward by one of the industry partners following an internal bidding process or be out-licensed. The three industry partners will also provide R&D expertise and additional resources to assist with the commercial evaluation and development of projects."[8]

Two funds for technology transfers were also recently established at Tel Aviv University. The first is the Momentum Fund, backed by Tata, Temasek, SanDisk, HNA EcoTech, and private international investors. Managed by the university's TTO, it is advised by venture capitalists and industry veterans who form a screening committee to pick the most suitable scientific discoveries for licensing or direct investing. A second Tel Aviv University fund, i3 Equity Partners, provide seed money and resources for promising early stage technology projects in the Internet of Things space. Investors in the fund include industry leaders General Electric, Microsoft, Qualcomm, Tata, and others. i3 Equity Partners runs in collaboration with the

---

[6] The first agreement was with the Chemistry Department at the University of Oxford followed by the University of Southampton, University of Leeds, and King's College London.

[7] https://www.pehub.com/2016/01/658857/ retrieved on 25 February, 2019.

[8] "UCL joins consortium to launch £40 million Apollo Therapeutics Fund," UCL News, 25 January 2016.

independent VC firm Pitango. As with Apollo Therapeutics, the goal of these funds is to include esteemed industry partners to establish leadership in a domain where the university is positioned to generate breakthrough technologies. With a goal to sponsor several seed and pre-seed start-ups annually, both funds will benefit selected companies with technology, tools, mentoring, business development, and office space on the university campus, as well as support from the partnering multinational corporations for technology validation, design, proof-of-concept, later stage investments, and ultimately, the purchase of mature technologies and distribution in high-potential markets, including China and India.

UNIVERSITY SCIENCE PARKS

One of the key enablers for the commercialization of disruptive technologies is the establishment of university science parks (also known as university technology "hubs" or "clusters"), which consist of groups of institutions and companies located within a common geography and dedicated to the same technological field.

First and foremost among these hubs is Silicon Valley, the brainchild of Frederick Terman, Stanford Dean of Engineering, who in 1951 spearheaded the creation of Stanford Industrial Park, whereby the university leased portions of its land to high-tech companies. The vision was to create a living community near the campus. Terman directed his students, including William Hewlett and David Packard, to locate their newly formed companies there. The symbiotic relationship between Stanford University and Silicon Valley was fortified through ongoing joint programs and Terman's vast network of exceptional alumni. The comprehensive approach succeeded beyond expectations and seeded an innovative mindset in the area that remains stronger than ever.

Korea's Daedeok Innopolis was built as a cluster of universities, government research institutes, private research institutes, and start-ups, and spans almost 70 square kilometers. There are about 100 research institutes within the park and over 1,000 private companies. It is also home to roughly 20 business incubators and over 30 Daedeok ventures have listed on KOSDAQ (Korea's NASDAQ equivalent).

Other notable examples of tech clusters elsewhere include Adlershof (Berlin), Sophia Antipolis (Southern France), Zhongguancun Science Park (Beijing), and Hsinchu Science Park (Taiwan). In the United Kingdom, "Silicon Fen" was developed as a software, electronics, and biotechnology hub around the University of Cambridge, and more recently, the White City Campus was created by Imperial College London to translate its academic research into viable innovations. Although science parks can also be built around companies, it is more effective to build them adjacent to campuses, sometimes even on the university land, as this provides better access to faculty and students. In addition, it is important that these clusters provide central services facilities (e.g., toxicology laboratories) as well as local professionals for legal and regulatory services, accelerators, housing infrastructure, and so on.

In order for a university science park to succeed, it must include several ingredients: cutting-edge science and technology, an entrepreneurial spirit, and the presence of mature companies. Such an environment facilitates collaboration, stability, and the exchange of ideas, resulting in a thriving local ecosystem and a spillover effect to the broader community in terms of job creation and talent attraction. Angel investors, VC firms and technology and medical companies tend to develop networks around science parks, thereby enhancing their visibility, and consequently, financing opportunities for the start-up companies. The result is a flywheel momentum, where venture enterprises from these locations have more favorable conditions to succeed. Governments also recognize science parks as drivers of economic growth, and in some cases, offer tax advantages or a friendly regulatory framework for these locations. At the same time, the mature companies involved provide complementary facilities to the university (e.g., equipment and laboratories through joint programs) as well as jobs to entrepreneurs or faculty in the later phases of their careers, and may become investors (or ultimately buyers) in the start-ups.

On the extreme opposite side of the spectrum lies the recent unheralded case of Carnegie Mellon University and the San Francisco-based ride-hailing company Uber. In February 2015, Uber announced a research collaboration with the university's renowned robotics research center and opened a facility adjacent to the university. Shortly after this announcement, the company hired away four of the institution's top robotics faculty and 36 other researchers and technicians. The results for Carnegie Mellon University were catastrophic: there has been no collaboration on a single project to date, and far more importantly, the university lost a quantity of world-class talent that is very difficult to replace.

UNIVERSITY-BASED ACCELERATORS [9]

Business accelerators are designed to help entrepreneurs in the very early stages of concept development in fleshing out their ideas and preparing to launch the business. With the myriad of existing business accelerators, what is the added value of a university-based accelerator (UBA)? After all, business acceleration is not directly relevant to the university's two traditional core functions of basic research and teaching. Therefore, it is helpful to consider the features that distinguish UBAs from commercial accelerators. First, UBAs tend to fill in the gap of the most nascent stages where scientific ideas are not yet ripe for support by commercial accelerators. Second, they often leverage facilities and equipment available at universities for deep science projects not provided by commercial accelerators. Third, being housed within a university can provide support in terms of receiving non-dilutive funding, such as government grants and philanthropy. Fourth, alumni networks are a major asset, and they usually prefer to support and volunteer for university-related activities compared to private sector initiatives.

Consider the case of the Creative Destruction Lab (CDL) at the University of Toronto. CDL recruited seven of the most successful entrepreneurs in Toronto (the so-called "G7 Fellows"), ones with proven experience in commercializing science-based technology and driving it to a substantial monetary success. Serving as mentors for seed-stage, science-based technology companies, the G7 Fellows set milestones for each company and regularly meet with entrepreneurs over a nine-month period in order to monitor progress and set new targets. Achieving the periodic goals has to be taken extremely seriously and participants are weeded out during the program, with less than half of those admitted completing it. Sessions include an all-day meeting every eight weeks as well as half-hour, bi-weekly calls between the mentor and the entrepreneur. In addition to providing guidance, the G7 Fellows use these sessions to develop an ongoing relationship with some of the entrepreneurs. The role of the lab staff is to perform the initial screening for admission to the program and guide the entrepreneurs toward achieving the goals set in their periodic meetings.

Typically, half way through the program, either ventures have been dropped or a G7 mentor declares his or her intention to become an investor. Such a declaration conveys "a strong positive signal to other investors in the tech community that a young entrepreneur has been identified by a seasoned one, who has followed

---

[9] This section draws on panel discussions at the Public Policy Forum on Venture Capital and Innovation, Quebec City, October 2014.

the former for several months (seen the movie, not only the picture) and become an anchor investor in his/her new venture."[10]

Again, a clear advantage of the UBA is access to laboratory equipment and to dedicated alumni both as mentors and as potential investors. However, these resources need to be managed very carefully so as to avoid cannibalizing resources or potential donors from core university functions and departments. In terms of measuring success, metrics to assess UBAs could include the number of teams supported, the number of start-ups transitioned to first-tier commercial accelerators, the number of those ultimately funded by VCs, the number of jobs created, an assessment of the ability of the accelerator to attract students to the university, and/or the quality of the overall program's reputation.

THE CASE OF STANFORD UNIVERSITY[11]

Stanford University provides an unparalleled case of deeply rooted entrepreneurial culture. The combination of its location within Silicon Valley and its own superb research makes the university a magnet for global talent. Faculty-student initiatives are natural, leading to a most vibrant and successful venture ecosystem. A 2012 study by the university estimated that all the companies formed by Stanford entrepreneurs generate a total global revenue of $2.7 trillion annually.[12]

Some of the current venture-promoting initiatives at Stanford include the following:

- **Business Association of Stanford Entrepreneurial Students (BASES):** This initiative carries out programs like the BASES $100,000 Startup Challenge, Entrepreneurial Thought Leaders Seminar, Startup Career Fair, Women in Entrepreneurship Summit, and Social Impact Week.

- **StartX:** This accelerator was created by students to generate collective intelligence and provide entrepreneurship education.

- **SPARK:** This program was launched by a senior professor on leave to start her company, and aims to provide education about the journey to convert research into a marketable product and implementation of drug development.

- **Biodesign:** This initiative offers support to entrepreneurs for improving healthcare around the world through technological innovation. Support is based on market needs, guiding students from problem identification to solution development and patent application.

- **TomKat Center:** This program provides funding to sustainable energy, transportation, and water innovations through the Innovation Transfer Program.

The Stanford Office of Technology Licensing (OTL), which is in charge of transferring technology to the industry, enters tailored license agreements with Stanford start-ups, targeting flexible terms that encourage

---

[10] Main Conclusions document of the Forum above, page 14.

[11] This section is based on Ku (2016) and her CIV2017HK presentation in April 2017.

[12] http://news.stanford.edu/news/2012/october/innovation-economic-impact-102412.html

growth while protecting the university's IP. From its inception in 1970 until 2017, the office processed over 11,500 cumulative disclosures and signed 6,500 license agreements.

OTL receives about 500 invention disclosures per year, resulting in 80–120 licenses, of which about 10–20% are for start-up companies and the rest for existing companies. As part of the license agreements, OTL often takes equity stakes in the start-ups; this occurred 351 times (of which 50% were active) between 1970 and April 2017. Start-ups are mostly from the School of Medicine and the School of Engineering. While the majority are ultimately unfruitful, some turn out to be remarkably successful, such as the one involving two students, Larry Page and Sergey Brin, who insisted that their search engine algorithm was superior so the university filed for a patent application. After Brin and Page went on to found Google, Stanford took a minor share in Google equity as partial consideration for the license, which has since generated over $340 million, primarily from sales of shares.

In total, as of 2017, OTL has generated nearly $1.9 billion in cumulative gross royalties. This amount was shared between the innovators, the research budget of the university, and the ongoing operational, legal, and patent registration and maintenance costs. Yet, as discussed above, the distribution is exceptionally skewed. Over $1.2 billion came from just three inventions out of the total of 11,500. Only 88 cases generated in excess of $1 million in cumulative royalties, and only 33 exceeded $5 million.

Looking forward, Stanford now emphasizes cross-disciplinary research collaborations (a "team science"). Its philosophy continues to be that start-ups provide a major bridge between research and development, but the university also recognizes the importance of working closely with existing corporations. Finally, it seeks more involvement with foundations.

SOUTH KOREA[13]

Recently, South Korea has seen a concerted effort to create an economy where science, technology, culture, and industry collaborate. This effort followed from a government vision to ignite a second driver of growth similar to the rapid economic growth that the country experienced in the second half of the 20th century, transforming South Korea from a developing economy to a highly developed one. The venture activity has been led by the Korea Advanced Institute of Science and Technology (KAIST) and Pohang University of Science and Technology (POSTECH), the former inspired by Stanford and the latter by the California Institute of Technology (Caltech).

One of KAIST's key characteristics is its engagement with industry, which involves embedding applied engineering into university practices. This practice is aided by having KAIST located in the Daedeok Innopolis technological park. KAIST graduates are highly sought after by the country's leading companies. The university also has a legacy of extremely successful entrepreneurs among its former graduates and a powerful alumni network; a track record of faculty and graduate start-ups, supported by incubation and acceleration programs; and business incubators that have supported over 500 new ventures and collaborate with about 100 industrial partners on average annually. Among KAIST incubated companies, more than 10 subsequently listed on KOSDAQ.

Similarly, POSTECH's model is based on industry collaboration, as its foundation is linked to steel company POSCO, one of Korea's largest multinationals. Inspired by Caltech, POSTECH was founded in

[13] This section draws on Lee (2016).

1986 as the most selective private university in South Korea. Students and faculty face extremely high hurdles for joining, and the institution's scientists are routinely among the country's most productive researchers. POSCO's founder set the ethos of collaboration between industry, private research institutes, and universities as the ideal model to advance science and technology, leading to POSCO's Research Institute of Industrial Science and Technology (RIST) and other centers for venture businesses. POSTECH has its own technology license and collaboration institute to facilitate the alliance between the university and industry.

KAIST and POSTECH demonstrate how to develop the right vision, partners, infrastructure, and policies to create world-leading universities in a short period of time. Knowledge transfer is enabled by supportive patrons, flagship science and engineering universities, and links to industry and applied research. However, technology in Korea is still very much channeled to the large corporations, and the country lags behind in its entrepreneurial culture, which makes it very different from California, Israel and other start-up hotbeds.

OTHER CASES[14]

From 2005 to 2009, Utah had a tech-savvy and tech-friendly governor who set encouraging technology among his top priorities. Under his leadership, significant new funding was dedicated to technology development. The University of Utah started a spin-off initiative that focused on building an environment with proactive leadership, a change of culture, and partnership with the local entrepreneurial community. It adhered to the motto "it takes a village" to support the growth of entrepreneurial activity and to nurture new ventures. At the pre-seed level, the university protected the IP of discoveries until viable prototypes and business models were identified. Its services also included incorporation, grant application, brand design, website development, accounting outsourcing, insurance protection, and facility infrastructure. The University of Utah later retained MIT to help support its growing start-ups. Federal grants were sourced, leading to $17 million Small Business Technology Transfer (STTR) awards. Ultimately, the program created over 100 spin-offs in five years from a baseline of zero. By the sixth year, 90% of these start-ups were still alive, and one company reached a valuation over $400 million by 2015.

However, the program was abruptly terminated in 2012 when the university's TTO was hired away by Ohio State University and the program director moved back to a faculty position at the business school. It is undeniably disheartening to see a program achieve so much success and then fade away without attaining sustainability.

The European Union has recognized the continent's insufficient tech venturing out of core sciences as an impediment toward sustainable economic growth and competitiveness. In 2008, the European Institute of Innovation and Technology (EIT) was created to support programs and collaboration "from idea to product, from the lab to market, and from student to entrepreneur." The EIT is organized around designated themes to promote innovation in key targeted areas (e.g., digital). It targets graduate, doctoral, and professional education, and fosters innovation by supporting entrepreneurs in identifying market demands, conducting R&D, and commercializing new products. More than 200 start-ups have been supported so far, representing a combined valuation of €1 billion.

---

[14] This section draws on the lessons from around the world that appear in the University Venture issue of the Coller Venture Review (2016). Specifically, articles by Krueger; Gelissen; Rajan and Jhunjhunwala; and Mwora.

In Indian mythology, the goddess Saraswathi, symbolizing education and learning, and the goddess Lakshmi, symbolizing commerce and entrepreneurship, always fight and avoid staying in the same place. This relationship serves as an apt metaphor for India's academic and business environments. While the pursuit of learning and scholarship has always been encouraged in India, Indian universities did not provide an environment conducive to ventures. In addition, Indian society is generally less tolerant of entrepreneurial failures, although this has started to change with the turn of the 21st century. Rajan and Jhunjhunwala (2016) report on the case of the Indian Institute of Technology Madras (IITM), one of the premier universities in India. IITM engages in all early stages: pre-seed, venture formation, mentoring, and support. It funds hundreds of projects per year with financial support from government agencies. In 2015/16 there were nearly 100 start-ups incubated at IITM, with 21 faculty members founding start-ups. Leveraging its strong alumni network, the organization maintains close relationships with the private sector to bring practical solutions to challenges faced during market penetration.

In Kenya, technology entrepreneurship has grown since 2010, when the government installed submarine fiber optic cable for fast and reliable Internet connectivity, and then further enhanced the technological infrastructure by introducing mobile money services, open source crowd-mapping, and a crisis reporting platform. The creation of the Nairobi Innovation Hub (iHub), followed by the rapid emergence of other innovation hubs and labs concentrated in Nairobi, earned the capital the moniker "Silicon Savannah." The two leading universities, Nairobi and Strathmore, had a major role in innovation in that area through their programs Computing for Development (C4D) and iBizAfrica, respectively. With a focus on mobile and information technology, these initiatives offer incubation, acceleration, and services for development and growth stages. The programs benefit from support from several university units and faculties on matters such as IP, information technology, energy research, and legal and business training and advisory services for start-ups.

Finally, Japan, like Korea, has seen innovation confined within its mammoth-size interlocking conglomerates, known as *keiretsu*. In a recent move to encourage technological entrepreneurship out of universities, the Japanese government created a regulatory system that permits and encourages national universities to invest in their home-grown start-up businesses. Accordingly, in 2015/16, four national universities were allocated 100 billion yen in commitments from the government to become hubs for creating start-up companies. This funding was used to create Tohoku University Venture Partners, the University of Tokyo Innovation Platform, Osaka University Venture Capital, and Kyoto University Innovation Capital.

CONCLUSION

Some of the venture-supporting instruments available to universities overlap with those of governments, such as the promotion of science parks. However, academia is positioned to act more directly, given its role in technological development, access to students and faculty on campus, and natural positioning to connect the public and private sectors. Some universities have indeed succeeded in leading innovation in certain areas; for example, Wisconsin-Madison, where primate and human stem cells were isolated for the first time; the University of Edinburgh, famous for genetic studies and the first cloning, Dolly the sheep; and Russia's Skolkovo Institute of Science and Technology on regenerative medicine.

In pursuit of a flourishing entrepreneurial environment, universities must deal with the misalignment between academic interests, oriented to research and knowledge dissemination, and the daily mundane efforts required to support a start-up. They face ongoing challenges, including a lack of a market-oriented approach and conflicts around IP. Moreover, faculty members must balance their time and efforts between academia and their privately owned ventures, and there is a genuine threat of universities losing their top talent to commercial or corporate ventures. An essential—but often overlooked—factor in creating a lasting impact is building an entrepreneurial buzz across the entire campus, beyond the labs. In light of these challenges, it is not surprising that only a few universities have managed to master the balancing act of combining supreme science and venturing. Yet, despite these difficulties, universities are a most promising platform to enable and cultivate a prosperous entrepreneurial ecosystem with immeasurable benefits for all involved parties.

REFERENCES

Gelissen, J. H. A (2016) "Europe's bid for a univenture breakthrough," *Coller Venture Review* 4: 92-101.

Krueger, N. (2016) "Utah's creation of a univenture oasis in the desert," *Coller Venture Review* 4: 32-41.

Ku, K. (2016) "Stanford's univenture secret sauce," *Coller Venture Review* 4: 22-31.

Lee, D. S. (2016) "Looking for a second miracle on the Han river," *Coller Venture Review* 4: 102-111.

Lerner, J. (2000) "ARCH venture partners," in: *Venture Capital & Private Equity: A Casebook*: 101-125.

Vincent, I. and A. McKenzie Mason (2010) "Venture funding for the university startup," *AUTM Technology Transfer Practice Manual,* Association of University Technology Managers https://www.autm.net/AUTMMain/media/ThirdEditionPDFs/V4/TTP_V4_VentureFund.pdf

Mworia, W.M. (2016) "Crafting a silicon savannah," *Coller Venture Review* 4: 56-65.

Rajan A.T. and A. Jhunjhunwala (2016) "One stroke, many colors – Univenture at IIT Madras, *Coller Venture Review* 4: 80-91.

In his own words: Don Rose, PhD., Director of KickStart Venture Services, University of North Carolina at Chapel Hill, and author of *Research to Revenue: A Practical Guide to University Start-Ups* (UNC Press)

Supporting and funding early-stage university start-up companies

Universities are a rich source of research-based innovation. Traditionally, these innovations have been commercialized by the licensing of the technology to an established company. With the rise of entrepreneurship in our society, and specifically on many campuses, an increasingly common route for commercialization is spinning out of a university start-up company. The challenge in commercializing university innovations via the start-up route is multifaceted:

- **Technology push:** Most university innovations are based on basic science, and are rarely developed in response to a specific customer need. Thus, we are usually pushing technology into the marketplace without a defined need.

- **Patent window:** The publication of scientific results by academic faculty is essential for tenure, grant applications, and student careers. But once the patent application has been filed by the university, the patent clock begins to tick. And since the innovation is very early in development, many years of the patent clock may tick before the product reaches the market.

- **Business literacy:** In spinning out university start-ups, two worlds collide: academia and business. These worlds have different incentives, motivations, languages, and expectations. Most science and engineering faculty and students lack the business literacy needed to navigate the commercial world. They end up confused and overwhelmed.

- **Attracting talent:** Given the lack of business literacy among faculty and student founders, it is imperative to bring the right technical and business talent into these start-ups. However, the high technical risk of university start-ups combined with their lack of funding keeps talented management from joining the start-up.

- **Funding for technology development:** Most of the innovations arising from university research are very early in the product development cycle. The technical readiness, being low, raises the risk of failure and deters those wanting to invest time and money in the commercialization process. Although de-risking of the innovation can be done in the university setting, federal grants do not often fund non-hypothesis driven technology development work. Equity-based investments are possible but, again, the risk is too high to attract angel investors or venture capitalists.

The first two challenges, *technology push* and *patent window*, are inherent in academic technology commercialization. There is not much we can do to address these. The latter three, *business literacy*, *attracting talent*, and *technology development funding* have solutions. However, most of the solutions must be led by the university. Let's unpack each of these challenges.

Enhancing Business Literacy for Academicians

At the University of North Carolina, we have explored a number of approaches to educating faculty and students to better understand the start-up process as well as general business fundamentals:

- **Faculty entrepreneur workshops:** A two-day workshop provides faculty and graduate students with an introduction to starting a company. A unique aspect of the workshop is to match the participant with a local entrepreneur, technologist, or business leader with domain expertise in the area of the innovation. This one-on-one coaching helps the participant prepare a plan going forward.

- **Book:** We wrote *Research to Revenue* as a practical guide to help faculty who want to understand this process in more depth (a secondary audience are entrepreneurs who are spinning a company out of the university for the first time). The goal of the book is to help the reader be a good consumer of, and make better decisions in, the start-up process.

- **Faculty entrepreneur fellows:** A program that we are just now beginning to implement (patterned after a similar program at the University of Utah) identifies faculty who have previously started a company. These faculty entrepreneur fellows receive training to increase their awareness of university policies and resources. By formally identifying these faculty, inexperienced faculty can reach out to peers for advice and guidance.

Attracting Talent

- **Advisers:** Many VC firms bring in entrepreneurs in residence (EIRs), many of whom have recently exited, to look for and eventually lead new deals. Universities often try a similar approach but there are significant differences. First, most university innovations are years away from funding, which is outside the tenure of most university EIRs. Second, what is needed at an early stage is not an executive who can raise money or even put together a business plan, but someone with technical domain expertise in the area of the invention who can answer two fundamental questions: Who cares? Will it work? At the University of North Carolina, we have tried the EIR approach but have moved to advisory panels for each (potential) start-up. These panels comprise local entrepreneurs, technologists, executives, and corporate scientists. They meet with the founding faculty once per quarter during the spinout process.

- **Micro-consulting projects:** We have developed a micro-consulting program that pays a local entrepreneur to take a deep dive into a technology to answer some specific questions: What is the customer need? How large is the market? What is the regulatory path? Who are the competitors? These consulting projects, which usually last two to four months, are paid engagements which not only build the business case but can also engage a business leader. The deep dive gives consultants the opportunity to do their own due diligence on start-up opportunities.

Funding for Technology Development

Funding for technology development is the biggest funding gap in spinning out a university innovation into a start-up. Any funding program for developing a university innovation must be bot integrated and stage appropriate. An integrated program allows for step-wise progression for the development of the innovation; stage-appropriate funding implies smaller funding at the earlier stage (higher risk) and greater funding at later stages (lower risk). At the University of North Carolina, we have deployed a number of funding mechanisms, some internal and some targeting external funding sources.

- **Technology development grants ($10,000–$30,000):** These grants help the faculty to de-risk the innovation by answering specific questions raised by potential licensees. Successful accomplishment of the goals of the project will enhance the licensability of the innovation, be it a start-up or an established company.

- **Technology commercialization awards ($25,000–$50,000):** These awards are given to the university start-up company to do proof-of-concept experiments and generate preliminary data for SBIR/STTR awards. They are reviewed by an outside panel. Beyond the funding, these awards give us the opportunity to help shape the strategy of the company in the early days through a dialogue around the application.

- **SBIR/STTR awards ($225,000–$1 million):** U.S. government agencies (e.g., NIH, NSF, etc.) set aside a small portion of their extramural budget for small companies to develop early stage, mostly university-derived, innovations. We have contracted with SBIR/STTR consulting companies to work with faculty members and their start-ups to write effective grant applications.

- **University venture fund:** The university has provided capital for a local VC firm to manage on behalf of the university. The agreement with the firm stipulates that it must invest the capital in university IP-based companies, selecting investments based on investment criteria and experience. The initial funding is $10 million, and funding is to be allocated in $100,000–$500,000 investments with the goal of investing a total of $1 million in promising start-ups.

In his own words: David Ai, J.D., M.S., M.B.A., Director of the Knowledge Transfer Office, City University of Hong Kong, and Chair of the Association of University Technology Managers (AUTM) Asia.

On the elusive success of technology transfer policy in China—two blind spots

As China tries to upgrade its technological competitiveness, to compensate for the loss of low labor rates as a competitive advantage, local governments at the city and provincial levels have been working hard to encourage the transfer of innovation from universities to industry players. With few exceptions (e.g., Shenzhen area and Tsinghua University Science Parks) these programs have not produced significant results. Why not? Perhaps one answer is that these efforts often fall into some rather predictable traps. Two very common blind spots that I have witnessed in the last three years are

- "We want to build the largest IP/innovation trading platform in the country (or the world)."
- "We want to start a large real estate project to accommodate and promote IP/innovation trading operations."

These two blind spots have driven many governments to spend their money and time on things that appear to be crucial, but in reality, do not deliver impact. Both are what I would call "hardware projects" without sufficient attention to the investment in "software," or human capital, which is the real issue.

First, IP rights and innovations are a unique "merchandise" and cannot be traded online easily like Gucci bags between many sellers and buyers. Each innovation is truly unique, by definition, so there is no referenceable "market" price. Further, IP transactions require deep due diligence, involving a long process to understand the needs and particulars of each side, which can take months of hard work before reaching a positive outcome. Finally, both parties of an IP transaction must also negotiate many terms, such as upfront payments, royalty rates, performance diligence, sublicensing rights, and so on, so the complexity of such transactions does not fit a simple ecommerce model.

Next, real estate projects do have their unique place in economic development for local governments in China. They offer a quick way for a local government to trade resources they control (land) for more liquid assets (floor space after the development, or cash), while leveraging external resources from real estate developers. IP trading or technology licensing requires little space, but that aspect has become merely an insignificant side note to the visible trophies—a shiny new building, for example—as a showcase of innovative accomplishment.

Such symptoms illustrate a "checklist mentality" behind the innovation agenda worldwide. By simply following several easy steps, any university or government can claim that it has accomplished a great deal in terms of promoting innovation. Indeed, we have witnessed some commercial operators rising to the occasion to fulfill such checklist requirements as an outsourced service, so the project leaders can claim "mission accomplished," and turn their attention to other issues.

As long as we are talking about checklists, let's add "sustainable and localized training on IP, technology licensing, and entrepreneurship" to the list. There is *nothing* more important than building human capital to encourage innovation. It is time for us to bring human capital back into the discussion of an innovation agenda.

To this end, we at City University of Hong Kong have started building a channel, between our base in Hong Kong and our mainland China market, through which international innovations can be systematically introduced into China. This channel is assisted not by artificial intelligence-based big data robots, but by real human experts who understand both sides of this channel. With a proposed new training institute on international technology transfer, we hope to illustrate that an innovation platform with significant human capital investments is the right model. As we have heard many times, after all, technology is about people!

Appendix: Selected disruptive innovations from university research

In medicine:

- Penicillin (Imperial College London)
- Polio vaccine (University of Pittsburgh)
- Insulin as a treatment for diabetes (University of Toronto)
- Tuberculosis antibiotics (Rutgers University)
- Vitamins A, B, and the enrichment of Vitamin D content (University of Wisconsin- Madison)
- Chemotherapy drugs (Michigan State University and Florida State University)
- Flu shots (University of Rochester)
- Blood preservation technique (Columbia University)
- X-ray (University of Freiburg, Germany)
- Ultrasound (University of Vienna and Glasgow University)
- CAT scan: full body CT scanner (Georgetown)
- MRI scanner (SUNY Downstate and University of Nottingham)
- Artificial heart (Wayne State University)
- Pacemaker (University of Minnesota)

In technology and computing:

- Solar power (MIT)
- Laser technology (Moscow State University)
- Richter scale (Caltech)
- Geiger counter (University of Manchester)

- Modern oil prospecting (MIT)

- Touchscreens (University of Illinois Urbana-Champaign)

- Graphene (University of Manchester)

- Lithium-ion batteries (MIT)

- Nanowire (Technion, Israel)

- Plasma screens (University of Illinois Urbana-Champaign)

- Liquid Crystal Display (LCD) screens (Kent State University)

- Polygraph (University of California Berkeley)

- Modern seat belt (Cornell University)

- ENIAC, the first fully functioning digital computer (University of Pennsylvania)

- Atanasoff-Berry computer (ABC), an earlier automatic electronic digital computer but not programmable, nor Turing-complete (Iowa State University)

- RSA cryptography (MIT and the Weitzman Institute in Israel)

- Linux (University of Helsinki)

- Android (Osaka University)

- VisiCalc, the first spreadsheet (Harvard with an MIT alumnus)

19 Venture Lending

For startups, cash is King, Queen, and Jack.
Anonymous

INTRODUCTION

For innovative entrepreneurial firms, gaining access to financial resources is a key challenge. In the arena of alternative investments, venture lending has emerged as an effective vehicle of financing promising start-ups with debt to complement and boost equity.[1] The use of debt over equity in such a high-risk environment is not intuitive and even paradoxical. After all, there is seemingly no logic in lending to a nascent business with negative cash flows, no collaterals, and no recourse, thereby taking equity risk for a debt return. Yet when utilized appropriately, venture debt can accelerate corporate growth while delaying the next equity round. For this reason, over the last couple decades, the use of venture lending has gained substantial prominence, growing to become an established industry. There are no formal figures for the size of the market of venture loans, but Fischer and de Rassenfosse (2012) estimate that the U.S. venture debt industry provides at least $3 billion to new ventures annually, or about one venture debt for every seven venture capital (VC) dollars invested.[2]

This chapter outlines the business model of venture lending in financing young entrepreneurial firms. It presents the concept and unique pragmatic aspects of venture lending, as well as its economic underpinning. We will discuss how venture loans are structured to incorporate incentives and economic considerations to reduce exposure to the high risks associated with start-up firms while compensating lenders with participation in the upside.

THE ROLE AND EVOLUTION OF VENTURE LOANS

Innovative start-ups develop products and services—mainly in core sectors such as technology, cleantech, and life sciences—which usually require a substantial upfront investment in research and development. Given the very high levels of risk that start-up companies face, the natural financing instrument is equity (whether preferred or common) rather than debt. Furthermore, in order to moderate the high risks associated with providing a large lump sum up front, funding is provided in stages, commonly referred to as "rounds." Whereas early rounds of capital are typically targeted for the development of core technologies and proof of

---

This chapter was co-authored with Lauren Talmor, Duke University School of Law.

[1] Consistent with practice, the terms "venture lending," "venture debt," and "venture loans" are used interchangeably.

[2] See also Ibrahim (2010). Precise figures are available for the listed venture debt providers. As of December 31, 2015, Hercules Capital, the largest non-bank venture lender in the United States, reported $5.7 billion in commitments since its 2004 inception, whereas Silicon Valley Bank reported $17 billion in loans—albeit only $1 billion was loaned to start-ups. Western Technology Investment (WTI) commits $400 million annually across approximately 100 new loans.

concept, later rounds are aimed at funding production and market penetration. Absent tangible assets and positive operational cash flows, bank debt is not a viable form of financing for new ventures.

Venture lending is a relatively new phenomenon in the world of debt financing. Its roots go back to the 1980s, when venture lending was first introduced as an extension of equipment leasing.[3] At the time, companies that entered into equipment leasing agreements were mostly capital-intensive hardware businesses (e.g., semiconductor fabrication companies). Other industries such as software were not as attractive to early equipment lessors due to concerns about the intangibility of the software technology and thus, the lack of material assets to collateralize a loan. As of the early 1990s, the venture lending industry has become more experienced in dealing with companies whose balance sheets are comprised of tangible assets of little collateral value (e.g., computer workstations) and intangible assets (e.g., software code and intellectual property (IP)). Because of this shift in the nature of VC-backed companies, the venture leasing business morphed into the venture lending business. The finance companies specializing in venture lending became comfortable with their ability to evaluate the current and future enterprise value of an early stage company. The use of venture loans became more and more prevalent, and it has evolved in conjunction with the dotcom boom. The burst of the dotcom bubble resulted in a major contraction to both VC and venture lending (notably, the disastrous collapse of the mighty Comdisco Inc.). Venture lending has since followed the swings of the high-tech sector as well as the recent global financial crisis. Today, it is an integral part of the venture ecosystem, where both companies and investors are far more prudent about their use of debt and its implications should they encounter difficult times.

Not only is venture debt for young technological companies becoming more prevalent as the industry grows, but the available pools of debt financing continue to expand as well. On the supply side, as venture loans are typically granted for a three- to four-year period, many venture lenders can recycle capital throughout their fund lives. From the demand side, since investment in start-ups is staged, venture capitalists are required to reserve sufficient capital ("dry powder") for future rounds of investment in their portfolio companies, which often calls for augmenting the equity injection with debt. Indeed, a growing number of high-profile growth stage companies use venture debt to complement equity. Although correlation does not imply causality, there is evidence that venture lending has been used in a disproportionally large number of successful companies. For instance, in 2012 alone, over 40% of the VC-backed companies that exited through IPOs that year had used venture debt at some point. The association with growth is evident from this figure, being five times larger than the 8% prevalence of debt among the entire population of VC-backed companies during the same year.[4] Today, the use of venture debt has grown significantly; it is estimated that at least 30% of high-growth companies receive debt financing (IFLR1000 2014). This sharp increase is not only due to organic growth in the market for venture debt, but has also resulted from a change in the regulatory environment whereby commercial debt has been rapidly replaced with non-bank credit. This trend has gained momentum following the Dodd-Frank Act and other legislative measures that impose stiffer regulations on commercial bank lending, thereby boosting non-bank credit lending.

---

[3] Early attempts to fund venture leasing by individuals were made by WTI and Equitec. Meier-Mitchell pioneered the current industry form of venture lending backed by intangibles. Using quantitative models attracted institutional investors and established the new asset as acceptable investment with legitimacy and permanence.

[4] http://www.xconomy.com/boston/2013/05/21/venture-debt-as-growth-capital-you-bet

VENTURE LOANS COMPARED WITH OTHER FORMS OF DEBT

Venture loans fill a gap in the debt market spectrum, serving as an effective financial instrument to complement VC investments in young and innovative firms. Whereas commercial debt (e.g., lines of credits, letters of credits, and other forms of bank debt) is subject to stipulations and covenants, the borrower can use venture loans with far less restriction. Venture debt is a useful source to fund activities such as product development, market penetration, or any other operational need. Due to fast changes taking place in the technological environment, new ventures do not necessarily need tangible assets to develop products and services. As mentioned, until the 1980s, virtually all young innovative firms were prohibited from accessing debt. Early stage companies could not have met the stringent conditions for receiving traditional bank loans. They failed to qualify for bank credit as they lacked tangible assets, a track record, stable revenues, or positive cash flows. Venture loans, being different from bank debt, fill the gap in the credit market by providing a new source of funding that was previously unavailable for early stage companies.

Venture loans are structured differently from traditional bank loans in terms of payment charges as well as other provisions. Interest rates for venture loans are higher, payment schedules differ, and there is an upside reward (sometimes referred to as "equity kicker") in the form of warrant coverage. Typically, this upside reward takes the form of warrants extended in proportion to the size of the loan, thereby providing for equity participation in case of a successful future exit. The warrants add to the total return on the loan, and thus increase the compensation for undertaking the high risk associated with venture loans.

Venture loans are also quite different from short-term credit such as convertible or bridge financing instruments. Convertible debt differs from venture debt in that it converts debt into equity in the next equity round. Unlike convertible debt, a venture loan remains as outstanding debt and is not meant to be converted into equity; this is lucidly captured through the phrase "no loan to own." Exhibit 1 summarizes the main differences between the terms of venture debt, convertible debt, and working capital facilities.

Exhibit 1: Comparing venture debt to other forms of debt

	Venture Debt	**Convertible Debt**	**Working Capital Line**
Description	A non-convertible, senior term loan that can be used like equity, and includes warrants	A loan that converts to stock in the next equity round, usually at a discount or with warrants	A revolving line of credit that is secured by working capital; may or may not include warrants
Repayment	Generally repaid in monthly payments over the life of the loan	None, converts to equity	Can flex up or down over the life of the loan, depending on the "borrowing base" securing the loan
Approximate Interest Rate	10-15%	3-8%	6-10%
Dilution	Generally a small fraction of equity (< 1%), due to warrants	Similar to equity, but can be more or less dilutive depending on valuation in the next round and specific terms	Minimal to none; may or may not include warrants
Default Clauses	Varies, but often limited to failure to repay	Generally none	Often includes MAC catch-all (any "material adverse change"), investor abandonment, etc.
Financial Covenants	Generally none	Generally none	Often bound to a minimum amount of cash, A/R, performance vs. plan, etc.

Source: Gordan, P. "Venture debt: A capital idea for startups," Kauffman Fellows Report 4, 2012.

VENTURE LENDING BUSINESS MODEL

Venture loans are individually structured financial instruments, which are repaid by the start-up firm through equal monthly payments consisting of principal and interest, often referred to as mortgage-type amortization.[5] Fees charged by the venture lender constitute further income components. The most common one is an upfront arrangement fee which typically amounts to up to 1.5% of the original loan amount. Moreover, an early repayment (prepayment) penalty is charged in case the borrower wishes to pay back the balance loan amount ahead of the arranged schedule; this happens when investors are able to achieve an exit earlier than planned. Prepayment penalties vary considerably depending upon competitive factors. In general, the venture lender expends significant time and effort and takes on risk when committing to the loan to the start-up company. Therefore, the lender needs the loan to be outstanding for the agreed-upon time in order to generate the interest earnings necessary to appropriately compensate for the risk and effort. If the interest earnings are unavailable due to a prepayment, the lender will structure the penalty to provide this compensation.

In addition, there are exit incentives, which typically consist of warrants that allow the lender the right to buy a previously agreed amount of company stocks or to receive a fixed payment in the event of an exit. The warrants have an expiration date that far exceeds the maturity date of the loan, thereby enabling the lender to share the upside even if that happens several years later in the life of the start-up company. While realizing a successful exit and sharing the upside is the ideal scenario to both the lender and the borrower, it is unfortunately not the prevailing scenario in the risky world of start-ups. Two more possible outcomes have to be considered. In the middle possible outcome, the loans plus interest are fully paid back, but the borrowing company ultimately fails to reach a material exit, so the warrants expire unexercised. Finally, the worst possible outcome is when a borrower gets into insolvency prior to a full repayment of the loan, in which case the lender gets paid principal and interest until the point where the borrower is no longer able to continue payments. Most often, such an outcome is preceded by a process of harsh negotiations over which the lender may reluctantly agree to restructure the loan, stretching out the remainder of the payment schedule in order to provide cash flow relief to the borrower. Often, the lender will expect the venture investors to provide some additional financial support to the distressed borrower in response to the cash flow relief. These negotiations therefore include three interested and adversarial parties: the lender, the investor, and the borrower. In the event of default, the lender, who is holding a senior lien on the company's assets, is able to partially recoup the unpaid share of the principal by selling off assets (whether tangible or intangible).

In general, a venture loan is considered and approved on the basis of the borrower's ability to pay it back rather than attempting to predict the value from a potential upside. The venture lender's task is to identify start-up companies that will survive long enough to repay the loan, as opposed to identifying companies that will ultimately achieve successful exits. Equity investors need to pick winners—but the venture lender needs to pick survivors. These are very different tasks. Upside from warrants is hugely uncertain, and although it could ultimately provide a meaningful boost to the loan return, it is in no way a rationale for consenting to take a significant downside risk. Risk exposure is mitigated in three stages. First, as with any other lending activity, a thorough credit analysis is undertaken to ensure that all risks are calculated and accounted for. Second, the design of the loan payments must be meticulously tailored to the company at hand, taking into consideration inflection points in the operational cash flows such as the prospect of potential licensing agreements, grants, and the formation of material strategic partnerships and expected future rounds of equity

---

[5] Sometimes a grace period is negotiated whereby only interest charges are paid during the first six months, while the amortized principal and interest start afterwards.

fundraising. Third, venture lenders continuously monitor the borrowing company's cash flow and remain closely informed through formal periodic reports and ad hoc conversations. Maintaining a constant dialogue with the company enables the venture debt provider to anticipate delays in payments and to take measured steps relatively early on.

Warrants as income sources for venture lenders

In practice, warrant coverage ranges from 3–20% of the original loan amount. The percentage varies primarily based on the stage of the business, geography, and market cyclicality. The warrants are usually issued at an exercise price equal to the last equity round and carry a price protection in case the subsequent qualified round occurs at a lower price (a "down round"). For example, consider a loan of US$1 million, with 15% warrant coverage and a strike price equal to the last round share price of US$0.75. In such a case, the company will issue 200,000 warrants at the above price to the venture lender at the time the loan is granted, with a long warrant maturity (e.g., 10 years).

Despite the obvious economic desirability of such warrants, they play no fundamental role in the lending decision. Warrants are nice to have but should never be the core consideration when evaluating a company. First and foremost, venture lending is a banking business which is focused on managing the downside risks and not on major upside potential. Warrant coverage is seen as a valuable additional income component for the lender's overall return that is aimed at compensating for the risk that lenders undertake, but it should not influence a specific credit decision. Venture loans are priced primarily as debt, and should only be evaluated as such when committed.

Risk reduction in venture lending contracts

Venture loans are usually structured as amortized loans where the borrower has to pay a fixed monthly amount (interest plus a portion of the principal) over a certain period (typically three years). Occasionally, there is a six-month grace period in which only interest payments are made by the company. The feature of monthly payments, as will be discussed later in greater depth, is a critical component of the loan structure since it aligns the economic interests of the different parties, thereby decreasing the lenders' risk.

Another mechanism used to reduce the lenders' capital at risk is to apportion the loan commitment into tranches. Often, those tranches are made contingent on pre-set milestones that the borrower has to achieve in order to qualify for the next portion of the venture loan. Milestones are usually based on events contemplated in the company's business plan, such as technological achievements (e.g., successfully passing clinical tests) or commercial ones (achieving agreed-upon revenues). Making tranches of the loan contingent on passing pre-agreed milestone targets links the outstanding size of the loan to the progress and value of the business, thus acting as the most direct mechanism to lessen credit risk.

To increase the likelihood of a loan repayment, venture lenders stipulate seniority over other lenders or investors in the company by including a clause titled "restriction of indebtedness" in the agreement. This clause restricts the borrower from undertaking new debt, or otherwise limits the total indebtedness to a certain amount (typically slightly above the level of the venture loan). Allowing further borrowing, even if it is subordinated to the venture loan, will introduce competing interests and complicate the capital structure. The additional cash flow burden reduces the borrower's margin for error and hence the soundness of the venture loan. Further, if there is too much debt in a company, it discourages venture investors from continuing to support a marginal company for three reasons: (1) all of the lenders will have a claim senior to the equity investors on the company's value in liquidation; (2) much of the new equity cash will go to debt service for the lenders and not to the growth of the company; and (3) the company may also be required to maintain a minimal level of cash at all times, so that it is able to meet its ordinary business obligations.

A key risk mitigation for the lender is the collateralization of the IP and tangible assets through a first priority lien (conversely, a negative pledge on the IP of the enterprise).[6] Since the value of fixed, tangible assets in highly innovative businesses such as software, Internet, or biotechnology is minimal, lenders need a lien on the IP as a protection in case of default. IP in young high-growth companies often consists of patents, software, and specialized technologies. The value of IP is usually determined by the industry and the specific market circumstances of each company. In start-ups, that value also depends heavily on the inventors and the people who are experts in these technologies. Thus, without employees who are very familiar with the relevant technologies, software and unpatented technologies are difficult to monetize in default. As such, IP collateralization acts mainly as a deterrent to the original owners or developers rather than a source of cash recovery for the lender.

IP in the form of patents is considered to be stronger collateral than unpatented knowhow. In reality, however, there is no great difference between the two, and the lender often finds it nearly impossible to monetize IP (be it patented or not) in a default of a start-up. The reason for this difficulty is that IP is typically built through a process of gradual innovation, as opposed to a single act of disruptive creativity. In a competing industry where multiple companies develop similar incremental knowhow in parallel, patent infringement is very hard to prevent; this is particularly true for the venture lender. As a financial institution, the lender operates from outside of the industry and hence, is unlikely to be aware of (let alone able to prove) incidents of patent infringement, whether intentional or innocent. Altogether, it is doubtful whether a venture lender is able to benefit from those intangible assets in bankruptcy, unless the defaulted enterprise is sold en bloc. Nevertheless, a blanket lien on all assets (including IP) is an effective tool to deter entrepreneurs from walking away from an indebted company only to have a fresh restart in a newly set similar business.

Although lenders do not take an active role in overseeing the borrower, they do maintain a material degree of monitoring through requiring it to routinely supply financial reports, bank statements, and minutes of board and shareholders meetings. In addition, the lender should engage in periodic conversations with management in order to keep a good grip on the business development and fundraising processes.

VENTURE FIRM PERSPECTIVE: EXTENDING THE CASH RUNWAY

Venture loans are used to provide further cash in order to accelerate growth (e.g., launch products, enter markets, and invest in employees and research and development) or achieve other milestones set by the board and the management of the company. Such activities entail a budgetary cash burn which the company must sustain. By receiving a venture loan, the start-up company is able to extend its cash runway toward achieving its growth targets. The VC loan therefore enables the company to postpone the next equity round to a later date, giving it more time to reach milestones indicative of its clear progress. Achieving milestones yields a

---

[6] A negative pledge is a contractual prohibition on granting a security interest in, or selling the IP to, any other party.

higher intrinsic valuation for the enterprise. Postponing the next equity round until a step-up in valuation can be attained lowers dilution for both the entrepreneur and any existing investors who do not pro rata participate in the next round. Despite the warrants granted to the lender, the use of venture debt as opposed to external equity is far less dilutive for a start-up company that has yet to achieve a meaningful jump in valuation—assuming that it does, in fact, successfully achieve its set milestones. Failure to achieve the milestones and reach a valuation step-up will make the venture debt somewhat dilutive, and can impede the company's ability to raise additional equity. Utilizing debt versus equity can provide start-up companies with the cash runway necessary to achieve the growth alluded to in their business plans, and reduce the future dilution.

Using a venture loan to increase the cash runway is also very beneficial if used as the last source of funding before achieving exit. The loan plays the same positive role of preventing dilution as it does when postponing a next round of external funding. In fact, some venture lenders specialize in making much larger loans to companies that have achieved market acceptance of their product or service. They lend to companies deemed to be in the "growth" stage (as opposed to the higher-risk "development" stage) and provide loans large enough to eliminate the final round of equity financing. These can be loans as large as $30 million.

So far, we have discussed the role of venture debt as a means of "buying" time in order to build more value in the business prior to the next round of equity funding or before exit; yet it must be noted that this is economically meaningful only if the next round is meant to include new investors. If the entire next round of funding comes from existing investors, then taking a venture loan is actually counterproductive. Not only would the principal have to be returned to the lender, but interest and other related debt-service costs would be incurred by the borrowing firm. Without benefiting from a diminished dilution, taking on debt as opposed to equity is less beneficial if the existing investors intend to fund the next equity round.

Ulterior motives from the venture capitalists' perspective include the use of leverage to reduce their exposure to the portfolio company. Sometimes the converse is true, if the VC firm wishes to deploy as much money as possible out of the door into a certain company and will reject venture debt so that the firm preserves the ability to invest more equity. The management team is diluted in this scenario, and that is a source of friction.

RELATIONSHIPS TRIANGLE: VENTURE CAPITALIST, START-UP, AND VENTURE LENDER

Most venture lenders require having at least one VC firm (and preferably two) as an investor in the start-up they consider backing. Why do venture lenders stipulate an existing or concurrent VC investment when screening companies for investment? Venture loans are relatively small in size and the lender strives to create a portfolio diversified over many companies. The modest upside of loans with warrants relative to that of equity investors means that it is not economically worthwhile, or even feasible, for lenders to provide mentorship or management direction, but that they would rather depend on the venture capitalists for guidance and stewardship of the investee companies. Venture capitalists provide monitoring and value-added services in order to accelerate the growth and development of their portfolio companies. Their overseeing role is critical to the lender since firms that apply for venture loans tend to be young, innovative start-ups that lack tangible collaterals. VC firms act to lower the risk exposure to the lender by applying their extensive experience in building enterprises to the growth and success of the particular company.

Director seats and preferential shareholders' voting rights enable VC firms to "stir the board" and influence the financing and strategic decisions of the young enterprise. Furthermore, companies backed by highly reputable venture capitalists perform better than companies backed by less reputable venture capitalists.[7] For those reasons, VC backing fulfils important functions for the lender in reducing risks associated with the venture loan.

By setting a prerequisite of VC backing, venture lenders effectively "free ride" on these services as part of their business model. There are other reasons why lenders formally demand a prior VC investment. First, equity rounds that are led by professional and experienced investors provide an arm's length valuation basis to set a credible strike price for the granted warrants. Second, when deciding whether to make a loan, and in further dealings with the borrowing company, it is essential for lenders that the counterparties are institutional investors that are there for the long haul, and whose credibility and reputation guide their conduct. This reliability is most helpful in the due diligence stage, where venture lenders may rely more heavily on the work already done by venture capitalists—specifically, the due diligence on the underlying technology and markets—and more readily assume that the books are correct (i.e., likelihood of fraud is low). The same applies later on when dealing with the company on an ongoing basis following the loan investment. In the absence of institutional investors, lenders may eventually find themselves dealing with a counterparty whose conduct is murky or unprofessional. In particular, should the company fall on hard times by either reaching default or requiring a loan renegotiation, professional conduct is vital—and could not be guaranteed if the only investors were private individuals. Thus, the presence of VC firms on the board significantly lessens counterparty risk.

Developing trust and credibility during difficult times establishes reliability and a bilateral need for building long-term relationships and repeated collaboration on multiple transactions. Consequently, the network created and frequent dialogue between VC firms and lenders strengthen the mutual business credibility of the parties and make actions during adverse times more amicable and predictable; this helps in easing credit risks, as well as providing further deal flow opportunities. The flip side is that reputational considerations require the lender to negotiate restructurings while being compelled to take into account the opposing interests of the equity investors, often leading the lender to relax credit terms as in order to preserve the important long-term relationship with the VC firm. The lender must perform a careful balancing act in these situations. Overall, building long-term relationships between the institutional suppliers of capital decreases moral hazards and interjects a professional code of conduct that facilitates a smoother loan renegotiation should the start-up fall on hard times.

With respect to the motivation and demand for venture loans, there are strong reasons for venture capitalists and other equity providers to seek loans for their portfolio companies. First, the inherent high risk of early stage investment prompts VC firms to adopt a diversification strategy, as opposed to investing in a small number of companies. This strategy is also economically efficient since it enables venture capitalists to spread and exert their skills and experience over a meaningful number of companies. Consequently, equity syndication within rounds and over time is very common in VC investment as a means of increasing diversification across more companies. Venture loans act to substitute some of the need to syndicate the equity, which often results in better economics, given the far less dilutive form of financing. Another motivation VC firms have for seeking venture loans for their portfolio companies is to reserve sufficient capital (dry powder) for future rounds of funding as investment in start-ups is staged. Venture loans act to alleviate some of the pressure for future reserves.

---

[7] See Nahata (2008).

Finally, venture lending produces a win-win situation in another rather interesting way. The more optimistic venture capitalists are about the prospects of certain portfolio companies, the more they would prefer debt over an external equity round, thereby sending a strong signal to the venture lender concerning the concurrent assessment of the business and its future prospects. All other things being equal, venture capitalists would prefer to seek venture loans for portfolio companies that they feel most confident about, as opposed to seeking external equity for their other companies.

HORIZON OF DISAPPOINTMENT AND THE DESIGN OF VENTURE LOANS

As discussed, investment in young and innovative firms is done in stages in order to reduce the magnitude of capital at risk. The uncommitted capital set aside by venture capitalists as a reserve for the future support of their portfolio companies is a first-order factor in the lender's consideration whether to grant a venture loan. For the majority of start-ups, further equity rounds, licensing agreements, or the prospect of an exit are the most likely means of repaying venture loans. Since there are typically no (or insufficient) positive operating cash flows in the short or mid-term, the continuing need for external financing in order to expand the business becomes the prime life buoy for the lender should the borrowing entity enter hazardous territory (i.e., enter the lender's so-called "watch list").

Therefore, a mandatory condition for granting a venture loan is that the company is backed by strong hands. When assessing the venture lending decision, analyzing the financial capabilities of the current investors and their genuine enthusiasm in further backing the company is as important as the business due diligence of the company itself. An important feature of venture loans is that even if the company falls on hard times, enough value may remain in the company so that current investors would be reluctant to allow the company to default on its service debt payments. An event of default is lethal to investors as it erases their entire past investment in the company and surrenders it to the lender. To minimize the chance of default, the venture loan transaction is structured according to several guidelines:

- **Size:** The loan must be sufficiently small in relation to the size of past investments and the company valuation as set in the latest round so as to not overwhelm the capital structure and discourage future equity investments

- **Tranching:** The loan is not granted as a lump sum, but rather, is tranched into multiple fundings over time with each funding requiring a specific milestone achievement. Tranching reduces the size of the loan principal extended in the riskiest stage of the company's development, thereby decreasing the lenders overall risk.

- **Dry powder:** Institutional investors in general—and VC firms in particular—usually need to state if they have reserved funds in order to follow on their investment in the company (even though that statement is not contractually binding).

- **Cash runway (mitigating front-end risk):** The borrowing company needs to show that it has enough cash runway prior to undertaking the loan (ideally, no less than nine months of runway). That assurance eliminates much of the risk of default during the first year, deferring the likelihood of default to the second or third year of loan maturity.

- **Principal amortization (mitigating back-end risk):** Since the loan is structured to be amortized, the likelihood of loan default at the third year should also be modest, as the remaining balance of the loan at that point is relatively small—roughly one-third of the original loan is still outstanding. For instance, for a US$2 million loan amortized over three years and bearing a 10% interest rate, the outstanding loan balance after two years would be US$734,000; this is a relatively modest sum compared to the value of the company when writing the loan, certainly in companies in which tens of millions of equity were invested, and where the loan due diligence provided enough positive indications about the company's ability to withstand its obligations.

The last point highlights a key principle in the economics of venture loans: the risk of the loan is not necessarily determined by the riskiness of the underlying business, or even its ultimate fate, but rather, is linked to the perceived intrinsic enterprise value during the life of the loan. This notion generates the somewhat paradoxical causality that early stage companies are often safer for lenders than more mature companies. Consider the drug discovery sector as an example. Although ultimately very risky, this sector is capital intensive and endowed with a high level of IP built from years of research and development at universities or other scientific institutions, as well as funding from government grants, endowments, or private sector investors. In such an environment, it is quite unlikely for a VC firm to let its portfolio company default during the early years of the business (i.e., before it is known whether the drug under development will work or not). This situation is referred to as a long "horizon of disappointment," and it provides the lender with a good cushion of risk mitigation—a situation that could be described as "strong hands." In contrast, an e-commerce or enterprise software company where the IP is less robust may be very risky to a lender, even if the company is more mature and cash generating. Should the fortunes of such a business change, equity investors' horizon of disappointment may be quite short if it is judged that any further equity injection would be "throwing good money after bad," thereby triggering a decision to shut down the business. This case could be described as one of "weak hands." There are additional scenarios which may be characterized as ones of either "strong hands" or "weak hands." For instance, a situation that could be described as "weak hands" is where a VC firm is less incentivized to inject further equity into a last remaining unrealized portfolio company in an otherwise very successful fund cohort.

Venture loans are designed so that the amortizing debt service payments are made at short intervals, typically monthly. The rationale emerges from the same mindset as outlined above. For equal monthly payments over three years, each payment constitutes a few percentages of the original principal of the loan. Continuing the previous illustration, the monthly payment comes out to be about US$65,000. Each month, the equity investors face the decision of whether to keep the borrower solvent enough to pay that rather modest sum and continue owning the business, or to default, thereby surrendering the business to the lender; this is the well-known analogy of equity investment to a call option, whereby every debt service payment results from a decision to keep the equity option alive until the next time payment is due. Alternatively, this could also be viewed as an equity holder decision not to exercise a put option (Merton 1974). Insights from option pricing theory tell us that the lower the monthly payment, the lower the chance of default, because the value of the option alive is always compared to the size of the payment that is concurrently due. Applying this rationale, if, for instance, we were to naively structure the loan on a semiannual amortization schedule, it would have multiplied the probability of default by a factor of approximately six.

GOVERNMENT VENTURE LENDING INCENTIVE PROGRAMS

There has been a growing movement in public sector efforts across the globe to design schemes and dedicate financial resources to foster local venture ecosystems. Policymakers' desire to support innovation stems from the fact that, despite the high risk involved in investing in new technology development, innovative companies are a major driver for long-term economic growth, attracting foreign capital, creating jobs, and boosting exports.

The majority of public financial support is in the form of grants, tax breaks, direct equity through competitive processes, and indirect equity through co-investing with VC funds. However, there are also incentive schemes through debt. These take two main forms: direct lending to start-ups and indirect support by augmenting and reducing the risk of private lending institutions.[8]

In addition to government lending support, many multinational organizations offer venture lending incentive programs. A notable program in this category is the InnovFin SME Guarantee facility, which is part of Horizon 2020, the EU framework for research and innovation. Through this scheme, the European Investment Fund (EIF) guarantees debt for innovative small and medium-sized enterprises (SMEs). The InnovFin SME Guarantee facility is deployed by eligible local banks and venture lending companies, which are chosen after a selective process. Once a financial intermediary is qualified by the EIF, it can then lend on favorable terms to innovative SMEs in the EU and associated countries. The scheme covers 50% of the losses incurred by the financial intermediaries on loans, leases, and guarantees between €25,000 and €7.5 million which they provide per SME company. Exhibit 2 presents the guiding criteria set by a leading British bank to qualify for a loan under the InnovFin SME Guarantee facility.

EMERGENCE OF VENTURE LOANS IN CHINA[9]

Like elsewhere in the world, the traditional credit culture of commercial banks in China is primarily designed to serve mature enterprises. Lacking fixed assets as collateral, early and growth stage enterprises do not typically pass the hurdle for obtaining commercial loans. To address the scarcity of debt funding for venture businesses, in April 2016, the China Banking Regulatory Commission, the Ministry of Science and Technology, and the People's Bank of China jointly issued the Guidance on Strengthening Innovation of Banking Institutions and Conducting Pilots of Combined Credit-Equity Investment for Technological Innovation-Based Enterprises and Start-Ups (the "Guidance"). In a simultaneous act, these authorities also announced the first batch of pilot projects that included five state-level independent innovation demonstration zones (e.g., Zhongguancun in Beijing and Zhangjiyang in Shanghai) and 10 participating banks

---

[8] Examples of direct lending mechanisms include the U.S. Small Business Administration loan program, France's SOFARIS, Austria's Finanzierungsgarantie-Gesellschaft Technology Financing Program, and the U.K. Startup Loan Scheme. Indirect lending incentive schemes include the U.K. Enterprise Finance Guarantee and the Singaporean Loan Insurance Scheme. See Klingler-Vidra (2014).

[9] This section is drawn from Beijing Private Equity Association (BPEA) Newsletter, Vol. 64 May 31, 2017.

which were qualified to extend venture loans, including China Development Bank, Bank of China, and Bank of Beijing.

The overriding bank regulatory environment is set by Article 43 of the Law of the People's Republic of China on Commercial Banks, which explicitly forbids commercial banks from making direct equity investments across mainland China. As a result, most large commercial banks in China have established equity investment arms through holding or controlling subsidiary companies. Often, the banks set offshore subsidiaries, which then invest equity locally by setting domestic subsidiaries.

For early stage equity investments, most commercial banks operate mainly by cooperating with VC funds. In this way, banks not only bypass regulatory restrictions on sharing equity returns in China, but also mitigate some of the risks since they recognize that VC firms are better equipped to screen early stage enterprises. Convertible loans or venture loans with warrants are arranged through the VC firm acting as an intermediary between the borrowing enterprise and the lending bank. Upon a monetization event of the venture business, the VC firm may convert the loan to equity or exercise the warrants and share the returns with the banks.

Given the stringent bank regulatory system with respect to risk control, and the lack of experience and successful track records among Chinese commercial banks, only a few of them offer venture loans at present; the industry is still in its infancy. It is hoped that the new Guidance discussed above will facilitate and uplift this type of venture funding.

Exhibit 2: guiding criteria for the UK InnovFin SME Guarantee facility

High-growth stage	Post-seed	Series A	Series B/C
Type of firm	Early stage, revenue-generating businesses	Scaled-up, moderately capitalized businesses	Scaled-up, well capitalized businesses
Revenue	over £250,000	£500,000–£5 million	over £5 million
Growth rate	over 100%	over 20%	over 20%
Funds raised	over £500,000	over £500,000	over £5 million
Purpose	Working capital	Working capital	General operational purposes
Enterprise value (EV)	--	over £5 million	over £25 million
Debt to EV	--	up to 10%	up to 10%
Product	Term loan	Term loan	Overdraft, term loan
Amount	over £100,000	up to £1 million	up to £5 million
Tenor (months)	12+	12+	12–36
Collateral	EIF InnovFin SME Guarantee Cross-guarantee & Debenture	EIF InnovFin SME Guarantee Cross-guarantee & Debenture	EIF InnovFin SME Guarantee Cross-guarantee & Debenture
Warrants to be taken	Yes	Yes	Yes

CONCLUSION

Venture loans aim at young technology companies that are not mature enough to qualify for bank debt. We have emphasized several contractual instruments that are used to lower the downside risk in venture lending, of which a key aspect is the underlying IP owned by a company and the possibility of its collateralization. Among the non-contractual features, a salient consideration is the presence of VC backing, which lessens the risk associated with the lack of positive cash flows and tangible assets. From the borrower perspective, venture debt extends the company's cash runway and enables it to postpone an external round of equity financing in order to achieve further business progress to justify a higher valuation. The next equity round would then be less dilutive for the current shareholders. This benefit should be balanced against the interest and other costs associated with the venture loan in evaluating the loan desirability. Interest and principal have to be paid on a relatively fast-paced schedule, and the borrowing enterprise must have a clear financing strategy and liquidity management in order to handle the debt burden appropriately.

The chapter started with a rather provocative view, pointing out the paradox in extending loans to high-risk and immature companies allegedly taking equity risk for debt-type return. However, if properly selected and managed, the interest rates and fees charged should cover the operational cost of running the venture lending business, as well as the occasional write-offs. As such, all incoming debt-service cash flows net out with the operational costs of the lender, leaving the latter with a portfolio of long-term warrants. Thus, the more astute view would be to consider venture lending as a highly disciplined factory of warrants. For example, a venture loan portfolio of $200 million with an average warrant coverage of 14% represents an equity stake equivalent to $28 million in VC-backed companies "for no investment," and without the trouble of value-added services. While the latter statement is economically true, venture lenders should be careful not to focus on the warrants when evaluating loan candidates. As noted, such a mindset could be hazardous, and so venture lenders should make their decisions based on the assessed ability of the borrower to return the loan, and the strength of the equity backers' commitment to pump additional funds into the business.

Venture lending is a hybrid of debt and equity, and as such, it captures a wide spectrum of financial and business elements. It employs economic concepts like option pricing and game theory when evaluating whether a company qualifies for a loan, and in designing the loan terms and repayment schedule.

REFERENCES

Fischer, T. and G. de Rassenfosse (2012) "Venture debt financing: Determinants of the lending decision," SSRN working paper, January.

Gordan, P. (2012) "Venture debt: A capital idea for startups," *Kauffman Fellows Report 4,* Kauffman Fellows Press.

Ibrahim, D.M. (2010) "Debt as venture capital," *University of Illinois Law Review,* 1169-1210.

International Financial Law Review 1000, "Latham & Watkins expands emerging company and venture capital practice," 2014.

Klingler-Vidra, R. (2014) "All politics is local: Sources of variance in the diffusion of venture capital policies," PhD thesis, London School of Economics, 2014. A synopsis appears in Venture Findings 1: 37-42.

Merton, R.C. (1974) "On the pricing of corporate debt: The risk structure of interest rates," *Journal of Finance*, Vol. 29(2): 449–470.

Nahata, R. (2008) "Venture capital reputation and investment performance," *Journal of Financial Economics*, Vol. 90(2): 127-151.

The industry view from Silicon Valley on current market trends

The current low-interest-rate environment has forced institutional and retail investors alike to chase yield wherever they can find it. Venture debt, with its (relatively) high cash-on-cash returns and warrant upside, has become a natural haven.

The venture business is becoming increasingly challenging as companies are taking longer to exit, crossover investors/mutual funds are investing in private companies (although this is slowing down now), and serial entrepreneurs are waiting longer than previously to raise their first institutional rounds—so the market is bifurcated between mega funds (e.g., NEA, Sequoia, Greylock) and micro VCs. These micro VCs are sole GP funds of less than $100 million that don't require board seats and are thought of as "entrepreneur friendly." Venture lending works very well symbiotically with these funds; they love the product and the mentorship that lenders provide entrepreneurs and nascent businesses.

The majority of exits are under $100 million. Of the total cases where we made on warrants involved exits that were greater than $100 million, and only 10% of those were IPOs. Venture lending has adjusted to these conditions by modifying the warrants. Now VC funds are insisting on "last or next," and many times even demand "any next round" when a company is believed to be overvalued, rather than just accepting the current/last round strike price. Sometimes the funds even include put options which kick in on a certain date or upon a change of control when the warrant doesn't have a clear baseline value.

INDEX

www.privatecapitalbook.com

Private Capital
Volume II: Investments
Copyright © 2020 by Eli Talmor and Florin Vasvari
Edited by Kontent360
Printed in the United Kingdom

ISBN 978-1-9162110-5-6